T0144602

ENCYCLOPEDIA OF COMPUTER SCIENCE AND TECHNOLOGY

VOLUME 23

ENCYCLOPEDIA OF COMPUTER SCIENCE AND TECHNOLOGY

EXECUTIVE EDITORS

Allen Kent   *James G. Williams*

UNIVERSITY OF PITTSBURGH
PITTSBURGH, PENNSYLVANIA

ADMINISTRATIVE EDITORS

Rosalind Kent   *Carolyn M. Hall*

PITTSBURGH, PENNSYLVANIA

VOLUME 23
SUPPLEMENT 8

MARCEL DEKKER, INC. • NEW YORK and BASEL

MARCEL DEKKER, INC.
270 Madison Avenue, New York, New York 10016

LIBRARY OF CONGRESS CATALOG CARD NUMBER: 74-29436
ISBN: 0-8247-2273-6

Current Printing (last digit):
10 9 8 7 6 5 4 3 2 1

PRINTED IN UNITED STATES OF AMERICA

CONTENTS OF VOLUME 23

CONTRIBUTORS TO VOLUME 23

STEPHEN J. ANDRIOLE, Department of Information Systems & Systems Engineering, George Mason University, Fairfax, Virginia: *Command and Control Decision-Aiding*

WILLIAM L. BENZON, Consultant, Troy, New York: *Visual Thinking*

WILLIAM E. BILES, Ph.D., P.E., Department of Industrial Engineering, University of Louisville, Louisville, Kentucky: *Manufacturing Systems Simulation*

AUSTIN BLAQUIERE, Professor, University of Paris, Laboratoire d'Automatique Theorique, Paris, France: *The Bellman Continuum*

JOHN M. CARROLL, Manager of User Interface Theory and Design, IBM T. J. Watson Research Center, Yorktown Heights, New York: *Interface Design Issues for Intelligent Advisory Systems*

SU-SHING CHEN, Department of Computer Science, University of North Carolina, Charlotte, North Carolina: *Spatial Information Processing: Representation and Reasoning*

LEON L. COOPER, Thomas J. Watson, Sr., Professor of Science, Co-Director, Center for Neural Science, Brown University, Department of Physics, Providence, Rhode Island: *Brain and Information Research*

ALAN G. LAW, Computer Science Department, University of Regina, Regina, Saskatchewan, Canada: *Approximation, Optimization, and Computing*

JEAN MC KENDREE, Member of Technical Staff, Human Interface Laboratory, MCC, Austin, Texas: *Interface Design Issues for Intelligent Advisory Systems*

STUART A. MC LEAN, School of Library and Information Science, University of Pittsburgh, Pittsburgh, Pennsylvania: *Object-Oriented Database Management Systems*

J. L. MATÉ,   Professor of Computer Sciences and Dean of the Facultdad de Informatica, Universidad Politecnica de Madrid, Madrid, Spain: *Knowledge Engineering Design and Construction of Expert Systems*

A. MEYSTEL, Ph.D.,   Department of Electrical and Computer Engineering, College of Engineering, Drexel University, Philadelphia, Pennsylvania: *Intelligent Control*

MICHAEL K. MOLLOY,   Department of Computer Science, Carnegie-Mellon University, Pittsburgh, Pennsylvania: *Performance Petri Nets*

ALI R. MONTAZEMI,   Associate Professor of Information Systems, Faculty of Business, McMaster University, Hamilton, Ontario, Canada: *Management Information Systems*

SERGEI NIRENBURG,   Center for Machine Translation, Carnegie-Mellon University, Pittsburgh, Pennsylvania: *Machine Translation*

JUAN PAZOS,   Professor of Computer Sciences and Vice Dean of the Facultdad of Informatica, Universidad Politecnica de Madrid, Madrid, Spain: *Knowledge Engineering Design and Construction of Expert Systems*

MARTIN PLAEHN,   Vice President, Research & Development, Template Graphics Software, Inc., San Diego, California: *PHIGS: Programmer's Hierarchical Interactive Graphics Standard*

MAURIZIO RAFANELLI, Ph.D.,   Consiglio Nazionale Delle Ricerche, IASI - CNR, Rome, Italy: *Statistical and Scientific Database Management Systems*

THOMAS G. RAY, Ph.D., P.E.,   President, Sportco, Inc., Minden, Louisiana: *Manufacturing Systems Simulation*

HANS J. SCHROEDER,   Laboratory "Signal Storage Technique", Physikalisch-Technische Bundesanstalt Braunschweig, Berlin, Federal Republic of Germany: *Magnetic Disks*

JOHN A. STANKOVIC, Ph.D.,   Associate Professor, Department of Computer and Information Science, University of Massachusetts, Amherst, Massachusetts: *Real-Time Computing*

GREGG ZEHR,   Hardware Project Manager, Macintosh, Apple Computer, Inc., Cupertino, California: *The Memory Management Unit*

ENCYCLOPEDIA OF COMPUTER SCIENCE AND TECHNOLOGY

VOLUME 23

APPROXIMATION, OPTIMIZATION, AND COMPUTING

INTRODUCTION

The fields of approximation, optimization, and computing encompass a wealth of mathematical material; they have enjoyed illustrious histories over the centuries and are now undergoing exciting developments as the twenty-first century approaches. The evolution of the modern computer has brought into focus many of their overlap regions. Techniques, applications, and expanding areas of research derive mutual benefits from the interactions, and they provide fundamental tools for tackling increasingly complex problems in the sciences, engineering, and medicine. This article addresses some of the interplay among the three fields. the familiar continuous, real-valued functions are used with the powerful inner product structure, to provide a setting in which approximation and optimization can be discussed together briefly, in conjunction with basic concepts of the computing for machine implementation. The initial focus in this introductory article is on continuous techniques, but a discrete-methods development parallels that using the continuous tools; there is a great deal of interplay between continuous and discrete methods in general.

APPROXIMATION AND INNER-PRODUCT OPTIMIZATION

Let $C[a, b]$ denote the set (vector space) of all continuous, real-valued functions defined on an interval $[a, b]$. In the field of Approximation theory, one of the most celebrated results from the classical analysis period in the later 1800s is attributed to Weierstrass: his theorem asserts that for any given $f \in C[a, b]$ and any $\epsilon > 0$, there exists a polynomial, p, such that

$$|f(x) - p(x)| < \epsilon$$

for every x in $[a, b]$. This measure of discrepancy is usually denoted by $|| \ ||_\infty$, called a *norm*. Thus, with

$$\|f - p\|_\infty = \max_{a \leq x \leq b} |f(x) - p(x)|,$$

Weierstrass' theorem asserts that any f in $C[a, b]$ can be approximated arbitrarily closely by a polynomial, using this *uniform* or *Tchebicheff* norm, $|| \ ||_\infty$. Other norms for assessing sizes of elements prove useful too, in a variety of approximation problems, and many different families of approximants might be considered also; others which have been and are employed extensively in $C[a, b]$ include rational functions and trigonometric functions. In the discussion below, a special kind of norm is employed, induced by an inner product. Consequently, such a norm inherits some particularly important properties and, as a result, approximation to an element with respect to this norm can be minimized (optimized). Furthermore, solution of a certain corresponding linear system produces this best approximation as well.

1

Definition

A (real) inner product on a set of elements $f, g, h, \ldots$, with (real) scalars $a, b, c, \ldots$, is a mapping $\langle \, , \, \rangle$ which associates with each pair of elements a (real) number, subject to the following properties:

$$\langle f, f \rangle \geq 0,$$

$$\langle f, f \rangle = 0 \text{ if, and only if, } f \equiv 0,$$

$$\langle f, g \rangle = \langle g, f \rangle, \text{ and}$$

$$\langle af + bg, h \rangle = a\langle f, h \rangle + b\langle g, h \rangle,$$

for any elements f, g, and h and any scalars a and b.

For example, on the set $C[a, b]$, if $w(x)$ is any selected, positive-valued, continuous "weight" function,

$$\langle f, g \rangle = \int_a^b f(x)g(x)w(x)dx \tag{1}$$

is an inner product. A second example may be given to show a discrete structure: let N be a chosen positive integer and let $x_j = j/N$, for $j = 0, 1, 2, \ldots, N-1$. Then one inner product on the set of real or complex sequences $\{f(x_0), f(x_1), \ldots, f(x_{N-1})\}$ is

$$\langle f, g \rangle = \sum_{j=0}^{N-1} f(x_j) \, \overline{g(x_j)}. \tag{2}$$

The celebrated Cauchy-Schwarz Inequality [1], that $|\langle f, g \rangle|^2 \leq \langle f, f \rangle \cdot \langle g, g \rangle$ holds for any pair of elements in any inner product space, may then be used to show that

$$\|f\| = \sqrt{\langle f, f \rangle} \tag{3}$$

is, indeed, a norm (specifically, it satisfies the *triangle inequality* $\|f + g\| \leq \|f\| + \|g\|$, just as does the uniform norm or any of the other norms). It is this class of norms which is employed below.

Suppose $g_1, g_2, \ldots, g_n$ are n linearly independent elements in $C[a, b]$ and let f be in $C[a, b]$. Consider the problem of determining scalars $c_1, c_2, \ldots, c_n$ such that

$$\left\| f - \sum_{j=1}^n c_j g_j \right\|^2 = \int_a^b \{f(x) - \sum_{j=1}^n c_j g_j(x)\}^2 w(x)dx$$

is minimized over all possible choices of the c_i. A successful approach is to seek a minimum of this expression in n variables by setting each of its n, first partial derivatives to zero. Since

$$\frac{\partial}{\partial c_i} \int_a^b [f(x) - \sum_{j=1}^n c_j g_j(x)]^2 w(x)dx = \int_a^b 2[f(x) - \sum_{j=1}^n c_j g_j(x)]g_i(x)w(x)dx,$$

equating this to zero yields that

$$\sum_{j=1}^{n} c_j \langle g_i, g_j \rangle = \langle f, g_i \rangle,$$

which is a single linear equation in unknowns $c_1, c_2, \ldots, c_n$. In summary then, it is necessary that

$$\begin{pmatrix} \langle g_1, g_1 \rangle & \langle g_1, g_2 \rangle & \cdots & \langle g_1, g_n \rangle \\ \langle g_2, g_1 \rangle & \langle g_2, g_2 \rangle & \cdots & \langle g_2, g_n \rangle \\ \vdots & \vdots & & \vdots \\ \langle g_n, g_1 \rangle & \langle g_n, g_2 \rangle & \cdots & \langle g_n, g_n \rangle \end{pmatrix} \begin{pmatrix} c_1 \\ c_2 \\ \vdots \\ c_n \end{pmatrix} = \begin{pmatrix} \langle f, g_1 \rangle \\ \langle f, g_2 \rangle \\ \vdots \\ \langle f, g_n \rangle \end{pmatrix}. \tag{4}$$

The solution of linear system (4) is the key to a wide class of *approximation/optimization* problems.

Theorem

Let $g_1, g_2, \ldots, g_n$ be n linearly independent elements in *any* inner product space, and let f be a member of the space. Then:

(a) The coefficient matrix in the corresponding linear system (4) is nonsingular, and

(b) $\|f - \sum_{j=1}^{n} c_j g_j\|$ is minimized if, and only if, $(c_1, c_2, \ldots, c_n)^T$ is the solution of (4).

The proof of this theorem can be given with elementary methods. First, suppose on the contrary that the column vector $(b_1, b_2, \ldots, b_n)^T$ is a nontrivial solution of the corresponding homogeneous system. Then

$$\sum_{i=1}^{n} b_i g_i$$

is not the zero element, since the g_i are linearly independent. But,

$$0 < \langle \sum_{i=1}^{n} b_i g_i, \sum_{j=1}^{n} b_j g_j \rangle = \sum_{i=1}^{n} b_i \left(\sum_{j=1}^{n} \langle g_i g_j \rangle b_j \right) = \sum_{i=1}^{n} b_i(0) = 0,$$

a contradiction. To establish (b) let $(c_1, c_2, \ldots, c_n)^T$ be the solution of (4), and let $(d_1, d_2, \ldots, d_n)^T$ denote any n-tuple. Introduce $\Delta c_i = d_i - c_i$ for $i = 1, 2, \ldots, n$. Then:

$$\|f - \sum_{i=1}^{n} d_i g_i\|^2 = \langle f - \sum_{i=1}^{n} c_i g_i - \sum_{i=1}^{n} \Delta c_i g_i, f - \sum_{j=1}^{n} c_j g_j - \sum_{j=1}^{n} \Delta c_j g_j \rangle$$

$$= \|f - \sum_{i=1}^{n} c_i g_i\|^2 + \|\sum_{i=1}^{n} \Delta c_i g_i\|^2 - 2\langle \sum_{i=1}^{n} \Delta c_i g_i, f - \sum_{j=1}^{n} c_j g_j \rangle.$$

This last expression is equal to $-2\sum_{i=1}^{n}\Delta c_i(\langle f, g_i\rangle - \sum_{j=1}^{n}\langle g_i, g_j,\rangle c_j)$ and hence is zero since the inner part is just a restatement of the i-th equation in (4). Consequently,

$$\|f - \sum_{i=1}^{n} d_i g_i\| \geq \|f - \sum_{i=1}^{n} c_i g_i\|,$$

with equality when, and only when, $\Delta c_i = 0$ for $i = 1, 2, \ldots, n$.

This is the key theorem in several varied areas of application, and it serves as a good focus for interplay among approximation, optimization, and computing. Simply, for any selected linearly independent set of basis elements g_i, and for any chosen (or, perhaps, sought) element f, the best (i.e., optimized) approximation to f from among the elements of the linear subspace generated by the g_i is $\sum_{i=1}^{n} c_i g_i$, where the c_i may be computed as the solution of the linear algebraic system (4).

There is a special case for (4) which has attracted attention of scientists for decades. Once the inner product $\langle\ ,\ \rangle$ is selected, if a set $\{g_1, g_2, \ldots, g_n\}$ can be found for which $\langle g_i, g_j\rangle = 0$ when $i \neq j$ (this is called *orthogonality*), then the coefficient matrix reduces to a simple diagonal matrix and (4) can be solved trivially, without a need to resort to a numerical linear system solver. In fact, if $\langle g_i g_j\rangle = 0$ when $i \neq j$, then the solution of (4) is

$$c_i = \frac{\langle f, g_i\rangle}{\langle g_i, g_i\rangle} \text{ for } i = 1, 2, 3, \ldots, n. \tag{5}$$

The c_i are called the *Fourier coefficients* of f, with respect to the orthogonal set $\{g_1, g_2, \ldots, g_n\}$, and their properties and a number of associated results may be found in Ref. *1*.

APPROXIMATION AND OPTIMIZATION, WITH COMPUTING

This basic theorem provides a wealth of material in connections among approximation, optimization, and computing. Three quite different examples are given here: the first employs polynomial approximants with an integral inner product and it brings out the fundamental problem of ill conditioning in the computation of solutions to linear systems. The second example touches on the classical (continuous) theory of Fourier series with the trigonometric approximants, and the third involves the discretization of Fourier techniques for current computational ideas, including the fast Fourier transform.

Example 1. In the space $C[0, 1]$, consider the inner product

$$\langle f, g\rangle = \int_0^1 f(x)g(x)dx,$$

and let $g_i(x) = x^{i-1}$ be the basic functions for $i = 1, 2, \ldots, n$. It is easy to check that $\langle g_i, g_j\rangle = 1/(i + j - 1)$, and hence the linear system (4) in this example becomes:

$$\begin{pmatrix} \frac{1}{1} & \frac{1}{2} & \frac{1}{3} & \cdots & \frac{1}{n} \\ \frac{1}{2} & \frac{1}{3} & \frac{1}{4} & \cdots & \frac{1}{n+1} \\ \vdots & \vdots & \vdots & & \vdots \\ \frac{1}{n} & \frac{1}{n+1} & \frac{1}{n+2} & \cdots & \frac{1}{2n-1} \end{pmatrix} \begin{pmatrix} c_1 \\ c_2 \\ \vdots \\ c_n \end{pmatrix} = \begin{pmatrix} \langle f, x^0\rangle \\ \langle f, x^1\rangle \\ \vdots \\ \langle f, x^{n-1}\rangle \end{pmatrix}. \tag{6}$$

Thus, $p_n(x) = c_1 + c_2 x + c_3 x^2 + \cdots + c_n x^{n-1}$ minimizes $\|f - p_n\|$. The Weierstrass theorem, incidentally, ensures that $\|f - p_n\|_\infty \to 0$ as $n \to \infty$ in the situation when $w(x)$ is a constant function.

The coefficient matrix in (6), called the *Hilbert matrix* of order n, is notoriously ill-conditioned. That is, numerical solution procedures for computing $(c_1, c_2, \ldots, c_n)$ are fraught with difficulties, and adverse effects of error accumulation increase as n increases. A clear discussion of conditioning may be found in Rice [2], and more detailed analyses appear elsewhere [3,4]. As an added complication in (6), the elements of the right-hand side might be available only through some numerical integration (approximation) procedure, thus introducing additional errors into an ill-conditioned system. Limited numerical success for a problem such as (6) may sometimes be found through use of software included with powerful packages such as IMSL.

The problem of conditioning may be avoided completely if a replacement set of g_i can be found which is orthogonal with respect to the inner product being used; with orthogonality, the system's solution would therefore be available immediately by (5). For polynomials, there is a vast amount of material concerning families which are orthogonal over different intervals of integration, and with different weights $w(x)$. The reader should refer to Volume 13 of this Encyclopedia for an overview of Special Functions, to Chihera [5] for a sound introduction to the field, or to the classic reference by Szego [6].

Example 2. In the space $C[-\pi, \pi]$, the set $\{1, \sin\ x, \cos\ x, \sin 2x, \cos 2x, \ldots\}$ provides an ideal choice for selection of the basis functions g_i, if the inner product being used is

$$\langle f, g \rangle = \int_{-\pi}^{\pi} f(x)g(x)dx \ .$$

For, if $m \neq n$, $\langle \sin\ mx, \sin\ nx \rangle = \langle \sin\ mx, \cos\ nx \rangle = \langle \cos\ mx, \cos\ nx \rangle = 0$, and this orthogonality again permits the immediate solution (5) of the linear system (4). In summary then, for f in $C[-\pi, \pi]$, and any selected positive integer n,

$$\int_{-\pi}^{\pi} \left[f(x) - \left\{ \frac{a_0}{2} + \sum_{k=1}^{n} a_k \cos\ kx + \sum_{k=1}^{n} b_k \sin\ kx \right\} \right]^2 dx$$

is minimized if, and only if,

$$a_k = \frac{1}{\pi} \int_{-\pi}^{\pi} f(x) \cos\ kx dx, k \geq 0$$

and

$$b_k = \frac{1}{\pi} \int_{-\pi}^{\pi} f(x) \sin\ kx dx, k \geq 1.$$

These last relations form a window to the massive area of Fourier theory which has developed from the classical analysis era in Approximation theory to the present. Analytic aspects are surveyed in this Encyclopedia (see Fourier Analysis in Volume 8), one of the many good introductory textbooks in the area is by Tolstov [7] and a classical reference which covers Fourier integrals as well is by Carslaw [8]. In this example, solution of the linear system (4) is trivial, but questions of convergence of the n-th Fourier sum (to its function) or questions of accurate/efficient calculation of the Fourier coefficients a_k and b_k are nontrivial.

Example 3. The third illustration included here has a different nature from the other two. Computer implementation of the classical Fourier techniques leads to the problems of discretization of nondiscrete structures; for example, an interval is often replaced by a finite set of points. The Fourier techniques, however, are sufficiently rich to warrant a great deal of separate development within the discrete settings themselves. The discrete (digitized) Fourier methods prove to be highly effective in several modern areas of research and application, including medical imaging, and the reader with an interest in such development is referred to "Radiology in Medicine" in Volume 12. Again, the Theorem from the last section plays a key role; the change from the other two examples being that the inner product structure employed now will be (2), for sequences, rather than one for functions continuous on an interval.

For a function $f(x)$ defined on $-\infty < x < \infty$, its Fourier transform is the function F defined by

$$F(u) = \int_{-\infty}^{\infty} f(x) e^{-2\pi i u x} dx .$$

The transform methods are particularly effective, for example, in solving certain types of ordinary and partial differential equations [9]. Suppose $f(x)$ vanishes outside of some interval, say outside of $0 \le x \le 1$. Then

$$F(u) = \int_0^1 f(x) e^{-2\pi i u x} dx \approx \sum_{j=0}^{N-1} f(j/N) e^{-2\pi i u j/N} \frac{1}{N} ,$$

the last approximation appearing as a Riemann sum for the integral, using as partition the points $x_j = j/N (j = 0, 1, \dots, N-1)$, for some selected positive integer N. With, now, the discrete inner product (2), it is straightforward to check that the functions $G_k(x) = \exp(2\pi i k x)$, for $k = 0, \pm 1, \pm 2, \dots, \pm(N-1)$, generate sequences which are orthogonal. That is,

$$\langle G_k, G_m \rangle = \sum_{j=0}^{N-1} \exp(2\pi i k \, j/N) \exp(-2\pi i m \, j/N) = 0$$

when $k \ne m$.

A usual subset of these orthogonal G_k which is employed is $\{G_0, G_1, G_2, \dots, G_{N-1}\}$. For this choice of basic functions g_i to accompany the inner product (2), minimization of the corresponding norm from among the linear combinations of the g_i can, again, be written explicitly from (5). The result is that the best linear combination

$$p(x) = \sum_{k=0}^{N-1} c_k G_k(x)$$

which minimizes

$$\left\| f - \sum_{k=0}^{N-1} c_k G_k \right\|^2 = \sum_{j=0}^{N-1} |f(j/N) - p(j/N)|^2$$

is the one with

$$c_k = \frac{\langle f, G_k \rangle}{\langle G_k, G_k \rangle}$$

That is, it is the one with

$$c_k = \frac{1}{N} \sum_{j=0}^{N-1} f(j/N) \exp(-2\pi i k j/N), \, k = 0, 1, 2, \ldots, N-1 . \tag{7}$$

It should be noted that each c_k in (7) may also be viewed as a Riemann sum approximation to $F(k)$, the continuous transform evaluated at k. The formula (7), which accepts sample data $\{f(0), f(1/N), f(2/N), \ldots, f((N-1)/N)\}$ and produces the sequence $\{c_0, c_1, c_2, \ldots, c_{N-1}\}$, represents the *discrete Fourier transform* of the input data. In terms of complex arithmetic (and disregarding the factor $1/N$), each c_k requires N multiplies and $N - 1$ adds for a total of $2N - 1$ operations; so, to compute all the $c_k (0 \leq k \leq N - 1)$ is an $O(N^2)$ process, using the form (7). Considerable attention has been given to more efficient computation of the c_k than $O(N^2)$ and a Fast Fourier Transform (FFT) algorithm is invariably employed now to compute the c_k using a process which is $O(N \log_2 N)$; CPU savings are dramatic, with processing speed-up factors of several hundreds possible.

The discrete Fourier transform (7) generalizes readily when the data are sampled from a function, f, of two, or more, variables, and it is the FFT computation of the c_k which leads to a wealth of practical digital imaging techniques. The recent book by Gonzalez and Wintz [10] provides an excellent state-of-the-art overview of this diverse field.

CONCLUDING REMARKS

The three examples given here illustrate some of the diversity of application possible within an area common to approximation, optimization, and computing. Each of these fields continues to evolve rapidly in concepts, techniques, and applications.

The settings for developments in Approximation frequently lie in a vector space with a norm, or at least a metric, structure. An excellent introductory overview, "Approximation Methods," appears in Volume 2 of this Encyclopedia. Fundamental references which provide a more extensive introduction to Approximation theory include Rice[11] and Cheney [12]. For the area of linear algebra and computations, Reference 13 provides a good introduction.

Areas of optimization are considerably varied in content, thrust, and techniques. Minimization using $\| \, \|_\infty$ on $C[a, b]$, for example, is different from that with an inner product norm—a good introduction to such Tchebicheff methods for *approximation /optimization* is given in Volume 4. In relation to Approximation theory, a variety of norms might also be employed for approximation of functions of one or more variables, the variables themselves possibly being of a more general nature [12]. There are, however, a number of other disciplines which involve some type of optimization, quite different in nature. Classical optimization, linear programming, nonlinear programming, or quadratic programming (see Volumes 5, 10, 11, or 12, respectively), for example, present other different mathematical or computational structures. Reference 14 is included for the reader who may wish to explore the basics of those areas further.

Computing is a burgeoning field, and scientific computing continues to evolve in a fundamental way with increasingly powerful hardware, diverse software, and emergence of parallel architectures. There are a number of excellent software libraries which are readily available commercially for mathematical and statistical routines, such as IMSL

[*15*] and NAG [*16*], and they provide a rich set of resources to call upon. For users wishing a deeper understanding of many modern scientific routines, numerous program listings and informative discussions, including extensive Fourier software, are collected in Ref. *17*.

REFERENCES

1. P. J. Davis, *Interpolation and Approximation*, Blaisdell, Waltham, MA, 1963.
2. J. R. Rice, *Matrix Computations and Mathematical Software*, McGraw-Hill, New York, 1981.
3. D. M. Young and R. T. Gregory, *A Survey of Numerical Mathematics*, Vols. I and II, Addison-Wesley, Reading, MA, 1973.
4. A. Ralston and H. S. Wilf, *Mathematical Methods for Digital Computers*, Vols. 1 and 2, Wiley, New York, 1960.
5. T. S. Chihara, *An Introduction to Orthogonal Polynomials*, Gordon and Breach, New York, 1978.
6. G. Szego, *Orthogonal Polynomials*, American Mathematical Society Colloquium Publications, Providence, RI, 1959.
7. G. P. Tolstov (Trans. R. A. Silverman), *Fourier Series*, Prentice-Hall, Englewood Cliffs, NJ, 1962.
8. H. S. Carslaw, *Introduction to the Theory of Fourier Series and Integrals*, 3rd. ed., Dover Publications, New York, 1930.
9. R. V. Churchill, *Operational Mathematics*, McGraw-Hill, New York, 1958.
10. R. C. Gonzalez and P. Wintz, *Digital Image Processing*, 2nd ed., Addison-Wesley, Reading MA, 1987.
11. J. R. Rice, *The Approximation of Functions*, Vols. 1 and 2, Addison-Wesley, Reading, MA, 1969.
12. E. W. Cheney, *Introduction to Approximation Theory*, McGraw-Hill, New York, 1966.
13. B. Noble, *Applied Linear Algebra*, Prentice-Hall, Englewood Cliffs, NJ, 1988.
14. G. S. G. Beveridge and R. S. Schechter, *Optimization: Theory and Practice*, McGraw-Hill, New York, 1970.
15. IMSL Inc., 2500 ParkWest Tower One, 2500 CityWest Boulevard, Houston, TX 77042.
16. NAG: Numerical Algorithms Group, Inc., 101 31st Street, Downers Grove, IL, 60515.
17. W. H. Press, B. P. Flannery, S. A. Teukolsky, and W. T. Vetterling, *Numerical Recipes: The Art of Scientific Computing*, Cambridge University Press, Cambridge, 1986.

ALAN G. LAW

THE BELLMAN CONTINUUM

INTRODUCTION

Richard Bellman, a most prolific and renowned mathematician of the United States, has made major contributions in pure mathematics and in numerous areas of applications: engineering, economics, medicine, energy, water resources, mathematical physics, operations research, management sciences, psychology, and sociology. This breadth of interests and this ability to contribute to so many fields at such a high level is rare indeed.

Throughout his years in science, Professor Bellman made a great many friends among his colleagues and students as well as among followers in the field of science. After he passed away, a group of his colleagues in the United States attempted to preserve his School. As one way to achieve this goal, they suggested holding an annual or biennial workshop: *the Bellman Continuum*. This workshop was envisioned as being interdisciplinary in nature, as a tribute to the achievement of Richard Bellman.

The first meeting was held at the University of Michigan, Ann Arbor, Michigan, in 1985 and the second was hosted by the Georgia Institute of Technology, Atlanta, Georgia, in 1986. The organizers thought that France might be a fine location for the third meeting, from both scientific and geographical points of view: Richard Bellman was very popular in Europe, especially in France. An additional strong motivation for this choice was the fact that the eighth International Conference Analysis and Optimization of Systems of INRIA was to be held in Antibes on June 8–10, 1988. It provided an ideal opportunity to take advantage of the presence of a large number of specialists from all parts of the world to organize a conference where a free exchange of ideas could take place.

In the first two meetings, the program had been dictated by the interdisciplinary nature of the workshop, with topics defined by the interest of the participants. The unifying theme incorporated scientific ideology and mathematical tools rather than specific fields of study. In the third meeting for scientific purposes to be explained later, the subject matter to be treated was limited, in view of the fact that facets of the areas defined below could change from one meeting to the next. The following topics, chosen in areas where research is very active and promising, in directions opened and explored by Richard Bellman, were selected:

Control of Uncertain Dynamical Systems
Control and Nonlinear Filtering of Quantum Mechanical Processes
Models and Control Policies for Biological Systems
Models and Control Policies in Economics and Social Systems

Since the Bellman Continuum is an homage to the memory of Richard Bellman, a recognition of his human and scientific influence throughout the world, and an attempt to strive forward in the directions he has shown, this brief introduction must be complemented at once by a few lines about some significant points of the scientific life of this mathematician.

RICHARD BELLMAN (1920–1984)

Vita

Richard Bellman was born on August 26, 1920 in New York City. He received the B. A. degree from Brooklyn College in 1941, the M. A. degree from the University of Wisconsin in 1943, and the Ph.D. degree from Princeton University in 1946, all in mathematics. He taught in the Departments of Mathematics of Princeton University and Stanford University from 1946 to 1952. From 1953 to 1965, he worked at RAND Corporation in Santa Monica, California. In 1965, he became Professor of Mathematics, Electrical Engineering, and Medicine at the University of Southern California. He held this position up to the end of his life.

His publications include over 600 research papers in technical journals, more than 30 books, and seven monographs. He has also been the Editor of two major journals, the *Journal of Mathematical Analysis and Applications* and the *Journal of Mathematical Biosciences,* and the Editor of two major book series, Mathematics in Science and Engineering and Modern Analytical and Computational Methods in Science and Mathematics, at Academic Press Inc. and American Elsevier Publishing Co., respectively.

His honors and awards include:

Norbert Wiener Prize, Applied Mathematics, American Mathematical Society and
    Society for Industrial and Applied Mathematics, 1970
Dickson Prize, Carnegie-Mellon University, 1970
Alza Distinguished Lectureship, Biomedical Engineering Society, 1972
Doctor of Science, University of Aberdeen, Scotland, 1973
Doctor of Law, University of Southern California, 1974
Doctor of Mathematics, University of Waterloo, Canada, 1975
Fellow, American Academy of Arts and Sciences, 1975
John Von Neumann Theory Prize, Institute of Management Sciences and Operations
    Research Society of America, 1976
Member, National Academy of Engineering, 1977
Member, National Academy of Science
Medal of Honor, Institute for Electrical and Electronic Engineers

An Outline of Bellman's Scientific Work

The scientific work of Professor Bellman started in stability theory, with the study of systems subject to small deterministic influences. This led him to the study of systems subject to large stochastic influence. These were first steps in modern control theory, an area in which he is one of the pioneers.

From the late 1940s on, Bellman became interested in the process of decision making. This led him to the theory of *dynamic programming,* which is probably his most popular work. Working alone, during a very short time period in the 1950s, he constructed one of the most powerful tools of modern control theory and applied it to the problems in numerous fields of engineering, mathematics, and science. His book, *Dynamic Programming,* published by Princeton University Press in 1957, "burst upon the scene" * with countless ideas for further research.

---

*Borrowed from C. T. Leondes, "An Appreciation of Professor Richard Bellman," *Journal of Optimization Theory and Applications, 32* (4),(December 1950). Special issue in homage to Professor Richard Bellman.

The work of Richard Bellman must be viewed in the light of the scientific revolution started by the advent of computers. Bellman was always very interested in obtaining answers through numerical techniques, and the great power of dynamic programming is due in large measure to its compatibility with the digital computer.

The crowning achievement of dynamic programming is *Bellman's principle of optimality* to which we shall return later. Not only does this principle provide a recursive type of calculation which is ideally suited for implementation on a digital computer, but it also lies at the confluence of great streams of the human thought which, from the origins of mechanics and, later, of thermodynamics, have led to the theories of relativity and quantum mechanics. Few physicists know that the early work of Louis de Broglie, in the infancy of quantum mechanics, is based on a principle of optimality: the "*principe de l'harmonie des phases*" akin to the one which Bellman was to formulate in its more general form thirty years later.

This aspect of Bellman's work illuminates general relativity as well. That Richard Bellman was aware of this is shown by a preliminary report of October 1977, *Differential Geometry and Dynamic Programming,* reviewed in a Notice of the American Mathematical Society (1978, No.2):

> An important characteristic of a surface is the shortest path between two points, a geodesic. This may be treated by the calculus of variations leading to well-known equations. It may also be treated by dynamic programming leading to new equations of initial value type.
>
> This is important in relativity theory since the path of a particle subject to no external forces is a geodesic.
>
> The methods of dynamic programming can also be used when there are constraints such as forbidden regions or bounds on the derivative.

Although dynamic programming is probably his best-known work, many other parts of his research have had a great influence as well, among them those on bang–bang control theory, quasilinearization techniques, the theory of differential equations, difference equations, differential–difference equations, inequalities, matrix theory, and application of computers to simulation.

On one hand, his work opens the way to new investigations of fundamental theoretical questions, and on the other hand, it provides efficient tools for solving actual applications. In addition, let us point out

> The wide range of his theoretical achievement
>
> The broad spectrum of his interest in the field of applications, which enabled him to develop research in border areas and in fields that cross departmental boundaries, such as economics, energy, water resources, ecological systems, mathematical physics, operations research, management sciences, psychology, and sociology.

Bellman's work in the medical field began in the 1960s, and it deserves special attention. The development of the computer made possible for the first time construction of realistic models in biology and medicine. Bellman's research had a strong influence on a rational approach to medical problems and the application of mathematics to medical problems had a strong influence on Bellman's research.

This brief outline of the achievements of Richard Bellman explains the interdisciplinary nature of the Bellman Continuum. it also explains the necessity of limiting the subject matter to be treated in each of its meetings.

A FEW MASTER LINES

Now, let us delve a bit further into the scientific outlines of Bellman's achievement. Since it covers so many fields, a survey would be far beyond the scope of this article. Instead of striving for an exhaustive view of the subject matter, we will focus our attention on a limited number of master lines of this work in the domain of optimal control. The questions the author of this article chooses to emphasize depend in a large measure on his concern. As this article is part of an Encyclopedia, the distortion thus introduced must be partly mended. It will be mended, we hope, by referring the reader to the notes section containing a documented bibliography. Accordingly, the interested reader will be given the possibility of going deeper into the matter. The author is indepted to Prof. Marzollo for his contribution to this Notes section.

As this article is directed primarily at a range of users, some of whom maybe relatively uninformed on the topic, we shall not provide technical details. the main questions will be introduced through simple examples, without any precise mathematical argument. Precise arguments can be found in the articles and books referred to in the notes, or in the books of Richard Bellman listed at the end.

Feedback Control

Richard Bellman noted that "If the language of science is mathematics, much of its prose and poetry is occupied by the theory of differential equations. Consequently, as new shapes loom on the scientific horizon, this theory is progressively enriched."*

The modern theory of optimal control is one of these new shapes which loomed on the horizon in the late 1950s and early 1960s. Among the early works in that area is bang–bang control theory, which we shall illustrate by an example. Bang–bang theory has been an important step in the theory of optimal control [1].

Let us consider a one-dimensional mechanical oscillator governed by the differential equation

$$\ddot{x}_1(t) + x_1(t) = 0 \tag{1}$$

The foregoing equation represents the law of motion of a mass point of unit mass m=1, subject to the opposing point force $S = -x_1$, along a straight line, where $x_1 = x_1(t)$ is the position of that point at the time t. Its velocity is $x_2 = \dot{x}_1(t)$. $x = (x_1, x_2)$ is the *state* of the system at the time t.

The fact that the system will oscillate indefinitely may not be desirable; we then attempt to modify or *control* its behavior. For instance, we may wish to reduce $x = (x_1, x_2)$ to zero, no matter what its state at the initial time t = 0.

One way to do this is to introduce a forcing function F, dependent in general upon time, into the system. The equation corresponding to (1) now has the form

---

*Borrowed from Richard Bellman, "New Directions of Research in the Theory of Differential Equations," in *Nonlinear Differential Equations and Nonlinear Mechanics,* (J. P. LaSalle and S. Lefschets, eds.), Academic Press, New York, 1963.

$$\ddot{x}_1(t) + x_1(t) = F(t) \tag{2}$$

The function F is to be chosen in some class of *admissible* functions of time and subject to various constraints, so as to force x(t) to follow the prescribed behavior as time evolves.

A fundamental idea of modern technology is that of *feedback control*. In place of considering the control function F to be merely a function of time, we regard it as a function of the current state of the system, that is, a function of x. When the control function is a function of time only, we say that the system is *open-loop*, whereas when the control function is a function of the current state, we say that the system is *closed-loop*.

Here, for instance, if we let $F(t) = -\dot{x}_1(t)$ Eq.(2) becomes

$$\ddot{x}_1(t) + \dot{x}_1(t) + x_1(t) = 0 \tag{3}$$

which is the equation of a damped oscillator.

Indeed, the controlled system is damped no matter what its initial state is, but it tends asymptotically to rest, i.e., as $t \to \infty$. We may wish to reduce x to zero in finite time and, better, *in the minimum time* [2].

One must take account of the fact that, for practical reasons, the control function (a force in our example) cannot be given arbitrarily large values. The function F is subject to *constraints* such as

$$| F(t) | \leq F_{max} , t \geq 0, \tag{4}$$

where F_{max} is a given constant.

In other words, the constraint set is compact. The study of such cases was an important novelty in the late 1950s [3].

An admissible control, subject to constraint [4], which transfers the state x (t) from a given initial state $x^0 = x(0)$ to zero in the minimum time, if it exists, is called an *optimal control* for the time optimal control problem stated above.

In that example, an optimal control can be shown to exist and to be unique: it is a piecewise constant function of the time with values in the set $\{- F_{max}, + F_{max}\}$. Such a control is called a *bang-bang control*.

Note that Eq.(2) can also be written as a system of two first-order equations, namely

$$\dot{x}_1(t) = x_2(t)$$

$$\dot{x}_2(t) = -x_1(t) + F(t) \tag{5}$$

The problem described above is one of the simplest ones in the theory of optimal control. It belongs to a large class of problems in which there are simple and natural restrictions upon the type of control which can be exerted upon a system.

More generally, the equations which govern the behavior of such systems are

$$\dot{x} = Ax + u, \qquad x(0) = c \tag{6}$$

where $x = (x_1, \ldots x_n) \in R^n$, $u = (u_1, \ldots u_m) \in R^m$, A is a constant matrix, and $u = u(t)$ or $u(x)$ (depending upon which interpretation is most convenient at the moment) is to be chosen subject to constraints such as

$$u_k^{min} \leq u_k(t) \leq u_k^{max} , k = 1, 2, \ldots n , t \geq 0 , \tag{7}$$

where u_k^{min} and u_k^{max} are given constants.

An extension of the foregoing problem is the one of minimizing a functional such as

$$J = \int_0^T [(x(t), Bx(t)) + (u(t), C\,u(t))]\, dt, \tag{8}$$

over all admissible control functions, where x and u are related by means of (6), with constraints such as (7).

A further extension is the one of minimizing a general functional such as

$$J = \int_0^T g(x(t),\, u(t))\, dt, \tag{9}$$

where x and u are related by means of differential equations

$$\dot{x} = f(x,\, u), \qquad x(0) = c, \tag{10}$$

with constraints upon x and u.

Many other extensions have been studied since the 1960s, among which those related to *impulsive control* and those related to *multicriteria decision making* [4] and *dynamic games* which have important applications, in particular in engineering, in the theory of management and in economics.

The example we have started with corresponds to one of the links in the scientific evolution which led, after World War II, to the theory of dynamic optimization starting from problems of minimum time. It shows how, initiated by technical motivations, a general theory can spring up and become an important part of the scientific culture of its time. On the one hand, the field of applications of the theory has rapidly spread; on the other hand, this spreading has been at the origin of an incredibly large number of abstract problems most interesting for mathematicians.

At this point, a few remarks may be in order. It is an historical fact that the theory of optimization was first motivated by operational research problems of military type [5]. However, when part of the theory was oriented toward concerns of the geometrical type, in the mid 1960s, it became clear that some of its essential notions were already at hand in the works of Carathéodory, Bouligand, Marchaud, and Zaremba, in the 1930s [6]. More obviously, the theory of optimization has connections with the calculus of variations. A number of works have been devoted to investigating possible equivalences between the two approaches. Fermat's problem of minimum time is older still. In this perspective, the modern theory of optimization loses its isolation and enters a long lineage of former mathematical works.

Bellman's Principle of Optimality and Dynamic Programming [7]

The great power and lasting value of dynamic programming is due in large measure to its compatibility with the digital computer. We shall limit the description of this method to certain finite multistage decision process problems, and, rather than speak abstractly of the particular type of process with which we are concerned, we present a simple illustrative example.

Consider the square network shown in Figure 1. We consider it as part of an infinite *network* and will refer to it as such in what follows. We use the term *vertices* for the points of intersection of the straight lines shown in the figure, and we label them by letters; we designate the line segments shown connecting certain vertices as *arcs*. There is associated with each vertex a pair of coordinates—say x_1, x_2—with respect to the reference system of figure 1.

A *state* of the decision process is characterized by x_1, x_2 and by the stage k of the process $k \in \{0, 1, \dots K\}$.

It is convenient to think of the state as a point at

$$x = (x_1, x_2, x_3) \in R^3$$

where $x_3 \in \{0, 1, \dots K\}$.

For $x = x^k = (x_1, x_2, k)$ we say that the state is at the *k*-th stage.

A *path* is an ordered set of states.

The state changes, that is, x may take on different values in R^3, as x_3 varies from 0 to K. The evolution of the state is governed by a set of difference equations. Here we shall suppose that these equations are

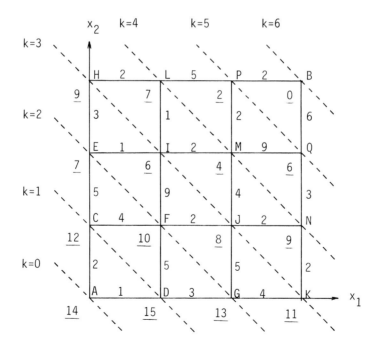

FIGURE 1.

$$x_1(k + 1) - x_1(k) = u_1(k)$$

$$x_2(k + 1) - x_2(k) = u_2(k)$$

$$x_3(k + 1) - x_3(k) = 1$$

where the *decision* $u(k) = (u_1(k), u_2(k))$ at the stage k is required to belong to the *admissible set of decisions* $\{(0, 1), (1, 0)\}$.

For instance, if $x_1^k = x_1(k)$, $x_2^k = x_2(k)$ are the coordinates of vertex F in Figure 1, the choice $u(k) = (0, 1)$ leads to vertex I with coordinates $x_1^{k+1} = x_1^k$, $x_2^{k+1} = x_2^k + 1$ at the stage k + 1. Likewise, the choice $u(k) = (1,0)$ leads to J at the stage k + 1.

A two-stage path of this kind induced by one of the decisions $(0, 1)$ or $(1, 0)$ through Eqs. (11) will be called a *move connecting* the two vertices $x(k)$ and $x(k+1)$.

In our example, we are interested in a set of *admissible paths*, that is, those paths generated by a sequence of decisions, emanating from the initial state $(A, k = 0)$, and ending at the terminal state $(B, k = K = 6)$. We shall say that such paths *connect* A and B.

Shown on the figure is a number associated with each arc, that is, associated with each move of the state corresponding to one of the decisions $(0, 1)$ or $(1, 0)$, which we shall call the *value* of the move. The value of a path is taken to be the sum of the values of its component moves.

Having described a sequential choice procedure, an example of optimal decision process problem is the following:

How shall we generate a sequence of decisions which produces an admissible path with minimum value?

This problem can be readily solved by using *Bellman's Principle of Optimality*, which asserts:

> An optimal sequence of decisions in a multistage decision process problem has the property that whatever the initial stage, state, and decision are, the remaining decisions must constitute an optimal sequence of decisions for the remaining problem, with the stage and state resulting from the first decision considered as initial conditions.[*]

The mathematical description of the reasoning is as follows:

We begin by introducing an auxiliary function V^* of the integer variables x_1, x_2. The function V^* is defined at the vertices (x_1, x_2) of the network as follows:

If there exists no path connecting the vertex (x_1, x_2) and the terminal vertex B, we let

$$V^* (x_1, x_2) = \infty.$$

Otherwise, we let

$$V^* (x_1, x_2) = \text{the value of a minimum value path}$$
$$\text{connecting the vertex } (x_1, x_2) \text{ and B.}$$

There may exist more than one such minimum-value path, however this value is unique because it is a minimum.

---

[*]R. Bellman and S. Dreyfus, *Applied Dynamic Programming*, Princeton University Press, Princeton, 1962.

Now, let $C_1(x_1, x_2)$ denote the value of the move connecting the vertices (x_1, x_2) and $(x_1 + 1, x_2)$ and let $C_2(x_1, x_2)$ denote the value of the move connecting the vertices (x_1, x_2) and $(x_1, x_2 + 1)$. These values correspond to the decisions $(1, 0)$ and $(0, 1)$, respectively.

Then, for any vertex (x_1, x_2) different from B, which can be connected with B by a path, the principle of optimality asserts the relation

$$V^*(x_1, x_2) = \min \begin{bmatrix} C_1(x_1, x_2) + V^*(x_1 + 1, x_2) \\ C_2(x_1, x_2) + V^*(x_1, x_2 + 1) \end{bmatrix}, \tag{12}$$

where $\min \begin{bmatrix} \alpha \\ \beta \end{bmatrix}$ denotes the smaller of the two real numbers α and β.

Equation (12) is a recurrence which allows the computation of $V^*(x_1, x_2)$ in an iterative fashion at any vertex (x_1, x_2) of the network where this value is finite, provided that the value of V^* at the end point B is known.

We take the value of V^* to be zero at the endpoint, that is

$$V^*(3, 3) = 0 \tag{13}$$

This choice requires a few arguments which we skip.

The relation (12) together with the boundary condition (13) is the *dynamic programming relation* for the problem stated above. The value of the function V^*, computed iteratively at each vertex of the network where it is finite, is shown on Figure 1.

Letting

$$L(x, u) = \begin{cases} C_1(x) & \text{for} \quad u = (1, 0) \\ C_2(x) & \text{for} \quad u = (0, 1) \end{cases}$$

at any vertex x of the network where V^* is finite, relation (12) can be easily seen to be equivalent to

$$\min_u [\, L(x, u) + V^*(x + u) - V^*(x)] = L(x, u^*) + V^*(x + u^*) - V^*(x) = 0 \tag{12'}$$

where u^* denotes an optimal decision at vertex x.

Note that, when the function V^* is known, an optimal path can be easily obtained by making use of the right-hand equality in (12').

The essence of dynamic programming is the embedding of the stated problem in a more general family of problems, each with a different initial stage and state. In most of the applications, the time of computation which dynamic programming requires increases according to a polynomial law, with the number n of stages, for large n, there is an enormous advantage with respect to the search for a minimum based on a listing of all the possible paths. This is what makes this method so powerful for applications [8].

Optimal Value Function

The function V^* introduced above plays a very important part in the theory of optimal control. It is called *optimal value function* or *Bellman's function*. As concerns practical applications, we have seen that it provides locally all the information needed for taking an optimal decision. In other words, if we know the current state of the system and the function V*, at least locally, we have all the data for taking an optimal decision. This feature extends the power of this theory to the level of concepts. It is correlated with geometric notions [9], which are well suited for a discussion of optimal control.

Since we have considered multistage processes first, we must now say a few words about dynamic programming in the case of systems whose state changes in a continuous manner over time [10]. Again, we shall rely on a simple example without rigorous mathematical arguments. This example is in the domain of mechanics.

Let the physical system under consideration be a particle (mass point), moving along a trajectory

$$x(t) = (x_1(t), x_2(t), x_3(t))$$

in the usual space, on some interval of time $[t_0, t_1]$. Knowing that the motion of that particle, when a number of classical assumptions are satisfied, obeys the Hamilton least action principle, provided that the interval of time $[t_0, t_1]$ is sufficiently small, one can easily put the basic equations on nonrelativistic as well as relativistic classical analytical mechanics of a particle in the form of a control problem.

In this control problem, the motion of the particle is governed by

$$\dot{x} = u, \qquad u = (u_1, u_2, u_3), \tag{14}$$

and a fictitious decisionmaker controls its evolution through his choice of a feedback control function u in an admissible set, so as to minimize the *cost* J

$$J = \int_{t_0}^{t_1} L(x(t), u(x(t), t), t)dt \tag{15}$$

subject to the end conditions

$$x(t_0) = x^0, \qquad x(t_1) = x^1$$

$L = L(x, u, t)$ is the *Lagrangian*. In one of the simplest nonrelativistic cases

$$L(x, u, t) = \frac{1}{2} mu^2 - U(x, t) \tag{16}$$

where m is the mass of the particle and U is a given potential function.

By an extension of the arguments of the previous section, the global condition of minimum which the cost must satisfy is replaced by a local condition. It is introduced through the auxiliary function V*: the optimal value function for the present problem. Provided that a number of mathematical assumptions are satisfied, this local condition is written as

$$\min_{u} \left[L(x, u, t) - (\partial V^* / \partial t) - \sum_{\alpha=1}^{3} (\partial V^* / \partial x_\alpha) u_\alpha \right] =$$

$$= L(x, u^*, t) - (\partial V^* / \partial t) - \sum_{\alpha=1}^{3} (\partial V^* / \partial x_\alpha) u_\alpha^* = 0 \tag{17}$$

This is the equation of *dynamic programming* for our problem. In particular, when L(x, u, t) is given by (16), we deduce from (17) that

$$u^*_\alpha = (1/m)\,(\partial V^* / \partial x_\alpha), \qquad \alpha = 1, 2, 3. \tag{18}$$

By substituting in (17) we obtain

$$(\partial V^* / \partial t) + \sum_{\alpha=1}^{3} (1/2\,m)\,(\partial V^* / \partial x_\alpha)^2 + U = 0 \tag{19}$$

which is the *equation of Hamilton–Jacobi* in classical nonrelativistic mechanics. This result is a general one if we put apart the case of nonholonomic constraints [*11*]: *In the dynamics of a mass-point [12,13], Bellman's function V* is identical with the function of Hamilton-Jacobi, usually denoted by S.*

At this point, a few comments are in order.

Einstein has emphasized the importance of geometry in mechanics. Louis de Broglie has strived to put quantum mechanics in the framework of optics [*14*] paying much attention to the geometrical optics approximation. Dynamic programming appears to be tightly related to geometry in such a way that it is not surprising that it fits so well with approaches to mechanics and optics[*15*]. It is especially useful in general relativity. It also fits pretty well with an alternative stochastic approach to quantum mechanics [*16*] which has no connections with the Schrödinger's program.

Since the 1960s it has become clear that a problem of optimal control can be transformed into a problem of differential geometry, with a method directly inspired by Huygens principle of geometrical optics. Prior work in calculus of variations which might be considered most closely related to that approach, and to dynamic programming, is probably that of Carathéodory (1935).

Let us return to our simple example.

(a) If we follow the particle along its path x = x(t) in R³, we see that the surface $F(t)$, defined by

$$F(t) = \{y : V^*(y, t) = V^*(x(t), t)\}$$

in R³, at time t, looks like a wave front which moves as time evolves and, at all times, the trajectory of the particle is normal to $F(t)$ (Fig. 2).

(b)   This picture needs be complemented by the space–time representation, in which we define the set of isocost surfaces $\{S(C)\}$ in R⁴:

$$S(C) = \{(x, t) : V^*(x, t) = C\},$$

where C is an arbitrary constant. For any given times t', t'', with $t' < t''$, the isocost surface $S(C')$ through point $(x(t''), t'')$ can be deduced from the isocost surface $S(C')$ through point $(x(t'), t')$ by a construction similar to one of Huygens in geometrical optics (Fig. 3). Thus, we recognize connections between our problem of optimal control and geometrical optics.

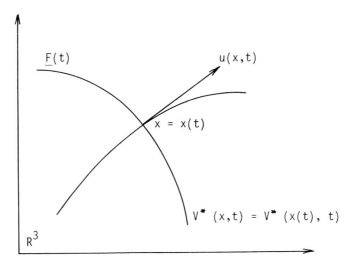

FIGURE 2.   Wave front *F*(t) and trajectory.

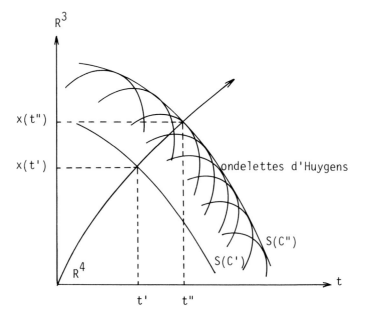

FIGURE 3.   Isocost surfaces. Construction of Huygens.

Reachable Set and Controllability: An Example in Relativistic Dynamics of a Mass Point

Now, let us consider the motion of a particle governed by the state Eq. (14), and replace in the cost integral (15) the previous Lagrangian by the new one given by

$$L(x, u, t) = -m_0 c^2 \sqrt{1 - u^2/c^2} \quad . \tag{20}$$

m_0 is the rest-mass of the particle and c is the velocity of light in the vacuum. Expression (20) comes from physical arguments in relativity (see e. g. Louis de Broglie [*17*]).

By using the relativistic Lagrangian given by (20) in the dynamic programming relation (17) we obtain, instead of (18), the new formulas

$$\partial V^* / \partial x_\alpha = \frac{m_0 \, u_\alpha}{\sqrt{1 - (u^2/c^2)}} \qquad \alpha = 1, 2, 3, \tag{21}$$

$$\partial V^* / \partial t = \frac{m_0 \, c^2}{\sqrt{1 - (u^2/c^2)}} \qquad , \text{ with } u = u^* \tag{22}$$

This is so because the minimum required by dynamic programming is then obtained at an interior point of the constraint set. (21) and (22) are the expressions for the components of the *momentum*, and for the *energy*, respectively, of the particle.

A detailed discussion of this problem would go beyond the scope of this article. However, we will sketch some of its features.

In (special) relativity, the speed of a mass-point cannot exceed c, so that our constraint set is defined by

$$\| u \| \le c \tag{23}$$

where $\| \, . \, \|$ denotes the Euclidian norm of a vector in R^3.

Since we are dealing not with an actual physical particle but with a *model* of it, we shall prefer the name *mass-point* to the one of particle. Since we need not care too much about m_0 which is a constant, for simplicity we shall consider a mass-point to be a point in R^4 which, itself, is a model of the physical space-time. Thus, time t is one of the coordinates of a mass-point in a rectangular coordinate system of R^4.

Due to the constraint (23), a mass-point emanating from (x^0, t_0), termed the *source*, cannot reach every point of R^4. The *reachable set* is shown in Figure 4. Letting $x^0 = 0$, $t_0 = 0$, this reachable set is the closed cone

$$g(x, t) = -ct + \sqrt{x_1^2 + x_2^2 + x_3^2} \le 0 \quad .$$

Its boundary $g(x, t) = 0$ is sometimes called *cone of light*.

In our example, Bellman's function V^* can be shown to be given by

$$V^*(x, t) = -m_0 c \sqrt{c^2 t^2 - (x_1^2 + x_2^2 + x_3^2)} \quad . \tag{24}$$

It vanishes on the cone of light.

A few isocost surfaces of the family $\{S(C)\}$, defined in the preceding paragraph are shown on Figure 4. Let us note without further comments that Figure 4 also illustrates a very simplified version of the cosmological phenomenon called "Big-Bang," in which each member of the isocost surfaces family represents a set of events which have the same "age" relative to the creation of the universe.

The problem described above belongs to a large class of problems associated with various state equations, various type of sources, various Lagrangians, and various constraints. As in our special case, the general theory has two purposes:

First, find the reachable set
Second, for any given point in the reachable set, find an optimal path emanating from
    the source and ending at that point

Problems of the first type belong to the class of *controllability problems*. For such problems, special attention is paid to trajectories which partly or entirely belong to the boundary of the reachable set.

Those of the second type are *optimal control problems* stricto sensu.

From the proof of the dynamic programming relation (17), it turns out that it is valid at interior points (x, t) of the reachable set only. At the boundary points of the reachable set, not belonging to the source, another relation holds, namely

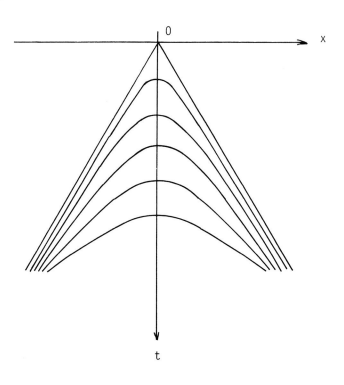

FIGURE 4.

$$\min_u \; [- (\partial g / \partial t) - \sum_{\alpha=1}^{3} (\partial g / \partial x\alpha) \, u\alpha] = \tag{25}$$

$$- (\partial g / \partial t) - \sum_{\alpha=1}^{3} (\partial g / \partial x\alpha) \, u^*_\alpha = 0$$

provided that proper mathematical assumptions are satisfied [*18*]. g is the function which is used in the representation of the boundary g(x, t) = 0 of the reachable set.

Since, in our example the constraint set is compact, the minimum in (25) need not be obtained by canceling the partial derivatives of the bracket, with respect to the uα.

Here as the minimum occurs at a boundary point of the constraint set one deduces from (25)

$$u^* = (c \; \mathrm{grad} \; g) / (\| \; \mathrm{grad} \; g \; \|). \tag{26}$$

By substituting in (25) one obtains

$$\frac{1}{c^2} (\partial g / \partial t)^2 - \| \; \mathrm{grad} \; g \; \|^2 = 0 \;, \tag{27}$$

which is the *equation of the eikonale* of geometrical optics.

A thorough study of problems of the class to which our example belongs, with more general assumptions, provides an interesting insight in geometrical optics, in the domain of general relativity [*15*].

NOTES

The reference numbers of these notes correspond to the ones of the Master Lines section.

1. For the first discussion of the "bang-bang" control, see I Flügge-Lotz *Discontinuous Automatic Control*, Princeton University Press, Princeton, 1953. More generally, for a good treatise on optimal control theory [including several aspects other than dynamic programming, such as the *Maximum Theorem* of Pontryagin (1956)], see E. B. Lee, and L. Marcus, *Foundations of Optimal Control Theory*, Wiley, New York, 1967.

2. For example, the open-loop minimal time problem with F(t) in an open interval is a particular case of the Meyer problem in the calculus of variations.

3. It seems appropriate to recall the interesting but relatively unknown attempts to extend the necessary conditions of the classical calculus of variations to the case of closed constraint sets. See the following papers, all of them by researchers of the Chicago school of calculus of variations, initiated by G. M. Bliss: F. A. Valentine, "The Problem of Lagrange with Differential Inequalities and Added Side Conditions," in *Contributions to the Calculus of Variations* 1933-1937, University of Chicago Press, Chicago, 1937; E. Mc Shane, "On Multipliers of Lagrange Problems," *Ann. J. Math.*, *61*, 809-819, (1939); M. R. Hestenes, *A General Problem in the Calculus of Variations with Applications to Paths of Least Time*, the RAND Corporation, R. M. -100, 1949 (this last paper contains a reformulation of the Bolza problem in calculus of variations in order to adapt it to an optimal control problem). The practical importance of optimal control theory with closed constraint sets was recognized by the aerospace industry (e. g., in the problem of letting a rocket reach its target in minimal time, with constraints on the rocket's acceleration). The theory was largely developed in the 1960s, as well as related numerical aspects.

4. For several aspects of this theory, see e.g., *Multicriteria Decision Making* (G. Leitmann, A. Marzollo, eds.), Springer, New York 1975.

5. We refer here, as everywhere in this article, to dynamic optimization. However, the same remark applies to static optimization, whose development was first motivated by operational research problems of military type, then economic and management problems. We recall the simplex method for solving linear programming problems, which was independently developed by Kantarovich in the Soviet Union and by G. Dantzig in the United States in the 1940s, and the Kuhn-Tucker multipliers method for nonlinear programming problems, which generalized, in 1951, the classical Lagrange method to problems with inequality constraints.

6. See Note 9.

7. R. E. Bellman introduces this denomination in his fundamental work *Dynamic Programming* (Princeton University Press, 1957), with reference to the decisions to be taken for steering optimally the state of a system to a target (hence the name "programming"); the time variable plays a role in the process (hence the adjective "dynamic"). Dynamic programming is distinct from "mathematical programming" (linear or nonlinear programming), which refers to methods for finding minima or maxima of functions in sets defined by given constraints, in case time does not play a role (hence the denomination "static programming").

8. In this example, for a square network with $(m + 1)$ vertices on each side ($n = 2\,m$ stages) the number of operations is the following:

> At each vertex where there is a choice between two decisions: (i.e., at each one of the m^2 vertices of a square network with m vertices on each side), 2 additions and 1 comparison.
> At each other vertex (i.e., at each one of 2m vertices): 1 addition.

Therefore, $2\,m^2 + 2\,m = 2\,(\frac{n}{2})^2 + n$ additions and $m^2 = (\frac{n}{2})^2$ comparisons. In our particular case, for $n = 6$, there are 24 additions to be executed. For large n, there is an enormous advantage with respect to the naïve method which consists in comparing the costs of all admissible paths between A and B. Taking into account the constraints on the controls, the number of such paths are obviously

$$\binom{n}{\frac{n}{2}} = \frac{n!}{\left(\frac{n}{2}\right)! \left(\frac{n}{2}\right)!}$$

and therefore the number of additions is

$$\frac{(n-1)!}{\left(\frac{n}{2}\right)! \left(\frac{n}{2}\right)!}$$

For $n = 20$, the simple enumeration method asks for more than 10^6 additions, whereas dynamic programming asks for 220. The difference in the number of comparisons is still larger.

9. The fundamental equation of dynamic programming may be considered as an extension of the "fundamental equations of the calculus of variations" by Carathéodory (see

C. Carathéodory, *Variations rechnung und partielle Differential-gleichnungen erster Ordnung*, Teubner, Leipzig, 1935, p. 208). From these equations one may deduce Hamilton-Jacobi's equation and most results of the classical calculus of variations. Historically, the inverse path was followed in classical calculus of variations and in mechanics, and it is also the one of most modern mechanics text: from the Hamilton principle, the Euler-Lagrange equations are derived, and from the latter, Hamilton's equations, and finally the Hamilton-Jacobi partial differential equations. For the relationship between the calculus of variations and dynamic programming (see e.g., S. E. Dreyfus, *Dynamic Programming and the Calculus of Variations*, Academic Press, New York, 1965).

For a theory of dynamic optimization based on geometrical concepts and related to dynamic programming, see A. Blaquière, G. Leitmann, "On the Theory of Optimal Process" in *Topics in Optimization* (G. Leitmann, ed.), Academic Press, New York, 1967. Some mathematical techniques on which this type of theory is based were developed in the 1930s. See A. Marchaud, "Sur les champs de demi-cones et equations différentielles du premier ordre," *Bull. Soc. Math. France, 62*, 1–13 (1934); S. K. Zaremba, "Sur les èquations au paratingent," *Bull. Sci. Math., 60*(2), 139–160 (1936).

10.   For a more in-depth analysis, see the already mentioned works, and also e.g., R. E. Bellman, *Introduction to the Mathematical Theory of Control Processes*, Vol. 1 (1967), Vol. 2 (1972), Academic Press, New York; D. H. Jacobsen, and D. A. Mayne, *Differential Dynamic Programming*, Elsevier Publishing Company, New York, 1970; R. E. Larson, and J. L. Casti, *Principles of Dynamic Programming*, Marcel Dekker, New York, 1978.

11.   See e.g., A. Blaquière and A. Marzollo, "Some Relations Between Optimal Control Theory and Classical Mechanics," in *Dynamical Systems and Microphysics, Geometry and Mechanics* (A. Avez, A. Blaquière, and A. Marzollo, eds.), Academic Press, New York, 1982.

12.   If the trajectory is not on the boundary of the reachable set (see following paragraph).

13.   The reader may note a fundamental difference between dynamic programming and the classical calculus of variations. In the problem of minimizing the cost integral (15) (with $\dot{x} = u$, $u = u(t)$) for given end conditions, following Euler, Lagrange, Weierstrass, all the methods of the calculus of variations have faced this problem by trying to find a $u^*(.)$ such that all "near" functions obtained by adding "small variations" to $u^*(.)$ give a noninferior value to the cost integral. Even when the problem consists in finding the minimal value of the cost, the interest is centered on the properties characterizing $u^*(.)$, and independent of the variations (stationarity conditions of Euler-Lagrange, necessary minimality conditions of Legendre for "weak" variations, necessary minimality conditions of Weierstrass for "strong" variations). This is natural since, with fixed-end conditions, the knowledge of $u^*(.)$ implies that of the optimal value of the cost, and not vice-versa.

On the contrary, in dynamic programming, the main interest is on the determination of the optimal value function V^*. In other words, instead of directly facing a given particular optimization problem, with fixed endpoints, in dynamic programming a whole family of optimization problems is considered. This family corresponds

i.   To every possible initial point and fixed terminal point; or
ii.   To every possible terminal point and fixed initial point.

(i) is illustrated by the discrete example given in this paper; and (ii) is illustrated by the continuous example.

In the discrete example, there is an alternative method of solution in which the specific problem is embedded in a family of problems with fixed initial vertex and various terminal vertices (see, e.g., S. E. Dreyfus, *Dynamic Programming and the Calculus of Variations*, Academic Press, New York, 1965).

Likewise, in the continuous example, there is an alternative method of solutions in which the given problem is embedded in a family of problems with fixed terminal point and various initial points. Then (17) is to be replaced by

$$\min_{u} \ [\ L(x, u, t) - (\partial V^* / \partial t) + \sum_{\alpha=1}^{3} (\partial V^* / \partial x\alpha) \, u\alpha] =$$

$$= L(x, u^*, t) - (\partial V^* / \partial t) + \sum_{\alpha=1}^{3} (\partial V^* / \partial x\alpha) \, u^*_{\alpha} = 0 \qquad (17')$$

Knowing the solution for the whole family of above mentioned problems, that is, knowing V*, one is able to solve every particular problem, including, of course, the given problem which corresponds to the given end points.

14.   See L. de Broglie, Thèse de Doctorat, Masson, 1924, reprinted in 1963, and e.g., "Thermodynamique relativiste et mécanique ondulatoire," *Ann. Inst. H. Poincaré,IX* (2), 103 (1968).

15.   See, e.g., A. Blaquière, "Optimality with Feedback Control in General Relativity," and A. Blaquière and M. Pauchard, "Reachability with Feedback Control in General Relativity," in *Dynamical Systems and Microphysics, Control Theory and Mechanics* (A. Blaquière and G. Leitmann, eds.), Academic Press, New York, 1984.

16.   See, e.g., K. Kime and A. Blaquiere, "From Two Stochastic Optimal Control Problems to the Schrödinger Equation," in Lecture Notes in Control Information Sciences 121, Modeling and Control of Systems in Engineering Quantum Mechanics, Economics, and Biosciences. (A. Blaquiere, ed.), Springer-Verlag, Berlin-Heidelberg, 1989.

17.   See L. de Broglie, *Une tentative d'interprètation causale et non-linéaire de la mècanique ondulatoire,* Gauthier-Villars, Paris 1956.

18.   The proof may be easily written by adapting to this case the one given in Chapter 6 of A. Blaquière, F. Gérard, and G. Leitmann, *Quantitative and Qualitative Games*, Academic Press, New York, 1969. In that reference, there is more than one "pilot" and more than one cost integral (game theory).

MEETINGS OF THE BELLMAN CONTINUUM

First Bellman Continuum

This first meeting was a three-day workshop organized by Professor Semyon Meerkov, of the University of Michigan, and Mrs. Nina Bellman, the widow of Richard Bellman, Santa Monica, California. It was held at the University of Michigan, Ann Arbor, on May 29–31, 1985.

The name Bellman Continuum was chosen by Prof. Meerkov and Mrs. Bellman, as an homage to the memory of Richard Bellman and to stress the expected continuity between his work and the scientific areas to be studied and developed in the successive meetings.

Attendance was by invitation only. About 20 scientists from the United States, France, Japan, and New Zealand participated in this meeting and gave presentations at the following sessions:

Mathematics
Systems and Computers
Medicine and Biology
Mathematics and Systems

Abstracts were distributed to all participants at the meeting.

Mrs. Bellman informed the participants concerning Richard Bellman's papers, books, unfinished manuscripts, and journals, stored at her home in Santa Monica, and extended a welcome to anyone interested in working with these papers to come and peruse them.

Second Bellman Continuum

The second meeting was a three-day workshop chaired by Dr. Augustine O. Esogbue of the School of Industrial and Systems Engineering at Georgia Institute of Technology Atlanta, Georgia.

It was held at the Georgia Institute of Technology, Atlanta, on June 23–25, 1986, in conjunction with a workshop on Dynamic Programming and Water Resources (June 25–27, 1986).

Further information can be obtained from the Chairman Dr. Augustine E. Esogbue.

Third Bellman Continuum

The first two meetings of the Bellman Continuum corresponded to a formative stage. They attracted scientific friends of Richard Bellman and a few scientists whose work has connections with his school.

We must praise both Prof. Semyon Meerkov and Mrs. Nina Bellman for their leadership role.

Also, we must praise the group of Professors of the United States:

George, Adomian, University of Georgia
Augustine Esogbue, Georgia Institute of Technology
Stanley Lee, Kansas State University
George Leitmann, University of California-Berkeley
Lotfi Zadeh, University of California-Berkeley

who participated in the organization of these first meetings, in particular Prof. Esogbue, who chaired the second conference.

This preliminary experience and Richard Bellman's popularity in Europe led them to expect that the third Bellman Continuum held in France might attract "new blood."

The Third Bellman Continuum organized by the Institut National de Recherche en Informatique et en Automatique (INRIA) and the University of Paris 7, was held on June 13–14, 1988, at the INRIA Research Center of Sophia-Antipolis, on the French Riviera, 6 miles Northwest of Antibes. It followed immediately the INRIA Eighth International Conference Analysis and Optimization of Systems, held at the Palais des Congrès of Antibes on June 8–10, 1988, and it preceded immediately the Third International Symposium on Differential Games and Applications, held at INRIA-Sophia Antipolis on June 16–17, 1988.

This workshop could not have taken place without the technical and financial assistance of INRIA, to whom we express our gratitude. Financial support from a number of national and international institutions listed below is gratefully acknowledged:

Institut National de Recherche en Informatique et en Automatique (INRIA)
Centre National de la Recherche Scientifique (CNRS)
European Research Office, United States Army (ERO USA)
Ministère des Affaires Etrangères (MAE)
Ministère de l'Education Nationale (MEN)
Ministère de la Recherche et de l'Enseignement Supérieur (MRES)
United Nations Educational, Scientific and Cultural Organization (UNESCO)
Université Paris 7 (UP7)
Association Française pour la Cybernétique Economique et Technique (AFCET):
    Collège Mathematique Appliques

The Third Bellman continuum was sponsored by:

Association Française pour la Cybernétique Economique et Technique (AFCET)
International Federation of Automatic Control (IFAC)
Technical Committee on Mathematics of Control
Technical Committee on Theory

The Organizing Committee was:

A. Blaquiere	Chairman, Université Paris 7, France
N. Bellman	Santa Monica, CA USA
A. Bensoussan	Université Paris-Dauphine/INRIA, France
P. Bernhard	INRIA-Sophia Antipolis, France
Th. Bricheteau	INRIA, France
A. Esogbue	GA Institute of Technology, Atlanta, GA USA
G. Feichtinger	Technical University Vienna, Austria
M. Fliess	Laboratoire des Signaux et Systèms, CNRS-ESE, France
A. Fossard	ENSAE, Toulouse, France
S. Lee	Kansas State University, Lawrence, KS USA
G. Leitmann	University of California, Berkeley, CA USA
S. Meerkov	University of Michigan, Ann Arbor, MI USA
M. Thoma	Technische Universität, Hannover, Federal Republic of Germany
L. Zadeh	University of California, Berkeley, CA USA

The program included invited and contributed lectures in the following areas:

Topic 1: Control of Uncertain Dynamical Systems, Neglected Dynamics
Topic 2: Control and Nonlinear Filtering of Quantum Mechanical Processes
Topic 3: Models and Control Policies for Biological Systems
Topic 4: Models and Control Policies in Economics and Social Systems

Keynote speakers were Prof. G. Leitmann, University of California, Berkeley, and Prof. S. K. Mitter, Massachusetts Institute of Technology.

Originally, it was thought that a gathering of a small number of specialists on an invited basis was sufficient for the purpose. However, the responses to our initial announcement surpassed our most optimistic estimate of the enthusiasm of workers in these areas. Subsequently, it was decided that we would edit the Proceedings of this workshop as a volume containing all the invited papers and selected contributed papers submitted to the workshop. This text has been published by Springer-Verlag in the Series "Lecture Notes in Control and Information Sciences."

Now, let us briefly outline the main scientific directions defined by the choice of the above topics.

Topic 1

Many systems in the "real" world are subject to human intervention and control. The first step in devising a control policy or strategy for the accomplishment of a desired end is the abstraction of the perceived salient features of the actual (physical, chemical, engineering, biological, economic, etc.) system. Such an abstraction is usually embodied in a *mathematical model*, e.g., ordinary differential equations, finite difference equations, partial differential equations, and so on. Mathematical models are always *uncertain*, partly because they are approximations involving unknown or partially known elements, and partly because they include elements which model uncertain effects in the real world.

Two avenues are open to the system analyst dealing with such uncertain mathematical models, a *statistical approach* and a *deterministic one*. In the program, emphasis was on the latter.

Among the questions studied:

Control of uncertain dynamical systems
Neglected dynamics
Neglected sensors/actuators
Uncertain systems including parts with "fast" and "slow" dynamics
Chaotic systems
Robust control
Fuzzy systems

Topic 2

A quantum mechanical control system is a quantum mechanical system with a time-varying part considered as a perturbation. Different kinds of problems can be studied on it: one can be interested in the time-varying part as a signal to be extracted from the measurements on the system. This is the *quantum-filtering problematic*, usually associated to the concept of *nondemolition measurements*. Also the time-varying part can be considered as purposeful control on the system, a *control problem* stricto sensu.

Quantum mechanical control theory is an essential step along the way from quantum physics to quantum technology.

Among the questions studied:

Analogy between mathematical problems of nonlinear filtering and quantum physics
Stochastic calculus of variations and quantum mechanics
Stochastic mechanics
Stochastic reciprocal processes in the sense of Bernstein-Jamison
Nondemolition filtering
Control of quantum processes

Topic 3

From the 1960s, Bellman recognized that many biological systems display a number of characteristics similar to those of the decision processes to which he had devoted much attention. He then turned his talents toward developing models and control policies for these systems. He published many excellent papers in this field and achieved recognition as one of the pioneers in bringing the strength of mathematics and computer science into the medical area. His original motivation was the cancer problem; it is still a mystery why the control mechanism of a cell suddenly fails.

Topic 3 followed along the line of this part of Bellman's work. At the level of a cell and of quantum processes in it, this topic is closely related to Topic 2.

Among the questions studied:

Application of the method of systems analysis, control theory, and simulation to the field of biology and medicine,

for example

Aspects of modeling and simulating tumor growth and treatment
Application of control theory to chemotherapy and radiotherapy
Application of the theory of impulse control to hypodermic injections
Identification in cardiology
Mathematical models for the regulation of agonist– antagonist pairs

Topic 4

One field of application of the mathematical theory of systems is in the overlapping areas of mathematical economics, econometrics, social sciences, and management science. Among the many questions studied in Topic 4, the following list is not exhaustive:

Differential games approaches
Theory of viability
Theory of cooperation, competition, threat strategies, dynamical coalitions
Optimization with infinite horizon
Theory and applications of impulse control
Optimal cycles in economics

The list of the lectures, in the two parallel sessions of the program, was the following:

Control of Uncertain Dynamical Systems

Controlling Singularly Perturbed Uncertain Dynamical Systems
    G. Leitmann (USA)
Solutions contingentes de l'equation d'Hamilton-Jacobi-Bellman
    H. Frankowska (Poland–France)
On Robust Control of Uncertain Linear Systems in the Absence of Matching Conditions
    H. Stalford (USA)
Singularly Perturbed Uncertain Systems and Dynamic Output Feedback Control
    E. P. Ryan and Z. B. Yaacob (UK)
Control of Uncertain Mechanical Systems with Robustness in the Presence of Unmodelled Flexibilities
    M. Corless (USA)
Asymptotic Linearization of Uncertain Multivariable Systems by Sliding Modes
    G. Bartolini and T. Zolezzi (Italy)

*Models and Control Policies for Biological Systems
and Ecosystems*

Automatique et régulation biologique
    D. Claude (France)
Computer Models Applied to Cancer Research
    W. Düchting (FRG)
Biological System Response Prediction by Application of Structure–Activity Model
    B. Jerman-Blazic, I. Fabic-Petrac (Yugoslavia), M. Randic (USA)
Periodic Control of Linear Time-Invariant Systems
    S. Meerkov (USA)
Cyclic Control in Ecosystems
    J. Bentsman (USA)
Self-Controlled Growth Policy for a Food Chain System
    G. Bojadziev (Canada)

Mathematics and Systems, Computational Bearings

Quasilinearization in Biological Systems Modeling
    E. S. Lee, K. M. Wang (USA)
A Three-Mirror Problem on Dynamic Programming
    S. Iwamoto (Japan)
Existence and Computation of Solutions for the Two-Dimensional Moment Problem
    G. Sonnevend (Hungary-FRG)
An Approximation Procedure for Stochastic Control Problems, Theory and
    Applications
    R. Gonzalez, (Argentina), E. Rofman (France)
Speculations on Possible Directions and Applications for the Decomposition Method
    G. Adomian (USA)
Fuzzy Arithmetics in Qualitative Reasoning
    D. Dubois, H. Prade (France)
Fuzzy Dynamic Programming: Theory and Applications
    A. Esogbue (USA)

This list is approximately the table of contents of the Proceedings published by Springer–Verlag. (*Lecture Notes in Control and Information Sciences* [2] *Modeling and Control of Systems in Engineering, Quantum Mechanics, Economics and Biosciences* (A. Blaquiere, ed.). Springer-Verlag, Berlin-Heidelburg, 1989.)

The Workshop was attended by 73 participants and observers from 18 countries (Austria, Argentina, Brazil, Canada, Finland, France, Germany, Great Britain, Hungary, Israël, Italy, Japan, The Netherlands, Poland, Soviet Union, Switzerland, United States, and Yugoslavia) and has been considered very successful in highlighting the current trends and perspectives of the new questions set forth in its program. The interdisciplinary exchange of ideas was attribute to the honor and much in the spirit of Richard A. Bellman.

Further information can be obtained from the Chairman

            Prof. A. Blaquiere
            Laboratoire d'Automatique Théorique, Tour 14–24
            Université Paris 7
            2 Place Jussieu
            75251 Paris Cedex 05, France

APPENDIX: BOOKS OF RICHARD BELLMAN

Bellman, R., *Stability Theory of Differential Equations*, McGraw-Hill, New York, 1953.

Bellman, R., *Dynamic Programming*, Princeton University Press, Princeton, 1957.

Bellman, R., Clark, C., Craft, C., Malcolm, D., and Ricciardi, F., *On Top Management Simulation*, American Management Association, New York, 1957.

Bellman, R., *Introduction to Matrix Analysis*, McGraw-Hill, New York, 1960.

Bellman, R., *Adaptive Control Processes: A Guided Tour*, Princeton University Press, Princeton, 1961.

Bellman, R., *Modern Mathematical Classics*, I, *Analysis*, Dover Publications, New York, 1961.

Bellman, R., and Beckenbach, E. F., *An Introduction to Inequalities*, Random House, New York, 1961.

Bellman, R., *A Brief Introduction to Theta Functions*, Holt, Rinehart, and Winston, New York, 1961.

Bellman, R., and Beckenbach, E. F., *Inequalities*, Springer-Verlag, Berlin, 1961.

Bellman, R., and Dreyfus, S., *Applied Dynamic Programming*, Princeton University Press, Princeton, 1962.

Bellman, R., and Cooke, K. L., *Differential–Difference Equations*, Academic Press, New York, 1963.

Bellman, R., and Kalaba, R., *Mathematical Trends in Control Theory*, Dover Publications, New York, 1963.

Bellman, R., Kalaba, R., and Prestrud, M., *Invariant Imbedding and Radiative Transfer in Slabs of Finite Thickness*, American Elsevier, New York, 1963.

Bellman, R., Kagiwada, H., Kalaba, R., and Prestrud, M., *Invariant Imbedding and Time-Dependent Processes*, American Elsevier, New York, 1964.

Bellman, R., and Kalaba, R., *Dynamic Programming and Modern Control Theory*, Academic Press, New York, 1965.

Bellman, R., *Quasilinearization and Nonlinear Boundary-Value Problems*, American Elsevier, New York, 1965.

Bellman, R., Kalaba, R., and Lockett, J., *Numerical Inversion of the Laplace Transform*, American Elsevier, New York, 1966.

Bellman, R., *Perturbation Techniques in Mathematics, Physics and Engineering*, Holt, Rinehart and Winston, New York, 1966.

Bellman, R., *Modern Elementary Differential Equations*, Addison-Wesley, Reading, MA, 1968.

Bellman, R., *Introduction to the Mathematical Theory of Control Processes*, Vol 1., Academic Press, New York, 1968.

Bellman, R., *Some Vistas of Modern Mathematics*, University of Kentucky Press, Lexington, 1968.

Bellman, R., *Methods of Nonlinear Analysis*, Vol. 1., Academic Press, New York, 1969.

Bellman, R., Cooke, K. L., and Lockett, J., *Algorithms, Graphs and Computers*, Academic Press, New York, 1970.

Bellman, R., *Introduction to the Mathematical Theory of Control Processes*, Vol. 2., Academic Press, New York, 1971.

Bellman, R., and Angel, E., *Dynamic Programming and Partial Differential Equations*, Academic Press, New York, 1972.

Bellman, R., and Borg, G., *Mathematics, Systems and Society*, Swedish Natural Sciences Research Council, Committee on Research in Economics, FEK Report No. 2, Berlingska Boktrycheriet, Lund, Sweden, 1972.

Bellman, R., *Methods of Nonlinear Analysis*, Vol. 2., Academic Press, New York, 1973.

Bellman, R., and Smith, C. P., *Simulation in Human Systems, Decision-Making in Psychotherapy*, John Wiley and Sons, New York, 1973.

Bellman, R., and Wing, G. M., *An Introduction to Invariant Imbedding*, John Wiley and Sons, New York, 1975.

Bellman, R., *Can Computers Think? An Introduction to Artificial Intelligence*, Boyd and Fraser, San Francisco, 1978.

Bellman, R., *Analytic Number Theory—An Introduction*, Addison-Wesley, Reading, MA, 1980.

Bellman, R., Esogbue, A., and Nabeshima, I., *Mathematical Aspects of Schedules and Application*, Pergamon, Elmsford, NY, 1981.

Bellman, R., and Roth, R. S., *Quasilinearization and the Identification Problem*, World Scientific, Singapore, 1983.

Bellman, R., *Eye of the Hurricane: An Autobiography*, World Scientific, Singapore, 1984.

Bellman, R., *Mathematics in Medicine*, World Scientific, Singapore, 1984.

Bellman, R., and Roth, R. S., *The Laplace Transform*, World Scientific, Singapore, 1984.

Bellman, R., and Adomian, G., *Partial Differential Equations: New Methods for their Treatment and Solution*, D. Reidel Publishing, Dordrecht, The Netherlands, 1984.

Bellman, R., and Roth, R. S., *Methods in Approximation*, D. Reidel Publishing, Dordrecht, The Netherlands, 1985.

Bellman, R., *Selective Computation*, World Scientific, Singapore, 1985.

Other References can be found in

The Bell Continuum, A Collection of the Works of Richard E. Bellman (Robert S. Roth, ed.), World Scientific, Singapore, 1986.

AUSTIN BLAQUIERE

BRAIN AND INFORMATION RESEARCH*

That most intriguing aspect of human memory: its persistence in spite of continual loss of individual neurons over the lifetime of the individual has led many workers to the concept of distributed memory [1–7]. For a distributed memory (more like a hologram than a photograph) possesses in a very natural way the property of relative invulnerability to the loss of storage units: individual memory sites hold superimposed information concerning many events. In order to obtain a single event, information must be gathered from many sites. Loss of individual units decreases signal-to-noise ratios but does not lose items of information.

Further, in contrast to modern computers that perform large numbers of sequential operations very rapidly and very accurately, the central nervous system works slowly and probably not with enormous accuracy on the level of individual units, with cycle times that cannot be shorter than a few milliseconds. However, we can make complex decisions in small parts of a second. This suggests very strongly that there is much parallel processing in the brain—an idea that is almost obvious on inspection of a component such as the retina.

It is now commonly thought that the synaptic junction may be a means to store information (memory, for example) as well as to transmit it from neuron to neuron. Large networks of neurons connected to other neurons via modifiable synaptic junctions provide the physiological substrate for the distributed parallel systems discussed here (Fig. 1).

The actual synaptic connections between one neuron and another are generally complex and redundant; we have idealized the network by replacing this multiplicity of synapses between axons and dendrites by a single ideal junction which summarizes logically the effect of all the synaptic contacts between the incoming axon branches from neuron j in the F bank and the dendrites of the outgoing neuron i in the G bank (Fig. 2).

Although the firing rate of a neuron depends in a complex and nonlinear fashion on the presynaptic potentials, there is usually a reasonably well-defined linear region in which some very interesting network properties are already evident. We, therefore, focus our attention on the region above threshold and below saturation for which the firing rate of neuron i in G, g_i, is mapped from the firing rates of all of the neurons f_j in F by:

$$g_i = \sum_{j=1}^{N} A_{ij}f_j \qquad (1)$$

In doing this we are regarding as important average firing rates, and time averages of the instantaneous signals in a neuron (or perhaps a small population of neurons). We are further using the known integrative properties of neurons.

We may then regard [A_{ij}] (the synaptic strengths of the N^2 ideal junctions) as a matrix or a mapping which takes us from a vector in the F space to one in the G space. This maps the

---

* This work was performed at Brown University with support from the Office of Naval Research's Special Focus Program on Learning and Memory.

35

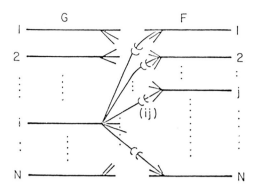

FIGURE 1.   An ideal distributed mapping. Each of the N input neurons in F is connected to each of the N output neurons in G by a single ideal junction. (Only the connections to i are drawn.)

neural activities $f = (f_1, f_2 \ldots f_N)$ in the F space into the neural activities $g = (g_1, \ldots g_N)$ in the G space and can be written in the compact form:

$$g = Af \tag{2}$$

It has been shown that the distributed mapping A can serve in a highly precise fashion as a memory that is content addressable and in which 'logic' is a result of association and an outcome of the nature of the memory itself [5].

The N^2 junctions, A_{ij}, contain the content of the distributed memory. It could be that a particular junction strength, A_{ij}, is composed of several different components with different lifetimes thought of as corresponding to different physiological or anatomical effects (e.g., changes in numbers of presynaptic vesicles, changes in numbers of postsynaptic receptors, changes in Ca^+ levels and/or availability, anatomical changes such as might occur in growth or shrinkage of spines). We then have the possibility that the actual memory content (even

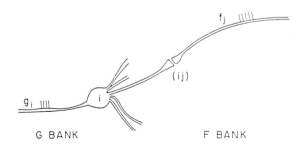

FIGURE 2.   An ideal synaptic junction.

in the absence of additional learning) will vary with time. For a two–component system we might have:

$$A_{ij}(t) = A_{ij}^{(long)} (t) + A_{ij}^{(short)} (t) \qquad (3)$$

where $A_{ij}(t)$ represents the memory at some time t, while $A_{ij}^{(long)}$ and $A_{ij}^{(short)}$ have long and short lifetimes. Thus in time $A_{ij}^{(short)}$, will decay, leaving $A_{ij}(t) = A_{ij}^{(long)}$. Whether what is in the short-term memory component is transferred to the long-term component might be determined by some global signal, depending on the interest of the information contained in the short-term component.

From this point of view, the site of long- and short-term memory can be essentially identical. At any given time there is a single memory. The distinction between long- and short-term memory is contained in the lifetime of the different components of A_{ij}.

We now ask how a mapping of the type A might be put into the network. The ij–th element of A,

$$A_{ij} = \sum_{\mu\nu} c_{\mu\nu} \; g_i^{\mu}, f_j^{\nu} \qquad (4)$$

is a weighted sum over the j components of all mapped signals f^{ν} and the i components of the responses g^{μ} appropriate for recollection or association. Such a form could be obtained by additions with each input f and output g to the element A_{ij}:

$$\delta A_{ij} \sim g_i f_j \qquad (5)$$

This δA_{ij} is proportional to the product of the differences between the actual and the spontaneous firing rates in the pre- and postsynaptic neurons i and j. (This is one realization of Hebb's form of synaptic modification [8].) The addition of such changes to A for all associations $g^{\mu} \times f^{\nu}$ results finally in a mapping with the properties discussed in the previous section.

Synaptic modification dependent on inputs alone, of the type already directly observed in Aplysia [9], is sufficient to construct a simple memory—one that distinguishes what has been seen from what has not, but does not easily separate one input from another. To construct a mapping of the form above, however, requires synaptic modification dependent on information that exists at different places on the neuron membrane: what we call two-(or higher-)point modification.

In order for this to take place, information must be communicated from, for example, the axon hillock to the synaptic junction to be modified. This implies the existence of a means of internal communication of information within a neuron—in the above example, in a direction opposite to the flow of electrical signals [5]. The junction ij, for example, must have information of the firing rate f_j (which is locally available) as well as the firing rate, g_i, which is somewhat removed (Fig. 3). One possibility could be that the integrated electrical signals from the dendrites produce a chemical or electrical response in the cell body which controls the spiking rate of the axon and at the same time communicates (e.g., by backward spiking) to the dendrite ends the information of the integrated slow potential.

The discussion above leads to a central issue: what is the principle of local organization that, acting in a large network, can produce the observed complex behavior of higher mental processes? There is no need to assume that such a mechanism—believed to involve

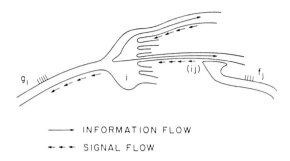

————▸ INFORMATION FLOW

◂ ◂ ◂ SIGNAL FLOW

FIGURE 3.   Two point modification.

synaptic modification—operates in exactly the same manner in all parts of the nervous system or in all animals. However, one would hope that certain fundamental similarities exist so that a detailed analysis of the properties of this mechanism in one preparation would lead to some conclusions that are generally applicable. We are interested in visual cortex because the vast amount of experimental work done in this area of the brain—particularly area 17 of cat and monkey—strongly indicate that one is observing a process of synaptic modification dependent on the information locally and globally available to the cortical cells.

Experimental work of the last generation, beginning with the path-breaking work of Hubel and Wiesel [*10,11*], has shown that there exist cells in visual cortex (areas 17, 18, and 19) of the adult cat that respond in a precise and highly tuned fashion to external patterns—in particular bars or edges of given orientation and moving in a given direction. Much further work has been taken to indicate that the number and response characteristics of such cortical cells can be modified [*12–15*]. It has been observed, in particular, that the relative number of cortical cells that are highly specific in their response to visual patterns varies in a very striking way with the visual experience of the animal during the critical period [*16–19*].

Most kittens first open their eyes at the end of the first week after birth. It is not easy to assess whether or not orientation-selective cells exist at that time in striate cortex: few cells are visually responsive and the response's main characteristics are generally "sluggishness" and "fatiguability." However, it is quite generally agreed that as soon as cortical cells are reliably visually stimulated (e.g., at 2 weeks), some are orientation selective, whatever the previous visual experience of the animal [*17–20*].

Orientation selectivity develops and extends to all visual cells in area 17 if the animal is reared, and behaves freely, in a normal visual environment (NR): complete "specification" and normal binocularity (about 80% of responsive cells) are reached at about 6 weeks of age [*19*]. However, if the animal is reared in total darkness from birth to the age of 6 weeks (DR), none or few orientation-selective cells are then recorded (0–15% depending on the authors and the classification criteria); however, the distribution of ocular dominance seems unaffected [*13,16–19,21*]. In animals whose eyelids have been sutured at birth, and which are thus binocularly deprived of pattern vision (BD), a somewhat higher proportion (12–50% of the visually excitable cells) are still orientation-selective at 6 weeks (and even beyond 24 months of age) and the proportion of binocular cells is less than normal [*22–26*].

Of all visual deprivation paradigms, putting one eye in a competitive advantage over the other has probably the most striking consequences. If monocular lid-suture (MD) is performed during a "critical" period (ranging from about 3 weeks to about 12 weeks), there is a rapid loss of binocularity to the profit of the open eye [22,27]. At this stage, opening the closed eye and closing the experienced one may result in a complete reversal or ocular dominance [23]. A disruption of binocularity that does not favor one of the eyes may be obtained, for example, by provoking an artificial strabismus [28] or by an alternating monocular occlusion, which gives both eyes an equal amount of visual stimulation [29]. In what follows, we call this uncorrelated rearing (UR).

These results seem to us to provide direct evidence for the modifiability of the response of single cells in the cortex of a higher mammal according to its visual experience. Depending on whether or not patterned visual information is part of the animal's experience, the specificity of the response of cortical neurons varies widely. Specificity increases with normal patterned experience. Deprived of normal patterned information (e.g., dark-reared or lid-sutured at birth), specificity decreases. Furthermore, even a short exposure to patterned information after six weeks of dark rearing can reverse the loss of specificity and produce an almost normal distribution of cells.

We do not claim and it is not necessary that all neurons in visual cortex be so modifiable. Nor is it necessary that modifiable neurons are especially important in producing the architecture of visual cortex. It is our hope that the general form of modifiability we require to construct distributed mappings manifests itself for at least some cells of visual cortex that are accessible to experiment. We thus make the conservative assumption that biological mechanisms, once established, will manifest themselves in more or less similar forms in different regions. If this is the case, modifiable individual neurons in visual cortex can provide evidence for such modification more generally.

Cortical neurons receive afferents from many sources. In visual cortex (layer 4, for example), the principle efferents are those from the lateral geniculate nucleus and from other cortical neurons. This leads to a complex network that we have analyzed in several stages.

In the first stage we consider a single neuron with inputs from both eyes (Fig. 4).

Here, d^l, d^r, m^l, m^r are inputs at synaptic junctions from left and right eyes. The output of this neuron (in the linear region) can be written:

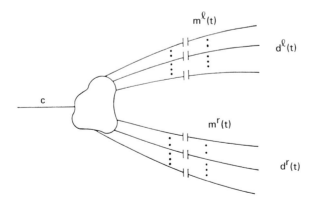

FIGURE 4. A model neuron.

$$c = m\rho \, d\rho + m^r \, d^r \tag{6}$$

This means that the neuron firing rate (in the linear region) is the sum of the inputs from the left eye multiplied by the appropriate left-eye synaptic weights plus the inputs from the right eye multiplied by the appropriate right-eye synaptic weights. Thus the neuron integrates signals from the left and right eyes.

According to the theory presented by Bienenstock, Cooper, and Munro [30], these synaptic weights modify as a function of local and global variables. To illustrate we consider the synaptic weight.

Its change in time, m_j, is given below:

$$m_j = F(d_j \ldots m_j \; ; d_k \ldots c; \bar{c} \ldots ; X,Y,Z) \tag{7}$$

Here variables such as $d_j \ldots m_j$ are designated local. These represent information (e.g., the incoming signal, d_j, and the strength of the synaptic junction, m_j) available locally at the synaptic junction, m_j. Variables such as $d_k \ldots c$ are designated quasilocal. These represent information (such as c, the firing rate of the cell, or d_k, the incoming signal to another synaptic junction) that is not locally available to the junction m_j but is physically connected to the junction by the cell body itself—thus necessitating some form of internal communication between various parts of the cell and its synaptic junctions. Variables such as $\bar{c}$ (the time-averaged output of the cell) are averaged local or quasilocal variables. Global variables are designated X, Y, Z. . . . These latter represent information (e.g., presence or absence of neurotransmitters such as norepinephrine or the average activity of large numbers of cortical cells) that is present in a similar fashion for all or a large number of cortical neurons (distinguished from local or quasilocal variables presumably carrying detailed information that varies from synapse to synapse).

In a form relevant to this discussion BCM modification can be written:

$$m_j = \phi(c, \bar{c} \; ; X, Y, Z \ldots)d_j \tag{8}$$

so that the j-th synaptic junction, m_j, changes its value in time as a function of quasilocal and time-averaged quasilocal variables, c and $\bar{c}$, as well as global variables, X, Y, Z, through the function, ϕ, and a function of the local variable d_j. The crucial function, ϕ, is shown in Figure 5.

What is of particular significance is the change of sign of ϕ at the modification threshold, Θ_M, and the nonlinear variation of Θ_M with the average output of the cell $\bar{c}$. In a simple situation:

$$\Theta_M = (\bar{c})^2 \tag{9}$$

The occurrence of negative and positive regions for ϕ drives the cell to selectivity in a normal' environment. This is so because the response of the cell is diminished to those patterns for which the output, c, is below threshold (ϕ negative) while the response is enhanced to those patterns for which the output, c, is above threshold (ϕ positive). The nonlinear variation of the threshold with the average output of the cell, $\bar{c}$, places the threshold so that it eventually separates one pattern from all of the rest. Further it provides the stability properties of the system.

A detailed analysis of the consequences of this form of modification is given in BCM. The results (as modified in the network analysis outlined next) are in general agreement

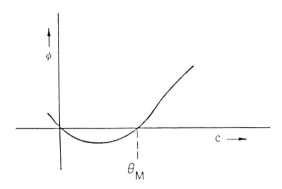

FIGURE 5.   The BCM modification function.

with what we might call classical experiments of the last generation. Neurons in normal (patterned) environments become selective and binocular. In various deprived environments (e.g., monocular or binocular deprivation) the theoretical behavior follows the experimental results.

To better confront these ideas with experiment, the single neuron discussed above must be placed in a network with anatomical and physiological features of the region of interest. For visual cortex this suggests a network in which inhibitory and excitatory cells receive input from the lateral geniculate nucleus (LGN) and from each other. A simplified form of such a network, a first-order representation of the anatomy and physiology of layer IV of cat visual cortex (Fig. 6) has been studied by Scofield and Cooper [*31*]. In a network generalization of Eq. (6), we write:

$$c_i = m_i^l \, d\rho + m_i^l \, d^r + \sum_j L_{ij} c_j \qquad (10)$$

where L_{ij} are the intracortical connections.

Analysis by Scofield and Cooper of the network along lines similar to that of the single cell analysis described above shows that under proper conditions on the intracortical synapses, the cells converge to states of maximum selectivity with respect to the environ-

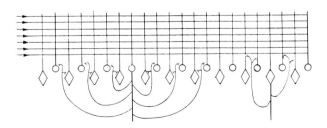

FIGURE 6.   A simplified neural network.

ment formed by the geniculate signals. Their conclusions are therefore similar to those of BCM with explicit further statements concerning the independent effects of excitatory and inhibitory neurons on selectivity and ocular dominance. For example, shutting off inhibitory cells lessens selectivity and alters ocular dominance. The inhibitory cells may be selective but there is no theoretical necessity that they be so.

A mean field approximation to the above network shows that if the average effect of intracortical connections results in inhibition of individual cells, then in monocular deprivation, the geniculocortical synapses to the cell will converge to non-zero states that give, as the result of stimulation of the closed eye, total responses that are zero [*32*]. However, the fact that the geniculocortical states are non-zero means that the removal of cortical inhibition through the chemical blocking of inhibitory synapses would uncover responses from previously nonresponsive cells. This result is in accord with the experimental observation of 'masked synapses' after the removal of the inhibitory effects of GABA with the blocking agent bicuculline [*33,34*].

An unexpected consequence of this theory is a connection between selectivity and ocular dominance. The analysis given in BCM and extended in the mean field network theory shows that in monocular deprivation, nonpreferred inputs presented to the open eye are a necessary part of the suppression of deprived eye responses. It follows that the more selective the cell is to the open eye (increasing the probability of nonpreferred inputs) the more the closed eye will be driven to zero, thus increasing the dominance of the open eye (Fig. 7a).

For an experimental test of these ideas it is important to determine what happens *during* the ocular dominance shift produced by monocular deprivation. An experiment in which monocular experience follows a period of dark rearing has been performed by Saul and Daniels (1986). Their results confirm the expected correlation between ocular dominance and selectivity (Fig. 7b) [*34a*].

One consequence of the network theory discussed above is that experimental results that have been obtained in visual cortex over the last generation can be explained primarily by modification of lateral geniculate (LGN) to cortex synapses with minimum changes among intracortical synapses. Thus the possibility is opened that most learning takes place in the LGN synapses. This somewhat surprising result has as one consequence the possibility of great simplification in the analysis of network modification.

An alternate hypothesis that has been considered for some time is that intracortical synapses bear heavy responsibility for modification in cortical circuitry during learning (see, e.g., Ref. 35). In particular, it has been suggested that ocular dominance shifts in monocular deprivation are due to increased activity of GABAergic neurons, the open eye suppressing the closed. Sillito documented in normal cats that visually unresponsive cells may be "unmasked" by iontophoretic bicuculline [*36*]. Thus, it is not unreasonable to speculate that many of the unresponsive cells in visually deprived kittens are being suppressed. Together, these data suggest as a possible hypothesis that in kitten striate cortex the GABAergic neurons respond to sensory deprivation by forming new synapses. This hypothesis implies that the density or strength of GABAergic synapses will increase in zones of cortex that are deprived of a normal thalamic input; in the case of monocular deprivation, these zones correspond to the closed-eye ocular dominance columns and to the monocular segment contralateral to the deprived eye. On the other hand, the theory described above suggests that there will be minimal response of GABAergic neurons to sensory deprivation. This hypothesis has been put to test in recent series of experiments [*37*].

To examine the distribution of GABAergic synapses, Bear et al., immunocytochemically localized GAD in sections of striate cortex [*37*]. While immunocytochemistry is not a

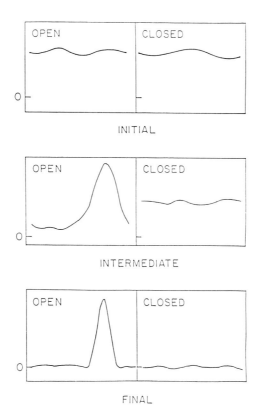

FIGURE 7a. Progression of development of selectivity and ocular dominance.

quantitative measure, they reasoned that changes restricted to deprived ocular dominance zones should be readily detected with this method. As a quantitative estimate of GABAergic synapse density, they biochemically measured GAD activity in homogenates of striate cortex.

They found no evidence for a change in the distribution of GAD-positive puncta in 12 unilaterally enucleated kittens. The band of layer IV puncta remained uniform even though the periods of monocular deprivation examined would all be sufficient to cause a physiological ocular dominance shift in striate cortex. GAD immunoreactivity was unchanged even under conditions that produced alterations in the level of the metabolic enzyme, cytochrome oxidase. Measurements of GAD activity showed no consistent or significant difference between either the binocular segments of enucleated and control kittens, or the monocular segments of enucleated animals.

This conclusion is in striking agreement with network analysis which, as mentioned above, suggests that inhibitory synapses are much less modified by experience than excitatory synapses. In addition to its implications for the 'site of learning,' such a hypothesis leads to important simplifications in the analysis of complex networks.

One of the most exciting of present projects is that of trying to find a molecular basis for synaptic modification. A molecular model for the BCM form of modification based on

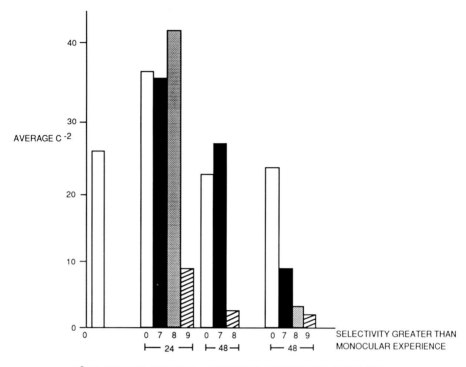

FIGURE 7b.   Average left eye $\overline{c^2}$ versus right eye selectivity and monocular experience.

NMDA receptors has been proposed. In this model the BCM modification threshold is identified with the voltage-dependent unblocking of the NMDA receptor channels. A consequence of this identification is the requirement that the voltage dependence must vary depending on the history of the cell activity.

Stated in this language many questions become of obvious interest. Among these: How long does it take to adjust to a new average firing rate? What does the molecular model say about the interaction of various neural transmitters? Can we connect those cells that modify with those acted on by modulators? (e.g., if inhibitory cells modify less, perhaps they are less acted on by modulators?). Do the same rules apply in the developmental period as apply to reorganization in adults?

You have been sufficiently warned about the hazards of making predictions; now I will venture to say a few words about the future. Imagine first that the problem of how the brain functions and organizes information has been solved. What would the consequences be? There could clearly be medical applications, possible means for treatment and amelioration of various physiological and psychological disorders. Also there would be new means for information processing—organization of computers. We could very likely duplicate electronically the information processing functions so that we would have available to us machines that would share our ability to learn and that could duplicate our processes of reasoning. Such devices would become standard components of what we today call computers.

I would guess that his would occur board by board—a gradual encroachment of intelligent components into conventional machines—somewhat like neo-cortex came to dominate the brain. The Aegis Combat System of the future will be dominated by such machines.

But will this problem be solved in our lifetime? When I began to work in this field about a decade ago, opinions were: an interesting problem but insoluble in our lifetime. Today, fashion has changed. Everyone talks about parallel processing, connection machines, and neural networks. What was heresy and put one in danger of being burned ten years ago has become received religion; but it is not sufficient to change religion. It is the details that count.

The object is to construct systems that can learn, that can modify their behavior depending upon their environment—and thus are to some extent self-organizing. But the details of the architecture that makes these systems function effectively is not self-organizing—that is what we must construct. It's not sufficient just to build hardware, connect elements, and see what happens with no real understanding of what might be accomplished. I hope that the current burst of enthusiasm for this field will not slacken if results do not come quite as quickly as sometimes promised.

REFERENCES

1. H. C. Longuet–Higgins, "Holographic Model of Temporal Recall," *Nature, 217*, 104 (1968).
2. H. C. Longuet–Higgins, "The Non–local Storage of Temporal Information," *Proc. R. Soc. Lond. (Biol.), 171*, 327–324 (1968).
3. J. A. Anderson, "Two Models for Memory Organization Using Interacting Traces," *Math. Biosci., 8,* 137–160 (1970).
4. J. A. Anderson, "Simple Neural Network Generating and Interactive Memory," *Math. Biosci., 14,* 197–220 (1972).
5. L. N. Cooper, "A Possible Organization of Animal Memory and Learning," in *Proc. Nobel Symposium on Collective Properties of Physical Systems* (B. Lindquist and S. Lindquist, eds.), Academic Press, New York, 1974 , pp. 252–264.
6. K. Pribam, M. Nuwer, and R. Baron, "The Holographic Hypothesis of Memory Structure in Brain Function and Perception," in *Contemporary Developments in Mathematical Psychology,* Vol. II. (D. H. Krautz, R. C. Atkinson, R. D. Luce, and P. Suppes, eds.), W. H. Freeman, San Francisco, 1974.
7. T. Kohonen, *Associative Memory: A System Theoretic Approach*, Springer–Verlag, Berlin, 1977.
8. D. O. Hebb, *The Organization of Behavior*, Wiley, New York, 1949, p. 62.
9. E. R. Kandel, *Cellular Basis of Behavior: An Introduction to Behavioral Neurobiology*, W. H. Freeman, San Francisco, 1976.
10. D. H. Hubel, and T. N. Wiesel, "Receptive Fields of Single Neurons in the Cat's Striate Cortex," *J. Physiol. (London), 148*, 574–591 (1959).
11. D. H. Hubel, and T. N. Wiesel, "Receptive Fields, Binocular Interactions and Functional Architecture in the Cat's Visual Cortex," *J. Physiol. (London), 160*, 106–154 (1962).
12. C. Blakemore, and G. F. Cooper, "Development of the Brain Depends on the Visual Environment," *Nature, 228,* 477–478 (1970).
13. C. Blakemore, and D. E. Mitchell, "Environmental Modification of the Visual Cortex and the Neural Basis of Learning and Memory," *Nature, 241*, 467 (1973).

14. H. V. B. Hirsch, and D. N. Spinelli, "Modification of the Distribution of Horizontally and Vertically Oriented Receptive Fields in Cats," *Exp. Brain Res., 13,* 509–527 (1971).

15. J. D. Pettigrew, and R. D. Freeman, "Visual Experience Without Lines: Effects on Developing Cortical Neurons," *Science, 182,* 599–601 (1973).

16. M. Imbert, and Y. Buisseret, "Receptive Field Characteristics and Plastic Properties of Visual Cortical Cells in Kittens Reared with or Without Visual Experience," *Exp. Brain Res., 22,* 2–36 (1975).

17. C. Blakemore, R. C. Van Sluyters, and J. A. Moyshon, "Synaptic Competition in the Kitten's Visual Cortex," *Cold Spring Harbor Symp. Quant. Biol., 40, The Synapse,* 601–609 (1975).

18. P. Buisseret and M. Imbert, "Visual Cortical Cells. Their Development Properties in Normal and Dark–Reared Kittens," *J. Physiol (London), 255,* 511–525 (1976).

19. Y. Fregnac, and M. Imbert, "Early Development of Visual Cortical Cells in Normal and Dark–Reared Kittens: Relationship Between Orientation Selectivity and Ocular Dominance," *J. Physiol (London), 278,* 27–44 (1978).

20. D. H. Hubel, and T. N. Wiesel, "Receptive Fields of Cells in Striate Cortex of Very Young Visually Inexperienced Kittens," *J. Neurophysiol., 26,* 994–1002 (1963).

21. A. G. Levanthal, and H. V. B. Hirsch, "Receptive Field Properties of Different Classes of Neurons in Visual Cortex of Normal and Dark–Reared Cat," *J. Neurophysiol., 43,* 1111 (1980).

22. T. N. Wiesel, and D. H. Hubel, "Comparisons of the Effects of Unilateral and Bilateral Eye Closure on Cortical Unit Responses in Kittens," *J. Neurophysiol., 28,* 1029–1040 (1965).

23. C. Blakemore, and R. C. Van Sluyters, "Reversal of the Physiological Effects of Monocular Deprivation in Kittens: Further Evidence for a Sensitive Period," *J. Physiol. (London), 237,* 195–216 (1974).

24. K. E. Kratz, and P. D. Spear, "Effects of Visual Deprivation and Alterations in Binocular Competition on Responses of Striate Cortex Neurons in the Cat," *J. Comp. Neurol., 170,* 141 (1976).

25. A. G. Levanthal, and H. V. B. Hirsch, "Effects of Early Experience upon Orientation Sensitivity and Binocularity of Neurons in Visual–Cortex of Cats," *Proc. Natl. Acad. Sci. (USA), 74*(3), 1272–1276 (1977).

26. D. W. Watkins, J. R. Wilson, and S. M. Sherman, "Receptive Field Properties of Neurons in Binocular and Monocular Segments of Striate Cortex in Cats Raised with Binocular Lid Suture," *J. Neurophysiol., 41,* 322 (1978).

27. T. N. Wiesel, and D. H. Hubel, "Single–Cell Responses in Striate Cortex of Kittens Deprives of Vision in One Eye," *J. Neurophysiol., 26,* 1003–1017 (1963).

28. D. H. Hubel , and T. N. Wiesel, "Binocular Interaction in Striate Cortex of Kittens Reared with Artificial Squint," *J. Neurophysiol., 28,* 1041–1059 (1965).

29. C. Blakemore, "The Conditions Required for the Maintenance of Binocularity in the Kitten's Visual Cortex," *J. Physiol., 261,* 423–444 (1976).

30. E. L. Bienenstock, L. N. Cooper, and P. W. Munro, "Theory for the Development of Neuron Selectivity: Orientation Specificity and Binocular Interaction in Visual Cortex," *J. Neurosci., 2,* 32–48 (1982).

31. C. L. Scofield, and L. N. Cooper, "Development and Properties of Neural Networks," *Contemp. Phy., 26*(2), 125–145 (1985).

32. L. N. Cooper, and C. L. Scofield, "Mean Field Approximation in Neural Networks," *Proc. Natl. Acad. Sci.*(USA), *85,* 1973 (1988).

33. F. H. Duffy, S. R. Snodgrass, J. L. Burchfiel, and J. L. Conway, "Bicuculline Reversal of Deprivation Amblyopia in the Cat," *Nature, 260*, 256–257 (1976).

34. A. M. Sillito, J. A. Kemp, and H. Patel, "Inhibitory Interactions Contributing to the Ocular Dominance of Monocularly Dominated Cells in the Normal Cat Striate Cortex," *Exp. Brain Res., 41,* 1–10 (1980).

34a. A. Saul, and J. Daniels, submitted for publication.

35. J. P. Rauschecker, and W. Singer, "The Effects of Early Visual Experience on the Cat's Visual Cortex and Their Possible Explanation by Hebb Synapses," *J. Physiol. (Lond.), 310*, 215–240 (1981).

36. A. M. Sillito, "The Contribution of Inhibitory Mechanisms to the Receptive Field Properties of Neurons in the Cat's Striate Cortex," *J. Physiol., 250*, 304–330 (1975).

37. M. F. Bear, D. E. Schmechel, and F. F. Ebner, "Glutamate Decarboxylase in the Striate Cortex of Normal and Monocularly Deprived Kittens," *J. Neurosci., 5*, 1262–1275 (1985).

LEON N. COOPER

COMMAND AND CONTROL DECISION-AIDING

THE CONCEPTUAL BACKDROP

Command and control (C^2) are elements of the force effectiveness process, as Figure 1 suggests, as well as a means for the enhancement of human performance. Figure 2 suggests that computer-based decision aids and support systems can support a number of activities, including C^2. This article concentrates simultaneously on C^2 and the decision aids and support systems used to enhance C^2. It presents some definitions of C^2 as well as information about C^2 decision-aiding technologies, the design and development of C^2 decision aids, and some of the more famous C^2 decision support systems.

What is Command and Control (C^2)?

Command and control (C^2) is the process by which military and civilian "commanders" exercise authority and direction over their human and material resources to accomplish tactical and strategic objectives [1]. C^2 is accomplished via the orchestrated implementation of a set of facilities, communication, personnel, equipment, and procedures for monitoring, forecasting, planning, directing, allocating resources, and generating options to achieve general and specific objectives. In industry, managers and corporate leaders identify market objectives and then mobilize resources to achieve them; in the military, commanders plan and execute complicated, phased operations to fulfill their missions. Commanders in industry mobilize factories, aggressive managers, line workers, and their natural and synthesized resources to produce superior products. Commanders in the military mobilize weapons, troops, and sophisticated communications apparati to defend and acquire territory and associated military and political objectives.

What is Command and Control (C^2) Decision Making?

Decision making lies at the heart of C^2. While commanders will always need data, information, and knowledge to inform their decisions, the decision-making process itself can be supported by C^2 decision support systems. Such systems support the "cognitive" functions of the commander. Some of these include the nature of threats, assessments about his or her organizational capabilities, and the identification of operational opportunities. C^2 decision support systems also recognize decision-making constraints, such as limited time and incomplete and ambiguous information.

Figure 3 suggests the range of C^2 decision support systems opportunities [2]. There are currently a variety of decision support systems that support decision making in the cells in the matrix. There are systems that support decision making at the National Military Command System level, for the Unified and Specified Commands, the Services and in the Field. Note also that Figure 3 indicates that there are strategic, theater, allied and tactical levels, and that decision making is presumed to be very different at various points along the war–peace continuum.

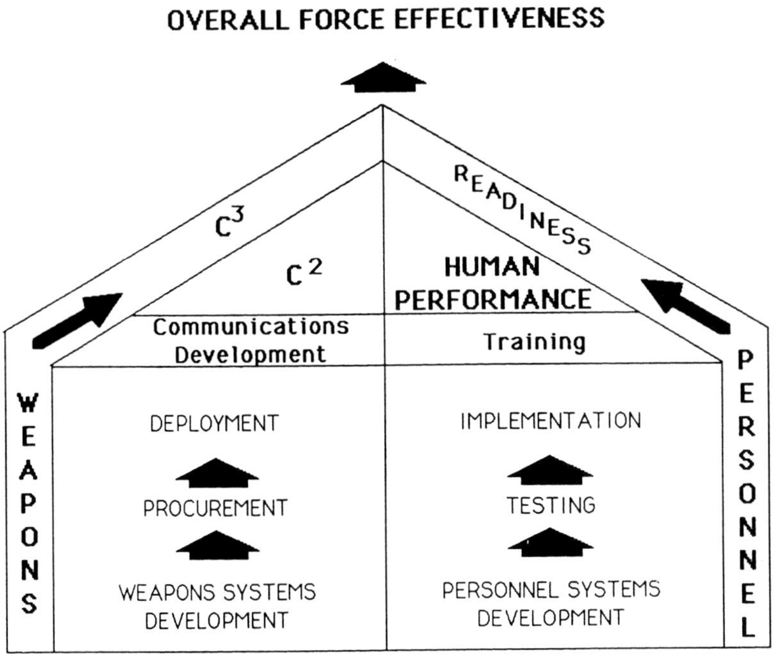

OVERALL FORCE EFFECTIVENESS

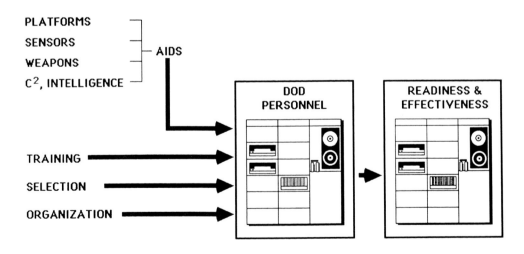

FIGURE 1.   The force effectiveness process.

FIGURE 2.   Range of computer-based support systems applications.

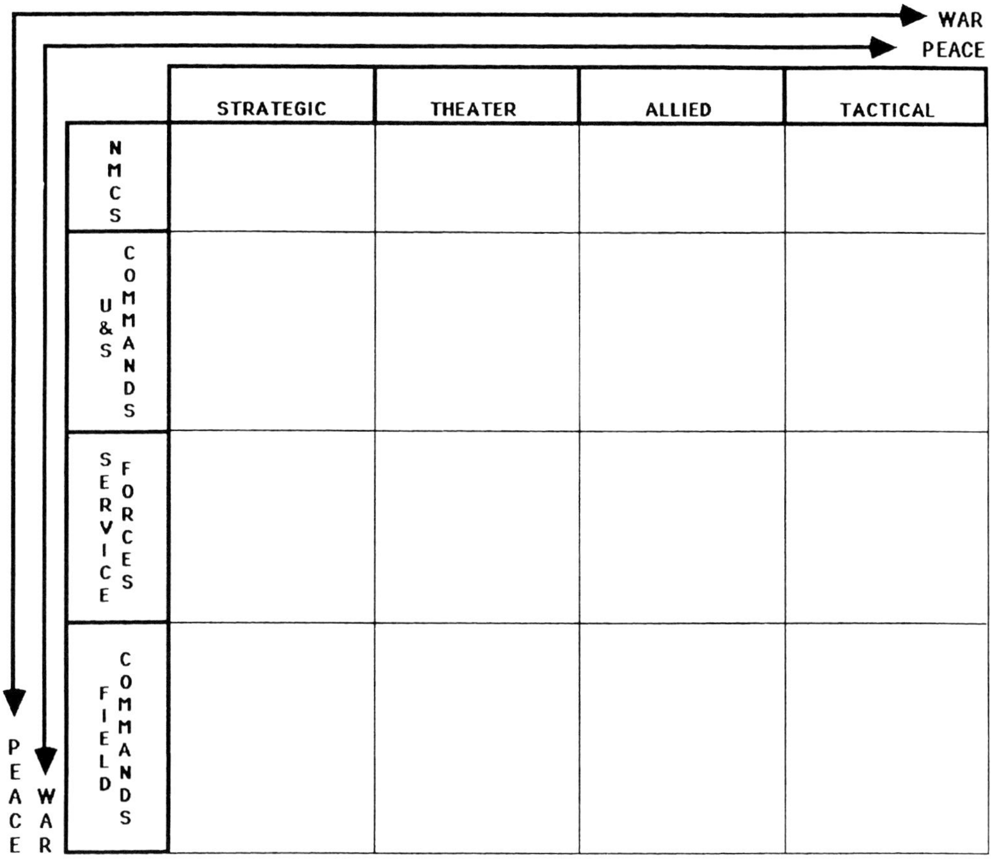

		STRATEGIC	THEATER	ALLIED	TACTICAL
	N M C S				
U & S	C O M M A N D S				
S E R V I C E	F O R C E S				
F I E L D	C O M M A N D S				

FIGURE 3.   C² decision-making matrix.

Figure 4 suggests the range of complexity of the C² decisions that a tactical flag commander must make. Commanders at all levels and in all branches of the military must solve similar problems and make the same kinds of decisions.

Decision Aids and Support Systems for Command and Control (C²)

Perhaps the best way to understand where C² decision aids and support systems can help the most is to identify the special problems that commanders routinely face. Some of these problems include:

    Suboptimal information management
            Information "overload"
            Difficulty finding key information
            Poor information presentation
            Incorrect information
            Ambiguous information
            Incomplete information

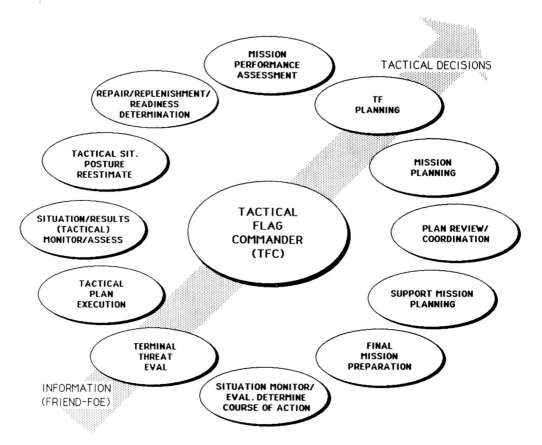

FIGURE 4.   Exemplar C² decision making.

> Limited option generation and implementation
>> Limited alternative generation
>> Suboptimal option evaluation
>> Limited scenario generation capabilities
>> Limited real-time simulation capabilities

These and additional problems are summarized in Figure 5, which also suggests where C² decision aids and support systems can yield the greatest payoff.

Beginning around 1979, a date that marks the advent of the widespread proliferation of microcomputers throughout the defense establishment, decision aids and larger support systems have been designed, developed, and applied to a variety of C² decision-making problems (see Case Studies for more details on several representative systems).

C² decision support systems help commanders discriminate among alternatives, simulate the implementation of options, and evaluate the impact of decisions made by commanders in various situations. They help commanders test assumptions, perform "what-if" analyses, and conduct decision-making "postmortems."

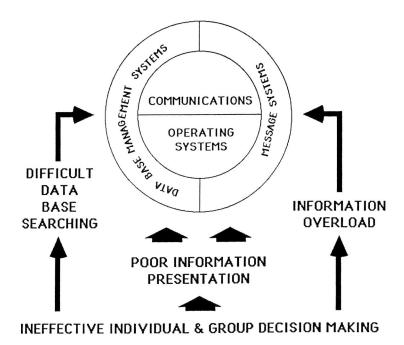

FIGURE 5. Opportunities for C² decision making.

DECISION-AIDING TECHNOLOGIES

Those who design and develop decision aids for C² call upon the social, behavioral, engineering, mathematical, computer, and management sciences. C² decision support systems design and development is multidisciplinary by nature and necessity. A variety of analytical methods and other tools and techniques are available to the designer of advanced C² systems. Figure 6 identifies the major decision-aiding technologies.

Analytical Methods for Interactive Decision Aiding

Designers of C² decision aid and support systems have a variety of analytical methods at their disposal. The key lies in the correct matching of analytical methods to problems [3]. There are several primary methods classes worth discussing here. They include decision analytic methods, operations research methods, methods derived from computer science and artificial intelligence, and methods derived from the field of human factors engineering.

Decision Analytic Methods

Some of the methods, tools, and techniques used to drive C² decision support systems include utility/value models, probability models, and mixed value–probability models [4].

Utility/value models come in a variety of forms. Some are based upon conventional cost-benefit models and assumptions. Some are based upon the treatment of value as "regret," that is, the "flip side" of utility, since many C² commanders perceive costs more viv-

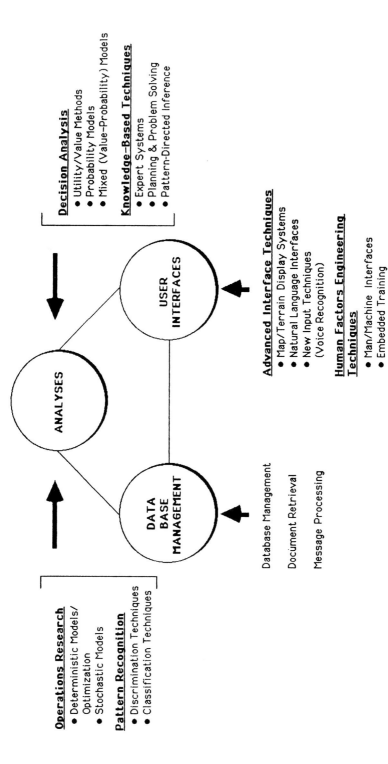

FIGURE 6.   Major decision-aiding technologies.

idly than benefits. Others are based upon multiattribute utility assessment (MAUA) models. MAUA models are powerful tools for assessing the relative value of alternative courses of action. The methodology is generic. It can be used to assess the relative value of courses of action, personnel, or objects and processes of any kind. In the civilian sector, MAUA models are used to assess the value of alternative sites for new factories, alternative business plans, and corporate jets. In the military, they are used to assess alternative tactical plans, the performance of competing weapons systems, and the value of alternative investments in high technology.

Probability models, including probability trees, influence diagrams, and Bayesian hierarchical inference models, identify data, indicators, events, and activities that when taken together predict the likelihood of single or multiple events. Figure 7, from the *Handbook for Decision Analysis* [4], presents a Bayesian hierarchical inference structure intended to determine the likelihood of a country developing a nuclear weapons capability. In its computer-based form, the model permits analysts to determine how new evidence affects the likelihood of a given country's intention to develop nuclear weapons. The model works via

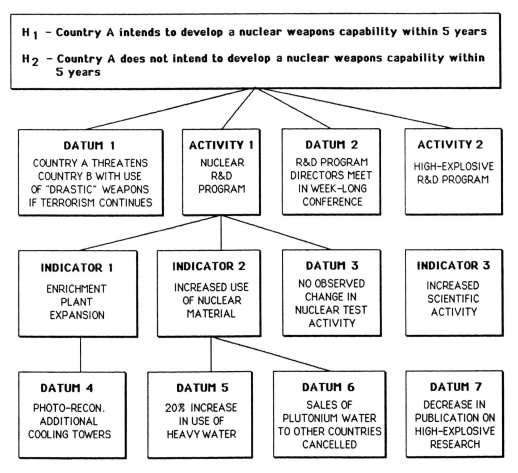

FIGURE 7. Bayesian hierarchical inference structure for nuclear weapons capability assessment.

assessments about relationships among data, indicators, and activities that chain react up the model to determine the probability of the hypotheses that sit at the top of the structure.

Mixed value–probability models often drive C^2 decision support systems. The most recognized form of the mixed model is the probability tree, which generates values for outcomes given the likelihood of events and the value of their occurrence.

Operations Research Methods

A number of tools and techniques comprise the range of operations research methods [5]. Several that deserve special mention include linear programming, dynamic programming, integer programming, queuing theory, aspects of system analysis, and even the classic quantitative–empirical inferential statistical methods.

Linear programming is representative of operations research methods that seek optimization. Linear programming methods can be applied to complicated resources allocation and optimization problems when the following conditions exist [5]:

- When the parameters of the problem constitute a linear function
- When alternative resource mixes are possible
- When the linear functions (and constraints) can be expressed mathematically
- When the mathematical relationships among variables can be mapped
- When resources are finite (and quantifiable)

Linear programming enables a problemsolver to optimize the allocation of resources according to a specific goal. There are two primary linear programming methods: the graphic method and the powerful and popular simplex method. The graphic method involves the plotting of the linear function and constraints in a multidimensional space and then solving the simultaneous equations of the plotted lines. The simplex method involves the implementation of an iterative mathematical process until the best solution is found.

Linear programming methods are flexible because they permit asset, constraint, and goal manipulation. Dynamic programming methods also account for time intervals.

These and related optimization methods can be used to solve a variety of C^2 problems, weapons assignment, equipment reliability assessments, production planning, and the numerous "assignment" problems that surround so many C^2 decisions.

Computer Science and Artificial Intelligence Methods

Computer science is a discipline with roots in information theory that links electronic data processing with data and models for data storage and retrieval. The tools and techniques of computer science make it possible to implement a variety of analytical methods that are more accurately located within one or more of the above categories. Pattern recognition, queuing, networking, inventory modeling, and simulation, while quite frequently considered computer science methods, really belong to the operations research community. Database management methods really belong to the management science community, while document retrieval methods belong to those who apply the tools and techniques of library and information science. The key to understanding the range of methods (from any of the classes) lies not in strict definitions of disciplines or fields of inquiry, but in the development of comprehensive, nonredundant taxonomies of methods. Ideally, such taxonomies will be anchored in the social, behavioral, engineering, computer, mathematical, and management sciences.

"Conventional" algorithmic methods refer to those used to collect, refine, store, route, process, and create data and information for specific problem-solving purposes. in many cases, this amounts to writing algorithms to implement decision analytic, operations research, or management science methods. On other occasions, it reduces to the development of tabular and graphic displays, while on still others, conventional computer science methods are applied to database housecleaning chores.

Artificial intelligence (AI) methods seek to identify, codify, and process knowledge. AI systems differ from conventional ones in a number of important ways. First, conventional systems store and manipulate data within some very specific processing boundaries. AI systems store and apply knowledge to a variety of unspecified problems within selected problem domains. AI systems can make inferences, implement rules of thumb, and solve problems in certain areas in much the same way humans solve problems.

The representation of knowledge is the mainstay of AI. There are a number of options available to the "knowledge engineer," the AI systems analyst with responsibility of converting problem-solving processes into executable software. The most popular knowledge representation technique is the rule, an "if– then" formalism that permits knowledge engineers to develop inferential strategies via some relatively simple expressions of knowledge. For example, if a tank will not start, it is possible to write a series of rules that represent the steps a diagnostician might take to solve the problem:

> If the engine will not start, then check the battery
> If the battery is OK, then check the solenoid
> If the solenoid is OK, then check the fuel tank
> If the fuel tank is full, then check the starter . . .

These simple rules might be expanded and reordered. Hundreds of rules can be used to perform complicated diagnostic, maintenance, and planning tasks.

Some other knowledge representation techniques include frames, inference networks, and object–attribute–value triplets [6].

All knowledge representation techniques strive to represent the processes by which inferences are made from generic knowledge structures. Once knowledge is represented it can be used to drive expert systems, natural language processing systems, robotic systems, and vision systems. Expert systems incarnate expert knowledge about problem solving; natural language systems permit free-form interaction with analytical algorithms; robotic systems use knowledge to identify objects and manipulate through complex environments; and vision systems intelligently process images and "see," recognize, and respond to their micro environments [7].

Human Factors Engineering Methods

In addition to the analytical methods discussed above are several classes of methods that the C^2 decision aid and support systems designer must understand. These include all those pertinent to the actual means by which the system is connected to its user. Here the reference is to the user-computer interaction routines, the use of appropriate displays, error handling, response time, and all those issues relevant to how easy the system is to use and productive it makes its user. All of these issues, tools, techniques, and methods fall under the general auspices of human factors engineering.

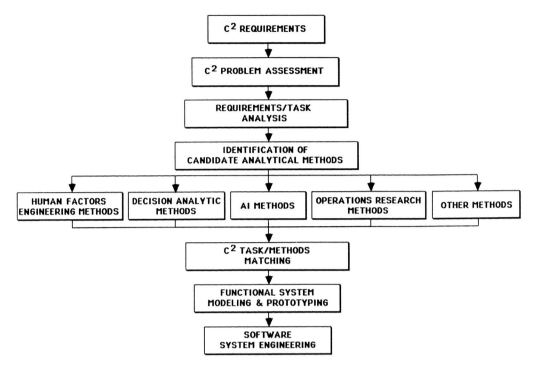

FIGURE 8.   The tasks/methods matching process.

The C² Tasks/Methods Matching Progress

Analytical methods are best exploited when they "match" a specific C² requirement. Figure 8 suggests that the selection of an analytical method cannot be made independent of the requirements the system under development is intended to satisfy. The tasks/methods matching step in the C² systems design and development process is critically important to the application of successful systems [9].

THE DESIGN AND DEVELOPMENT OF C² DECISION AIDS AND SUPPORT SYSTEMS

The design and development of decision support systems intended for use by relatively in-experienced computer users to solve analytical problems is fundamentally different from the design and development of systems intended to provide inventory control support to frequent users. Those that design and develop C² decision aids and support systems have, accordingly, perfected their requirements analysis techniques. Many of these techniques rely upon the structured interviewing of commanders to determine their decision-making needs. C² decision support systems designers have also endorsed the "rapid prototyping" approach to systems design, since it is so difficult to capture C² decision–making require-ments the first time. C² systems designers thus build several working prototypes of their systems to help validate requirements before proceeding with full-scale system development. Finally, the C^2 decision aids community has devoted a great deal of attention to how systems can be evaluated.

C^2 Decision-Making Requirements Analysis

Designers of C^2 decision aids and support systems identify and refine decision-making requirements by employing a number of methods. They include survey and questionnaire methods, methods based upon interviews and (direct and indirect) observation, and simulation and gaming-based methods.

The key to C^2 requirements analysis lies in the identification of the essential decision-making tasks, tasks that when well-performed can significantly enhance C^2 decision-making performance.

Requirements analysis is employed to identify not only critical C^2 decision-making tasks, but profiles of the users and organization in which the system will reside as well. User profiles, tasks profiles, and profiles of the organization comprise the requirements equation, as suggested in Figure 9.

Figure 9 presents a three-dimensional requirements matrix that illustrates the intersection of tasks, users, and organizational characteristics. Each cell in the matrix represents a requirements challenge. The tasks in the matrix are generic; in practice, a C^2 requirements analyst would convert those generic tasks into very specific tasks (pertaining to, for example, resource allocation problems, tactical planning, and target value analysis). Perhaps the same requirements analyst would specify users in greater detail than simply inexperienced/experienced/infrequent user/frequent user. Organizational–doctrinal characteristics might also be specified in greater detail. Regardless of the level of detail (and the methods used to achieve it) the requirements matrix suggests that prudent designers of C^2 decision aids and support systems deal with all three dimensions of the requirements challenge.

C^2 System Modeling and Prototyping

Figure 10 presents the C^2 systems design and development process via prototyping. Prototyping is sanctioned by the C^2 design community because it is so difficult to identify and refine C^2 requirements (especially decision-making requirements) the first time through the requirements process. The prototyping premise calls for the design and development of a working model of the decision support system under development, the solicitation of reactions to the model from prospective users, and the refinement of the model when requirements can be validated. Prototyping calls for iteration. It also calls for the development of two kinds of prototype system: "throwaway" and "evolutionary" systems. Throwaway systems are used when requirements are especially difficult to capture; evolutionary ones are used when C^2 requirements are less elusive. (Once requirements begin to emerge, throwaway prototypes evolve into evolutionary ones.)

C^2 Systems Evaluation

C^2 decision aids and decision support systems are evaluated somewhat more comprehensively than conventional software systems. The reason why is simple. C^2 decision aids and support systems are inherently user oriented. Evaluations of their performance must therefore attempt to measure the extent to which the system supports requirements, interfaces well with its users, supports the organizational mission it is intended to serve, contains efficient algorithms, can be maintained, and is (well or badly) documented. In other words,

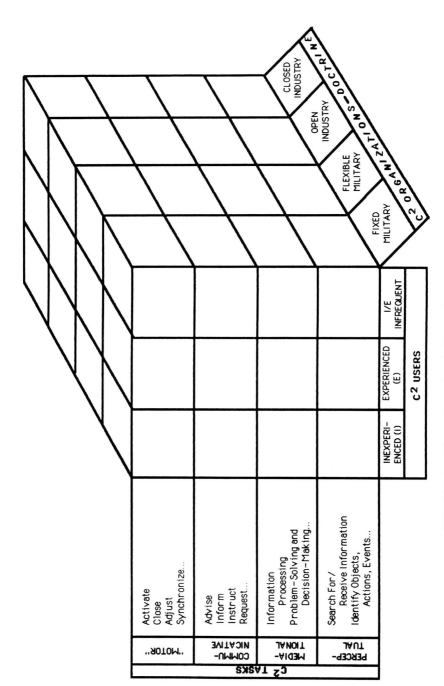

FIGURE 9.   Three-dimensional C² requirements matrix.

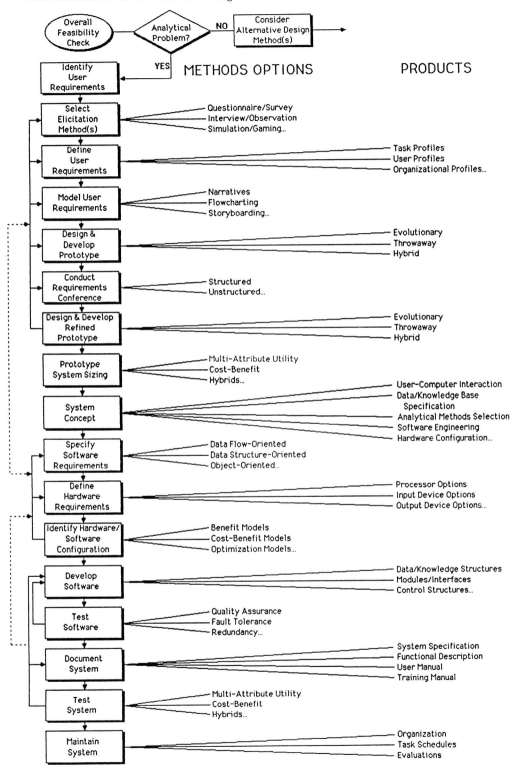

FIGURE 10.   C² system design and development process via prototyping

decision aids and support systems evaluation deals with all of the conventional software performance issues as well as those that pertain to how well or badly the system serves its users and organizations.

One of the very best approaches to the evaluation of decision aids and support systems belongs to Adelman and Donnell [*10*]. Figure 11 presents this multiattribute utility assessment structure for the evaluation of decision aids and support systems. note the orientation to users, organizations, and accuracy. In a fullblown decision aid evaluation this structure would be used in conjunction with a conventional software quality assurance model to determine how well the system supports users and operates.

CASE STUDIES IN THE DESIGN, DEVELOPMENT, AND APPLICATION OF C² DECISION AIDS AND SUPPORT SYSTEMS

C² decision aids and support systems have been applied to a range of C² problems. Many of these systems have remained as prototypes, since they were intended only to demonstrate or prove a concept. Many others, however, have enjoyed operational success.

Some Working Prototypes

CONSCREEN [*11*]

CONSCREEN is a prototype system designed to assist tactical planners in the identification and evaluation of alternative courses of action. The method that it uses is multiattribute utility assessment. The system calls for the user to evaluate a number of courses of action vis-a-vis a set of criteria designed to measure each course of action's desirability criterion by criterion. Figure 12 presents the criteria in the multiattribute utility structure [*11*] used by planners to evaluate alternative courses of action. After planners assess the alternative courses of action, the system calculates the plans overall utility, or value to the planner. The system generates a rank ordering of plans according to the extent to which they satisfy the criteria.

OB1KB [*12*]

OB1KB is an expert system that helps tacticians manage the order of battle. OB1KB uses rules to help commanders make real-time battle management decisions. The system uses a graphic (map-based) interface intended to widen the communications bandwidth between the system's knowledge base and users. The specific tasks that the prototype performs include tracking enemy movements, the identification of enemy location and disposition, and generating estimates of the battlefield situation.

KNOBS [*13*]

KNOBS (Knowledge-Based System) assists tactical Air Force commanders in mission planning, specifically, offensive counterair mission planning. The system assists commanders in the allocation of their resources, selecting the weapons that should be matched with known targets, prioritizing the air tactics that should be used, and the assessment of the impact of constraints, such as adversary behavior and weather. KNOBS is knowledge based, that is, it uses a knowledge base comprised of frames and rules about mission planning.

0.0 Overall Utility

1.0 Aid/User Interface
1.1 Match with Personnel
1.1.1 Training & technical background
1.1.2 Work style, workload, and interest
1.1.3 Operational needs
1.2 Aid characteristics
1.2.1 General
1.2.1.1 Ease of use
1.2.1.2 Understanding Aid's processes
1.2.1.3 Ease of training
1.2.1.4 Response time
1.2.2 Specific
1.2.2.1 User interface
1.2.2.2 Completeness of data files
1.2.2.3 Accuracy of expert judgements
1.2.2.4 Ability to modify judgements
1.2.2.5 Understanding of Aid's algorithms
1.2.2.6 Utility of graphs
1.2.2.7 Utility of print-outs
1.2.2.8 Understanding of text

2.0 User/Aid Organization
2.1 Efficiency Factors
2.1.1 Acceptability of time for
2.1.1.1 Task accomplishment
2.1.1.2 Data management
2.1.1.3 Set-up requirements
2.1.2 Perceived reliability under average battle conditions
2.1.2.1 Skill availability
2.1.2.2 Hardware availability
2.2 Match with organizational factors
2.2.1 Effect on organizational procedures and structure
2.2.2 Effect on other people's position in the organization
2.2.2.1 Political acceptability
2.2.2.2 Other people's workload
2.2.3 Effect on information flow
2.2.4 Side effects
2.2.4.1 Value in performing other tasks
2.2.4.2 Value to related organizations
2.2.4.3 Training value

3.0 Organization/Environment
3.1 Decision Accuracy
3.2 Match between Aid's technical approach and problem's requirements
3.3 Decision process quality
3.3.1 Quality of framework for incorporating judgement
3.3.2 Range of alternatives
3.3.3 Range of objectives
3.3.4 Weighting of consequences of alternatives
3.3.5 Assessment of consequences of alternatives
3.3.6 Re-examination of decision-making process
3.3.7 Use of information
3.3.8 Consideration of implementation and contingency plans
3.3.9 Effect on group discussions
3.3.10 Effect on decision maker's confidence

FIGURE 11. Multiattribute utility assessment structure for C^2 decision aids/support systems evaluation.

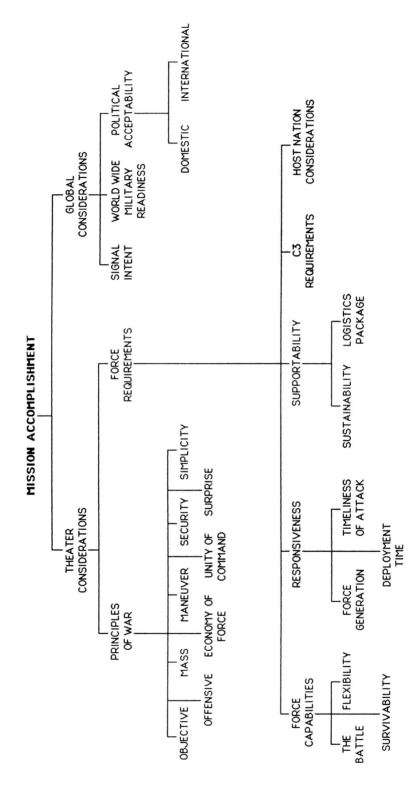

FIGURE 12.   Multiattribute utility assessment structure for the evaluation of alternate tactical plans.

Operational Decision Aids and Support Systems

Decision aids and support systems are used by commanders in a number of environments. They are used to assess the value of alternative targets. They are used for complex route planning. They are used to match weapons to targets. Many of these systems are "embedded" in much larger weapons systems, while others "stand alone" as adjuncts to larger systems.

Several prototypes have led to the issuance of "required operational capability" memoranda which have, in turn, produced support for the development of full-scale decision aids and larger support systems. In the late 1970s, for example, the U.S. European Command (EUCOM) required the capability to perform real-time decision analyses of complicated tactical option selection problems. This requirement led to the development of several systems for EUCOM use.

The U.S. Air Force is embedding decision aids in cockpits as well as in the tactical air commands. The Navy is using decision aids for the placement of sonar buoys, for battle management planning, and for distributed decision making.

The Worldwide Military Command and Control System (WWMCCS) embeds a variety of decision aids; indeed, aspects of WWMCCS and the WWMCCS Information System (WIS) constitute an extremely large decision support system.

Decision aids and support systems are used in the intelligence community to estimate adversary intentions, forecast international crises, and assess the likelihood of new weapons programs in selected countries.

NEXT GENERATION DECISION AIDS FOR C^2

Decision aids for C^2 will continue to evolve. It is safe to predict advances in analytical methodology that will expand the range of problems amenable to computer-based decision aids and support systems. It is also safe to predict that users will continue to clamor for powerful real-time support.

Methods like artificial intelligence, biocybernetics, neural network modeling, and cognitive profiling will emerge in the 1990s as significant forces in the design and development of decision aids. On the implementation side, we can expect the refinement of parallel processors, distributed processors, and processors that can assure reliability and security.

Strategic and tactical decision aiding in the year 2000 will be highly distributed, exceedingly embedded, heavily "behavioral," and "faster than doctrine." The last point is important because the operational community has yet to address the issues connected with the use of systems that may be incompatible with what commanders are taught in the service schools and military experience and doctrine. Technology will continue to affect the evolution and interpretation of doctrine. The use of high technology-based decision aids and support systems will help define this evolution.

In fact, we can expect the integration of a variety of findings (from many disciplines) into a single conceptual architecture for and intelligent, adaptive decision support system concept, as suggested in Figure 13 [*14*].

It is important to note that the design, development, and use of decision aids and support systems for C^2 is not confined to the United States military community. The Soviet Union and a number of European countries have integrated decision aids into their force structures [*15*]. As the pace of battle quickens—due largely to advanced weapons systems' capabilities—the need for real-time decision support is rising.

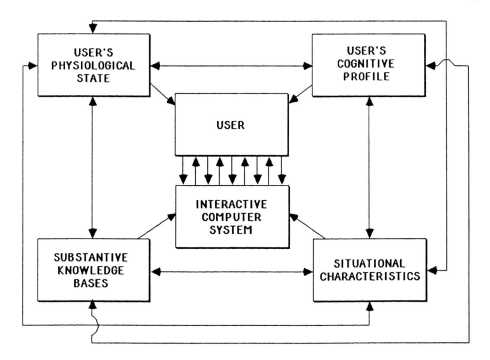

FIGURE 13.   Next generation decision aid system concept.

Finally, as the next generation of users moves into the operational community, we can expect an acceleration of the integration of decision aids and support systems into the operational community. As suggested above, real battlefield requirements will certainly contribute to the acceleration; however, another more powerful change is also occurring in the user community. Whereas just a few short years ago users were extremely inexperienced with analytical computing, future users will have had enormous exposure to computing long before they go into the field. While it is impossible to determine the precise impact of this change, there is no question that the impact will be felt. Opportunities for the design, development, application, and evaluation of C^2 decision aids and support systems can only be expected to rise.

REFERENCES

1. S. J. Andriole, and G. W. Hopple, "They're Only Human: Decision-Makers in Command and Control," *Signal,* 61–66 (October 1984).
2. S. J. Andriole, *Interactive Decision Aids and Support Systems for Strategic and Tactical Command and Control,* International Information Systems, Inc., Marshall, VA, 1987.
3. S. J. Andriole, *Handbook for the Design and Development of Interactive Decision Support Systems*, Petrocelli Books, Inc., Princeton, 1988.
4. S. Barclay, R. V. Brown, C. W. Kelly, III, C. R. Peterson, L. D. Phillips, and J. Selvidge, *Handbook for Decision Analysis*, Decisions and Designs, Inc., McLean, VA, 1977.

5. R. J. Thierauf, *An Introductory Approach to Operations Research,* John Wiley and Sons, New York, 1978.
6. S. J. Andriole (ed.), *Applications in Artificial Intelligence,* Petrocelli Books, Inc., Princeton, 1986.
7. S. J. Andriole, and G. W. Hopple, *Artificial Intelligence and National Defense: Progress and Prospects,* Lexington Books, Lexington, MA, 1988.
8. D. A. Norman and S. W. Draper (eds.), *User Centered System Design,* Lawrence Erlbaum Associates, Hillsdale, NJ, 1986.
9. S. J. Andriole, "Methodologies for Computer-Assisted Decision-Making: A Matrix-Based Requirements/Methods matching Strategy, " in *Advances in Man-Machine Research,* Vol. 5 (W. B. Rouse, ed.), Jai Press, Inc., forthcoming.
10. L. Adelman, and M. L. Donnell, "Evaluating Decision Support Systems: A General Framework and Case Study," in *Microcomputer Decision Support Systems: Design, Implementation and Evaluation* (S. J. Andriole, ed.), QED Information Sciences, Inc., Wellesley, MA, 1986, pp. 285–309.
11. A. W. Martin, R. M. Esoda, and R. M. Gulick, *CONSCREEN—A Contingency Planning Aid,* Decisions and Designs, Inc., McLean VA, 1983.
12. A. H. Weiss, "An Order of Battle Adviser," *Signal,* 91–95 (November 1986).
13. A. J. Tachmindji, and E. L. Lafferty, "Artificial Intelligence for Air Force Tactical Planning," *Signal,* 110–114 (June 1986).
14. S. J. Andriole, "The Design of Microcomputer-Based Personal Decision-Aiding Systems, " *IEEE Trans. Systems, Man and Cybernetics, 12,* 463–469 (1982).
15. J. K. Grange, "Cybernetics and Automation in Soviet Troop Control," *Signal,* 93–96 (December 1984).

BIBLIOGRAPHY

Andriole, S. J. (ed.), *High Technology Initiatives in C3I,* AFCEA AFCEA International Press, Fairfax, VA, 1986.

Andriole, S. J. (ed.), *Microcomputer Decision Support Systems: Design, Implementation and Evaluation,* QED Information Sciences, Inc., Wellesley, MA, 1986.

Andriole, S. J. (ed.), *Artificial Intelligence and National Defense: Applications to C3I and Beyond,* AFCEA International Press, Fairfax, VA, 1987.

Andriole, S. J., and S. M. Halpin (eds.), *Information Technology for Command and Control,* Special of the *IEEE Trans. Systems, Man Cybernetics, 16* (November/December 1986).

Boyes, J. L. (ed.), *Issues in C3I Program Management,* AFCEA International Press, Fairfax, VA, 1984.

Boyes, J. L., and S. J. Andriole (eds.), *Principles of Command and Control,* AFCEA International Press, Fairfax, VA, 1988.

STEPHEN J. ANDRIOLE

INTELLIGENT CONTROL

COMPUTER CONTROL SYSTEMS: NEW PARADIGM HAS EMERGED

New Tendencies in the Development of Control Theory

A new area of systems engineering endeavor has emerged, which can be considered an intersection of Artificial Intelligence, Operation Research, and Control Theory, and which is actively spurred and stimulated by the advances in Computer Science (see Fig. 1).

Early control theory was aiming toward "regulation" and stable operation of machines, and toward providing stable and accurate operation of dynamical systems with feedback, and eventually toward providing required functioning of any preassigned *object of control* including machines in a variety of environments, man–machine systems, and even human teams, economical systems, etc. In the latter incarnation, control theory was understood to be a tool of much broader conceptual entities such as *general theory of systems, cybernetics*, etc.

Control theory turned out to be more viable than these general conceptual entities, primarily because the community of specialists in control theory were always associating themselves with a well-established mathematical apparatus of differential and integral calculi (later enhanced by methodology of linear algebra and other domains of mathematics), and with a concrete customer who understood this mathematical apparatus (and/or believed in it). Yet there was always a definite dissatisfaction with the results and orientation of control theory.

Conventional control deals with a broad variety of problems using a spectrum of devices starting with speed regulators in the early steam engines, and ending with stabilizing a goal-oriented group of spacecraft. However, the following problems are unequivocally considered to be difficult to solve in the paradigm of conventional control theory:

Optimal control of nonlinear systems
Optimum control of stochastic systems
Control of 6DOF multilink manipulators
Control of redundant systems
Control of autonomous robots
Control of systems with multisensor feedback information
On-line control of systems with incomplete initial knowledge of the model and/or of
    the environment
Control of systems under human supervision, etc.

An opportunity to view all these systems in a different, unconventional way has arisen as a result of the broad application of computers, and in particular, industrial computer systems equipped with a variety of transducer-sensors. All of the systems listed above need a loop which would contain the intelligent means capable of dealing with a number of complicated problems: *perception* for organizing a diversified information set coming from a

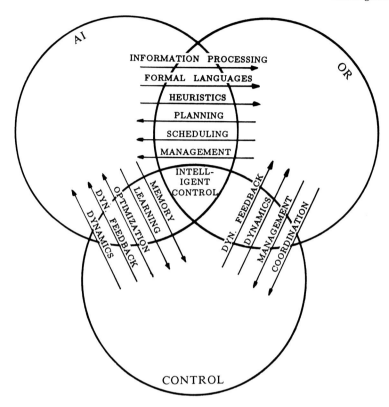

FIGURE 1.   Intelligent control as a part of its scientific paradigm.

multiplicity of sensors, *knowledge base* for enabling the system not only to interpret the results of perception but also to put them in a perspective necessary for determining strategies, and policies of future operation as well as to submit all necessary information for planning/control processes, *planner/controller* to generate proper control sequences, and so on (Fig. 2).

Most of the users in various areas of application have become active in using computer systems, and they have grown accustomed to solving problems by "programming whatever they need." Indeed, computers gave users a long-awaited opportunity to switch from the devices based upon analytical models to the class of devices browsing the memory and searching for the precomputed instruction. On the other hand, man–machine interfaces are broadly based upon use of natural language, linguistical models and algorithms easily compatible with widespread interfaces. The time has come for changing the paradigm.

For a long time, specialists in the area of control had a general feeling that there was a need to formulate the difference between two important entities: the first is so-called *control theory* (conventional), or *theory of automatic control*, and the second elusive entity which is always around and differs drastically from the conventional control theory. This other entity tends to utilize unconventional approaches, to expand out of the domain of integral and differential calculi, into a number of other domains starting with automata theory and ending in linguistics, fuzzy sets, neural networks, and so on.

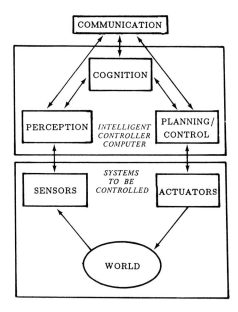

FIGURE 2. Closed loop of a typical intelligent controller.

Conventional Control

A paradigm of conventional control theory treats subjects of interest in view of a particular aspect of their behavior, which can be represented by the apparatus of differential and integral calculi, theory of differential equations, linear algebra, and vector analysis. This is the method of formulating problems according to conventional control theory (e.g., by R. Kalman, 1969). It starts with a definition of a system.

Definition. A system Σ, $\Delta \supset \Sigma$ is a mathematical structure $(T, X, U, \Omega, Y, \Gamma, \varphi, \eta)$ defined by the following axioms:

1. Existence.   There exist a given time set T, a state set X, a set of input values U, a nonempty set of acceptable input functions (or command sequence, or control)
    $$\Omega = \{\omega : T \to U\},$$
    a set of output values Y, and a set of output functions
    $$\Gamma = \{\gamma : T \to Y\}.$$
2. Direction of time.   T is an ordered subset of the reals.
3. Organization.   There exist a state–transition function (or trajectory of motion, or solution curve)
    $$\varphi : T \times T \times X \times \Omega \to X$$

whose value is the state t∈ T resulting at time t∈ T from the initial state (or event) x = x(τ) at the initial time τ∈ T under the action of the input ω∈ Ω. This function has the following properties:

    a.   Direction of time. Function φ is defined for all $t \geq \tau$ (not for all $t < \tau$).

    b.   Consistency. Function φ(t;τ,x,ω) = x for all τ∈ T, all x∈ X, and all ω∈ Ω.

    c.   Nested concatenation, or composition. For any $t_1 < t_2 < t_3$ the following holds

$$\varphi(t_3 \; ; \; t_1, x, \omega) = \varphi(t_3;t_2, \varphi(t_2;t_1,x,\omega),\omega)$$

    for all x∈ X, and for all ω∈ Ω.

    d.   Causality. If ω_1, $\omega_2 \in \Omega$ and $\omega_1 = \omega_2$, then $\varphi(t;\tau,x,\omega_1) = \varphi(t;\tau,x,\omega_2)$.

4.   Transfer function mapping. There exist a map $\eta : T \times X \rightarrow Y$ which defines the output $y(t) = \eta(t,x(t))$.

Several generations of control scientists turned out to be imprisoned within this rigid cage of this model of the reality. One can see immediately that a very strict structure is required from the beginning in which the sets of input, output, and states are clearly separated and given in advance. No negotiation is presumed as a part of the future control operation, no overlapping among the sets is presumed. The system does not contain any notion of *goal of operation* as a part of the structure. However, this might not be required at this stage: it does have the set for control, but we have not yet discussed how this set will be applied.

In reality, we are interested in defining the state-transition function not only *after* but also *before* the definite moment in time ($t \geq \tau$). Otherwise the problems of prediction, the most important problems in the domain of contemporary real systems to be controlled, are made more difficult to resolve.

Axioms 1 through 3 imply that the time scale of the system should be preselected. Another way of dealing with the system model can be introduced which does not require the time scale of the system to be displayed. Interestingly enough, there is a tacit presumption that this concatenation (see the property "c") should be unique, which is an extremely rigid requirement. It actually excludes from consideration all redundant systems where a multiplicity of concatenations can be found.

This set of definitions and axioms is usually supplemented by a demand of stationarity, linearity, and smoothness. Properties of the state-transition function lead to the following theorem. Every system Δ with a state-transition function defined as shown above, and with the norm ‖ω‖ = sup‖u(t)‖ has a transition function in a form

$$\frac{dx}{dt} = f(t, x, \pi^t \omega),$$

where operator π^t is a mapping, $\Omega \rightarrow U$ is derived from $\omega \rightarrow u(t) = \omega(t)$. The suggestion to select π^t in a form $\pi^t: \omega \rightarrow (u(t), u'(t),...,u^{(n)}(t))$ (by L. Zadeh, C. Desoer, 1963) is rejected which further narrows the domain of systems under consideration. In the case of a smooth, linear, finite dimension case, the transition function obeys the simplified relations. (The simplification is determined by selecting norms of the corresponding spaces with no derivatives of the time functions for controls. Only now are we coming to realize that the expectation of L. Zadeh and C. Desoer might be quite right, we are dealing now with systems which need a norm based upon all sets of $u(t)$, $u'(t),...,u^{(n)}(t)$).

$$\frac{dx}{dt} = F(t)\, x\ + G(t)\, u(t),$$
$$y = H(t)\, x(t),$$

where F(t) and G(t) are parts of the expression f(t,x,u(t)) = F(t)x + G(t) u(t), H(t) is a mapping T → {p × n matrices}, which is obtained from the equation

$$y(t) = \eta(t,x(t)) = H(t)x(t),$$

T = R^1, and X,U are normed spaces, F(t) is a mapping F:T → {n × n matrices}, G(t) is a mapping G:T → {n × m matrices}, n is a dimensionality of states x∈ R^n, m is a dimensionality of controls u∈ R^m, p is a dimensionality of outputs y∈ R^p. Proper adjustments and modifications are being made for a variety of cases: discrete systems, systems with nonvarying parameters, etc.

The control law in conventional control is defined as mapping k:T × X → U which puts in correspondence x(t) and u(t) for each moment of time. So, in this formulation we do not define how the control law corresponds to any of the control requirements. The standard problem of control is defined as follows: for each event from the set of initial events (t0,x0) the control should be determined u(•) which transforms this initial event into the goal set, and minimizes the cost functional simultaneously (P. Falb, 1969).

Another definition of a control problem has a clear reference to the *conventional control theory* (J. J. D'Azzo, C. H. Houpis, 1981). The control problem is recommended to be divided into the following steps: (1) establishing a set of performance, (2) writing down the performance specifications, (3) formulating a model of the system in a form of a set of differential equations, (4) *using conventional control theory*, find the performance of the original system, and if it does not satisfy the list of requirements, then *cascade* or *feedback compensation* must be added to improve the response, (5) using modern control theory, assign the entire eigenstructure, or the necessary structure to be designed to minimize the specified performance index (which is understood to be a quadratic performance index). In general, one can easily see a surprising lack of uniformity in the existing views on the *control problem*.

The following definition of control law can be considered consistent with the practice of control [1]: *control of a process implies driving the process to effectively attain a prespecified* goal. One can see that the notion of goal is included in this definition.

Issues of Dissatisfaction with Conventional Control Theory

We can see that the latter definition says nothing about the system or its model. This is remarkable! Indeed, the system per se is beyond the scope of our interest. The body of conventional control offers a model of a system, and then proposes methods of dealing with this formal body within the boundaries of the model selected. The user is more interested in the theory of control which would be invariant of the model of system. What we are interested in (together with the user), is a *process under consideration*, and a *goal we must drive this process toward.*

Given the above example of a classical approach to control problems, the following issues characteristic for the conventional control theory can be focused upon.

a.   Model is considered to be the source of the theories for problem solving, not vice versa. (Let us take the existing mathematical theory, and let us see what are the resembling control problems—this is the business of control theory.) As a result, one can take a book in control theory, and not be able to tell it from a book on the theory of differential equations, or on linear algebra, or on the theory of linear operators.

b.   The problems of control are being formulated and solved not to the extent of the need of the user, but to the extent of intrinsic capabilities of the existing analytical and computational apparatus. (This is what I can do, and I really do not care whether this contrivance can solve your real problem, or not.) The researchers in control area do not want to deal with the so called ill-posed problems. Luckily, the theory of ill-posed problems appears to have brought about a standardization of a class of problems in the area of linear operators. After this the word "ill-posed problem" is understood as a scientific term in the theory of linear operators. In the meantime, all of the real problems of control are actually ill-posed problems, no matter what kind of mathematical model was offered for their solution.

c.   Formulation of the control problem is considered to be a prerogative of the "control person," and not a result of the dialog between the " user" and the "control person." (How can I talk to him when he cannot identify his electronic carburetor neither with rings nor with ideals?). Thus, the technical requirements, and their negotiation is not considered to be a part of solving the problem of control. Dealing with the "natural " cost functions is considered to be outside of control theory. Eventually, the reality of existing cost functions is usually not negotiated, and the designers of control systems often live in the imaginary world of minimization of doubtful(although solvable) quadratic forms. Optimum controllers are traditionally considered to the degree of minimizing the average quadratic error. Time minimization is not considered to be an attractive problem. In general, optimization problems are carefully avoided.

d.   Planning is not considered to be a part of the control problem and is left to the AI people (or to the user). (They should plan, I will just track the motion along with their plan.) References to planning are primarily found in articles on dynamic programming, which ties dynamic programming even more closely to the corresponding AI methodologies (e.g., search, etc.). Other areas of control theory prefer someone external to plan the motion trajectory in advance (preferably, off-line). The results of planning are then considered a part of control problem formulation. In the meantime, the intrinsic linkage between planning and control is perceived in all control problems.

Planning per se is considered to be a topic intrinsic to AI; it seems to be more linguistically inclined, and treats subjects which are being omitted from the classical paradigm of conventional control theory. Formulating the goal of the operation seems to be a topic which appeals to the AI specialist. Cost function is a topic of focus within the operation research (OR) theory. Search algorithms with heuristics are developed by specialists in AI or OR. The only light expansion in the search processes and "planning" is known within the theory of dynamic programming.

e.   Problems of dealing with information are beyond the scope of existing control theory. (Everything should come to me in the form of parameters, variables, or controls—no matter how you do it!.) A significant innovation took place when K.-S. Fu started talking openly about control systems with recognition in the loop. Processes of recognition can affect the control process drastically since the vocabulary of the controller may depend on the recognition results. In general, computers have opened much broader horizons to control specialists dealing with information.

f. Adaptive and learning systems, neural networks, and other imitation brain processes, fuzzy controllers, linguistic controllers, fractal dimension in control, and so on. (In my time, "fuzzy system" meant failure!.) This list starts with items which are accepted as part of control theory, and winds toward much more esoteric areas which are needed by contemporary computer controllers, generated by this need, and cannot be considered strictly legitimate tools of control theory. Some of these topics are taken care of outside of the control discipline. For example, if probabilistic processes with insufficient knowledge of probabilistic characteristics are present within the system, then the dynamics of controlled motion, conditions of stability for such a motion, and minimization of the average quadratic error of such a motion cannot be done legitimately by the control theory methods. So people use these methods illegitimately. Generally, they prefer to apply a number of new ("practical") techniques, running the gamut from woo-doo (introduced by a programmer) methods to some very bright interesting ideas which deserve to be considered seriously.

INTELLIGENT CONTROL; CONTROL THEORY, AI, AND OR BLENDED BY COMPUTER SCIENCE METHODOLOGY

A Change from Dealing with Isolated Problems to Dealing with a Problem as a Part of Its Environment

Control theory focused traditionally on control system (CS) which is supposed to provide operation of a plant (PL) satisfying some requirements (Fig. 3) CS is meant to exist separately from PL, and the flow of controls U is presumed to be generated by CS as something that can be interpreted as a "feedforward" control (FW). External "feedback" (EFB) was to be designed as the ultimate result of the efforts of a control engineer involved in the process of creation of CS. This was the case in the beginning. Very soon, however, it was understood that the plant in turn affects the control system as a kind of internal feedback (IFB). The necessity to constantly explicate plant during the process of control design,

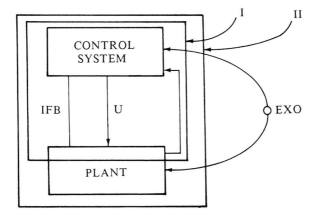

FIGURE 3. Focus of concentration in control theory.

resulted in the conclusion that PL should be represented as a part of CS, and "to design the controller" means "to design the feedback." Surely, the exosystem (EXO) affects both of them. So, instead of concentrating on (I), the control engineers went on with analysis and design of the whole combination (II).

Here it turned out that the methodology of computer science tends to shift the preference in selection of the formal apparatus of model representation. The system is usually decomposed into a plant and a controller. The convenience of DI model (i.e., a model based upon premises and apparatus of differential and integral calculi) obtained as a result of this decomposition, is paid for by tremendous loss of "unstructured" information. In AI methodology, even mathematically unstructured information can be retained within the logical, or linguistical (or similar) systems of representation. However, the elegance and strength of integral/differential models can hardly be utilized within an AI framework in a direct way.

The apparatus of differential and integral calculi (DIC) was a powerful tool that virtually has predetermined the system of representation. Although any problem was initially formulated in a language of technological application (LTA), the bulk of LTA knowledge (negotiated initially with a user) could not be utilized in the problem-solving process because of the constraints imposed by the DIC language, which is always less diversified than LTA language. So, it became a tradition that any set of technical requirements to the future CS as well as a description of the reality of PL, would be translated first from the "language of the engineer," or *LTA representation*, to the lingo of *DIC representation*. After the problem is solved within DIC representation, the solution ought to be translated back to real world language. This process of consecutive translation of the situation from one language into another language is shown in Figure 4.

Undoubtedly, the following inclusion holds: $TR_{LTA} \supset TR_{DIC}$ which determines the same situation with representations of the output of the design process $CSS_{LTA} \supset CSS_{DIC}$. Certainly, one would also have to comply with the reality that DIC techniques could resolve only limited problems. Thus, the control theory has adopted the following custom: only problems that could be solved within the DIC language domain would be attempted. Several decades of this situation led to the exponentially increasing number of various solutions obtained within DIC representation for various problems. However, the actual number of solutions assuming a translation into LTA representation is not as impressive. All LTA activities were done by users. And these users now turned out to be programmers. This had a substantial impact on both the computer and the control specialists. As a result, a variety of technologies appeared, demanding from control systems built upon the LTA representation, that they must not be abridged by the process of mapping the set of technical requirements from LTA representation into DIC representation. These technologies include a variety of computer systems: intelligent machines and robots, flexible and integrated manufacturing systems, autonomous devices including autonomous mobile systems, intelligent systems of control and communication like C^3I (not to mention SDI and similar systems). All of these systems are also equipped by a multiplicity of sensors (including vision), and operate with no human involvement. The problem of translating everything into the paradigm of DIC language seemed formidable. There was a practical necessity of using anything available: in this case, LTA representation. LTA technologies are supported by a powerful engineering tool: the computer, which is coming to be viewed in a broader context than merely a support system for computations (Fig. 5). Taking the limited subset of robots as an example, one can easily understand that DIC representation cannot satisfactorily resolve the problems that arise in this area. Computers are not well suited to DIC representation. Indeed, it is well known that the complete system of linear

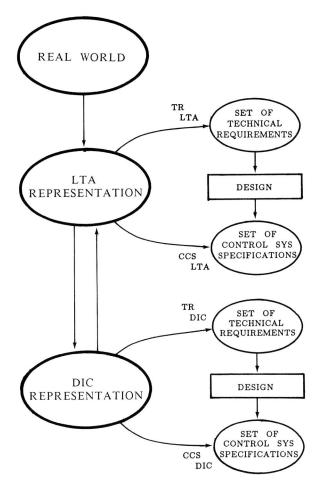

FIGURE 4.   Design based on two different representations.

deterministic differential equations is cumbersome; written for a rigid 6DOF multilink manipulator, efforts to adapt this system have been unsuccessful (although the prototype manipulator is severely simplified, all its parameters are not and cannot be known accurately, nonlinearities and coupling are neglected, errors are magnified by the process of solution, and so on).

Complexity of a System to be Controlled, and Complexity of the Computer Controller

The plant system PL is being driven by CS with the help of a multiple (generally) set of actuators A, under the condition of uncertainty of PL and A parameters (which are known only partially). Since each of the actuators can be associated with a "subsystem" or a "subassembly" of the system, a hierarchical or similar decomposition of the overall system is expected (Fig. 6). After decomposition is completed, the lower levels contain too many information units to be used in the design of the higher levels. Talking about "parameters"

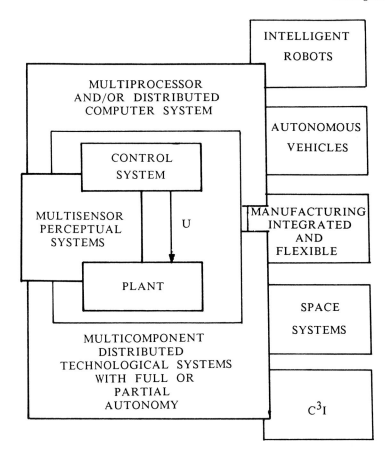

FIGURE 5.   New technological paradigm.

presumes the existence of some model (a mathematical one, usually, in DIC representation), which might not be the case. The knowledge of PL explicated from the LTA representation is frequently presented in such a way that the resulting PL model in DIC representation turns out to be quite rudimentary, or at least, too simplistic. Adaptive controllers seemed to offer a good solution, however, they also tried to confine the richness of the system in a DIC structure of the primary nonadaptive controller. Therefore, sophisticated users turned to the AI models because production systems do not require any model simplification.

The remaining knowledge (if one does not want to lose it) can be taken care of by using the available AI methods (linguistic representations, production systems, etc.). The uncertainties cannot be judged using the existing probabilistic models, since the information does not exist for building such models. New information about the PL parameters should be obtained during plant operation, thus the discovery of the new plant models is an expected part of control procedure. The variety of the expected operation modes should be taken into account and the processes of operation under all possible conditions must be considered. Even for a simple multilink manipulator, one cannot easily answer the question what is the "best" case of operation, what is the "worst" case, and whether there is any hypothetical "average" case which could be accepted as a "design" case. EXO is becoming a part of PL. On the other hand, it is clear by a multiplicity of

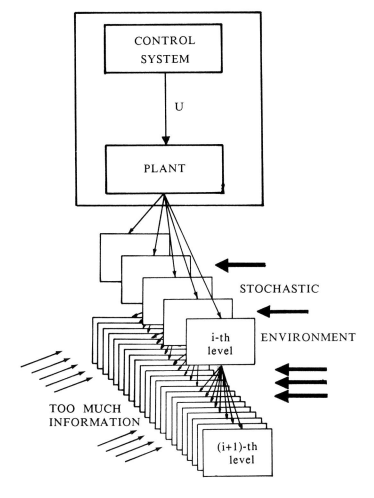

FIGURE 6. Hierarchical decomposition of the system.

controllers since it has many actuators. This *multiactuation* is becoming an important issue in the problem of intelligent control theory.

Exosystem and Multiactuation as Parts of the Overall Problem

Information about EXO often is not available early in its implementation. This information should be recognized within the reality of EXO, and should then be dealt with in proper fashion. This information includes facts of varying degrees of importance (resolution?), which should be processed in different ways. Thus the idea emerges of studying the reality of EXO under different resolutions depending on our interest in the details. Consistency is found for the overall system by using different parts of EXO considered under different resolutions.

The easiest way to establish consistency, is to consider the EXO as a hierarchy of decomposition in parts, or resolutional hierarchy (this concept coincides with the *frame* concept in AI). This is how the perceptual subsystem delivers the EXO to the controller. The hierarchy of EXO is quite similar to the hierarchy of PL: the bulk of the information (knowledge?) about the world, or the *world description* should be decomposed (tessellated) into a hierarchical resolution set of parts (Fig. 7). The mechanism of the new knowledge acquisition is provided by a system of multiple sensors, their signals must be integrated in order to enrich our knowledge of EXO; in other words, EXO should be constantly *perceived*. Perception of EXO should be considered a part of normal system operation; thus learning is a natural procedure which requires recognition of familiar features and objects as well as discovery of unfamiliar entities and concepts.

On the other hand, since most of the systems are multiactuator systems [*4*], their actuators must be assigned individual controllers, and each of them should be dealt with as an individual control system within its *scope of attention*. At the same time, the complete multiactuator system can be considered as an object of control: a single system is supposed to coordinate the activities of the multiple controller subsystems. A separate controller submits to the *coordinator* a control assignment, which is obtained at a higher level of the control hierarchy (lower level of resolution), and deals with the objects, parameters, variables, and controls formulated at a higher level of generality.

Thus, we come to the hierarchically intelligent controller which has organization, coordination, and hardware control levels (see Fig. 8) as described in by Saridis [*2,3*]. The

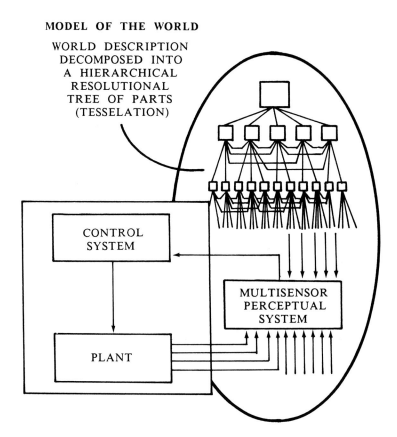

FIGURE 7.   Multisensor perceptual system and its inner knowledge representation.

organization level accepts and interprets the input commands and related feedback from the system, defines the tasks to be executed, and segments it into subtasks in their appropriate order of execution [5]. At the organization level, appropriate *translation and decision schemata* linguistically implement the desirable functions [6, 7]. The coordination level receives instructions from the organizer and feedback information for each subtask to be executed and coordinates execution at the lowest level. The lowest level control process usually involves the execution of a certain motion and requires besides the knowledge of the mathematical model of the process, the assignment of end conditions and a performance criterion (cost function) defined by the coordinator [8].

Problem Formulation Is Also a Part of the Control Problem

Finally, as a rule, the task is posed imprecisely, the description of many functions to be provided by a computer control system is incomplete, and the expected situations of the operation are given to a control engineer by the user in an approximate way. In many cases, this is determined by the possibility of transferring the knowledge of a user to the designer (control engineer). In many cases, it is determined by intractability of the problem as it appears to the user. The control engineer is designing a substantial part of the future system (starting with task formulation and ending with actuators operation).

However, often this control engineer is not familiar with the context of operation. Long ago, it was understood that the design of the control process was a tradeoff with the parameters of the system. Later, it became clear that it was a tradeoff with the model as well as the actual structure of the system. Now we know that the tradeoff includes the processes of task formulation. Moreover, the negotiation of the task-set is part of design. We can

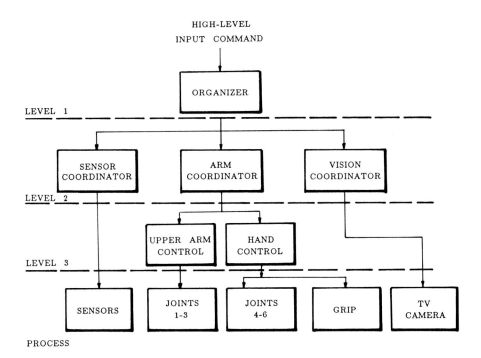

FIGURE 8.   Hierarchical intellegent control system.

expect that in future systems, the continuous process of task negotiation will be a part of the computer control system (Fig. 9).

INTELLIGENT CONTROLLER

Considering all of these factors together, the concept of intelligent controller emerges as a combination of : (a) methodology of modeling the system with a hybrid DIC/LTA representation, (b) a hierarchical model of imprecise and incomplete plant, (c) hierarchical and incomplete knowledge of the exosystem delivered by multiple sensors, which is being reorganized constantly in the process of learning, (d) task negotiation as a part of the computer control system as well as the control process (see Fig. 10). A number of techniques have been devised in, and developed for this particular paradigm of consideration (theory of hierarchical control, entropy methods for hierarchical controller design, principle of increasing precision with decreasing intelligence, etc.). A number of potentially applicable results within this paradigm include theory of team control, theory of fuzzy sets, and systems. Many developments of control theory are specifically for use in

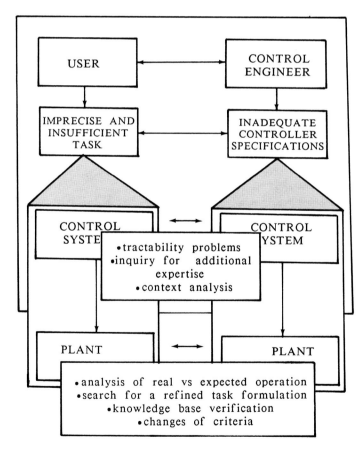

FIGURE 9.   Structure of the "user–control engineer" negotiations.

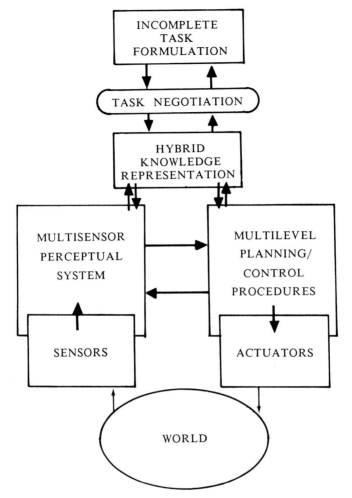

FIGURE 10.   Structure of intellegent controller.

control systems (learning and self–organizing systems, neural networks, knowledge-based, linguistical, and cognitive controllers).

NEW DISCIPLINE: INTELLIGENT CONTROL

Blend of the Disciplines: Control Theory, AI, OR

So, how is it possible to control the motion, and more generally, the development of any kind of system, independently of their complexity, independently of our capability of separating it from the environment and localizing it, independently of the context, independently of the forms of knowledge available, and the methods for its representation? It cannot be done using control theory alone. While powerful, its tools are restricted by the self-imposed myopic constraints of the designer and hidden within the mechanism of DIC representation.

Nor can Artificial Intelligence theory (is there any?) accomplish the task: AI surrenders when time-dependent dynamic processes are involved. It divorces itself from the ideas of stability, controllability, and others. Neither Control Theory not AI can operate out of the OR paradigm: its queues and game situations are typical for the variety of applications. Intelligent Control tends to fuse these three disciplines together when necessary. The alloy seems to be powerful and flexible. Analysis of published reports in the area of Intelligent Control over the period of 1983–1988 shows that many of the articles were theoretically interesting, and useful in application, yet they could not be viewed in the framework of the conventional control theory.

Intelligent Control as a discipline, is expected to provide generalization of the existing control discipline on the basis of

Combined analysis of the plant and its control criteria, with the system of goals, and metagoals which determine the process of negotiations through the overall design procedure

Processes of multisensor operation with information (knowledge) integration and recognition in the loop

Man–machine cooperative activities, including imitation and substitution of the human operator

Computer structures representing the above-mentioned elements

Here we are in the dark as to the situation in the area of Intelligent Control. None of the elements mentioned above is supported by substantial research and analysis. There is no established terminology identifiable with the area of Intelligent Control. The word "intelligent" is used in a variety of contexts with different nuances of meaning which contributes to confusion in a number of cases. There is a tremendous inertia of following the conventional recommendations and views which is hindering the development of intelligent control ideas and methods.

A new area of the system science Intelligent Control is emerging at the cross section of a number of important scientific disciplines: automatic control, artificial intelligence, and operation research. Interest in this discipline began about a decade ago, however, the "birthdate" of Intelligent Control can be alluded to as the date of the first meeting of scientists interested in Intelligent Control (August 1985, Troy, NY). This meeting testified to the existence of substantial interest in this phenomenon. At the first meeting, the principles of Intelligent Control as a discipline were established. After the first meeting, the IEEE Technical Committee on Intelligent Control was organized. About two hundred IEEE members joined the new committee. An interesting discussion within the IEEE Technical Committee on Intelligent Control is in progress, dedicated to defining Intelligent Control as well as to constructing a possible syllabus of courses on Intelligent Control.

At the second meeting, further discussions demonstrated continued growth of interest in the new emerging discipline (Philadelphia, January 1987). The second meeting derived from the principles obtained at the first, approaches some specifics, and highlights many future perspectives. This meeting had more sponsors, and broader participation (the first meeting comprised only U.S. participants; the second included representatives from Europe, Japan, and several developing nations). The third international conference (Washington, D.C., August 1988) demonstrated a number of conventions in terminology as being accepted by most participants; several hundred scientists became members of the Technical Committee.

Dealing with Knowledge: A Distinctive Trait of Intelligent Control

The category of "knowledge" cannot be considered a prerogative solely of computer science anymore. Knowledge is becoming a "key player" for intelligent control systems ("knowledge-based controllers"). Knowledge can be defined as the function of removing uncertainty in the operation of an intelligent machine [9]. Saridis proposed to measure knowledge by the entropy, and to use the rate of knowledge as a measure of intelligence of the machine. The following rates are of importance: throughput, blockage, coordination, internal decision, and noise. Knowledge requires taking care of the following activities: perception, representation, cognition, reasoning, and decision making (including planning/control).

One of the most powerful ideas of Intelligent Control, is that of establishing a direct link between the organization of knowledge and the structure of the Intelligent Controller. In conventional control theory, knowledge is involved in the structure of the controller, and in the processes of control only implicitly. We are not yet used to working with this matter (knowledge). Yet, we can foresee the drastic changes in the design and control methodologies linked with knowledge as a control agent.

This is why research in the area of Intelligent Control centers around two major topics linked with knowledge

Knowledge Implementation: structures of intelligent control systems
Knowledge Evaluation: observations and computations in intelligent control

The process of removing the uncertainty in the execution of various tasks can be characterized by *precision* [9]. Since the value of precision is limited at each hierarchical level, the control hierarchy can always be associated with the resolutional hierarchy [10–12]. Resolution of knowledge representation strongly affects all subsystems of the system shown in Figure 10.

THE STRUCTURE AND THE SUBJECTS OF INTELLIGENT CONTROL THEORY

The word "intelligent control" was coined by the late K.-S. Fu [13–15], who dedicated the last decade of his life to research and analysis of various aspects of the nonconventional control systems. The definition of Intelligent Control has appeared initially in Ref. *1*, where the property of "Intelligence" is being linked with the capability of a system to expose a variety of features which traditionally had been out of the scope of specialists in conventional control theory: decision making, games, image recognition, adaptation to the uncertain media, self-organization, planning and scheduling of operations, etc. Even the very process of control problem formulation is visualized in an unconventional way: no preferred mathematical model is presumed, most of the information is presented in a descriptive manner, and the initial assumptions are being challenged during the whole process of problem solving, and then during the process of control.

It became clear also that any actual advances in AI, robotics, and in general, in intelligent machines, can be achieved only on the basis of control application of particular AI methods in robots and other intelligent machines [2]. The same ideas are valid for CAD-CAM, large space systems, flexible manufacturing, unmanned systems, telepresence devices, autonomous vehicles, etc. During the last decade, the extensive development of new technologies based upon computer application and linked with robotics and integrated manufacturing in industry, intelligent warfare, and C[3]I in military systems, space technologies, etc., has generated a number of new extensions for the area of Intelligent Control. Fusing multisensor outputs, employing visual feedback, observing different parts of the same process at different levels of control hierarchy, all have helped create a new type of controller: controllers with recognition in the loop [*13–15*].

Once the term recognition became acceptable, other terms followed; the main one is knowledge. It becomes clear that a closed mathematical model is not to be placed in the center of analysis and synthesis of control systems and processes, but rather, a system of *world representation* based upon a broader knowledge of the operation to be performed, and the context of the performance. The structure of the intelligent controller as an object of analysis of the theory of Intelligent Control will be discussed below (Figs. 2, 8, 10).

The multiple advantages of semiotic systems of world representation gave birth to a new type of control system: a system with linguistical control. From numerical control, liguistical controllers evolved to control by concepts. An advanced type of learning process: namely, conceptual learning linked with creation of new concepts, has attracted the attention of specialists in learning, and stimulated interest in utilization of learning properties in controllers [*3*].

A strong link between Intelligent Control and Operation Research theory became obvious with the appearance of systems with adaptive control and self–organization [*1*]. Now, with rule-based and other knowledge-based controllers indicating that Production Systems, given thorough treatment in the area of Artificial Intelligence, become a legitimate part of computer-based controllers, the merger of all of them: AI, OR, and Control Theory, seems unavoidable within the framework of the Theory of Intelligent Control [*3,16–18*].

Synthesis of the theory of Intelligent Control is not expected to be just a mechanical gathering and combining of all the related theoretical "gadgets" from the literature. A number of forgotten or overlooked ideas can fertilize existing theories. For example, the problem of negation is becoming increasingly important in systems of knowledge representation for intelligent control. The "power of veto" (M. Pedelty, 1963) can be understood in a sense apart from a trivial logical negation. (Interestingly enough, the use of the generalized negation is considered a major stage in the evolution of human intelligence.)

The appearance of this new discipline is not being met with cheers by everybody. It is well known that many of AI, OR, and Control specialists are not leaning toward any merger among these disciplines. It seems much easier to build a theory around the model than to build a model to satisfy the conclusions from the theory. However, it is clear now that this merger is unavoidable, since the results of this merger are long awaited in robotics, integrated manufacturing, computer-aided design, and many other areas.

Intelligent Control does not aim to achieve incremental development of a definite formal tool as happened in the theory of conventional control, which is developing all possible implications from the theory of differential and integral equations, and is doing so in a rigidly consistent manner. The goal of Intelligent Control is rather to achieve a more adequate satisfaction of real requirements in real environment by a consistent blending of a variety of scientific formal theories and methods borrowed from different scientific domains. It is expected that the scientific consistency of Intelligent Control as a discipline will be provided by a consistency of the functioning system for which the problem has been solved, so to speak, consistency on a metalevel of its representation.

MAJOR THEORETICAL ISSUES OF THE INTELLIGENT CONTROL THEORY

Ill-Posedness of Real Problems

The problems of control in reality are usually ill-posed. Ill-posed problems arise almost always when the experimental data are to be used to construct a model of reality. Assume the model of system is expected to be constructed in the form $Au = f$, $f \in F$, where $A:D_A \supset U \rightarrow F$ is an operator with a nonempty domain of definition D_A, in a metric space U, with a range in a metric space F. The ill-posed problem is on hand when the conditions of solvability, uniqueness, and stability are not satisfied. (Solvability requires that the range of the value Q_A of the operator A coincide with F; uniqueness requires that the equality $Au_1 = Au_2$ for any $u_1, u_2 \in D_A$ should imply the equality $u_1 = u_2$; and the stability condition requires that the inverse operator A^{-1} be continuous on F [19]). An important class of ill-posed problems is generated by random errors in the input information, or by a stochastic nature of the source of information [20]. *Well-posedness* (A. Tikhonov, 1943) is achieved by using a concept of narrowing of region of definition of the primary operator. The problem is said to be well-posed in the Tikhonov sense if:

It is known a priori a solution u of the problem which belongs to the specified set M, $D_A \supset M$, and the solution u is unique in the class M

Infinitely small variations of the solution u correspond to infinitely small variations of the right-side f in ($Au = f$) retaining the solution in the class M

Regularization of the ill-posed problems is based on the idea that the minimum deviations of the f values can be stabilized by using some auxiliary nonnegative functional satisfying some additional parametric conditions (A. Tikhonov, 1963, 1965). These ideas are important since they attract our attention to the processes in the vicinity of the solution. It means that the model in the vicinity can be be different from the model in-the-large. This in turn implies a powerful conclusion about *nested set models* (since the consideration about a couple vicinity model-model-in-the-large, can be repeated recursively).

Nested Models of Information Acquisition, Estimation, Identification, Representation, and Control

It is tempting to consider this nested set of models as a phenomenon of a general type which is linked with the general laws of efficient information processing systems with limited computer power [18]. Any methodology of successive approximation suggests a need in using nested representation system with consecutive refinement of the resolution of information top-down [21]. The advantages of successive approximations were the focus of R. Bellman's early works [22] as related to the control problems with limited storage.

A class of dynamic systems is being successfully solved by using so-called *multigrid* methods. Nested hierarchical representation of information with its consecutive retrieval properties (top-down estimation, identification, and control) is becoming commonplace in information systems and databases. It seems that the models of *scattering* in estimation theory are kindred to the general framework of nested hierarchical models of representation, information acquisition, estimation, identification, and control. One can expect that merger between these methods with multiple time-scale analysis is inevitable [23,24].

However, this conceptual scheme is not appropriate within the structure of conventional control theory. Obviously, the upper levels of the nested hierarchy with their

pyramid   nested   multiboard
                      knowledge base   planning/control
vision computer   computer   computer

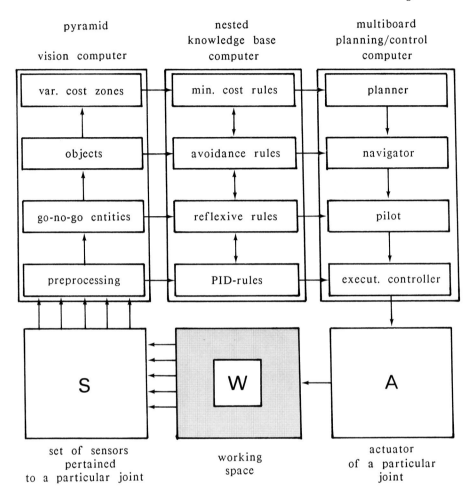

FIGURE 11.   Nested multiloop structure.

low resolution of state representation and slower time scales coincide with activities typical for nondynamic planning with its vague results and approximate recommendations. Clearly, the lower the level, the higher the accuracy and the faster the time scale (i.e., more dynamic model is being considered). This gradual change from the planning processes toward real-time control is becoming clearer to researchers and control engineers.

Nested Hierarchy of Control Loops

Given the considerations above, one can transform the loop shown in Figure 10 into the nested hierarchy of control loops (see Fig. 11). This phenomenon can help us to consider planning/control as a joint recursive process, and to build all other algorithms for dealing with information and knowledge, in a similar manner. One can see that while the loops are independent control-wise, they are linked together correspondingly within the vertical structures of representation for perception, knowledge organization, and planning/control. This vertical linkage provides consistency of the overall controller operation. In the conventional controller, the flow of control information is never coordinated with similar processes at other levels of resolution (from above, and from below) as well as at the other time scales.

It was demonstrated [*10,12*] that nested hierarchy of knowledge (which is organized according to the degree of certainty and belief), implies a nested hierarchy of decisionmaking processes. This leads to a similar nested hierarchical structure of a controller. Nested hierarchical controllers turned out to be successful in the initial efforts in the area of autonomous robotics. Three-level NHC with a module based on Planner-Navigator-Pilot system, is currently employed in several versions of mobile autonomous robots. However, no nested control loops were introduced at that time, and the key significance of processing at different resolutions at each hierarchical level was not completely understood.

The multiresolutional loops of the controller shown in Figure 11 can be considered an entity ("intelligent module"). This entity is built upon two interrelated knowledge bases: one, carrying the entity relationship structure of the word representation, and another, defining planning/control operations upon this structure.

Negotiation of Cost Function Among the Loops

One of the first approaches proposed as a successful decision-making process upon nested hierarchical structures, was suggested by Y. C. Ho and K.-C. Chu [*24–26*]: that, in certain cases, the dynamic problem to an equivalent static team decision problem, and for LQG cases in particular, the optimal control problem can be expressed as a linear function of the observed data. T. Yoshikava (1973, 1978) has demonstrated that, in a discrete time system with N control stations, the (partially) nested information structure of Ho and Chu can be represented as a one-step delay-sharing information structure, and the algorithm of dynamic programming (DP) is applicable. DP seems to be the most appropriate and perspective method for the following reasons:

1. Most of the systems we are dealing with in the intelligent control area are substantially nonlinear, coupled, and cumbersome: off-line precomputation of table look-up would be expected for control of such a systems.
2. DP as a graph search allows for enhancement by a number of heuristic methods which are intended to make the algorithms more computationally efficient.

Selection of the proper system of cost functionals is becoming important. Few cost assignment strategies are available that can be considered "tractable," and confirmed by substantial experience of broad application. One possible alternative is the strategy of cost assignment in which the total cost of the node selection ("feasibility of the node expansion") C_f is divided in two parts

$$C_f = C_g + C_h \qquad \text{(P. E. Hart, N. J. Nilsson, B. Rafael, 1968)}$$

where C_g is the cost from the initial node to the one of the set of generated nodes candidates, and C_h is an evaluation of the cost from the node candidate to the goal.

When no additional information is available, one should determine the minimum possible value of distance between the candidate node and the goal, using the accepted metric of the space of the search. This strategy leads efficiently to the optimum solution. Another strategy, known from the Stackelberg games is "leader-follower" strategy. Its recommendations coincide with the heuristic of A* algorithm: the upper bound of the minimum cost should be selected for comparison of alternatives. In a nested hierarchy these recommendations determine the *envelope of independent decision-making*.

The nested resolutional (by generalization) world representation (e.g., category of "knowledge" C_{gk}) corresponds to the nested resolutional (by attention) world representation (e.g., category of "knowledge" C_{ak}) as follows

$$\dots \supset C_{gk,i-1} \supset C_{gk,i} \supset C_{gk,i+1} \supset \dots$$
$$\downarrow \qquad \downarrow \qquad \downarrow$$
$$\dots \subset C_{ak,1-1} \subset C_{ak,i} \subset C_{ak,i+1} \subset \dots$$

which is the major basis of nested decision-making processes upon these hierarchies A rule of ordering the decisions follows on the basis of nesting and the policy of decision making. Given a nested world representation

$$S_1 \supset S_2 \supset S_3 \supset \dots \supset S_i$$

and a set of cost functionals for these representations, based upon accepted decision making policy, the set of decisions will constitute a nested hierarchy

$$D_p(S_1) \supset D_p(S_2) \supset D_p(S_3) \supset \dots \supset D_p(S_i)$$

(proof and related commutative diagrams are given in Ref. *12*).

Planning in the Loop

Planning is traditionally considered to be a process which is performed separately from the process of control This is acceptable for the vast multiplicity of systems where planning can be performed off-line, and the process of control can be initiated given a set of highly generalized units of knowledge together with a number of unchangeable goals. By lowering the level of generalization and keeping the certainty and belief within the required limits of the level resolution, we can build in a hierarchy of nested planning processes. In this hierarchy, the desirable trajectory determined at the higher level arrives at the lower level as a *fuzzy envelope of operation* (FEO). New planning is being done within FEO at a higher resolution.

This decoupling of the decision-making upper levels (or *off-line stages*) from the lower levels of decision making and immediate performance (or *on-line stages*) is probably the most characteristic property for distinguishing the planning stages from the control stages of operation as well as for distinguishing the corresponding subsystems or any device where constant human involvement is presumed. This decoupling does not take place in the intelligent control system: planning and control are inseparable parts of the unified HNC. Planning and control are linked by the intermediate level of decision making which deals with processes which require knowledge use at a definite level of generalization, but after processes of updating are completed.

Attention-driven planning means that at this intermediate level, the results of the ongoing motion affect the results of generalization (since the system of "Perception" initiates processes of information updating). We name planning processes *navigation* per se at the level of "Planning-control" subsystem where the results of real-time updating become crucial for successful planning. The nested hierarchy of perception does not require hierarchy of sensors, although it does not preclude any acceptable hardware solution. Nested hierarchy at the preprocessing stage is viewed as a result of sequential zooming, or the focusing of attention. Zooming must be based upon focusing of attention, otherwise the constraint of the limited computing power would not be satisfied. (One can see that this concept can be interpreted within the framework of existing theories of image organization and interpretation.)

The processes of planning should be performed at each level, and cumulatively, should constitute a nested hierarchy of mutually consistent results. The whole problem must be solved based upon a new set of premises pertaining to knowledge-based motion control of autonomous systems and using other means of solution. The new premises generate new promises, and new strategies of planning for a hierarchical nested intelligent module can be devised within the structure of the intelligent controller.

Planning processes determine the desirable motion goals and/or trajectories (with increased precision at lower levels of planning) without actually moving. Thus, planning is expected to generate the input to the control system in the form of a description of the state (or the sequence of states) to be achieved during the operation. This means, that the system of planning must actually *predict* the motion trajectory which should be admissible, and at the same time it should provide the desirable value of the cost function.

Joint planning/control process means that the control system input is to be determined as a result of planning. Finally, it means that, in the autonomous control system, planning and control should be considered as a hierarchically joint knowledge-based process (and/or system) because of their intrinsic interactive character and mutual influence. This principle of planning/control inseparability is totally consistent with existing theory and practice of design and implementation of hierarchical intelligent systems.

All of the planning–control levels of the mechanism of knowledge-based navigation interact vertically via recursion of the algorithms of sequential production providing sequential refinement top-down, and correctional replanning bottom-up. Functioning of the hierarchical production systems of perception, and planning-control, is supported by vertical interaction of levels in the "knowledge base" via aggregation and decomposition based upon preassigned values of resolution per level. So, the thesaurus as well as context, exist as a result of internal processes of self-organization within the body of knowledge.

On the contrary, the two subsystems: perception-knowledge base and knowledge base-planning/control (shown in Fig. 10) are viewed in the theory of intelligent control, as *vertical nested knowledge processing hierarchies with horizontal interaction per level.* Indeed, all new knowledge acquired should be organized, the list of primitives in operation must be verified and updated. This procedure is done at a horizontal level and exercises the control algorithms. In the latter case, the map of the world as well as the list of rules to deal with this map are becoming an object of heuristic discretization and search.

Prediction, on the other hand, should be obtained before the actual motion starts, and information on the world at this stage is usually incomplete. Thus, the contingencies must be contemplated based upon construction of plausible situations for which the uncertain variables and parameters should be estimated. Synthesis of contingencies is more efficient if the zones of state space are eliminated where the search should not be done. Most of these zones are determined by constraints and the dynamic model of intelligent control system. Interestingly enough, the dynamic models should be different for different levels of the intelligent controller system: the higher the level of nested hierarchy the lower is the influence of the dynamic processes linked with motion. Clearly, the role of the control subsystem is presumed to be a *compensatory* one; the uncertainties of the initial information, and the inconsistencies of the cost function formulation should not diminish the expectations of the desirable results of motion conveyed to the control system in the form of the plausible situations. The specifics of any intermediate stage between the planning and control (here it has been named traditionally "navigator") is reflected in the specifics of dealing with the knowledge base, which is being constantly updated at this level.

The *contingency motion trajectories* which are obtained as a result of planning (and subsequently, as a result of navigation) must be considered as a set of alternative tasks for control, and is to be input to the controller. Thus, the more successful planning (i.e., the better the uncertainties have been handled at the stage of planning, and the closer the preplanned trajectory is to the potential optimum control trajectory), the easier will be the compensatory role of the conventional controller, which is presumed to be at the bottom of the planning-control hierarchy.

Perception Stratified by Resolution

In the subsystem P (perception), the information mapped from the world is stored and organized. The process of organization presumes the process of recursive generalization: the "whole" at the input in P is many times stratified by resolution.

We will name "phaneron" the array of information which is coming into P from the whole multiplicity of sensors. (The term "phaneron" was introduced by C. S. Pierce for the totality of information which can be called *phenomenal world*). Phaneron is not structured at the moment of arrival, it should be recognized and identified within ER structure. These processes are broadly discussed in the literature, and the importance of such phenomena as "attention," and "resolution" is emphasized often in the literature on computer vision.

Separation in levels appeared to be a natural phenomenon linked with the properties of attention, and its intrinsic links with the process of generalization. In fact, generalization is required for the efficient use of computing resources and allocation, and attention is one of its tools. Thus, the new class labels which are created by the process of generalization, are being considered as new primitives of the upper level of world representation. This rule: the class labels of the lower level are considered as primitives for the higher level, is one of the laws of the mechanism of nested hierarchy.

The results of this identification (a snapshot of the world) contain information, parts of which can be different than the previous snapshot, and part will be the same (e.g., about relations among objects and/or their properties). Thus identification can be accomplished only in the context, i.e., in constant interaction with another body of information (thesaural knowledge base). This affects the set of preprocessing procedures which are separate from the rest of the intelligent module primarily because of the initial experience of manufacturing of the computer vision systems. Proper allocation of the information contained within phaneron should be simultaneous with the process of finding phaneron structure (or image interpretation).

Nested Dynamic Programming

The principle of optimality of Bellman can be stated as follows for stochastic problems: at all times, no matter present information and past decisions, the remaining decisions must constitute an optimal policy with regard to the current information set. Bar-Shalom (1981) has shown that in the cases of incompletely observed Markov process, stochastic dynamic programming can be applied. The sequence of "planning-navigating-piloting (or guidance) actuator control (or execution)" appears as a direct result of the nested hierarchical search in the structure of information under consideration. The method of nested dynamic programming (NDP) follows from the commutative diagrams and analysis given in Ref. 12. It states that the optimum control should be found by consecutive top-down and bottom-up procedures, based on the following rules.

> *Rule 1.* NDP should be performed first at the most general level of information system with complete (available) world representation.

This will obviously lead to a very fuzzy solution from the view of the lowest level of the system ("actuator"). However, this provides substantial advantages later: the substantial part of the world will be excluded later from consideration at the lower levels.

> *Rule 2.* NDP is being performed consecutively level after level top down. The subspace of the search at each of the consecutive lower levels is constrained by the solution at the preceding upper level recomputed to the resolution of the next lower level.

The area which for the upper level was considered as the optimum solution, is considered at the lower level as the stripe (zone) of independent decision making. However, due to the additional information which appears at a given level during the performance, the optimum solution of the lower level may require seeking beyond the envelope of independent decision making. Rule 3 is to be applied in this case.

> *Rule 3.* When during the actual motion, due to the new information, the optimum trajectory determined at a given level must violate the assigned boundaries, this new information should be submitted to the upper level (proper generalization must be performed, and the information structure must be updated). This generates a new top-down NDP process.
> *Rule 4.* When arrival of the new information is bounded (e.g., by a "limit of vision"), then the recursion of nested process of planning is being done with consecutive process of subgoals creation.

The nested hierarchy of maps $\{m_i\}, i = 1,2\ldots$ is the input for the planning/control system. Actually, this nested hierarchy is being generated in the process of interaction between the subsystems M and C. Let us demonstrate how this process of interaction proceeds:

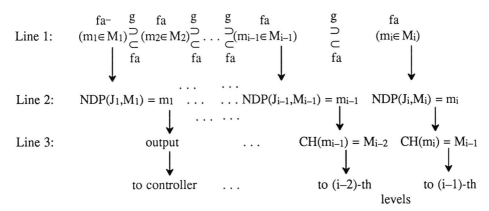

Line 1 shows two nested hierarchies: one based on generalization (of maps $\{M_i\}$) and another on focus of attention (of maps $\{m_i\}$). Hierarchy of sets is obtained from the hierarchy of sets of applying the NDP algorithm per level (line 2). To do this, a nested hierarchy is added to the nested hierarchy. In order to compute a set, the results of applying

NDP per level, are enhanced up to the meaningful consistent map partition; one possible algorithm for this is "convex hull." This system is then at the closed loop level to top-down level and after convergence, the system of controller commands is obtained.

Levels of the control algorithm constitute the nested hierarchy of the "team players" which uses the "initial scope," constraints, and cost functional refined by the upper level in order to submit the results for the lower level.

REPRESENTATION IN INTELLIGENT CONTROL

The prevailing environment of blending computer science with control theory has changed the methodology of representation. AI, OR, and control theory, traditionally had different approaches to the problem of world representation. In the past, the problem of adequate world representation was given limited attention in the control theory. Models based upon differential and integral calculi (DIC representation) were considered a major tool for dealing with control problems. Goals and control strategies are frequently described implicitly. In systems of Intelligent Control this traditional representation is becoming inadequate for problem solving.

General Issues of System Representation

In conventional control theory, the system is considered a collection of ordered pairs of time functions representing inputs and outputs. A minimal amount of past information is given which is required to completely describe the future behavior of the system. Thus a set of integral/differential equations is presumed to be analyzed. This apparatus entails acceptance of a multiplicity of conventions which restrict both shape of the processes and the character of the relationships among the processes and the system.

System Modeling and Identification

Certainly, the plant as well as the controller are only approximations. For many practical cases, this simplification is acceptable. The process of modeling is based upon identification of a structural system. Interestingly, the need of rigidly introduced structural or parametric identification procedure was never fully appreciated out of the context of the advanced control systems with self-identification. In the meantime, the need for the rigid approach to system identification is becoming of paramount importance, otherwise the subsequent steps in applying all means of control methodology will fail to be supported by the system representation which must be based on the same initial premises.

Analytical Models of Various Order

Based on decomposition of the systems (usually performed on intuitive level), DIC models are built which are very complex and of a high order even in comparatively simple cases. A number of order reduction techniques are known. The most powerful is based on an "elegant" process of decomposing the system in such a way that the subsystems either have a very low order or assume representation in a matrix form, allowing for an easy computational model. All of these techniques use experience-based heuristics. Thus, the AI-related liberal methods of dealing with the problem description, from the very beginning, permeates this (pertaining to DIC models) seemingly rigid approach to representation. Since the heuristics are never (or very seldom) devised explicitly, the researcher loses the opportunity to continuously verify the adequacy of representation at the different stages of the process or design.

Nonanalytical Models Based Upon
Differential and Integral Calculi

In many cases, DIC models cannot provide for a closed form solution, or generate an elegant computational model which substitutes the closed form solution. Then the computational models are applied which require a kind of on-line, or even off-line simulation of the system. This happens frequently when an integration should be done, when the structure of the system is changed in time, when the automata are simulated, and so on. The boolean nonanalytical controllers are surprisingly similar to production systems borrowed from AI. Algorithms of dynamic programming can be related to OR with the same confidence as they are presently related to the area of Control Theory.

General Concept of Nested Hierarchical Representation of Knowledge for Intelligent Control Systems

The concept of nested hierarchical knowledge representation (NHKR) is instrumental in Intelligent Control theory. All hierarchical systems of knowledge representation, as well as all hierarchical control structures are based on this concept. This concept embraces methodologies of nested hierarchical refinement, multigrid methods, etc. The well-known *principle of increasing accuracy with decreasing intelligence* in the hierarchical control system [5,9] is linked with the concept of nested hierarchical knowledge representation. In order to relate this concept to the existing structures of information representation, we will also use the term: *Multiresolutional (pyramidal) representation of spatial knowledge.* (The latter term is often used in the area of computer vision and image processing (see S. Tanimoto, T. Pavlidis [1975], and L. Uhr [1972]). However, we are considering information about the world *only* as a possible source of control knowledge.) The aspect of multiresolutional (pyramidal) representation of knowledge which is of interest to Intelligent Control, is the relation between the resolution of representation, and the ability of the system to recognize (identify). Analysis of the process of information acquisition (e.g., perception) confirms the affinity of the information organization to the structure of NHKR.

There is a remarkable correspondence between the idea of multiresolutional ideas of visual hierarchy, and the ideas of nested hierarchical control. Indeed, it is impossible to compute the control sequence at the highest resolution of representation: the time of computation is too large. It is also impossible to use the quick results of computations obtained at the lowest level of resolution: the results are too vague. It is acceptable though, to scan through all resolution levels top down gradually driven from one level to another by the attention focus, and to refine the initial vague (and quick) results, with search only in the vicinity of the unclear results before its clarification. It is clear also that the phenomenon of resolutional nesting can be employed successfully in both cases: pictorial and/or conceptual. Then the processes of *lateral search* are invoked for image recognition and interpretation, and as we expect, for planning/control purposes.

Thesaural Knowledge Base: Semantic Networks with Context-Oriented Interpretation

This technique is even more important from the view that the treatment of pictorial information as well as the treatment of semantic networks, can be done using the same methodology. Both pictorial and semantic networks then can be considered as look-up tables (LUT) [e.g., tables of rules for the production system (for the image interpretation, for the motion control, etc.)]. It seems reasonable to extend the principle of multiresolutional knowledge organization to the domain of semantic networks, and then to perform the lateral search procedures at the resolutional level of the semantic network. Recent results by D. Waltz (1985) seem to follow this direction of development.

Thus LUT can be considered as an *ordered* list of clauses (certainly, logic is presumed to be multivalued with fuzzy and/or probabilistic assigning of quantitative data). LUT can be presented as a graph. Quantitative values assigned to clauses are to be understood as the costs of edges in the graph. Since any logical implication can be interpreted as *casual directionality* the graphs can be directed ones. We will be interested in defining strings of vertices or paths in the semantic graph in which the binary relation "is connected to" has a *value of strength* and can be interpreted as a relevance relation, and therefore, the edges of the semantic network are inducing the network partitions in *relevance classes*. Relevance differs from equivalence only by the absence of transitivity among its properties. Relevance is more general relation than equivalence because it assumes interpretation for a substantially larger set of real cases and situations, and includes equivalence as a particular case. All LUTs, semantic, as well as pictorial, can be represented as the relevance graphs. Each set of rules is in fact a set of relevance statements. Two vertices belong to the same relevance class if the value of strength exceeds the threshold value.

If only one threshold is considered, then relevance class coincides with equivalence class. However, we will consider the same sets under different threshold values later. This will obviously induce a set of nested relevance classes. Hence, due to the bonds between each pair of variables or words in a vocabulary, the relevance classes are generated. Clustering the information into the relevance classes is absolutely equivalent to the segmentation of pictorial information, and can employ criteria proven successful in this area (e.g., maximization of the likelihood of belonging to a definite cluster).

An important question is: where is the graph representation to be taken from? The answer is contained in the definition and description of the graph structure: LUTs are the source for the graph representation (with all the above mentioned prerequisites for LUTs). Eventually, elements and components of the graph are obtained as a result of questioning the other representations of the system, including the analytical representation, test results, verbal descriptions of relevant domains of the world, humans-experts, etc. (Nested LUTs are being used explicitly in a number of expert systems.)

Knowledge represented in the Intelligent Controller contains at least two parts: thesaurus and context. Thesaurus is maintained independently of a particular operation to be performed, and it constitutes the "wisdom," "education," and "experience" of the Intelligent Controller. Context is determined by the task within a domain of thesaurus, and can be considered as a "map" of the world in which the operation must be designated together with the list of rules pertaining to this map. Map of the world is extracted from the thesauri according to the concept. Thesaural knowledge bases (TKB) are actually based upon declarative and implicative knowledge which should be contained in the global thesaurus of the system where all definitions, explanations, and interpretations are stored.

TKB are considered to be a collection of relevance statements which are considered to be the well-formed formulae (WFF) for decision-support systems of various kinds. It is clear that knowledge consists of discretes which are later referred to as units of knowledge and are interpreted as relevance statements determined as a part of the overall relational graph. When we talk about knowledge, it is represented knowledge that is actually meant (i.e., we are not interested here in discussing the nature of the reality represented within the system of world representation). It is generally accepted that engineers deal with two types of knowledge: declarative, and procedural. No one knows exactly what the difference is between these two types, however, one can assume that procedural knowledge is information about the operators applicable to the declarative knowledge (i.e., what are the procedures which could be applied to the knowledge units given in TKB). One can find in the literature another explanation which relates the term "procedure" to "action" within the system. We include the actions within the system, to the domain of declarative knowledge by simple substitution of the action verbs by the corresponding nouns.

Each declarative WFF can belong to one of two groups: *existential* (statement of existence) including statements of objects and relations among them, and *transitive* (statement of change). Both of these units of knowledge, are presented in implicative form (clauses). It seems reasonable to describe the TKB representation constantly discussing the analogy among the linguistical (logical, AI), set theoretical on one hand, and on the other hand, vector analytical manners of describing situations (which do not differ in essence). So, when we use the term "variable", and "mapping", the terms "statement of existence", and "statement of connection" are meant simultaneously. In the algebra language, statements of existence are understood as *variables* (x, y, z,. . .), and statements of connections among them as individual *mappings* (x → y, x → z,. . .).

Knowledge Organization for Control Purposes

Theory of control-oriented knowledge organization is considered as a part of the Intelligent Controller. This theory focuses upon development of models of knowledge bases for motion, structures of algorithms, and design of systems for optimum motion of autonomous or semiautonomous systems. Intelligent Control theory makes use of the fact that the similarities among the existing structures of control (most of which are knowledge-based) for autonomous robots reveal a number of inner mechanisms of goal-oriented dealing with knowledge, as a part of Intelligent Controller functioning.

Roughly speaking, any Intelligent Controller is organized as a team of human decisionmakers which allow for using many efficient solutions developed for human teams, e.g., Stackelberger strategies with leader–followers, etc. The theory of team control was developed with direct orientation for application in human teams. It turns out, that the important application of the theory of team control can be determined within the area of robotics, where Intelligent Controller belongs. Like the theory of teams, theory of Intelligent Controller deals with coordinated activities of decisionmakers operating under definite strategies, developing decisions under conditions which require that they coordinate their decision-making policies. Like team theory, Intelligent Controller theory requires a definite information structure. Unlike team theory, however, Intelligent Controller deals with computers, controllers, and mechanical machines, not with humans.

Intelligent Controller is a relatively new area of application for control theory as well as for the theory of knowledge bases. Terminology, definitions, techniques, or solid results are unknown in the area of Intelligent Controller. There is as yet, no consistent theory for dealing with descriptive, poorly structured knowledge for self-programmed robot control. Nevertheless, it is clear that properly utilized expertise of prior operations can serve as a convenient and productive tool for building efficient controllers. It would be improper to reject any attempts to find nonstandard control recommendations related to this domain of control technologies. It is especially important for autonomous intelligent robots, where an operation is possible only on the basis of huge arrays of coded expertise and the conventional control solutions cannot be utilized because they do not operate in real time. In all cases, controls are considered to be realizable if an efficient procedure of computation can be arranged which enables real-time operation of Intelligent Controller. Thus, emphasis is on solutions which do not lead to NP hard problems. The problem of representing control systems in a form which will allow for tractable solutions is of substantial interest. In knowledge-based controllers, this problem has a specific content: information structure which should be suited to proper knowledge quantization.

General Characterization of D Structure

Descriptive world representation (D structure) can be formalized as a global semantic network, or a list of all possible labels and relations among them. D structure is considered to be the result of statistical texts decomposition, where the texts are understood as all available papers, documents, expert accounts, or other passive sources which are relevant to the problem of control. The texts are presumed to be interpretable within a definite context of the problem, and the problem is supposed to be understandable within a definite Universe of Discourse (UOD). UOD is represented by words and expressions given in thesaural form which is not a part of the formal D structure, but is available for the user, and is being used for its interpretation.

Passive sources of knowledge are those which are not a part of the controller, and are not subject to dynamic interaction with the controller. Given a passive source, D structure is a list of relations between each couple of labels, and this list is believed to represent all pertinent knowledge from the texts. Since the global D structure is an abstraction, one would be interested in constructing a local D structure which has sense only in the context of a particular problem, and is subject to further decomposition in even more local D structures relevant to the higher resolution of the chosen subsets of the context. D structure can be considered a connected list of valued statements about relations among labels and it can be characterized by the following properties.

1. The list is open-ended, new relationships can be added to the list during the process of design problem solving as well as during the process of control of the functioning system (learning). Each label, and each relation is independently characterized by a number designating the significance of the label, or the relation. This significance value is obtained taking to account (a) the statistics of the label usage in the representative texts, and (b) the expert opinion.

2. The operation of generalization is introduced in this list, which function is to organize into classes all of the labels as well as all of the relationships among them. New labels are assigned to the titles of classes and these labels are included in the initial list (closure). Actually, these new labels are expected to exist within the initial complete list of the properly built D structure (completeness).

3. Each relation stated within the list may be considered a meaning-generator. Meaning-generator is expected to generate statements which have not been mentioned in the initial context, and possibly, have not been meant. This presumes reference to the associative memory, which is contained in the context. Each statement which can be received from the D structure carries not only explicit information (interpretation within the thesaurus), but also the implications from the statement which can be generated from the associative memory. Associative memory is not necessarily available in existing knowledge-based controllers, but it should be. A search (e.g., browsing) procedure leads to the implicit knowledge extraction from the associative memory.

4. After the global (abstract) D structure is built, it is not referred to any problem or procedure. An additional effort is required to refer this structure to some abstract reference frame, and to locate within this global data structure a problem-oriented subset of the data structure to be controlled within the reference frame. The abstract reference frame is selected in order to describe the labels as combinations of real properties. Relations between them still hold, and each label becomes not just a word, but a point in a

multidimensional description space (D space). Each relation in this D structure, in turn, should be put in a D space in order to be utilized for problem solving.

5.   This system of references, or reference frame can be constructed in the form of a multidimensional coordinate system for an imaginary vector space. Each label is then assumed to have a number of dimensions. This reminds us that each label is being represented as a set of properties, or eventually as a set of words (variables). Each property (word, variable) can definitely be quantitatively evaluated.

6.   In order to create a list of axes, we analyze the hypergraph of the D structure, because every label should be represented there which is capable of affecting the control situation. The list of axes necessary to describe a particular label is the list of all of the other labels connected to the label of consideration (the total hypergraph). Each label is defined only by other labels, and cannot have a dimension that is not described by a label.

7.   The information imposed is limited by the hardware (cost, complexity of the architecture, and the time of computation) as well as by the software (complexity of the algorithm). These factors are determined, in part, by the level of connectivity of the D structure (2^n relations for n nodes if the description is complete). In practice, the number of relationships can be limited on the basis of the task at hand. This will be determined essentially by the highest (finest) level of resolution of representation. Resolution, in turn, is determined by the minimum distinguishable cell (word) of representation at the level of primitives.

Mathematical Properties of the D Structure

The following mathematical properties can be sought for in a D structure.

D-structure is a field (partially ordered) or a quadruple (Δ, +, •, $\Rightarrow$) where Δ is an *abelian* group under addition, with identity element e, + and • are the operations, and $\Rightarrow$ is a set of relationships of (weak, partial) order. (A group is abelian if the operation (•) is commutative (a • b = b • a), where the notation = means "congruence." Two elements are considered to be congruent if their component elements are equivalent, and if corresponding relations between each couple of components are equivalent; equivalence is a relation which is reflexive, transitive, and symmetrical, for equivalence we use notation $\leftrightarrow$. A *monoid* with every element *invertible*, is a group. A monoid is an ordered triplet (W,•, $\Rightarrow$) where W is a set of partially ordered ($\Rightarrow$) subsets (posets) of valued words, and (•) is an associative binary operation).

Minimal poset is any couple of words connected by a relation $\Rightarrow$ and are named a statement (or a rule) in a D structure. Valued words are defined as a symbol (label) and a real number associated with this symbol. A binary relation $\Rightarrow_i$ on any H subset of W(W$\supset$H) is a rule because it "decides" whether or not ($a\Rightarrow_ib$) for any given a,b$\in$ W. Elements of the monoid are words which can be characterized by a set of other words evaluated by a real number. In other words, there is a mapping from the space of words into the space of real numbers. Later we will use this peculiarity of words utilized as elements of the D structure to establish a vector space for D structure representation.

Any relation is considered a valued statement (a statement associated with a real number). The field Δ contains a variety of subsets with different relations $\Rightarrow_i$. The types of these relations will be discussed later. A word (label) is a latice since it is a poset, and supremum and infinum exist for all subsets of the word. We can see that each element of the D structure (a word) is a set of other words which are also elements of the D structure. Each of these words is, in turn, a set of words which are also elements of the D structure. This recursion provides for a nested hierarchical law of the word's interpretation. If the number of recursive decompositions to be done is limited (local D structure is considered), then we receive a hierarchy of the world representation. The limited set of the top words is determined by the problem formulation.

If D structure is a group, then a nonempty subset H of D structure is said to be a subgroup if for all x,y∈ H, x • y ∈ H, and x⁻¹∈ H where x⁻¹ is the inverse of x∈ Δ. There is a unique element e∈ Δ such that ea = a = ae for any element a∈ Δ. For each a∈ Δ there is a⁻¹∈ Δ such that a⁻¹a = e = aa⁻¹. A group product should be viewed as a mapping m:Δ x Δ→ Δ (Notation → is used for mapping). Order on Δ is compatible with the operations of addition and multiplication in the following sense: for all a,b,c∈ Δ, b ⇒ c implies a + b ⇒ a + c and if a ⇒ e, then b ⇒ c implies ab ⇒ ac.

Operations on the D Structure

Addition is interpreted as *concatenation* (or minimum cost concatenation), which is defined as a path (minimum cost) in Δ from x to y (x,y∈ Δ). Path (minimum cost) is understood as a string of statements in a D structure (related couples of words) x ⇒ a, a ⇒ b, . . . ,m ⇒ n, n ⇒ y which is designated as a string of nodes describing the path in its sequence (x,a,b, . . . ,m,n,y). This path serves for evaluation of the statement of relationship between the initial and final nodes of the path. Concatenation of two strings designates a path (minimum cost) between the initial word and a final word using both strings as mandatory components. For concatenation, we will use a notation P (which alludes to path).

Multiplication is interpreted as amalgamation, which is defined as generation of a V formation in D structure. Similar to concatenation, one can provide for minimum cost amalgamation. A V formation in D structure is defined as a pair of lattices (words) a,b∈ Δ with a lattice c∈ Δ , which is a sublattice of both a and b (i.e., a ⊃ c, b ⊃ c) which means also that a ∩ b = c. Amalgamation is a class generating procedure: the lattice c is the class generating property. Therefore we will refer to this procedure as to an operation generalization and will use a notation G (which alludes to generalization).

Class Generation by Amalgamation: Belonging to a Meaningful Cluster

D structure can be interpreted as an ε-net (A. N. Kolmogorov, 1953) at a definite resolution, and as a system of nested ε-nets with different scale where scale is defined as a ratio between resolution at a level and resolution at the lowest level. Clearly, each of the larger tiles at the upper level is a "generalization" for the set of smaller tiles at the lower level of the hierarchy. Selection of one of the tiles at the upper level (focusing attention) entails selection of a definite subset of smaller tiles at the lower level.

We would assume that the ε-net can be constructed of any type of world description technique. Description can be quantitative, and can represent a measure for a definite measurable variable, then the ε-net demonstrated the structure of relationships among the measured discretes of this world representation. Description, also can be quantitative, e.g., linguistical, and the ε-net will convey the knowledge of relationships among the labels, or words denoting the objects and processes of the world. We will consider this structure of knowledge representation to be common in both cases, and will name it D structure (descriptive structure).

The term "generalization" is not yet defined properly; at this stage, we will assume this loose explanation for generalization as if we are dealing with an operator of unifying separated units of knowledge in a set. We would like to stress the fact that the inclusions X⊃X⊃x shown in this hierarchy of the tile embeddings, have important and broad meaning than just "scaling of the size." The inclusion predicate ⊃ has a meaning of "belonging to a class." In the case of spatial knowledge, this belonging is related to some spatial neighborhood where the space is understood as physical space. However, one can talk about state space, space of weighted properties, and so on, and the notion of "belonging to a class of some spatial neighborhood" becomes closer to a meaning of "generalization" as it is understood in the discipline of logic. Then discretization of the state space will contribute simultaneously to (a) minimum required interval of consideration, (b) hierarchy of classes of belonging to a meaningful neighborhood.

Relations among the larger tiles at the upper level can be considered as generalizing representation of the corresponding relations among the tiles of the corresponding subsets at the lower level. This implies not only that properties of this tile per se, are generalized, but also its relationships with the other tiles.

Class generation is based upon Principle of Abstraction: there exist a set such that

$$(\forall x)[x \in H \leftrightarrow f(x)]$$

where $\Delta \supset H$,

$$f(.) \text{ is a WFF with one variable,}$$

which means that if a WFF about some property is formulated, a set H can be found such that all members of this set have this property (class generating property). It is our intention to represent knowledge in such a way that every WFF in a broad sense (for a class), is a generalization for a WFF of a concrete instantiation (for a member of this class). Thus, a set is considered to belong to a class iff it has a class generating property of this particular class, i.e.,

$$a \in \{x | f(x)\} \leftrightarrow f(a).$$

In other words, any WFF can be restated as a statement of belonging to a definite class. Thus, having D structure which represents all existing (and potential) classes within the knowledge of the system, we actually have all WFFs which can be stated, or all rules of functioning and control. Any statement represented in D structure implies partitioning, since it can be adequately represented iff existence of the object is put in direct correspondence with its belonging to a definite class or to a set of classes. This belonging is to be evaluated by a membership function.

Accuracy and Resolution of the D Structure

The field of the D structure (partially ordered) is a quadruple $(\Delta, P, G, \Rightarrow)$ where Δ is an abelian group under concatenation, with identity element e. A group is indeed abelian because the operation G is commutative (aGb = bGa). A monoid is an ordered pair (Δ, G) where Δ is a set of partially ordered subsets (posets) of words, and G is an associative binary operation. Two words connected by a relation $\Rightarrow$ are named a statement (or a rule) in a D structure (notice that each statement can be interpreted as a clause). A binary relation $\Rightarrow_i b)$ for any given a,b ∈ H. The field of the D structure contains a variety of subsets with different relations $\Rightarrow_i$. The types of these relations will be discussed later. A word is a lattice since it is a poset, and supremum and infinum exist for all subsets of the word. Each word x entails its negation ($\neg$) which is considered a compliment in the UOD (anything else but x). We will use a notation $\neg x = x^{-1}$.

If (Δ, G) is a group, then a nonempty subset H (context) of the D structure (universe of discourse) is said to be a subgroup if for all $x, y \in$ H, $xGy \in$ H (since H is now UOD for the word x) where x^{-1} is the negation (inverse) of $x \in$ F. There is a unique element $e \in \Delta$(e is ¬ UOD) such that $eGa = a = aGe$ for any element $a \in$ F. For each $a \in$ F there is $a^{-1} \in$ F such that $a^{-1}Ga = e = aGa^{-1}$. A group product should be viewed as a mapping $m:\Delta x\Delta \rightarrow \Delta$.

Let us interpret the order in our field by determining the relationships $\Rightarrow$i exercised in the D structure. Order on Δ is compatible with the operations of concatenation and generalization in the following sense: for all $a,b,c\Delta, b \Rightarrow c$ implies $aPb \Rightarrow aPc$ and if $a \Rightarrow e$, then $b \Rightarrow c$ implies $aGb \Rightarrow aGc$.

The state space for analysis and problem solving for knowledge-based control is a vector space over the field Δ of our D structure, which is an extension of a field corresponding to the D structure. Vector space R^n is a set of all n-tuples of real numbers, and D structure is supposed to be mapped into R^n

$$\Delta \rightarrow R^n$$

This mapping is supposed to be an order-preserving mapping, i.e., isomorphism. If the conditions are provided for these two spaces to be Hilbert spaces, then they are isomorphic (since any two Hilbert spaces are isomorphic).

Labeling the class presumes dealing with this class as a primitive at the given level of consideration. Moreover, this class (now, also a primitive) is being again clustered in classes of the higher level. In order to deal with class as with a primitive we have to neglect the inner content of this class (which might be reflected as new properties of the new primitive but with no mention of the initial primitives with their properties). The levels of the hierarchy of representation (since they are created by a mechanism of generalization) are dealing with the same world given with different level of richness in submitting specific details, level of coarseness (fineness). We will name this characteristics of world representation at the level, resolution ,which is a measure of distinguishability of the vectors in the state space.

Uncertainties

Two major sources of uncertainties are known: when the structure of a plant and the underlying physical laws are unknown or partially unknown, or when parameters of the plant, process, and environment are unknown or partially unknown. In the prevailing multiplicity of cases the states of the system, its parameters, and the controlled and uncontrolled inputs, can be assigned to a set of values only with a certain probability, while some parameters or inputs are random. In such cases the future behavior of the system can only be described with a certain probability and the system is called stochastic.

In all of these cases, the importance of some weakly defined procedure such as "decision making " grows. When the number of uncertainties is substantial, the credibility of DIC models, especially models of high order, is very low. The topic of uncertainties representation can reveal the most important criteria of applicability for both DIC representation and the D structure. Analysis of the comparative area of application of these two methods of representation has not been completed. Future research will show the relations between these two methods, will demonstrate when both methods are adequate, and when they cannot be used interchangeably.

THEORY OF CONTROL REVISITED

A variety of issues can be illustrative for the cluster of research, development, and application activities unified under the label "intelligent control." We are touching here upon some of these issues which can complement the above analysis of the situation in the area.

Feedback Concept

The totality of this great concept should be given new and proper interpretation based on a broad experience of dealing with different approaches (including conventional and intelligent controllers in computer-based realization). In the framework of "intelligent control" the differences between feedback and feedforward is becoming elusive. Indeed, considering the so-called "feedforward" concept, one can easily see that: (a) it contains elements of "early" planning, (b) the feedback signal is presumed; it is not merely absent. Thus, the combination of planning based upon some expectation of the process, with the measurement of real states of the plant, control system, and environment is to be understood as the expected advancement of a simple feedback concept. Feedback control utilizing this principle, employs explicitly the on-line algorithms of control. This type of control has been considerably researched and a large number of algorithms exist in the literature. Off-line (time-consuming) algorithms, usually require the use of look-up tables, a recent development. Further feedback compensation is presumed since the error is allowed which exceeds the requirements of the user, the results of control are considered planning for the subsequent tracking.

Optimum Control

Intelligent Controllers help in understanding that there are no nonoptimum controls. Any system to be controlled should be controlled under some conditions of strong or weak optimality with regard to time, accuracy, energy, or any other types of gains and losses that can be of interest to the user and/or designer. Even if the problem of optimality is not explicit, it is always implied. Specialists in control theory should not take advantage of the user by selecting the criterion of optimality in the form of desideratum for the control specialist. Interestingly enough, the LQG period in the history of Control Theory, together with numerous achievements, brought a number obstacles to the present development of the theory of optimum control. Harvesting results of conveniently, selected "desideratum," the researchers shy away from exploration of any criterion of optimality other than those based upon quadratic form. Multiple criterion optimization is not given proper attention: it is too "context-dependent," too gravitated toward OR and AI.

    Thus, when the problem of optimization is posed at a level of substantial complexity, heuristics are introduced for proper approximation of the control representation. The rigidity of the theory applied and the solution obtained, turned out to be ephemeral. Success in application of quasioptimal search algorithms led to a resurgence of interest in dynamic programming. It is tempting to consider Pontryagin principle to be a qualitative result rather than an analytical result of using variational methods. Criteria of performance are usually based upon introduction of some performance criteria which behave similar to utility function. "Time," "error," and "energy consumption" are the major factors of concern. The efficiency of the system (linked with losses of energy in the components of the system) provides an accurate measure of the system reliability.

    Most of the rules of optimality are traditionally introduced by control and OR theorists. Admissible controls were introduced in the optimum control theory. Theory of "utility" was first employed in OR. In large-scale systems, the use of OR methodologies, with all of their "Pareto-optimal-policies," and risk assessments, so undesirable in conventional discipline of control, is unavoidable.

Neurons, Automata, Networks, Learning

McCulloch-Pitts (MCP) Neuron. The analogy between the automata and human structure of intelligence turned out to be stronger than was initially meant to be. The MCP neuron, and other similar elementary elements are the basis of building the contemporary multiprocessor computer systems. Postproduction systems happen to be an appropriate theoretical tool of dealing with problems formulated for systems based on MCP neuron.

Automata with Memory. From the scientific point of view, the theory of automata turned out to be most appropriate to describe the "anthropomorphic" properties of multiprocessor computer systems, in particular, learning. Theory of automata is a legitimate development of the mathematical theory of computer languages (including postproduction systems). In the 1960s, automata theory was considered a part of control theory (e.g., M. Arbib, 1963). Now that the limits of LQG paradigm are clear to the engineering community, automata theory as a control tool is resurrected within the theory of intelligent control.

Perceptrons and Neural Networks. The problem of learning and self-organization was first discussed within the "control" community. However, the means for the solution was determined in the late 1970s within the AI community. Early perceptrons (F. Rosenblatt, 1958) could not succeed without an adequate computer base. Currently, all diversifications of the perceptron devices are labeled as neural networks. These are the natural, if not the best expected, components for the intelligent control systems with adaptation and learning properties. Clearly, the D structure can be considered a special model for a class of neural networks, or multilayer nonlinear perceptrons.

Adaptive and Self-Organizing Control: Control with Learning and Recognition. The term "adaptive control" was borrowed from psychology and physiology to indicate a "behavioristic" approach to control. Adaptive systems are based on various heuristic principles of dealing with uncertainties. The property of self-organization is somewhat anthropomorphic. Learning is considered to be synonymous with the property of interest. The difference between the two types of learning (quantitative and conceptual) only now is becoming a focus of interest. The drastic difference between the qualitative adjustment, and a trigger effect of concept creation is not yet receiving enough attention.

Here the role of "observer" should be especially emphasized. The hypothesis of a need for a multiple modality of sensors for conceptual learning makes the systems with a single sensory modality appropriate only for quantitative learning. In the observer with multiple sensory modalities two strategies can be considered: with sequential application of modalities in an a priori planned sequence, and with series/parallel application of sensory modalities in a sequence of input information. Certainly, the theory of "observers" as it is presented now within the modern control theory, should be substantially developed and changed when the systems are being developed into the domain of intelligent control.

"Esoteric" Controllers: Linguistic Through Cognitive Ones

Linguistic and Knowledge-Based Control. The variety of options to represent the system and to manipulate with the representation seems to be very fruitful in the case of linguistic systems. Reasoning instead of computing upon QEM (quantitative evolutionary models) turned out to be not only attractive, but also productive. Instead of estimating quantitative changes, we can reason about changes! D structure is definitely a legitimate model of processes in this type of controllers.

Fuzzy Systems and Fuzzy Controllers. There is not much difference between linguistic and fuzzy controllers. The distinction is in the area of using quantitative and qualitative methods. The fuzzy sets and systems theory opens up a number of promising opportunities to the further use linguistical representation for a very effective quantitative control based upon a reasoning system as well as QEM.

Cognitive Controllers. When the knowledge base is very large, and the perception is very diversified, the operation of the Intelligent Controller comes close to human cognition. The key issue here is to organize knowledge in such a way as to allow for finding the interpretations of new *states* (world descriptions) leading to the new task formulation. Hierarchical systems with hierarchical perception and knowledge bases bear close semblance to human cognitive activities. There are many metaphorical models of human cognition. However, they lack the sense of orientation for use in systems of Intelligent Control. Researchers should be warned against direct absorption of cognitive psychology terms which can be loaded with inappropriate connotation.

Interaction Between AI, OR, and Control Theory

Intelligent Control theory does exist. However, as yet, it has not been presented in a rigid and consistent form. The main statements, techniques, and applications are disseminated in different sources within various areas. It has acquired almost everything from the conventional areas of science, and is held together by the orientation function defined in Ref. *1*.

Control Function and Properties Implanted in AI Procedures. "Control" is an intrinsic component of the production system. It is interpreted as a mechanism of arranging and scheduling of rules application. For a specialist in Control Theory, the "rules" together with "control," are equivalent to a control system. The interrelatedness of control concepts in AI and Control Theory is a matter for further investigation. Functions of the control algorithm correspond to a definition of Intelligent Control. The control strategies are considered to be a part of a rule base updated as a result of constant evaluation of the circumstances under pressures of "external" criteria and preferability concepts generated at the moment. Thus, the optimality requirement could mean different operation under different circumstances, i.e. different subset of the rule base.

Control Orientation of GPS. GPS (General Problem Solver) is traditionally understood as a system advisor. However, its advice can be considered as an "input" for a "lower level controller."

a. Production rules in a "situation–action" form. GPS and many other production systems have the input and output in a "situation–action" form, where the situation is understood as the state description, and the "action" is the control.

b. Hierarchical Production Systems (HPS). HPS is obtained from a conventional production system by a recursive interpretation of the "control part" as a "rule part" of the upper level.

c. Inference Engines and Decision Making Discriminators. Inference engines (i.e., a production system) generate output after the preferential alternative of the "action" is obtained. The decision-making discriminator is an internal component of a production system.

Elements of Control in the Theory of Planning. Plannings is understood as a technique of finding proper controls on the basis of forecasting the states and comparing the forecast with the desirable state development. The hierarchical system description based upon the hierarchy of resolution of the world representation, is traditional in the theory of planning. The "nesting" of controls found for all of the levels satisfies the consistency requirements. Planning is analyzed within a framework of "feedback–feedforward" duality, and within the concept of production system.

AI, OR, and Control Theory Functions Mutually Implant Each Other. OR exercises heuristics, rules' hierarchies, and logical representations in the same degree as is done in Control Theory. Most of the axioms and assumptions concerned with flows of events and theories of queues are based upon heuristics. Optimization, scheduling, and coordination are elements common for OR and Control Theory.

Heuristics in Intelligent Control

Heuristic Strategies of Algorithms. All of the search algorithms initially created in OR (branch-and-bound method, and other algorithms of search) are based upon a multiplicity of search heuristics, and are utilized in the theory of dynamic programming. All major ideas of linear, nonlinear, and dynamic programming are based upon AI-like heuristic constructions (including methods of decomposition and aggregation).

The variety of systems models employed by Control Theory are as heuristical as most of the AI constructions: (a) structuring the models, (b) order reduction, (c) devising inputs, outputs, states, etc. Especially as it affects the results of the analysis when model structuring, framing, or criteria based upon linguistical models are used (not always explicitly) in posing the problem.

Control algorithms, in most cases, are based upon linguistical construction, hidden underlying logical structures, which often are not analyzed. Selection among various alternatives, qualitative and/or quantitative discrimination, is a valuable control function which does not receive sufficient attention within Control Theory.

    a. Discrimination functions are introduced in the form of postulates; the logical structures behind them are not always clearly perceived.
    b. Switching times, bang-bang control have an interesting inner logical structure, a set of implicitly accepted rules assumptions, and heuristics underlying the algorithms; this subject is not analyzed sufficiently.

Specifics of Intelligent Controllers

The standard situation in a hierarchical system is when redundancies, recognition, learning, and so on, are considered at each level of the hierarchy.

Principle of Increasing Precision with Decreasing Intelligence. This principle is intended to legitimize the simultaneous consideration of the representations at different resolutions (frame decomposition) nested hierarchy of resolutions, and horizons of planning. The most precise of all levels, the lower level controller, has the least redundancy, the most accuracy, and the lower necessity in using the "choice" feature.

Different Levels of AI Applications at Different Levels of Intelligence. Anthropomorphic structures (such as "Planner," "Navigator," "Pilot") illustrate that the structures of AI application are different at different levels. The lower the level is, the higher is the application of conventional control theory, and the lower is the application of AI. Coordination functions at different levels are understood as the functions of aggregating the subtask performance at the level of decomposition. These functions are strongly related to the AI techniques.

Man–Machine Communication. A semi-intelligent operation can be expected, which requires constant communication with a human operator, or operator involvement from time to time. Linguistic Commands Recognition should be associated with the linguistics of the knowledge base, logic of the controller, and the communication media. The language of interaction with the operator should be selected in a way to intensify the operation of the system.

Interaction with the environment is based upon multiple sensory systems of perception, presumed to be required for systems of intelligent control. Multisensory fusion should be able to deal with incomplete and dynamic information. The redundancy therefore becomes a property which helps to perform recognition, generalization, decomposition, and creation of hypotheses.

Updating the World Representation. This process makes multisensory fusion, especially the use of vision sensors, very important. World map updating is done via the process of recognition. It is found that such systems add a number of new properties. The task and the world map become a result of coordinated decomposition of problem-oriented knowledge base.

Coordinated Motion Control. The problem of coordinating several robots in a cooperative function (robotic team control) is not the only possible example of application. Any joint operation of systems and devices constitutes a problem of cooperation, or antagonistic activities. Two types of cooperation can be delineated: cooperating systems which belong to the same coordinator, or systems belonging to two or more different coordinators.

Determining Real-Time Assignment. The mechanism of constant problem decomposition and aggregation ends up with determining the real-time assignment for the lower level controller, which is to be represented according to specifications in a form of D1 model, logical structure, etc.

Structure of Intelligent Control. The structures of Intelligent Control should reflect the specifications of the intelligent machines requiring this type of operation. The following groups of intelligent machines are presently known: intelligent robots-manipulators, mobile autonomous systems, CAD/CAM systems, aircrafts, spaceships, missiles, etc. A thorough analysis of specifications is required to determine the sets of specifications mentioned above.

Structures with Properties of Intelligence. Renewed effort is required to consider all of the following structures in the framework of the theory of Intelligent Control.

a. Structures with learning capabilities. The existing theory of quantitative learning should be supplemented by a task to implant property of recognition.

b. Structures with adaptation. Conventional systems of adaptation can be improved substantially, based upon learning with recognition.

c. Structures with self-organization. These activities must not be programmed. The "self" of the system is to define the method of updating the knowledge base of the system.

d. Structures with concept creation. The need for concept creation is clear in view of the evolution of learning systems (conceptual vs. quantitative learning). Thus, some elements of "creativity" should characterize any intelligent control system. However, humanlike operation as defined in intelligent control, cannot encompass all components included in the term "creativity."

On the other hand, it is becoming clear that the dubious and yet possible field of "creative control" will no longer remain untouched. Indeed, the treatment of "generator of images" by U. Grenander in the framework of rigid mathematical theory seems to be a natural outgrowth of his analysis of distribution of groups, which in an interesting way predates the theory of fuzzy sets and systems within the body of category theory.

Many recent reports are directly or indirectly contemplating the foundations of the theory of concept creation applicable to the theory of Intelligent Control.

- e. Structures with autonomous operation. Autonomous systems constitute the next step of development in systems of Intelligent Control.
- f. Structures with cooperation. As stated earlier, the cooperation is meant as a goal-oriented interaction within the team (of robots, arms, legs, etc.).
- g. Structures with self-reproduction. Self-reproduction can appear to be economically feasible during long-term missions.

Concept of "Planner-Navigator-Pilot." An example of a Cognitive Intelligent Controller with this structure is described in Ref. *11*. The possibility of intuitive functions in intelligent controllers should be expected in systems with large self-organizing knowledge bases and conceptual learning. This can be considered a next stage of development in the area of Intelligent Control.

Computer Systems for Intelligent Control

Fifth-Generation Computers as a Base for Developing Systems of Intelligent Control. Taking into account expectations for fifth-generation computers, they are the most appropriate computer base for Intelligent Controllers.

Computer-Performer. Clearly, Intelligent Control systems must deal with redundant and simultaneously, incomplete information on the process, the internal states, and the environment. On the other hand, some of this information can be contradictory. The knowledge base should be able to handle these properties of information and maintain the image of the process as well as the image of the universe of discourse. Decomposition and aggregation (generalization) should be done on-line, i.e., pixel-wise structure of the world, as well as the processing and convenience of principles other than that of Von-Neuman.

At the present time, we can discuss the different results using intelligent control systems in the following different "breeds" of computers: Computer-thinker Logically, Computer-thinker Creatively, and Computer with Self-awareness. The distinctions can be developed only upon a very diversified hierarchical knowledge base with self-organization.

Information–Intensive Systems. Self-organizing, self-developing knowledge bases are desirable basics for information-intensive systems (IIS). The structure of IIS should possess the properties of concept creation and goal-oriented knowledge reorganization.

Languages and Architectures for Intelligent Control. This topic should be considered as one of the most important points of emphasis in the future development of Intelligent Control-oriented computer architectures.

Hierarchical nested control theory not only generates the conceptual architectures of cognitive controllers for autonomous robots, but also suggests a number of preferable computer architectures as well as techniques of dealing with problems of the system arising from existing architectures.

REFERENCES

1. G. N. Saridis, *Self-Organizing Control of Stochastic systems*, Marcel Dekker, New York, 1977.

2. G. N. Saridis, "Intelligent Robotic Control," *IEEE Trans. Auto. Control, AC-28*(5) (1983).
3. G. N. Saridis, "Toward the Realization of Intelligent Controls," *Proc. IEE, 67*(8) (1979).
4. A. Meystel, "Intelligent Control of a Multiactuator Systems," *IFAC Information Control Problems in Manufacturing Technology 1982*, D. E. Hardt (ed.), Pergamon Press, Oxford and New York, 1983.
5. G. N. Saridis, "Intelligent Control for Robotics and Advanced Automation," in *Advances in Automation and Robotics*, Vol. 1, JAI Press Inc., New York, 1985.
6. J. H. Graham, and G. N. Saridis, "Linguistic Design Structures for Hierarchical Systems, *IEEE Trans. Sys., Man, Cybernet., SMC-12*(3) (1982).
7. G. N. Saridis, J. Graham, and G. Lee, "An Integrated Syntactic Approach, and Suboptimal Control for Manipulators and Prostheses," Proceedings of 18th CDC, Ft. Lauderdale, FL, 1979.
8. G. N. Saridis, and C.-S. G. Lee, "An Approximation Theory of Optimal Control for Trainable Manipulators," *IEEE Trans. Sys., Man, Cybernet., Smc-9* (1979).
9. G. N. Saridis, "An Integrated Theory of Intelligent Machines by Expressing the Control Performance as Entropy," in *Control-Theory and Advanced Technology*, Vol. 1, No. 2, MITA Press, Tokyo, 1985.
10. A. Meystel, "Nested Hierarchical Intelligent Module for Automatic Generation of Control Strategies," in *Languages for Sensor-Based Control in Robotics*, Vol. 29, U. Rembold, and K. Hormann (eds.), NATO ASI Series, Springer-Verlag, Berlin, 1987.
11. A. Meystel, "Knowledge-based Controller for Intelligent Mobile Robots," in *Artificial Intelligence and Man-Machine Systems*, Vol. 80, H. Winter (ed.), Series Lecture Notes in Control and Information Systems, Springer Verlag, Berlin, 1986.
12. A. Meystel, "Planning in a Hierarchical Nested Controller for Autonomous Robots," Proceedings of the 25th IEEE Conference on Decision and Control, Athens, Greece, 1986.
13. K. S. Fu, "Learning Control Systems," in *Advances in Information System Science*, J. T. Tou (ed.), Plenum Press, New York, 1969.
14. R. S. Fu, "Learning Control Systems—Review and Outlook," *IEEE Trans. Auto. Contr., AC-15* (1970).
15. K. S. Fu, "Learning Control Systems and Intelligent Control Systems: An Intersection of Artificial Intelligence and Automatic Control," *IEEE Trans. Auto. Cont., AC-16* (1971).
16. G. N. Saridis, "Foundations of the Theory of Intelligent Controls," Proceedings of the IEEE Symposium on Intelligent Control, Troy, NY, 1985.
17. G. N. Saridis, "Knowledge Implementation: Structures of Intelligent Control Systems," Proceedings of the IEEE Symposium on Intelligent Control, Philadelphia, PA, 1987.
18. A. Meystel, "Intelligent Control: Issues and Perspectives," Proceedings of the IEEE Symposium on Intelligent Control, Troy, NY, 1985.
19. J. Hadamard, "Sur les problemes aux derivees partieliesphysique," *Bull. Univ. Princeton, 13*, 49–52 (1902).
20. A. M. Fedotov, *Linear Ill-Posed Problems with Random Errors in the Input Information*, Nauka. Cib. Affiliation, Novosibirsk (1982) (in Russian).
21. G. Meinardus, *Approximation of Functions: Theory and Numerical Methods*, Springer-Verlag, New York, 1967.

22. R. Bellman, "Successive Approximations and Computer Storage Problems in Ordinary Differential Equations," *Comm. ACM, 4* (1961).

23. A. Iftar, F. Khorrami, and U. Ozguner, "A Comparison of Multiple Time-Scale Analysis and Overlapping Decomposition," Proc. of the Int'l Conf. on Systems, Man, and f11. D. Graupe, in *Identification of Systems*, Van Nostrand Reinhold, New York, 1972.

24. M. Coderch, et al., "Hierarchical Aggregation of Linear Systems with Multiple Time Scales," *IEEE Trans. Auto. Cont., AC-28*(11), 1983.

25. Y. C. Ho, and K.-C. Chu, "Team Decision Theory and Information Structures in Optimal Control Problems," Parts I and 2, *IEEE Trans. Auto. Cont., AC-17* (1972).

26. Y. C. Ho, and K.-C. Chu, "On the Equivalence of Information Structures in Static and Dynamic Teams," *IEEE Trans. Auto. Cont., AC-18*, 187–188 (1973).

27. Y. C. Ho, and K.-C. Chu, "Information Structure in Dynamic Multi-Person Control Problems," *Automatics, 10*, 341–345 (1974).

A. MEYSTEL

INTERFACE DESIGN ISSUES FOR INTELLIGENT ADVISORY SYSTEMS

INTRODUCTION

Two empirical phenomena have structured much recent research on human–computer interaction: (1) people have considerable trouble learning to use computer systems [1,2], and (2) their skill tends to asymptote at relative mediocrity [3–5]. Underlying these two factors there appears to be a conspiracy of reasonable strategies for learning and performance in a practical domain which have the surprising effect of undermining the motivation required to learn and to perfect skills [6].

The situation can be sketched as follows. People want to use computer equipment because they want to get something accomplished. This is all to the good in that it gives users a focus for their activity with a system, and it increases their likelihood of receiving concrete reinforcement from their work. On the other hand, this very orientation also reduces incentive to spend any time merely learning about the system. After all, engaging in activity (via on-line tutorials or programmed self-instruction manuals) effectively requires the learner to cease working. This dichotomy between learning and working inclines new users to try to skip training altogether, or to skip around in a training sequence, sometimes with disastrous consequences. And it inclines more experienced users to stagnate; when situations occur that could be more effectively handled by new procedures, they are likely to stick with the procedures they already know, regardless of their efficacy.

Recently, many researchers have rallied to the suggestion that the motivational "cost" of learning and skill improvement could be reduced by means of intelligent system monitors [7]. This could mitigate the learning versus working conflict by better integrating the time and effort spent on learning with actual use of the system itself. This "advice-giving" approach contrasts with the more typical drill and practice style of contemporary on-line tutorials and the confusing verbosity of typical context-insensitive help commands [8]. On-line tutorials and helps can incorporate monitoring and adjusting to the user's specific needs, as evidenced in behavior, but characteristically maintain a sharp separation between learning and working that can undermine the user's motivation to make use of training and help materials.

We present a structured overview of current proposals for advice-giving systems. We have three specific goals. First, we would like to review the literature. Research in this area in expanding rapidly and the time has arrived when "intelligent" monitoring technology is practical. This makes it important to structure and assess the research literature now.

Second, our particular orientation is to consider requirements for such systems from a behavioral standpoint. One striking lesson in recent computer science is that our capability to build a new system technology is only one condition for the potential "real success" of the technology. Mere technological feasibility must be augmented by empirical study of whether and how people will find new a technology useful and tractable. It is clear that intelligent user monitoring is such an area. It is pointless to build such facilities unless we take into account behavioral requirements on their usefulness and usability. Ideally, such an assessment can be made even before the new technology is completely developed [9–11].

Our third goal is to extract the themes and conclusions in this research that can help to direct future work. To lay our cards on the table from the outset: we believe, based on our study of the current literature, that far too little behavioral work has been invested to date in design research on advisory systems. This is ironic since one of the chief practical motivations for such systems is to produce advisory capabilities that effectively support the needs of human users. Indeed, this lack of attention to usability is increasingly being identified as a key reason for the limited impact that expert systems technology has had on real computing [12,13].

We have organized our discussion of the literature into two major topic areas: the knowledge involved in giving advice, and the contingencies for and content of effective advice.

ADVISORY KNOWLEDGE

Advice-giving systems will need to have knowledge if their advice is to be worth anything. What will it mean for a system to have knowledge? What does an advisory system need to know about? How much does it need to know? How is it supposed to get this knowledge? Philosophers can rest easy; in the current state of the art, having knowledge—applied to a computer system—is merely storing information and being able to act on the basis of that information. Advice-giving systems are distinguished chiefly in that they store information about a system, about commands, conditions, procedures, etc. They can access this information and provide it to a user as on-line training and help. This puts the philosophical issues to rest, but it awakens a host of technical issues.

In the editing environment in which this report was composed, the command "help split" evokes six screens of information defining the editing command *split*. The system has stored knowledge about itself and can provide this knowledge on request. True advisory systems will have to know about more than merely their own dialog conventions. They will have to know about advice giving, about the tasks they are to be used for, and about the ways that users can vary. For example, our editor might be enhanced to know to respond differently to "help split" depending on whether a text file or a Pascal program is being edited. [For review of the state of the art in help systems, see Refs. 8,14.]

We consider these types of knowledge under three headings: general skills, domain knowledge, and user models. General skills include knowledge about things like tutoring styles and natural language—knowledge areas that transcend the particular system, the user, and the tasks for which the user employs the system. Domain knowledge (as in the example of elaborating "help split") incorporates specific task information. A user model is what the system knows about the person interacting with it. We review the ways that current work has addressed these three levels in turn.

General Skills

General skills are often cited as being important, but are far less frequently discussed. There is a good reason for this. General skills encompass knowledge of such things as advisory strategies and natural language. These topics are vast and intricate; our understanding of them is very incomplete. Accordingly, it is not surprising that we have been unable to satisfactorily codify these knowledge domains in advisory systems.

Advisory Strategies

How can advice be given effectively? Given a particular advisory strategy, how can the strategy be modified effectively on the basis of feedback from an advisee? Sleeman and

Brown [*15*], in the Introduction to their well-known anthology on intelligent tutoring systems, label the need for explicitly describing different advisory strategies as "critical," but the articles in their book do not, in fact, address this issue. Clancy [*16*], for example, takes it as a significant advance that his GUIDON system architecturally separates the domain knowledge base from the advisory strategies—underscoring the importance of the latter. He [*16*, p. 205] specifically calls attention to the question of evaluating the strategies, but leaves the question open.

Typically, researchers have opted for a single, particular advisory style offering little or no empirical rationale. For example, many tutoring systems have employed a Socratic style in which the system poses questions and the user is expected to provide answers [*16*, p. *219*; *17,18*]. It is likely that this is an effective style for interactive tutoring, particularly for highly structured knowledge fields, but it is also significant that no evidence has been offered to demonstrate this possibility. More worrisome perhaps is the possibility that the Socratic style is adopted for tutorially irrelevant reasons. Giving the system control of the dialog by allowing *it* to Socratically pose all the questions allows a simple question-list knowledge-structure with very locally defined tutorial states [*19*].

One important trade-off is that system control of advisory dialog may undermine usability. Coombs and Alty [*20*] analyzed actual interactions of computer consultants working on problems that users presented. They found that the flow of information tended to be one way: after the user posed an initial question, the advisor assumed control of the interaction. Advisors rarely included explanations or checks that the user really understood the advice. Users often criticized advisors for "not making the information meaningful" (p. 407). Advisory interactions that were judged successful by users tended to be ones in which the advisory strategy allowed shared control of the dialog [*12*]. In face-to-face advisory interactions, users often present claims to advisors instead of asking questions in part, we believe, to share in the control of the dialog [*21*].

Learning-by-doing environments comprise the other major advisory design that has been implemented experimentally [*22,23*]. In this approach the user can more freely initiate actions. The user's move is compared with an expert move, generated by the system, and feedback is provided to shape the user's responses toward the expert prototype. This approach places more initiative, and therefore more control, in the hands of the user than does the Socratic approach. However, allowing this increased flexibility in user interaction may entail more demanding knowledge requirements of the system. The system must know all the ways a user's actions can depart from those of the normative expert, and the particular significance of each potential departure.

Generally, learning-by-doing environments have been developed for playing educational games in which the state-space of possible move combinations is relatively small. Several investigators have developed empirically based taxonomies of "bugs" [*22–24*] or of "object-related misconceptions" [*25*]. But these taxonomies are very domain dependent and hence may not capture general knowledge about strategies for error correction or the development of expertise by means of advisory guidance [*cf., 26*].

Neither the Socratic nor the learning-by-doing approach enjoys much systematic empirical validation [but, *cf., 24*]. A researcher's choice of advisory strategy remains largely a matter of fiat. Kimball [*19*, p. 283], for example, explicitly rejects the approach of learning-by-doing environments for the domain of posed math problems but offers no empirical rationale. It is also notable that both approaches are always applied unilaterally in current tutoring systems. Current systems are not able to reason about tutoring per se and to dynamically select situationally appropriate tutoring strategies.

Fischer et al. [*27*; see also *28*] have acknowledged the need for a variety of advisory strategies. They distinguish between active and passive strategies for help: on the active strategy, the system interrupts the dialog to provide advisory commentary on the user's actions, on the passive strategy the user must explicitly request advice. Unfortunately, they have not shown empirically how either of their advisory strategies were specifically called for on behavioral grounds or how implementing them in fact proved useful to people. Direct behavioral work is beginning to provide descriptions of what successful advising is like (often analyzing the behavior of human advisors). We return to this later.

Natural Language

As in the case of advisory strategies, there has been a general recognition of the importance of general skill in natural language to successful advisory interfaces [*29*]. But the problem has often been finessed rather than confronted. Systems like those described by Coombs and Alty [*12*] and by Goldstein [*30*], for example, appear to have little or no natural language capability. Fischer et al.'s [*27*] Passivist system merely slices out keywords in the style of Weizenbaum's [*31*] Eliza. Sleeman's [*32*] ACE system parses with simple argument templates, a very rough and inevitably fragile and domain-specific approach. What are the behavioral consequences when the user inadvertently foils the template and resultingly gets garbage advice from the system? The risk, as Brown et al. [*22*, p. 244] observe, is that arbitrarily approximate treatments of natural language may cause more problems than they solve.

Malhotra and Sheridan [*10*; see also *33*] adopted an empirical approach to this problem by simulating an order writing and invoicing system that could answer questions and respond to commands in English. In their studies, the user-system dialog was filtered by the experimenter who could intervene behind the scenes to enhance the apparent natural language capabilities of the system. In this way, Malhotra and Sheridan were able to study the behavioral requirements for natural language capabilities in a system without actually implementing them. Over half of the sentences produced by their subjects instantiated a small set of structural templates. However, more than a third of the sentences produced were classified as not syntactically analyzable.

Chin [*34*] has more recently employed this empirical approach to study a simulation of the UNIX Consultant [*35*]. He found that over a quarter of the queries submitted to the simulated consultant incorporated contextual syntactic constructs, such as ellipsis, anaphora, indirect speech acts, and grammatically incomplete clauses. However, the rate of contextual constructs in a control group querying a human consultant was nearly double this. These results suggest, on the one hand, that natural language interface facilities need to be able to interpret contextual constructs, but that, on the other hand, people may voluntarily restrict the contextual complexity of their queries when interacting with an advisory system.

Chin and Malhotra and Sheridan provide an alternative to natural language restrictions motivated chiefly by ease of implementation. They raise the theoretical issue of how to more comprehensively characterize the nature of appropriate natural language restriction. Finally, they begin to provide methods for analyzing the cost-benefit trade-offs in general skill requirements for advisory systems (e.g., how much does a particular enhancement in natural language capability actually enhance the usability of an advisory interface?), a critical issue if these systems are to be practical in any near term.

Behavioral work has also helped to expose problem areas in natural language interfaces. For example, Ogden and Brooks [*36*] showed that while users had relatively little trouble learning a syntactic restriction that reference to target should precede search criterion (e.g., "List names of history majors"), they had significant problems learning vocabulary restrictions (e.g., that table names, column names, and data entries must be nouns). Furnas et al. [*37*] reported that the terms users select to refer to entities are extremely diverse, suggesting that extensive aliasing support would be required for users to experience the referencing capabilities of the system as natural language. With respect to advisory systems, it is problematic that when users are most in need of help, they may be least able to observe restrictions in making a query [*38*].

General skill areas, like advisory strategies and natural language, are clearly amenable to behavioral study. Hopefully, simulation techniques like those of Malhotra and Sheridan [*10*] and Chin [*34*] and direct behavioral investigations like that of Coombs and Alty [*12,20*] will come to be more widely employed in the exploration of general knowledge requirements for advisory systems.

Domain Knowledge

In our "help split" example, we described an on-line help system that could refer to heuristic knowledge about the tasks it supported in determining how to respond to help requests. However, we described a domain knowledge capability of extremely limited scope. Many diagnoses that might be made by an advisory system about a user's intentions would require examining and extracting a pattern from a sequence of user activity [*23*, p. 96]. They would require looking not merely at the state the user has arrived in, but at the entire process that the user traversed in getting there [*39*].

Toward a Theory of Domains

Lurking around all work on domain knowledge is the disturbing possibility that the research outcomes will be too strictly domain-specific. Many of the domains that have been investigated in studies developing advisory systems for interactive tutoring are extremely simple. VanLehn [*40*, p. 9] described his own domain of interest (subtraction) as "dry, formal and disconnected from everyday interests." This raises a general question about the adequacy of the solutions proposed: will they extend to more complex and typical areas of knowledge? It is also notable that much extant work has focused on what one might call declarative, as opposed to procedural, domains. Procedural domains include the interactive use of systems, program composition, and debugging. The meteorological domain studied by Stevens et al. [*17*], for example, includes underlying mechanisms of cause and effect, but no procedures. This raises the question of how the Stevens et al. analysis of multiple knowledge representations might extend to a procedural domain: for example, what is the scriptal/functional distinction in such a domain?

What kinds of domains are there? Naturally enough, computer science application work has focused attention on procedural domains [e.g., programming plans and bugs; *41*]. At an extreme from these are declarative domains, such as the knowledge people have about typing pages, knowledge they are able to exploit in what-you-see-is-what-you-get text editors [for discussion of user interface metaphors, see Ref. *42*]. People also have functional knowledge, for example, about spreadsheet constraints, and interactive knowledge about cooperative work and communication, knowledge they use in electronic mail applications, for example. These categories are suggested merely for the sake of discussion. We need to better articulate a taxonomy of domains that expresses the similarities and contrasts between types of domains. This taxonomy must reflect the significant empirical contrasts between types of domains, and in doing so would clarify what sorts of domain knowledge theories we have at present, and what sorts we do not have [*43–45*].

Advisory domains tend to be quite fuzzy. In our studies, advisors reported that a substantial proportion of the queries they handled actually were outside their "official" area of responsibility [*46,47*]. These misclassified queries were not random; for example, a text consultant was frequently asked about printer hardware and editors, even though text consultants were officially responsible only for formatting. Hence, adequately representing domain knowledge in an advisory system probably entails representing appropriate peripheral knowledge as well.

Psychological Pertinence

Theories of domain knowledge are intended to be psychologically pertinent analyses, producing interpretations of what the user experiences and undertakes that match the interpretations the user would make, namely in terms of the user's intentions.

Fitter [*48*, p. 341], for example, argues that in order to be useful to people a system must represent its knowledge *as people know it* [see also Refs. *29,49*]:

1. The underlying process which the computer is performing should model the processes which are directly pertinent to the user in a manner compatible with the user's own model of the process
2. The communication language (or user interface) should be designed so as to reveal underlying processes as vividly as possible

More recently, Wenger [*50*] argued that since the main purpose of advisory systems is the communication of knowledge, domain knowledge must be represented transparently for people. The rub, of course, is to accurately carry out these prescriptions in given cases (and to be able to know that you have done so). What does it mean to model a system's operation and interface on processes pertinent to the user? What is the user's internalized mental model of the system after all?

These are difficult questions. The extant research literature in psychology provides little basis for deriving serious mental models of complex task domains [*51*], and virtually no direct behavioral research either informs claims about psychological pertinence or has been brought to bear on evaluating these claims [see also Ref. *52*]. However, it is possible that the psychological theory and its application can develop together. For example, McKendree and Zaback [*53*] recently developed an advisory system for a statistics application that incorporates a production system task model similar to that developed by Kieras and Polson [*54*] in laboratory studies of users. However, they found that their planner needed to be able to generate alternative courses of action, thus suggesting avenues for development in the Kieras and Polson model.

It is worrisome, however, to find that some researchers merely assume that these questions are settled. Jagodzinski [*49*, p. 218 f.), for example, states "Since the inception of computers there has been a continuous movement in programming away from methods which reflect the working of the computer towards methods which correspond more closely with human cognitive processes." In a very rough, intuitive sense, this claim seems correct. But as a summary of the state of research, it is a meaningless promise of optimistic intentions, lacking any serious probing of what "human cognitive processes" might refer to.

A fruitful alternative approach to focusing on mimicking human domain knowledge is to focus on the apparent discrepancies between human cognition and computational knowledge techniques. For example, Kidd and Cooper [*13*] called attention to the mismatch between the exhaustive backward chaining strategy for drawing out connections in a database and what they call the "quick stab" strategy, perhaps more typical of how people try to draw out such connections. Kidd and Cooper did not analyze this discrepancy in much detail or study its empirical consequences directly, but their suggestion clarifies how to get started in identifying relevant human cognitive processes.

Multiple Representations

Fikes [55] and Stevens et al. [17] raised the important possibility that multiple representations of a domain are necessary. The idea is that any single domain representation will not provide enough basis and flexibility to support effective advising. Fikes contrasted rote description, functional description, and procedure teleology description. Rote description focuses only on the steps of a procedure and the desired result. Functional description includes also a rationale for each step—its dependency relations with other steps and its contribution to the desired result. Procedure teleology extends this rationale to the procedure itself; it describes the task that the procedure is designed to achieve and the function that each step in the procedure plays. A limitation of Fikes' work is that it proceeds from a purely a priori standpoint: the specific empirical consequences of his notion of procedure teleology remain unclear.

Stevens et al. [17] developed the multiple representations thesis more concretely in the context of an empirical investigation. They studied the domain of meteorological knowledge. People were taught facts about weather (Oregon is wet) and the mechanisms that underlie these facts. They identified two relevant levels of knowledge: scriptal knowledge, expressing situationally grounded, causal relations, and function knowledge, expressing a more abstract, qualitative model. They found that scriptal knowledge governed the sequencing of major topics in an advisory dialog, while functional knowledge governed the finer structure of advisory interaction. Unfortunately, their work rested on an ad hoc sample of pedagogical anecdotes. Stevens et al. present little systematic evidence that their distinction actually underlies a significant distinction in human thought, one significant enough to constrain the design of advisory systems. Nevertheless, this work is empirical and suggests an interesting direction for further work in knowledge representation.

The Grain of Analysis

As in the case of general skill, it is often claimed that representing more domain knowledge is a key to better advisory systems. For example, Stevens et al. [17, p. 22] who represented their knowledge domain in two separate formats, suggested that additional multiple representations would be necessary. In a similar vein, VanLehn [40, p. 23] concluded that his own progress would have been greater had he represented domain knowledge at a finer grain—that of processes underlying procedural bugs rather than that of bugs themselves. Indeed, it is a typical move in work with knowledge-based systems to predict that more could be achieved if only more knowledge and finer grain knowledge were represented.

Rich [56] proposed that a convenient grain of representation for domain knowledge is the level of statements in the system code. She conjectured that if an advisory facility could examine system code, statement by statement, it could find answers to what she took to be the principal types of user queries ("what causes this outcome?", "what will happen if I do this?", and "what is the difference between these two ways of doing it?"). This is an interesting proposal if only because it relinquishes the requirement of psychological pertinence that most researchers have placed on their views of domain knowledge. However, it is important to bear in mind that Rich did not demonstrate that her proposal really could produce a feasible domain representation, with respect to answering the user query types she enumerated. Moreover, she did not establish that these query types are in fact exhaustive, or even typical, of the queries users actually want advice for.

Reiser et al. [57] gave a user-based rationale for selecting Lisp atoms as the grain of analysis for an intelligent tutoring system for Lisp. They argued that a finer grain (e.g., keystrokes) would often underdetermine specific errors and thus underdetermine specific tutorial advice. A larger grain, however, would delay feedback past the point when specific errors could have been classified, and therefore allow the user to unproductively perservere in the error state. Perhaps also, by focusing on a single and salient grain of resolution for domain knowledge representation (like the Lisp atom) the system might present a more consistent advisory style to the user. However, selecting the atom as the grain may be a two-edged sword: providing advice at the atom level means that the system might overlook or misadvise on problems which, in fact, pertain to higher levels of program structure or which involve conceptual tangles of several lower level problems.

Instead of stuffing more domain knowledge into advisory systems, we might ask: how little domain knowledge, and at how large a grain, can still provide any leverage to advice-giving? Such an approach is largely complementary to the bulk of extant research; it would focus relatively more attention on projecting dialog fluency and the appearance of some advisory competency and relatively less on the organization and access of very large knowledge databases. Thus, instead of storing the components processes underlying 500 bugs, we might store a dozen prototype scenarios to roughly classify user situations and advise at that grain. Classic demonstrations such as Weizenbaum's [31] Eliza suggest the power that mere appearances can exert on people. Our work on scenario machines (reviewed below) has also explored this direction.

User Models

Referring once again to our "help split" example, we might consider enhancing the system by maintaining a record of a given user's work patterns and help calls for use in diagnosing the nature of a future help call by that user (or by any user). A special concern here of course is that the computer not be, or be seen as, spying on the user (e.g., to benchmark worker productivity). However, to provide individually and situationally pertinent advice, the system may need to analyze user activity. Developing and maintaining predictive user models has been seen as critical for advisory systems [15,58].

Vocabulary Analysis

How is a user model to be constructed and updated? Can the system merely ask the user to indicate a skill level? It seems unlikely that the responsibility for determining skill level can effectively be placed with the user. A simple partitioning into "novices" and "experts" is probably not adequate [59]; but offering more categories might make the self-classification task difficult and unreliable. People are notoriously bad at accurately describing their own information needs [60,61]. Will the system need to be able to infer the user's skill level (and the user's specific problems and concerns) from actions and responses? This seems to be a more adequate approach, but it is clearly also more demanding on the system.

Rich [61] describes an advisory facility for a document formatting system which embodies a simple but interesting approach. In her system, a user's skill level was determined by a keyword analysis of the vocabulary employed in help calls. Each text formatting command had associated with it a hierarchical structure of explanations ranging from general to technical, couched in vocabulary that reflected the degree of complexity involved. The skill level diagnosed in the user's help call determined the vocabulary level of the explanation produced by the system.

One problem with this approach is that it is not clear how diagnostic the vocabulary in a help call really is: an utter novice probably won't pose very technical queries, but a user with considerable experience might still use relatively general vocabulary and therefore get advice at too elementary a level. No behavioral assessment of the vocabulary analysis approach has been made yet.

Behavior Analysis

Perhaps a more direct route to automatically diagnosing user skill is to monitor and evaluate the user's actual behavior. Much of this work has focused on monitoring and evaluating user errors. For example, Coombs and Alty [*12*] stored prototypical error patterns as a normative user model for users of a Prolog environment. When particular users generated patterns of behavior that matched a stored prototype, relevant corrective advice was produced. We would prefer to have more than a mere list of attested error types to direct a behavior analysis. We would like to have a more general, or abstract, taxonomy of error, and more importantly, theoretical understanding of why errors occur.

Earlier we referred to work on the concept of knowledge "bugs," or systematic departures of a user model from an ideal model [*22–24*]. A bug is defined to be the least variant of a correct skill [*24*], that is, the smallest change in a correct procedure that would make it into an error. Bug theorists stress that this level of analysis is more abstract than that of prototypical error patterns. The latter are merely elements of the stream of behavior. Bugs, however, are seen as knowledge hypotheses: error, characteristic nonoptimalities, and even correct performances could all be evidence of a particular bug hypothesis. Systems like BUGGY and DEBUGGY try to recognize bugs and compositions of bugs in a person's work. Recognized bugs comprise a level of analysis of the user's skill, and a basis for generating specific advice.

Unfortunately, research on behavior analysis is still quite inconclusive. For example, more than five years of development work on bug diagnosis for the domain of simple arithmetic managed to analyze only a third of actual learner errors. Perhaps a more worrisome fact is that no principles have been isolated that distinguish correctly analyzed learner errors from those misanalyzed vis-a-vis bugs. Even though bugs are viewed as abstract hypotheses, there is no systematic theory of bugs (and of course this applies a fortiori to inventories of error prototypes). An inventory of bugs or errors is an inventory of mini-theories of a person's knowledge, but there is no systemic constraint on this taxonomy. Conversely, a view of learning as a process of debugging "least variants" in performance is still no richer than the simple accretion of stimulus–response connections. This is not merely a limitation in the theory. It is a practical limitation. Since particular inventory of bugs or error prototypes develops on a case by case basis without any overarching framework, each new case is virtually a tabula rasa. From a practical standpoint this is a crippling limitation.

Perhaps current approaches to knowledge bugs are at too low a level to understand cognitive skill. One could certainly drop the requirement that bugs differentiate "least variants" in performance. Such "higher level" bugs might comprise a more efficacious, as well as more tractable, grain of theoretical analysis. (Indeed, higher level bugs might coextend better with the level of error prototypes, and thus be a more empirically straightforward level as well.) Finally, it is clear that in many cases analyses of user error must explicitly incorporate the intention the user had in making the error [*62*]. Thus, behavioral analysis, in the sense of bugs and error prototypes, may need to become cognitive analysis [*63*].

Normative Models

A simple approach is to develop and refer to a normative user model, a single description, intended to apply to all. An example of this is the training wheels interface studied by Carroll and Carrithers [*64*], which hardcoded the assumption that new users of a word processing application would not need to access specific advanced system functions. When users attempt to access these functions, they are informed that the functions are not available to them.

The training wheels design was based on empirical research indicating that new users often access advanced function by mistake, and then become distracted and confused by the consequences. Nevertheless, a limitation with this approach is that if users' actual goals should fail to accord with the normative model, they could become frustrated with the implicit and inflexible guidance it provides. Reiser et al. [57] employed a normative model with prescribed goals in the Lisp tutor, but adjusted rendered advice dynamically in response to specific user actions. Error correction advice was adjusted to suit the manner in which an error was committed; users could also request specific clarifications or explanations. A limitation of such approaches lies in the fact that functionally equivalent knowledge can still be psychologically distinct [65].

An ambitious approach to adjusting advice is to incorporate both a normative reference model and a user-specific model of a given individual. For example, Sleeman and Brown [15, p. 5] discuss the use of an ideal expert model, a user-specific model, and a comparison of performance outputs of the two models as a basis for generating advice. Goldstein [30, p. 67] criticized this approach for assuming that the knowledge of the novice can be viewed as a simple subset of the knowledge of the expert, and that the transition from novice to expert consists of nothing more than the accretion of knowledge, gradually and ballistically minimizing the performance differential between the two models. Goldstein's discussion echoes critiques of the accretion learning theories of stimulus–response psychology [66] by contemporary theorists in artificial intelligence [67] and cognitive learning [68], who view learning as incorporating radical cognitive restructuring.

The possibility that the relation between novice and expert skill is more intricate and perhaps more erratic than merely the number of learned connections is consistent with an empirical test of the ideal normative model approach. Sleeman [32] employed an ideal expert model in designing a system to coach algebra. The model made relevant diagnoses for less than half of the errors that actually occurred in an algebra tutoring situation, and made the correct diagnosis on only half of those. The Lisp tutor of Reiser et al. [57] introduced a variation on ideal normative models in which the "ideal" model was not that of an ideal expert, but rather that of a ideal learner—an advanced student [69]. Reiser et al., [57] stored a list of productions as an ideal student model, and annotated this list based on the given individual's monitored performance to indicate which productions were assumed to have been learned. This system correctly diagnosed 45 to 80 percent of user errors.

Individual Differences

Coming at these problems from the top down, instead of from the bottom up, we might begin with a general analysis of individual differences and deduce from this patterns of errors or bugs that are diagnostic. This strategy holds the promise of providing an integrating framework that could help to generalize the case by case behavior taxonomies across task domains and systems.

The user modeling that underlies design of advisory systems has typically presumed that users are homogeneous in relevant ways. Of course, everyone also clearly sees that a better alternative would be to tailor interface presentation for individual differences [61]. We agree that individual differences may figure importantly into future advice-giving technology, but we also believe that the area is virtually undeveloped at present. It makes sense to say that people have diverse styles and needs for information. And it seems that people who provide information to others (e.g., reference librarians, people giving directions) do not make adjustments based on some reckoning of individual difference [70]. Therefore, it does seem reasonable to predict that computer systems may need to incorporate capacities for such accommodation to individuals. What seems unclear at present is just what the relevant dimensions of this accommodation are.

Many of the examples discussed are quite unconvincing. On one hand, many of the individual difference categories that are discussed are extremely general (like sex and Rich's stereotypes like " intellectual feminist"). The problem with these categories is relating them in focused ways to significant aspects of human information processing. To wit, do intellectual feminists have different advisory needs?

On the other hand, more specific individual difference categories often provide little real design implication. For example, in making a case for considering individual differences in interface design, Rich [*61*, p. 200] calls attention to studies by Card et al. [*71*], indicating that keystrokes per task should be minimized in designing word processing interactions for experts, and to studies by Ledgard et al. [*72*], indicating that English-like, full-word commands should be used in designing word processing interactions for novices. She calls these " conflicting requirements," but it is not at all clear that they do conflict, even for a specific level of user experience (i.e., Card et al. clearly view keystroke estimates of complexity as approximations, and Ledgard et al. in fact used very *brief* full-word commands).

An interesting, and increasingly relevant, individual difference is the user's experience with other systems, including specific expectations about functions, vocabulary, predicted errors, and confusions. For example, Rosson [*73*] found that the number of different full-screen text editors a person had previously used predicted other user characteristics (range of program function keys used in editing). As in the other areas we have examined here, individual differences seem ripe for empirical investigation although little has been done as yet.

Knowledge Bounds

How much knowledge is enough? Clearly, it is sound to argue that more explicit knowledge about advisory strategies, more natural language capability, more content knowledge about given domains and more extensive user modeling of individual users could make interactive advisory systems more effective. However, this detaches the issues from the problem context that gave them meaning. It is the constraints and limitations placed on knowledge representations that give this work scientific interest. Moreover, developing advisory systems is more than an exercise in knowledge representation; it has an engineering aspect. This latter aspect is also overlooked if we merely conclude that adding more of every type of knowledge will lead to better advisory systems.

Carroll and Aaronson [*74*] simulated an intelligent advisory system for a commercially developed database and report application. The simulation provided system-initiated (active) help in response to diagnosable errors. By design, the simulation had only bounded intelligence: it was intended to model a system not a human advisor. In some cases the system's limited knowledge, clashed with user expectations. When it did so, it tended to lose. For example, one user jumped to the conclusion that he could create a database by editing items in an existent database. He was wrong in this and made a long series of errors, each of which the system correctly pointed out, with suggestions for correction. He rejected these because he was sure he knew what to do. Intelligent beings are like this of course. The point is that we cannot now anticipate the clashes between the user intelligence we all have and the advisory intelligence we hope to build. Adding more intelligence is not an adequate way to think about this issue: we cannot now build systems that are intelligent in the sense

- What advisory strategies are there?

- Under what conditions are different strategies effective?

- How can different strategies be integrated?

- In what specific ways can natural language enhance system usability?

- In what ways do people voluntarily restrict their use of natural language when interacting with a recognition facility?

- How can a user's mental model of a task domain be incorporated into an advisory system?

- What properties of domain models, and at what grain of analysis, are most important for generating advice?

- How can we generalize advisory techniques across different task domains?

- Can user models that incorporate learning transitions and trajectories (as well as end states) be developed?

- Are there application areas for which normative modeling approaches will be adequate?

- How should individual user models be incorporated into advisory systems?

- What behaviors and self-descriptions can be collected to build user models?

- What differences in individual users are important for advice, and how can they be addressed through design?

FIGURE 1 Examples of advisory knowledge issues.

that people are, we may never be able to do this. The more concrete research question is how can we help people deal with bounded intelligence?

A key direction in which knowledge requirements work needs to move is in placing constraints and limitations on knowledge representations, and in measuring and evaluating the ensuing behavioral consequences. In the theoretical arena, this means going beyond inventories of knowledge elements to theories of knowledge structures; it means developing a theory of domains, and better theories of particular domains—empirically testable theories; it means understanding advisory strategies and restricted natural language capabilities so that alternatives can be explicitly characterized, contrasted, and evaluated, not merely selected or rejected on intuitive grounds.

In the practical arena, we need to look not merely at how to implement more comprehensive approaches, but at the consequences of self-limited approaches, solutions which are more technically feasible and which may be good bargains in advisory effectiveness. We have explored a research and training tool called a "scenario machine" [75,76]. The scenario machine encodes a series of goals and tasks for the user to accomplish with the system. The system makes each succeeding task seem plausible as the user works through the programmed scenario via information incidentally presented (e.g., the user receives electronic mail containing a query about a bulletin board item which must in turn be accessed and examined to answer the query). It can provide advisory dialog about the current goals, the steps of a procedure being executed, or other information relevant to the current task. The scenario which the user traverses is designed to include the fundamental functions of the systems, those functions users will need to have understood when they are engaged in actual use of the system. This sort of approach allows the system to provide very appropriate and context-sensitive advice without explicitly representing knowledge about the domain or dynamically inferring the user's goals.

When considering a topic like "knowledge requirements," one might be inclined to see it as a "formal" issue (as artificial intelligence, more than human factors). We do not agree with this. In fact, looking over the current literature, it is striking that many of the questions we have raised (and for the most part had to leave open) could *only* be resolved by making behavioral measurements of people using current research prototypes.

ADVISORY DIALOG

The knowledge requirements for advice giving are a foundation but in some sense also merely preliminaries to the "real" problem of giving advice. For even granting that the system knows the right sorts of things, that it has all the right answers and skills, how should these be structured and deployed in an advisory dialog? What should the system say? And when? We divide our discussion of this into three subsections. First, we examine the issues of establishing, and inevitably sharing, initiative in an advisory dialog between a system and a user. Second, we discuss architectures and styles for providing advice. Finally, we consider the scope of advice rendered.

Initiative

The simple "help split" example we have referred to several times assumes that the user will explicitly request the system to provide advice by issuing a command. This is quite typical in the commercial state of the art. The user must take full initiative in requesting advice. We could imagine dropping this assumption: the system could directly monitor the user's activities, that is, keep a log of every user action, analyze this log, and then initiate advisory dialog. Indeed, when one speaks of advisory systems, the implication is that initiative is at least shared in part with the system.

A number of issues arise immediately. For example, what level of user activity should be monitored, that is, what classes of events should be logged? The system could log every single keystroke event, or it could log events at a higher level (e.g., exemplars of a closed class of taxonomized errors). How should advice be delivered? The system could merely suggest more efficient or more correct ways to use the system, for example, through verbal feedback, or it could compel the user to do things in these alternate ways. These two contrasting approaches rather severely modulate what it means to give "advice."

System Monitoring

In current advisory systems, the most typical class of user actions to monitor for is errors. This makes good intuitive sense. After all, it is in the context of an error that users need most to be advised. It seems reasonable to assume that in attempting to recover from an error a user is motivated to attend to and to use advice. As such, error monitoring provides good grounds for feasibility demonstrations.

The key problem in error monitoring is defining what is to be taken as an error. There are simple cases: in a factual domain, if the user asserts false facts, then he or she has made an error and can be corrected and tutored. Even in procedural domains there are fairly simple cases: The user who specifies a directory that does not exist is probably making an error. One who selects Printing before having created any printable data is also probably making an error. The user who selects Application Customizing at the first logon and prior to any other selection is probably making an error, and could be directed to first try out some simpler function—but maybe it's not an error. The user who queues and requeues the same print job over and over without ever operating the printer is also probably making an error, and could be coached on using the printer—but maybe the user really wanted to queue up several identical print jobs.

A user action is often an error only with respect to specific user goals. For example, the user who queued and requeued the same print job without printing was making an "error" only under the assumption that his or her operative goal was in fact to print the job out. If the goal was to fill up the queue, the entire action sequence might have been not merely correct but optimized. Thus, the problem in error monitoring becomes one of diagnosing errors based on inferred goals [62]. And the cross-product space of user actions and user goals in an interactive procedural domain like programming or word processing is potentially vast. Carroll and Aaronson [74] encountered problems in making correct error diagnoses even in what seemed to be clear cases. For example, one user was browsing a passive help system and trying out interaction techniques described there. In doing so, he committed an error and triggered a message from the simulated intelligent help system. Because he was operating in a what-if mode, and had in that spirit deliberately made the error, he was merely annoyed with the help, commenting, "Well, I've already guessed that!" To serve this user, the advisory system would have had to discriminate "browsing and experimenting" from "really trying."

The situation is even worse than this in that such errors and apparent errors tangle in sequences of user behavior. A typically correct user action executed in the context of a prior error may need to be interpreted as a consequent error. For example, correctly operating the printer could be an error if the goal is to print Document A and, via some other error, Document B was queued for printing before Document A was queued. It is an error because in this context correctly operating the printer will cause Document B to print. In the Carroll and Aaronson [74] study, one user misspecified a zip code field length in designing a data template, in the course of fixing this, he accidentally added two blank data records to this file. Though both errors were diagnosable, unstacking them systematically required domain knowledge beyond the deliberately imposed bounds of the system's intelligence.

Error monitoring is facilitated to the extent that the user's actions are predictable, or directly prescribed. Indeed, this is why so much work on advisory systems has focused on intelligent tutorials rather than on intelligent help systems. Tutorials provide the system with a more restricted domain of action to diagnose. Nevertheless, this also makes clear that work on advisory systems will need to develop both in the direction of monitoring for user problems other than overt errors [e.g., for problematic or merely inefficient patterns of use; 5] and for errors in real contexts of use (i.e., outside of tutorial environments). Shrager and Finin [77] describe an advisory system that monitored actual use and suggested more optimal methods to users. However, monitoring and analyzing "free" user activity is daunting. Quinn and Russell [78] evaluated an advisor for a copier system, noting significant problems in synchronizing the analysis of the user's state, the presentation of advice, and the user's state when the advice actually arrived.

User Discovery

Brown et al. [22, p. 228] report that, in their experience developing interactive tutoring systems, large amounts of system-initiated intervention was quite often deleterious. They argue that it is often better to leave the user alone, especially if the problem seems small. However, they also suggest that no advice be given if the learner gets too far off track [24, p. 96], arguing that it is unclear what sort of advice to give in such cases anyway. This is probably the best available wisdom, but it underscores the lack of depth in our current understanding: What is too far off the track? What is a small problem? What is too much system-initiated intervention? These are empirical questions that await systematic investigation.

System-initiated advice, however relevant to the user's situation, could still be a distraction to the user if the user's current goal is something other than attending to advice. This was identified as a major problem in the Carroll and Aaronson [74] study, yet it is difficult to imagine how an advisory system could recognize when the user will be receptive to help and when unreceptive. Fischer et al. [27] acknowledged this problem and employed a simple time-out approach; in their system advisory interruptions occur with an arbitrarily bounded maximum frequency. Carroll and Kay [75, see also next subsection] experimentally contrasted several approaches to intelligent prompting in a scenario machine. For example, in one version users received prompting advice, telling them exactly what to do in the current system state to avoid making errors at all. Other versions gave feedback advice, telling the user how to recover when an error had been committed. One version gave both prompting advice, directing the user what to do, and feedback advice, directing the user how to recover from errors committed. Interestingly, the people who were trained on this latter version performed most poorly in transfer of learning tasks, suggesting [with Brown et al. (22)] that too much advice can in fact be deleterious.

The approaches of Fischer et al. and Carroll and Kay control the amount and variety of advisory information provided, but the control they provide is not responsive to specific details of the user's situation. They do not try to distinguish cases of welcomed interruption from advisory harassment. Proponents of "discovery learning" often advocate waiting until the user explicitly asks for help before offering feedback [79]. When the system provides advice in response to a user-initiated request, it is more likely that in fact the user has the current goal of attending to the advice. The practical problem with current user-initiated advice facilities is that they often require lengthy and tedious prompting dialog interaction [13]. There is a need for work on schemes for streamlining system response protocols for user-initiated advice requests.

Taking an even stronger discovery learning approach, we might consider downside aspects of providing advice at all. It is often argued that providing information to people is in many cases less effective than allowing them to discover it on their own initiative [80]. The discovery approach takes advantage of opportunistic learning, that is, making the most of each unique personal experience. On the other hand, allowing the user to wander with minimal guidance in an exploratory learning mode may also be undesirable, for example, in terms of learning rate [81, but cf; 82]. It is also a question of whether very intricate skills could be "discovered" efficiently (compare inventing the calculus with learning it).

This possibility may interact with the type of interface under consideration. Discovery learning is perhaps more feasible for a menu interface [82] than for a command interface: the former explicitly list current options that can be tried and provide many implicit cues as well (e.g., in what the names of the options suggest). Interfaces designed around active forms [83,84] provide even more implicit advice to the user about what can be done from a given system state and the results entrained. These and other techniques, such as dynamically highlighting and/or relocating currently important display areas, might be thought of as providing "soft" advice to the user. Masson et al. [85] found that users working with a direct manipulation [86] version of an interface often perseverated on incorrect responses, in contrast to those using a command line version. They suggested that the direct manipulation interface evoked repetition of errors by failing to preserve a visual record of previous actions. The command line system records in teletype, and hence provides cues to curtail such perseveration.

The trade-off between rigid advisory guidance and discovery approaches may also be sensitive to level of experience. Elkerton [87] reported that very inexperienced users were sometimes confused by highly interactive, mixed-initiative dialog. Fischer and Stevens [88] noticed this in designing their System Assistant, which attempts to advise on rebooting a computer after a crash. The system incorporates a rigid question asking dialog as well as a facility in which users can volunteer information about the state of the computer. Novices seemed comfortable with the former dialog structure, but more experienced users preferred the latter. This may limit the utility of discovery approached for very inexperienced users.

Consequences

Advice-giving has consequences. At the very least, information is represented, and hopefully imparted. The user can attend to it, be distracted by it, even ignore it. Many other types of consequences are possible: the available function of the system can change when advice is given to implicitly compel the user to follow the advice, the user could be placed in a special system mode where the advice could be explored without risk of causing further errors or other complications.

Confirmation Dialog

Beyond merely presenting information, an advice-giving facility can modulate the system's control structure. For example, when the user can be diagnosed as having made an error or when the user is perhaps one command away from taking an action with potentially dangerous consequences, the system can enter into a "confirmation dialog." The system interrupts the user's session and poses questions which the user must answer before being permitted to continue with the session, for example, "Type Y if the information you are about to transmit is nonproprietary, or anything else to cancel the command." A well-known cliche example is the confirmation question "Are you sure you want to delete all your files?" The objective of such confirmation dialog, of course, is to force the user to rethink recent actions, immediate options, and possible consequences.

Many systems request confirmation for fatal errors (like the erase all files example). Cuff [88a], in a review of work on database retrieval systems for casual users, discusses this sort of protective mechanism as being desirable but does not specify how or when it should be invoked. Gable and Paige [29], also in a review of the literature, recommended that a confirmation approach be adopted in which the user is given immediate feedback by the system, but always has the prerogative to heed it or reject it. The argument in principle that a user be forced to confirm an intention to erase all files sounds comforting, but can we simply rest assured that the type of user who would erroneously issue the command in the first place will adequately appreciate the severity of the consequences when they are briefly reviewed in a confirmation prompt? We need to know how the approach works and, perhaps more important, when and how it is likely to fail.

Blocking Control

In the confirmation approach, the user's access to the system is temporarily interrupted by the advisory prompt. A more severe intervention is blocking: a portion of the system's function is rendered conditionally inaccessible to the user. Carroll and Carrithers [*64*] studied a training wheels system in which certain system states were blocked off: those that were problematic consequences of errors (the state of having an unprintable character in a textfile) and those that often led to error (prematurely selecting advanced functions). When the user selected these, a message was presented stating that they were not available in the training wheels version of the system. This blocking approach has the undesirable side effect of profoundly interrupting the user. If the system has misdiagnosed the situation and no error in fact occurred, or if the user intended to do what was indicated even though it was unorthodox, the consequences of blocking progress would be extremely frustrating. The blocking approach may be most appropriate to new users whose goals may be more limited (and therefore more easily anticipated or recognized) and who may be less sensitive to interruption in the flow of system control. For new users, Carroll and Carrithers showed that the approach led to more efficient learning of a word processing application.

The blocking approach has also been used in conjunction with various types of intelligent advisory dialog. Lewis and Anderson [*89*] studied people learning to play a logic-based computer game. They found that feedback immediately after an error was the most effective in learning the game's operators. They found also that people learned to recognize dead-end situations better if they were allowed to encounter them. Allowing people to actually "see" the consequences of an error they would have made (and to easily back out of or avoid these consequences) is an important type of advisory information, and one uniquely enabled by advisory systems. These two findings suggest that advice should be presented immediately after an error is made, but that the user should also be allowed to see what the consequences of the error would be (or would have been), before being blocked, allowed to correct the error and make the correct move [see also Ref. *58*].

Woolf et al. [*28*] have also adopted this approach in their Recovery Boiler Tutor. Students work through scenarios for 20 tutoring situations, receiving feedback only when they begin to progress away from the goal state. Carroll and Kay [*75*] and McKendree and Carroll [*76*] combined blocking with various kinds of advisory information in their scenario machine studies. The blocking idea has been developed more completely and with more empirical investigation than is the case with most advisory dialog techniques. However, most of the work has examined only demonstration systems, raising the further question of how far the ideas can be extended.

Automatic Correction

Perhaps at another extreme from blocking progress and providing confirmation dialog is the approach of automatic correction. In this approach when the user makes an error, the system interprets it as a correct next response and allows progress to continue uninterrupted. Thus, we might imagine a user who misexecutes "split" being automatically provided with a correct command form—without ever having to go through any explicit "help split" request. Interlisp's Do What I Mean (DWIM) facility [*90*] automatically resolves incorrect input and suggests a correction to the user (usually through nothing more sophisticated than spelling correction). However, in cases for which the correction is classified as "obvious" the system simply makes the correction without requesting explicit confirmation. Clearly, this approach might be convenient for experienced and sophisticated users, particularly when applied to mundane and common slips. However, the particular conditions under which the approach could be effective for such users have not been determined.

Two behavioral studies suggest that the automatic correction approach may also have a use in the design of training interfaces for new users. We earlier described research by Carroll and Kay [75] contrasting alternate versions of a training system. The best training design of those they evaluated, both from the standpoint of training time and success in a transfer of learning task was one with automatic correction: as the novice worked through a training scenario, errors were interpreted as the next correct action. Earlier work by Hillen [91] with an on-line manual reached the same conclusion. How far these curious findings can be extended is an open question (although it seems clear the approach must break down in the limit).

Protected Modes

All of the approaches we have considered to this point provide advice within the context of interaction with the actual system itself. Many of them involve altering the control structure of the system. An alternative is to create a special mode within which the user can work out problems and receive advice. For example, Jaagodzinsky [49] described a "reconnoiter mode" in which the actions of system commands are simulated without actually altering any of the user's data. A user who has a problem could switch into reconnoiter mode, resolve the problem by harmlessly trying things out, and then return to the actual system environment to continue a work session. Such an idea was implemented in a text-processing system called NLS-SCHOLAR, in which the user could ask a "What if.." question which would create a temporary copy of the current file and carry out the hypothetical action without affecting the actual workspace [92], and in the SIGMA message processing service [93].

These approaches leave to the user the responsibility for initiating a reconnoiter or what-if session, but we might elaborate them to imagine the system suggesting such advisory subsessions when potential user errors are detected. A problem with these approaches is that by placing the advisory subsession within a special mode, we risk inviting the confusion users typically encounter in having to keep track of different modes of operation [94,95]. Indeed, Clark [96] reported that users he observed sometimes forgot the underlying concern that motivated a help request in the course of switching from problem solving to learning mode. The growing availability of undo facilities suggests an interesting reconciliation of the utility for protected modes with the problem of mode changing: the actual system environment can become a protected environment for trying things out.

It seems likely that the bottom line regarding the management of initiative and consequences in the design of advisory systems is that all the approaches we have inventoried here (and no doubt the several we missed) can play useful roles. There is nothing wrong with this conclusion for the moment as long as one bears in mind how far it is from where we need to go if there is going to be a principled basis for designing such systems. We need to investigate the conditions under which each technique is most useful; we need to understand the design trade-offs; we need to do all this empirically and systematically.

Scope

We have referred to error recovery dialog, but without focusing on exactly what information should be provided in this dialog. DWIM automatic correction [90] provides no explicit information. But information could be provided to help the user identify the specific error that triggers advisory intervention. We could help the user better understand what he or she is trying to do (in the sense of a goal), or to better understand how to do it (the concrete steps that facilitate accomplishing the goal), or perhaps to better understand the larger context within which this work and the particular task at hand are taking place.

We examine the issues of advisory scope in three parts. First, we look at various levels at which advisory dialog can be couched: methods, goals, examples. Second, we consider how the appropriate scope of advice-giving might vary as a function of the user's current situation, including the problem-solving context in which the user is working. Finally, we briefly consider the question of managing metacommunicative aspects of dialog to help motivate the user to pay attention to advice.

Methods

Step-level advice can be presented very directly, as literal directions, to users. There is a degree of consensus about traditional help systems that the focus of presented information should be on *how* to do something, in concise and direct instructions, in contrast to more abstract or general explanations and descriptions [91]. Step-level dialog has also been advocated for intelligent advisory facilities [23, p. 92; 39, p. 152]. Burton and Brown say explicitly that they hoped to implicitly suggest appropriate goals to users through the language in which the appropriate steps were presented.

One problem with this approach is that it magnifies the costs of any mistaken diagnosis the system might make. For if the system misdiagnoses the user's situation and suggests the wrong next step, the user could quite possibly be thrown far off the track by the advice given (all the succeeding advised steps will be wrong too). A complementary problem arises if the suggested next step (even though correct) is far from what the user expected. The user could follow it by rote but without any new understanding of the system. An alternative would be to reverse the strategy of Burton and Brown, implicitly suggesting steps by explicitly advising goals.

Goals

Fikes [55] argued that a rote description of steps, though it may help a person perform in some routine situations, does not provide sufficient basis for problemsolving when the specified sequence of steps fails to produce the intended result. He developed the notion of a "procedure teleology," a functional description of (1) the task to be achieved and (2) each step in the procedure. This will allow the user to recognize situations where a procedure might not be appropriate and will support reformulation of new plans. An alternative approach is to advise directly on goals. Human advisors focus a great deal of attention on communicating and clarifying goals [97]. When they fail to do this, their clients are dissatisfied [20]. Users in studies of simulated advisory systems request goal-based rationales for advice [38], and sometimes reject advice that fails to appear relevant to their goals [74]. The learning demands of goal-level advice might be greater than those for step-level advice, since the learner is not told what to do at the level of actions, but for this reason the learning might also be more cognitively elaborated and robust [58,82].

In the scenario machine work [75,76] we found that goal-level advice was in fact more technically tractable than step-level advice. Because of the constraints of a task scenario and its inherent goal structure, it was straightforward to predict what the user might be trying to do. It was far less clear how a given user might decide to try to achieve the goals. We also found that goal-level advice was more useful to users [76]. McKendree [98] and Singley [99] found goal-level advice to be very useful in tutorial situations.

An even more technically tractable approach might be to provide only *implicit* goal-level advice, and then require the user to generate appropriate steps from this. The training wheels systems studied by Carroll and Carrithers [64] merely advised the user that a selected function was not available during training (their system blocked selected functions that were judged to have been prematurely selected, based on the user's experience and current task). This level of advice did not directly help the user decide what to try instead. The user had to generate a new goal in view of the task he or she was trying to accomplish and the blocking message, and then derive the specific steps to achieve that goal.

Examples

Edmonds [*100*] stressed how unwise it can be to specify very general-level objectives in detail because these goals will quite likely change as a function of the user's experience. For example, the vocabulary in which users understand system-relevant goals may change radically with their experience. Edmonds concluded that the means of attaining goals should be specified first since they are more stable. He specifically suggested that this step-level information could be presented by means of an example designed to facilitate analogical mapping to the user's current situation [*101*].

The RABBIT system [*83*] allows users to query a database through successive reformulation of an example target instance. However, presenting step-level advice through examples can also be problematic. It is notoriously difficult to differentiate those aspects of an example that generalize to an analogical domain from those that do not [*102*]. The advice may become ambiguous.

Work at Carnegie-Mellon has addressed the problem of presenting and managing goals explicitly to escape the sorts of problems Edmonds raised. In these schemes goals are logged and posted on the display as work progresses [*58,98,99,103*].

Clearly, advice and even examples can be provided at a variety of levels. A person could be advised exactly what step to carry out next, merely given information about appropriate goals and allowed to derive a course of action from this, or provided with examples that model appropriate goals, plans, and actions. A goal could be suggested or exemplified when behavior (or an explicit help request) indicates that the user has lost track of the path in a complex procedure. But a step could be employed when the indication is that the user is pretty much on track but has made a small slip. It seems plausible that strategies for advice giving might need to vary according to the needs of the user and the nature of the task. For example, Paris [*104*] built a system which emphasized components and mechanisms of an object if the user was judged to be experienced, but operational and causal relations if the user was judged to be a novice. Unfortunately, no behavioral work has addressed this question yet.

Adjusting Advice

Jackson and Lafrere [*7*] urge that the type of advice provided should indeed vary as a function of the level of the task. Well-specified tasks may require no more than descriptive information support of the type found in many conventional help systems. Animated demonstrations of system function may be more appropriate for tasks requiring the integration of subprocedures, while even more open-ended tasks might require dynamically generated intelligent advice. Although Jackson and Lafrere cited no specific empirical backing, or psychological reasoning, for these suggestions their view is consistent with the few behavioral studies of advice-giving that have been published. McCoy [*25*] discussed anecdotes in which experts corrected misconceptions about the attribute mappings among objects. In her examples, the experts provided more information than was necessary to expose the particular misconception; the additional information often served to establish the correct conception by raising questions about new issues.

McKendree et al. [*95*] studied a more procedural domain than McCoy; computer programming in Lisp. Advisor/learner diads worked through a series of typical programming problems in an unconstrained tutoring situation. The content of the advisory dialog was analyzed in terms of the goals and methods employed by the advisors. This analysis showed that the advisors tended to vary the content of their help according to a judgement of the "seriousness" of the misconception. A minor slip or syntactic error may elicit only enough information from the advisor to correct the immediate problem. However, a learner response which indicated something more serious to the advisor might evoke more extensive explanation, examples and questions. Again, though, it was not clear in this analysis just what information the advisors used to determine "seriousness."

Pollack [105] solicited electronic bulletin board queries pertaining to a computer mail system. She noted that advice-seekers do not always have well-formed plans about what they need to know, for example, they ask about actions that are impossible with respect to the system. A consequence of this, in her study, was that advisors sometimes respond with an action not asked for, an alternate plan. Pollack directed these observations at the "appropriate query assumption" of Allen and Perault [106], the assumption that the user always has a well-formed plan and will ask an appropriate question. This result suggests that advice-giving cannot presuppose the well-formedness, vis-a-vis a domain, of a request for advice. Hill and Miller [38] simulated an interactive intelligent advisory system with a human advisor. In this situation, they found that the advisors often focused on ensuring that the immediate goals and queries articulated by clients were compatible with longer range goals, as inferred from previous user queries and actions. In some case, the advice addressed these long-term considerations *instead* of answering an immediate, but perhaps inappropriate, query.

Aaronson and Carroll [107] analyzed actual advisory interactions with a system in which human advisors received queries and made responses to their user-clients by means of electronic mail. This system created an interesting "one-shot" advisory environment: clients and advisors never met face to face and each interaction consisted of a single query and a single response. Several distinctive strategies emerged from the characteristics of this situation. For example, about half the queries omitted details the advisor needed in order to respond. Advisors dealt with these incomplete queries by making assumptions about the user goal underlying the query or by providing multiple solutions to cover the range of possible queries the user might have had in mind (among other strategies).

Advising the Process

It is daunting, but also clear, that the entire situation in which the user is interacting defines the user's advisory needs. Several researchers have emphasized the importance of directing advice to *processes* involved in problem solving, rather than concentrating only on a solution to the immediate problem. This has, for example, been isolated as a major deficiency in bug analyses of users' knowledge and performance. Genesereth [39] argued that in order to correctly analyze the bugs in a user's procedure, the entire problem-solving process must be analyzed, not merely local segments (e.g., the activity immediately preceding the manifestation of a bug).

Coombs and Alty [12,20] found that consultants often attended too little to the organization of the advisory process: advisors assumed control of the dialog as soon as possible and permitted only a one-way flow of information; they rarely included explanations of the larger problem context; they rarely checked that the users really understood the advice given. These problems appeared to interact with the sophistication of the user, however. In advising relatively sophisticated users, advisors did tend to give explanations, and to share control of the advisory interaction to a greater extent. These latter interactions were also viewed by the users as being more successful.

These more successful advisory interactions often seemed to have little obvious structure; they seemed more rambling. More information seemed to be given than was really necessary. However, in debriefing sessions with the users and consultants, the motivations often became more apparent. The large information exchange served to make explicit the inferences involved in problem solving and allowed the user to participate through monitoring and feedback. The end result was to encourage "problem solving through mutual understanding" in which the user worked through his problem with the help of the advisor. They concluded that a guidance system should "support rather than direct problem solving. This support should mainly be in the form of assistance in building and evaluating concepts in the problem area" [*12*, p. 27]. Thus, like Fikes, they conclude that advice which evolves with the user's knowledge about the processes, steps and purpose of the task will hold the user in better stead when other problems are encountered [see also Ref. *13*]

Our analysis of advisory interactions between computer consultants and users also supports these conclusions. We found that ostensibly successful advisory interactions often did not codify a solution per se, rather the "solution" took the form of an enumeration of strategies and plans to pursue, along with the elimination of other courses of action judged to be less promising [*108*]. We also found that one of the chief mechanisms through which advice is generated is the posing of verificational questions by *client*: "All I do is read from standard input; is it that simple?" Thus, to an extent, "giving advice" merely means getting explicit encouragement for a solution one already knows [*21*].

Attitude and Motivation

Although we have focused here on procedures, goals, and steps as levels for advice giving, it is important to bear in mind the larger context within which advice giving takes place. It is quite possible that the most important elements ineffective advice lie beyond providing more correct and complete information. Alty and Coombs [*109*] made an empirical survey of the advice and information needs of users at a university computing center and found that one of the principal bases of user satisfaction with the center's help desk service was the personal human contact it provided. Similar points have been stressed by Eason [*110,111*].

It is obvious that attitudes toward computers, toward the particular system, and toward the system advisory dialogs will influence the user's ability to use and learn the system effectively. Several demonstration systems have explicitly addressed this. For example, Burton and Brown [*23*, p. 89] provided positive encouragement as well as critique feedback in WEST, to help motivate users. However, these attempts to address motivational and attitudinal issues have rested on intuitive analyses of what these factors are and how they should be addressed. Malone [*112*] and Carroll [*113*] suggested that motivational elements used in computer games, such as fantasy, challenge, and safety in risk taking, might be incorporated into user interface dialog designs to produce more intrinsically interesting system dialogs. However, to date this work has not actually resulted in new dialog designs.

Summary

People often need advice when they are solving problems. Current work on advisory systems has focused on system-initiated advice giving in the context of user error. This is probably an excellent choice; it is intuitively the type of situation in which people might be receptive to advice and therefore one in which we can get the leverage to demonstrate feasibility.

The shortcomings of current research center on two issues: First, the particular demonstration systems that have been developed and described in the literature have sam-

- Under what conditions should a system take initiative in advisory dialog?

- Are there heuristics for advising error tangles that cannot be fully diagnosed?

- How can we provide opportunities for discovery learning and yet still ensure adequate advisory support?

- How can access to protected modes be engineered to avoid mode-changing usability problems?

- When are obtrusive advice-giving approaches, like blocking and automatic correction, more appropriate than mere information presentation?

- How can blocking be used with sophisticated users?

- How can automatic correction be used for nontrivial problems?

- At what level of problem detail should advisory dialog be couched (e.g., should it advise goals or steps), and under what conditions?

- How can we develop a more comprehensive theory of user goals in intelligent advisory systems?

- In what presentation vocabulary should advisory dialog be couched (e.g., examples, demonstration, explanations, procedures)?

- What are the specific usability benefits and costs of adjusting the content and presentation of advice dynamically?

- How can we advise the problem solving process and not merely comment on the outcomes of that process?

- How can metacommunication in advisory dialog be used to motivate users to attend?

FIGURE 2 Examples of advisory dialog issues.

pled the space of advisory interaction somewhat haphazardly. What level should advice be provided at: goals, steps, examples? What consequences should accompany advice: blocking, correction, special modes? How should advice be timed with respect to a triggering event such as an error? How much advice should be given? What dynamic aspects of advice-giving strategies are important?

A second class of shortcoming is that virtually none of the current work has been subjected to any systematic empirical study: advisory systems (Fig. 2) *ought* to help people solve their problems but we have no solid basis yet for believing this has really been achieved. Indeed, Coombs and Alty [12] have recently posed the interesting question of why—now that demonstration advisory systems are available—this technology still has yet to be used much in real application. They raise the possibility that this failure is due to a fundamental lack of usability. Similar points are made by Kidd and Cooper [13].

Behavioral evidence suggests that many forms of communication are used spontaneously in advice giving [*17,20,97*]. However, there have been no systematic investigations of the effectiveness of various styles nor of the interaction with context or type of misunderstanding. This expertise in domain-specific problem solving and methods of teaching has been abstracted through experience which is very limited in the case of automated systems. Advisory systems which have been built generally employ only one of these strategies or perhaps a few of them chosen randomly to vary advisory style. It is necessary to combine intuitions and behavioral studies to systematize more effective advising.

THE RESEARCH AGENDA

We have tried to capture and taxonomize some of the key issues in design of advisory systems, both from an a priori viewpoint and from the standpoint of the state of the art. What can we learn from this? We have not found a well-developed paradigmatic endeavor with a high structured and generally agreed upon set of standard issues and a set of clear research successes. But this is not surprising. The area of advice giving is a frontier in both cognitive science and computer science.

In our view, the chief lessons to be drawn bear on managing the research agenda. Too much energy is being directed at existence demonstrations—the design and implementation of limited-scale advisory technology. This is an appropriate early objective to have, and it is still relevant to investigate by implementation whether current small-scale advisory systems will scale up for large and complex, real applications. However, very little systematic effort has been directed at exploring the behavioral issues pertaining to advisory systems. Indeed, the study of advisory systems is very fragmented: system researchers don't worry enough about the usability of their demonstration systems, behavioral researchers don't worry enough about implementation issues, and developers of real advisory systems cannot make use of the research. This could be a critical deficiency: even if current questions of technical possibility were to be settled with overwhelmingly impressive software, we would still be gambling on the intuition that the type of advisory facilities developed would be usable, even desirable, to real people.

To avoid this gamble two items need to be promoted on the research agenda for advisory systems: we need a psychological theory of advice and advising, and we need behavioral methodology to assess the actual success of demonstration advisory systems. We consider these in turn.

Toward a Theory of Advice Giving

One approach to experimental computer science is to build a reasonable working system through which to explore, discover, and understand the principles of the system's operation. This is an important research method and it has become important as rapid prototyping tools have become more powerful, flexible, and widely available. A limitation of this approach is that in any area of system design with direct implications for the user interface, this method is underconstrained. Moreover, it has become ever clearer that every aspect of system design has direct implications for the user interface. Accordingly, the approach of building experimental demonstration systems must be augmented to include usability considerations [*114*].

How can this be accomplished? The starting point must be a general understanding of what advice is, how people generate and deliver advice, and how people make use of advice in the context of problems. We do not have such a general understanding now. Indeed, much of our current understanding of advice and advice giving (like our understanding of usability generally) is either too high level or too low level. High-level principles like "Advice should be relevant," or "Represent and communicate information about the system as people do," remind one of the famous but vacuous maxim "Know the user." Neither is very deep or very useful. Conversely though, principles can be codified at too low a level. Much current discussion of demonstration advisory systems offers design principles evaluated only casually in the context of a single system. But because each of these systems differ in innumerable and unsystematic ways, they really cannot be compared, contrasted, or generalized with any confidence.

Useful principles will be applicable in a variety of domains and yet provide guidance for specific content and structure. One such principle might be "Advice should be presented in a vocabulary of system-independent goals." This principle is strong enough to be falsifiable, and to really constrain the design of advice facilities. Another principle which could be useful and which is empirically testable is "Give immediate feedback when an error is detected." Exactly how this should be done is still a question. Should the user be blocked from any further progress? Allowed to see consequences? We do not claim these principles exemplify the best we can hope for, or even that they are correct (the evidence for them is still too limited). Rather, we are suggesting that such principles are the *least* we should settle for; they are a start. Clearly, there is a lot of work to be done before we will have anything to seriously call a theory of advice, but as we have seen, studies directed at this are beginning to appear.

Measuring Advisory Effectiveness

Advisory systems are obviously intended to find practical application. Indeed, the chief rationale for providing an advisory capability is to help users become more successful and effective. But, as we have tried to stress, good intentions are just not enough. Developing a theory of advice is a key to going beyond mere good intentions, but even this is no guarantee that what was designed to be an effective advice facility *is*, in fact, an effective advice facility. Unfortunately, even when the problem is acknowledged, the solution offered can be useless: "implement . . . in a sensible way" [*115*]. This is not a methodology, it merely underscores the current lack of methodology.

We need to develop, codify, and routinize the use of behavioral evaluation techniques within the development process for advisory systems. We surely do not mean to suggest that there is a wealth of rich and powerful behavioral methodology that can now be taken off the shelf to improve advisory interfaces. There are in fact a variety of techniques (some of which have been referred to in this report; see also [*116*]. However, their effectiveness in helping to guide real, complex system projects is still something we have too little experience with to be able to confidently evaluate [but see recent case studies *117–120*]. Appropriate methods have to be constructed or adapted to this area.

One recommendation we would make is that researchers try to strike a balance between getting "hard" behavioral data that might be convenient to quantify and summarize, and "softer" behavioral data that might be relatively more illuminating in helping to guide redesign [*121*]. For example, Reiser et al. [*57*] focused considerable attention on behavioral evaluation and were able to report very encouraging overall statistics for the behavioral efficacy of their Lisp tutor. However, they fail to report any qualitative details: For which error types did the tutor fail? How much of the power of their tutorial design was derived from the user-initiated Clarify and Explain keys and how much from the system-initiated tutorial? We need to know, of course, that advisory designs can really work, and this can be assessed quantitatively. But it is the qualitative measurements that will guide further research developments.

Once we accept the suggestion that the effectiveness of advice facilities be measured (and not merely insisted on), we can seriously ask whether given advisory systems are cost effective with respect to others. If one approach was 90 percent as effective as an alternative, but cost a tenth as much (in terms of development time and computing resources), it might be a good deal. We referred earlier to the scenario machine approach, which encodes knowledge about a domain at a very large grain (that of a computer user action path). Such systems do not break knowledge down into procedural atoms and cannot generate inferences to respond dynamically, but their behavioral utility has already been systematically demonstrated. A scenario machine is cheap, but assessing its effectiveness will involve consideration of user and task specifics.

The research area of advisory systems is vital to a science of user interface design. The area must represent a variety of technologies; knowledge engineering and dialog management are two key ones we have looked at in this review. But success in designing intelligent systems for training and help will finally depend on usability. And as we have argued, the area has not yet incorporated a serious psychological theory base or empirical methodology. Rectifying this will probably involve inventing psychological theory and method as much as it will assimilating existing theory and method. But the effort could be richly rewarded: advice giving could become the first successful domain for intelligent interfaces.

ACKNOWLEDGMENT

We thank Amy Aaronson, Robert Campbell, Richard Herder, Jakob Nielsen, Mary Beth Rosson, Ted Selker, Jeff Shrager, and John Thomas for comments on an earlier draft of this manuscript. Many of the thoughts incorporated into the final draft grew out of the discussions of a reading group we participated in that also included Amy Aaronson, John Black, Keith Bergendorff, Richard Catrambone, Nancy Grischkowsky, Richard Herder, Joeann Paige, Robert Mack, Jakob Nielsen, John Richards, Mary Beth Rosson, Linda Tetzlaff, John Thomas, and Ken Williamson. An earlier version of this report appeared as Carroll and McKendree [*122*].

REFERENCES

1. R. L. Mack, C. H. Lewis, and J. M. Carroll, "Learning to Use Office Systems: Problems and Prospects," *ACM Trans. Office Inform. Sys., 1,* 254–271 (1983)
2. M. Mantei, and N. Haskell, "Autobiography of a First–time Discretionary Microcomputer User," in *Proceedings of CHI'83 Human Factors in Computing Systems,* Boston, December 12–15, ACM, New York, 1983, pp. 286–290.
3. J. Nielsen, R. L. Mack, K. Bergendorff, and N. L. Grischkowsky, "Integrated Software Usage in the Professional Work Environment: Evidence from Questionnaires and Interviews," in *Proceedings of CHI'86 Human Factors in Computing Systems,* Boston, April 13–17, ACM, New York, 1985, pp. 162–167.
4. B. Pope, "A Study of Where Users Spend Their Time Using VM/CMS," *IBM Res. Rep.,* RC 10953 (1985).
5. M. B. Rosson, "Patterns of Experience in Text Editing," in *Proceedings of CHI'83 Human Factors in Computing Systems,* Boston, December 12–15, ACM, New York, 1983, pp. 171–175.

6. J. M. Carroll, and M. B. Rosson, "The Paradox of the Active User," in *Interfacing Thought: Cognitive Aspects of Human–Computer Interaction* (J. M. Carroll, ed.), Bradford Books/MIT Press, Cambridge, MA, 1987.

7. P. Jackson, and P. La Frere, "On the Application of Rule-Based Techniques to the Design of Advice-Giving Systems," *Int. J. Man–Machine Studies, 20,* 63–86 (1984).

8. R. C. Houghton, "Online Help Systems: A Conspectus," *Comm. ACM, 27,* 126–133 (1984).

9. J. D. Gould, J. Conti, and T. Hovanyecz, "Composing Letters with a Simulated Listening Typewriter," *Comm. ACM, 26*(4), 295–308 (1983).

10. A. Malhotra, and P. S. Sheridan, "Experimental Determination of Design Requirements for a Program Explanation System," *IBM Res. Rep.*, RC 5831 (1976).

11. M. B. Rosson, and N. M. Mellen, "Behavioral Issues in Speech-Based Remote Information Retrieval," in *Proceedings of AVIOS 85* (L. Lermon, ed.) AVIOS, San Francisco, 1985.

12. M. J. Coombs, and J. L. Alty, "Expert Systems: An Alternate Paradigm," *Int. J. Man–Machine Studies, 20,* 21–43 (1984).

13. A. L. Kidd, and M. B. Cooper, "Man-Machine Interface Issues in the Construction and Use of an Expert System," *Int. J. Man–Machine Studies, 22,* 91–102 (1985).

14. N. S. Borenstein, "The Design and Evaluation of On-Line Help Systems," Ph.D. dissertation, Carnegie-Mellon University, Technical Report, CMU-CS-85-151 (1985).

15. D. Sleeman, and J. S. Brown (eds.), *Intelligent Tutoring Systems,* Academic Press, New York, 1982.

16. W. J. Clancy, "Tutoring Rules for Guiding a Case Method Dialog," in *Intelligent Tutoring Systems* (D. Sleeman and J. S. Brown, eds.), Academic Press, New York, 1982, pp. 201–225.

17. A. Stevens, A. Collins, and S. E. Goldin, "Misconceptions in Students' Understanding," in *Intelligent Tutoring Systems* (D. Sleeman and J. S. Brown, eds.), Academic Press, New York, 1982, pp. 13–24.

18. B. Woolf, and D. D. McDonald, "Building a Computer Tutor: Design Issues," *IEEE Comput.,* 61–73 (September 1984).

19. R. Kimball, "A Self-Improving Tutor for Symbolic Integration," in *Intelligent Tutoring Systems* (D. Sleeman and J. S. Brown, eds.), Academic Press, New York, 1982, pp. 283–307.

20. M. J. Coombs, and J. L. Alty, "Face-to-Face Guidance of University Computer Users–II: Characterizing Advisory Interactions," *Int. J. Man–Machine Studies, 12,* 407–429 (1980).

21. A. P. Aaronson, and J. M. Carroll, "The Answer is in the Question: A Protocol Study of Intelligent Help," *Behav. Inform. Technol., 6,* 393–402 (1987).

22. J. S. Brown, R. R. Burton, and J. de Kleer, "Pedagogical, Natural Language and Knowledge Engineering Techniques in SOPHIE I, II, and III," in *Intelligent Tutoring Systems* (D. Sleeman and J. S. Brown, eds.), Academic Press, New York, 1982, pp. 227–282.

23. R. Burton, and J. S. Brown, "An Investigation of Computer Coaching for Informal Learning Activities," in *Intelligent Tutoring Systems* (D. Sleeman and J. S. Brown, eds.), Academic Press, New York, 1982, pp. 79–89.

24. R. R. Burton, "Diagnosing Bugs in a Simple Procedural Skill," in *Intelligent Tutoring Systems* (D. Sleeman and J. S. Brown, eds.), Academic Press, New York, 1982, pp. 157–183.

25. K. F. McCoy, "Correcting Misconceptions: What to Say When the User is Mistaken," in *Proceedings of CHI'83 Human Factors in Computing Systems,* Boston, December 12–15, ACM, New York, 1983, pp. 197–201.
26. D. A. Norman, "Categorization of Action Slips," *Psychol. Rev., 88,* 1–15 (1981).
27. G. Fischer, A. Lemke, and T. Schwab, "Knowledge-Based Help Systems," in *Proceedings of CHI'85 Human Factors in Computing Systems*, San Francisco, April 14–17, ACM, New York, 1985, pp. 161–167.
28. B. Woolf, D. Blegan, J. H. Jansen, and A. Verloop, "Teaching a Complex Industrial Process," COINS Technical Report 86-24, University of Massachusetts (1986).
29. A. Gable, and C. V. Page, "The Use of Artificial Intelligence Techniques in Computer-Assisted Instruction: An Overview," *Int. J. Man–Machine Studies, 12,* 259–282 (1980).
30. I. P. Goldstein, "The Genetic Graph: A Representation for the Evolution of Procedural Knowledge," in *Intelligent Tutoring Systems* (D. Sleeman and J. S. Brown, eds.), Academic Press, New York, 1982, pp. 51–77.
31. J. Weizenbaum, "ELIZA—A Computer Program for the Study of Natural Language Communication Between Man and Machines," *Comm. ACM, 9,* 36–45 (1966).
32. D. Sleeman, "Assessing Aspects of Competence in Basic Algebra," in *Intelligent Tutoring Systems* (D. Sleeman and J. S. Brown, eds.), Academic Press, New York, 1982, pp. 185–199.
33. J. C. Thomas, "A Method for Studying Natural Language Dialog," *IBM Res. Rep.,* RC 5882 (1976).
34. D. Chin, "An Analysis of Scripts Generated in Writing Between Users and Computer Consultants," *Proc. National Computer Conf., 53,* 637–642 (1984).
35. R. Wilensky, Y. Arens, and D. Chin, "Talking to UNIX in English: An Overview of UC," *Comm. ACM, 27*(6), 574–593 (1984).
36. W. C. Ogden, and S. R. Brooks, "Query Languages for the Casual User: Exploring the Middle Ground Between Formal and Natural Languages," in *CHI'83: Human Factors in Computing Systems* (A. Janda, ed.), ACM, New York, 1983, pp. 161–165.
37. G. W. Furnas, T. K. Landauer, L. M. Gomex, and S. T. Dumais, "The Vocabulary Problem in Human-System Communication," *Comm. ACM, 30,* 964–971 (1987).
38. W. C. Hill, and J. R. Miller, "Justified Advice: A semi–naturalistic Study of Advisory Strategies, in *Proceedings of CHI'88 Human Factors in Computing Systems*, Washington, DC, May, ACM, New York, 1988.
39. M. R. Genesereth, "The Role of Plans in Intelligent Teaching Systems," in *Intelligent Tutoring Systems* (D. Sleeman and J. S. Brown, eds.), Academic Press, New York, 1982, pp. 137–155.
40. K. VanLehn, "Bugs Are Not Enough: Empirical Studies of Bugs, Impasses and Repairs in Procedural Skills," Xerox PARC Technical Report CISII, (1981).
41. J. C. Spohrer, and E. Soloway, "Novice Mistakes: Are the Folk Wisdoms Correct?," *Comm. ACM, 29,* 624–632 (1986).
42. J. M. Carroll, R. L. Mack, and W. A. Kellogg, "Interface, Metaphors and User Interface Design," in *Handbook of Human Computer Interaction* (M. Helander, ed.), North Holland, Amsterdam, 1988.
43. H. Gardner, *Frames of Mind: The Theory of Multiple Intelligences*, Basic Books, New York, 1983.
44. D. E. Rumelhart, and D. A. Norman, "Representation in Memory," in *Steven's Handbook of Psychology* (R. C. Atkinson, R. J. Hernstein, G. Lindzey, and R. D. Luce, eds.), John Wiley, New York, 1986.

45. E. Turiel, and P. Davidson, "Heterogeneity, Inconsistency, and Asynchrony in the Development of Cognitive Structures," in *Stage and Structure: Reopening the Debate* (I. Levin, ed.), Ablex, Norwood, NJ, 1986, pp. 106–143.

46. A. P. Aaronson, and J. M. Carroll, "Understanding Intelligent Help: A Protocol Analysis of Advisory Interactions," *IBM Res. Rep.*, RC 13059 (1987).

47. J. McKendree, E. A. McAuliffe, and J. M. Carroll "When All Else Fails: Problems Brought to a Text Consultant," *IBM Res. Rep.*, RC 11639 (1986).

48. M. Fitter, "Towards More "Natural' Interactive Systems," *Int. J. Man–Machine Studies, 11*, 339–350 (1979).

49. A. P. Jagodzinski, "A Theoretical Basis for the Representation of On-line Computer Systems to Naive Users," *Int. J. Man–Machine Studies, 18*, 215–252 (1983).

50. E. Wenger, *Artificial Intelligence and Tutoring Systems: Computational and Cognitive Approaches to the Communication of Knowledge*, Morgan Kaufman, Los Altos, 1987.

51. J. M. Carroll, "Satisfaction Conditions for Mental Models," *Contemp. Psychol., 30*(9), 693–695 (1985).

52. J. M. Carroll, and J. R. Olson, "Mental Models in Human-Computer Interaction: Research Issues About What the User of Software Knows," in *Handbook of Human Computer Interaction* (M. Helander, ed.), North Holland, Amsterdam, 1988.

53. J. McKendree, and J. Zaback, "Planning for Advising," in *Proceedings of CHI '88 Human Factors in Computing Systems*, Washington, DC, May, ACM, New York, 1988.

54. D. E. Kieras, and P. G. Polson, "An Approach to the Formal Analysis of User Complexity," *Int. J. Man–Machine Studies, 22*, 365–394 (1985).

55. R. E. Fikes, "Automating the Problem Solving in Procedural Office Work," AFIPS Office Automation Conference, Houston, TX, March 23–25, *Proceedings*, AFIPS Press, Reston, VA, 1981, pp. 367–369.

56. E. Rich, "Programs as Data for Their Help Systems," National Computer Conference, Houston, TX, June 7–10, *Proceedings*, AFIPS Press, Reston, VA, 1982, pp. 481–485.

57. B. J. Reiser, J. R. Anderson, and R. G. Farrell, "Dynamic Student Modelling in an Intelligent Tutor for Lisp Programming," IJCAI, Los Angeles, August 18–23, *Proceedings*, Morgan Kaufmann, Los Altos, CA, 1985, pp. 8–14.

58. J. R. Anderson, "Cognitive Psychology and Intelligent Tutoring," Cognitive Science Society Conference, Boulder, CO, June 28–30, *Proceedings*, 1984, pp. 37–43.

59. S. W. Draper, "The Nature of Expertise in UNIX," in *Human–Computer Interaction–Interact '84* (B. Schackel, ed.), North Holland, New York, 1985, pp. 465–472.

60. R. Nisbett, and T. Wilson, "Telling More Than We Can Know: Verbal Reports on Mental Processes," *Psychol. Rev., 84*, 231–259 (1977).

61. E. Rich, "Users are Individuals: Individualizing User Models," *Int. J. Man–Machine Studies, 18*, 199–214 (1983).

62. W. L. Johnson, S. Draper, and E. Soloway, "Classifying Bugs is a Tricky Business," in *7th Annual NASA/Goddard Workshop on Software Engineering*, Baltimore, December 1, NASA/Goddard, Greenbelt, MD, 1982.

63. K. VanLehn, "Felicity Conditions for Human Skill Acquisition: Validating an AI-Based Theory," Xerox PARC Technical Report, CIS-21 (1983).

64. J. M. Caroll, and C. Carrithers, "Training Wheels in a User Interface," *Comm. ACM, 27*(8), 800–806 (1984).

65. H. A. Simon, "The Functional Equivalence of Problem Solving Skills," *Cog. Psychol., 7*, 268–288 (1975).

66. E. L. Thorndike, "The Psychology of Learning," in *Educational Psychology,* Vol. 11, Teachers College of Columbia University, New York, 1913.

67. S. Papert, "The Role of Artificial Intelligence in Psychology," in *Language and Learning: The Debate Between Jean Piaget and Noam Chomsky* (M. Piattelli–Palmarini, ed.), Harvard University Press, Cambridge, 1980.

68. D. Klahr, "Transition Processes in Cognitive Development," in *Mechanisms in Cognitive Development* (R. J. Sternberg, ed.), W. H. Freeman, San Francisco, 1984.

69. J. R. Anderson, R. Farrell, and R. Sauers, "Learning to Program in Lisp,," *Cog. Sci., 8,* 87–129 (1984).

70. R. M. Krauss, and S. Glucksberg, "Social and Nonsocial Speech," *Sci. Am., 236,* 100–105 (1977).

71. S. J. Card, T. P. Moran, and A. Newell, *The Psychology of Human–Computer Interaction,* Lawrence Erlbaum, Hillsdale, NJ, 1983.

72. H. Ledgard, J. Whiteside, A. Singer, and W. Seymour, "The Natural Language of Interactive Systems," *Comm. ACM, 23,* 556–563 (1980).

73. M. B. Rosson, "The Role of Experience in Editing," in *Human–Computer Interaction—Interact '84* (B. Schackel, ed.), North Holland, New York, 1985, pp. 45–50.

74. J. M. Carroll, and A. P. Aaronson, "Learning By Doing with Simulated Intelligent Help, *Copmm. ACM, 31,* 1064–1079 (1988).

75. J. M. Carroll, and D. S. Kay, "Prompting, Feedback and Error Correction in the Design of a Scenario Machine," in *Proceedings of CHI'85 Human Factors in Computing Systems,* San Francisco, April 14–17, ACM, New York, 1985, pp. 149–153.

76. J. McKendree, and J. M. Carroll, "Impact of Feedback Content in Initial Learning of an Office System," in *Proceeding of INTERACT '87, The Second IFIP Conference on Human–Computer Interaction,* Stuttgart, September, Elsevier Science Publishers, North-Holland, 1987, pp. 855–859.

77. J. Shrager, and T. Finin, "An Expert System That Volunteers Advice," in *Proceedings of the National Conference on Artificial Intelligence,* Pittsburgh, August 18–20, 1982, pp. 339–340.

78. L. Quinn, and D. M. Russell, "Intelligent Interfaces: User Models and Planners," in *Proceedings, CHI '86 Human Factors in Computing Sytems,* Boston, ACM, New York, 1986.

79. M. T. Elson-Cook, "Design Considerations of an Intelligent Teaching System for Programming Languages," in *Human–Computer Interaction—Interact '84* (B. Schackel, ed.), North Holland, New York, 1985, pp. 409–414.

80. L. S. Shulman, and E. R. Keislar (eds.), *Learning by Discovery: A Critical Appraisal,* Rand McNally and Company, Chicago, 1966.

81. R. F. Dearden, "Instruction and Learning By Discovery," in *The Concept of Education* (R. S. Peters, ed.), Humanities Press, Atlantic Highlands, NJ, 1967.

82. J. M. Carroll, R. L. Mack, C. H. Lewis, N. L. Grischkowsky, and S. R. Robertson, "Exploring Exploring a Word Processor," *Human Comput. Interaction, 1,* 283–307 (1985).

83. M. D. Williams, "What Makes RABBIT Run?," *Intl J. Man–Machine Studies, 21,* 333–352 (1984).

84. M. Zloff, "Query-by-Example: A Data Base Language," *IBM Sys. J., 16,* 324–343 (1977).

85. M. E. J. Masson, W. C. Hill, J. Conner, and R. Guindon, "Misconceived Misconceptions?," in *Proceedings of CHI '88 Human Factors in Computing Systems,* Washington, DC, May, ACM, New York, 1988.

86. B. Shneiderman, "Direct Manipulation: A Step Beyond Programming Languages," *IEEE Computer,* 16 (1983).

87. J. Elkerton, "Online Aiding for Human-Computer Interfaces," in *Handbook of Human–Computer Interaction* (M. Helander, ed.), North Holland, Amsterdam, 1988.

88. G. Fischer, and C. Stevens, "Volunteering Information—Enhancing the Communication Capabilities of Knowledge-Based Systems," in *Proceedings of INTERACT '87, The Second IFIP Conference on Human–Computer Interaction*, Stuttgart, September, Elsevier Science Publishers, North–Holland, 1987.

88a. R. N. Cuff, "On Casual Users," *Lit. J. Man-Machine Stud., 12*, 163–187 (1980).

89. M. L. Lewis, and J. R. Anderson, "Discrimination of Operator Schemata in Problem Solving: Learning from Examples," *Cognitive Psychol., 17*, 26–65 (1985).

90. W. Teitelman, and L. Masinter, "The Interlisp Programming Environment," *Computer, 14*(4), 25–34 (1981).

91. J. R. C. Hillen, "Comparison of Four Different Self-Paced Manuals," *IBM Hursley Human Factors Laboratory*, HF047 (1981).

92. M. C. Grignetti, C. Hausmann, and L. Gould, "An "Intelligent" On-line Assistant and Tutor: NLS SCHOLAR," in *Proceedings of the National Computer Conference, 44*, Anaheim, CA, May 19–22, AFIPS Press, Reston, VA, 1974, pp. 775–781.

93. J. Rothenberg, "On-line Tutorials and Documentation for the SIGMA Message Service, *Proceedings of the National Computer Conference*, New York, June 4–7, AFIPS Press, Reston, VA, 1979, pp. 863–867.

94. M. Good, "Etude and the Folklore of User Interface Design," *Sigplan Notices, 16*(6), 34–43 (1981).

95. M. Newman, and F. Sproull, *Principles of Interactive Computer Graphics,* 2nd Ed., McGraw-Hill, New York, 1979.

96. I. A. Clark, "Software Simulation as a Tool for Usable Product Design," *IBM Sys. J., 20*(3), 272–293 (1981).

97. J. McKendree, B. J. Reiser, and J. R. Anderson, "Tutoring Goals and Strategies in the Instruction of Programming Skills," Cognitive Science Society Conference, Boulder, CO, June 28–30, *Proceedings* (1984) pp. 252–254.

98. J. McKendree, "Effective Feedback Content for Tutoring Complex Skills," Ph.D. dissertation, Phychology Deptartment, Carnegie-Mellon University (1987).

99. K. Singley, "Developing Models of Skill Acquisition in the Context of Intelligent Tutoring Systems," Ph.D. dissertation, Psychology Department, Carnegie-Mellon University (1986).

100. E. A. Edmonds, "Adaptive Man–Computer Interfaces," in *Computing Skills and the User Interface* (M. J. Coombs and J. F. Alty, eds.), Academic Press, New York, 1981, pp. 389–426.

101. E. L. Rissland, E. Valcarce, and K. Ashley, "Explaining and Arguing with Examples," *Proceedings of the National Computer Conference*, Morgan Kaufmann, Los Altos, CA, 1983.

102. K. J. Holyoak, "Analogical Thinking and Human Intelligence," in *Advances in the Psychology of Human Intelligence*, Vol. 2 (R. J. Sternberg, ed.), Lawrence Erlbaum, Hillsdale, NJ, 1983.

103. J. R. Anderson, and E. Skwareki, "The Automated Tutoring of Introductory Computer Programming," *Comm. ACM, 29*, 842–849 (1986).

104. C. L. Paris, "Combining Discourse Strategies to Generate Descriptions to Users Along a Naive/Expert Spectrum," in *Proceedings of the Tenth International Joint Conference on Artificial Intelligence*, Milan, Italy, Morgan Kaufmann, Los Altos, CA, 1987, pp. 626–632.

105. M. E. Pollack, "Information Sought and Information Provided: An Empirical Study of User/Expert Dialogs," in *Proceedings of CHI'85 Human Factors in Computing Systems*, San Francisco, April 14–17, ACM, New York, 1985, pp. 155–159.

106. J. F. Allen, and C. R. Perault, "Analyzing the Intention of Utterances," *Artif. Intell., 15,* 143–178 (1980).

107. A. P. Aaronson, and J. M. Carroll, "Intelligent Help in a One-Shot Dialog: A Protocol Study," in *CHI+GI'87: Human Factors in Computing Systems and Graphics Interface* (J. M. Carroll and P. P. Tanner, eds.) ACM, New York, 1987, pp. 163–168.

108. J. McKendree, and J. M. Carroll, "Advising Roles of a Computer Consultant," in *Proceedings of CHI'86 Human Factors in Computing Systems*, Boston, April 13–17, ACM, New York, 1986, pp. 35–40.

109. J. L. Alty, and M. J. Coombs, "University Computing Advisory Services: The Study of the Man–Computer Interface," *Software—Prac. Exp., 10,* 919–934 (1980).

110. K. D. Eason, "The Manager as a Computer User," *Appl. Ergonomics, 5,* 9–14 (1974).

111. K. D. Eason, "Dialogue Design Implications of Task Allocation Between Man and Computer," *Ergonomics, 23,* 881–891 (1980).

112. T. W. Malone, "Toward a Theory of Intrinsically Motivating Instruction," *Cognitive Sci., 4,* 333–369 (1981).

113. J. M. Carroll, "The Adventure of Getting to Know a Computer," *IEEE Comput., 15*(11), 49–58 (1982).

114. J. M. Carroll, and M. B. Rosson, "Usability Specifications as a Tool in Iterative Development," in *Advances in Human–Computer Interaction* (H. R. Hartson, ed.), Ablex Publishing, Norwood, NJ, 1985.

115. K. S. Jones, "Proposals for R&D in Intelligent Knowledge Based Systems," *J. Inform. Sci., 8,* 139–147 (1984).

116. N. S. Anderson, and J. R. Olson, (eds.), "Methods for Designing Software to Fit Human Needs and Capabilities," *Proceedings of the National Research Council Workshop on Software Human Factors*, National Academy Press, Washington, DC, 1985.

117. W. L. Bewley, T. L. Roberts, D. Schroit, and W. L. Verplank, "Human Factors Testing in the Design of Xerox's 8010 "Star" Office Workstation," in *Proceedings of CHI'83 Human Factors in Computing Systems*, Boston, December 12–15, ACM, New York, 1983, pp. 72–77.

118. J. D. Gould, S. J. Boies, S. Levy, J. T. Richards, and J. Schoonard, "The 1984 Olympic Message System: A Test of Behavioral Principles of System Design," *Comm. ACM, 30,* 758–769 (1985).

119. J. M. Carroll, P. S. Smith-Kerker, J. R. Ford, and S. A. Mazur-Rimetz, "The Minimal Manual," *Human Computer Interaction, 4,* 123–153 (1987–88).

120. M. Good, J. Whiteside, D. Wixon, and S. Jones, "Building a User-Derived Interface," *Comm. ACM, 27*(10), 1032–1043 (1984).

121. J. M. Carroll, and R. L. Campbell, "Softening Up Hard Science: Reply to Newell and Card," *Human Comput. Interact., 2,* 227–249 (1986).

122. J. M. Carroll, and J. E. McKendree, "Interface Design Issues for Advice-Giving Expert Systems," *Comm. ACM, 30,* 14–31 (1987).

JOHN M. CARROLL

JEAN McKENDREE

KNOWLEDGE ENGINEERING DESIGN AND CONSTRUCTION OF EXPERT SYSTEMS

KNOWLEDGE AND ITS ENGINEERING

The search for knowledge is as old as the history of humanity; without knowledge we cannot control the objects in our surrounding. As Sun Tse declared in the 5th century B.C., that which allows the sovereign to know and the good general to intuit, to expect, and anticipate, what is beyond the ordinary run of mortals, is forward knowledge. Bacon summed it up in his famous statement, "knowledge is power," as did Eco [1].

For his part, Bell [2] establishes that in postindustrial societies information is the resource which has undergone the greatest change, as a means of providing knowledge which is its strategic resource and whose principal axiom is the codification of this knowledge. This knowledge can be public and/or private. Public knowledge is that which appears in published form and is made up of first principles, axioms, laws, and definitions independent of the subject matter, that is, general theories. Private knowledge is usually the knowledge that experts in a particular area have internalized and use in their daily work, and comprises facts relevant to the subject matter, heuristics, and beliefs.

The only currently known way of codifying both public and the expert's private knowledge is by using the techniques of artificial intelligence (AI) comprising the so called knowledge-based systems. When the knowledge which is incorporated in these systems is basically obtained from human experts, these systems are called expert systems (ES) [3]. An ES can be described as an advanced computer program which simulates the thought process of a human expert in a particular field, by providing a computerized advisor which is efficient, clever, inexpensive, and capable of explaining its behavior and using an expert's heuristics to work with both quantative and qualitative information.

All this knowledge in its most general form (Fig. 1), is encompassed by ES in the so called knowledge bases [4], which are separated from the inference processes which they handle, this, perhaps, being the most conspicuous structural characteristic of these systems.

The process of designing and making operative knowledge-based systems in general, and in particular, the ES, is known as knowledge engineering.

The unique nature of this engineering is that it needs to call upon specialized judgments and expert behavior, which go beyond what is generally associated with standard software development projects. Consequently, knowledge/information engineers must have a capacity for carrying out the following tasks, which are outlined in Figure 2 [5]:

1. Evaluating and recognizing potential applications, diagnosing those which are trivial before investing serious efforts trying to analyze them.
2. Extracting private knowledge from the experts and public knowledge from wherever it exists.
3. Carrying out a thorough analysis before attempting implementation.

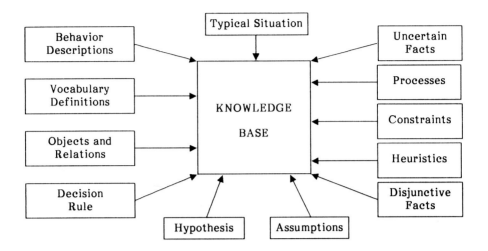

FIGURE 1   An ES knowledge base containing different types of knowledge, facts, and information.

4.   Designing, constructing, and verifying knowledge base(s), by selecting suitable representations of knowledge. Designing and constructing problem-solving models and subsequently verifying them.
5.   Defining the space problem, that is, the states and the operators necessary for carrying out the search. When problems are properly structured these elements are known. When problems are badly structured, some of these elements are missing or not known.
6.   Relaxing some restrictions.
7.   Using heuristics to reduce the search space.
8.   Using reduction techniques or breaking down into subproblems if the problem is too big and complex.
9.   Using learning techniques and analogies, that is, using previous knowledge.
10. Choosing the right tool to successfully complete the previous tasks.

The linking of these tasks appears in the following section on methodology.

METHODOLOGY FOR CONSTRUCTING EXPERT SYSTEMS

Introduction

According to Nietzsche [6], "the most precious wealth is methods." Descartes [7], the great methodologist, stated in rule IV of his "Regulae ad Directioem Ingenii": "Method is necessary for investigating the truth." For these reasons, we present here, a method which will lead to the creation and operation of an expert system. This method, called IDEAL, an acronym of the phases which make it up (in Spanish, *I*dentificacion, *D*esarrollo, *E*jecución, *A*ctuacón, *L*ogro), and whose structural arrangement appears in Figure 3 [8], contains the following phases:

1.   *I*dentification and selection of the application and conception of the solution

INPUTS

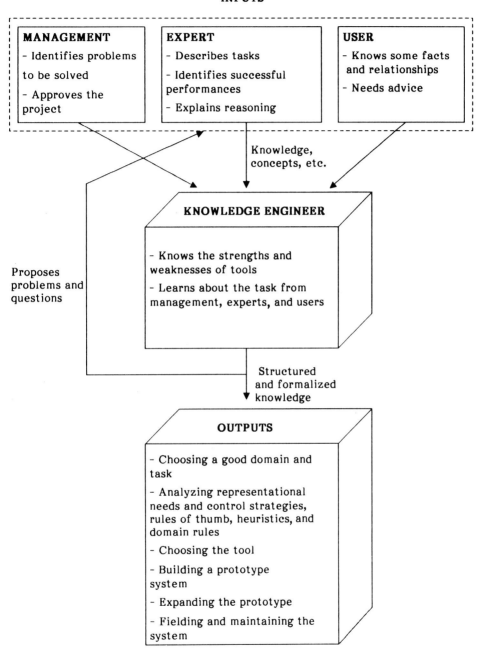

FIGURE 2   The roles of the knowledge engineer.

2. *D*evelopment of the prototype(s)
3. *E*xecution and construction of the complete system
4. *A*chieving the integration of the system with previous ones and assimilation of technology

Figure 3 shows the factors which influence negatively the correct functioning of the method, on the left, linked by dotted lines to the boxes which represent the different phases. It is necessary to overcome or at least mitigate these negative influences in order to achieve success. On the right, linked to the boxes by continuous lines, are the positive, dynamic elements of the whole process.

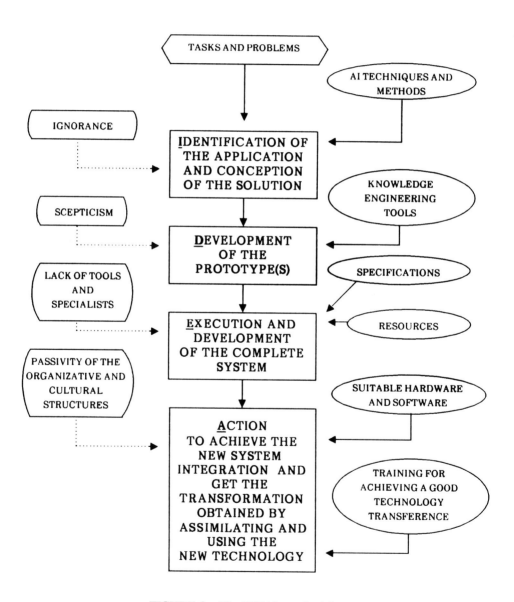

FIGURE 3   The IDEAL methodology.

Phase I: Selection of the Application

We must consider two types of questions in this phase:

Direct Questions

Artificial Intelligence users find it very difficult to describe, in general, the characteristics that allow a problem to be adequately resolved by an ES. However, the first question to be answered by an organization considering the development of an ES is: Will the ES approach be able to work efficiently in a specific problem?

Although there is no easy clear cut answer to this significant question, it is not that difficult to define some behavioral guidelines that have proved acceptable. ES technology should be considered only when its development is possible, adequate, and justified in a given situation.

Conditions for the features of a specific problem to be addressed by an ES are summarized in three heuristic rules:

1. If truly genuine experts are willing to provide the necessary experience in a cooperative effort to reach a mutually agreeable solution, and are capable of creating their own working methods and procedures to establish cases, and if the task has been properly structured, and is not very difficult, requiring simple cognitive expertise, and, finally it is either an R&D or practical case (but not both), then ES development is possible.
2. If experts must function in hostile, hard, and ungratifying environments, or there is a lack or excess of human experts, or expertise is needed in different places at the same time, if a high tax on investment recovery is expected, or there are no alternative solutions, or conventional, algorithmic programming is neither possible nor satisfactory, then building an ES is justified.
3. If the task is complex and requires basically symbolic manipulation and heuristic solutions, and it is or can be reduced to a manageable size, and has practical value, if basic research to find solutions is not necessary, and the amount of required knowledge is large enough to necessitate the use of a database, and the ES can satisfy long-term needs, and if the effects of its introduction can be planned for and if the countered ES building project does not interfere with other projects, then building an ES is appropriate.

Indirect or Collateral Questions

It is not enough to determine whether the problem can be treated with knowledge engineering technology, so that it can be solved in the everyday environment. In addition to basic technical considerations, we must take into account other questions which, if they are obviated, can inhibit the use of this technology. These questions are summarized in a fourth heuristic rule that tries to guarantee the system's success.

4. If managers are aware of the project and are eager to accept it, with realistic expectations, and the required changes in the standard procedures are minimal and the end users are willing to accept the introduction of ES and are assured that the results do not have political consequences, then in a stable domain where global project goals have been adequately integrated, and an appropriate technology transference has been done, the success of the project is guaranteed.

A project which intends to automate the above-mentioned methodology, is being developed in the Artificial Intelligence Laboratory of the Facultad de Informática (Universidad Politécnica de Madrid). The precise methodology and application are being defined at this writing.

Phase II: Prototype(s) Development

If the problems fulfill all Phase I requirements declared in the above heuristics rules, the next step will be the ES development. ES developers do not follow a set of well-defined steps to build the system, as the inherent complexity of the project is not conducive to a pre-established stepwise approach. For that reason, we think the wisest methodology is an evolutionary and exploratory approach.

As Waterman [9] states, in a sophisticated and utilitarian way, ES evolve similarly as do their building tools. An ES usually begins as a small experimental prototype to prove problem feasibility, to reassure funding sources, and to verify some ideas about the problem definition, scope, and representation. Many ES become research prototypes of medium size, capable of presenting acceptable evidence from a number of test cases. Others develop to medium/large size when they are revised through verification in the step of real problemsolving in the user community. Under these circumstances, they become field prototypes. When reliable, the prototype offers good services and friendly interfaces, when the program has been thoroughly tested and is large enough, it can be reimplemented in a more efficient and portable language to increase its speed and reduce its storage requirements. Lately, some of these prototypes have found use in the commercial area.

The incremental approach means that the system itself can help in the development effort and builders can take advantage of what they learn when implementing the initial aspects and the different developed prototypes.

There is no doubt that it is sometimes advisable to redesign or reimplement the problem. For example, if the knowledge base reaches an unmanageable size or control, becomes slow and more difficult, then the knowledge engineer and the expert should reexamine the problem and perhaps redesign the initial representation scheme.

Prototype(s) Development Stages

Although we cannot specify the exact steps to be followed in building an ES, we can describe the different stages of system development, as well as the different activities of each stage. To this effect [9,10] a prototype development can be considered as a set of five highly independent and overlapped phases: definition, conceptualization, formalization, implementation, and verification. Nevertheless, although from a didactic point of view, it is convenient to distinguish these five phases (Fig. 4), there is no simple way to describe them in an adequate fashion.

Definition. During this phase, knowledge engineers and experts determine the problem features. In order to do so, they must identify the problem itself: its type and scope; the participants in the development process; a collection of test cases to justify the prototype adequate operations; and the necessary resources (related to time-consuming, computing facilities and experts availability). Then, the aims or goals of the prototype to be built up, and how services can be improved and expertise be distributed must be described. Finally, the criteria for success, determining the actual final users, with detailed examples of the problems and the acceptable solutions for them must be established.

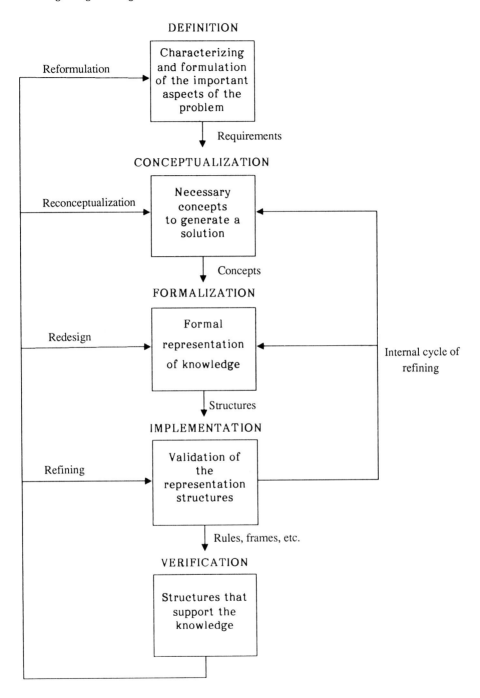

FIGURE 4   Phases in the ES development.

Of all those activities, developers find the identification of the problem and its adequate scope to be the most difficult; usually the proposed problem is too big or complex and must first be reduced to a manageable size.

Knowledge Conceptualization. Once the domain has been identified, the next step is to clearly define the concept of knowledge. Obtaining the knowledge necessary to build an efficient ES and structure it so that it can be utilized, usually hinders the development of an ES. Up to now, there has been no automatic method of doing this, with the exception of some simple aids aimed at building ES, which are able to extract rules from examples. It is necessary, therefore, to consider how the knowledge engineer gets the knowledge from the expert.

The knowledge engineer and the expert must combine their efforts to solve specific problems. In general, the experts have difficulties in expressing the methods or rules which they use to solve a specific problem within a general frame of knowledge. This is because they are inclined to establish their own conclusions and the reasoning used by them in general terms, which is too extensive to permit an effective analysis by computer. The expert is supposed to have the elements of basic knowledge and to be able to combine such elements so fast that it is difficult to describe the processing and link of each step, as it can even ignore the individual steps. These aspects represent "the paradox of experience," which can be defined by saying that the best qualified experts are unable to describe the knowledge which they use in solving the problems.

Expert knowledge appears to be compiled, that is, remade and reduced to a minimal and presented in an efficient form, which makes it more difficult to extract. When the experts solve problems within their experience, they recognize new situations as a state of things with which they are already familiar as shown in Fig. 5 [9]. However, when experts face new situations, they behave like intelligent neophytes. They are inclined to apply (Fig. 6) general principles and deductive steps which provide causal links among several steps within a sequence for the solution of problems.

There are two approaches or groups of methods to measure the rendering of services and to discover the experience: observation or experimental methods and intuitive methods. The experimental method entails observing the expert solving realistic problems, taking care not to say or do anything that may influence the approach of the expert. Protocols of thought are often used. The knowledge engineer analyzes a transcription of the session once it has ended, possibly with the help of the expert. This approach encounters practical difficulties due to huge gaps in the description of the process. The researcher has great difficulty in filling those gaps, and, if he forces the expert to be more explicit, the line of the reasoning achieved may perhaps not reflect the solution techniques actually used. Having developed a certain sense of what a problem is, the knowledge engineer may start to describe , in a semiformal language, what he or she thinks is happening in the sessions held to try to resolve the problem.

The intuitive method depends on the introspective analysis of the expert regarding the field. In some cases the knowledge engineer surveys or interacts with the experts in order to familiarize himself with their methods of solution, and becomes a pseudoexpert, developing a representation of the experience which is later verified with the experts. In other cases, the real expert acts as a constructor of theories about his own behavior and tries to directly incorporate them into an information system. The problem lies with the difficulties the experts encounter in describing the real techniques used. In these cases, a useful approach may consist in the fact that the computer may support procedures for general solutions to specific cases starting from the basis of solutions given by it or by the experts. This approach is closely related to long-term work carried out regarding learning.

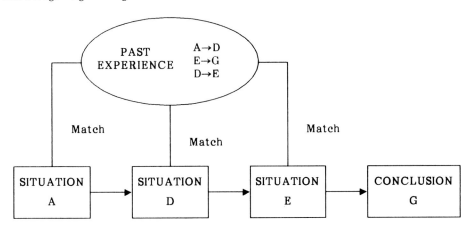

FIGURE 5   Problem-solving by an expert system in a familiar situation.

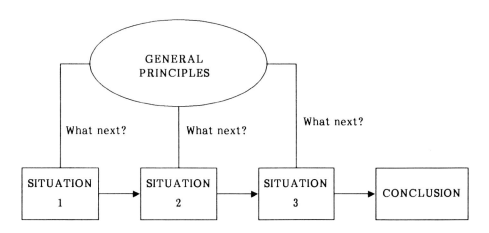

FIGURE 6   Problem-solving by an expert system in a novel situation.

In general, the knowledge engineer will rely on the technique of the interview (Fig. 7), which combines the two former approaches. For example, the expert will engage in introspection while he solves a problem; speaking aloud about the way he does it. The knowledge engineer will orient him whenever it is deemed necessary, raising important questions to encourage and support the expert, suggesting possible reasons and hypothesizing concepts and rules.

Once the prototype is operative, the expert will examine and criticize each rule, and evaluate the control strategies utilized in order to select them. In this way, justifications for each rule which the system may subsequently use to explain its operation can be included.

A capable knowledge engineer can use some of the techniques described to "decompile" the knowledge. The more capable he or she is, the more clearly will the final system show the real heuristics and procedures of the expert.

Another technique used is analysis of protocol. This technique is aimed at producing models of the systems for the resolution of problems, and it was described by Newell and Simon [12] and, more recently, by Ericson and Simon [12]. In this case, the behavior of the expert is recorded while he works on the solution of a problem, and this protocol is transcribed and analyzed, in order to finally convert it into a set of production rules which transforms a state into the following state. At present, analysis of the protocol is made in two phases. In phase one, definite problems are presented to the expert, who is asked to verbalize all the decisions he made in arriving at a solution; this list provides the negative influences outlined in Figure 3. In phase two, each sequence of these formerly recorded actions is reexamined in concurrence with the expert, who is asked to explain the basis for those decisions. The expert must also explain why alternative actions, which seemed to him or her to be equivalent, or, at least, possible were discarded. The answers provide the negative conditions which conform to the right side of the rule (Fig. 3). The protocols may provide

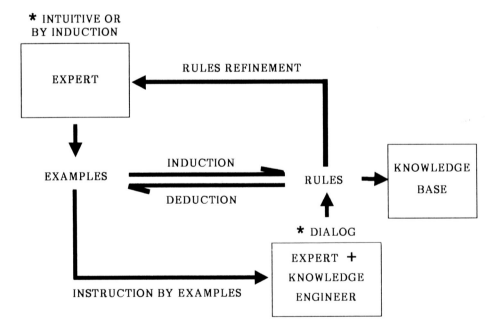

FIGURE 7   Combining approaches by the interview technique.

useful heuristics or facts which the knowledge engineer may use either directly as knowledge or indirectly as metaknowledge, and key data on the thought processes of the expert which might not have arisen during the interviews.

A third technique entails multidimensional scaling, which seems to be appropriate when a certain number of intrinsically related concepts are involved, which are not easily identifiable by beginners and for which experience consists in being qualified to distinguish them. The method produces a set of dimensions which define the space containing the objects of general knowledge and differentiate certain objects from others.

Finally, a fourth technique is based on the classification of concepts. The experts, besides having detailed knowledge of specialized fields, have a global structural knowledge about general knowledge. This metaknowledge is very useful when a great quantity of information must be organized. A version of this technique is to obtain a set of concepts which broadly cover the general knowledge; each concept is then transferred to a card, and the expert is asked to classify them into groups describing common characteristics of each group. The group can be compared to form a hierarchy.

The Figure 8 [3] chart furnishes a guide to the different types of knowledge and the techniques applicable for their capture.

The initial sessions of knowledge acquisition lead to the creation of a knowledge design document [13], which must emphasize: the different arenas in the design, the dependence among the arenas, and a detailed enumeration of the different elements of the knowledge such as procedures, restrictions, heuristics, etc. This document is crucial to define and verify the knowledge which is eventually incorporated into the system. Circulating this document among the experts helps to avoid omissions and to detect and correct errors. This document can be used experimentally to solve new design problems but must be strictly followed.

Formalization and definition of the Computational Architecture or Design of the Structures for Organizing the Knowledge. This phase implies expressing the key concepts and the relations in a formal way, habitually within the framework suggested by a knowledge engineering tool. In this way, the knowledge engineer(s) should have

Knowledge type	Possible technique to be used
Concepts and relationships	Documents reading or study Multidimensional scaling techniques
Routine procedures	Protocol analysis Task analysis
Facts and heuristics	Incidental protocols Structured interviews Proof and memory techniques
Classificatory knowledge	Themes classification Multidimensional scaling

FIGURE 8   Relation among knowledge types and applicable techniques.

formulated some ideas about the appropriate tools to be used to resolve the problem before starting the formalization period. Strict objectivity in this phase is necessary in order to let the real facts dictate the tool to be chosen, and to not allow the preferences or preconceived ideas of each knowledge engineer or existing resources within his reach to override the facts. To this effect, a conventional attitude is to consider only the task to be developed in order to choose the tool. This can lead to a wrong choice, because it is necessary as well to consider the phase of the methodology for the construction of an ES which is being performed, and who is to use the tool. For example, the same methodology cannot be used in the period of acquisition of knowledge as in the period of integration of the system into another wider one. For each definite activity there is a tool which is the most appropriate. That is, the requirements for a tool do not exist "a priori," but they are derived from the person who is going to use it, how it will be used, and from the stage at which work is being done. Because of the large number of attributes, some of them contradictory, no one tool can possess all the attributes necessary for all purposes. Consequently, a tool should be portable and compatible in knowledge representation with other products; in this way, an ES can be developed with the tools most suitable for each user in each task. Two major groups of tools can be distinguished: hardware and software (Fig. 9) [*14*].

Knowledge engineering hardware tools. In order to develop a tool which supports AI processing, it is necessary to keep in mind the requirements of the applications in this general knowledge. To this end, unlike conventional numeric algorithms, most AI applications, and in particular, ES present several characteristics:

a. Symbolic processing with primitive operations (such as classification, comparison, operations on sets) or, at a higher level, operations on models such as phases, charts, or images.

b. Nondeterministic computations, because it is impossible to plan, with the information available, the procedures that must be performed and completed. In general, search, use of incomplete specified functions, or heuristics to reduce the search space are necessary.

c. Dynamic performance, because in general, new data and function structures can crop up when the problem is solved, and on the other hand, the maximum size of a given structure can be so large that memory space must be dynamically assigned and freed after the problem is solved.

d. Significant potential capacity for parallel and distributed computation may be needed to concurrently process a set of necessary and independent tasks (conjunctive parallelism or "AND"), or tasks on a point of nondeterministic decision, typical in AI (disjunctive parallelism or "OR").

e. Knowledge management, in order to reduce complexity, avoid an exhaustive search, or handle a large quantity of knowledge which is often uncertain.

f. Open systems, as the knowledge to solve the problem can be incomplete and an open perspective is necessary to enable continuous refinements and acquisition of new knowledge.

The choice of a computer to support a given AI application, should be based upon a series of considerations:

Representation, concerning the knowledge and the methods to solve the problems and the means to represent it. The level of representation is an important element in the design process and suggests whether or not a given problem can be solved in a reasonable length of time. To this end, it is necessary to consider the utilization of metaknowledge, knowledge about the knowledge in the domain, and its organization within the hierarchy. The use of metaknowledge, whose highest level representative is common sense knowledge, enables integration of different representation schemes and programming paradigms. The choice of an adequate representation of the knowledge is important and it is necessary to carry out valuations as to the quantity of necessary memory, time, expected use of the knowledge, etc. Finally, a computer oriented to a given AI language will inherit all the characteristics and limitations of the language which implements it.

Control, related to the detection of dependence and parallelism within the problems; it is necessary to consider the truth maintenance, since a great number of AI applications are characterized by a lack of consistency and complete knowledge at the representation level. The control mechanisms are also engaged in the reorganization and composition of the knowledge base and AI programs, to make processing more efficient. Due to nondeterminism of the problems, these can be, in general, decomposed into a large number of smaller tasks. Another objective of the control system is to select the tasks ready to be assigned to usable processors.

Processing, special purpose computers can be classified into the following architectures; microlevel, to support AI processing, with fundamental designs with AI applications to perform basic operations such as comparisons, set intersections, etc.; macrolevel, intermediate level which can be built starting from the former level and can execute more complex operations; system level, oriented toward one or more languages and knowledge representation schemes supporting its specific characteristics. Specific systems can be singled out to support languages of production rules, frames, semantic networks, and special applications such as robotics or comprehension of natural language. Figure 9 depicts a taxonomic study of AI machines; some are real and others are conceptual representations. However, at present, it is also possible to use conventional machines to develop an ES.

A great number of the parallel architectures are "connectionist"; therefore, the collection of permanent knowledge pieces of the system is stored as a model of connections or strong connections among the elements of the process interact, instead of being passively located in memory waiting for the central processing unit to look for it. Connectionism, though somewhat debated among the AI community, is a current research trend, owing to the possible similarity between the connectionist networks and the human neural networks.

Knowledge engineering software tools. In the research on design and construction of ES, it appears at present to be primordial to determine the essential qualities that a good tool must have in order to carry out its function. Among the basic criteria are the following:

1.   Epistemology and modularity, to represent and support different forms of knowledge and introduce pieces of knowledge in any order.

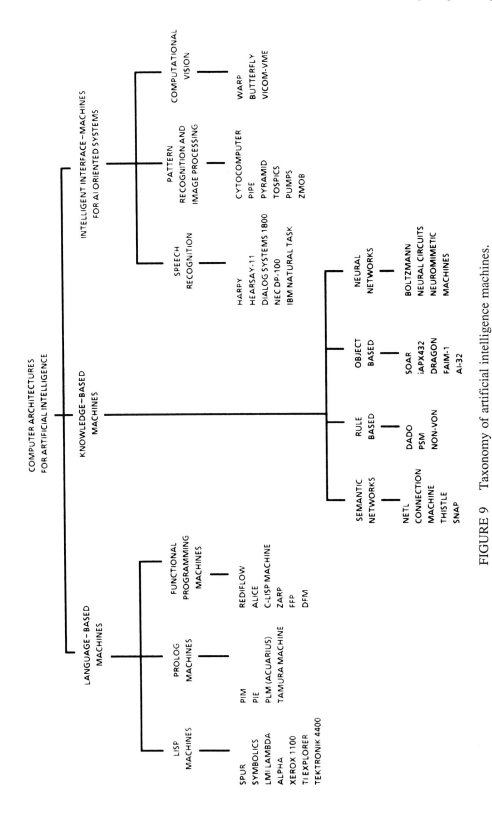

FIGURE 9   Taxonomy of artificial intelligence machines.

2.   Ease of use, so that experts may interact in a natural way, and the knowledge engineer may pay special attention to the product without being concerned about programming complexity.
3.   Inference and control, or how to represent the concepts, and which aids are available.
4.   Capacity to rapidly create a prototype in order to check the task effectiveness and verify that the basic problem scope and representation scheme is correct, also paying sufficient attention to system performance speed.
5.   Gradual, nonsudden, degradation of the tool, as problems grow more difficult, keeping in mind, that the best tool during the development phase may not be the best to produce the final version.
6.   Rendering of services, such as speed, ease, size, etc.
7.   Development power and increasing capacity, to balance flexibility, facility, and speed of development with efficiency and adaptability to the problem needs.
8.   Friendly support of the user facilities and interfaces, to save time and money and to allow non-data-processing users to use it without difficulty.
9.   Pragmatism, in relation to items such as cost, efficiency, use when being developed, incorporation into the present system, time, etc.
10. Universality, to use the tool in different application types.
11. Reliability of the tool, according to the number of users, and the reputation as being strong and well debugged.
12. Maintenance, taking into consideration that a tool which has to be maintained by oneself during the ES development must never be acquired.

Figure 10 shows, according to the task, the bases used in order to select a tool for building an ES. As mentioned, sometimes the tool chosen for the development phase will not be the most adequate for working exploitation. Figure 11 shows the considerations to be taken into account in choosing a tool, regarding user performance and development phase.

Some of the most popular tools are ART (Automatic Reasoning Tool), KC (Knowledge Craft), and KEE (Knowledge Engineering Environment); these are the most powerful and versatile tools. They offer very flexible ES development environment, as well as different paradigms for representing knowledge. These and other existing commercial tools features are summarized in Table 1. In relation to the three most important ones, and as a summary, it can be said that ART seems to be currently the most adequate tool for complex applications, for which it provides nonmonotonic reasoning capacities, that is, it can go on changing, in accordance with the different information that is being received based on temporary points of view, treatment of uncertainty, etc. Its greatest strengths are its great power and high integration. Its greatest drawback is its price, 50% higher than its competitors; it is also difficult to learn and to handle.

For its part, KC presents the most powerful and varied knowledge representation. KC has contexts which are very useful in effecting sophisticated reasoning, although they are neither so efficient nor so well integrated as ART points of view, nor does it have a truth maintenance system. KC's main disadvantages are its limited facility for integration; in fact it seems that it was built by combining components that were independent, furthermore, it is difficult to learn and use. It has some advantages: its good understanding between its representation power and its capacity to solve problems; in addition its opening enables the user to access most of its internal characteristics.

Apart from its integration capability, KEE's most outstanding feature is that is easy to learn and use because of its powerful user interface. Its weakness lies in its low inferential

TABLE 1 Attributes of Some Commercial Expert System Building Tools

Name	Art 3.0	Kee 3.0	Knowledge Craft	Picon	S.1	ES Environment Vm/Mvs	Envi-Sage	KES	M.1	Nexpert Object	Pers. consultant +	EXSYS 3.0	Expert Edge	ESP Frame Engine	Insight 2+	TIMM	Rule Master	KDS 3	1st Class
Functional Uses																			
Classification	X	X	X	X	X	X	X	X	X	X	X	X	X	X	X	X	X	X	X
Design	X	X	X		X					X				X			X	X	X
Planning scheduling	X	X	X							X						X	X	X	
Process control	X	X	X	X						X						X	X	X	
Knowledge Representation																			
Rules								X	X			X							
Structured rules	X	X	X	X	X	X	X			cataloged	X		X	X	X		X		X
Certainty factors					X	X	X	X	X		X	X	X		X	X	X	X	X
Max. number of rules									1000	2000	800	5000			2000			16,000 from 4000 examples	
Frames with inheritance	X	X	X	X	No inherit.					X	X			X				X	
Object-oriented	X	X	X	X										X					
Logic	X	X	X		X									X					X
Examples																			
Structured examples																X	X	X	X
Procedures	X	X	X		X	X	X	X		X	X			X					
Inference engine																			
Forward chaining	X (Goal rules)	X	X	X	FR	X	X	X		X	X	X		X	X		X	X	X
Backward chaining	Goal rules	X	X	X	X	X	X	X	X	X	X	X	X	X	X	X	X	X	X
Demons	X		X	X	X	X	X		X	X	X			X					
Blackboard type	X	X		X						X				X				X	X
Time modeling	X	X		X															
Truth maintenance	X	X								X			X	X				X	
Meta control	X	X	X	X	X	X	X		X	X	X			X					
Logic	X	X	X		X					X				X					
Induction																X	X	X	X
Mathematical calculations	X	X	X	X	X	X	X	X	X	X	X	X	X	X	X	X	X	X	X
Contexts: viewpoints and worlds	X	X	X	X						X								X	
Pattern Matching																			
Variables	X	X	X	X	X			X	X	X	X	Numeric	Numeric	Numeric &	Numeric		X		Numeric
Literals	X	X	X	X						X			Numeric	Strings					& logical
Sequences	X		X	X								X							
Segments	X		X	X			X	X											
Wildcards	X												X						X
Developer Interface																			
KB creation: Word processing	X		X		X	X	X	X	X	X	X	X	X	X					X
Line entry		X	X	X	X	X	X	X		X	X	X	X	X	X	X	X	X	X

Feature	Values (left → right)
KB editor	X X X X X X X X X X X X
Menus	X X X X X X X X X X X X X
Check for consistency	X X X X X X X X
Graphic representations of KB	X X X X X X X X X X X X X
Inference tracking	X X X X X X X X X X X X X X
Graphics utilities for building end-user interfaces	X e X X X X X
Screen format utilities	X X X X X X X X X X X X X
Graphics simulation	X X e
capabilities	(Extra Cost)(Extra Cost) e X X X X X e
Why?	X X X X X X X X X X X X X X X X X X
How?	X X X X X X X X X X X X X X X X X X
Explanation expansion	X X X X X X X X X X X X X X X X X X
On-line help	X X X X X X X X X X X X X X X X
Sintaxis help	X X X X X X X X X X X X X X
Tools extensible	X X X X X X X X X X X X X X X X X
Language of tool	COM LISPCOM LISPCOM LISPZETA LISP LISP C PASCAL PASCAL C LISP C PROLOG 2T.PASCAL FORTRAN 8086 PASCAL
Compilable	incremen incremen incremen X incremen X incremen X incremen X incremen X X X Assembly X
Other language requirements	— C COMPILER —
Operating system	COM LISPCOM LISPCOM LISP LISP VMS, UNEX CMS GDDM UNEX, VMSVM/CMS VM/CMS OR MVS VMS ULTRIX MSDOS ON PC MSDOS VMS MSDOS MSDOS MSDOS MSDOS MSDOS DOS 3.0 UNEX, VMS MSDOS
Computers Supported	
Symbolics	X X X X X
LMI	X X X X
TI Explorer	X X X X
VAX	X X VMS ULTRIX X VMS ULTRIX X
Xerox	X X AT X AT X
IBM PC	X X X X X X
Macintosh	X X X
TI Prog	X X X X X
Apollo	X X X
Sun	X X X X X
IBM 370	X X X
Otros	X X X X X X X
Systems Interface	
Languages hooks	Via host Computer Via host Math Via host Math PASCAL etc. C C.PASCAL LISP C PROLOG MOST PASCAL BASIC ANY
Databases hooks	Via host Computer Via host Math Via host Math X X DBASEIIIDBASE III X Via Host Computer X X READS ASSEMBLY LANG. X DBASEII

TABLE 1 (Continued)

Name	Art 3.0	Kee 3.0	Knowledge Craft	Picon	S.1	ES Environment Vm/Mvs	Envi-Sage	KES	M.1	Nexpert Object	Pers. consultant +	EXSYS 3.0	Expert Edge	ESP Frame Engine	Insight 2+	TIMM	Rule Master	KDS 3	1st Class
End User Interface																			
Screen capabilities — Line	X	X	X	X	X	X	X	X		X	X	X	X	X	X	X		X	X
Menu	X	X	X	X	X	X	X	X	X	X	X	e	X	X			X	X	e
Graphics	X	X	X	X	e			e		X	e							X	
Simulation	X	SIMKIT Simulation extra cost	Simulation extra cost	X	e	e	e			X									
Why?	X	X	X	X	X	X	X	X	X	X	X	X	X	X	X		X	X	X
How?	X	X	X	X	X	X	X	X	X	X	X	X	X	X	X	X	X	X	X
Help	X	X	X	X	X	X	X	X	X	X	X	X	X	X	X			X	
Initial pruning	X	X						X			X	X	X		X			X	
Multiple solutions	X	X	X	X	X	X	X	X		X	X	X	X		X			X	
Examples saved			X							X	X	X	X	X		X		X	X
Multiple and uncertain user resp. o.k.	X	X	X	X	X	X	X	X	X		X	X	X		X	X	X	X	
What if	X	X	X	X	X	X	X	X	X	X	X	X	X		X	X		X	X
Company	Inference	Intellicorp	Carnegie Group	LMI	Teknowledge	IBM	Sys Design S/W	Software Arch & Engr.	Teknowledge	Neuron Data	TI	Ensys. Ca intel.	Human Edge	Exp. Sys Inter	Level-5A	GRC	Radian	KDS Sys	Progr in Motion
Cost (1st unit)	$65k	$52k includ. training	$50k includ training	$60k	$52k 1use mac $45k	$35k	$25k on VAX $25k on	$4k pc $7k WkStns	$5k	$5k PC-AT $3k MAC	$3k	$395 PC ??? VAX	$2500 Adv $4000 Pro	$895	$485	$19k PC $19k others	$995 PC $5k Wk Stn $175k VAX	1495	$495
Run time system cost	$1-8k	PC Host VAX $20k + 0.54/PC	None yet		$9.5k	$25k	10% of develop. sys		$50	$1k	$75 First unit	One time free	$50	By agreement	Nego.	No fee	$100PC $500 UNIX VMS	Based on quality	No fee

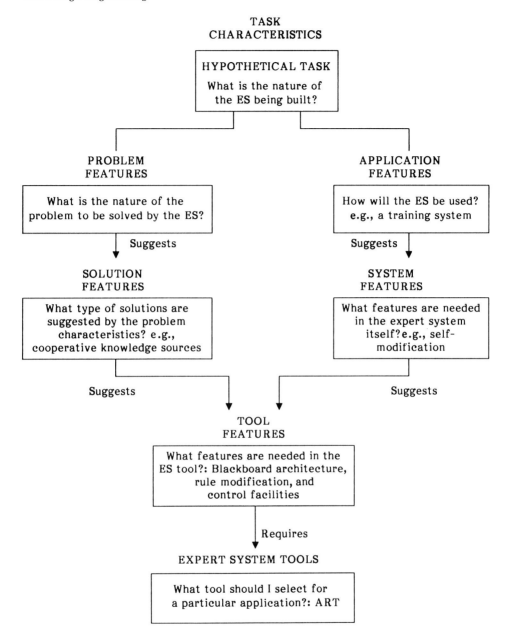

FIGURE 10   Basis for selecting an expert system tool, depending on a particular application.

	I. Knowledge Acquisition	II. Prototypes Development	III. Complete System	IV. Integration	V. Learning
1. Student	(a) Important: -Knowledge intuitive representations -Low cost -Casual user interface (b) Secondary: -Multiple schemes for knowledge representation -Those schemes integration -Default values processing	(b) Secondary: -Default values processing			(a) Main: -Knowledge intuitive representations -Low cost hardware and software -Casual user interface -Default values processing (b) Secondary: -Easy explanation facility -Examples
2. Expert	(a) Important: -Knowledge intuitive representations -Knowledge liaison support -Knowledge base verifier (b) Secondary: -Knowledge inductive acquisition -Default values -Domain-specific expertise	(a) Important: -Explanation facilities -Knowledge base completeness and consistency verification -Aids for knowledge inductive acquisition (b) Secondary: -Inclusion of domain expertise - Knowledge base verifier -Default values processing	(a) Main: -Explanation facilities -Knowledge base completeness and consistency verification (b) Secondary: -Knowledge base verifier	(a) Important: -Explanation facilities -Knowledge base completeness and consistency verification (b) Secondary: -Knowledge base verifier	(a) Main: -Knowledge intuitive representations -Expert interface -Knowledge base verifier -Examples (b) Secondary: -Default values processing -Knowledge inductive acquisition -Casual user interface -Low cost hardware and software -Training and support

					(Main)
3. Knowledge Engineer	(a) Important: -Multiple schemes for knowledge representation -Those schemes integration -Helps in the selection of the representation -Helps in compiling knowledge -Facility for knowledge base verifying (b) Secondary: -Knowledge completeness and consistency verification -Default values -Explanation facility -Helps in brainstorming -Helps in knowledge inductive acquisition -Migration capability	(a) Important: -Default values processing -Inclusion of domain expertise -Knowledge completeness and consistency verification -Helps in compiling knowledge -Knowledge base verifier (b) Secondary -Migration capability -Explanation facilities	(a) Important: -Knowledge completeness and consistency verification -Support for large search spaces -Multiple and integrated schemes for knowledge representation -Uncertainty processing -Belief maintenance (b) Secondary: -Migration capability -Explanation facilities -Changeable inference engine	(a) Important: -Knowledge completeness and consistency verification -Support for large search spaces -Multiple and integrated schemes for knowledge representation -Uncertainty processing -Belief maintenance (b) Secondary: -Migration capability -Explanation facilities -Changeable inference engine	(a) Main: -Default values processing -Multiple representation schemes -Casual user interface -Representation schemes integration (b) Secondary -Good documentation -Adequate examples -Training and support -Low-cost hardware and software
4. Artificial Intelligence Programmer	(a) Important -Simulation interface capability -Graphic support (b) Secondary: -Casual user interface -Friendly developer interface -Interface with popular productivity tools	(a) Important: -Simulation interface capability -Large search spaces -External languages and products bridges -Modularity -Graphic support -User interface equipment development (b) Secondary: -Friendly development interface	(a) Important; -High services: speed and storage capacity -External languages and products bridges -Modularity -Powerful debugging tools -Unnecessary features omission -Modular development of the user interface -Graphic support (b) Secondary: -Friendly development interface -Portable to different hardware, including PCs		(a) Main: -Good documentation -Default values processing -Casual user interface -Examples (b) Secondary: -Low-cost hardware and software -Access to source code -Multiple schemes for knowledge representation -Multiple reasoning paradigms -Training and support

FIGURE 11   User and development phase depending considerations for selecting a tool

characteristics and its slowness, and that its scope seems to be limited to the construction of prototype and not very complex applications. However, newer versions appear to have overcome or at least diminished these limitations. It has also announced an interface facility to access more easily and rapidly conventional databases.

In addition to these characteristics, knowledge engineering tools must have another quality which is growing increasingly important: the integration, showing two sides; first, to avoid giving the impression like KC, of having been built by combining separate components, in such a way that they may dispose of a series of more powerful complementary tools. Second, to facilitate the interfaces with other systems.

Knowledge representation. Another highly important question in the prototype development phase is knowledge representation. To deserve such a qualified adjective, an "intelligent" system must incorporate the necessary knowledge concerning the decisions it must make. There is no theory for knowledge representation that claims that the fitness of certain formalisms for fixed applications is measured by its effectiveness and efficiency, but it is generally accepted that the components which must appear in a representation are as follows:

> Objects, that is, representation, description, and categories of objects
> Events and actions, since part of the knowledge consists of facts about objects
> Performances, or how to do things, how events will occur
> Generalization and abstraction, which seem to constitute the learning capacity nucleus
> Reasoning metalevel, or use of knowledge about knowledge

The diversity of developed techniques is embodied in two large groups: declarative and procedural. No system exploits knowledge in either of the two forms excluding the other. A declarative knowledge without procedures to handle it does not seem to be possible, nor plausible, and vice versa, the existence of procedures without anything to be handled.

The declarative and procedural representations are alternative strategies to obtain the same results, but each represents special characteristics which make it more adequate in certain cases. If the facts are independent and changing, the declarative approaches are more transparent or easier to understand and to maintain due to its modularity. For experts and users, the declarative approach is more comfortable to use. On the contrary, the procedural representations are more efficient and easier to maintain. The trace of procedure is more comfortable to follow, because the instructional flow can be examined easily. Knowledge engineers generally prefer a procedural approach.

Declarative techniques permit information to be specified without establishing any hypothesis of the form in which it will be used. The emphasis falls on the process to which it is to be submitted, that is, "what." In this case, knowledge is represented as a static collection of facts and a set of general procedures to handle them. Each fact is stored once independent of the different forms in which it can be used. As can be seen, it is a very modifiable, flexible system and it may lead to a considerable saving of resources as well as to certainty in deductions. Semantic networks and predicate calculus are some of the most often used declarative techniques.

On the other hand, procedural techniques give more emphasis to the manner of carrying out the cations which represent a particle of knowledge. As with algorithmic programming languages, emphasis is on the form in which a problem is going to solved, that is, the "how." Here knowledge is represented by procedures to be used later; in this way, the representation of knowledge as heuristic or not well adjusted to simple declarative schemes (e.g., probabilistic reasoning) is easier. This kind of system allows more direct development of its line of reasoning by using domain-specific heuristics to avoid non-natural reasoning lines, on the other hand, it is endowed with a facility for codifying and understanding the reasoning process itself. Rule-based systems are usually discussed as procedural schemes; while frames and scripts are considered to be mixed. All of these will be studied separately hereinafter.

Predicate calculus. The first attempt to build intelligent systems used first-order predicate calculus as representation, for its expressive power and well-defined semantics. Let us suppose that we want to represent: John gives Mary a pencil. John is Mary's friend. Using a predicate logic-based formalism, such as Prolog, these two sentences are represented as follows:

gives (John, Mary, pencil)   person (John)
friend (John, Mary)   person (Mary)
                                    physical object (pencil)

Logic seems a natural way for expressing certain notions, as it frequently corresponds to intuitive understanding; such notions are easy to modify, which facilitates experimentation. It is accurate, that is, there are standard methods for determining the meaning of an expression. It is flexible, as it is not subordinated to the process types which really make deductions. Finally, it is modular, as the knowledge may increasingly grow as new facts are discovered and added. Unfortunately, there is no effective process which decides whether a particular arbitrary sentence is a logical consequence of an arbitrary knowledge base; moreover, the small grain size of these structures is inadequate for representing individual complex objects and relations among them. These problems led to the development of semantic networks, and of object-oriented and frame-based knowledge representation languages. Predicate calculus is formally equivalent to those other formalisms, but it has been substituted by them due to the aforementioned difficulties and is less efficient in implementation. In other words, all the representation formalisms are formally equivalent but, pragmatically considered, quite different.

Production rules. As soon as the first steps were taken in AI, representation and treatment by traditional algorithms of AI problems and their solutions began to be questioned. Traditional programs have, as an essential characteristic, their sequential character. This is not adequate in situations in which the environment can change and it is necessary to simulate human answers to its stimulus. Thus the idea of using data as a part of the program which runs the operation arose. These ideas gave way to the advent of production rule-based systems which belong to a more general type of system, called "pattern-directed inference systems."

A rule-based system generally has three basic components: a facts base or working memory, which contains a set of data with the world, environment and program information; a set of rules or rules base; and a control strategy, rule interpreter or inference engine, which links the system work cycles. A production rule is an expression as:

IF A THEN B

The premise, A, expresses the rule-firing conditions. It generally consists of several elemental conditions. The conclusion, B, indicates the new fact or facts which can be deducted from the hypothesis.

One of the most important characteristics that the rules must present is the approximate character [*15*]. Knowledge-based systems handle data obtained from experience, which can only be known in an approximate way. That is, production rules do not reflect logical implications, only expert convictions. This can be understood by associating with each rule, a certainty factor or credibility coefficient which reflects the higher or lower confidence degree which the expert associates with each rule.

It is necessary to work such rules in such a way to avoid deducing invalid results. To do so different models of "approximate" calculus have been proposed: probability, plausibility, modal (which includes the notion of necessary or possible fact); non-monotonic, which manages the lack of time permanence; and fuzzy calculus. The last fundamental idea is to define characteristic functions (CF), that are continuous in the (0,1) interval, unlike those of classic set theory, that were defined for the set A as FA (x) = 1, x $\in$ A; FA (x) = 0, x $\notin$ A. In this way, the approximation concept can be introduced within a frame that remains formal. Then, uncertain and fuzzy facts can be handled using the production rules.

The main advantages of rule-based systems are modularity, which allows addition, removal, or modification of rules freely, and uniformity, as information is encoded in production rules. The disadvantages which derive form these advantages are inefficiency and opacity, or difficulty in following the control flow when solving a problem.

Semantic networks. Production rules do not represent declarative knowledge, such as relations among domain objects, in a natural way. As mentioned, semantic networks arose from the search for alternatives to represent knowledge. This formalism groups different components which share a common notation in order to refer to the elements of the representation:

1. Nodes, which habitually represent objects, concepts, or situations in the domain, and
2. Arc, linking nodes, which represent relations among them.

But nodes and arcs, can have associated labels. For example, the semantic network of Figure 12 [*16*] can be used to represent sentences mentioned in speaking about the computation of predicates, where "the" means element of; "ss" means superset, and "arg" means argument. Arch labeling preserves the semantics of the relations. There is no set limit as to the types of relations to be used to maintain the sense of the assertions which one wishes to model, however excessive linking types may lead to inefficient functioning of the interpreter of the semantic network. Therefore, it is necessary to show some restraint in the number of relations.

The more widely used processes correspond to:

1. Generalizations: "is-a(n)," which places an entity into relation with a more general one
2. Aggregation: "part-of," which links an object with its components
3. Classification: "member-of," which links an object with a generic type

The deficits of representation by semantic networks are the lack of an adequate and universally known terminology, and the lack of formal and adequate semantics. The main advantage is its graphic charm, which makes it rapidly comprehensible.

Although it is useful to think of semantic networks using the graphic notations, they cannot be represented within the computer in this way. Some type of structure of

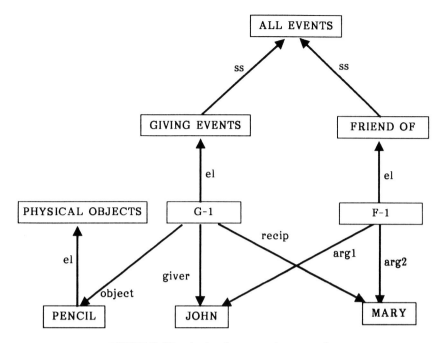

FIGURE 12   A simple semantic network.

"attribute-value" memory is typically used. For example, in LISP, each node would be an atom, the links would be the characteristics, and the nodes at the other end of the links would be the values.

Frames are also representation formalisms oriented to structured objects. The notion of frame was introduced by Minsky [17]. A frame is a structure to represent stereotyped situations. Each frame is associated with different types of information. Part of this information relates to how to use the frame. The other part relates to what is expected to happen next, and, in particular, to what to do if these expectations are not confirmed.

One can think of a frame as a network of nodes and relations. The "high-levels" of the frame are fixed, and they represent things which are always true in respect to the situation assumed. The "lower levels" have a lot of terminals or "slots," which must be filled by specific data. The collections of related frames are joined in frame systems. The effects of important actions are shown by means of transformations between the frames of the system. These are used to cut costs in certain types of computations, to represent changes of emphasis and attention, and to show the effectiveness of the "image." Some slots can be filled with assignments by default. Thus the frame can contain a great number of details whose assumption is not specifically justified by the situation.

The two sentences of the last example could be represented by the frames in Figure 13 [3]. in this example, several types of knowledge are represented. The "type" slot is used to establish a hierarchical hereditary characteristic among frames, which, in turn, permits information from a "parent" frame to be obtained so that the "children" may inherit (it is similar to the linkage "is-a" of a representation in a semantic network). The slots can have a complex structure in some systems, similar to a frame. Other times, the slot contains an indication or expectation about which types of values it can take.

A variant of frames, scripts, are especially designed to represent sequences of events.

Name	G-1
Type	Giving-Event
Giver	John
Recip	Mary
Object	Pencil

Name	John
Type	Person
Address	...
...	...
...	...

Name	Pencil
Type	Physical-Obj
Color	...
Length	...
...	...

Name	F-1
Type	Friend-of
Arg1	John
Arg2	Mary
...	...

Name	Mary
Type	Person
Address	...
...	...
...	...

FIGURE 13   An example of representation with frames.

Figure 14 [*3*] presents a summary of the main types of formalisms of knowledge representation, with the typical techniques of reasoning associated with them, as well as the main inconveniences of each one.

Use of the knowledge: reasoning and control. The inferences engine fulfills a task which corresponds to the control of the operation of the pieces of knowledge. It then expresses a certain type of reasoning, a paradigm which can be characterized at different levels.

1. For intellectual progress with respect to the solution of problems, global functioning of the system can be cited as reasoning of the following types: "hypothesis and verification," reductio ad absurdum, reasoning for spreading of restrictions, reasoning by analogy, and reasoning by decomposition of problems into simpler subproblems.
2. In the conceptual aspect one tries to visualize the space search targeted for exploration. There are essentially two types of search spaces: the space of states and the space of problems.
3. Regarding the more operative aspect, reasoning can be characterized in a syntactic manner for the qualifications of forward and backward chaining.
4. Regarding search, it is possible to characterize how the inference engine builds the graph of states or problems and also how it runs over it. When a decision is to be taken, that is, at the moment of choosing a rule, the inference engine can use different strategies in order to make this choice: depth (e.g., hill-climbing, reverse), or extent (search in beam, separation, and progressive valuation).

Rule-based systems can be divided into two categories based on the syntax of the rules and their control structure:

REPRESENTATION	TYPICAL REASONING TECHNIQUES	DRAWBACKS
Rules for knowledge of experience	Forward and or backward chaining	General but unstructured
Semantic networks for casual knowledge	Markers propagation	What a link is
Frames for mixed knowledge	Procedural link	The clue is to find the semantic particles

FIGURE 14   Knowledge representation types.

Systems run by the antecedent, or with forward chaining, in which, when the antecedent is true, the consequent is processed, and the associated actions are performed

Systems run by the consequent; in this case, the cataloguing of performance of the rules is led by backward chaining, implying matching of the consequents of the rules with the assertions to be tested.

The control strategy in a rule-based system contains the control knowledge, and is nothing more than a "general model for problem solving." This strategy links the working cycles; each cycle consists of two phases:

1. Decision or rule selection phase:
   (a) Restriction consists of exploiting, whenever possible, the general pieces of knowledge, dividing the facts and rules into families; determining which of their subsets deserve to be compared at the moment so that the comparison stage may be as fast as possible.
   (b) Matching wherein, the database is examined in order to select the subset of candidate rules to be fired. That subset is called the conflict set.
   (c) Conflict resolution, where the rules to be fired are fixed. For this purpose, there exist several approaches: selecting the first rule that matches the context, the one with a higher priority according to the criteria defined by the programmer, the most specific one, any of them, or even none, that is exploring the rules with a pseudoparallelism that will become actual using the future parallel computers.
2. Action, firing, or deduction phase. In this phase, the inference engine controls the execution of the selected rule. Using forward chaining, it usually introduces, removes, or modifies data in the base. Using backward chaining, it introduces the rule premises as subgoals in the base.

The cycle is repeated until the goal fact is added (with forward chaining) or all the subgoals are verified within the base (with backward chaining). It also stops in both cases when no rule can be fired.

In order to explain both reasoning mechanisms, let us suppose that we have the following set of rules:

```
1: IF B and D and E   THEN F
2: IF D and G        THEN A
3: IF C and F        THEN A
4: IF B              THEN X
5: IF D              THEN E
6: IF A and X        THEN H
7: IF C              THEN D
8: IF X and C        THEN A
9: IF X and B        THEN D
```

and the following database:

>   Known facts: B,C
>   Goal: H

In forward chaining, reasoning starts with the known facts, applying rules until the goal is deduced. In this way, X and D can be deduced from B and C using rule 4 and 7, respectively. When one rule is fired, new facts are added to the base. Figure 15 shows the tree that describes this way of reasoning for the example presented. The arcs represent applied rules, and the nodes represent different database states. The dashed arcs are matched but not fired rules. The strategy used to select rules is to choose the first applicable one.

When reasoning uses backward chaining, it begins with the goal (H), trying to introduce equivalent subgoals, that must be verified. In this way, H is replaced, using rule 6, by subgoals A and X, which are the new goals to be considered. In turn, A can be verified using one of these rules: 2, 3, or 8. If it fails, for example, if G cannot be deduced here in any way, it is necessary to go back, and the last rule disregarded is tried. Figure 16 shows this way of reasoning for the former example.

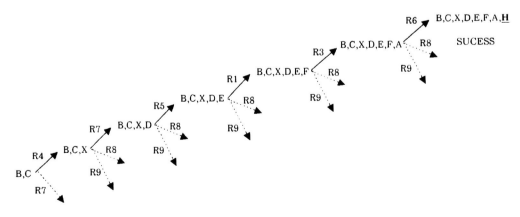

FIGURE 15   Example of forward chaining

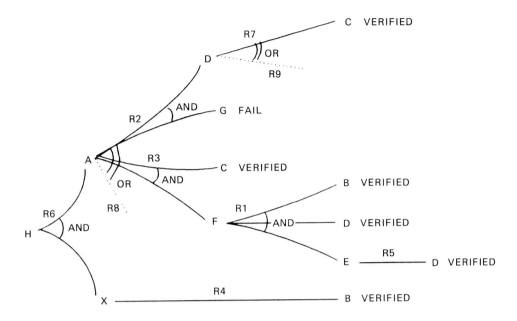

FIGURE 16   Example of backward chaining.

Matching is the most widely used reasoning mechanism with structured objects, such as frames and semantic networks. This operation is analogous to predicate calculus unification [16]. It is fundamental to the structured objects as the global database of a production system.

Matching works on semantic networks as follows: a network fragment that represents a sketch of the object or fact is built and then compared with the network in the database to see if such an object exists. The variable nodes are bounded to the values they should have for the matching to be perfect.

Continuing with the example presented, suppose that we want to ask the question "Who gives Mary the pencil?." This could be presented by the network fragment in Figure 17. That fragment is compared with the database network, searching for a G node with an "object" link to PENCIL and a (recipient) link to MARY. When it is found, the node pointed by its "giver" link is returned as the answer. The matcher could also infer network structures not explicitly present.

The same question could be presented by the Figure 18 goal frame and answered by matching it with the Figure 13 fact frame G1.

Within the deductive operations that can be used for reasoning with semantic networks and frames are delineations, inheritance, and net and frame rules. Implications that assert properties about every member of a set by a special kind of object (frame or network) are called delineation entities. These entities can be used in the forward direction to create new fact frames or networks or to add properties to the existing ones.

In many applications, the structured objects denoting individuals of sets, form a taxonomic hierarchy. Consider the example semantic network. Learning that Mary is a person, we could use the delineations (together with some set theory) to make several forward inferences. Specifically, we could derive that Mary breathes, has two arms, etc. The

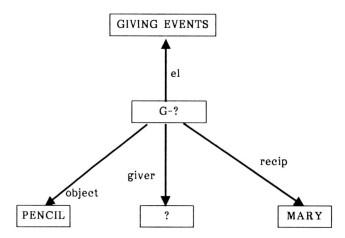

FIGURE 17   Semantic network piece to query a database.

system works as if an object automatically inherits all of the necessary features from its sets and supersets. Marker propagation is a frequently used mechanism for handling inheritance in semantic networks. The marker marks the node which he or she wants to know something about, and the mark begins spreading across the network through certain links, depending on the kind of problem or question to be solved.

A frame inherits the slot values from other frames of which it is a subclass or instance. Once a frame has been selected to express the current context or situation, the main process, when reasoning with frames, frequently consists simply in satisfying its slots requirements. Inherited and default values are relatively easy to fill; to a great extent; the power of the frames representation is based on them, as any new frame expressing the situation can use the values fixed by former experience without having to compute them again. When information has to be deduced, procedures associated with the slots provide a means of specifying adequate methods that can take advantage of the current context, namely, "domain-specific heuristic." In other words, general problem-solving methods can be complemented with domain-specific knowledge.

Semantic networks and frames formalisms can be used as a basis for rule-based systems. On occasion, as in KEE, rules themselves are represented and structured as frames.

Name	x
Type	Giving-Events
Giver	y
Recipient	Mary
Object	Pencil

FIGURE 18   Frame to answer the question: Who gives Mary a book?

Underlying the declarative structure of frames (the way static facts are organized), there exists a dynamic or procedural aspect in frames. In particular, procedures that direct the system reasoning or behavior can be attached to the slots in order to solve problems.

Active values are procedures or rule sets attached to the delineation frame slots, that are fired when reading or modifying the slot value. These procedures implement events or data directed processing, since they run only when certain data or events appear. As the structure suggests, frame-based systems are useful in domains in which expectations of the data form or content are very important for solving problems such as visual scenes interpretation or speech recognition. The slots have attached procedures that only work when certain events occur. "If-needed" procedures run when the slot information is needed, but the slot is empty. "If-added" procedures run when new information is stored in the slot. Finally, "if-deleted" procedures run only when the slot information is deleted.

Besides representation and use of knowledge about objects and relations, it is necessary to take into consideration control knowledge. Experts in several fields, such as medicine or mathematics, who may not be familiar with computers, have found it rather convenient and natural to express their skills in the form of predicates and rules. But it is also necessary to supply deduction systems with control knowledge. Efficient control strategies are rather complex and incorporating them into computer control programs requires great skill. Ideally, the design of control strategy should be left to the AI expert. However, domain-specific control knowledge is usually very important to the program. Therefore, it is interesting that the experts frequently furnish such knowledge as well as declarative and procedural knowledge. Some different ways to embody control knowledge are:

1. Metarules. The metarule notion to reflect higher level knowledge, that is control knowledge, was introduced by Davis in TEIRESIAS. In TEIRESIAS [*17*], metarules work with object-level inference rules and deduce how to use these rules in given situations. They represent strategies for using object-level knowledge. Their syntax is identical to that of the production rules, so that they can use the same reasoning mechanisms, and knowledge is encoded uniformly in all the levels. They allow the reordering of a rule set that leads to an objective. They are metarules due not to any syntactic detail, but to the fact that they express "knowledge about knowledge."

   A metarule is an indication about how to reason in a given situation and, therefore, it provides useful advice for selecting the rules to be applied to improve program performance. For example, [*18*]:

   > IF the culture was not obtained from a sterile source, and there are rules which mention in their antecedent a previous organism which can be the same as the present one,
   > THEN there exists an evidence (1.0) that none of them is going to be useful.

   Interest in this rule lies in the fact that a past but only superficially healed infection, can appear again a month later at the latest. Therefore, one way of deducing the identity of the organism causing the infection is to make reference to former infections. However, this line of reasoning is not valid if the infection culture was made in such a way that the sample is not sterile. In this case, it has no interest to deduce the present organism identity, starting from the previous one.

2. Agenda. Another control mechanism in knowledge-based systems is the agenda. An agenda is a list of the tasks that the system can carry out. Each task generally

is associated with a list of reasons which caused it to be proposed, and a coefficient or measure of its usefulness. A system controlled by an agenda operates selecting from the agenda the most interesting task and carrying it out, allocating resources (time and space) depending on its importance or interest. When a task runs, it will probably generate new tasks, which will have to be incorporated into the agenda [*19*]. This selection-operation sequence is cyclically repeated.

3. Blackboard [*20*]. This mechanism organizes and controls individual, and perhaps different, components, called knowledge sources. A blackboard is a natural process of using different knowledge types in a unique system. To explain the methodology, imagine a large blank blackboard, and group of people around it trying to compose a puzzle. Each person has one piece of the puzzle, and the person who thinks that he or she possesses a "promising" piece places it. If any of the available pieces held by other players fits in with the pieces already in place; it is properly placed, moving closer to a solution.

The puzzle can be solved in complete silence; there is no need for direct communication among the group members. Neither is there an established order in which to place the pieces; that is why this control is called opportunistic. If you want to put an order in the process, it is necessary to use a monitor that reviews all the pieces available for placement and selects one of them; this necessitates some criterion or strategy that can be defined "a priori" or dynamically as long as it keeps on solving the problem.

Implementation. During this phase the knowledge engineer(s) put the formalized knowledge into a computer program with proven capabilities. Building a program requires:

Contents: data structures, inference rules, and control strategies to solve the problem.
Form, specified by the tool chosen in order to develop the system.
Integration, which implies combining and reorganizing different elements of knowledge to delete wrong global comparisons.

This stage should be performed rapidly, since one reason for implementing the initial prototype is to verify the effectiveness of the design decisions made during the first development phases. This means that there is a high probability for the initial code to be revised or rejected during the development.

Though it is sometimes a stage by itself, it is at this stage that development is usually carried out. This development is one of the most important aspects, and usually takes longer in the case of an ES, particularly when the aim is to compare that interface and, if possible, improve those to which the users are accustomed. An adequate interface helps considerably in system acceptance.

Verification. Verification implies evaluating the prototype performance and usefulness and, if necessary, revising it. The expert, specifically, evaluates the prototype and helps the knowledge engineer with the eventual, though probable, revision. Examples performed by the prototype should be verified on several problems in order to evaluate its performance and usefulness. This evaluation can reveal problems with the representation scheme, such as forgotten concepts and relations, knowledge represented at the wrong level of detail, or manageable control mechanisms. Such problems can compel the constructors to "recycle" the system through the different development phases, reformulating the concepts, improving the inference rules, and revising the control flow.

On the other hand, questions that the system asks of the user in an unintelligent or unnatural way, reduces his confidence in the system. Consequently, the system explanations must be able to adequately describe how and why the conclusions have been reached, and the test problems must cover the domain handling typical cases, testing the limitations of the difficult cases expected.

The system must be debugged and verified in a laboratory environment before it can be extended to verifying real tests. Final users require something more than just performance or high quality; they also want a rapid, reliable, system that is easy to use and understand. In addition, its failures must be recoverable. Obviously, then the ES needs to be subject to considerable test verification before being ready for commercial use.

Phase III. Production or Development of the Complete System

Once everyone is satisfied with the final version of the prototype, it can be extended to a complete or in-production phases ES. Among the activities necessary to develop the complete system are the following:

Implementing the Central Structure or Nucleus of the Complete System

Recently, it has been asserted that it is better to disregard the prototype. It is likely that the different prototypes will only emphasize the need for restarting the basic design of the knowledge base and sometimes, the entire development process. Among the modifications usually necessitated, we can find the exact list of objects, attributes, and relationships included in the system, the hierarchical relations adjustment, and variations of ways in which inference and heuristics are handled. Finally, while the prototype may be successful, the initial knowledge representation structures and the facts used eventually need to be modified.

Extending the Knowledge Base Previously Obtained

This may turn out to be the main work to be carried out in the construction of a whole system. If the knowledge base is to be enlarged, it is necessary to add a great number of heuristic cases, which generally and usually increase the depth of the system. It may also be decided to incorporate new rules which handle additional subproblems or other aspects not originally contemplated before the work of the experts.

Tailoring the Interface to the Final User's Needs

This interface enables the ES to provide the user with information and if necessary, to obtain information. Considerable attention must be paid to the introduction of sentences and explanations that may aid the user in following the logic of the ES and, at the same time the system must make it easier and natural for the user to ask and obtain any detail he wishes from the system. The use of graphical representation is very helpful and can be a key to the success of the system.

Monitoring and Evaluation of the Performance of the Developed System

A new interface must enable the expert to introduce different cases to inspect the system reasoning and go over a given case step by step, asking why certain particular or no particular rules are followed, and to identify in this way those items in which additional specific knowledge is required in order that the system may reach an adequate conclusion. On the other hand, at this point of the development, the experts have sufficient mastery with respect to the introduction of rules, that they proceed with inserting new rules into the system. In this way, the transfer of the system control of the knowledge engineers to the system itself or to the experts is facilitated, so that they may be engaged in perfecting, elaborating, and completing the maintenance of the system by themselves.

Phase IV. Integration and Maintenance in the Production Regime

It is not enough to build a good ES that works correctly in an isolated way; it is necessary to integrate it into the working environment in which it will continue operating. The aim of integration is not to make significant changes in the ES, but to include those procedures which may be necessary to make the ES function coordinatingly with the existing systems, either expert systems or conventional ones, within an organization. Among the activities to be carried out in this stage, the following can be included:

Organization of the Transfer of Technology

When the ES is ready for integrated functioning, the knowledge engineers must make sure that the experts, the users, and the system personnel who are going to use and maintain the system really understand it. The experience gained by this time now seems to indicate that the experts are willing to accept the system rapidly, once they are convinced that it can provide them with really useful advise. However, convincing those who are not experts raises all the problems and challenges associated with the introduction of a new technological system in the environment of an organization. Success in this aspect depends on the care with which the planning of this task is carried out, on the quantity and extent of communication among the different parties, and on adequate opportunities provided to discuss change. In short, everything that has been pointed out in the indirect questions explained in Phase I.

Establishment of Interfaces of the ES with Different Software, Hardware, and Other Systems

This is another objective to be fulfilled in the integration process. An ES may need to obtain information from measurement instruments or other hardware systems, or to access systems of databases or even to require data and information from persons. Objectives can also include perfecting factors which depend on the time within the system, so that it may function in a faster and efficient way, or that the physical characteristics of the hardware may be improved, if the system has to function in nongeneralized process environments. The "transportable character" of the code generated in the development of the ES to a production code is closely related to integration.

Improved Performance of the Resulting Global System

Once the ES is integrated within a larger system, it is necessary to improve the performance of the global system, which will undoubtedly be disturbed by the introduction of the ES. Factors such as response time and transactional ease are pertinent here, since, if they are not accounted for adequately, it is not possible to say that the system is in production. In this regard, it is also necessary to consider the functional perfection of the interfaces to facilitate the operating and handling of the global system for the final users.

System Maintenance

Maintenance consists, on one hand, in training the personnel who will be responsible for its care and, on the other hand, in making the system flexible for adaptation to dynamic environments. When a system is translated into a language different than the development language, to facilitate speed and transportability, its flexible character is sacrificed. This can become acceptable if the system has captured all the knowledge within the working domain and if the knowledge is not going to be modified in the near future. On the contrary, if an ES has been designed just because the working domain is being modified, it will be necessary to maintain the system within the development environment, which provides a continuous maintenance activity.

CONCLUSION

A method verified in different fields has been presented: medicine, banking, public administration, teaching, industry, defense, and legislation; and to carry out different tasks: monitoring, diagnostic, planning, interpretation, prediction, etc. This method is to be used as a procedure manual to serve as the guideline for carrying out the entire process rather than as something to be followed in an imperative way. In other words, it must be seen as an initial facility rather than as a condition which is imposed. Viewed in this way, and through the experience accumulated in the development of more than a dozen ES, it is a guarantee that the knowledge engineering project will be successful.

Finally, it is necessary to point out that an important item, as far as knowledge engineering is concerned, which, hic et nunc is not going to be developed here due to obvious space limitations, is the training of the knowledge engineers. However, we must point out that it is not enough to be adept in the construction techniques of ES to become a good knowledge engineer; equally important are psychological, interpersonal, and social factors; these factors have not been given adequate attention by universities; hopefully, this will change in the future.

REFERENCES

1. H. Eco, "Intelectuales y Poder," *Diario 16*, Madrid, (November 28, 1986).
2. D. Bell, "The Microelectronics Revolution," in *The Social Framework of the Information Society*, M.L. Dertouzos and J. Moses (Eds.), MIT Press, Cambridge, MA, 1979.
3. J.L. Maté and J. Pazos, *Ingenieria del Conocimiento. Diseño y Construcción de Sistemas Expertos*, Sociedad para Estudios Pedagógicos Argentinos, Serie Inform ática, Córdoba, Argentina, 1988.
4. R. Fikes and T. Kehler, "The Role of Frame-Based Representation in Reasoning," *ACM Comm.* 28 (9) (1985).
5. P. Harmon and D. King, *Expert Systems*, John Wiley & Sons, New York, 1985.
6. F. Nietzsche, *Así habló Zaratusta*, Ediciones Orbis, Barcelona, 1982.
7. R. Descartes, *Discurso del Método* . . . Ed. Porrua, México, 1977.
8. J. Pazos, "Methodolgía IDEAL para el Diseño e Implementación de Sistemas Expertos," Jornadas RANK XEROX sobre sistemas Expertos., Madrid, 1986.
9. D.A. Waterman, *A Guide to Expert Systems*, Addison-Wesley, Reading, MA, 1986.

10. F. Hayes-Roth, D.A. Waterman, and D.B. Lenat (Eds.), *Building Expert Systems*, Addison-Wesley, Reading, MA, 1977.

11. A. Newell and H.A. Simon, *Human Problem Solving*, Prentice Hall, Englewood Cliff, NJ, 1972.

12. K.A. Ericson and H.A. Simon, *Protocol Analysis. Verbal Reports as Data*, The MIT Press, Cambridge, MA, 1984.

13. D.G. Borrow, et al, *"Expert Systems: Perils and Promise,"* *Comm. ACM*, *29*(9)(1986).

14. K. Hwang, J. Ghosh, and R. Chowkwangon, "Computer Architectures for Artificial Intelligence Processing," *Computers IEEE*, January (1987).

15. J. Pazos, *Intelligencia Artificial. Programación Heurística*, Parainfo, Madrid, 1987.

16. N. Nilsson, *Principles of Artificial Intelligence*, Tioga, Palo Alto, CA, 1980.

17. M. Minsky, "A Framework for Representing Knowledge," in *The Psychology of Computer Vision*, P. Winston (Ed.) McGraw-Hill, New York, 1975.

18. R. Davis and D.B. Lenat, *Knowledge-Based System in Artificial Intelligence*, McGraw-Hill, New York, 1982.

19. J.G. Carbonell, *Criterios para el éxito en la Construcción de Sistemas Expertos*, Facultad de Informática, Madrid, 1986.

20. L.D. Erman, et al., "The Hearsay II Speech-Understanding System: Integrating Knowledge to Resolve Uncertainty," *Computing Surveys*,12(2)(1980).

J.L. MATÉ

J. PAZOS

MACHINE TRANSLATION

The field of machine translation (MT) has had a long and turbulent history. Indeed, it was the first nonnumerical application suggested in the 1940s for the then nascent field of computer science. Within a few years, more than two dozen MT projects had been organized in the United States and in Europe. Research and development continued until the early 1960s, when it became clear that a high-quality, fully automated translation system could not be developed within the then current state of the art. This realization led to the cut-off of research support by the United States government and signified the end of the early MT paradigm. In the late 1970s, research and development in MT intensified significantly, especially in Europe and Japan. From then, until the present, the number of MT projects has continued to grow. Among the contributing factors to this renascence are the enormous improvement in the quality of computer hardware and software, realistic expectations, and progress in such essential for MT areas as theoretical and computational linguistics and artificial intelligence (AI). At present MT is a vibrant research and development topic, actively pursued in the United States, Japan, and Europe. A number of good surveys of the history of machine translation are available, notably, Zarechnak [1] and especially Hutchins [2], who discusses the topic in considerable detail. For additional descriptions of current issues in the field, see, e.g., Nirenburg [2a].

HISTORY OF MT RESEARCH

In the late 1940s MT seemed a very attractive and feasible application of computer technology. This opinion was bolstered by the following considerations. First, in the era of information explosion translation became a very important business. As in every other business, automation is supposed to enhance efficiency. Second, translation is a common task regularly performed by humans. Therefore, the specification of the task is relatively straightforward: the conceptual design of a potential MT system can be modeled after the organization of the translation process performed by humans. Third, the dictionary lookup, which may account for a very significant part of the time spent on translation, can be reduced to an insignificant level when on-line dictionaries are used. Finally, spectacular successes of cryptography during World War II called for applying its methods to other fields. Translation could indeed be understood as a code-breaking task ("When I look at an article in Russian, I say: 'This is really written in English, but it has been coded in some strange symbols. I will now proceed to decode',") [3], and this was yet another impetus to the development of MT. Feasibility considerations tended to be influenced by the perception of translation as a common everyday task, performed with relative ease by humans. Such was the rationale behind the exciting development of MT research from the late 1940s until the early 1960s.

It is customary to consider the so-called Weaver memorandum as the starting point of research in MT. In 1949, Warren Weaver, then a Vice President of the Rockefeller Foundation, distributed 200 copies of a letter in which he suggested the concept of MT to some of the people who could have an interest in developing it. Even though the memorandum was predominantly a strategic document, several important theoretical and methodological issues were discussed in it, including the problem of multiple meanings of linguistic units, the logical basis of language, the influence of cryptography, and the necessity to analyze language universals. Not all of the scientific ideas in the memorandum were appropriate and useful (notably, the entire cryptographic angle soon proved to be inapplicable), but it aroused significant scientific and public interest in the concept of MT. In 1948, the University of London team led by Andrew Booth and Richard Richens was the only one to carry out research and experiments in MT. In the first two years after the Weaver memorandum, work on MT started in earnest at a number of scientific research institutions in the United States, including the Massachusetts Institute of Technology, the University of Washington, the University of California at Los Angeles, the RAND corporation, the National Bureau of Standards, Harvard University, and Georgetown University.

The major concepts, topics, and processes of MT—such as morphological and syntactic analysis, pre- and postediting, homograph resolution, interlingual representation of meaning, work in restricted vocabularies, automating dictionary look-up, etc.—were first defined and debated at that time. The first scientific conference on MT was held in 1952 at MIT, and the first public demonstration of a translation program took place in 1954 at Georgetown University.

The Georgetown experiment involved translating 49 Russian sentences, selected from texts on chemistry, into English. The dictionary included about 250 words, and the Russian grammar consisted of only six rules. No pre-editing of the source language sentences was required, and the output was of adequate quality. This experiment was perceived by the general public and sponsors of scientific research as strong evidence for the feasibility of MT. The wide publicity and resonance of this experiment has also led to the establishment of MT projects outside the United States, notably, in the Soviet Union.

Through the 1950s and into the following decade, research in MT continued and grew. The requirements of this application gave an impetus to significant theoretical developments in linguistics and what would later become known as the discipline of artificial intelligence. The quality of actual translations, however, still remained largely below an acceptable level and required extensive postediting, as can be seen from the following example, an excerpt from a 1962 demonstration of the Georgetown GAT system, translated from the Russian original:

> By by one from the first practical applications of logical capabilities of machines was their utilization for the translation of texts from an one tongue on other. Linguistic differences represent the serious hindrance on a way for the development of cultural, social, political, and scientific connections between nations. Automation of the process of a translation, the application of machines, with a help which possible to effect a translation without a knowledge of a corresponding foreign tongue, would be by an important step forward in the decision of this problem.

Still, researchers in MT remained largely optimistic about the prospects of the field. "The translation machine. . ."—wrote Emile Delavenay in 1960—"is now on our doorstep. In order to set it to work, it remains to complete the *exploration of linguistic data*." When Yehoshua Bar Hillel published his critique of contemporary MT research [4,5], his was a minority opinion. Bar Hillel's central claim was that fully automatic high-quality machine translation was unattainable because of the inability of building computer programs for lexical disambiguation. His now famous example was the following paragraph:

Little John was looking for his toy box. Finally, he found it. *The box was in the pen.* John was very happy.

The word "pen" in the emphasized sentence above has at least two meanings; a writing pen and a playpen. Bar Hillel's conclusion was that "no existing or imaginable program will enable an electronic computer to determine that the word *pen* in the given sentence within the given context has the second of the above meanings."

Since Bar Hillel was one of the early champions of MT and had intimate knowledge of the research in the field, his critique has had a wide resonance in the public attitudes toward MT as well as among its sponsors in U.S. government and industry. Coupled with the increased difficulty of problems facing MT research after the initial successes, and notwithstanding the fact that many of the then current projects (notably at Georgetown and IBM) pursued exactly the type of MT research recommended by Bar Hillel, namely, a combination of machine translation with human postediting, this criticism started the process of reassessment of attitudes toward the field. The reassessment culminated in the publication in 1966 of a report by the influential Automatic Language Processing Advisory Committee organized in 1964 by the National Academy of Sciences. The ALPAC [6] report, as it came to be known, was critical of the state of the art in MT and recommended drastic reductions in the level of support for MT research. The ALPAC report was sharply (and appropriately) criticized as biased and inaccurate. Many of its assessments, however, were correct, especially those dealing with the evaluation of practicality of MT research. In retrospect, the strongest negative effect of ALPAC was not so much the reduction in funding as the damage to the status of MT as a scientific endeavor in the United States.

The early MT projects, indeed, failed to reach their stated goal of building systems of good quality, fully automated translation in broad domains. The principal mistake of the early MT workers was, however, one of judgment: the complexity of the conceptual problem of natural language understanding was underestimated. The variety and the sheer amount of knowledge that must be used in any solution of this problem proved to be enormous, so that the success of MT as an application became dependent on the solution of this problem. It would take more than fifteen years for MT to start a scientific comeback.

While the ALPAC report effectively brought MT programs in the United States to a halt, research and development continued in several scientific groups in the Soviet Union, Canada, Germany, France, and Italy, as well as in a small number of commercial institutions in the United States. Notable achievements of MT in the 15 years after the ALPAC report included the development and everyday use of the first unquestionably successful MT system, TAUM-Meteo, developed at the University of Montreal, Canada, and used routinely to translate weather reports from English into French. The MT program Systran has been used during the *Soyuz–Apollo* space experiment in 1975, and in the following year was officially adopted as a translation tool of the European Economic Community (EEC).

The beginning of the revival of MT as a scientific discipline and an application of linguistic and computer technology must, however, be traced to the establishment of the Eurotra project and the MT effort in Japan. Begun in 1978, Eurotra is an ambitious, well-supported project aimed at providing MT capability among all official languages of the EEC (Danish, Dutch, English, French, German, Greek, Italian, Portuguese, and Spanish). At present, Eurotra employs about 160 researchers in a number of national groups and at the project headquarters in Luxembourg. The current generation of Japanese MT efforts started around 1980, supported both by the government (notably, within the Fifth Generation Computing project) and by industry.

The above developments gradually led to a revival of MT research in the United States. In 1983, the National Science Foundation approved a research grant, albeit a small one, for MT work, the first such action in two decades. MT activities at various scientific meetings have significantly intensified, and several conferences devoted specifically to MT have been organized recently. New research groups have been set up, notably, the Center for Machine Translation at Carnegie-Mellon University, with a staff of about 30. The importance of MT has been underscored by the resonance of MT Summit and MT Summit II, a congress, held in Japan in 1987, and in West Germany in 1989, respectively, which attracted researchers, users and sponsors of MT from all over the world, members of academia, governmental institutions, industrial entities, and multinational bodies, such as EEC. The general mood of the conference was one of optimism and the realization that the need for MT in modern world is even more pressing than it was 40 years ago.

The new optimism of MT researchers and sponsors is based on spectacular advances in computer technology (drastic improvements in processing speed and memory capacity, advances in computer architecture, emergence of database technology, development of high-level programming languages, and interactive programming environments, etc.) and computational linguistics (in particular, techniques for morphological and syntactic analysis and synthesis of natural language texts). Advances in automatic processing of meaning and techniques of human-computer interaction are also an important component of the current MT paradigms. With the knowledge of the past difficulties, and therefore, with a realistic assessment of the possibilities of MT technology application, the current MT projects are well equipped to produce a new wave of scientifically nontrivial and practically adequate machine translation systems both to compete and to cooperate with humans in translating a wide variety of scientific, industrial, official, journalistic, and other texts.

MACHINE TRANSLATION TECHNIQUES

The task of MT can be defined very simply:

1. Obtain a text in one language (SL, for sourcelanguage) and understand its meaning
2. Produce a text in another language (TL, for target language), so that the meaning of the TL text is the same as the meaning of the SL text

The successful completion of the former task is a prerequisite for the latter. We will therefore concentrate at first on the understanding facet of MT work. A number of important questions can be raised at this point:

1. How does one set out to extract the meaning of a text?
2. How does one represent the meaning of a text?
3. What *is* this meaning?
4. Is it absolutely necessary to extract it (or at least *all* of it) in order to translate?

Question 3 is a basic problem in linguistics and philosophy of language. We cannot even circumscribe all of its facets here. We will have to take a more operational approach to discussing the problem of the meaning of MT. Question 2 relates to the problem of knowledge representation, either in the style it is done in artificial intelligence or in a more traditional sense, as in lexicography. Question 1 highlights the computational problems of such an enterprise as MT. All the above are difficult problems, and no definitive solutions have been suggested at this stage of the development of the field of computational linguistics and AI. It is in this light that one must interpret Question 4. Is there a possibility that success in a particular application area, such as MT, is not contingent on producing workable solutions for the above problems? The rest of this section is devoted to a discussion of the depth of meaning analysis necessary for determining the translation of a text.

Human translators use dictionaries as sources of information about SL and TL. The type of dictionary that is most often used by humans is the bilingual dictionary, which incorporates correspondence units of SL and TL. By design, this SL–TL mapping seeks to preserve meaning. And, since meaning is the invariant between the SL and TL texts in translation, such dictionaries must serve the purpose adequately. An important point to remember, however, is that bilingual dictionaries, as we know them, are designed for human use. People possess a great ability to "make sense" of language units. This makes the task of the lexicographer simpler in that not all aspects of meaning have to be absolutely laid out; people will be able to understand even a flawed explanation. The situation is quite different when the dictionary is used by a computer program. Let us illustrate the types of dictionaries and processing modules that will become necessary in this case.

BUILDING AN MT SYSTEM

Suppose the system obtains the German text (1) as input.

(1) Das Buch liegt auf dem Tisch.

The English translation of (1) is (2).

(2) The book is on the table.

The dictionary necessary to perform this translation is as follows:

German	English
auf	on
Buch	book
das	the
dem	the
liegt	is
Tisch	table

The translation program supplied is one that substitutes the English words for their German counterparts, one by one. Do we have an MT system? Yes, a system of machine translation of the German sentence (1) into English. Indeed, it is only under certain constraints that "liegen" should be translated as "be." Can we use the same system to go from English into German? No, because we have a one-to-many relationship from "the" to "das" and "dem." Our knowledge, as recorded in the dictionary, is insufficient to resolve this ambiguity, and we have no additional knowledge to help us make the proper choice. This is the first time we observe that MT research can be viewed as a process of accumulating knowledge that facilitates making correct choices of output. Now, to translate (2) into Russian, we will need the dictionary as follows:

English	Russian
a	#
book	kniga
is	#
on	na
table	stole
the	#

Sentence (2) will be, therefore, translated into Russian as (3).

(3) Kniga na stole.

Interestingly enough, (3) is also the translation of (4):

(4) The book is on a table.

The above suggests, somewhat unexpectedly, that the articles do not have meaning in English. This, of course, is not true. We will return to the question of how the articles influence the translation later. Note also that the Russian word "stole" is in fact one of 10 different words (corresponding to different case and number values) that will in real texts correspond to the English "table" in its meaning of a piece of furniture. We will not, however, discuss morphological analysis here. Morphological analyzers have been built for many languages, including such morphologically rich ones as Hebrew or Finnish.

Once again, we can see that it is impossible to use the same dictionary for a back translation of (3) into English. There is no indication where to put (if at all) the words that correspond to zero strings in Russian. This example shows that more knowledge has to be introduced into the system. For instance, the fact that class nouns, when used in their singular forms in English sentences, must be preceded by an article (a, the), a demonstrative (this, that . . .), a possessive (e.g., my, their), a question-word (e.g., what, which, whose), or the quantifier one. This is a part of the knowledge about the syntax of English.

The knowledge and difficulties described above were well known to the early MT researchers. One way of coping with these problems for them was to build the so-called "direct" translation systems that were specifically designed with a particular SL and a particular TL, and in which analysis of TL actually depended on what the TL was. Most of the early MT systems were direct, and the large production-level systems of the 1970s, such as Systran or Spanam, were also built on this principle. The rules on which they operated can be exemplified by the following excerpt from the set of rules used in the Ramo-Woolridge Russian-English MT project (quoted from Hutchins, [2] and slightly edited to facilitate understanding):

If in the SL text the word DO follows within eight words of OT in any sentence, translate the Russian OT as the English FROM and the Russian DO as the English TO

If in the SL text ZA is followed by a symbol, translate it into English as PER, otherwise, as FOR or DURING

To translate the Russian NET do the following: if OF was inserted into the TL before a potential genitive at the beginning of a word block preceding or following NET, suppress the English equivalent for NET and substitute THERE IS NO for OF

In general, the processing in direct translation systems is organized as illustrated in Figure 1.

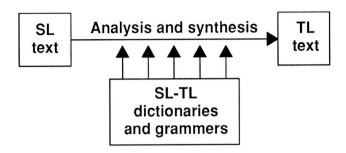

FIGURE 1.

In an advanced direct translation system the processing is typically divided into many sequential steps, most of them are language pair-specific. The following is the set of processes used by Systran for translating a SL sentence:

1. Morphological analysis of SL words
2. Resolution of homographs based on grammatical categories of words in immediate context
3. Detection of compound nouns (e.g., error message)
4. Identification of the boundaries of noun and verb groups and other phrases
5. Identification of dependency relations (agreement, government, parataxis) inside phrases
6. Identification of conjunction (including punctuation) and conjoined phrases (needed, e.g., to determine that in a phrase such as "old men and women" the conjoined elements are the two nouns, while the adjective modifies the entire conjunction, not just the noun "men")
7. Identification of the functional structure of the sentence, primarily, of its subject and predicate
8. Analysis of prepositional phrases
9. Translation of idiomatic expressions
10. Translation of prepositions
11. Resolution of remaining translation ambiguties, using the information in the main bilingual dictionary
12. Translation of remaining lexical units
13. Word order rearrangement

The above process uses a type of syntactic knowledge that was not tapped in our earlier examples, specifically, the knowledge of lexical categories of words. However, unlike in earlier MT systems, we can now derive the syntactic structure of SL texts within a theoretically motivated framework of generative grammar. The knowledge of the syntactic structure of (5) helps us to decide whether "coach" is a noun or a verb; "lost," a verb or an adjective; "set," a noun, a verb, or an adjective. The knowledge of English syntax is sufficient to eliminate this 12-way ambiguity and choose the correct reading. This type of knowledge is recorded in a "grammar" of a SL in a modern MT system. A special processing unit (a syntactic parser) applies this knowledge to the input text and produces its syntactic structure. The dictionary now can have a separate entry for every distinct syntactic

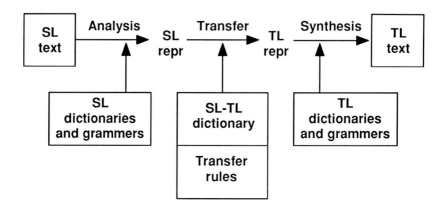

FIGURE 2.

reading of an SL word (so that, e.g., "set" will appear as the head of three entries, one each for this word's syntactic meaning of noun, adjective, and verb).

(5) The coach lost a set.

With the development of generative grammar methods for representing the syntactic structure of natural language sentences, it became clear for MT researchers that such analysis is best done based on the SL information alone, without a reference to a particular TL. The architecture of MT systems underwent a change, and the so-called *transfer* approach supplanted the direct translation paradigm. The architecture of a typical transfer MT system is illustrated in Figure 2. The process of translation in the transfer paradigm consists of three stages:

- Analysis of SL text
- SL—TL transfer
- Synthesis of TL text.

At the first stage, the SL text is analyzed, most often, morphologically and syntactically, without any reference to a particular TL language. A grammar of SL is used as the main source of knowledge. The result of this stage is typically a syntactic structure of the sentences in the input text, usually represented as a tree. Figure 3 shows some of the tree structures that can be used for representing the results of syntactic analysis of (5).

The results of analysis disambiguate the SL text to the point when it is easier for the transfer stage mechanisms to substitute lexical units and syntactic structures of SL by their counterparts in TL. Transfer processes rely on the information stored in bilingual SL–TL dictionaries and special transfer grammars that contain data about correspondences of syntactic structures in a particular SL–TL pair. Finally, the TL synthesis stage is responsible essentially for linearizing the TL trees obtained after transfer, according to the rules of a TL grammar.

Unfortunately, in some cases, syntactic knowledge is not sufficient for disambiguation. Thus, on purely syntactic grounds it is impossible to determine whether in (6a) the conjunction connects two nouns or a noun and a noun modified by an adjective (i.e.,

(1)

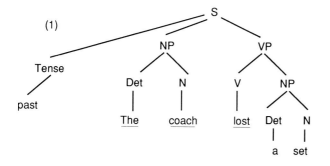

(2)

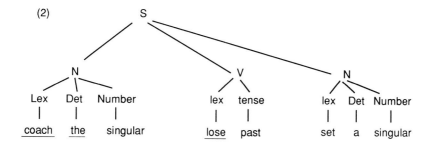

FIGURE 3.

conjunction connects two nouns or a noun and a noun modified by an adjective (i.e., whether the chairs are also white). Note that one cannot neglect to extract this type of knowledge, because the form of a potential translation may depend on the intended meaning. Thus (6a) will be translated into Hebrew as either (6b) or (6c).

(6a) White tables and chairs
(b) Shulhanot levanim vekisaot: (white tables) and (chairs)
(c) Shulhanot vekisaot levanim: White (tables) and (chairs)

Further types of ambiguities that syntactic knowledge fails to take care of include prepositional phrase attachment and decomposition of noun–noun compounds in English.

Even more profound evidence of the insufficiency of syntactic analysis for MT is presented by the commonplace lexical–semantic ambiguity of natural language. Thus, in a standard English–Russian dictionary the words "coach," "lose," and "set" from (5), in their correct syntactic meanings, detected by the syntactic analysis, have 6, 10, and 34 readings, respectively. This is a 2040-way ambiguity. (Incidentally, even though syntactic disambiguation leaves us with this multiple ambiguity, syntactic analysis is still very useful. After all, if the correct parts of speech are not detected, the number of readings for the three words is 11,15, 96, respectively, producing a 15,840-way ambiguity.)

It certainly says something about the disambiguating powers of humans that we can effortlessly assign this sentence a single meaning, with the only source of uncertainty in whether the game played was tennis, squash, or racquetball.

```
    Coach  lost   set    total
ways ambiguous, syntactically and semantically
     11    15     96     15840
ways ambiguous, syntactic ambiguity eliminated
      6    10     34     2040
```

As another example, consider the Russian sentence (7).

(7) Novaja partija byla luchshe vo vsex otnoshenijax

Taken out of context, this sentence does not contain any clue as to the appropriate meaning of the highly polysemous Russian word *partija*. The texts in (8) illustrate the correct translations when the context is provided.

(8a) [The old Liberal Center was too doctrinaire for his taste.] The new party was better in all respects.
(b) [The previous consignment contained substandard supplies.] The new batch was better in all respects.
(c) [In the previous game he did not notice a fork that cost him a rook, and lost.] The new game was better in all respects.

The choice of the appropriate TL correlate was facilitated for humans by the context. A Russian–English dictionary that would be able to distinguish the alternatives will have to have special context identification markers, as in (9). These context markers are semantic in nature. They suffice for human translators. MT systems should, however, possess special means of identifying the semantic context and acting upon its recognition. This task has been a central concern of the subfield of natural language processing within AI, and was found to require much more information to be stored in the computer than simply the semantic markers such as those in (9) or those used in the dictionaries of such MT systems as Metal. In addition, the set of semantic markers should be made consistent and expressive enough to cover all the necessary shades of meaning in a particular domain of discourse, since even the descriptions of the same objects will require different granularity of distinctions for translating texts in different domains of discourse. Thus, describing the concept of land in a political context will be different from the description of the same concept in the domain of, say, agronomy.

(9) *Partija,* noun, feminine. 1. (political) party; 2. (commerce) batch; 3. (chess) game.

In order to automate semantic analysis one must, first of all, devise a principled way of representing the meaning of the input text with the help of a complete system of semantic markers and then provide rules of using such a representation to extract the necessary knowledge about the context. The large number of semantic markers necessary to describe a reasonably rich subworld, the fact that they stand in well-defined relationships to other markers, and the total absence of any natural language material in the representation are characteristics of AI-oriented approaches to meaning extraction. The notations used in AI systems are rich enough to be called semantic interpretation languages. In AI they are called knowledge representation languages; in MT they are traditionally called *interlinguae*. If the analysis module of an MT system can produce a representation of an SL text in terms of a natural language-independent interlingua (IL), and the synthesis module of such a system can obtain this IL text as input and produce a TL text, then the transfer stage of the MT process can be avoided. Moreover, bilingual dictionaries will be rendered superfluous, since SL and TL will not be in any direct contact. And this means that once an IL text is produced from a certain input it can then be used to generate texts in any number of TLs, thus facilitating multilingual MT. A significant economy of effort ensues, due to the fact that there will be no need to compile bilingual dictionaries and transfer grammars for each SL/TL pair, but instead only two dictionaries for each natural language: one for the SL-IL translation and the other for the IL-TL translation. This economy of effort is illustrated in Figure 4.

In general, the interlingua approach can be considered a logical extension of the transfer approach, where the "length" of the transfer stage has shrunk to become a point (cf. Fig. 5).

MT researchers understood the advantages of the interlingua approach to MT very early. However, the task of semantic interpretation of SL texts has proved too difficult for the early MT efforts. One of the first attempts to use semantic analysis, that is, to use a knowledge representation language in MT, was made within the Yale AI school. The Conceptual Dependency knowledge representation language [e.g., 7] was used to represent the meaning of the input sentence. The experimental MT systems that were built in this school used background knowledge about the world to infer information not explicitly mentioned in the input sentence, in order to be able to disambiguate it. This background knowledge usually described typical complex event sequences, called "scripts," that are common in certain subworlds. Thus, the knowledge that the event described in (5) belongs to the $TENNIS script, helps disambiguate this sentence completely by suggesting the

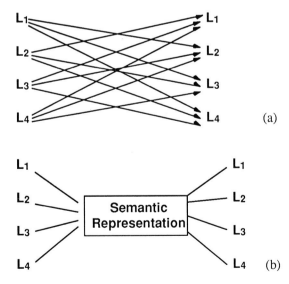

FIGURE 4. (a) Transfer approach: N(N–1) processes. (b) Interlingua approach: 2N processes. For N = 72, transfer = 5,112, interlingua = 144 processes.

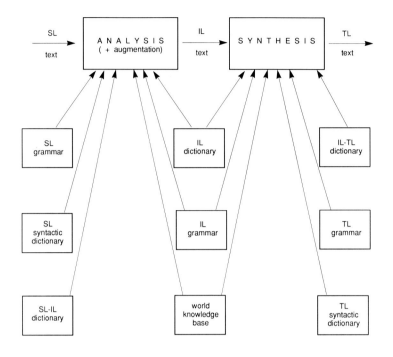

FIGURE 5.

appropriate readings for the words "coach" and "set." Once the meanings of the input sentence have been represented in the interlingua, with the help of scripts and using conceptual dependency, a set of discrimination nets, with choice points marked by particular units of semantic knowledge, are used at the generation stage of the system to connect interlingua meanings and TL words and phrases.

Schematically, the process of translation in such systems can be illustrated as follows [we use the example from Ref. 8]. Suppose, for instance, that the sentence (9) has been supplied as the input to the translation program. The sentence will be analyzed (translated into the conceptual dependency language) as (10). The dictionary that the analyzer will use will connect the English verb "hit" with a "frame" in which there will be a slot for "action," occupied by the marker PROPEL (which is not to be interpreted as an English word!) and a slot for "force" which will be filled by the marker ABOVE-AVERAGE. The slots for "agent," "object," and "instrument" will be listed in the dictionary without fillers. It is the responsibility of the analyzer to create an interlingua structure for the new event, using the representation of "hit," taken from the dictionary, as its nucleus, and to find fillers for the slots that are unoccupied. It is predominantly for the purpose of identifying these slot fillers that the system uses scripts and other background knowledge.

(9) Mary hit John.

(10) (event EV001
            (action PROPEL)
            (agent MARY)
            (object JOHN)

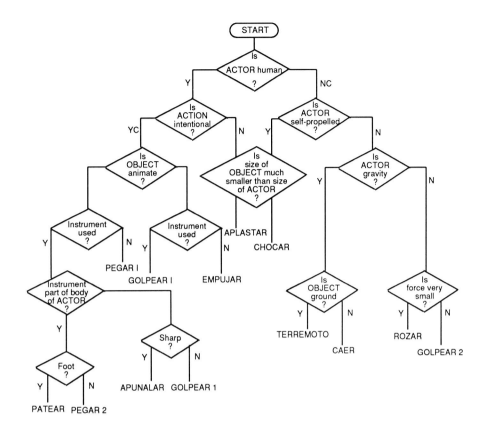

FIGURE 6.

(instrument *UNKNOWN*)
(force *ABOVE-AVERAGE*)
(intentionality *POSITIVE*))

In order to translate (10) into Spanish, a discrimination net such as that in Figure 6 must be used. The aim is to choose the appropriate verb to render the IL action PROPEL in Spanish.

In the case of generating (10) *pegar* will be chosen.

The kind of analysis performed by this type of system is, however, far from sufficient. A number of choices still remain unresolved even at this level of semantic processing. It appears that the script information alone is insufficient to resolve all the text ambiguities. Additional types of choices remain unaccounted for. Let us briefly illustrate them.

If (11) is uttered by a boss in a conversation with a subordinate, it should be translated into Russian as (12); if it is uttered in a conversation between a homeowner and a reluctant housepainter, it should rather be translated as (13). This example highlights the influence of the speech act character of the utterance (an order in the first case; a plea in the second) on the representation of its meaning and, therefore, its eventual translation.

(11) Will you please start working on the project?
(12) Bud'te dobry, nachnite rabotu nad proektom.
(13) Ne mogli by vy nachat' rabotu nad proektom?

In a standard conceptual analysis system, all six Russian sentences in (14) will be assigned the same meaning. The word order permutations are, however, significant in that they contribute to the meaning of the sentence. In (15) the English translations of the nonemphatic readings of the sentences in (14) are listed. The sentences in (15) differ in what is considered (by the speaker) already known and what is considered new information in these sentences. Establishing these distinctions is known as thematic analysis of text. Note that, while in Russian these distinctions are marked by word order, in English word order is accompanied by the choice of indefinite and definite articles (indefinite articles typically introduce noun phrases that are new). Thus, we find that English articles do, after all, carry a meaning. Note that in (14a) the new information can be either the prepositional phrase *v komnatu* or the entire verb phrase *voshel v komnatu*. In the former case the indefinite article must be used; in the latter, the definite. The remaining ambiguity in (14f) is of a different origin: the new information in it is that the man came into a/the room and not into some other place.

(14) (a) Chelovek voshel v komnatu
      (b) V komnatu voshel chelovek
      (c) Voshel chelovek v komnatu
      (d) Voshel v komnatu chelovek
      (e) V komnatu chelovek voshel
      (f) Chelovek v komnatu voshel
(15) (a) The man came into a/the room
      (b) Into the room came a man
      (c) Came the man into the room
      (d) A man came into the room
      (e) It was a man that came into the room
      (f) It was into a/the room that the man came

Sometimes it is difficult or impossible, while processing a text, to evoke a standard script or even a more general memory organization packet (MOP) that relates texts with typical abstract settings and events remembered from past experience. But it may help enormously if just the subworld to which the text belongs could be determined. Thus, (16) [9] will be translated in two clearly distinct manners depending on whether the text belongs to the subworld of jail or prizefighting. Of course, it is not an easy task to detect the subworld automatically.

(16) Rocky slowly got up from the mat, planning his escape. He hesitated a moment and thought. Things were not going well. What bothered him most was being held, especially since the charge against him had been weak. He considered his present situation. The lock that held him was strong, but he thought he could break it.

One must also have means of understanding elliptic construction. Ellipsis is an ordinary and necessary feature of all input texts, not an aberration. Thus, one has to be able to understand (17) if it appears in a text after (18). Special types of knowledge and processing arrangements are necessary for this task.

(17) Six, to be precise.

(18) There are several flights from Atlanta to Pittsburgh on Tuesday.

The problem of anaphoric reference also involves a number of knowledge-based choices. Knowledge is needed for the computer to be able to find the referents for "there" and "they" in (19), as well as the beginning of the list of problems referred to there. Note that one cannot, in the general case, translate (19) without understanding, that is, simply using corresponding pronouns in TL. This is because in some languages additional choices have to be explicitly made. For example, translating (19) into Hebrew, one will have to make a choice between the masculine and the feminine gender form of "they." In order to do this, one has to determine the anaphoric referent for the pronoun. Anaphoric phenomena cover not only pronouns but also definite noun phrases. In order to translate (20) [*10*, p. 56], one has to understand that all the italicized noun phrases in this text refer to one concept token. Indeed, a straightforward translation of this passage into, say, Russian would be difficult. A human translator would not use *ispanec* (Russian for Spaniard) to translate the noun phrase in the last sentence. It will be similarly impossible to translate the indefinite noun phrase *a man* as such into Russian if complete understanding of coreference relation in this text is not achieved.

(19) There they found many additional problems.

(20) Priest is charged with Pope attack.

(Lisbon, May 14) *A dissident Spanish priest* was charged here today with attempting to murder the Pope. *Juan Fernandez Krohn, aged 32,* was arrested after *a man armed with a bayonet* approached the Pope while he was saying prayers at Fatima on Wednesday night. According to the police, *Fernandez* told the investigating magistrates today *he* trained for the past six months for the assault. *He* was alleged to have claimed the Pope 'looked furious' on hearing *the priest's* criticism of his handling of the church's affairs. If found guilty, *the Spaniard* faces a prison sentence of 15–20 years.

The Times, May 15, 1982.

It is at approximately this level of understanding of the input text meaning that the number of its legal readings becomes comparable with that recognized by human translators. The state of the art in the field is such, however, that no actual or even experimental MT system at present can detect all or even many of the facets of the semantic, contextual and rhetorical meaning. Potentially, however, there are additional levels of sophistication that can be added to an MT system. Thus, for instance, style considerations will often be important during the generation stage of the operation of an MT system. The study of these factors (one can call it computational stylistics) has not yet come into the focus of attention of the MT research community. Natural language generation as such has been extensively studied in the context of dialogue, question–answering systems (most often, to generate computer responses in the natural language front ends of database systems). Work on powerful MT generators has been begun only very recently.

Another possible avenue of research, which is still an uncharted terra incognita, is the study of the craft of the human translator as an expert task. Translators are experts. In this age of expert systems it is unlikely that no thought be given to studying the process of translation from this point of view. Some difficulties arise, of course. One important questions is, whether the expertise of the translator transcends the knowledge of the two languages and the knowledge of the subject of the translation. If the answer is yes, then the expert system approach may prove interesting, because it will be a way of extracting this additional knowledge and learning to use it in a computer system. Naturally, it may prove impossible to extract that knowledge efficiently. It seems, however, that such knowledge exists: we intuitively believe that experienced translators know how to do translations better than novices. This may have to do with their ability to express their understanding of the SL text better. Indeed, it is the case that the translatorial agencies consider it more important for a (human) translator to know TL better than SL.

THE CHOICES

The deeper the desired level of analysis of a text, the more difficult it is to achieve with the help of computers, and, therefore, given the state of the art in the field, the less feasible it is at present to build an MT system that benefits from that level of analysis. Indeed, even syntactic parsers and grammars of sufficient generality cannot be taken off the shelf and used without major modifications. Semantic analyzers are scarce and provide at best a partial coverage of the world of concepts necessary for translation. Modules capable of analyzing the rhetorical content of the utterance or its discourse structure are even more remote. A significant amount of research is currently under way on the problems of semantic and pragmatic analysis of natural language. But this research is predominantly theoretical.

Is there a possibility to simplify or avoid complete analysis and still achieve tangible results in MT? The answer is a qualified yes. There are two major avenues of circumventing the problem of completely automatic disambiguation. First, one can restrict the grammar and the vocabulary of the input text in such a way that most of the ambiguity is thus eliminated. This is the sublanguage or subworld approach to MT. Second, one can drop the requirement of complete automation and allow humans to get involved in the translation process. As we will see, there are a number of ways in which this process of machine-*aided* translation can be organized. The difference between these approaches is not only in the tactics of interspersing the automated and manual steps in the process of translation, but also in the nature of the subtasks for which humans are responsible.

Those who contemplate building an MT system must weigh the particular requirements in terms of quality, allowed development time and breadth of coverage of their projects before deciding what level of automation is the most appropriate for them. A simplified rule of thumb is: the less time allowed for research and development, the shallower the analysis module and, therefore, the deeper the involvement of humans in the translation process.

Restricting the Ambiguity of SI Text

The best example of the sublanguage approach is the operational MT system TAUM-Meteo, developed at the University of Montreal and delivered to the Canadian Weather Service for everyday routine translations of weather reports from English into French. The system operates very successfully, practically without human intervention. Its vocabulary consists of about 1500 items, about half of which are place names. The syntactic constructions that occur in the variant of English used as SL in TAUM-Meteo constitute a relatively small subset of English syntactic constructions. There is very little semantic ambiguity in the system, since it is always expected that ambiguous words are used in the context of their meanings which belongs to the subworld of weather phenomena (for instance, the word front in TAUM-Meteo will be understood unequivocally as a weather front). Finding well-delineated, self-sufficient and useful small sublanguages is a very difficult task, and this is one reason why the success of TAUM-Meteo was not repeated by any other operational system.

Partial Automation of Translation

The demand for MT is high and growing, most of it in subject areas whose corresponding sublanguages are much richer, and, consequently, less feasible, than that of weather forecasts (as the Montreal group quickly learned when they tried, with quite limited success, to extend their system to the subject area of aircraft maintenance manuals). To deal with the demand for automation of translation today one has to think of ways of using the knowledge and knowhow already available in the field to provide a certain degree of automation of the translation process. Practically all operational and experimental MT systems feature some human involvement, and it is safe to say that in the immediate future one can expect this involvement to decrease but not to disappear completely.

There are two major classification dimensions for MT systems featuring partial automation. They may be classified according to:

1. The actual share of work performed by humans rather than the computer (the degree of automation)
2. The strategy of human involvement: whether the humans work on the text *before, during* or *after* the computer deals with it (there is, of course the possibility of combining some or all of these three strategies)

In accordance with the degree of automation involved, MT systems range from relatively simple interactive editing and dictionary look-up tools for the use of human translators (the type of activity supported by such systems is known as machine-aided human translation, MAHT) to quite sophisticated systems, most of them still experimental, that involve syntactic and sometimes even semantic analysis and provide a much higher level of automation of the translation process (these systems perform human-aided machine translation, HAMT). The achievement of fully automated good quality translation remains a distant but, for some projects, persistent goal.

The philosophy of the MAHT approach is best expounded by Alan Melby of Brigham Young University. He recognizes three levels of human-computer interaction in developing what he calls a translator workstation. Level One Workstation, the least sophisticated one, essentially presupposes a complete and convenient word processing environment with convenient means of accessing on-line dictionaries and encyclopedias. Level Two Workstation adds the spelling checks, concordances and text dictionaries and presupposes that the text to be translated is in machine-readable form. Level Three Workstation involves a degree of automatic processing, including, possibly, some analysis. Melby is not specific about what particular means are available at this level, but it is clear that such a workstation is somewhere in between MAHT and HAMT.

With respect to the strategy of human involvement, the three basic possibilities have come to be known as preediting, postediting, and interactive editing. A human preeditor reads the input text and modifies it in such a way that the MT system is able to process it automatically. Difficult and overly ambiguous words and phrases are replaced with those that the editor knows the program will handle. A human posteditor obtains the output from an MT system and eliminates all inaccuracies and errors in it. An interactive editor engages in a dialogue with the MT system, in which the human resolves ambiguities that the machine is not capable of resolving itself. It is, of course, necessary to build a special interface to maintain the dialogue. The types of questions asked can also vary: the computer may ask the human to provide a TL correlate for an ambiguous SL unit or may ask to be provided with the meaning of an SL unit, in the language in which the meanings are represented in the system.

Interactive editing has become a viable alternative with the development, over the past decade, of sophisticated interactive programming environments. A disambiguation-oriented dialogue can include interactions as follows:

The word 'pen' means:

1) a writing pen
2) a play pen

NUMBER>>

To resolve referential ambiguity, a system can ask a question in the following manner:

The word 'she' refers to

1) 'Cathy'
2) 'my mother'
3) 'the sailboat'

NUMBER>>

The interactive word sense disambiguation can indeed be accomplished relatively easily. The referential ambiguity, though, will present a problem, because the program will have to be able to find the candidate (pronominal and other) referents, which is a nontrivial task in itself. The design of the interactive component to perform syntactic disambiguation may be difficult and the component itself, cost ineffective simply because it is not an everyday task for a human to compare syntactic structure trees. Semantic analysis, however, has a stronger disambiguating power and, therefore, syntactic disambiguation can be rendered unnecessary in an interediting system that relies on human intervention to choose the appropriate word senses.

Until very recently human intervention in the process of MT predominantly took the form of postediting, whereby the product of an MT system is submitted for editing by a human editor, exactly like human translations are in better translatorial agencies. (Preediting the SL text before submitting it to an MT program has also been discussed and used.) The important feature of this approach is that the posteditor is not required to know SL. In practice, however, many of the outputs of such systems come in such a garbled way that it becomes a major problem to edit them without dipping into the SL text.

In the systems that espouse the HAMT strategy with postediting (and a majority of current experimental systems belong to this group) feasibility and cost effectiveness become the major criteria for success. The postediting approach is based on the premise that MT can (and should) be performed without a complete understanding of SL texts by the computer. This belief is justified in terms of feasibility. What this approach means is that an MT system is essentially an aid in human-controlled translation.

The quality and depth of the disambiguation process, as determined by the quality of underlying conceptual models of language and world used in an MT system is an alternative criterion on the basis of which MT systems can be judged. If one accepts the position that the nature of human involvement should be not in correcting the (errorful) texts produced by the system, but rather provide the system with additional disambiguation knowledge that was not recorded in its knowledge base, one becomes able to judge an MT systems in terms of the latter criterion. The methodological basis for this approach is in the interactive editing approach with the dialogue aimed at gaining disambiguation knowledge, not the TL correlates that will be eventually obtained based on this knowledge. This approach is compatible with the research strategy of gradual movement toward fully automated translation and, therefore, its success depends on significant advances in basic research; the former approach is more of the engineering variety in that it aims at partial automation within the realm of what is feasible today. However, the postediting approach already produces results that are considered adequate for a number of purposes, while no large-scale system based on deep understanding has yet been put into operation. The tension between these two positions enlivens the MT research and development scene of the 1990s.

REFERENCES

1. M. Zarechnak, "The History of Machine Translation," in *Machine Translation* (B. Henisz-Dostert, R. R. McDonald, and M. Zarechnak, eds.), Mouton, The Hague, 1979.

2. J. Hutchins, *Machine Translation. Past, Present, Future,* Ellis Horwood Publishers, Chichester, England, 1986.

2a. S. Nirenburg (ed.), *Machine Translation: Theoretical and Methodological Issues,* Cambridge University Press, Cambridge, 1987.

3. W. Weaver, Translation, reprinted in *Machine Translation of Languages* (W. N. Locke and A. D. Booth, eds.), MIT Press, Cambridge, pp. 15-23.

4. Y. Bar Hillel, "Report on the State of Machine Translation in the United States and Britain," The Hebrew University of Jerusalem, Technical Report (1959).

5. Y. Bar Hillel, "The Present Status of Automatic Translation of Languages," *Adv. Comput., 1*, 91-163 (1960).

6. ALPAC, 1966.

7. R. Schank, *Conceptual Information Processing,* North Holland, Amsterdam, 1975.

8. J. G. Carbonell, R. E. Cullingford, and A. V. Gershman, "Steps Toward Knowledge-Based Machine Translation," *IEEE Transactions on Pattern Analysis and Machine Intelligence*, 1981.

9. R. Anderson, R. Reynolds, D. Schallert, and E. Goetz, "Frameworks for Comprehending Discourse," *Am. Educ. Res. J., 14*, 367-381 (1977).

10. G. Brown and G. Yule, *Discourse Analysis,* Cambridge University Press, Cambridge, 1983.

SERGEI NIRENBURG

MAGNETIC DISKS

INTRODUCTION

In the field of information processing, mainly two kinds of media are used for magnetic storage of data: magnetic tapes which move longitudinally and rotating magnetic disks. Their precursors were magnetic drums (i.e., rotating cylinders). The advantage of magnetic disks (compared with tapes) is a short access time combined with high storage capacities. In the future another group of rotating media will become more important: optical and magneto-optical disks (erasable and nonerasable).

CLASSIFICATION

Common Properties

Properties common to all types of magnetic disks and drives are as follows:

Disks are flat circular plates (rigid or flexible) coated on both sides with a magnetizable layer which has various properties (coating thickness, coercivity, lubrication).

Recording is performed in concentric tracks, unlike a record where there is only one "track" in a spiral line. The number of tracks is a significant parameter indicating the capacity and it varies over a wide range. Another parameter often used but less significant is the track density (i.e., the number of tracks per unit of radial length), expressed in tracks per mm (tpmm) or tracks per inch (tpi).

Each track has a track number, beginning with track 00 which is normally the outermost track.

A pair of tracks on each side of a disk with the same track number is called a cylinder. In the case of disk packs a cylinder consists of several tracks. For double-sided diskettes, two tracks with the same track number are called a "cylinder" though in this case the track radii are different and the geometric configuration is unlike a cylinder.

Each track is divided into sectors. These are small numbered parts of a track in which one data block can be stored.

One of the main characteristics of a drive for magnetic disks is the access time. This is the time interval between the instant where a call for data is initiated and the instant at which the delivery of data is available for transfer. The access time is mainly determined by the rotation speed and the time needed to move the magnetic head from one track to another.

Different Properties

Magnetic disks differ in several aspects

Construction:	rigid disks or flexible disks
Size:	various diameters
Configuration:	single disks; disk cartridges; disk packs
Operation:	removable disks; nonremovable, fixed disks; rotating speed
Storage capacity:	formatted capacity; unformatted capacity
Standardization:	standardized; nonstandardized

In the following sections some of these characteristics are described in more detail.

CONSTRUCTION

The "classical"type of rigid disk is that where the magnetic heads fly relatively "high" above the disk surface. The flight height amounts to approximately $2\,\mu m$ ($80\,\mu in$). The flight condition evolves automatically due to the high speed of the rotating disk surface relative to the heads.

There are very strict requirements on the flatness and other surface properties. Sterile conditions are necessary for manufacture and operation. Even the smallest particles of dust can cause a "head crash," which normally damages not only the head itself but also one or several of the tracks on the recording surface. When this occurs, the disk can no longer be used and lost data may be very difficult to recover. The second type of rigid disk is the "Winchester disk," introduced around 1973. The surface of these disks is lubricated. The lubricant added to the coating material allows the head to be in contact with the disk surface during the head loading or unloading period. The head slides on the surface for "takeoff" and "landing." The flight height during normal operation is $\sim 0.4\,\mu m$ ($16\,\mu in.$), which, compared with that of the "classical" type, is considerably smaller. Winchester disks are consequently very sensitive to dust and must be well protected against any particle contamination by hermetic sealing of the housing. These disks are widely used for mass storage in personal computers, for instance.

Flexible disks have several designations. The "official" one used in standardization is the "Flexible Disk Cartridge" (FDC). Besides "floppy disk," in recent years the term "diskette" has become more and more popular.

Normal diskettes operate in the "in contact condition," that is, one or both heads are in direct contact with the medium. A good head-to-disk contact is an important prerequisite for correct write and read operations.

Comparing both head-to-medium conditions, the flying head for rigid disks and the head in contact with the surface of diskettes, the following can be stated: Contact means friction and consequently wear either of the head and/or of the coated surface, and as a result, the lifetime of heads and diskettes is limited. This is not the case for flying heads. Their lifetime and that of the medium is theoretically unlimited. Rigid disks are therefore more reliable.

SIZES

The diameters of the rigid disks most commonly used are: 356 (14), 266 (10.5), 230 (9), 200 (8), 130 (5.25), and 90 mm (3.5 in). The diameters of standardized diskettes are 200 (8), 130 (5.25), and 90 mm (3.5 in).

CONFIGURATIONS

Magnetic disks can be arranged in different configurations. Single disks are mainly used as fixed disks; such a disk cannot be removed from its drive. Removable single disks are always contained in a cartridge of which there are two types: top loaded and front loaded. A removable assembly of several magnetic disks is called a disk pack. Standardized disk packs contain up to 12 single disks. Fixed disks can also be composed of several disks which are not removable.

OPERATION

Removable disks can be mounted on and removed from either drive 1 or drive 2. In other words, removable disks can be used in different drives or data processing systems. A prerequisite for a general data interchange is, however, standardization, which does not exist for modern disks. In many cases, data interchange is restricted to the system of one manufacturer. Disk packs, disk cartridges, and diskettes belong to the group of removable disks. Nonremovable disks are fixed disks, usually of the Winchester type. One or several magnetic disks remain permanently installed in their drive. There are also "removable fixed" disks on the market. In this case, the fixed disk together with its drive can be removed from the system. This is a convenient solution if secret or confidential data stored on a fixed disk are to be protected. A significant operation parameter is the rotational speed. For standardized removable disk cartridges and disk packs, the number of revolutions is 2400 per minute. This figure is higher for fixed disks usually in the order of 3600 per minute.

   For flexible disk cartridges the number of revolutions is considerably lower: 200 mm (8in): 360/min, 130 mm (5.25 in); 300/min and 360/min, and 90 mm (3.5 in): 300/min and 600/min.

STORAGE CAPACITY

Seen from the users point of view, capacity is one of the most important characteristics. It indicates the amount of data which can be stored on a disk, normally expressed in bytes, kbytes, or Mbytes. It should, however, be noted that capacities are stated or calculated in two different ways and consequently, there are two different figures.

   The "unformatted capacity" of a disk is a fictitious figure; it does not indicate the real data capacity. Since this figure is always greater than that of the "formatted capacity," it is widely used in advertising. For the user, however, only the "formatted capacity" is important, as this figure tells him exactly what amount of data he really can store on his disk.

   What is the difference between these two kinds of specifications and how can the capacities be calculated?

Unformatted Capacity

The unformatted capacity is the maximum number possible of recordable bytes, disregarding any formatting. This means that it is assumed that each track is continuously and completely recorded with "zeros" or "ones" (depending on the recording method). The unformatted capacity of a disk is therefore the product of:

> The maximum number of bytes per track ×
> The number of tracks ×
> The number of recordable sides

The only minor problem is in calculating the number of bytes per track. For all standardized diskettes, the linear recording density is specified as: the number of flux transitions per radiant (ftprad). For modern modes of recording, for instance, modified frequency modulation (MFM), one flux transition represents one bit. A group of eight bits is a byte. The radian is the unit of angle. As opposed to the more popular unit, the degree, one radian corresponds to 360° divided by 2π. So the number of flux transitions for a track equivalent to one complete revolution of the disk, is therefore calculated as follows:

$$\frac{\text{flux transitions}}{\text{track}} = \frac{\text{flux transitions}}{\text{rad}} \times 2\pi = \frac{\text{bits}}{\text{track}}$$

$$\frac{\text{bytes}}{\text{track}} = \frac{1}{8} \frac{\text{bits}}{\text{track}}$$

There is a practical example: The unformatted capacity C_u of the 2 Mbyte 90 mm (3.5 in) diskette (15,916 ftprad, 80 tracks 2 sides) is:

$$C_u = \frac{2\pi \times 15,916 \times 80 \times 2}{8} = 2,000,063 \text{ bytes} \approx 2 \text{ Mbytes}$$

In some cases specifications for the linear density of magnetic disks are given in bits per mm (bpmm) or bits per inch (bpi). Such information is rather meaningless since at least for "normal" recording methods the density always depends on the track diameter. The density is lowest in the outermost track and highest in the innermost track. If a density is stated in bpi, it only makes sense in combination with an indicated track.

Formatted Capacity

For a certain standardized format, the real formatted capacity is the product of

> the number of data bytes per sector ×
> the number of sectors per track ×
> the number of tracks per side ×
> the number of sides

For the 2 Mbyte 90 mm (3.5 in) diskette using the standardized MS-DOS (Micro Soft Disk-Operating System) format, the formatted capacity C_f is

$$C_f = 512 \times 18 \times 80 \times 2 = 1,474,560 \text{ bytes} \approx 1.47 \text{ Mbyte}$$

For this type of diskette the formatted capacity is only 74% of the unformatted capacity.

STANDARDIZATION OF MAGNETIC DISKS

Why Standardization?

When standardized materials are mentioned, everyone thinks first of screws or writing paper formats. This is correct, since all interchangeable material must be standardized, otherwise no interchange is possible, so there are many standards for magnetic media. These standards have two main purposes:

> Specifications of the unrecorded media (dimensional magnetic and other physical characteristics) make physical interchange possible on different drives and also enable national and international trade to be carried on.
> Standards for recorded media in combination with labeling standards (recording methods, track layout, codes, format and labeling, file structure) enable data to be interchanged between data processing systems.

There are no standards for drives. All requirements needed by manufacturers for drives or magnetic heads are contained in the media standards.

Standardization Organizations

On the international level there are two organizations dealing with standardization in this field:

> The International Organization for Standardization (ISO)
> The International Electrotechnical Commission (IEC)

Until 1987, the Technical Committee TC97 (information processing systems) of ISO was responsible for the standardization of rigid and flexible disks. As the tasks of both international organizations were intermixed with regard to information processing, a new joint technical committee (JTC) was founded in 1988 (ISO/IEC/JTC1 "Information Technology").

On the national level there are several standardization institutes in different countries. In the United States, for instance, there is the American National Standards Institute (ANSI). National standards for magnetic disks and diskettes are more or less based on international standards. The trend in all countries is to make them identical with ISO standards, in recognition of the fact that differences will always cause problems.

The standards of the European Computer Manufacturers Association (ECMA) are also well known. These are normally created in a relatively short time, at least compared with the time-consuming procedures at ISO. In many cases, ECMA Standards are therefore "forerunners" of ISO standards and consequently, also of the national standards which follow. These ECMA standards are of great importance even though ECMA is not an "official" organization like ISO or IEC.

Sometimes, "de facto standards" or "industry standards" are mentioned, but it is not clear what is really meant by this. These expressions are sometimes used in cases where "normal" standards do not exist.

Extent of Standardization

The standards for the older types of magnetic disks and the standards for diskettes specify "minimum requirements for full data interchange." What is data interchange? It is not only the classical or typical case where a disk is demounted from a drive of system A, moved to another system B and mounted here on a drive in order to read the data written on system A. Interchange problems may for instance, also occur in operating a single PC in which a diskette-drive has to be replaced. In this case the new drive must be able to read the data written on the old drive.

The task of standardization is therefore to specify all the requirements for the magnetic disk and indirectly also for the drive, its write and read-electronic, the controllers, etc. The following may serve as an example: The standard for the 90 mm (3.5 in) diskette comprises more than 100 dimensions. Each dimension has a tolerance and even under worst-case conditions concerning the tolerances, influences of temperature and humidity, each diskette must work properly when interchanged.

For modern types of Winchester disks no standards exist either for the magnetic characteristics of the unrecorded disk, for the track format, or for labeling only. For the dimensions, other disks or diskettes serve as a pattern.

Standardized Magnetic Disks

There are two groups of disks which are standardized:

Removable rigid disks (disk cartridges, disk packs) as used in professional systems (e.g., in computing or data processing centers). For standardized types see Table 1.

Flexible disks, mainly used in personal computers and other small systems (word processing, CAD, CAM, CIM applications). For standardized types see Table 2.

PRESENT STATE OF TECHNOLOGY AND OUTLOOK

From the beginning of magnetic recording technology, the following trends have been observed: Smaller dimensions of the media, higher packing densities and capacities while at the same time, maintaining or—if possible—improving the reliability and all this at lower prices.

Dimensions

The progress made in recent years regarding magnetic disks is evident. The dimensions of rigid disks were reduced from 356 mm to (14 in) to 90 mm (3.5 in), and of flexible disks from 200 mm (8 in) to 90 mm (3.5 in).

What is to be expected in the future? Further miniaturization of the media only makes sense in a few cases. For instance, smaller diskettes[50 mm (2 in)] are used in the portable PCs or lap tops, where, however, the size of the drives, their weight and power consumption are probably more important than the size of the medium itself.

Packing Densities and Capacities

For rigid disks of the Winchester type, further progress in increasing the capacities may be expected. Memory technology is rapidly changing and magnetic disks have not yet reached their capacity peak. There are several possible ways to achieve higher storage capacities:

Increasing the linear recording density, that is, the number of flux transitions or recorded bits per unit of length along a track. In this case limits were recognized as far as conventional recording methods and coating materials are concerned. Certain technological innovations, like new head techniques (e.g., thin film or magnetoresistive heads) and new recording techniques (vertical recording) in combination with high coercitive coating (thin film media) made further progress possible or will do so in the future. For the time being, the highest linear densities are to ~ 1200 bits per mm (bpmm) [31,000 bits per inch (bpi)].

Increasing the track density. Higher densities of the tracks (i.e., smaller track widths and smaller distances between the tracks), can only be achieved using sophisticated servo track techniques to position the heads and keep them exactly on track. Optical techniques for the head positioning have also been announced. All this implies extremely high precision of the drive mechanism. At present fixed disks with a track density of 55 tracks/mm (tpmm) [1400 tracks per inch (tpi)] are on the market.

The first two ways mentioned serve to increase the physical bit density per area [cm^2 (in^2)]. A new technique using glass substrate instead of aluminum for rigid disks would also improve the areal density, as a smoother surface would induce the heads to fly closer to the surface. The Winchester technology started in 1973 with an areal density of 0.26 Mbits/cm^2 (1.7 Mbits/in^2). In 1988 the maximum areal density ran up to ~ 6 Mbits per cm^2 (40 Mbits/in^2). Experts predict that this density will increase by a factor of 3 within the next 5 years.

Another way to increase the formatted capacity of fixed disks is to take advantage of the fact that using conventional track formats (constant number of sectors per track), the linear density at the outer tracks is considerably lower than that of the inner tracks. More effective recording methods (constant density or zone bit recording) and also encoding schemes ["Run length limited" code (RLL)] or data compression techniques result in higher capacities.

The following are a few examples of the storage capacities (unformatted) of fixed disks as of 1988:

90 mm (3.5 in), 2 disks: 50 Mbyte
130 mm (5.25 in), 8 disks: 765 Mbyte
200 mm (8 in) packs: close to 1 Gigabyte

TABLE 1. Standardized Rigid Magnetic Disks

ISO Standard	ANSI Standard	Size	Designation	Characteristics	
Unlubricated disks					
2864	X3.46–1983	356 mm	Six -disk pack	Capacity	7Mbytes
				Tracks	200
3561	–	14 in	Track format	Recording density	1100 bpi
3562	–	356 mm	Single disk cartridge (top loaded)	Capacity	5 Mbytes
				Tracks	200
3563	–	14 in	Track format	Recording density	2200 bpi
3564	X3.58–1984	356 mm	Eleven–disk pack	Capacity	54 Mbytes
				Tracks	400
		14 in		Recording density	2200 bpi
4337	X3.63–1981	356 mm	Twelve–disk pack	Capacity	100 Mbytes
				Tracks	404
		14 in		Recording density	4040 bpi
5653	X3.64–1981	356 mm	Twelve–disk pack	Capacity	200 Mbytes
				Tracks	808
		14 in		Recording density	4040 bpi
6902	–	356 mm	Single–disk	Capacity	$\approx$ 20 Mbytes
		266 mm		Tracks	$\approx$ 800
		14 in		Recording density	4040 bpi
		10.5 in			
	X3.52–1987		Single–disk cartridge (front loaded)	Recording density	2200 bpi

Model	Standard	Size	Type	Specification	Value
	X3.89–1981		Single–disk cartridge (front loaded) double density	Recording density	200 tpi
				Recording density	2200 bpi
	X3.76–1981		Single–disk cartridge (top loaded)	Recording density	200 tpi
				Recording density	4400 bpi

Lubricated disks

Model	Standard	Size	Type	Specification	Value
6901	X3.112–1984	356 mm / 14 in	Single disk	Capacity	≈ 50 Mbytes
				Tracks	≈ 800
				Recording density	≈ 10,000 bpi
7297	X3.120–1984	200 mm / 8 in	Single disk	Capacity	≈ 70 Mbytes
				Tracks	≈ 1650
				Recording density	≈ 20,000 bpi
7298	X3.119–1984	210 mm / 8.3 in.	Single disk	Capacity	≈ 50 Mbytes
				Tracks	≈ 800
				Recording density	≈ 20,000 bpi
7929	X3.128–1986	130 mm / 5.25 in	Single disk	Capacity	≈ 38 Mbytes
				Tracks	≈ 1200
				Recording density	≈ 15,000 bpi
	X3.115–1984	356 mm / 14 in	Trident pack	Capacity	≈ 80 Mbytes
				Track density	≈ 370 tpi
				Recording density	≈ 6000 bpi
8679	X3.155–1987	5.25 in	Removable cartridge		

Note: Capacity figures are based on the unformatted capacity for both sides of a disk. For most of the disk types standards for the track format do not exist.

For the lubricated disks the figures for capacity, number of tracks, and recording density are approximated.

TABLE 2. Standardized Flexible Disk Cartridges (Unrecorded) and Their New International Designations

Type No.	ISO Standard	ANSI Standard	Size mm (in)	Sides	Tracks per Side	Unformatted Capacity	Formatted Capacity[b]
ISO 101	5654/1	X3.73–1980	200 (8)	1	77	0.4	0.246
ISO 102	7065/1	X3.121–1984	200 (8)	2	77	1.6	1.136[c]
ISO 201	6596/1	X3.82–1980	130 (5.25)	1	40	0.125	0.073
ISO 202	7487/1	X3.125–1985	130 (5.25)	2	40	0.5	0.368[d]
ISO 203	8378/1	X3.126–1986	130 (5.25)	2	80	1.0	0.737[d]
ISO 204	8630/1	X3.162[a]	130 (5.25)	2	80	1.6	1.228[d]
ISO 301	8860/1	X3.137[a]	90 (3.5)	2	80	1.0	0.737[d]
ISO 302	9529/1	[a]	90 (3.5)	2	80	2.0	1.474[d]

[a]In preparation.
[b]The formatted capacity depends on the format used.
[c]For 512 data bytes per sector.
[d]Figures based on "Format B" (MSDOS).

Access Time

Further progress is also to be expected concerning the access time. The average seek time for drives manufactured in 1988 is in the order of 16–25 ms. In the future this time could possibly be reduced to 10 ms.

Reliability

Measures of the reliability of magnetic disks and drives are the "Mean time between failures" (MTBF) and the "bit error rate." Some of the figures indicated in the data sheets of drive manufacturers are given here:

> The MTBF, defined as "for a stated period in the life of a drive mean value of time (in hours) between consecutive failures under stated conditions" amounts to 20,000 to 50,000 "power on hours" (POH). (50,000 hours correspond to 5.7 years).

Such figures look very good, however, the user should know that "Mean" time means that 50% of the drives will exceed the time stated without failure. He can only hope that his drive belongs to this half and not to the other one.

> The bit error rate is a measure of the quality of a drive. It indicates the number of erroneous bits per read bits. Some typical figures are:
>
> Soft error rate: 1 in $10^{10} \ldots 10^{11}$ bits read
> Hard (permanent) error rate: 1 in $10^{12} \ldots 10^{13}$ bits read

Costs

Increasing packing densities and storage capacities of magnetic disks result in falling costs. The usual way to indicate costs for memory devices is to give the price per capacity in Mbyte.

In 1980, one Mbyte cost US$185. At that time the areal density amounted to 0.15 Mbits/cm^2 (1 Mbit/in^2). In 1988 the costs were in the order of US$6 per Mbyte and the estimated price in 1993 will be US$1.75 per Mbyte.

BIBLIOGRAPHY

Cloke, B., *EDN*, 199–220 (March 1987).
Memory and Storage, Time-Life Books, Richmond, VA, 1987.
Ohr, S., *Electr. Des.*, 55–58 (September 1986).
Seither, M., *Mini-Micro Systems*, 23–26 (February 1987).
Special reports, *Electronics*, *61*, 52–81 (August 1988).
Standards of the American National Standards Institute (ANSI), see Table 1. 1430 Broadway, New York, NY 10018.
Standards of the International Organization of Standardization (ISO), see Table 1; ISO, P.O. Box 56, Geneva Switzerland.
Williams, T. *Computer Design*, 49–55 (February 1988).

HANS J. SCHROEDER

MANAGEMENT INFORMATION SYSTEMS

INTRODUCTION

In recent years, the concept of management information systems (MIS) has aroused considerable interest. This interest can be attributed to the availability of a growing number of increasingly flexible and inexpensive systems now on the market. The newly developed hardware and software undoubtedly provides an opportunity to address the problem of rising office costs without requiring huge capital expenditure. However, the diffusion of information technology must be managed with care. Otherwise, the generation of undesirable side effects could compromise organizational activities.

Critical pressures exist, which necessitate well-managed information resources [1]. Some of these pressures are described below:

Rapid Changes in Technology

Technical and cost characteristics of hardware and software continue to evolve rapidly, offering substantially different and profitable approaches to application development. As technology changes, however, to ensure that an organization does not fall unwittingly into a proliferation of incompatible systems, planning becomes increasingly important.

Personnel Scarcity

The scarcity of trained, perceptive analysts and programmers, coupled with the long training cycles needed to make them fully effective, is a major restraining factor in the development of information systems.

Scarcity of Other Organizational Resources

Limited financial and managerial resources is another critical factor. Information systems provide only one of the many strategic investment opportunities available to a company, and cash invested in information systems is often at the expense of other critical areas. Hence, a review of both the effectiveness and the efficiency of these expenditures is a matter of some importance, being a critical limiting factor in setting up new projects, particularly in companies where profit and cost are significant factors.

To manage information resources, therefore, one needs insight into certain key questions: (1) How is computer technology absorbed into an organization? (2) What problems are encountered in absorbing these technologies? (3) What strategies exist for providing a better fit between the organization's information needs and the available technology? (4) How can the effectiveness of an organization's computer-based information systems (CBIS) be identified and measured?

These issues are discussed herein. First, the methodologies and frameworks proposed for describing the issues affecting the management of information resources are presented. Next, the processes involved in identifying the information needs of the organization are described. Then issues impacting on the methods used to make cost–benefit analyses of information systems, which leads to the choice of a specific CBIS for design and development, are presented. The methods and procedures involved in systems analysis, design, and implementation are of major importance and are discussed next. Successful implementation of CBIS is becoming increasingly dependent on the evolution of the software engineering environment, which is described in a subsequent section. The final section is a discussion of issues needing further investigation to achieve more effective management of information resources.

MANAGEMENT OF INFORMATION SYSTEMS

Computer-based information technology is generally regarded as a major tool in achieving high levels of office productivity. The increased sophistication and expectations of decisionmakers has made management of an organization's information resources an even greater challenge. Broadly speaking, it can be said that the goal of a computer-based information system (CBIS) is to provide decisionmakers with information, at all levels, and in all functions. This information is necessary to assist management make timely and effective decisions in planning, executing, and controlling their activities.

Information can come from a variety of sources and in a variety of formats. Whatever its form, a properly designed CBIS should have the ability to *anticipate* the information needs of DMs and to *make* information readily available as needs arise. However, in any organization, success of a CBIS depends on the processes involved in information technology assessment and adoption (ITAA). "Assessment" and "adoption" refer to the organizational policies and the strategies and to the tasks employed, either explicitly or otherwise, in the effort to identify, acquire, and diffuse the appropriate technology. Several models that deal with this issue from different angles can be identified such as (1) organizational context variables affecting the successful operation of the CBIS, (2) stage theory, and (3) the theory of diffusion of technology. These are discussed below.

Organizational Context Model

Design, development, implementation, and management of information systems depend on a variety of interacting factors [2–6]. The influence of these factors varies among different organizations and even among the different units within an organization. Questions raised by these factors are "What are the prime influencing factors affecting success of CBIS?" and "How do these factors interact and influence a successful operation of CBIS?" In their search for an answer to these questions, Ein–Dor and Segev [3] identified ten organizational variables that directly or indirectly influence the success of CBIS. These variables are organizational size, organizational maturity, organizational structure, organizational time frame, the psychological climate in the organization toward CBIS, the extraorganizational situation, organizational resources, rank and location of the responsible executive, and the steering committee. Montazemi [6] investigated the effects of eight such factors on end-user satisfaction and found that end users in less centralized firms are more satisfied with their CBIS. This may be because less centralized firms are in greater need of integration devices. Furthermore, because they have diverse needs, and they formalize goals, less centralized organizations require information systems that are tailored to the needs of individual decisionmakers. Increased complexity of decisions and more intricate coordination needs require more specialized systems analysts to perform in-depth information system planning. During the development phase of CBIS, the presence of systems analysts and the degree to which they perform pertinent analysis tends to have a positive influence on end-user participation. In turn, mutual cooperation tends to have a positive influence on an end user's level of computer literacy, on satisfaction with the application software developed, and on mutual understanding of the problems and limitations inherent within an information systems environment.

Stage Theory

A popular, although scientifically not well grounded, evolution of information systems in any organization is represented by the stage model introduced by Gibson and Nolan [7]. They contend that, in the evolution of information systems in any organization, one can identify four distinct stages (i.e., initiation, expansion, formalization, and maturity).

By categorizing the evolution of information resources into stages, the possibility of sorting and, consequently, managing CBIS more easily is a salient consideration. Within this framework, the growth of information systems resources (EDP) is explained in light of the following:

1. Growth in computer applications
2. Growth in the specialization of EDP personnel
3. Growth in formal management techniques and organization

Stage one (initiation) occurs when computerization is implemented for the purpose of providing tangible cost savings (e.g., savings made in personnel by automating a payroll system). However, only rarely at this point does senior management assess the long-term impact of computerization on either personnel, the organization, or on its strategy.

Stage two is identified as a period of rapid "expansion." The result is an unplanned and exponential rise in expenditure on hardware, software, and personnel. Characterized by the growth of responsibilities of EDP facilities, this stage achieves little in the setting of project priorities or of making plans. During this period a crisis is believed to occur, which forces top management to become aware of the explosive growth and costs of the activity. Usually a decision is made to rationalize and to coordinate the entire organization's EDP effort.

At stage three, management attempts to slow down runaway computer costs by "formalizing" the operation. This stage frequently initiates a formal management reporting system for computer operation, new charge-out systems, and the establishment of elaborate quality control measures. To manage the involved processes effectively, it is suggested that organizations centralize certain components of their resources, install a steering committee, and assign systems analysts throughout the company to ensure that users' needs are being adequately met.

Stage four identifies the maturity of the information systems. During this stage, most MIS development funding is devoted to applications touching directly on critical business operations. The relationship between EDP and end user is both subtle and complex, and the integration of specialized and internally differentiated EDP resources into the company as a whole is not easy. Integration requires that the MIS manager take steps to achieve mutual understanding of his/her objectives, not only with senior management, but also with functional managers at the vice presidential level. Steering committees can play an important role here, by assuming responsibility for determining project priorities and encouraging new techniques, policies, and changes within the MIS department.

Diffusion of New Technology

McFarlan et al.'s [8] model of how change occurs in an organization is somewhat different. Their theory is addressed not to the stages of the evolution of an EDP department but rather to the phases by which an organization can manage the diffusion of new technology [1,8–10]. Their model segments the diffusion processes into four phases as follows:

Phase 1. Technology Identification and Investment.

The emphasis is on learning and applying the new technology. Staff skills are built by means of pilot studies. At this phase, experience is assumed to be so limited that participants are not perceived as able to grasp long-term implications. Lack of management attention, incompetent project management, and/or poor choices in vendors or hardware can cause stagnation and impede progress to more advanced phases.

Phase 2. Experimentation, Learning, and Adaption.

This phase focuses on raising user awareness of the new technology and the problems it can solve by building on past experience. Success at this point generally leads to an increase in the number of requests for service. Staff and skill requirements, equipment acquisition, and the generation of appropriate financial data are assessed at this point. During this phase, care must be taken to remain flexible because it is now that the encouragement of innovative applications is essential. In many cases, this is the time when the most advantageous adaptations are developed. These new developments may differ drastically from those originally conceived of during the first phase, but if managers are not allowed to develop and refine their understanding, stagnation can easily occur and halt progress.

Phase 3. Rationalization and Management.

This phase is characterized by the pursuit of short-term efficiency measures. Management and operational control are sought, rather than strategic emphasis of the preceding phase. At this time, management controls are implemented to monitor the growth of new resources. Activities center on upgrading staff knowledge, reorganizing to allow the development of further projects, determining appropriate technology, and implementing the new technology in a cost-effective manner. As at the previous stage, care must be taken to avoid overstandardization, that may result in stagnation.

Phase 4. Widespread Technology Transfer.

Now the benefits and experience of the new technology are disseminated to other units within the organization. The technology base is installed, learning is relatively complete, and long-term analysis and planning are emphasized.

Huff and Munro [11] studied the assessment of information technology from a different perspective. They maintain that there are six phases involved in describing the ITAA process and that these can be distinguished as follows:

1. Awareness: The innovation is first heard of but full information about it is lacking
2. Interest: Missing information is deliberately sought out
3. Evaluation: Use of the innovation is mentally considered and a decision is made whether or not to try it
4. Trial: Practical, usually small-scale testing is made to assess the value of the innovation to the present and future situation

5. Implementation: The trial is extended to the first full use of the innovation; usually this involves only one, or a few, subunits of the organization
6. Diffusion: The innovation is extended, together with possible modification, to additional organizational units

The six possible interest groups that play decisive role in the process of the ITAA can be categorized as follows:

1. Users: Direct users of the technology
2. Influencers: Those who influence the buying process
3. Deciders: Those with final authority
4. Gatekeepers: Those in a position to provide special information, regarding either the technology per se or its application
5. Planners: Those who plan the implementation and perform the technology assessment
6. Sponsors: Those who provide senior-level support for the technology adoption

Four distinct models relating to the way in which the overall ITAA process is performed in an organization can be identified as (1) issue driven, (2) technology driven, (3) opportunistic model, and (4) normative ideal.

In an *issue-driven* environment, the process is closely geared to corporate and systems planning processes. For any given issue, the actual mechanism for carrying out the ITAA process often takes the form of a small study team which performs an information search via literature, vendor contacts, internal gatekeepers, as well as via counterparts in other organizations, and so forth. Outside the realm of the current issue, the search being ad hoc is incomplete; thus, the possibility of overlooking worthwhile opportunities is high. However, a major advantage of this approach is that high degrees of organizational slack and flexibility are not required as the approach is relatively well structured.

In a *technology-driven* organization, the ITAA sequence progresses from identification of an interesting technology to the location of an organizational problem to which it can be applied. Firms that follow this approach are usually well endowed with both technical gatekeepers and an information systems staff; basically, such organizations are better informed as to what is newly available, as well as to what information technology is still experimental. The success factor associated with the technology-driven approach is the need for thorough scanning of the many sources of information about new technology, as well as the requirement for a relatively large amount of organizational slack and flexibility within the information systems department to free up the time required for the scanning activities.

Organizations that follow the *opportunistic model* are deliberately not comprehensive with respect to either their issue identification (planning processes) or their technology identification process. Such firms typically perform some technology scanning, but in an ad hoc way. There is no large expenditure of resources in either planning or in information technology scanning and evaluation. There is also a lower need for specialist skills, such as planners and technical or applications gatekeepers. The ability to recognize opportunities for bringing together appropriate information technology with issues is paramount. The major problem is the risk of overlooking important issues or technological solutions.

In the *normative ideal* model, the ITAA process begins with a comprehensive assessment of the current information services environment and the future goals of the organization with regard to information services. Assessment is carried out to the level of current and future applications. Forecasts of the availability of new technology are then reviewed. The major strength of this model is that it is, in principle, comprehensive with respect to both information technology and organizational issues, problems, and opportunities. The weakness of the model is its high cost due to required organizational and technological reviews.

The above discussion serves to indicate the complexity of issues involved in the management of CBIS. The question arises as to what procedures should be followed in order to (1) recognize the information needs of decisionmakers and (2) to choose the appropriate technology to make information readily available as needs arise. Focusing on this questions, those techniques necessary to recognize an organization's information needs are presented next.

INFORMATION REQUIREMENTS ANALYSIS

In any organization, the information needs of decisionmakers are many and varied. However, most often, resources assigned to satisfying these needs are limited. Thus, information needs must be grouped together in such a way that each system (cluster) can be developed within time and cost constraints. Assessing information requirements should be viewed as a process active over the entire life cycle of a CBIS. Frequently, it is the most necessary component of system development, since in this context, the criticality of its role is most apparent. To this end, an organization's information requirements can be best identified in phases as follows [12]:

1. Organizational analysis
2. Strategy-to-requirement transformation
3. Logical system design
4. Logical-to-physical transformation
5. Systems implementation

Organization Analysis

Organizational analysis allows examination of the mission and nature of an organization and its environment. It is argued [13] that an effective strategic information systems planning process must provide (1) definition of key markets (within the firm) for CBIS products and services; (2) internal consistency, particularly between the strategic business plan and strategic CBIS plan; and (3) a means to assess the validity of the planning process. To this end, the critical success factor (CSF) method can be used to develop a means/ends relationship that focuses the CBIS strategy on areas critical to meeting these strategic goals [13]. The critical success factor method can be identified as a top/down approach that links critical organizational goals to a set of critical information requirements needed by individual decisionmakers in the organization. The CFS methodology comprises a three-step process: (1) interviews with relevant managers and key staff; (2) group sessions to evaluate and characterize relevant CSF; and (3) feedback, critique, and adoption of these CSFs to provide a final CSF statement.

Strategy-to-Requirement Transformation

Strategy-to-requirement transformation models the information system architecture (ISA) to represent the information flow requirements of an entire organization. The ISA relates the organizational processes that must be performed to those data classes required by specific processes. Modeling for the ISA consists of the following activities:

    1. Global entity relation modeling
    2. Conceptual data modeling
    3. Process modeling
    4. Data/process integration

At minimum, a logical modeling process for ISA (1) addresses the needs of all users of data processing services and (2) minimizes any redundancy in data and process modeling across the organization. The resulting ISA is used as the basis for performing logical systems design and for establishing commitment for system implementation.

Logical System Design

Using the logical model provided by phase two, the third phase, logical systems design, takes care of data design, applications, and geographic architectures. Essentially, data architecture represents a blueprint of the databases that should be designed from the standpoint of the whole organization. Application architecture defines the application areas necessary to support ISA and the relationships that exist between those applications. Geographic architecture defines where applications will run, where databases will be located, and what communication links are needed between them.

    The logical design for these architectures consists of the following components:

    1. Entity/relation diagram (ERD) and global ERD
    2. A complete, consistent semantic data modeling which includes: entities (objects), properties, relationships (is-a, is-part-of), functional dependencies, events and actions, data item set (keys)
    3. Directories and dictionaries
    4. Process model
    5. Operational mode
    6. Dialogue and communications procedures

Logical-to-Physical Transformation

This fourth phase of information requirements analysis is the basis for directing the implementation of a set of systems. This includes the following activities:

    Decomposing data, application, and geographic architectures into subsystems (portfolio of applications)
    Deciding on the detailed design of each subsystem
    Making commitments to priorities and schedules for subsystems implementation

System Implementation

The final phase implementation of individual systems as identified in phase four. At this stage, the organization has an overall view of its information requirements as well as the blueprints of the information systems architecture. Each system must be subjected to a feasibility study, systems analysis, general systems design, detailed systems design, systems implementation, operation, maintenance, and evaluation. Several methodologies and techniques have been proposed to perform feasibility studies, to evaluate the underlying information systems, and conduct systems analysis and design. These issues will be looked at next.

COST–BENEFIT ANALYSIS IN INFORMATION SYSTEMS

Decisions that require the allocation of scarce resources to the development of a specific information system are important and directly affect the success of an information system. Two basic tenets for measuring the success of an information system can be identified as the overall cost incurred by the organization and the benefits received from it. The comparison of cost and value required prior to system development differs from comparisons undertaken to justify amendments to the system. This latter comparison, in turn, differs significantly from the ongoing comparison required to ensure that the value yielded continues to exceed cost.

The five principal steps in the technique of cost–benefit analysis are discussed below.

Selecting the Analyst

The analyst can be selected from the regular members of the organization at large. A second choice is to hire an outside consultant. Reputable consultants have the skills and experience required to perform a viable analysis, but they can be expensive, their work of variable quality, and their activities disruptive to the normal operation of the organization.

Identifying and Selecting the Alternatives

This process consists of specifying the objectives (e.g., better inventory control) and determining how to attain them. Performed properly, this step requires that all alternatives unacceptable for political or other reasons be discarded and that levels of performance for the remaining alternatives be determined.

Identifying and Measuring Benefits and Costs

Costs can usually be expressed in dollars: the purchase price of hardware and software, cost of staffs, rent for space, and so on. On the other hand, benefits take the form of tangibles such as cost savings, cost avoidance, and improved operational performance. Then again, intangible benefits include improved decisionmaking, enhanced morale, and better service to clients. The greatest problem with intangible benefits is that of assigning a value to information. All information has potential value, but this remains an unknown until the information is used to make a decision. Only then can its value be calculated as the difference in the expected value of the decision with and without the information. Even so this simple notion is hard to apply because value placed on a decision may be unreliable.

For any information system, a set of tangible and a set of intangible costs and benefits can be identified. Tangible cost/benefits are the easiest to identify and are amenable to standard measurements [14]. However, intangible cost/benefits are difficult to identify and measure with precision. The complexity of this issue has resulted in the upsurge of a variety of measurement techniques [15] such as follows: (1) MIS usage estimation, (2) user satisfaction, (3) incremental performance in decision-making effectiveness, (4) information economics, (5) utility analysis, (6) the analytic hierarchy approach, and (7) the information attribute examination; each of these has its own strengths and weaknesses [14–18].

Comparing Alternatives

This step consists of three tasks: converting the measures of costs and benefits to common units (e.g., dollars); establishing a discount rate for the undertaking; and calculating the present value of the alternatives.

Performing the Analysis

This step selects a criterion of comparison and applies it to present values for various alternatives. For a fair comparison, the outcome from alternative solutions must be standardized and alternatives compared over the same time period. Five possible criteria used to compare alternatives when performing cost–benefit analyses follow:

1. Maximization of benefits for given costs
2. Minimization of costs for a given level of benefits
3. Maximization of the ratio of benefits over costs
4. Maximization of the net benefits (present value of benefits minus present value of costs)
5. Maximization of the internal rate of return on the investment

SYSTEMS ANALYSIS AND DESIGN

Systems analysis is an approach to, and the development of, a body of techniques for analyzing the likely consequences of alternate decisions within the context of a given system. Necco et al. [19] identified six approaches that have been used over the years to develop CBIS in organizations: traditional/classical approach; systems development life cycle approach; structured approach; automated approach; prototyping approach; and information center approach. A brief description of these approaches is presented next.

Traditional/Classical Approach

The traditional/classical approach to systems analysis and design can be described as how the products of the phases of a systems development life cycle are documented. The primary documentation tools used in this approach are narrative descriptions, systems and program flowcharts, file layouts, and input/output layouts.

Systems Development/Life Cycle Approach

In general terms, the systems development life cycle (SDLC) approach can be described as a way to break a systems project into phases, activities, and tasks designed to complete a given project. In essence, a development life cycle is a structured way of producing all elements required by a system. Figure 1 represents a relatively sophisticated version of this the current and dominant view. This "waterfall model" carries developmental processes through eight stages: (1) system feasibility, (2) software plans and requirements, (3) product design, (4) detailed design, (5) code, (6) integration, (7) implementation, and (8) operations and maintenance. Validation or verification at each stage marks the transition to the next stage; recycling to earlier stages takes place as necessary [20].

Current belief is that the SDLC approach is widely used, but that a standard way to break systems projects into phases does not prevail [19,21]. Despite the lack of consensus about its structure, the SDLC approach is well suited for use in the development of CBIS and the specific phases, activities, and tasks that depend on the types of systems project and the information systems environment in the organization.

Steps involved in an SDLC can be identified as follows:

Systems Overview: An investigation of the nature of the problem and the undertaking of a brief appraisal as to its suitability for computer processing.

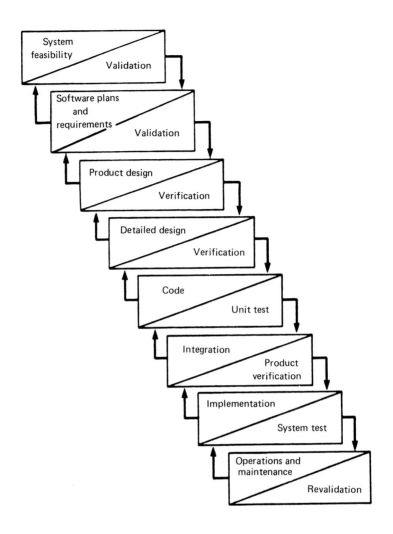

FIGURE 1.   The waterfall model of the software life cycle from ref. 20, by permission of Prentice Hall, Inc.

Systems Design: A detailed consideration of user requirements and the proposal of a number of outline solutions.

Systems Creation: The core of the development process (e.g., computer systems design, manual systems design, test programs, security design, system testing, etc.); this is the stage in which the majority of elements required to utilize the system are created.

System Implementation: Implementation of the organizational changes necessary to fully utilize the newly developed system.

In the 1970s the need to manage the process of SDLC for building CBIS prompted some organizations to market products under the rubric of systems development methodologies (SDM). Included in the SDM package is a description of the tasks to be performed during each activity within a phase, the content of end products to be delivered at the end of an activity and/or phase, and all the necessary formats for the program, system, and user documentation [22]. Additionally, some SDM products integrate the use of the structured methods with the management of the system development life cycle [23].

Structured Approach

The structured approach to systems analysis and design comprises concepts and tools. Several structured techniques exist to help an analyst model an organization at the requirement/determination level. These techniques include structured analysis and design technique [24]; data flow diagram [25]; business information analysis technique [26]; and interpretive structured modeling software [27]. The main concepts in the structured approach are to decompose system complexity and to describe systems in terms of data flow diagrams, structure charts, data dictionaries, and a process description. Systems are analyzed and designed from the abstract to the detailed level. Data flow diagrams and structured charts are developed for each level into which a system is partitioned. Diagrams are supported by a data dictionary that describes data stores, data flows, and data elements.

Automated Approach

Concurrent with the development of structured methods, computerized systems, which support many of the tasks performed in systems analysis and design, have been developed. Software packages such as Excelerator support the development and maintenance of data flow diagrams, structure charts, and other graphical techniques. This software package also includes the development of a related data dictionary and various analysis tools to assist in ensuring that such documentation is correct, complete, and consistent [28].

Prototyping Approach

Information systems can be designed based on the information requirements of a specific organizational task, irrespective of who performs it. This type of strategy is useful when the task is highly structured (e.g., payroll system). In this case, the system analyst exhibits a completely rational view of decisionmaking, and can assume complete control over design options and can predict the outcomes of every design decision. However, when a task is semi- or ill-structured, the information system should represent the specific requirements of individual decisionmakers. The complexity of such tasks requires that the systems analyst and the decisionmaker work together to define the characteristics of the underlying information systems. Iterative design reduces the possibility of a communication gap between the analyst and the decisionmaker. It is usual to first develop a simplified version of the required system and allow the decisionmaker to interact with it to identify areas needing improvement. Next, the prototype is refined in accordance with the comments of the decisionmaker. The improved prototype is again presented to the decisionmaker who may identify further change(s) and/or additions to be made to the system. This process continues until lack of improvement becomes apparent and/or incurred costs exceed the benefits to be received from the system.

The success of prototyping depends on the rules and procedures elicited from decisionmaker(s) and/or experts. The problem associated from eliciting this type of knowledge can arise from several sources, for example, limitation of verbal data, unelicitable knowledge, and the use of inappropriate elicitation techniques [29]. It is a misconception to suppose that knowledge can be directly captured from a domain expert. Lack of validity in verbal data can arise from nine sources:

1. Inexperience in self-reporting techniques
2. Reconstruction/theorizing rather than accurate reporting ("gap-filling")
3. Inaccessibility of procedural knowledge
4. Ineffability of certain events or internal representations
5. Ecological validity in the elicitation context (e.g., giving a verbal protocol on an unrepresentative task)
6. The taken-for-grantedness of highly familiar knowledge
7. Straightforward forgetting of relevant information
8. Ambiguities in verbalizations
9. Secrecy and deliberate underreporting

A partial solution to the problem of invalid verbal data lies in the iterative, feedback-driven nature of prototyping methodology. Prototyping can reduce the aforementioned difficulties; however, the problem of unelicitable (tacit) knowledge still remains. Tacit knowledge comprises the inferences and global knowledge that provide a nonarticulable framework for human reasoning [30,31]. Machine induction of decision rules from examples supplied and classified by the expert can compensate for the bottleneck [32]. Once it is accepted that, even within a single specialist domain, expertise can comprise several distinctive types of knowledge, the need for a variety of elicitation techniques becomes evident [33]. Knowledge elicitation techniques can be identified as follows [29]: (1) interviews, (2) verbal protocols, (3) machine induction, (4) observational studies, (5) conceptual sorting, and (6) multidimensional scaling (MDS).

Interviewing, this most familiar and widely used methodology for knowledge elicitation can take may forms. Asking an expert to give an introductory lecture about the task domain is one way, or an interview can incorporate the techniques of cognitive psychology for probing memory such as "critical incidental reports." Additionally, the interview may follow a questioning plan predetermined by the knowledge engineer, or be unstructured.

Verbal protocol analysis requires the expert to give a commentary on what he or she is thinking about while working through a typical decision problem. A recording is made of this "verbal protocol," which is then transcribed and analyzed. Myers et al. [34] have proposed highlighting the substantive knowledge in the transcript using a text editor and coding it directly into rules to form a prototype.

Machine-induced rules often have little resemblance to those elicited from human experts by other means. However, machine induction as a technique for facilitating cognitive emulation is appropriate for two reasons. First, the large example sets fed in as raw data are selected and preclassified by human experts, thereby reflecting their conceptualization of a domain. Second, when favorable conditions prevail and a complete or highly representative set of examples is available, induced rules can approximate human rules.

Observational studies are similar to verbal protocols, except that no inference from a secondary activity (i.e., giving a verbal report) is present. This type of study can take such forms as video recording, or the audio recording of phone conversations between engineers and remote users. Whatever the medium, transcripts require detailed analysis if useful knowledge is to be extracted.

Conceptual sorting is a technique of cognitive psychologists. At its simplest, the task can involve (a) obtaining a set of concepts that roughly cover a domain (from a textbook or glossary); (b) transferring each concept to a card; (c) asking an expert to sort cards into several groups, identifying what each group has in common; and (d) iteratively combining these groups to form a hierarchy.

Multidimensional scaling (MDS) techniques are used to identify perceived similarities and differences in a set of concepts. The reperatory grid is one such technique that has been transferred successfully to knowledge engineering [*32,35*]. In contrast to conceptual sorting, which helps identify the broad conceptual structure, MDS can uncover those fine discriminations between closely related concepts that experts make and which novices find difficult to make.

Information Center Approach

Reputed to have been originated by IBM, Canada, the information center approach to the development of CBIS addresses the problem of applications development and maintenance backlogs which exists in many organizations. In this approach, a staff of data processing specialists is organized to assist end users with developing their own computer applications. The main technology supporting this concept is that of the fourth-generation computer program.

Information centers can complement the traditional data processing department, reduce the systems development and maintenance effort, and control the proliferation of microcomputers throughout organizations. The principal issues in the use of information centers in organizations is probably focused in the relationship of the information center to the traditional data processing department, the type of applications appropriate for user development, and the responsibilities of pertinent staff members and users of the developed systems. To satisfy the information requirements of end users, the strategy followed during the systems analysis and design phase may consist of a combination of the above methodologies. To this end, satisfaction of end users with their CBIS largely depends on the accuracy with which the systems analysis and design phase can identify the needs and provide the appropriate tools to capture required information and to present them to the decisionmakers in a timely fashion. Recent trends in software development tools have made the realization of these goals possible. This is discussed next.

SOFTWARE ENGINEERING ENVIRONMENT

The fundamental objective of software engineering is to provide sound engineering principles, practice, and tools in support of all phases of a software life cycle. For a quarter of a century, commercial computing languages have evolved slowly. The first generation was machine language. There was no interpreter or compiler to translate the language into a different form, therefore, this task fell to the programmer, who had to use a binary notation for coding application programs. The second generation of programming language, which came into use in the mid-1950s, was symbolic assembly language. Assembly language utilized macros to lessen the tedious of programming. Nonetheless, assembly language was still far distant from human natural language, and therefore, it was a complex media within which to develop application programs. Third-generation programming language (high-level language) came into use in the 1960s. Third-generation languages (e.g., FORTRAN, COBOL, BASIC, PL/I, ADA) had moved a step closer to natural language. English words were used and formulae were expressed in mathematical notation.

Nevertheless, third-generation languages were still too complex for the end users to develop their own application software. In response to these problems, fourth-generation languages (4GL) were created to meet the following objectives [36]:

1. Speedier application-building process
2. To facilitate application and program changes, thus reducing maintenance cost
3. To generate bug-free code from high-level expressions of requirement
4. To make languages user friendly so that end users could solve their own problems and put computer to work

A variety of 4GLs are on the market which are intended to achieve the above objectives. However, due to the lack of standardization, currently available 4GLs offer a variety of options, in that they can support both procedural and nonprocedural codings. The major difference between procedural and nonprocedural languages is that nonprocedural languages require the programmer to instruct the computer by specifying desired results, rather than by specifying intermediate procedures to achieve that result. Ease of programming makes rapid prototyping possible. To increase the capability of the 4GLs in developing situation-specific macros, some 4GL programming languages also include a procedural language environment. Another attractive feature of 4GLs is their ability to support database management systems (DBMS) as well as graphical interface. These tools become especially important in a decision support system (DSS) environment. In general, the following can be identified as the desirable features of 4GLs [37]:

> Simple queries
> Simple queries and updates
> Complex queries
> Complex queries and updates
> Database creation
> Intelligent database operations, where the change of one value in the database causes
>   other operations to occur automatically
> Generation of data entry screens for key entry operations
> A procedural language
> Spreadsheet manipulation
> Multidimensional matrix manipulation
> Report generation
> Graphics generation
> Graphics manipulation
> Decision support for what-if questions
> Mathematical analysis tools
> Financial analysis tools
> Other decision support tools
> Text manipulation
> Electronic mailbox

A simple 4GL is an electronic spread sheet. More powerful 4GLs on the market include Focus, IFPS, RAMIS II, and SYSTEM W. Systems such as Focus provide a powerful general-purpose DSS generation environment, while, IFPS or System W are more applicable for the support of financial systems.

We have now entered the fifth-generation era where the commercialization of expert system developments, derived from artificial intelligence (AI) research, has launched a new industry. By virtue of their flamboyance the expressions "AI" and "expert systems" have captured the imagination that gave rise to an expanding wave of activity and, concomitantly, to unrealistic expectations about the state of the art. The term "expert system" refers to a computer program that applies a substantial knowledge of specific areas of expertise to a problem-solving process. Underlying the application system that captures the expert system is an assumption concerning the nature of an expert's decision processes (i.e., expertise) exercised within a particular application domain. As a concept, expertise involves two crucial factors: the first is its narrow scope when applied by an individual (or possibly a small group) and the second is its excellence in performance. Designing an expert system entails making explicit those details of a model of competence implicit in a domain of knowledge. The closer the expert system is to capturing this underlying model, the more satisfactory the system will be. It is possible to identify various tools and techniques with the inherent ability to elicit and to represent expert knowledge in the form of a computer program [*32,38–43*]. The basic components of expert systems are the inference engine, the knowledge base, the user–system interface, the explanation facility, and the knowledge acquisition facility. These components can either be supported by AI languages and/or by expert systems shells.

The three most popular AI languages are LISP, PROLOG, and OPS5. LISP (LISt Processor) developed in 1958, at the Massachusetts Institute of Technology by McCarthy, was the first symbolic processing language. The use of lists, collections of items contained within parentheses, which represent the association between symbols, was the key to efficient symbolic processing. While LISP-based systems are predominantly developed and used in the United States, PROLOG is more favored in Europe and Japan. PROLOG (PROgramming in LOGic) was developed in 1973 in France by Alain Colmerauer at the University of Marseilles. As its name indicates, PROLOG supports logic-based knowledge representation and programming methods in terms of facts and rules. PROLOG incorporates a wide range of features, including a control mechanism, built-in predicates, and effective debugging facilities. OPS5 (Official Production System 5), originally developed at Carnegie–Mellon University, is a knowledge engineering language able to support the rule-based representation method. It incorporates a pattern matcher, an interpreter that includes a forwardchaining mechanism, and various programming tools such as editing and debugging tools.

Although AI programming languages can be effectively used to program complex decision processes, the trend is to make use of expert systems shells. At present, the better known expert system shells include ART, KEE, Knowledge Craft, Nexpert object, GURU, and Personal Consultant. Expert systems shells reduce the programming requirements by incorporating a combination of the following inferencing strategies: backward chaining, forward chaining, breadth first search, depth first search, heuristic search, problem reduction, pattern matching, hierarchical control, unification, and event-driven control. Ease of use makes expert systems shells an especially attractive tool for rapid prototyping. Expert system shells support a combination of the following components:

1. Knowledge engineers' development aids
2. Knowledge acquisition aids
3. Knowledge data management tools
4. Inference engines
5. User–system interface
6. Explanation facilities
7. Language interfaces

DISCUSSION

Owing to rapid technological change as well as to the increasing sophistication of end users, management of CBIS is becoming ever more complex and challenging. As a result, increased effort has been directed toward management of CBIS. In turn, new insights into factors affecting the success of CBIS have been made; tools, methodologies, and frameworks for information requirements analysis, systems analysis, and software engineering have been much improved. Nevertheless, some major concerns still need to be attended to. Several techniques and frameworks to enable the management of information resources were presented here. However, a major deficiency is the absence of a unifying approach which can draw upon these frameworks in order to guide the MIS practitioner when he/she attempts to manage a company's information resources.

Furthermore, the need for supporting ill-structured decision processes is on the increase [44]. However, current knowledge of engineering methodologies for knowledge engineering and software for model building needs to be improved in order to meet the level of sophistication sought in both decision support systems and expert systems. The available tools and techniques of knowledge engineering can be of use for automatic decision processes. Although little is known about how to extract deep knowledge, this is the building block of intelligent reasoning [45,46].

Not only is the acquisition of knowledge important, but how that information is presented to the end user is essential to a successful CBIS [6]. Recently, there has been an upsurge of interest in the effectiveness of information presentation modes, and although the purpose of this type of research is varied, the underlying philosophy remains the same; the major trust being how to answer the question of how different modes of presenting information (i.e., in graphical, tabular, or textual) can influence human behavior in terms of the reception of information, its processing, and reaction to a decision environment. Despite the presence of an extensive number of studies dealing with graphical and other visual displays, the cognitive effects of different modes of presentation on the process of decisionmaking is still uncertain [47].

REFERENCES

1. F. W. McFarlan and J. L. McKenney, *Harvard Bus. Rev., 60,* 109–119 (1983).
2. B. DeBrabander and G. Thiers, *Mgmt. Sci., 30,* 137–155 (1984).
3. P. Ein-Dor and L. E. Segev, *Mgmt. Sci., 24,* 1067–1077 (1978).
4. J. L. King and K. L. Kraemer, *Comm. ACM, 27,* 466–475 (1984).
5. R. O. Mason and I. Mitroff, *Mgmt. Sci., 19,* 475–487 (1973).
6. A. R. Montazemi, *MIS Q., 12,* 238–256 (1988).
7. C. F. Gibson and R. L. Nolan, in *Catching Up with the Computer Revolution* (L. Salerno, ed.), John Wiley & Sons Inc., New York, 1983, pp. 25–43.
8. F. W. McFarlan, J. L. McKenney, and P. Pyburn, *Harvard Bus. Rev., 61,* 145–156 (1983).
9. F. W. McFarlan, *Harvard Bus. Rev., 62,* 98–103 (1984).
10. L. Raho, J. A. Belohlav, and K. D. Fiedler, *MIS Q., 11,* 46–57 (1987).
11. S. Huff and M. Munro, *MIS Q., 9,* 327–339 (1985).
12. R. D. Hackathorn and J. Karimi, *MIS Q., 12,* 203–222 (1988).
13. J. H. Henderson and G. Sifonis, *MIS Q., 12,* 187–202 (1988).
14. J. L. King and E. L. Schrems, *Comput. Surv., 10,* 19–34 (1978).
15. A. Srinivasan, *MIS Q., 9,* 243–253 (1985).
16. R. H. Irving, C. A. Higgins, and F. R. Safayeni, *Comm. ACM, 26,* 785–793 (1983).

17. B. Ives, M. H. Olson, and J. J. Baroudi, *Comm. ACM, 26,* 785–793 (1983).
18. A. Money, D. Tromp, and T. Wegner, *MIS Q., 12,* 222–236 (1988).
19. C. R. Necco, C. L. Gordon, and N. W. Tsai, *MIS Q., 11,* 460–476 (1987).
20. B. Boehm, *Software Engineering Economics,* Prentice-Hall, Englewood Cliffs, NJ, 1981.
21. R. G. Murdick, *J. Systems Mgmt., 21,* 22–26 (1970).
22. D. King, *Current Practices in Software Development,* Yourdon Press, New York, 1984.
23. A. F. Case, Jr., *Information Systems Development: Principles of Computer-Aided Software Engineering,* Prentice-Hall, Englewood Cliffs, NJ, 1986.
24. D. T. Ross and K. E. Schoman, Jr., *IEEE Trans. Software Eng., SE-3,* 22–40 (1977).
25. C. Gane and T. Sarson, *Structured Systems Analysis: Tools and Techniques,* Prentice-Hall, Englewood Cliffs, NJ, 1979.
26. W. M. Carlson, *Database, 10,* 3–9 (1979).
27. J. V. Hansen, L. J. McKell, and L. E. Metiger, *Mgmt. Sci., 25,* 1069–1081 (1979).
28. J. L. Whitten and L. D. Bentley, *Using Excelerator for Systems Analysis & Design,* Times Mirror/Mosby College Publishing, St. Louis, 1987.
29. P. E. Slatter, *Building Expert Systems: Cognitive Emulation,* Ellis Horwood Ltd, Chichester, 1987.
30. M. A. Boden, *Artificial Intelligence and Natural Man,* Harvester, Brighton, 1977.
31. H. M. Collins, R. H. Green, and R. C. Draper, in *Expert System 85* (M. Merry, ed.), Cambridge University Press, Cambridge, 1985.
32. J. Boose, *Expertise Transfer for Expert System Design,* Elsevier, New York, 1986.
33. J. G. Gammack and R. M. Young, in *Research and Developments in Expert Systems* (M. A. Bramer, ed.), Cambridge University Press, Cambridge, 1984.
34. C. D. Myers, J. Fox, S. M. Pegram, and M. G. Greaves, in *Expert Systems 83* (J. Fox, ed.), Churchill College, Cambridge, 1983.
35. M. L. G. Shaw and B. R. Gains, in *Expert Systems 83* (J. Fox, ed.), Churchill College, Cambridge, 1983.
36. J. Martin, *Fourth-Generation Languages,* Vol. I, *Principles,* Prentice-Hall, Englewood Cliffs, NJ, 1985.
37. J. Martin and J. Leben, *Fourth Generation Languages,* Vol. II, *Representative 4GLs,* Prentice-Hall, Englewood Cliffs, NJ, 1986.
38. B. R. Gains, *INFOR: Special Issue Intelligence Integration, 26,* 256–285 (1988).
39. F. Hayes-Roth, D. A. Waterman, and D. B. Lenat, *Building Expert Systems,* Addison-Wesley, Reading, MA, 1983.
40. J. Martin and S. Oxman, *Building Expert Systems: A Tutorial,* Prentice Hall, Englewood Cliffs, NJ, 1988.
41. J. J. Sviokla, *Database, 17,* 5–19 (1986).
42. J. J. Sviokla, *Database, 18,* 5–16 (1986).
43. G. Wright and P. Ayton, *Decision Support Systems, 3,* 13–26 (1987).
44. A. R. Montazemi, D. W. Conrath, and C. A. Higgins, *IEEE Trans. Systems, Man and Cybernetics, SMC-17,* 771–779 (1987).
45. B. R. Gaines, *Int. J. Man-Machine Studies, 26,* 453–472 (1987).
46. A. R. Montazemi and D. W. Conrath, *MIS Q., 10,* 44–55 (1986).
47. A. R. Montazemi and S. Wang, *J. Mgmt. Inform. Sys., 5,* 102–127 (1989).

ALI R. MONTAZEMI

MANUFACTURING SYSTEMS SIMULATION

INTRODUCTION

The application of simulation to manufacturing systems is a challenging task. Although the mechanisms of the simulation process are well developed, manufacturing is a field with a challenging spectrum of problems for the application of those mechanisms. Here we introduce the concepts of simulation, and of certain manufacturing systems, explore these concepts at an introductory level, and relate the application of simulation to manufacturing.

The effort to accomplish these ends will begin first by looking at the concept of a system. Next, manufacturing systems will be considered. Third, an effort will be made to introduce the operations research/management science modeling philosophy as it relates to simulation models. Then simulation will be examined as a modeling tool and its various approaches will be considered. Finally, we will show several approaches to the application of simulation to manufacturing systems and to the development of manufacturing systems models. The most capable commercially available simulation software will be described in connection with manufacturing systems simulation.

Systems and Subsystems

A common dictionary definition of a system is a "regularly interacting or interdependent group of items forming a unified whole" [1]. Another view of a system is that of a circumscribed sector of reality upon which we focus analysis in order to achieve some objective. Therefore, the concept of a system is a relative thing. For our purpose, we shall adopt the following definition of a system: a collection of entities interacting together over time toward the realization of one or more goals.

An *entity* is an object or an item that has a separate existence. An entity is characterized by a set of *attributes*. The role and behavior of an entity in a system is a function of its attributes. The three requirements for a system are then (1) entities, (2) relationships or interactions between entities, and (3) knowledge of the relationships between the entities and their attributes. A subsystem can then be defined from the Latin meaning of the prefix, sub, together with the previously defined word systems. 'Sub' means that which stands under, beneath, or below. A subsystem would then be an improper subset, in mathematical terms, of the entities of the system that would still meet the requirements for a system. It would be a system contained within a system.

It is in this light of systems knowledge that an approach will be made to manufacturing systems. The systems chosen for analysis will always be a part of some larger system or it would not exist.

Manufacturing Systems

The term manufacture actually means "made by hand." This is as opposed to *usufacture*—"the use of that which was made," i.e., that which occurred in nature. A more current and common meaning of manufacture would probably be "produced by transformation, alteration or reconfiguration of physical or chemical properties of the component raw materials." The intent here is to disabuse the reader of any requirement in the manufacturing process for the "made by hand" requirement of the old definition as being a literal requirement. It is meant, rather, as a case appearing in apposition to "occurring naturally." We shall focus on manufacturing as processes involving physical and/or chemical transformations applied to naturally occurring, processed, or synthetic materials.

A manufacturing system is then the set of processes by which the raw material input is transformed, altered, or reconfigured in its physical or chemical properties to produce an end product. This system is composed of the interacting and interrelated entities that make up the processes of materials transformation necessary to accomplish a specified end result in the product transformation.

Manufacturing systems exist at four levels. The first, and most basic of these is the *materials transformation level*. This is the level of the machine, or the level at which the material is changed from one form or state to another. Here concern is focused on the machine, the material, and the process through which the material is passed. Examples include machining a metal part and producing a plastic part by injection molding.

The second level of the manufacturing system is the *process control level*. At this level concern is for the integration of machines, and their control, to accomplish manufacturing specifications. It may involve automatic controls or computerized controls on the process. The objective is, however, to produce a quantity of product of a desired quality. Examples include the CNC program for machining a part and the control procedure for determining the proper time to eject a plastic part from the mold.

The third level of process control is the *production planning and control level*—the integration of a time horizon and production requirements for that horizon into the process. At this level, technical requirements are subsumed and the process is considered in an abstract manner. Examples include planning the number of metal parts to be machined on a CNC machine, and the number of plastic parts to be molded in a run on an injection molding machine.

The fourth level of a manufacturing system is the *strategic planning and control level*. This level is a basic policy-making level. It is concerned with what systems to use, in producing what products, at what time horizon in the future. This level is more abstract than the production planning and control level in that is deals with the future and with policy making rather than details of system operation.

Simulation can be applied at each level of this hierarchy of levels in a manufacturing system. A given simulation study might focus on any level, or on two or more adjacent levels. But it is not likely that a simulation study would be so encompassing as to involve all four levels at once.

The Overlays in Manufacturing Systems

These levels of manufacturing systems are essentially representations of the same system from different perspectives and for different purposes. The levels can be thought of in terms of transparent overlays on a system diagram. They can be peeled off one level at a time until the desired problem area has been located. At the time of definition of the specific system problem, levels of the overall system can be added if required, for the purposes of the analysis. The possibilities for analysis in such a framework are great. At the materials transformation level, an examination can be made of the operation of a single machine or of a machine and material interaction. Material flow can be analyzed through some set of machines, area of manufacturing or through the complete process.

Adding the process control level to the materials transformation level increases greatly the possibilities for problem studies. The process control level relates to the interpretation and control of the materials transformation level. This level involves the process monitoring and control and quality control efforts. Studies in this area would involve such problems as the effects on process throughput of changes in quality standards or the effects of component integration on process flow, or other variations.

Adding the complexity of the production planning and control level to the system generates a new vista for problem study and definition. The effects of the superimposition of schedules on the materials transformation level as it is integrated by the process control mechanisms can be evaluated.

By adding back complexity or by removing unneeded complexity, the problem can be isolated and studied within a meaningful level of process and system control relationships. This knowledge, coupled with the understanding of the simulation modeling approach, can enable a researcher to develop a meaningful solution to very complex problems.

Classes of Manufacturing

Among the many classes of manufacturing there are three that constitute the bulk of installed systems. There are job shops, batch production shops, and manufacturing flow shops.

A job shop is a manufacturing process characterized by a layout that groups like machines together. It normally produces high-cost, one-of-a-kind items or very low volume items. Its layout requires that the job be brought to the proper machine in sequence. It involves a high degree of material handling, which contributes to the high unit cost of production.

Batch production shops are a variation of job shops. If there is some specialization there may be a degree of process orientation in this type shop. This is done to reduce material handling and lower unit costs of production. This shop maintains its flexibility, however, by a lack of systems integration and the lack of a required flow path for a product. This lack of systems integration allows for changes in the processing steps and provides a great deal of flexibility.

The manufacturing flow shop is a mass production setup for low unit cost, highly specialized production, and minimum material handling cost. Machines or processing equipment are placed where needed to minimize time requirements in production. Ideally the product flows smoothly from input to final inspection with a minimum of manual handling and manual effort.

In manufacturing operations various combinations of these types of systems are found. A system chosen for study might be one of these types, a combination of these types or a subsystem of one of the types. Modern "flexible manufacturing systems," or FMS, attempt to automate the batch production facility by bringing to it many of the characteristics and advantages of the manufacturing flow shop.

The Operations Research/Management Science Approach

The approach of the operations researcher or management scientist is to construct a *model* of a situation in order to study a system. Models are of several types. Among these are iconic, analog, and symbolic models. Models are constructed to represent entities or groups of entities in the real world systems together with their interactions. The process of constructing the model to represent a situation is called *modeling*.

The degree to which the model captures the essence of the real world situation it has been constructed to represent is known as the *fidelity* of the model. A low fidelity (truth) model would be one that is not an accurate representation of its real world counterpart. Conversely, the term high fidelity, which has long been used in the area of sound recording, means high-quality reproduction of the situation that the model was constructed to represent. A model with low fidelity is called an abstract model. Similarly, a model with a low level of abstraction is a model with good fidelity.

A model is deemed valid if it has good fidelity. In complex models, it is possible to have good component fidelity and yet have errors in modeled interactions. In this case the system model would not be valid. The process of validation is that of checking the model and its interacting components to ascertain that they combine to provide an accurate representation of reality. This process is most often involved with simulation models. Simple symbolic models require little validation. In simulation this validation can involve program testing, testing generated random variates, subjective model validation as well as historical validation.

The Value of Systems Modeling in Manufacturing

A model is a representation of a true situation at some level of abstraction. If the model is an accurate representation in the primary areas of concern to the modeler it can provide information of value. The use of the model allows the situation modeled to be changed at will, in whatever manner desired, to evaluate the effects of the various changes. Such changes would upset the real world situation. They would encounter resistance on the part of personnel involved who feel threatened by change. The many changes would be extremely costly to the extent that in most cases this cost would be prohibitive. With the model, the changes can be made with no resistance on the part of personnel and at very reasonable cost. The studies done can be used to develop a single program or pattern for change that would give results that are desired. Upon developing this objective and obtaining management agreement for its implementation, a single change or program of change can be implemented. This can minimize the expensive part of systems evolution, i.e.,the study of the effects of change to determine which change should be made.

The procedure of modeling systems for study is very cost effective. This effectiveness comes from the savings that accrue from improved system performance at a relatively low cost of defining programs, procedures, or policies through the modeling process. It also greatly reduces the time required to evaluate the effect of proposed changes, as computer studies typically require far less elapsed time than experimentation with the real world system.

Simulation as a Tool of the OR/MS Approach

Simulation means "to cause to act like." It is defined as the development of a mathematical–logical model of a system and the experimental manipulation of the model on a digital computer. Two basic steps in simulation are cited in this definition: (1) model development and (2) experimentation. Model development involves the construction of a mathematical–logical representation of the system, and the preparation of a computer program that allows the model to mimic the behavior of the system. Once we have a valid model for the system, the second phase of a simulation study takes place; *experimentation* with the model to determine how the system responds to changes in the levels of the several input variables.

A model is the means we choose to capture the important features of the system under study. The model must possess some representation of the entities or objects in the system, and reflect the activities in which these entities engage.

The steps in a simulation study are as follows:

1. Problem formulation. A statement of the problem that is to be solved. This includes a general description of the system to be studied and a preliminary definition of the boundaries of that system.
2. Setting objectives. A delineation of the questions that are to be answered by the simulation study. This step allows further definition of the systems and its boundaries.
3. Model building. The process of capturing the essential features of a system in terms of its entities, the attributes or characteristics of each entity, the activities in which these entities engage, and the set of possible states in which the system can be found.
4. Data collection. Gathering data and information which will allow the modeler to develop the essential description of each of the system entities, and developing probability distributions for the important system parameters.
5. Coding. The process of translating the system model into a computer program which can be executed on an available processor.
6. Verification. The process of ascertaining that the computer program performs properly.
7. Validation. The process of ascertaining that the model mimics the real system, by comparing the behavior of the model to that of the real system where the system can be observed, and altering the model to improve its ability to represent the real system. The combined steps of verification and validation are crucial to establishing the credibility of the model, so that decisions reached about the system on the basis of the simulation study can be supported with confidence.
8. Experiment design. Determining the alternatives that can be evaluated through simulation, choosing the important input variables and their appropriate levels, selecting the length of the simulation run and the number of replications.
9. Production run and analysis. Assessing the effects of the chosen input variables on the selected measures of system performance, and determining whether more runs are needed.
10. Simulation report. Documenting the simulation program, reporting the results of the simulation study, and making recommendations about the real system on the basis of the simulation study. The implementation of these recommendations is usually the result of a decision by the appropriate manager in the organization.

This approach should be followed regardless of the application context of the simulation modeling effort. Law [2] describes the application of this approach to manufacturing systems specifically.

Simulation Approaches

There are three common approaches or orientations to the simulation of systems. These approaches involve the manner in which the system being simulated is viewed. This first orientation is the event type. This approach models the changes that take place in the system when events occur. A modeler defines the events that take place in the systems and the changes that occur with these events.

The activity-scanning orientation approach involves describing activities in which system entities are involved and specifying the requisites for starting and ending activities. This technique is used primarily in continuous systems simulation.

The process orientation approach involves the succession of activities, delays, and events associated with particular categories of entities. Logic is developed to handle these patterns of activities. The logic is defined in a higher level simulation language with a single statement. Then these different statements can be arranged to simulate the movement of entities through the system being represented.

Now that we have introduced the basic concepts of a system, a manufacturing system, and simulation modeling, we shall turn to the approaches we can take to simulating manufacturing systems.

SIMULATION OF MANUFACTURING SYSTEMS

The development of a manufacturing system simulation model begins with the selection of a suitable language into which to translate the conceptual model. Despite the widespread availability of very capable simulation languages and even highly specialized "canned" simulation programs for manufacturing, by far the largest number of simulations are developed in one of the high-level, general-purpose languages such as FORTRAN or PASCAL. This section describes the basic concepts involved in developing a simulation model of a manufacturing system, and discusses some of the general and specialized languages used to implement these concepts.

Developing Manufacturing Systems Models

The concepts of a system and a model of a system were discussed in the previous section. Before a conceptual model can be translated into a simulation program, a given "view of the world" must be adopted. This section describes a general concept of simulation modeling that is used for most of the languages that will be discussed here, but states these principles in terms typically associated with manufacturing systems.

System   A collection of entities (e.g., machines, workparts, operators, etc.) that interact together over time toward the realization of one or more goals.

Model   An abstract representation of a system, usually containing mathematical and/or logical relationships which describe the system in terms of states, entities and their attributes, resources, sets, events, activities, delays, and processes.

System state   A collection of variables that contain all the information necessary to describe the system at any time (e.g., the operational status of each of the machines in the system).

Entity   Any object or component in the system which requires explicit representation in the model (e.g., machines, workparts, operators, mechanics).

Attributes   The properties of a given entity (e.g., priority of a given job-order, the time a workpart entered the system, the quality status of a part).

Resource   A special class of entity which provides some form of service for a primary entity (e.g., a machine or a maintenance mechanic).

Set   A collection of associated entities, ordered in some logical fashion (e.g., a queue of workparts at a machine).

Event   An instantaneous occurrence that alters the state of the system (e.g., the arrival of a batch of workparts at a machine, or the failure of a machine).

Activity   A duration of time of specified length which is known at the beginning of the activity (e.g., the time to failure of a machine, the repair time of a failed machine).

Delay   A duration of time of unspecified length which is known only at the end of the delay (e.g., the time a workpart spends in queue waiting for service).

Process   A succession of activities, delays and events encountered by a primary entity as it courses through the systems (e.g., a workpart moving through a flexible manufacturing cell).

A distinction is made here between a "primary entity" and a "resource." A primary entity is one that represents the objective of the manufacturing system, such as a workpart or an assembly. A resource is an entity that performs an action on a primary entity or on other resources. For example, a machine (resource) performs an operation on a workpart (primary entity). A maintenance mechanic (resource) repairs a failed machine (resource). Some simulation languages (e.g., GASP-IV [3]) make no such distinction between primary entities and resources, classifying all of them as simply "entities." SIMAN [4] is an example of a language that requires such a distinction, however.

Languages Available for Simulation

The basic categories of languages used in simulation are high-level languaes (FORTRAN, PASCAL, C, etc), general-purpose simulation languages (GASP-IV [3], SLAM-II [5], SIMAN [4], etc.), and special-purpose simulation programs (PASAMS [6], XCELL [7], etc.). This section discusses the role of each of these in simulation modeling.

High-Level Languages

It is a probably a safe assertion that there are more computer simulation models developed in the high-level programming languages than in any other type of simulation modeling tool. The widespread availability of FORTRAN on the earlier mainframe computers made it perhaps the most popular of all languages for encoding simulation models.

A high-level language is a computer language that appears more like a human language than a machine language and is designed to be used on many different types of computers. A high-level language uses a compiler to translate it into machine language. Machine languages are unique to the computer for which they are designed. A program consisting of a set of instruction is prepared in the high-level language, compiled to produce a corresponding set of machine-language instructions, and executed on the computer. Examples of high-level alnguages are FORTRAN, PASCAL, BASIC, and C.

FORTRAN, is an acronym for FORmula TRANslator, and was designed around the needs of scientists and engineers who use computers primarily to perform large numerical calculations. The first commercially available high-level language, FORTRAN remains probably the best known and most widely applied of all programming languages. The current standard FORTRAN language is FORTRAN 77, which is described in the document ANSI X3.9–1978. Etter [8] and Pruett [9] give excellent descriptions of the FORTRAN language and its applications.

A classic early treatment of simulation was that by Tocher [10]. McMillan and Gonzalez [11], in another classic text dealing with computer approaches to decision models, illustrated FORTRAN approaches to simulation modeling. Schmidt and Taylor [12] described how to encode all of the essential simulation function in FORTRAN, and illustrated its use in such standard industrial engineering applications as queueing, inventory control, reliability, and maintenance. As an example of a manufacturing simulation model developed in FORTRAN, Savsar and Biles [*13*] presented a 600-line program for a model of an automated production flow line. This model allows the user to enter a set of data describing the flow line under study, simulate the system until selected statistical criteria are satisfied, and obtain output giving specific recommendations for productivity improvement. It is especially useful in evaluating the effects on production throughput of storage capacity along the production line as well as maintenance policies.

PASCAL is a high-level programming language which was developed to be highly structured, easily readable, and as unambiguous as possible. It was intended primarily as a teaching language, a truly standard language that would be inexpensive and easy to implement on any computer. A primary advantage of PASCAL in the early development of microcomputers was that it required less memory than FORTRAN and was therefore implementable on 64K machines. Vasudev and Biles [*14*] described a generalized microcomputer-based simulation language using PASCAL as the base language. The primary thrust of this development was to make possible simulation modeling on small-memory microcomputers, an objective that has become much less important as the cost of larger memories (512K and more) has dropped. Biles and Bathina [*6*] developed PASAMS, a PASCAL-based simulation model of automated manufacturing systems, which allows the user to completely describe the manufacturing configuration from input data, simulate a specified period of production, and obtain output showing the effects of the selected decision variables on production throughput and machine utilization. An important feature of such a simulation program is that it allows the user to evaluate alternative material handling options in setting up flexible manufacturing cells. This evaluation can take place in almost real time at the outset of the cell setup for the next batch of production.

The emergence of UNIX, an operating systems developed by Bell Laboratories in the late 1970s, also promoted C as a high-level language [*15*]. C which derived its name because it was the successor of two earlier languages A and B developed at Bell Laboratories, is the base language into which UNIX is encoded, and thus has advantages for applications on those computers which use UNIX as the operating language. C was a natural for 8-bit computers, as it required a much smaller machine-language instruction set than other high-level languages, but is finding many applications on larger machines because of its many efficiencies.

BASIC (Beginner's All-Purpose Symbolic Instruction Code) is another example of a high-level language that has found increased favor since the advent of microcomputers. Developed primarily as an instructional tool, BASIC is simple and easy to learn, but provides a poor basis for understanding programming. Nor is it very useful for simulation modeling, as it is an interpretative language and requires excessively long run times.

Despite their widespread use as programming languages in science and technology, and indeed their extensive use in simulation modeling, the high-level languages have several drawbacks in terms of simulation model development. Foremost is the need to encode subprograms for standard simulation functions, such as random number and random variate generation, file management, statistics collection and reporting. The general-purpose simulation languages, on the other hand, provide those basic functions that are repeated in almost every simulation modeling effort. The next section examines the more important of these general-purpose simulation languages.

General-Purpose Simulation Languages

Several languages have been developed to facilitate most of the common functions needed in simulation, including time advance, adding and removing entities from sets or files, managing the event list, generating random numbers and random variates, collecting statistics, and generating a standard report. The programmer must provide those features that are unique to the model of the systems he or she seeks to analyze.

The most prominent general-purpose simulation languages are GASP-IV, SIMSCRIPT, GPSS, SLAM, and SIMAN. GASP-IV is an event-oriented language, whereas GPSS is a process-oriented language. SIMSCRIPT-II.5, SLAM-II, and SIMAN offer the programmer a choice between these two modeling orientations.

This section describes these general-purpose simulation languages and their use in modeling manufacturing systems .

GASP-IV [3] is a collection of FORTRAN subroutines designed to facilitate an event-scheduling approach to simulation modeling using programs written in FORTRAN. It consists of more than 30 subroutines and functions for all the standard facilities required in simulation modeling. The programmer must provide a main program, an initialization routine, event routines, and, if desired, a problem-specific report generator. An essential requirement from the programmer is a subroutine called EVNTS, which directs program control to a particular event subroutine providing the logic corresponding to the changes in systems state which accompany the occurrence of the event. The main program must have a statement "CALL GASP" to start the simulation. Subroutine GASP determines the next event in the event calendar, and calls Subroutine EVNTS with the index NEXT to specify the imminent event. GASP-IV not only allows discrete-event modeling, but continuous and combined discrete/continuous modeling as well. SLAM-II, which is discussed later, retains all of the modeling features of GASP-IV.

SIMSCRIPT II.5 [16] is a general-purpose simulation language with facilities specifically designed to aid in the development of a discrete-event simulation model. As a simulation language, it allows the event-scheduling or the process-interaction point of view. As a scientific language, it is at least as powerful as FORTRAN, PL/1, ALGOL, or PASCAL. Many programming tasks can be done more efficiently (i.e., less programmer time) in SIMSCRIPT than in FORTRAN. A SIMSCRIPT program can be written in English-like statements in free format style; such a program is almost self-documenting and can be easily explained to a nonprogrammer. As with GASP-IV, SIMSCRIPT provides automatic maintenance of the future event list and the time-advance/event-scheduling algorithm, automatic maintenance of sets including the operations of adding and removing entities from sets, automatic collection of requested statistics, and random number and random variate generation.

SIMSCRIPT was initially developed by the RAND corporation in the 1960s, and was originally FORTRAN-based. SIMSCRIPT II.5, the latest version of the language, is owned by CACI, Inc. (Los Angeles, CA.). It is available for most large computer systems and can be leased or purchased through CACI. It has the capability to allow a process interaction approach, as well as the event-scheduling approach to be described here, and an extention is available to allow continuous simulation.

The world view taken by SIMSCRIPT II.5 is based on entities, attributes, and sets. Entities are classified as being either permanent or temporary. Permanent entities represent objects in a system that will remain in the system for the duration of the simulation. Examples include a fixed number of machines in a manufacturing cell model, or a fixed number of carriers in a material handling model. Temporary entities represent objects, such as workparts in a manufacturing model, which "arrive" to the system, remain for awhile, and then "leave" the system. The number of temporary entities active in the model may vary considerably over the course of the simulation. Entities may have attributes, and associated entities may belong to a set.

A SIMSCRIPT program consists of a preamble, a main program, event routines, and ordinary subroutines. As mentioned, the time-advance routine, random variate generation routines, and statistics-gathering routines are provided automatically. The preamble gives a static description of the system by defining all entities, their attributes, and the sets to which they may belong. It also defines the global variables, which are used to partially define system state, and lists the statistics to be collected on certain variables. A large collection of variables are automatically maintained. For example, TIME.V represents the simulation clock. If QUEUE is the name of a set, N.QUEUE is the number of entities in a set. The main program reads the value of input parameters, initializes the system state, and generates the first events. The event routines are automatically called by the time-advance subroutine, which in turn is activated by the statement "START SIMULATION" in the main program. Ordinary subroutines may be called from any event routine or the main program.

GPSS [17]   is a highly structured, special-purpose simulation language using the process interaction approach. It is oriented toward queueing simulations. A block diagram provides a description of the system. Temporary entities called transactions are created and may be pictured as flowing through the block diagram. Thus, GPSS can be used for any situation in which entities (e.g., workparts) can be viewed as passing through a system (e.g., a network of queues). GPSS is not a procedural language, such as FORTRAN or SIMSCRIPT; it is a structured method for describing certain types of systems . The GPSS processor then takes this description (i.e., the block diagram) and automatically performs a simulation. The time-advance/event-scheduling mechanism is transparent to the user.

GPSS (General Purpose Simulation Systems) was originally developed by Geoffrey Gordon of IBM in about 1960. It is available in some form for most large computer systems . An introduction to GPSS can be found in Schriber [17]. The latest and most powerful implementation of GPSS, GPSS/H, was developed by Henriksen [18] of Wolverine Software (Falls Church, VA).

Since the 1960s, GPSS has probably been the most widely used discrete-event simulation language. Two reasons for this popularity are the ease of learning the language and the relatively short time required for building a complex model. On the other hand, GPSS has several shortcomings, some of which may lead the programmer to unwittingly develop invalid models. GPSS/H has eliminated most of these shortcomings.

The two main concepts in GPSS are transactions and blocks. A *block* can be represented by a pictorial symbol or a single statement in the GPSS language. There are over 40 standard blocks in GPSS. Each block represents a specific action or event that can occur in a typical systems. These blocks are arranged into a block diagram which represents a process. *Transactions* representing active, dynamic entities may be pictured as flowing through the block diagram. Every path that a transaction can take through the system must be represented in the block diagram, which can have branches. The limited resources of a system are represented by the predefined GPSS entities, facilities, and storages. A *facility* is essentially a single server. A *storage* is a group of parallel servers. Statistics are automatically collected on the utilization of facilities and storages. In addition, queue and table entities are available to collect statistics on waiting lines or transit times.

The following example, taken from Schriber [19], illustrates the application of GPSS to a one-line, one-server queueing system. Castings are sent to a drilling machine, where each casting is to have a single hole drilled in it. The interarrival time of castings at the machine is uniformly distributed over the interval 15.0 ± 4.5 minutes. The time required to drill a hole in the casting is also uniformly distributed, over the interval 13.5 ± 3.0 minutes. Castings are processed in first-come, first-served order. This systems is modeled in GPSS, with statistics collected on three output variables: (a) the time required to process 100 castings; (b) the average number of castings in line; and (c) the average time castings spend waiting in line.

Figure 1 shows the GPSS block diagram for this model. Figure 2 presents the GPSS model file, which translates the block diagram into program statements that are intelligible to the GPSS processor. Figure 3 shows selected simulation output for the processing of 100 castings. Table 1 gives the results of eight independent replications of the model, with point estimates for the three output variables. Table 2 gives the 90% confidence intervals for the three output variables.

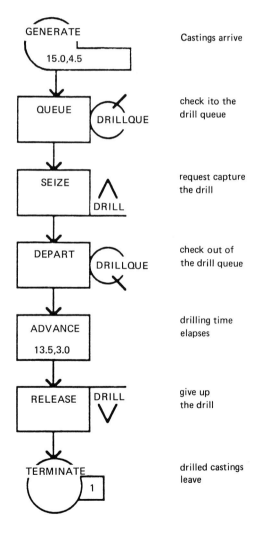

FIGURE 1   GPSS block diagram for a one line, one-server queueing system (from Ref. 19).

STMT NO.	I	LABEL	1 0	OPERATION	2 1	OPERANDS ⟶
1 →				SIMULATE		
2 →	*					
3 →	*••					
4 →	*	Model Segment 1 (Movement of Castings Through the System)				•
5 →	*••					
6 →	*					
7 →				GENERATE		15.0,4.5 castings arrive
8 →				QUEUE		DRILLQUE check into the drill queue
9 →				SEIZE		DRILL request/capture the drill
10 →				DEPART		DRILLQUE check out of the drill queue
11 →				ADVANCE		13.5,3.0 drilling time elapses
12 →				RELEASE		DRILL give up the drill
13 →				TERMINATE		1 drilled castings leave
14 →	*					
15 →	*••					
16 →	*	Run-Control Statements				•
17 →	*••					
18 →	*					
19 →				START		100 start the simulation
20 →	*					
21 →				END		end of model-file execution

FIGURE 2   GPSS model file for Figure 1 block diagram (from Ref. 19).

This example not only illustrates the application of GPSS to a typical, small-scale manufacturing system, but it also shows how the simulation output is analyzed statistically.

SLAM-II [5] is a FORTRAN-based, general-purpose simulation language which allows an event-scheduling or process interaction orientation, or a combination of both approaches. The event-scheduling portion of SLAM-II is quite similar to GASP-IV, which was described earlier. The process interaction portion of SLAM-II is similar in many respects to GPSS. This section briefly describes the process interaction portion of SLAM-II, which is marketed by Pritsker and Associates, Inc. (West Lafayette, IN).

To use the process interaction approach of SLAM-II, the analyst develops a network consisting of nodes and branches, which represents the processes in the system. The objects flowing through the system are called entities. The SLAM-II definition of an entity is analogous to a GPSS transaction. Such entities are dynamic; they flow through a process. Recall that a process is the sequence of events and activities that confront an entity as it flows through a system. A complete SLAM-II network model of a system represents all possible paths that an entity can take as it passes through the system. To run the model, the simulator translates the network representation directly into computer statements which are input to

---

RELATIVE CLOCK: 1488.9629   ABSOLUTE CLOCK: 1488.9629

(a) Clock Values

BLOCK	CURRENT	TOTAL
1	1	101
2		101
3		100
4		100
5		100
6		100
7		100
8		100
9		100

(b) Block Counts

(1) FACILITY	(2) TOTAL TIME	(3) AVAIL TIME	(4) UNAVL TIME	(5) ENTRIES	(6) AVERAGE TIME/XACT	(7) CURRENT STATUS	(8) PERCENT AVAIL	(9) SEIZING XACT	(10) PREEMPTING XACT
	--AVG-UTIL-DURING--								
DRILL	.917			100	13.655	AVAIL	100.0		

(c) Server Statistics

(1) QUEUE	(2) MAXIMUM CONTENTS	(3) AVERAGE CONTENTS	(4) TOTAL ENTRIES	(5) ZERO ENTRIES	(6) PERCENT ZEROS	(7) AVERAGE TIME/UNIT	(8) $AVERAGE TIME/UNIT	(9) QTABLE NUMBER
DRILLQUE	2	.215	101	42	41.6	3.172	5.430	

(d) Queue Statistics

(1) RANDOM STREAM	(2) ANTITHETIC VARIATES	(3) INITIAL POSITION	(4) CURRENT POSITION	(5) SAMPLE COUNT	(6) CHI-SQUARE UNIFORMITY
1	OFF	100000	100202	202	0.70

(e) Random-Number Generator Statistics

FIGURE 3   Selected simulation output from GPSS model in Figure 2 (from Ref. 19).

TABLE 1   Summary Statistics for Eight Independent Replications with the One-Line, One-Server Model.

Replication Number	Time to Drill 100 Castings	Castings Waiting for the Drill	
		Average No. Waiting	Average Time Spent Waiting
1	1489.0	0.215	3.172
2	1544.7	0.130	1.995
3	1488.6	0.193	2.851
4	1522.8	0.064	0.970
5	1507.8	0.199	3.001
6	1527.5	0.110	1.667
7	1561.2	0.049	0.770
8	1503.0	0.152	2.259
Mean	1518.1	0.139	2.090
Standard deviation	2597.0	0.062	0.910

Source: From Ref. 19.

TABLE 2   90% Confidence Intervals Resulting from Table 1 Replications

Time to Drill 100 Castings	Castings Waiting for the Drill	
	Average No. Waiting	Average Time Spent Waiting
[1499.5, 1536.7]	[0.094, 0.184]	[1.434, 2.737]

Source: From Ref. 19.

the SLAM-II processor. SLAM-II automatically handles the event-scheduling, time advance algorithm, file operations such as the addition and deletion of entities, the collection of numerous statistics, and the generation of random samples. With its automatic file handling, SLAM-II can easily manage queues on FIFO or a LIFO basis, or entities can be ranked and served in order of some attribute such as priority. Unlike GPSS, SLAM-II has built-in random variate generators for a wide variety of statistical distributions.

A SLAM-II network consists of branches and nodes. A branch represents the passage of time; that is, it represents an activity. In addition, a branch may represent a limited number of servers. A branch is coded as an ACTIVITY statement. Nodes are used to represent the arrival event (CREATE node), delays or conditional waits (QUEUE node), the departure event (TERMINATE node), and other typical system actions.

The following problem, from Pritsker [5], illustrates the SLAM-II simulation modeling approach. Assembled television sets move through a series of testing stations in the final stage of their production. At the last of these stations, the vertical control setting on the TV sets is tested. If the setting is found be functioning improperly, the set is routed to an adjustment station where the necessary adjustment is made. After adjustment, the TV set is cycled back to the last inspection station where it is again inspected. TV sets passing the final inspection are routed to the packing area. Figure 4 is a schematic diagram of the inspection/adjustment process.

Figure 5 shows the SLAM-II network corresponding to the TV inspection adjustment process. The first node is a CREATE node, which models the arrival process of TV sets to the final inspection station. Interarrival time is uniformly distributed between 3.5 and 7.5 minutes. The node labeled INSP is a QUEUE node, which holds TV sets awaiting inspection. The branch emanating from the INSP QUEUE node represents the inspection activity. As the labeling shows, Activity 1 has 2 parallel servers, each performing inspections according to a uniform distribution between 6.0 and 12.0 minutes. Entities which arrive to the INSP QUEUE node when both servers are busy are stored in file 1, as indicated by the number 1 on the QUEUE node symbol. Following inspection, the entities move to a GOON node where they are probabilistically routed to either the adjustor, with probability 0.15, or to packing, with probability 0.85. Those going to the adjustor move to the ADJT QUEUE node. The adjustment activity is Activity 2, which is uniformly distributed between 20.0 and 40.0 minutes, with entities routed back to the INSP QUEUE node. Activity 2 is performed by a single server as indicated by the absence of a circle with the number of servers enclosed. Entities routed to packing move to a COLCT node, which collects interval statistics

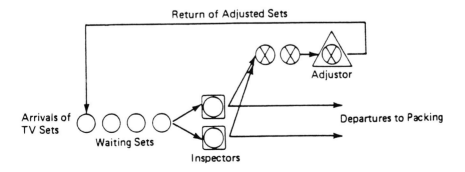

FIGURE 4   Schematic diagram of television set inspection/adjustment model (from Ref. 57).

on the variable corresponding to the time the entity spent in the system. The entities are then terminated. Figure 6 gives the network statement model for the TV set inspection and adjustment process. Figure 7 presents a summary report for this simulation. The analyst can also specify an optional trace of all or part of the simulation run.

SIMAN [4]   is a combined discrete/continuous simulation language for modeling general systems, although it has been designed to be especially applicable to manufacturing systems. SIMAN allows the programmer to employ either a process orientation or an event-scheduling approach to discrete simulation model development.

A useful feature of SIMAN is that it distinguishes between the system model frame and the experimental frame. The system model frame defines the static and dynamic characteristics of the system. In comparison, the experimental frame defines the experimental conditions under which the model is run to generate specific output data. For a given model, there can be many experimental frames resulting in many sets of output data.

The primary modeling orientation for SIMAN is the process view, in which a block diagram is constructed depicting the sequence of queues, activities, and delays encountered by an entity as it proceeds through the system. If an event orientation is used, a set of FORTRAN subprograms is used to augment or replace the block diagram. If the model contains continuous features, a set of differential/difference equations is encoded in subroutine STATE.

The following example, taken from Pegden [4], illustrates the application of SIMAN to a manufacturing system. This problem shows not only the process oriented approach to discrete-event simulation, but continuous modeling as well.

Steel ingots arrive to a soaking pit furnace in a steel plant where they are heated so that they can be rolled in the next stage of the process. The ingots arrive according to a Poisson process with a mean interarrival time of 2.25 hours.

There are ten soaking pits in the furnace. When an ingot arrives to the furnace, it is placed into a pit if one is available; otherwise it is placed in the cold ingot bank to wait for a free pit. The initial temperature of an arriving ingot is uniformly distributed between 400 and 500 °F. However, all ingots that are put into the cold ingot bank are assumed to have a temperature of 400° F on insertion into the soaking pit.

When an ingot is inserted into the furnace, it reduces the furnace temperature by the difference between the furnace temperature and the ingot temperature, divided by the number of ingots in the furnace. The furnace is heated according to the following differential equation:

$$\dot{F} = (2600 - F) \times .2$$

where F is the furnace temperature. The temperature change of the ingots as they are heated by the furnace is described by the following differential equation:

$$\dot{P}_j = (F - P_j) \times h_j$$

where P_j is the temperature of the ingot in the jth pit. The notations $\dot{F}$ and P_j represents the time derivatives dF/dt and dP_j/dt, respectively.

The variable h_j is the heating coefficient of the ingot in the jth pit and is equal to 1 plus a sample from a normal distrubition with a mean of .05 and a standard deviation of .01.

The ingots are heated in the furnace until the hottest ingot reaches 2200 °F. Then all ingots with a temperature greater than 2000°F are removed.

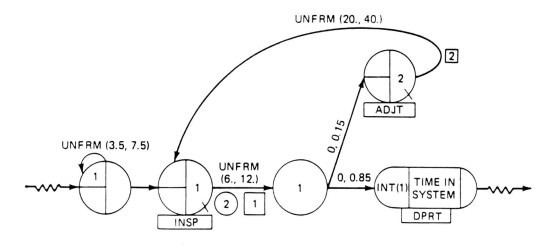

FIGURE 5   SLAM-II network of TV inspection adjustment model (from Ref. 5).

```
1   GEN,OREILLY,TV INSP. AND ADJUST.,6/25/83,1;
2   LIMITS,2,2,50;
3   NETWORK;
4        CREATE,UNFRM(3.5,7.5),,1;               CREATE TELEVISIONS
5   INSP QUEUE(1);                               INSPECTION QUEUE
6        ACT(2)/1,UNFRM(6.,12.);                 INSPECTION
7        GOON;
8        ACT,,.85,DPRT;                          85  DEPART
9        ACT,,.15,ADJT;                          15  ARE RE-ADJUSTED
10  ADJT QUEUE(2);                               ADJUST QUEUE
11       ACT/2,UNFRM(20.,40.),,INSP;             ADJUSTMENT
12  DPRT COLCT,INT(1),TIME IN SYSTEM;            COLLECT STATISTICS
13       TERM;
14       END;
15  INIT,0,480;
16  ;
17  ;   WRITE A TEXT TRACE FROM TIME 0 TO TIME 60,
18  ;    PRINT THE VALUE OF ATRIB(1), NNQ(1), AND NNQ(2)
19  MONTR,TRACE,0,60,ATRIB(1),NNQ(1),NNQ(2);
20  FIN;
```

FIGURE 6   Network statement model of TV inspection/ adjustment problem of Figure 5 (from Ref. 5).

SLAM II SUMMARY REPORT

SIMULATION PROJECT TV INSP. AND ADJUST.

BY OREILLY

RUN NUMBER 1 OF 1

DATE 6/25/1983

CURRENT TIME   0.4800E+03
STATISTICAL ARRAYS CLEARED AT TIME   0.0000E+00

** STATISTICS FOR VARIABLES BASED ON OBSERVATION **

	MEAN VALUE	STANDARD DEVIATION	COEFF. OF VARIATION	MINIMUM VALUE	MAXIMUM VALUE	NUMBER OF OBSERVATIONS
TIME IN SYSTEM	0.2663E+02	0.3591E+02	0.1348E+01	0.6381E+01	0.1622E+03	84

** FILE STATISTICS **

FILE NUMBER	ASSOC NODE LABEL/TYPE	AVERAGE LENGTH	STANDARD DEVIATION	MAXIMUM LENGTH	CURRENT LENGTH	AVERAGE WAITING TIME
1	INSP QUEUE	0.8515	0.7756	3	0	4.0465
2	ADJT QUEUE	1.4651	1.1945	4	1	46.8822
3	CALENDER	3.9019	0.4912	6	4	4.7177

** SERVICE ACTIVITY STATISTICS **

ACTIVITY INDEX	START NODE OR ACTIVITY LABEL	SERVER CAPACITY	AVERAGE UTILIZATION	STANDARD DEVIATION	CURRENT UTILIZATION	AVERAGE BLOCKAGE	MAXIMUM IDLE TIME/SERVERS	MAXIMUM BUSY TIME/SERVERS	ENTITY COUNT
1	INSPECTION	2	1.9059	0.2920	2	0.0000	2.0000	2.0000	99
2	ADJUSTMENT	1	0.8710	0.3352	1	0.0000	48.3651	245.4028	13

FIGURE 7   SLAM–II Summary report for TV inspection / adjustment model (from Ref. 5).

This system is simulated for 100 hours to determine the utilization of the furnace, the heating time for the ingots, the temperature of the furnace, and the number of ingots in the cold bank. The initial furnace temperature is 1100°F.

This example is modeled using the combined discrete/continuous features of SIMAN. The flow of ingots through the system is modeled using a block diagram and the ingot and furnace temperatures are modeled as continuous state variables.

We begin the development of the continuous component of the model by making an equivalence between the problem variables and elements of the SIMAN arrays S and D. We let S(J) for J equal to 1 through 10 represent the temperature of the ingot in the *j*-th pit, with a value of zero indicating the pit is empty. The temperature of the furnace is represented by S(11) and the variable S(12) is the temperature of the hottest ingot. These variables are summarized below:

$$S(J) = P_j \qquad\qquad j = 1, \ldots, 10$$

$$D(J) = \dot{P}_j \qquad\qquad j = 1, \ldots, 10$$

$$S(11) = F$$

$$D(11) = \dot{F}$$

$$S(12) = \max_{j} \; P_j \qquad\qquad j = 1, \ldots, 10$$

$$X(J) = h_j \qquad\qquad j = 1, \ldots, 10$$

Subroutine STATE for this example is shown in Figure 8. Initially, S(12) is set to 0.0. Within the DO loop, the temperature of each ingot is tested against S(12), and in each case where the temperature exceeds S(12), S(12) is reset to the ingot temperature. In this way, S(12) will be returned as the maximum ingot temperature. The last statement in the DO loop computes the rate of change of the temperature for each ingot. Following the DO loop, the rate of change of the furnace temperature is computed.

The block diagram listing is shown in Figure 9. The discrete model consists of two segments that will be described seperately. The entities in the first segment represent the ingots flowing through the system. The ingots are generated at the CREATE block and their arrival time to the system is marked in attribute 1. The ingots wait in file 1 at the QUEUE block for one unit of the resource PIT that is assigned a capacity of 10 in the experimental frame. Once the ingot seizes a PIT, the index of the available pit is determined using the FINDJ block to test for X (J) equal to zero that indicates pit J is empty. X(J) is then set to the heating coefficient for the ingot and S(J) is assigned the initial ingot temperature. A test is then made at the BRANCH block to determine if the ingot waited in the cold ingot bank. If the current time TNOW is greater than the mark time A(1), the ingot has waited in the cold ingot bank and is therefore branched to the block labeled COLDBANK where the temperature of the ingot is reset to 400 and attribute 1 is remarked at the current time. In either case, the ingots arrive to the ASSIGN block labeled FURNACE, where the furnace temperature S(11) is reduced by the difference between the furnace temperature and the ingot temperature, divided by the number of ingots in the furnace. The ingot then enters the QUEUE block where it waits in file 2 until signal number J is received. Following receipt of signal J the PIT is released and the heating time for the ingot is recorded.

```
        SUBROUTINE STATE
        COMMON/SIM/D(50) , DL(50) , S(50) , SL(50) , X(50) , DTNOW, TNOW, TFIN, J,
        NRUN
C
        S(12) = 0.0
        DO 10 I = 1, 10
        IF (S(I). GT.S(12))   S(12) = S(I)
10      D(I) = (S(11) – S(I)) * X(I)
        D(11) = (2600.0 – S(11)) * .2
        RETURN
        END
```

FIGURE 8   Subroutine STATE for SIMAN model of the soaking pit furnace model (from Ref. 4).

		BEGIN	
10		CREATE: EX(1,1): MARK(1);	CREATE ARRIVING INGOTS
20		QUEUE, 1;	QUEUE IN FILE 1
30		SEIZE: PIT;	SEIZE A PIT
40		FINDJ, 1, 10:X(J) . EQ.0;	FIND THE FIRST FREE PIT
50		ASSIGN: X(J) = RN(2,1) + .1;	ASSIGN THE HEATING COEFF.
60		ASSIGN: S(J) = UN(3,1);	ASSIGN THE INGOT INIT. TEMP.
70		BRANCH, 1:	
		IF, TNOW. GT.A(1), COLDBANK:	
		ELSE, FURNACE;	TEST FOR INGOT IN COLDBANK
80	COLDBANK	ASSIGN:S(J) = 400:MARK(1);	RESET INGOT TEMP. TO 400
90	FURNACE	ASSIGN:S(11) = S(11)–	
		(S(11) – S(J))/NR(1);	REDUCE FURNACE TEMP.
100		QUEUE, 2;	QUEUE IN FILE 2
110		WAIT:J;	HEAT UP UNTIL SIGNAL
120		RELEASE:PIT;	RELEASE THE PIT
130		TALLY:1, INT(1): DISPOSE;	RECORD HEATING TIME
	;		
140		DETECT:S(12),P,2200;	DETECT MAX PIT TEMP CROSSING
150		ASSIGN: J=0;	INITIALIZE SEARCH.INDEX
160	NEXTJ	ASSIGN: J=J+1;	INCREMENT SEARCH INDEX
170		BRANCH:	
		IF, S(J) .GT. 2000, RELEASE:	
		IF, J.LT.10, NEXTJ;	TEST FOR RELEASE OF INGOT
180	RELEASE	SIGNAL: J;	SIGNAL END OF HEATUP
190		ASSIGN:X(J) = 0;	RESET HEATING COEFF. TO 0
200		ASSIGN:S(J) = 0: DISPOSE;	RESET INGOT TEMP. TO 0
	END;		

FIGURE 9   SIMAN model block listing for soaking pit furnace operation (from Ref. 4).

```
         BEGIN;

10       PROJECT, PIT FURNACE, PEGDEN, 4/30/81;
20       DISCRETE, 50, 1, 2;
30       CONTINUOUS, 11, 1, .01, 1, .1;
40       INITIALIZE, S(11) = 1100;
50       PARAMETERS: 1, 2.25:2, .05, .01:3, 400, 500;
60       TALLIES: 1, HEATING TIME;
70       DSTAT: 1, NQ(1), COLDBANK QUEUE: 2, NQ(2), FURNACE UTIL;
80       CSTAT: 1, S(11), FURNACE TEMP;
90       RESOURCES: 1, PIT, 10;
100      REPLICATE, 1, 0, 100;
         END;
```

FIGURE 10

The second model segment monitors the temperature of the ingots and releases ingots from the furnace by signaling an end of the heatup operation represented by the WAIT block in the first model segment. The DETECT block monitors the hottest ingot temperature whenever 2200 °F is crossed in the positive direction. A search is then made over the index J from 1 to 10 to release all ingots having a temperature greater than 2000°F. For each ingot released a copy of the entity is branched to the SIGNAL block labeled RELEASE where a signal is sent to end the WAIT operation for pit J, the heating coefficient X(J) is set to 0. To indicate pit J is empty the temperature S(J) of the ingot in pit J is set to 0.

The experiment listing for this example is shown in Figure 10. The CONTINUOUS element specifies that the model uses 11 differential equations and 1 state equation. Based on this specification, SIMAN interprets the values for D(1) through D(11) over time to obtain the values for S(1) through S(11).

The SIMAN Summary Report for this example is shown in Figure 11. During the 100-hour simulation, 30 ingots completed processing with an average heating time of 19.36 hours. During this period, the average furnace utilization was 7.2 and there was a maximum of 5 ingots in the cold bank queue. The average furnace temperature was 2012°F.

Specialized Simulation Languages

In addition to the high-level programming languages such as FORTRAN, PASCAL, BASIC, and C, the general-purpose simulation languages such as GASP-IV, GPSS, SIMSCRIPT II.5, SLAM-II, and SIMAN, there are any number of highly specialized simulation products that enable a user to model manufacturing systems. Biles and Bathina [6] described PASAMS, a PASCAL-based computer simulation model of flexible manufacturing systems. PASAMS is a compact, flexible program that is ideally suited for low-cost microcomputers. The user interacts with the program to develop and simulate a model of a system containing machines, robots, conveyors, automated guided vehicles (AGVs), workparts, and assemblies. The user is freed from the task of learning a programming language or simulation language, and instead describes the systems in terms of its real

SIMAN SUMMARY REPORT

RUN 1 OF 1

PROJECT : PIT FURNACE
ANALYST : PEGDEN
DATE   : 4/30/1981
RUN ENDED AT TIME   .1000E + 03

TALLY VARIABLES

NUMBER IDENTIFIER	AVERAGE	STANDARD DEVIATION	MINIMUM VALUE	MAXIMUM VALUE	NUMBER OF OBS.
1 HEATING TIME	.1936E + 02	.5428E + 01	.1126E + 02	.2824E + 02	30

DISCRETE CHANGE VARIABLES

NUMBER IDENTIFIER	AVERAGE	STANDARD DEVIATION	MINIMUM VALUE	MAXIMUM VALUE	TIME PERIOD
1 COLDBANK QUEUE	.5102E + 00	.1227E + 01	0.	.5000E + 01	.1000E +03
2 FURNACE UTIL	.7199E + 01	.2937E + 01	0.	.1000E + 02	.1000E + 03

CONTINUOUS CHANGE VARIABLES

NUMBER IDENTIFIER	AVERAGE	STANDARD DEVIATION	MINIMUM VALUE	MAXIMUM VALUE	TIME PERIOD
1 FURNACE TEMP	.2012E + 04	.4469E + 03	.4378E + 03	.2556E +04	.1000E + 03

FIGURE 11   SIMAN summary report for soaking pit furnace operation (from Ref. 4).

components. The disadvantage of this highly specialized approach is that it cannot be readily applied to other types of systems.

XCELL+ [7] is another highly specialized approach to modeling manufacturing system. It employs a combination of computer graphics and a menu-driven data entry system. As shown in Figure 12, XCELL+ relies heavily on a schematic graphical model of the manufacturing system. It uses symbolic graphics rather than realistic pictorial graphics, but does use color to increase the amount of information that can be displayed effectively at one time.

Animated Graphics in Manufacturing Simulation

The advent of moderately priced color graphics monitors has brought about a plethora of animated graphics packages for computer simulation. Some of the commercially available animated graphics packages, and the simulation languages they support are listed below:

- MINUTEMAN Software's GPSS/PC, Version 2, provides built-in graphic and animation features
- Auto-Simulations, Inc. offers AUTOGRAM, which supports animated graphics on GPSS/H
- Systems Modeling's CINEMA provides animated graphics for SIMAN
- Pritsker and Associates' TESS supports SLAM-II and GPSS/H
- CACI's SIMFACTORY provides graphical animation for SIMSCRIPT II.5

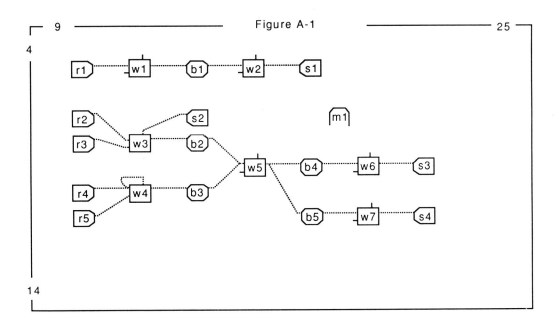

FIGURE 12 XCELL + block scheme for factory model (from Ref. 7).

REFERENCES

1. H. B. Woolf, (ed.), *Webster's New Collegiate Dictionary*, G. and C. Merriam Company, Springfield, MA, 1981.
2. A. M. Law, "Simulation of Manufacturing Systems," in *Proc. 1981 Winter Simulation Conference*, Atlanta, 1987, pp. 631–643.
3. A. A. B. Pritsker, *The GASP-IV Simulation Language*, John Wiley, New York, 1974.
4. C. D. Pegden, *Introduction to SIMAN*, Systems Modeling Corp., State College, PA, 1985.
5. A. A. B. Pritsker, *The SLAM-II Simulation Language*, Systems Publishing Company, West Lafayette, IN, 1985.
6. W. E. Biles and V. R. Bathina, "PASAMS: Pascal Simulation and Analysis of Manufacturing Systems," *Material Flow*, *3*, 1986, pp. 99–112.
7. R. Conway, W. L. Maxwell, J. O. McLain, and S. L. Worona, *User's Guide to XCELL + Factory Modeling System*, Scientific Press, Redwood City, CA, 1987.
8. D. M., Etter, *Structured FORTRAN 77 for Engineers and Scientists*. Benjamin/Cummins Publishing Co., San Francisco CA, 1987.
9. J. M. Pruett, *Fundamentals of Programming with FORTRAN 77*, Instrument Society of America, Research Triangle Park, NC, 1987.
10. K. D. Tocher, *The Art of Simulation*, Van Nostrand, Princeton, 1963.
11. C. McMillan and R. F. Gonzalez, *Systems Analysis, A Computer Approach to Decision Models*, Richard D. Irwin, Inc., Homewood, IL, 1965.
12. J. W. Schmidt, and R. E. Taylor, *Simulation Analysis of Industrial Systems* , Richard D. Irwin, Homewood, IL, 1970.
13. M. Savsar, and W. E. Biles, "Simulation Analysis of Automated Production Flow Lines," *Material Flow*, 2, 191–201. 1985.
14. V. K. Vasudev, and W. E. Biles, "Microcomputer-Based Modeling and Simulation," *Eur. J. Oper. Res., 24*, 30–36. (1986).
15. B. Kernighan, and D. Ritchie, *The C Programming Language*, 2nd Ed., Prentice-Hall, Englewood Cliffs, NJ, 1988.
16. H. M. Markowitz, P. J. Kiviat, and R. Valenzuela, *Simscript II.5 Programming Language*, CACI, Inc. Los Angeles, CA, 1987.
17. T. J. Schriber, *Simulation Using GPSS*, John Wiley, New York, 1974.
18. J. Henriksen, *The GPSS/H Simulation Language*, Wolverine Software, Falls Church, VA, 1984.
19. T. J. Schriber, "Perspectives on Simulation Using GPSS," in *Proc. 1987 Winter Simulation Conference*, Atlanta, 1987, pp. 112–125.

WILLIAM E. BILES

THOMAS G. RAY

THE MEMORY MANAGEMENT UNIT

INTRODUCTION

The memory management unit (MMU) is a hardware device that extends the CPU architecture to provide very low-level hardware support for advanced operating system software features, including virtual memory, multitasking, and data security. This article describes what an MMU is, and how it fits into the architecture of a computer system. We then discuss the characteristics of an MMU that are important to the operating system and give several examples of commercially available MMUs.

A major function of an operating system is to control access to the computer system's hardware resources. The operating system's memory management routines control a critical resource: memory.

THE MEMORY HIERARCHY

Most computer systems include a hierarchy of memory types that work together to form what looks like "the memory" to a program running on the CPU. This hierarchy can be modeled by a central processing unit (CPU), an MMU, and four types of memory (Fig. 1). The fact that there are several layers memory hierarchy is of no real interest to an end user; the divisions are invisible. The system architect, however, will mix and match from this model to design a memory system that hits a price/performance target.

An important MMU service is support for virtual memory. Virtual memory systems allow secondary memory to act like slow primary memory. This creates the illusion that the system includes a huge amount of memory when, in fact, there may be a small amount of random access memory (RAM) and a large hard disk.

This has two advantages, first it means that the system can run a program which is actually larger than the amount of available physical memory. For example, a system may include 2 Mbytes of RAM and still be able to run a 4 Mbyte program that accesses a 10 Mb data base stored on a 200 Mbyte hard disk. Second, it means that application programs do not have to be modified to match a particular memory configuration.

Another important function provided by all MMU designs is the ability to relocate a program to another part of memory, according to a set of preassigned translation rules. This relocation is done in hardware, without requiring any modification to the application software. A multitasking operating system can then switch from one program to another by simply reconfiguring the MMU's translation registers, without reloading the entire program. This ability to quickly switch between several programs allows a system to run several programs concurrently and is referred to as multitasking.

Figure 2 shows how an MMU with several programs running under a multitasking operating system performs this translation. Before a program is run on a system with an MMU, the operating system configures the MMU such that the user's program is relocated to an unused section of memory. The program then begins execution, unaware of the

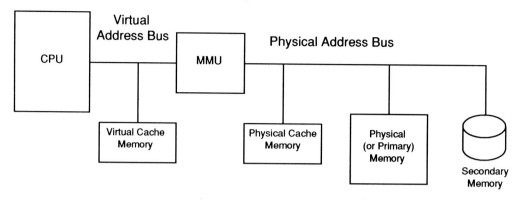

Block Diagram of Memory Hierarchy

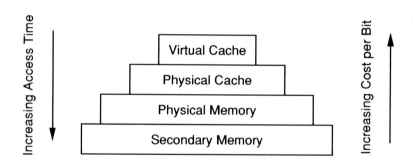

Memory Hierarchy- Access Time vs. Cost

FIGURE 1   System model includes a hierarchy of memory types.

MMU's actions. For example, a program may be compiled and linked to run starting at location 400, but if that location in physical memory is being used for some other purpose, the operating system can configure the MMU hardware to convert all the program's memory references to some other, unused section of memory. If the MMU did not provide the translation function, the compiler would have to somehow know physical addresses of the entire runtime system, and these addresses are unknown at compile time.

The MMU can enforce data security mechanisms. Since the MMU is in series with all CPU to memory accesses, it can provide data security by preempting unauthorized read or write cycles.

The MMU hardware provides these services by dividing physical memory into smaller pieces and assigning translation descriptors to these pieces. The operating system can then manipulate these descriptors to control the memory hierarchy and provide virtual memory, multitasking, and data security functions. The details of how the MMU hardware divides memory are described below.

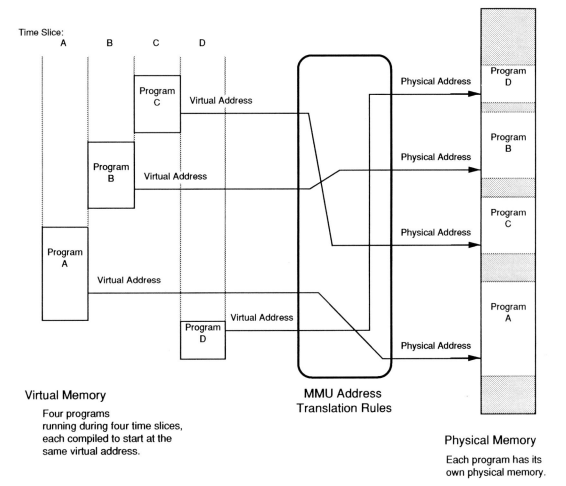

FIGURE 2   MMU translates virtual addresses into physical memory.

MMU HARDWARE DESCRIPTION

In a system that does not include an MMU, the CPU is attached directly to primary memory as shown in Figure 3. This figure also includes the state and timing diagrams for a memory read cycle. When the CPU wants to get data from the memory, it puts an address on the address bus and sends a strobe control to memory; then the memory puts the requested data on the data bus and returns an acknowledge to the CPU.

A system which includes an MMU is shown in Figure 4. Notice that the state diagram has two new states labeled MMU and TLB. When the CPU wants to read data from memory, it sends out a virtual address and strobe to the MMU. The MMU checks the translation lookaside buffer (TLB) to see if it already knows how to translate this virtual address into a physical address. If the information is in the TLB, then the MMU generates the physical address and sends a strobe to the memory. The memory then completes the cycle by returning data and an acknowledge to the CPU.

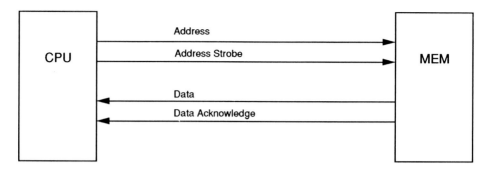

Block Diagram

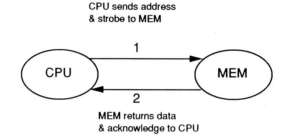

State Diagram

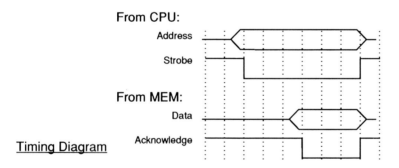

Timing Diagram

FIGURE 3   Typical system without MMU.

If the translation information is not in the TLB, then the MMU must search through tables of translation descriptors stored in main memory. When it finds the correct descriptor, it loads it into the TLB. Once the information is in the TLB, the MMU can generate a physical address and send a strobe to the memory. The memory then completes the cycle by returning data and an acknowledge to the CPU. The descriptor tables are stored in a tree structure in primary memory and the process of searching through the descriptor tables is called an MMU tablewalk. The tablewalk is done entirely by hardware internal to the MMU.

The translation process does change the hardware timing. The MMU does not assert the physical address strobe until it has received the virtual address strobe and had time to

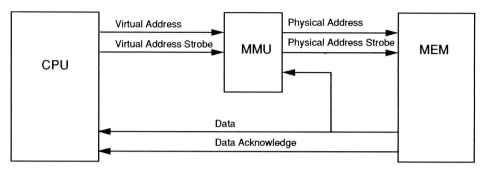

Block Diagram

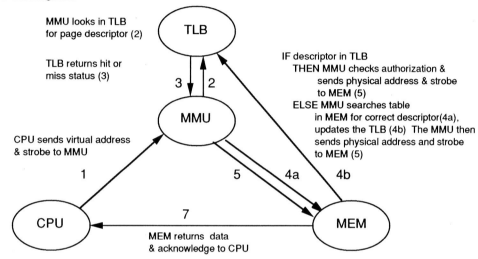

State Diagram

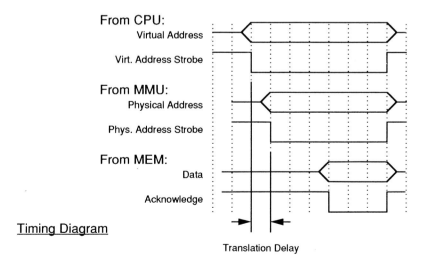

Timing Diagram

FIGURE 4   Typical system with MMU.

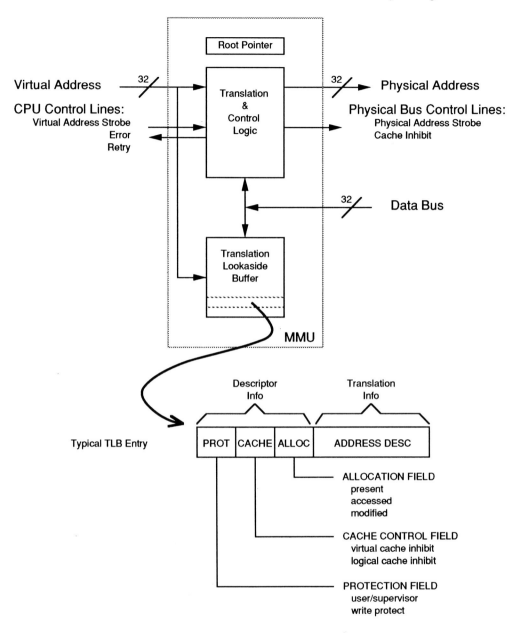

FIGURE 5   MMU block diagram.

access the TLB and put the physical address on the bus. This translation delay is marked on the timing diagram and effectively slows the CPU's memory access time. If the translation delay is too great, it may drastically hurt system performance as the CPU has to insert wait states. Microprocessors that include the MMU on the same chip as the CPU are usually able to shorten the translation delay enough that cycle times are not affected. If the MMU is external to the CPU, a system designer may have to use a faster memory design to make up for the translation delay or add a virtual cache to reduce the effects of the translation delay.

The block diagram of an MMU is shown in Figure 5. Notice that it has three interfaces to 32-bit buses; the virtual address bus and the physical address bus are used during translation and the data bus is used by the MMU to load data from the memory into the TLB at the end of a tablewalk. The root pointer register tells the control logic the location of the descriptor tree base in physical memory; where to begin the table walk. The TLB is a small cache memory that stores descriptors for recently translated addresses.

The TLB must be designed to provide high hit rates so that the time spent doing MMU tablewalks does not degrade system performance. The system designer must consider such issues as cache organization and replacement policies, and cope with the classic cache problems of address synonyms and stale data.

To avoid the time lost to translation delays, the TLB cache is addressed by the virtual address bus. Address synonyms occur because multiple virtual addresses describe different physical locations. For example, as program A is running, the TLB fills with the appropriate descriptors. When program B begins to run in the same virtual address space, the TLB can't distinguish whether the virtual address is coming from program A or B and may provide incorrect descriptor information. To avoid this problem, the operating system must invalidate the TLB before program B begins to run. Stale TLB data can occur when the CPU writes memory in order to modify a descriptor. Notice that the CPU might update a descriptor which is already in the TLB, the data in the TLB copy of the desciptor is then "stale" since it does not agree with descriptor in memory. Again, to avoid this problem, the operating system must invalidate the TLB after it modifies descriptor tables. Stale data can also occur in a multiprocessor system. This situation is discussed later.

Entries in the TLB can be divided into two parts: the translation information that allows the MMU to perform the virtual to physical translation and the descriptor information that assigns special attributes to each of those smaller pieces.

The TLB entry in Figure 5, shows these two parts. The descriptor information includes three fields which support special operating system functions.

The protection field is divided into two smaller fields which the operating system can program to insure system integrity. The write protect field can be set to stop illegal or unintentional write cycles. It can also be used to support operating system functions such as copy on write. The user/supervisor bit can be programmed to directly support the operating system model user and kernel modes, so that a process running in user mode can access user data and instructions, but the MMU will stop any attempted access to kernel instructions or data.

The cache control field allows the operating system to set cache inhibit bits for the caches. The cache inhibit bit must be set for areas of memory which are used for certain special uses such as memory mapped I/O devices. Data which is shared among several processes or several processors may have to be marked as cache inhibited to avoid cache coherence problems.

The allocation field provides hardware support for virtual memory. The present bit is set by the operating system when information is moved from secondary memory into primary memory. If the CPU tries to access an area which does not have the present bit set, the MMU stops the access and sends a signal to the CPU that forces a branch to an operating system routine. This routine moves data from secondary memory into primary memory and sets the present bit. Once the missing information has been moved into memory, the CPU can continue execution.

The accessed bit is set by the MMU when it loads the descriptor into the TLB. The modified bit is set by the MMU if the CPU does a write to the area of memory referred to by the descriptor. The operating system can use these two bits when it needs to reclaim memory for another use. Although the MMU sets these bits, the operating system memory management routines must clear them when system dynamics require it. For example, the operating system may clear the accessed bit, then check it later to determine if the page has been used recently by any applications programs. If it has not, the operating system may decide to reclaim that memory for use by another program. If the modified bit is set, this indicates an area of memory has been updated. Now the updated memory must be copied back to secondary memory before it can be reclaimed, or the most recent updates will be lost. The translation portion of the TLB entry includes address description information which allows the MMU translation logic to generate the high order physical address bits. Two translation schemes are described in detail below.

TRANSLATION SCHEMES

Two well-established translation mechanisms have become popular in a wide variety of systems. Each provides good flexibility and can be implemented with a modest amount of MMU hardware. These two translation schemes, segmented translation and paged translation, are described below.

Segmented translation allows memory to be partitioned into variable sized pieces called segments. The mechanism for segmented translation is shown in Figure 6. In this example, the upper bits of the address are called the segment number and the lower bits are called the segment displacement. The segment number is used to address into a table of descriptors. The descriptor includes a base address which is the starting address of the segment in physical memory. The descriptor also includes a length attribute. The segment offset should be smaller than the length, if it is not, the memory cycle is aborted and an error is indicated. Assuming that there is not an error, the translation is completed by arithmetically adding the segment offset to the base address. Physical memory can now be divided into 256 variable sized segments. Each segment can be from one to 64 Kbytes long.

Although variable segment size allows memory allocation to fit memory requests better, it leads to a problem called external fragmentation. This problem is unique to segmented MMUs and occurs when variable sized segments leave holes in physical memory which are too small for practical use.

Figure 7 shows how paged translation works. In this example, the MMU divides the virtual address into two parts, the upper bits are called the segment number and the lower bits are called the page index. The page index, which determines the page size, is passed directly through the MMU to form the lower part of the physical address. The segment number is used as an address into a segment table. The data out of the segment table is called the page address and forms the upper is used as an address into a segment table. The data out of the segment table is called the page address and forms the upper part of the physical address. Logically then, a memory location is described by a 13-bit offset into one of 2048 pages. While physically, memory is divided into 2k pages which have a fixed size of 8Kbytes.

Since pages have a fixed size, requests for memory that are smaller than the page size result in wasted memory. This phenomenon is called internal fragmentation. For example, suppose that a program needs 1Kbyte of storage for its data. When it is run it will be assigned one 4K segment. The other 3K is a memory fragment which cannot be used by any other program.

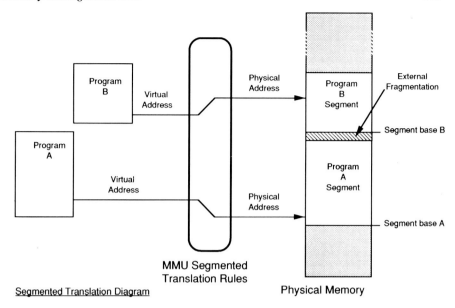

Segmented Translation Diagram

MMU Segmented
Translation Rules

Physical Memory

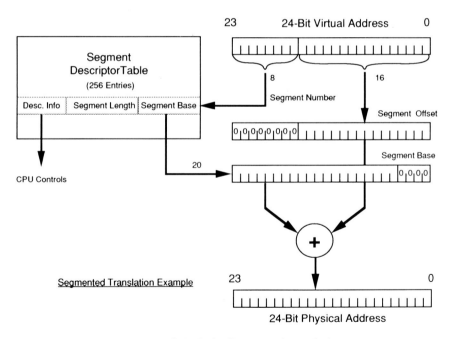

Segmented Translation Example

FIGURE 6   Segmented translation.

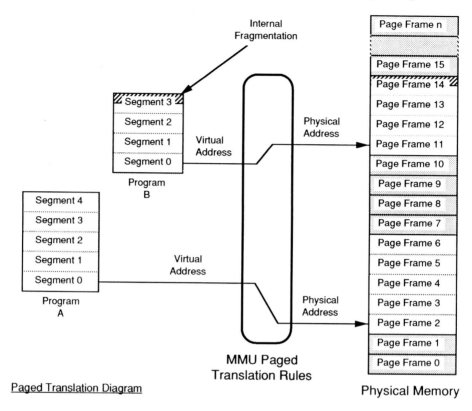

Paged Translation Diagram

MMU Paged Translation Rules

Physical Memory

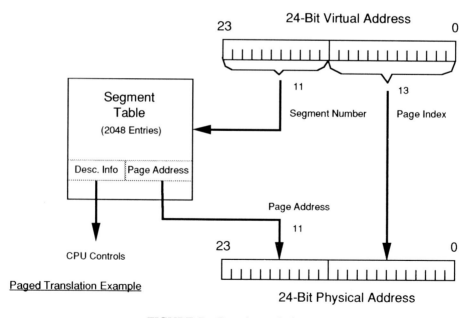

Paged Translation Example

FIGURE 7   Paged translation

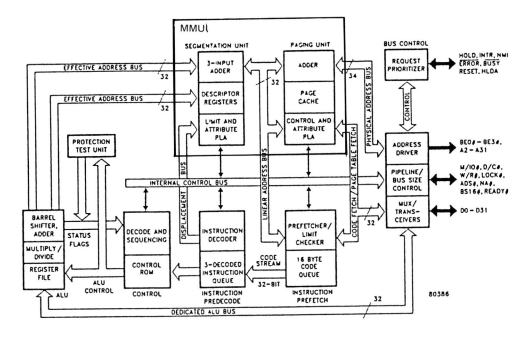

FIGURE 8   Intel microprocessor and MMU block diagram.

In both translation schemes, the MMU divides physical memory into smaller pieces and assigns descriptor information to each piece. The operating system can then use these attributes to control access to memory and provide important system features.

COMMERCIALLY AVAILABLE MMUS

The Intel 80386 microprocessor includes a CPU and an MMU in a single 132-pin pin grid array package. The block diagram of the 80386 is shown in Figure 8 [*1*]. The MMU architecture includes both a segmentation unit and paging unit.

The 80386 translation mechanism is detailed in Figure 9. The segmentation unit first translates the virtual address into a physical address. The segmentation unit allows variable size segments which can be as large as 4 gigabytes. The paging unit has a fixed two-level translation algorithm and a page size of 4K. The paging unit also includes a 32-entry TLB. The TLB is organized as a four-way set associative cache. When the TLB is full and it must find room for a new entry, the control logic implements a true LRU (least recently used) replacement algorithm to select the oldest entry for replacement.

The 80386 supports virtual memory. Present bits in the page descriptors notify the CPU if a page is in primary or secondary memory (see Fig. 10). The page descriptor also includes additional bits which the operating system can use to support page replacement

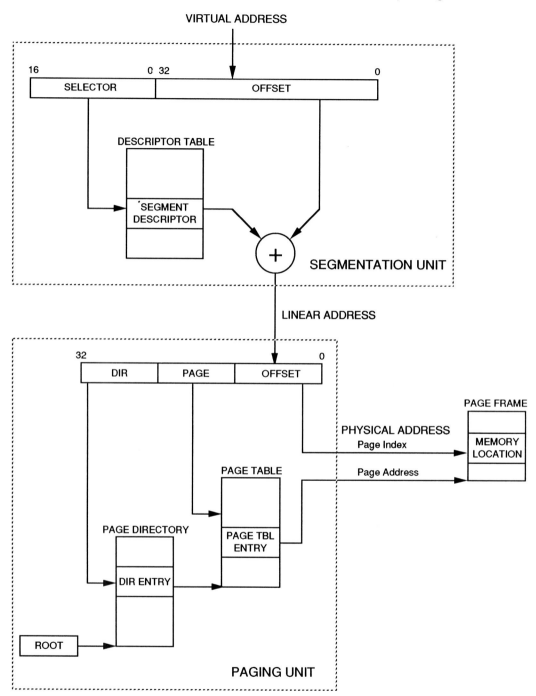

FIGURE 9   80386 MMU combines segmentation and paging translation.

31   12 11   0

PAGE FRAME ADDRESS 31..12	AVAIL	00	D	A	00	U / S	U / W	P

P   -PRESENT
R/S   -READ/WRITE
U/S   -USER/SUPERVISOR
A   -ACCESSED
D   -DIRTY
AVAIL   -AVAILABLE FOR SYSTEMS PROGRAMMER USE

NOTE: 0 INDICATES INTEL RESERVED. DO NOT DEFINE

FIGURE 10   Format of 80386 page table entry.

algorithms. There are *accessed* and *dirty* bits which are set by the MMU while programs are running. There is also a three-bit AVAIL field which the operating system can use, and these bits are typically used for aging information.

The Motorola 68030 combines a CPU, virtual cache, and MMU into a single chip. In the 68030 architecture, the MMU is defined as a coprocessor with its own register model and extensions to the instruction set. The block diagram of the 68030 is shown in Figure 11 [2].

The 68030 MMU implements a paged translation mechanism. The paging unit has a programmable translation algorithm which can have one to five levels of translation. The page size can also be programmed to be 256 to 32K bytes. There are also two transparent translation registers which can map separate blocks of memory directly, without translation. Figure 12 shows examples of 68030 translation tables.

The TLB (called the address translation cache in Motorola literature) is a 22-entry, fully associative cache and uses a pseudo-LRU replacement algorithm. The 68030's MMU architecture includes support for virtual memory support. The page descriptors are similar to those shown for the 80386.

Both the 80386 and 68030 integrate the MMU and CPU into a single chip. This allows improved performance by eliminating the effects of the translation delay, and reduces cost by eliminating the large, high pin-count package normally associated with an external MMU.

The last example shows the Motorola 88000 RISC processor. The block diagram for single processor system in Figure 13 [3]. Notice that the 88100 microprocessor is an example of a Harvard architecture, since it includes separate buses for the instruction and data paths. Two 88200 cache and MMU (or CMMU) devices are required, one for each of the buses. These physical caches are multiplexed to share a single path to primary memory.

The 88000 uses a paged translation mechanism which is similar to the 68030, however, the TLB architecture does include a unique feature which is designed to improve performance in a multiprocessor configuration.

The stale data problem described above involved a single processor system. Another cause for stale data is possible in a multiprocessor system. It occurs when several MMUs have copies of the same descriptor in their own local TLBs. If one processor then changes a page descriptor in physical memory, it can invalidate its own TLB but the data in the other TLBs is now stale. The 88200 CMMU allows a graceful solution to this problem by

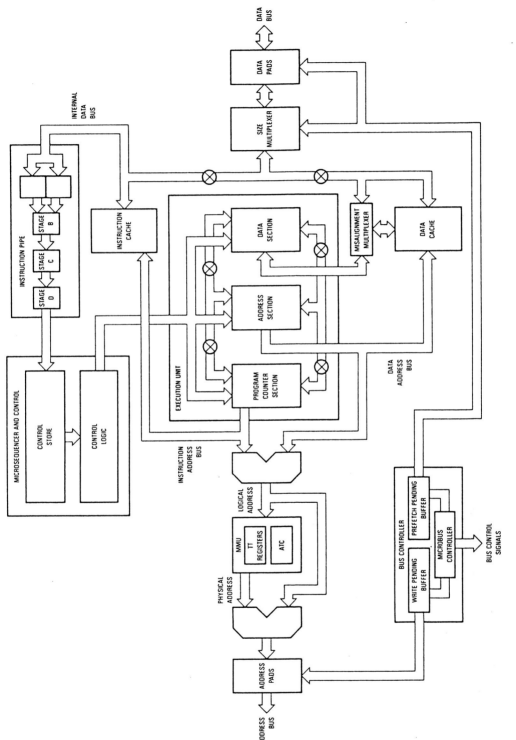

FIGURE 11   Motorola 68030 microprocessor and MMU block diagram.

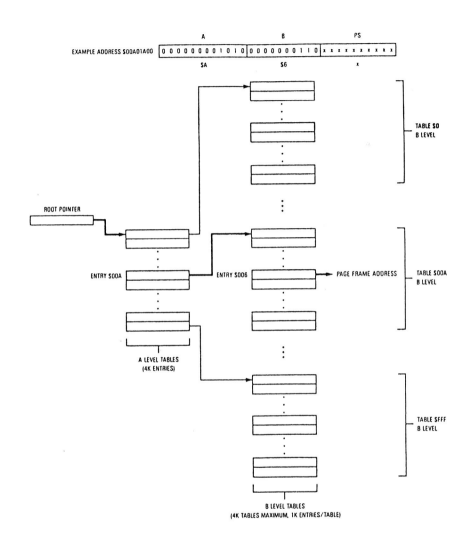

Two Level Translation Tree

FIGURE 12a   68030 Translation tables can be programmed for various configurations.

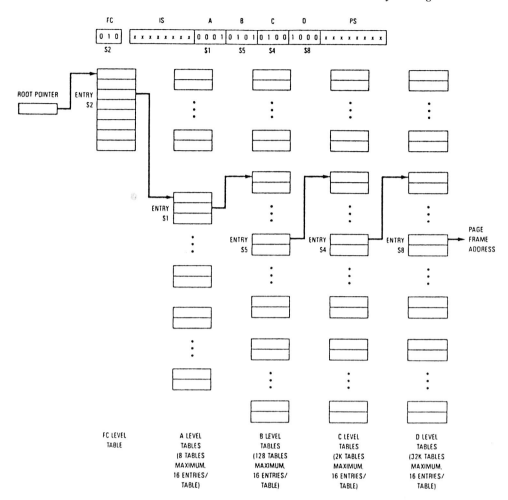

Five Level Translation Tree

FIGURE 12b

allowing remote invalidation of other TLBs (as shown in Fig. 14). As this illustration shows, when one of the processors changes a page descriptor in physical memory and flushes its own TLB, it can then send a command to other TLBs which will invalidate their (now stale) entries.

BIBLIOGRAPHIC NOTES

An extensive survey and bibliography can be found elsewhere [4]. A detailed discussion of the entire memory hierarchy, including cache/TLB design and performance issues are covered in a text by Pohm [5]. A discussion of MMU design options and cache/MMU interaction can be found in Cho [6]. Alexander et al. [7] compare the performance of various TLB architectures in the UNIX environment. Dixon [8] and Wood et al. [9] propose combining the MMU and cache functions. Memory management issues related to

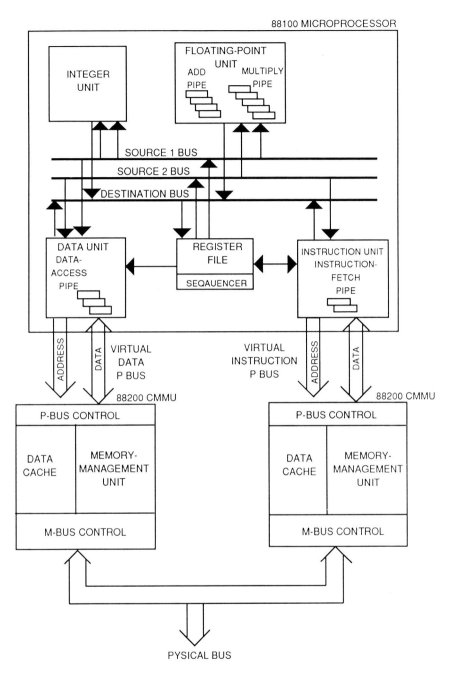

FIGURE 13   Motorola 88000 RISC Microprocessor and MMU block diagram.

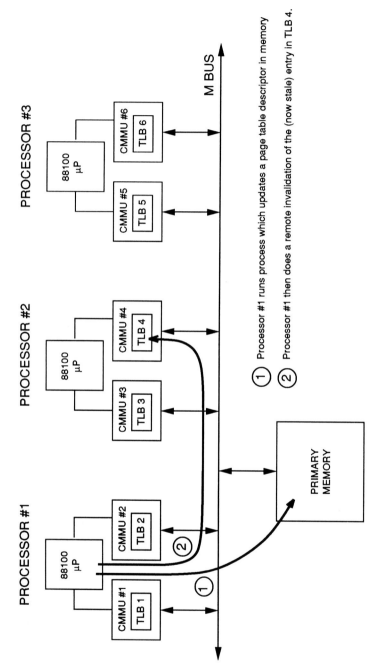

FIGURE 14   The 88000 multiprocessor architecture supports remote TLB invalidation.

multiprocessors and parallel operating systems are covered by Rashid et al. [*10*]. Baer [*11*] describes MMU theory in more depth, including discussion of an algorithim developed to simplify allocation in segmented systems (p. 298). An alternative to the classical MMU described here in proposed by Thakkar and Knowles [*12*].

OS/2's segmented memory management is discussed in Heller [*13*]. Strategies developed for porting UNIX to the 80386 are discussed in Hensler and Sarno [*14*]. A detailed description of the UNIX system can be found in Bach [*16*]. The VAX/VMS operating system and MMU hardware are described in Levy and Lipmon [*16*].

REFERENCES

1. Intel Corp., *80386 High Performance 32-bit Microprocessor with Integrated Memory Management*, Intel Corporation, Santa Clara, CA, 1986.
2. Motorola Inc., *MC68030 Enhanced 32-Bit Microprocessor User's Manual*, Motorola Inc., Austin, TX, 1987.
3. Motorola Inc., *MC88200 Data Sheet,* Motorola Inc., Austin, TX, 1988.
4. B. Furht and V. Milutinovic, "A Survey of Microprocessor Architectures for Memory Management," *Computer* (March 1987).
5. A. V. Pohm, and O. P. Agrawal, *High-Speed Memory Systems*, Reston Publishing Company, Inc., Reston, VA, 1983.
6. J. Cho, A. J. Smith, and H. Sachs, "The Memory Architecture and the Cache and MMU for the Fairchild Clipper Processor," UC Berkeley Computer Science Division Technical Report Number UCB/CSD 86/289, April 1985.
7. C. Alexander, W. Keshlear, and F. Briggs, "Translation Buffer Performance in a UNIX Environment," *ACM Computer Archit. News*, 13 (5), (1985).
8. P. Dixon, "Page Associative Caches on Futurebus", *Microprocessors Microsystems* (April 1988).
9. D. Wood, S. Eggers, G. Gibson, M. Hill, J. Pendleton, S. Ritchie, G. Taylor, R. Katz, and D. Patterson, "An In-Cache Address Translation Mechanism," *Proc. 13th International Symposium on Computer Architecture*, Tokyo, June 1986.
10. R. Rashid, A. Tevanian, Jr., M. Young, D. Golub, R. Baron, D. Black, W. J. Bolosky, and J. Chew, "Machine-Independent Virtual Memory Management for Paged Uniprocessor and Multiprocessor Architecture," *IEEE Transact. Computers* (August 1988).
11. J. L. Baer, *Computer Systems Architecture,* Computer Science Press, Inc., 1980, p. 298.
12. S. Thakkar and A. Knowles, "A High Performance Memory Management Scheme," *Computer* (May 1986).
13. V. Heller, "OS//2 Virtual Memory Management," *Byte* (April 1988).
14. C. Hensler and K. Sarno, "Marrying UNIX and the 80386," *Byte* (April 1988).
15. M. J. Bach, *The Design of the UNIX Operating System*, Prentice-Hall, Inc., Englewood Cliffs, NJ, 1986.
16. H. Levy and P. Lipman, "Virtual Memory Management in the VAX/VMS Operating System,"*Computer* (March 1982).

GREGG ZEHR

OBJECT-ORIENTED DATABASE MANAGEMENT SYSTEMS

> Some members of (the data processing) community have been so overwhelmed by the success of a certain technology for processing data that they have confused this technology with the natural semantics of information. They have forgotten any other way to think of information except as regimented hordes of rigidly structured data codes—in short, the mentality of the punched card.
>
> William Kent, *Data and Reality* (1978)

INTRODUCTION

In the current world of business computing, database management systems (DBMS) provide the basic model of data storage and retrieval. Records of fixed formats, field name addressing of data, and key value identification of entities have come to define the DBMS paradigm and have functionally delimited the realm of business computer applications. While these combined concepts allow for a high degree of data independence, or distinction between data storage and application programming, they also limit the range of functionality of DBMS.

Over the past five years, an alternative data model has emerged that promises to expand the functionality of DBMS to areas that do not fit into the rows and columns of record–oriented DBMS. Object–oriented database management systems (OODBMS) and the OODB they organize have found application in such dynamic environments as engineering, software development, and document management.

In the following paragraphs, I will define OODB, describe how they have been implemented and applied, and indicate how they will probably affect the future of information management over the next decade. The first section is an introduction to what database management systems are, and why they need to be modified. The next section relates database theory and programming languages to the development of the object–oriented model. The third section, the bulk of the article, gives an overview of various commercial and experimental projects that may be considered to be OODBMS. Three of these, Hewlett–Packard's IRIS, Servio–Logic's GemStone, and MCC's ORION, are explored in some detail. A series of other designs are considered under a couple of different "model" umbrellas. Finally, the fourth section summarizes the state of the art of object–oriented databases.

Although this report does not claim to represent the state of the art in database management systems in general, it is important to note that, recently, there seems to have been a general shift in the interests of the database community (i.e., ACM's SIGMOD). It used to be that most of the activity seemed to be in the areas of relational theory, dependency theory, and transaction modeling; the focus now seems to be on expanding the capabilities of DBMS to meet the needs of new user communities [1,2]. In this sense, it would be difficult to find a more timely or significant issue in the area of databases, or of information management, than the present topic.

WHY ARE OBJECT-ORIENTED DATABASES NEEDED?

The DBMS model of data presents a clerk's view of the world; every referenced entity has a fixed number of descriptive characteristics and the values for those attributes may be listed in a ledger [3]. Despite the simplicity and intuitiveness of this tabular model, as an information source its usefulness is severely limited. While charts and tables make sense in the financial and sports sections, newspaper publishers know that readers want text, drawings, and photographs in the rest of the paper. Database designers, on the other hand, seem to assume that if tables work for accounting packages, they will work for all applications. Unfortunately for them, most of the world does not fit into tables very well.

Researchers have identified several broad areas that are clearly beyond the scope of conventional database management systems. These include computer–aided design (CAD) systems, document and multimedia information systems (generically known as office information systems; OIS), and software design systems (computer–aided software engineering; CASE). A casual study of this list can reveal some interesting similarities which, although not definitive, indicate why traditional DBMS are not adequate.

First, most of these applications either store the actual entities or very complete representations of the entities of interest. A document database actually contains the document, not just a description and location of an external object. Similarly, a CAD DBMS contains drawings, and CASE databases contain program modules [3,4]. Standard databases generally do not allow storage of large objects, and attempts to reduce large objects, such as putting vector coordinates from CAD drawings into relational databases, suffer noticeably in performance.

Second, these applications generally require dynamic objects. They change over time, and their actual value is dependent upon the time in question. Users may inquire about the same object's state at different times, requiring some sort of version control. Multiple users may be involved, calling for the ability to create concurrent versions and separate edition paths.

Third, broad categories of objects hold some attributes in common, but to make finer distinctions between types you must recognize attributes specific to subcategories. For example, an entity of type Publication may generally be said to have an Author and a Title, but to know more about the item, you need to know what type of Publication it is. Books don't have journal titles or issue numbers, and journal articles don't have ISBN numbers. In these application areas, specialization of data definitions form a hierarchy in which the most general class is found at the root, and each level down represents a refinement marked by adding attributes. Instances of this can be found at any level. The identification of an instance with a type is known as classification. When traversed upward, specification relationships are usually known as IS–A links. Read this way, the association is called generalization.

Fourth, objects in these areas are often comprised of a hierarchy of parts which are nonexclusive and can be changed on the fly. The engine drawing that fits into the drawing of a Chevy may be the same drawing found as part of a Oldsmobile. This same paragraph may be part of a state–of–the–art paper, a dissertation proposal, and a dissertation. This circumstance is a clue that the tree structures of the hierarchical model, or even the strict CLASS and IS-A relationships of some object–oriented systems will be inadequate. Support for lattice structures in which a node may have more than one parent will be essential [*23*]. Equally important will be a clear distinction between generalization (IS-A) and aggregation (IS-PART-OF) relationships.

Finally, operations upon these structures will often go by the same names, but in reality they may be performing quite different actions. The program that moves a paragraph within a text and the one that moves a diagram across the screen may both be called Move, but the code will be quite different from one to the other. To keep the convenience of a generic Move call, yet have it operate differently depending upon the data involved, requires either a complex Move program that tests data types and contains routines for all possible results, or else the ability to affix appropriate Move program modules to the data itself. In the case where the program is affixed to the data, a picture that receives a request to Move will invoke its own Move procedure, and the paragraph that receives the same message will run a completely different routine. For large databases with user-defined types, a complex type-testing program may be impractical, if not impossible. Therefore, the object-oriented approach of attaching procedures to data objects becomes a practical alternative.

Each of these requirements corresponds to ideas that are well known in the programming language community as object-oriented programming (OOP). In our context, they will often appear in their respective OOP terms:

1. Object-identity. Each object is addressable by its OID
2. Versions. Multiple states of objects may exist simultaneously
3. Compound objects and inheritance. Objects are typed with methods
4. Composite objects. Structures may exist with many member objects
5. Message Passing and Polymorphism. Each object executes its own procedures to respond to messages passed to it

For the time being, we will also state that any system that satisfies each of these requirements is an object-oriented system.

Most object-oriented systems create volatile environments, which means that when the environment ceases to exist because the program stops or the machine is shut down, the objects are gone as well. Usually some provision is made to store the environment, but the objects have no form unless that environment is reconstructed. Persistent data are objects that have structure and values independent of the programs that use them. In traditional data processing, persistent data exists in the form of files. An object-oriented system that incorporates persistent representations of objects is an object-oriented database (OODB).

Data Management Systems Characteristics

Data Independence

The value of database management systems comes from their capability to shift the semantics of data from the programs that use them to the structures that store them. Before databases were introduced, and even today in many cases, if you wanted to know what a piece of data in a file "meant," that is what it was used for, you had to either look at the programs that used the file, or look it up in a dog-eared notebook of data definitions. To ask for the phone number from the current record is a meaningless question if the record has no structure, or has a structure that is not known.

Database management systems, on the other hand, allow data independence in the sense that programs and users may access data on the basis of knowing the field name. Physical storage is completely hidden from the user. The modification of data structures should require no programmatic alterations in applications. This is accomplished by storing information about the data with the data itself in the form of compiled schemas, system tables, or data dictionaries. Query languages such as SQL which use this meta-data now make it possible to pose ad hoc inquiries without writing a whole new application program.

Because the structure of data is separate from the application programs, a central repository of data definitions is possible that may be utilized by all users and programs. To ensure compatibility with organization policies and existing applications, this data dictionary should be carefully regulated. This responsibility usually belongs to a person or group with the function of database administration (DBA).

Database Structures

Data in databases are partitioned into groups of records that share identical formats, referred to variously as data sets, tables, or relations. Generally these sets are referred to as entity types, and some form of connection between entity types will represent the real world relationships between them. Currently there are three basic models of database structuring that serve to define almost all commercially available database management systems: hierarchical, network, and relational.

In hierarchical databases, records of one type that may be said to be dependent upon another type, such as Employees working for a Company, will be stored in close physical proximity to one another. The dependent records are grouped with one another to form a hierarchical data structure, or tree. For example, COMPANY XYZ in Pittsburgh has three departments, D1, D2, D3 with respective managers M1, M2, M3. Various employees–work for the various departments. The hierarchical records might look like:

XYZ Pittsburgh | D1 M1 E1 E2 E3 | D2 M2 E4 E5 | D3 M3 E6 E7 E8

It is important to note that without additional support through linking or indexing, the only feasible access point for data retrieval is through the uppermost key, the root of the tree.

When logical pointers, or record numbers, are used to link data sets together, the database is of the network model. In this model, real-world relationships are mirrored in the database by these connections between sets. Using the XYZ example, one network database implementation might have three sets of COMPANY, DEPARTMENT, and EMPLOYEE which are all connected by physical links. COMPANY XYZ would contain in its record a record number of the DEPARTMENT record D1. DEPARTMENT D1 would hold a NEXT pointer to form a linklist with D2 and also a pointer to the E1 EMPLOYEE record, which would be the head of a linklist of E1, E2, and E3.

Relational databases are sets of tables that form relationships through applying algebraic set operations on common data values. Relationships are somewhat intuitive in that they are recognizable through common data values. COMPANY XYZ in Pittsburgh must be the same company XYZ listed in the COMPANY-DEPARTMENT table as the owner of department D1:

COMPANY
COMP   CITY
xyz   pittsburgh

COMPANY-DEPARTMENT

COMP	DEPT
xyz	d1
xyz	d2
xyz	d3

DEPARTMENT

DEPT	MANAGER
d1	m1
d2	m2
d3	m3

The processes that go into decomposing tables to accurately model the entities and dependencies of the database are collectively known as normalization. A database designed to work consistently within the operations of relational algebra (i.e., algebraic set operations such as Union, Intersection, etc.) is said to be in third normal form, or 3NF.

Transaction Management

A database transaction is an atomic sequence of database events that will either commit their changes to the database as a unit or will make no changes at all. For efficient use of a database, many transactions must be allowed to execute simultaneously without leaving the database in an inconsistent state. Transactions must be guaranteed that data they access will not be modified by another transaction during their lifetime, nor that data they update will be overwritten. To implement this, most DBMS use locking strategies that prevent multiple transactions from interfering with each other's use of the data, while allowing concurrent access for inquiry activities.

A schedule of interleaved transactions is said to be serializable if there is a sequence of executions that return the same result as the schedule does. Protocols such as two-phase locking have been incorporated into DBMS to insure serializability, thus making efficient concurrent access possible and secure.

One issue about locking that will play a role in considering object-oriented databases is granularity of locking. This refers to whether a lock is being placed upon an entire database, a single table, a physical page, or a specific record. Obviously, to encourage concurrent access a low-level lock would be encouraged, but the price for lower levels comes in overhead to maintain extensive lock tables and slower access since each operation at the low level must check locks. With high-level locking, however, transactions sit waiting to retrieve information not remotely related to the current lock-holding transaction.

Database Integrity and Security

Authorization schemes can be built into database management systems that grant permission to access data to certain users or applications, while denying it to others. Depending on the type of database, this authorization may also be subject to granularity, such as allowing read-access at the set level, or prohibiting write-access to certain fields.

Database integrity usually refers to consistency within a database, such as making sure that if one data value appears, it must appear elsewhere in the database. For example, if a student is registered for a class, the student must also appear in the master registration file. For hierarchical and network model databases, this type of integrity is usually built in to the structure, but with the advent of the relational model it has become an issue that DBAs must be conscious of.

Backup and Recovery Procedures

Database recovery is usually linked to the issues of transaction management, because the biggest problems with restoring databases after either system or media failure stem from incomplete transactions. Data may be restored to a fixed point in time through backing up the data, copying it to another medium or device, however restoration of transactions that occur between backup and failure, requires other mechanisms. Primary among these is logging, where at every transaction the events are recorded on a separate medium. This may take the form of logging the previous state before a transaction, known as UNDO, or the commands and data that make up the transaction, known as REDO. Under certain circumstances, either or both may be used to restore data lost during system failure.

Other Database Models

Three models, hierarchical, relational, and network, were presented earlier as the current state of database technology. This is not to say alternatives have not been explored. In fact, many of the proposals of earlier researchers have led to the object-oriented models currently under discussion. Among these are the entity relationship model, the functional database model, and the set theoretic database model.

Entity Relationship Model. Chen's [6] entity relationship model has been widely adopted as a database design tool, but there is no scheme for actually implementing it as a database management system. Instead, it is a high-level approach to data modeling that could theoretically be placed on top of any system that organizes data into fixed formats. The basic notion is that entities, or objects of interest, and relationships between objects are two different concepts, and should be treated as such. Recognition of this forces the database designer to study how tables or datasets connect to one another, and whether or not all interactions between data elements are accurately reflected in their data model. This model directly addresses the ambiguity of the relational model where relationships and entity attributes are stored in exactly the same ways (i.e., as tables), and only a knowledgeable user can reliably pick out the semantics of each [7].

Functional Data Model. The functional database model (FDM) [8] is a close sibling of the relational model's notion of functional dependencies. Under the FDM, all data are retrieved as the result of a function, so that one sees database retrieval phrased in terms of AGE(STUDENTID("Smith")). The advantage of the functional model is that some data may be calculated, some may be stored in tables, or some may be retrieved from some other source, yet to the user it is completely transparent.

Set-Theoretic Data Model. This model [9] builds objects as labeled sets, which gives a simple path syntax and offers a simple, consistent, set calculus. The labeled sets serve two purposes not allowed by the relational mode. First, the label becomes a tuple surrogate, meaning that tuples are possible, violating the relational rules for first normal form. Second, sets of unspecified length are allowed and are theoretically stored as a unit, rather than recreating them through algebraic operations. For example, one company, Acme might have a data definition:

Acme:{Departments:{A12:{Name:'Sales',Managers:{'Nathen','Roberts'},
Budget:142000}},
{A16:{Name:'Research',Managers:{'Carter'}, Budget:256500}, . . .}.

Here, the labeled departments A12 and A16 identify compound objects, while managers may have one or more values. Both of these capabilities are contrary to relational normalization. STDM is a highly flexible system; most other traditional data models, such as relational and hierarchical, are easily modeled under STDM. On the other hand, it gains much of its flexibility from being entirely untyped, and thus loses the advantages for applications systems that strongly typed languages offer.

Object-Oriented Systems

Object-Oriented Programming

Object-oriented databases represent an intersection between the study of databases and the study of programming languages. It is from the latter of these two areas that the concept of object orientation developed, coming from he introduction of the abstract data type (ADT). ADTs are encapsulated data structures: they have a private store of data elements and a public interface of functions that can access that store. In object-oriented programming, encapsulation is combined with inheritance and message passing to construct languages where objects are typed according to functions they own, which they inherit from their class membership. Objects "run" their functions upon receipt of messages [10].

The first place an independent object appeared in programming languages was SIMULA. Smalltalk, CommonLISP with Objects (CLOS), C++, and Actors are among the more popular object-oriented programming languages, but it seems that new ones are being introduced monthly. The definition of object-oriented varies considerably as one moves from language to language, so it is useful to spell out the range of differences before going much further.

Inheritance usually is hierarchical, but the strictness of the hierarchy is variable. Some languages, such as Smalltalk, treat inheritance as strictly a specialization of classes, where each subclass is a subset of one parent class. Other languages allow for multiple inheritance, or mix-ins, so a class may be a subclass of two divergent classes. An example of multiple inheritance might be a CarForSale, which shares the methods and data of a MotorVehicle, but also shares the methods and data of a CommercialProduct. Thus, any instance of this class would have fields representing both NumberOfWheels and Price. To completely subvert attempts to define inheritance, there are also Actor-based object-oriented systems that use prototypes and delegation of methods in horizontal attachments instead of any hierarchy at all.

Class can refer to either a protocol of methods and a set of class variables or it can refer to the group of objects that share those characteristics. If referencing a membership, does it also include members of subclasses? This question is of special importance when attempting to design indexing systems and deciding whether or not to create one index for each subclass or a general index.

Message passing is also an ambiguous concept. Some languages treat messages as objects which are explicitly "send"ed from one object to another, while others treat them as little more than functions and arguments. When applied to databases, this arises as an issue when determining where a method is executed; against the data in secondary storage, against some assigned active object in primary memory, or in some shadow copy of the object.

Objects in Databases

Object-oriented programming generally takes place in a single-user environment where the objects are only required while the programming environment is in use. Any objects that do not fit into primary memory are either not allowed or parts of the environment are paged out to virtual memory. The significant aspect is that the objects exist within the environment, and any or all manipulation of objects requires manipulation of the whole environment.

Object-oriented databases should bring objects into memory only when invoked, and should be able to do so completely and efficiently. Most researchers argue that this should be a transparent operation. Objects from dynamic store and objects from the disk should not be handled any differently as far as the user is concerned. In implementation this is not so easy, as it requires "pointer swizzling" (switching back and forth between pointers to memory and pointers to disk).[1] If the hash tables or indexes to manage this are too large, performance suffers.

Class Definition

One of the most current topics in OODB is that of schema evolution. This debate is over the issue of when classes should be defined: fixed at compilation time, modifiable only to add new objects, or active objects may change. If classes change, what are the implications for data that have already been stored, and are changes inherited by all subclasses? Do changes include deletion? Banerjee et al. [11] have devised a useful set of constraints to determine which modifications are semantically consistent.

One approach, which may be the most practical, is to have classes fixed early in the database design. If for example, an office only uses certain general classes of documents such as invoices, letters, and reports, then why do they need the overhead that a dynamic schema modification utility would require? There is some concern that in changing environments, class definitions could outgrow their usefulness and this poses a bigger threat than having strictly defined classes. Products such as Smalltalk use Browser utilities to allow the designer to examine available classes. At some point (300 classes has been suggested), even the Browser becomes difficult for a user to handle [4].

Access of Data

As will be apparent from the descriptions in the next section, there is some disagreement about how one should be able to access data in an OODB. The techniques of small object-oriented systems where users use object identifiers easily will not work well across large databases. In large systems used over lengthy time periods, identifiers are easy to lose or forget. Access by attribute values is a minimal requirement of OODBS.

To implement attribute value access with any efficiency, it is necessary to violate the notion of a public interface. Method execution for each potential candidate could be very

---

[1] The term "pointer swizzling" came from a USENET news article contributed by J. Orenstien from Object Design Inc.

costly. Thus, indexes must have entry to the private stores of each object, and requests for indexes must be limited to class variables.

Indexing also poses the problem of granularity of indexes. If Vehicle is indexed, does the index retrieve all instances of class Vehicle, or instances of Car, Truck, and Bus as well? Simulation experimentation [*12*] has provided some data on the relative efficiency of multilevel indexes versus single-level indexes, indicating that the nature of potential queries is the determining factor.

Object-Oriented Database Implementations

Here we consider several attempts to implement the concepts of object-oriented programming in a database management system. The first three of these, IRIS, ORION, and GemStone are covered in some detail. Next, a selection of some DBMSs based upon the language C++ is briefly discussed. A final section introduces an alternative paradigm, extensible databases, which some researchers are offering either as a substitute for OODBMSs or as a platform for building customized OODBs.

The three major object-oriented database management systems (IRIS, ORION, and GemStone) have been the subjects of many articles over the past few years. In a way, they represent paradigms in the field, being well known and easily recognized models of what OODBs can be. The plurality of paradigms should be emphasized here, for these three systems have little in common with each other in their implementations. IRIS is an object-oriented frontend for a relational database, which is a technique popular in the scholarly literature, but difficult to consider as a contrast to the relational model. ORION is based upon a CommonLISP foundation, and resembles some of the expert system shells that have come out of research done in artificial intelligence, such as Knowledge Craft and KEE. The major distinction ORION offers over them is large-scale secondary storage object management. GemStone originated out of the merging of a set theoretical data model and the object-oriented programming language Smalltalk. Of the three, GemStone is the only one currently available commercially.

The remaining database systems outlined in this section are primarily examples of work being done in universities and research labs following a common model. That they all choose C++ as a foundation provides a common thread among them. Even though C++ was probably chosen because of the large potential customer base already committed to programming in C or C++, the fact that several distinct developers have found C++ an appropriate platform for developing persistent storage of objects underscores one of the major themes of current OODBMS research: seamless integration of primary and secondary storage within a single programming language.

IRIS–HP Labs

IRIS is a prototype "next-generation" database management system that has been under development at Hewlett-Packard Laboratories since 1984 [*13–18*]. Its object-oriented interfaces sit on top of a relational foundation to implement a highly flexible experimental environment. In addition to a set of C functions that provide programmatic links to C and Lisp, there is also an interactive query interface that is a true extension of SQL called OSQL. IRIS incorporates most of the hallmarks of object-oriented programming: classes and instances, inheritance, methods, and object identity. The one significant omission, message passing, is replaced by function calls. This one modification allows for almost seamless integration of IRIS with existing programming languages, foreign databases, and distributed systems.

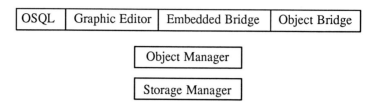

FIGURE 1.   IRIS architecture.

The IRIS Architecture. The bottom layer of the IRIS system is the Iris storage manager, which is ALLBASE (HP-SQL in Fishman [*15*], HPs relational/network (tables plus parent–child pointers) DBMS. ALLBASE handles all of the administrative functions of the database such as creation and deletion of relations, transaction management, logging, recovery, and buffer management. Cursor access of tuples (one at a time rather than table) simplifies the retrieval, updating, insertion, and deletion of individual tuples. Extensions to the storage subsystem proposed early in IRIS's development included long-term transaction management, extensible types, and multimedia objects. Some of these goals seem to have moved from storage issues to foreign function problems. Each will be discussed fully in a later section.

The next layer upward is the object manager. This is the heart of the system that handles schema definition, data manipulation, and query processing. In the object manager, data that are presented in terms of object, types, and functions are restructured to meet the storage manager's vocabulary of tuples, relations, and constraints. Schematically, the object manager and the storage manager are independent of one another, although for performance purposes in implementation they are tightly coupled. Even so, the relational substructure is completely hidden from all IRIS interface modules.

The top level consists of four interface packages. OSQL is an interactive query processor which extends SQL to allow access by identity rather than attribute value. For example, instead of:

        SELECT S.PHONE
          FROM STUDENTS
          WHERE S.NAME = "Smith"

one asks:

        SELECT PHONE(smith1).

The graphic editor is an interactive browser that allows the user to traverse type and interobject structures. The remaining two interfaces are experimental bridges to Lisp and C. Three types of language interfaces have been developed for each language. One is simply a traditional embedding of OSQL. The second is an encapsulation of the IRIS DBMS as a programming language object which has methods as defined in the object manager's C subroutines. Third is an experimental platform for treating database objects as persistent versions of the programming languages' own defined objects.   This provides a programming environment in which differences between dynamic and persistent objects are almost invisible.

IRIS Objects. Objects form the basic unit of access in IRIS. Each object has its own systemwide OID (Object IDentifier). Objects have properties, which are defined in terms of functions. A property may be a literal object, such as a string or a number, or it may be another object. For example, the property NAME for a person might be the literal object "Smith," while the property FATHER for the same person would be the OID of another person whose value for NAME may or may not be "Smith." At the theoretical level, IRIS makes no distinction between functions that retrieve stored data, functions that compute values, or functions that return values from other programs or machines.

Objects that share properties, or more formally, the functions that define properties, are said to be of the same type. Types are essentially the same as classes in other object-oriented systems, that is they are named collections of objects. Functions are implemented on a type, so that two objects of the same type will utilize the same function to return a property. Types are structured to allow simple inheritance and multiple inheritance, forming a nonrooted directed acyclic graph. A CAR may be a subtype of MACHINES, PASSENGER-VEHICLES, and PURCHASED-GOODS, and as such, would inherit all properties of all of these supertypes. Each instance of CAR would have functional values for each of the fields associated with each of these types, such as HORSEPOWER, NUMBER-OF-PASSENGERS, and PRICE, respectively. Under CAR there might also be subtypes, such as SEDAN and STATIONWAGON.

Polymorphism, or function name overloading, is permitted. Conflict resolution, for those cases that arise when the same function name is inherited from two sources, is based first upon specificity of inheritance and failing that, upon user-defined rules.

IRIS offers a dynamic environment in terms of type definition. Types may be added and deleted, and instances may have new types applied or removed over time. A graduating senior might have been of type STUDENT with such properties as CLASS or QPA, but upon graduation and employment may drop the STUDENT type and pick up an EMPLOYEE type, with a whole new set of properties (i.e., DEPT or SALARY). The one restructuring that is not yet allowed in IRIS is the creation of new subtype–supertype relations among existing types.

IRIS Functions. Functions and queries in IRIS are compiled into trees of relational algebra operations, which are then optimized by the object manager. At the bottom of the tree are leaves which may either be table lookups of stored functions or references to foreign functions. Higher nodes represent combinations of subtrees which are linked by operations such as cross-product, filter, and project (equivalent to join, select, and project in relational algebra). These are specified by derived functions and queries, and may be optimized by generating more efficient but semantically equivalent trees.

The simplest form of IRIS functions are those that look up stored data, or property functions. A function such as AGE(OID) is a table lookup that returns an integer given an object. Functions such as these are automatically reversible, so one could do an OSQL query such as: SELECT NAME(S) for each S where AGE(S) = 30. Functions are distinguished through constraints as to whether they are optional or required and single-valued [TEACHER(COURSE] or multivalued [STUDENT(COURSE]. An optional command CLUSTER may direct that certain properties be stored in the same table for ease of access.

Lyngbaek and Vianu [17] studied the relationship between the IRIS model of data and the underlying relational structures for stored functions and found several advantages of this mapping. Among these are the idea that existing relational data can be readily accessed by the IRIS system and that the powerful theoretical tools of the relational model can be used to formulate the semantics of the IRIS model. One clear disadvantage, which is true of most complex structures placed upon relational foundations, is the overhead of joining.

Derived functions are stored and implemented as IRIS queries in terms of other functions, just like a VIEW in relational databases such as Ingres. In some cases, a materialized derived function can be used to create a temporary stored version of a function frequently accessed. As mentioned before, these are compiled as relational algebra trees, and may be optimized at run-time in accordance with (proposed) user-defined optimization rules. Reduction of duplicate lookups, minimization of join operations, and knowledge of the domain can be utilized during development of optimization procedures.

Foreign functions are functions that access data or processes outside of the IRIS environment. These may be calls to other programs or databases, or calls to other machines and operating systems. The IRIS foreign function protocol is a set of programs to answer the five function calls: ALLOC, OPEN, NEXT, CLOSE, and DEALLOC. ALLOC and DEALLOC set up buffers for communications and destroy them when finished, OPEN and CLOSE initiate the activity in the foreign process, and NEXT is used to step through the returned data one object at a time. The five programs of the protocol are black boxes that the IRIS query processor invokes for any foreign functions, so operations such as setting up communications channels and formatting data must be handled by the programs to meet IRIS's expectations.

As examples of how foreign functions may be used, Conners and Lyngbaek [*14*] presented a model of a stockbroker's IRIS database which contains relevant information about customers and holdings. The broker also subscribes to a database which contains current information on stock values, and a tickertape service that gives current market activity. Queries to the IRIS database may include questions such as current value of holdings, or current value compared with this month's low price. Foreign functions may transparently access the stock database or the tickertape service to derive up-to-date information without actually storing the data in the broker's system.

Foreign functions are bound by the constraints of parameter passing and linking, common to subroutine library systems. A message-passing architecture would possibly be a more flexible arrangement than maintaining remote access programs as part of the IRIS architecture. One possible compromise that HP is exploring is building two-way data communications modules directly into IRIS so that the individual functions would not have to assume that responsibility. This would reduce the amount of work required to implement a foreign function, and one would expect it to increase the flexibility of operations that may be invoked.

IRIS OSQL and the Graphic Editor. Beech [*13*] listed several reasons why SQL was chosen as a base language as opposed to creating a new language. The OSQL designers felt it would be "socially irresponsible" as well as inexpedient to start from scratch when a suitable foundation already existed, for which many of the problems of implementing a new language had already been solved. The practice of embedding SQL also meant that preprocessors for host language access were also already available. Finally, as Lyngbaek and Vianu [*17*] already established, the relationships between relational databases and IRIS are significant and an SQL interface can only encourage this line of research.

One key element of SQL that was modified for OSQL is the FROM clause. In SQL the FROM serves to bind variables to tables, identifies tables to be searched, and establishes the scoping of the variable names. Since OSQL accesses instances of types instead of tables, the semantics of FROM would be misleading. Instead, OSQL uses FOR EACH, as in:

```
SELECT NAME, ADDRESS
FOR EACH SUPPLIER
WHERE CITY = 'Palo Alto';
```

One may also retrieve an object in its entirety and bind it to a variable, in contrast to the SQL operation of retrieving each value of a field separately.

Creating objects in OSQL is similar to creating tuples in SQL, in that just as one has to create a table and then identify an occurrence in SQL, in OSQL one creates a type and then defines an instance. An example

```
CREATE TYPE STUDENT SUBTYPE OF PERSON
(SID CHAR(6) REQUIRED,
CLASS_YEAR CHAR(2),
QPA REAL,
MAJOR DEPARTMENT,
ADVISOR FACULTY
);
```

Since STUDENT now inherits all functions of PERSON, properties such as NAME, ADDRESS, and PHONE would also be built in to the type STUDENT. Note that the type for MAJOR and ADVISOR are references to other object types, so that accessing information about the advisor would return the advisor object instead of just the name.

The properties of an object listed in a CREATE statement are implicit stored functions in object-oriented terminology, but IRIS actually generates a table that corresponds to the type definition. Derived functions, also known as intentional functions, are set up with a CREATE FUNCTION statement. To generate a list of students and advisors in a department, a CREATE FUNCTION would look like:

```
CREATE FUNCTION STUDENTADVISOR
(DEPARTMENT D) -> SET OF <CHAR(20),CHAR(20)>
SELECT NAME(S), NAME(ADVISOR(S))
FOR EACH STUDENTS
WHERE DEPARTMENT(S) = D;
```

IRIS as a Global Data Manager (GDM). Because of its foreign function capabilities, IRIS can also be used as an object manager to integrate data from many sources, including separate servers. As a case in point, imagine a collection of documents already stored in some previously established format on disk. An object class for these documents may be defined which has as its method protocol IRIS foreign functions capable of presenting, deleting, and modifying this text format. IRIS objects are then created of this type which contain only the parameters necessary to activate the methods with the appropriate functions. A user accessing the object would see it as just another IRIS object, while the original storage locations and formats do not have to change.

This use of IRIS as a global data manager underscores the advantage of being able to incorporate foreign functions. One can easily imagine the ability to "create" new objects composed of many individual objects that exist in distant locations and inconsistent formats, perhaps including information that is somehow calculated on the fly or responsive to real-time conditions of the system. Most significantly, all of this is accomplished while allowing the source objects to remain autonomous, not coerced to meet some arbitrary IRIS formatting requirements for either their data or their schemas.

ORION–MCC

ORION developed out of work being done at MCC on multimedia databases [*19*] and multiversion CAD systems [*20*]. The current implementation is a single-user system written in CommonLISP, developed on a Symbolics 3600 LISP machine and ported to Unix on a Sun workstation. As a research platform, ORION has provided opportunities for detailed study of specific challenges of object-oriented database implementation in areas such as transaction management, multimedia data management, composite object semantics, dynamic schema evolution, and access authorization strategies [5,11,12,21–24].

Objects in ORION. ORION is built upon a library of apparently static relationships or methods; data definitions are presented as attribute lists rather than operation declarations. None of the available literature discusses how new methods are implemented in ORION beyond the simple level of query specification. Attributes that may be used to build object definitions are either set or scalar and must be either a primitive class type (character, integer, string) or of a domain of some class (e.g., PERSON). A class is a grouping of objects with the same type definition, which is defined within the class lattice; a rooted directed acyclic graph in which OBJECT is the root class. Some attributes of a class may be shared-value attributes, of which all members have the same value and a change to the variable is reflected by each object of that class. Other attributes may be declared as default value variables, where each object starts out with the same value, but changes are only apparent to the local variable.

Typing within classes is not necessarily strong typing. An attribute may be of a superclass domain, so any of the subclasses may be used to fill the slot. For example, if PartID is defined as type PRIMITIVE, then its value may be of type integer, character, string, or some other PRIMITIVE type. An attribute of type PERSON may hold values that are object identifiers of STUDENT, EMPLOYEE, MANAGER, TAXPAYER, or CONGRESSMAN. Although classes may be subclasses of more than one class, and inherit from all superclasses, an instance (object) may belong to only one class. This was a performance decision, allowing the implementation not to have to follow multiple inheritance paths upon presentation of an object.

Accessing Objects. The languages of ORION are not thoroughly discussed in the literature, but they seem to be based upon the CommonLISP formats for object-oriented systems. The format to define a class looks like:

```
(make-class 'Vehicle: superclasses nil
   :attributes '(
      (Manufacturer:    domain Company)
      (Body         : domain AutoBody

                        :composite true


                  :exclusive true
                  :dependent nil)
      (Drivetrain      :domain AutoDrivetrain
                  :composite true
                  :exclusive true
                  :dependent nil)
      etc.))
```

A query also resembles a LISP statement, such as:

```
(select 'Vehicle '(and(equal Manufacturer name "Ford")
            (< Owner Age 20).
```

It is entirely possible that the frontend is still a collection of functions written in CommonLISP, so that ORION actually has no language of its own at this point. A graphic schema editor has been developed, but no discussion of it has appeared at this point.

The Architecture of ORION. The overall architecture of ORION consists of four basic modules. The message handler is responsible for invoking methods given messages and parameters (actually predicates and parameters). Methods may be either system-defined functions for meta-data operations such as creating and deleting instances, value access methods for retrieving data from declared attributes, or user-defined methods.

The second module is the object subsystem which controls schema evolution, version control, query optimization, and multimedia information management. Most of these topics will be discussed in more detail at a later point, but a few words on query optimization are appropriate here.

Compound queries present several alternative retrieval strategies. One basic division is between strategies that start with a class and find all instances matching a query, known as forward traversal, and those that start with instances of some attribute value and traverse upward to establish membership in classes, or backward traversal. In an object-oriented database, inappropriate selection of a strategy can seriously degrade retrieval efficiency. In ORION, the basic job of the query optimizer is knowing when to use which strategy, and how to combine them for the best results.

The third module of the ORION architecture is the storage subsystem. Here allocation and deallocation of disk space is maintained, objects are found on disk pages, and indexes are implemented. On disk, an object looks like a collection of attributes which are either primitive data values, pointers to other objects, or multimedia data descriptors. Multimedia data descriptors are pointers to multimedia records, which are large blocks of text, bit maps, or other byte streams stored elsewhere on the medium in an area maintained by a multimedia free list.

The final module is the transaction subsystem. Parts of this subsystem include a concurrency manager which handles the lock tables and a recovery manager which keeps the transaction log. In recent years, these have been among the most carefully studied functions of ORION. For relational databases, there is a large body of literature formalizing concurrency and recovery which simply does not exist for object-oriented systems. The ORION team has spent a great deal of effort attempting this formalism starting with placing a relational-type locking and logging system on top of ORION and developing it to act more appropriately in an object-oriented environment. Problems such as locking classes with

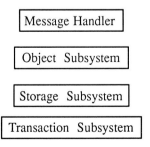

FIGURE 2. ORION architecture.

multiple inheritance (lattices) and versioning underscore the differences between the two database models.

Transactions in ORION. Although ORION is presented as a single-user system, it does allow multiple sessions and multiple windows on the same session. These features require a full-blown concurrency management system. ORION uses a timeout-based locking system, under which any transaction currently waiting on a lock to either read or write will either get it within the specified time or will be aborted and rolled back. All locks are released whenever a transaction commits or aborts.

For locking any specified object, three paths of granularity must be considered. First, the class membership hierarchy of the object must be locked with INTENT locks for either READ or WRITE operations. Second, any indexes to the attributes of the object must be locked, or more accurately, at a minimum those pages of the indexes that are effected by the action will be locked. Finally, those objects that are members of composite objects must lock the clusters they belong to. ORION treats composite objects as single lockable units.

Under recent modifications to the composite object structures, the whole locking system has been reevaluated [5]. Previously, an object could only belong to one composite object, such as when EngineBlockID could only exist in one instance of Automobile. The [5] revision supports the possibility that a paragraph or part drawing might appear as a component of several different objects, as is common in CAD and OIS applications. This is mainly accomplished by expanding the locking matrix to differentiate between composite objects that have exclusive member objects and those that have shared members.

A session is described as a set of transactions enacted serially, though not in any fixed sequence, so there is only one active transaction per session. The reasoning behind sessions is that in CAD applications there is a need for a model for long transactions, and the ORION group wants to be able to support a differentiation between atomic transactions and sets of activities so they could implement a long transaction module. Multiple windows allow a user to proceed to other processing while a current transaction is waiting on a lock. Since multiple windows all look in on the same session, the user has access to the same locks as the transaction currently waiting.

Data is written out to disk immediately upon a commit, so an UNDO log is sufficient for data recovery; either a transaction committed or it did not. Either way, incomplete data will not appear in the database. Hypothetical transactions are those that are allowed to access data (taking read locks only) which make no updates upon commit. "What if?" scenarios are one use for hypothetical locks, since extensive changes may appear to be made to the database to answer a query, yet none of the updates will be reflected in the permanent object store.

Versions in ORION. ORION supports multiple versions of objects by a hierarchical system of object version status levels: transient, working, and generic. When a user accesses an object, a transient version is created from either the single generic version of the object or a specified working version. For any given object there is only one generic version which is the root of the hierarchy. It is a data structure that contains a default version number, a next-version number, a count of current working versions, and a set of version descriptors for the working versions. Each version descriptor includes a version number, the id of the versioned object, and a list of descriptors to child versions. Binding of versions may be either static, pointing to an object id and a version number, or dynamic, pointing to the generic version which references the default version number. Transient versions can be updated and can be promoted to working versions. Working versions cannot be updated, only deleted. Any working version may be pointed to by the generic version as the current default version. Conflicts between modifications to transient versions of the same working version are resolved by a dual timestamp system of change notification and change approval timestamps.

Multimedia Information in ORION. ORION manipulates both one- and two-dimensional data as long byte strings to be accessed through appropriate presentation methods. As mentioned above, ORION stores multimedia data in a secondary memory space separate from its own structures. Hypothetically, it would not take major changes to apply ORION's multimedia capabilities to existing data stored in non-ORION maintained areas. ORION's view of the multimedia data is that of a multimedia record descriptor. The descriptor owns all access methods, stores the physical disk locations, and is the unit of logging. Changes made to multimedia data are considered to be either allocation of a new storage space or deletion of a previously allocated one, so modifications appear to ORION only as new pointers in the record descriptor and a rearranging of the free space chain.

The access methods for most standard presentation devices and stored multimedia object types have already been included in ORION. The resulting message-passing protocol generates an open byte-stream directly from disk to the presentation program with minimal copying of data from storage to primary memory. The hierarchy of objects that represent presentation devices and the hierarchy of presentation object types allow room for expansion if one wants to introduce new data types or new hardware to the system.

GemStone and OPAL from Servio-Logic

Servio-Logic has been actively researching object-oriented databases since 1983. They began their research with a set theoretic data model [9] but eventually chose to model a DBMS on the programming language Smalltalk-80. The resulting product, GemStone and its programming language OPAL, was one of the first commercially available OODBMSs [25–28].

The designers of GemStone had several goals in mind when developing their product. First among these was the notion of intentional semantics. Type definitions should be separate from object instantiation, and should include protocols of operations that may apply to instances of the defined type. This notion is best illustrated by the contrast with relational databases, in which a schema instantiates a relation at the time it is defined, and all operations are defined at the database level (i.e., the relational calculus) without any mechanisms for defining type-specific operations on relations. In a relational database, the available operations do not vary from table to table; join, project, and select are defined as operations to perform on the type TABLE. Whether each tuple represents an instance of STUDENT, AUTOMOBILE, or BANKTRANSACTION, the available operations are the same.

A second major goal was entity identity, under which data representing any entity can be referenced as a unit. Data values may change, some values may not exist, but the identity of the object will remain constant. Two distinct entities may have the same set of values, as in often found in engineering environments where, for example, two gates might have identical characteristics yet be functionally quite different. Through entity identity, compound items are easily supported and flexible, arbitrary, variations in structure are possible. This leads to more powerful data modeling than traditional database models permit; objects that are better able to model real-world relationships and changes.

Other goals were stated in terms of improvements over existing object-oriented programming environments, such as Smalltalk-80. Their system should avoid arbitrary (primary memory) limits on schemas and data items. With the incorporation of persistent data, explicit storage of historic states should be available, as should standard functions of

DBMSs: transaction management, concurrency, recovery capabilities, and authorization control.

Finally, OPAL was designed to provide a single language capable of managing secondary storage, providing general computational services, and acting as a system command language with as much transparency as possible. Borrowing from Smalltalk-80, they began with a language well-suited to rapid prototyping and a set of hardware object definitions to act as a foundation for system control.

Structure of GemStone. GemStone, like Smalltalk, is based on the three concepts of object, message, and class. An object is defined as a private memory with a public interface: instance variables that reference other objects, and methods that present and manipulate the privately held values. Objects are created as instances of some class. Classes are hierarchical, stemming from a root Object. Multiple inheritance is not allowed in Smalltalk or in GemStone.

Methods are invoked by message passing between objects. Methods are written in OPAL, and are attached to classes and thus to objects through inheritance. OPAL's message format is

<receiver> <message>

where the contents of <message> will be some method name and a set of optional arguments. Most messages return some object and may or may not alter the private data of the receiver. Messages are classified unary, binary, and keyword, depending upon the argument formats. A unary message is an operation that acts upon an object with no argument list, as in

4 negated

which will return a value –4. Binary operations are usually arithmetic operators or comparisons:

8 + 3
3 < 5
emp1 salary < emp2 salary (note: salary is unary, < is binary)

Keyword operators have specialized argument lists in which argument names appear before the actual argument:

anArray at 3 put: 'Ross' (selector is 'at:put:').

which would put the word 'Ross' into the third position of the data structure anArray.

On the surface, OPAL bears a close resemblance to Smalltalk. This similarity is maintained at the Executor level of the two-part GemStone architecture. The Executor controls sessions in GemStone, handling communications between GemStone and any host software, and managing a compiler and interpreter for each active user. Methods are compiled into sequences of byte codes, which the Executor activates when called upon to do so.

The second level of the GemStone architecture is the object manager which serves the same function as a Smalltalk object memory, but operates on a much larger scale. The additional overhead of secondary storage management and handling of concurrent accesses significantly expand the role of the object manager. This, coupled with the problems presented by potentially huge object lists (2 ^31 objects) and virtually unlimited object sizes (2 ^31 instance variables), acutely differentiate the two object handling systems.

Under the object manager implementation, objects come in five basic storage formats: self-identifying (primitive; Character, SmallInt, Boolean, etc.), byte (e.g., String, Float), named (instance variables holding object-ids), indexed (arrays), and nonsequenceable collections (sets). Although classes define object structures, classes themselves are not data access structures. Usually, if one wants an actual grouping of objects, it must be generated explicitly as a bag or a set. As a nonsequenceable collection of a given type, such a group may be indexed on class variables. Instances of subclasses are included in OPAL indexing as well as instances of the primary class. Dependency lists are maintained to insure that update and concurrency controls apply to indexes as well as data objects.

In addition to object element names and values, objects are stored with timestamps to accommodate versioning. GemStone uses an optimistic concurrency control policy, under which changes are only made apparent to other sessions upon commitment of a transaction. Shadowing of data ties versioning and concurrency issues together. As data are modified, a shadow object is created. When a commit occurs, the shadow object becomes the primary and the new object pointer and timestamp are added to the appropriate association lists.

Each user of GemStone has a dictionary list of known objects. Any user may have access to several of these dictionaries, and dictionaries may be shared among users. Authorization is handled through user name and password. A user may be authorized to access a group of objects with read-only privileges, read-write capability, or given no access at all.

Distributed GemStone. GemStone can be set up as a centralized server for a network of workstations. Methods may be either executed on the server, where a GemStone object is manipulated in permanent storage, or on the client workstation as an execution on a Smalltalk object. These two forms of method execution are known as proxies and deputies. Whether a system designer chooses one or the other is not always an easy decision. Factors such as competition among processes for objects, available bandwidth, and relative speeds of execution among machines must all be taken into account. In no case, however, is the permanent storage distributed to any storage other than that under control of the centralized GemStone server.

OPAL is a general, uniform, language for GemStone. In it, data may be defined (DDL), accessed, and updated (DML), extended transactions may be written, and the operating system utilities are available. Distributed systems often require access to other languages. To meet this requirement, GemStone has procedural interface modules (PIM) to implement remote procedure calls to GemStone from Either C or Pascal. Built around the general datatypes of the OOP (object-oriented pointer) and untyped buffers of fixed length, calls may be made to GemStone from a procedural language and the contents of objects returned through buffers. Servio tested their system successfully by interfacing GemStone with remote PCs running Microsoft Windows.

Three C++ Databases

R2D2: Karlsruhe and IBM. R2D2 comes from the University of Karlsruhe and the IBM Scientific Center at Heidelberg. It is a continuation of work done on the NF2 (Non-First Normal Form) data model in the AIM-P project. The goal behind R2D2 has been an engineering database system, so some of the particular needs of engineering systems are reflected in its design [29,30].

The designers of R2D2 aimed for a system that would be able to marry the benefits of both structurally and behavioral object-oriented systems. In their terminology, a structurally object-oriented database is one which maintains complex structures of hierarchical definitions and composite units. Behavioral object-oriented databases, on the other hand, are those that hide structures behind public access functions. They tend to be much more user or application oriented, with little concern for storage structures. By building a functional database language on top of the structurally object-oriented database AIM-P, the R2D2 group demonstrated that the two approaches can compliment one another.

The NF2 relations allowed attributes to have values which were other relations, thus permitting compound structures which are not possible in a pure relational design. In AIM-P these were implemented as small objects of "minidirectories" that would appear as separate objects which would consist of pointers in a tree, in which the leaves would be pointers to external data records. Tables (unordered sets of records), and Lists (ordered sets) were both accommodated for. Ordered sets of records, also a non-relational concept, made composite structures possible.

In R2D2 the goal is integration of the structural elements of AIM-P with behavioral elements at all levels: query, transaction/recovery management, programming, and storage. Because engineering operations involve very large objects, efficiency is also of prime concern. To implement an efficient system, the designers utilized a client/server model with local caching. Objects are retrieved as complete units, "checked out," from the server model which holds the public database. From that point on, the object is available to the user's application without returning to the server. Objects that are updated must be "checked in" back to the server to enact the update and confirm the consistency. Read and Update locks prevent conflicts between updates.

Objects are created as ADTs by specifying private internal variables and a list of access functions. The functions may be multivalued, accepting parameter lists and returning sets or vectors. Access to the data is through a query language similar to SQL or through an extended Pascal. Pascal data types are the visible structures to users, so every fetched object must be translated from a storage structure to the appropriate Pascal structure. A preprocessor handles this conversion.

ODE: AT&T Bell Labs. ODE (object database and environment) is currently an experimental system at AT&T Bell Laboratories and is based upon the language C++. Unlike C++, instances of objects may be specified to be persistent, thus giving database capabilities to the object-oriented language [31].

The programming language for ODE is called O++, and it is basically an extension of C++. In addition to the capability for persistent objects, O++ enhances C++ with triggers, constraints, versioning, and clustering as data manipulation tools. The query facility of O++ also goes beyond that of C++ with the iterative structures of for . . . suchthat and forall . . . suchthat which allow for SQL-like queries to be applied to large clusters of similarly typed objects.

C++ defines objects as instances of a type class. Each class specification consists of data items and functions. Public items and functions form the interface for the class, while private elements are only available to the functions defined within the class. For example, an object person might have a private data item "agevar," defined as an integer, and a public function "age()" whose sole purpose is to present the contents of "agevar" to object methods. Classes are hierarchical, and multiple inheritance is supported under C++. Ambiguities of common function names are resolved by explicit qualification. In C++, objects are instantiated by a command of "new":

```
stockitem *sip;
. . .
sip = new stockitem(initial values);
```

Objects are removed with a "delete" command.

O++ uses "new" and "delete" for volatile (primary storage) objects, and has "pnew" and "pdelete" for objects of persistent storage. Pointers to persistent objects are qualified at definition:

```
persistent stockitem *psip;
. . .
psip = pnew stockitem (initial values);
```

This close association with the established handling of volatile storage encourages the impression that O++ is not so much a database manipulation language as a merging of database capabilities into an object-oriented language.

Clustering in ODE can be applied to all objects of a specific type, or only those objects of a type that share some collective characteristics. It is not clear whether clustering can be applied to objects of different types, such as one might find in a document of CAD environment. In order to approximate the functionality of a relational database's join operations, O++ offers cluster operations for . . . suchthat and forall . . . suchthat. These iterate over all members of a specified cluster, matching each object against a condition. To retrieve all "junior" class members in the cluster of type student "IS" (IS majors) who have QPAs over 3.0, the code would read:

```
class student{
    public:
    Name;
    char sex;
    real QPA;
    Name class;
};
. . .
for s in "IS"
    suchthat (s->class = = Name("junior") && s->QPA . 3.0)
    printf("%s\n",s->name);
```

Forall works the same, except when iterating over a type it will also iterate over types inherited from the named class.

Constraints and triggers act upon some condition appearing in the database. Constraints reject a transaction (abort and rollback) if the stated condition is violated, such as if one tried to enter a driver born after 1973. Triggers may be perpetual or one time only, and are activated if some condition becomes true, as in if class size exceeds 30 generate a new section.

Vbase: Now OB2 From ONTOLOGIC Inc. VBASE (now available as OB2) from Ontologic, Inc. is a commercial object-oriented system with persistent storage. Its roots are in the language CLU, an MIT implementation of abstract data typing (ADTs) [32]. As such, its main objective is a high degree of integration between a procedural programming language and strongly typed objects.

Strong typing was chosen over the nontyping of object-oriented languages like Smalltalk because of the advantages it offers for building large systems. For one, error checking based upon type incompatibility can take place at compile time, making it easier to debug and making product releases more secure. This also means that instead of spending time at run-time dynamically binding methods most binding can be statically established at compile time, making for a faster program. Finally, program specification with fixed types enforces consistencies in large systems that user naming conventions do not.

Objects in VBASE are defined by a Type Definition Language (TDL) which bears a strong resemblance to type definitions in Pascal or Algol. It is block structured, allowing definition of types within types, arbitrary groupings, and support for path traversal. Aggregate objects, enumerated types, type variants, and unions are features of structured programming languages that are also included in TDL to maximize the potential for user-defined typing and polymorphism. Objects do have statically defined properties which automatically generate their own access methods. Syntactically, properties are defined separately from operations, although operation definitions may be provided by the user to supercede the default definitions.

Operations are written in a superset of C called a C Object Processor (COP) (recent advertisements indicate that this has since been replaced by C++). COP is also used for writing application programs for the VBASE database. A program or operation invokes a COP operation like a C function call, where the type of the objects int he parameter list will determine which version of the method to invoke. For example, the call Entity$Print(some-Object) would use different code depending on whether someObject was an integer, a string, or an enumerated type. Operations may be built in wrapper fashion, so that a subtype's definition is an elaboration upon the supertype's method without repeating the super method's code.

Inversing is handled simply by VBASE, so that operations such as ComponentOF and Component may be defined together, and will always return answers consistent with one another. One-to-many and many-to-many relationships can be easily maintained with this capability.

In VBASE all objects are persistent unless explicitly deleted. All operations, therefore, are database operations, and must be subject to the same constraints as other DBMS activities. Multiple concurrent processing, backup and recovery, and access control are all included in the design. In addition to these, VBASE offers two features that go beyond most DBMSs, clustering and triggers. Clustering allows the suer to specify where a newly created object may be stored in order to improve disk usage and reduce access times for objects commonly retrieved together. Triggers are operations that are invoked automatically upon matching some condition in the database, such as issuing a part order when QuantityOnHand falls below some point.

Extensible Databases

Before ending this discussion of prominent OODBMSs, some mention should be made about the area of extensible databases. Because they are not strictly object oriented, they are beyond the scope of this paper. However, they are so often either included among the OODBs or offered as alternative strategies so a few words are appropriate here.

The two leading extensible database models are POSTGRES and EXODUS, from University of California at Berkeley, and University of Wisconsin, respectively. POSTGRES is a central relational database with a large set of extensions that give it flexibility beyond the relational model. Among the added features are a capability to use nested tuples to allow compound object definitions; rule processing and stored procedures to simplify implementation of triggers and constraints; and state storage with timestamping to make versioning possible [*33–35*].

EXODUS is neither relational nor object oriented, but is instead a toolkit capable of modeling either of these models, or any of many others. A standardized storage system is provided, under which the basic unit is a "storage object," identifiable as a page and slot-number pair. Storage objects may shrink or grow to any size available on the medium. Versioning, locking, and recovery are all handled by the storage system [*36*]. In the EXTRA database built with the EXODUS tools, ADTs were supported with functions and operators. Complex objects with shared subobjects in a lattice structure were also included [*37*].

CONCLUSIONS

The current state of the art in object-oriented database systems is one in which much of the promise has been substantiated, but there is still little agreement of what the final product will look like. It has been shown that alternatives to the standard database models are better suited to certain applications than their predecessors. Those applications are characterized by large stored objects of complex structures, shared usage of subobjects, need for versions of data, and type-specific procedures.

The major areas of research are those where the most variation exists between the models presented. Among these are schema evolution, indexing strategies, transparency of persistent/dynamic object operations, inheritance structures, composite objects and data sharing, locking of shared objects and version paths, and interfacing with external languages and systems.

Schema evolution involves the ability to add new classes, to redefine relationships between classes, and to modify class definitions. Most researchers concede that adding new classes is an operation that should be readily available to users and is reasonable to implement. Redefining relationships and modification of existing classes, on the other hand, require strict protocols to insure database integrity. Whether or not these capabilities are worth the extra overhead is still an open question. Possible avenues for research involve efficient implementation algorithms for the evolution protocols, or domain-specific rule bases for narrowing down the semantics of these protocols.

Another problem area that could benefit from some domain knowledge is the selection of indexing strategies. The question here is at what depth of class membership is an index most efficient. Should an index order members only of the immediate class, or of all subclasses? If one is looking up a type DOCUMENT for the keyword "database," then they are probably interested in finding their topic in subclasses ARTICLE, REPORT, and ABSTRACT as well. Is this best handled with a global DOCUMENT index, an algorithm to search single-level child indexes of the parent class, or a set of rules forcing the user to make the decision? In what domains is a deep search more common than a single-level search?

Pointer swizzling, or the transparent manipulation of objects between primary and secondary memory, presents some difficult technical questions. In fact, this is a feature that traditional databases have never had and one would be hard-pressed to identify a demand for it outside of the academic research community. Purists call for this transparency as a way of overcoming "impedance mismatch" between language and storage to create "seamless integration" of program and data. Would this alter the way users viewed the data or dramatically change application programming in the object-oriented environment?

Inheritance structures still vary from system to system largely because the simplicity of implementing a strict hierarchy contrasts so severely with the difficulties of allowing multiple inheritance. In both cases, traversal is performed by the user during schema development and the system during method lookups. The additional time and complexity of multiple inheritance structures is likely to be intimidating to the user, and also a drain on system performance. Again, one must ask how often a user actually requires multiple inheritance within a specified application environment, and whether or not it is worth the tradeoffs.

It is clear that within OODB applications, there are some that require the ability for an object to belong to more than one structure, and some that must constrain ownership to one at a time. ENGINE12345 may be the physical motor that drives MYCAR, and can only be in one place at a time. However, the drawing for that ENGINE may appear as part of many different drawings of car models. Research into the semantics of composite structures and their applications is just beginning in the database field.

Several different schemes for locking objects and for creating versions of objects and for creating versions of objects have appeared in the implementations discussed here. A question remains, however, as to whether or not a simple check-out, check-in system is sufficient for a large object management system, or simply a stop-gap until a better algorithm comes along. Is it possible to implement a check-out system or even a user-specified versioning system and maintain any transparency of storage structures? Perhaps most important in terms of potential customer needs is the question of how much physical storage must be sacrificed to keep object versions and are there non-time-consuming algorithmic alternatives?

Finally, one common concern among implementations is how well can they interact with existing resources. In a large user environment, OODBs have the potential of organizing data from many sources such as distributed file servers, relational databases, user profiling data, and various input and output devices. To work in this role, they must be able to execute external procedures and store those procedures with the appropriate object representations. Various strategies to do this have been proposed, but their relative merits and shortcomings have yet to be collectively analyzed and compared. The notion of a global object manager is still one of the most powerful attractions of the OODBMS, but its potential is just beginning to be recognized. The possibilities in this area must be examined further.

Among the questions that seem to be on the horizon, it is clear one will be when is a extensible toolkit a useful alternative, or at the other extreme, when is a domain-specific object-oriented database all that is needed? Do users need the full functionality of run-time definition of classes and methods, or would previously compiled database schemas be more efficient? Despite the opportunities in researching complete flexibility, when OODBs hit the marketplace, users might find that they are only using a small subset of the capabilities anyway. Hopefully someone will ask these questions before users have made their decisions.

REFERENCES

1. P. U. Berstein, U. Dayal, D. DeWitt, D. Gawlick, J. Gray, M. Jarke, B. Lindsay, P. Lockemann, D. Maier, E. Neuhold, A. Reuter, L. Rowe, H. Shek, J. Schmidt, M. Schrefl, and M. Stonebraker, "The Luguna Beach Report: Future Directions in DBMS Research," *SIGMOD Rec.,18*(1), 17–26 (1986).
2. D. McLeod, "1988 VLDB Panel on 'Future Directions in DBMS Research': A Brief, Informal Summary," *SIGMOD Rec., 18*(1), 27–30 (1989).
3. S. Zdonik, "Object Management System Concepts," Second ACM–SIGOA Conference on Office Information Systems, Toronto, Canada (C. A. Ellis, ed.), 1984, 152–160.

4. O. M. Nierstrasz and D. C. Tsichritzis, "Integrated Office Systems," in *Object-Oriented Concepts, Databases, and Applications* (W. Kim and F. Lochovsky, eds.), ACM Press, Reading, MA, 1989.

5. W. Kim, E. Bertino, and J. Garza, "Composite Objects Revisited," in *Proceedings of ACM SIGMOD Annual Conference*, Portland, OR, ACM, New York, 1989, pp. 337–347.

6. P. Chen, "The Entity-Relationship Model—Toward a Unified View of Data," in *Readings in Database Systems* (M. Stonebraker, ed.), Morgan-Kaufaman, San Mateo, CA, 1988.

7. W. Kent, *Data and Reality: Basic Assumptions in Data Processing Reconsidered,* North-Holland, Amsterdam, 1978.

8. D. Shipman, "The Functional Data Model and the Data Language DAPLEX," in *Reading in Database Systems* (M. Stonebraker, ed.), Morgan-Kaufman, San Mateo, CA, 1988.

9. G. Copeland and D. Maier, "Making Smalltalk a Database System," in *Readings in Database Systems* (M. Stonebraker, ed.), Morgan-Kaufman, San Mateo, CA, 1988.

10. M. Stefik and G. Bobrow, "Object-Oriented Programming: Themes and Variations," *AI Magazine,* 6(4), 40–62 (1985).

11. J. Banerjee, W. Kim, H. Kim, and H. Korth, "Semantics and Implementation of Schema Evolution in Object-Oriented Databases," *Proceedings of ACM SIGMOD Annual Conference,* San Francisco, ACM, New York, 1987, pp. 311–322.

12. W. Kim, K. Kim, and A. Dale, "Indexing Techniques for Object-Oriented Databases," in *Object-Oriented Concepts, Databases, and Applications* (W. Kim and F. Lochovsky, eds.), ACM Press, Reading, MA, 1989.

13. D. Beech, "A Foundation for Evolution from Relational to Object Databases," in *Advances in Database Technology—EDBT'88* (J. W. Schmidt, S. Ceri, M. Missikoff,eds.), Springer Verlag, Berlin, 1988.

14. T. Connors and P> Lyngbaek, "Providing Uniform Access to Heterogeneous Information Bases," in *Advances in Object-Oriented Database Systems* (K. R. Dittrich, ed.), Springer-Verlag, Berlin, 1988.

15. D. H. Fishman, J. Annevelink, E. Chow, T. Connors, J. W. Davis, W. Hasan, C. G. Hoch, W. Kent, S. Leichner, P. Lyngbaek, B. Mahbod, M. A. Neimat, T. Risch, M. C. Shan, and W. K. Wilkinson, "Overview of the Iris DBMS," in *Object-Oriented Concepts, Databases, and Applications* (W. Kim and F. Lochovsky, eds.), ACM Press, Reading, MA, 1989.

16. D. H. Fishman, D. Beech, H. P. Cate, E. C. Chow, T. Connors, J. W. Davis, N. Derrett, C. G. Hoch, W. Kent, P. Lyngbaek, B. Mahbod, M. A. Neimat, T. A. Ryan, and M. C. Shan, "Iris: An Object-Oriented Database Management Systems," *ACM Trans. Office Inform. Sys.* (TOIS), 5(1), 48–69 (1987).

17. P. Lyngbaek and V. Vianu, "Mapping a Semantic Database Model to the Relational Model," in *Proceedings of ACM SIGMOD Annual Conference*, San Francisco, CA, 1987, ACM, New York, pp. 132-142.

18. M. Shan, "Optimal Plan Search in a Rule–based Query Optimizer," in *Advances in Database Technology—EDBT'88* (J. W. Schmidt, S. Ceri, and M. Missikoff, eds.), Springer Verlag, Berlin, 1988.

19. D. Woelk, W. Kim, and W. Luther, "An Object-Oriented Approach to Multimedia Databases,"in *Proceedings of ACM SIGMOD Annual Conference*, Washington, D.C., ACM, New York, 1986, pp. 311–325.

20. H. Chou and W. Kim, "A Unifying Framework for Version Control in a CAD Environment,"in *Proceedings Twelfth International Conference on Very Large Databases*, Kyoto, Japan, Morgan Kaufman, San Mateo, CA,1986, pp. 336–344.

21. J. Garza, and W. Kim, "Transaction Management in an Object-Oriented Database System," *Proceedings of ACM SIGMOD Anual Conference*, Chicago, IL, 1988, pp 37–45.

22. W. Kim, J. Banerjee, H. Chou, J. Garza, and D. Woelk, "Composite Object Support in an Object-Oriented Database System," OOPSLA'87 Object-Oriented Programming Systems, Languages, and Applications Conference Proceedings, *SIGPLAN Notices, 22*(12), 118–125 (1987).

23. W. Kim, N. Ballou, H. Chou, J. Garza, and D. Woelk, "Features of the ORION Object-Oriented Database System," in *Object-Oriented Concepts, Databases, and Applications* (W. Kim and F. Lochovsky, eds.), ACM Press, Reading, MA, 1989.

24. F. Rabitti, D. Woelk, and W. Kim, "A Model of Authorization for Object-Oriented and Semantic Databases," in *Advances in Database Technology—EDBT '88* (J. W. Schmidt, S. Ceri, and M. Missikoff, eds.), Springer Verlag, Berlin, 1988.

25. R. Bretl, D. Maier, A. Otis, J. Penney, B. Schuchardt, J. Stein, E. H. Williams, and M. Williams, "The GemStone Data Management System," in *Object-Oriented Concepts, Databases, and Applications* (W. Kim and F. Lochovsky, eds.), ACM Press, Reading, MA, 1989.

26. D. Penney and J. Stein, "Class Modification in the GemStone Object-Oriented DBMS," OOPSLA '87 Object-Oriented Programming Systems, Languages, and Applications Conference Proceedings, *SIGPLAN Notices, 22*(12), 111–117 (1987).

27. A. Purdy, B. Schuchardt, and D. Maier, "Integrating an Object Server with Other Worlds," *ACM Trans. Office Inform. Sys.* (TOIS), *5*(1), 27–47, (1987).

28. J. Ullman, *Principles of Database and Knowledge-Base Systems,* Volume I, Computer Science Press, Rockville, MD, 1988.

29. A. Kemper, P. Lockemann, and M. Wallrath, "An Object-Oriented Database System for Engineering Applications," in *Proceedings of ACM SIGMOD Annual Conference*, San Francisco, ACM New York, 1987, pp. 299–310.

30. A. Kemper and M. Wallrath, "A Uniform Concept for Storing and Manipulating Engineering Objects," in *Advances in Object-Oriented Database Systems* (K. R. Dittrich, ed.), Springer-Verlag, Berlin, 1988.

31. R. Agrawal and N. H. Gehani, "ODE (Object Database and Environment: The Language and the Data Model," *Proceedings of the ACM SIGMOD Annual Conference,* Portland, OR, ACM, New York, 1989, pp. 36–45.

32. T. Andrews and C. Harris, "Combining Language and Database Advances in An Object-Oriented Development Environment," OOPSLA '87 Object-Oriented Programming Systems, Languages, and Applications Conference Proceedings, *SIGPLAN Notices, 22*(12), 430–440 (1987).

33. M. Stonebraker, "The Design of the POSTGRES Storage System," in *Readings in Database Systems* (M. Stonebraker, ed.), Morgan-Kaufman, San Mateo, CA, 1988.

34. M. Stonebraker, E. Hanson, and C. Hong, "The Design of the POSTGRES Rules System," in *Readings in Database Systems* (M. Stonebraker, ed.), Morgan-Kaufman, San Mateo, CA, 1988.

35. M. Stonebraker and L. Rowe, "The Design of Postgres," in *Proceedings of ACM SIGMOD Annual Conference*, Washington, D.C., ACM, New York, 1986, pp. 340-355.

36. M. Carey, D. DeWitt, J. Richardson, and E. Shekita, "Storage Management for Objects in EXODUS," in *Object-Oriented Concepts, Databases, and Applications* (W. Kim and F. Lochovsky, eds.), ACM Press, Reading, MA, 1989.

37. M. Carey, D. DeWitt, and S. Vandenberg, "A Data Model and Query Languages for EXODUS," in *Proceedings of ACM SIGMOD Annual Conference*, Chicago, ACM, New York, 1988, pp. 413–423.

STUART A. McLEAN

PERFORMANCE PETRI NETS

INTRODUCTION

The performance evaluation of a computer system can follow two basic approaches. First, if the system already exists, direct measurements of some properties are possible. Second, if the system does not already exist or the particular scenario of interest is too difficult, expensive, or dangerous to create, a model of the system can be studied. However, the modeling of a system is always a tradeoff between the complexity of solution and the accuracy of the model.

Historically, the performance of a computer system was modeled with a network of queues [1–3] or a simulation [1, 4, 5]. With the increasing interest in parallel and distributed system architectures, those techniques proved to be too complex to solve or too cumbersome to specify. As an alternative, models based upon the Petri net [6–14] drew some attention. These models allowed a more natural representation of concurrency and blocking which are inherent to distributed and parallel systems.

THE UNDERLYING MODEL: A PETRI NET

The Petri net model, developed by Carl A. Petri [15], is an automaton with two types of nodes, transitions and places, which are connected by direct arcs. Places are often used to represent conditions in the system being modeled while transitions are used to represent events that can occur to modify the conditions. The state of the Petri net is defined by the use of tokens which reside in places to represent the holding of conditions. The particular pattern of tokens in places is called the marking of the Petri net. A transition is considered enabled (able to fire) when there is at least one token on each of the places that have an arc directed to the transition. When a transition actually fires, it removes one token from all the places with arcs directed from the place to that transition and places a token on each of the places with an arc directed from that transition to the place.

> **Definition 1**: A *Petri net* is a bipartite graph [16–18] with nodes P (places), T (transitions), input and output arcs A, and an initial marking M_0.

$$PN \triangleq (P,T,A,M_0)$$

$$P = \{p_1,p_2, \ldots ,p_n\}$$

$$T = \{t_1,t_2, \ldots ,t_m\} \tag{1}$$

$$A \subset \{P \times T\} \cup \{T \times P\}$$

$$M_0 = \{m_1^0 ,m_2^0 , \ldots ,m_n\}$$

Definition 2: Define for a Petri net *PN* the set function *IP* (i.e., preset *t* [18]) of input places for a transition *t* as *IP* (*t*) $\triangleq$ {*p*|(*p* ,*t*)∈*A*}.

Definition 3: Define for a Petri net *PN* the set function *OP* (i.e., postset *t** [18]) of output places for transition *t* as *OP*(*t*) $\triangleq$ {*p*|(*t* ,*p*)∈*A*}.

Definition 4: Define for a Petri net *PN* the set function *IT* (i.e., preset *p* [18]) of input transitions for a place *p* as *IT*(*p*) $\triangleq$ {*t*|(*t* ,*p*)∈*A*}.

Definition 5: Define for a Petri net *PN* the set function *OT* (i.e., postset *p** [18]) of output transitions for a place *p* as *OT*(*p*) $\triangleq$ {*t*|(*p* ,*t*)∈*A*}.

The definitions of the input and output functions given here are for nets without parallel arcs. If parallel (multiple arcs) are used these functions are defined on bags rather than sets.

The marking may be viewed as a mapping from the set of places *P* to the natural numbers *N*.

$$M:P \rightarrow N \text{ where } M(p_i) = m_i \qquad \text{for } i = 1,2, \ldots , n \qquad (2)$$

Definition 6: a transition is considered *enabled* when each and every one of its input places have one or more tokens (i.e., $\forall p \in IP(t), M(p) > 0$).

The enabling of a transition can be considered as the holding of conditions required by the event the transition represents. An extension to normal Petri nets adds an inhibitor arc from places to transitions which does a zero test. If there are any tokens in the input place of an inhibitor arc, then the transition is disabled. (Inhibitor arcs are normally drawn like regular arcs, except the arrowhead is replaced by a circle.)

Definition 7: A transition is said to have *fired* when it removes one token from all of its input places and places one additional token in all of its output places (i.e., $\forall p \in IP(t)$, $M_{i+1}(p) = M_i (p) - 1$ and $\forall p \in OP(t)$, $M_{i+1}(p) = M_i(p) + 1$), thus changing the marking function.

A firing of a transition changes one marking into another marking. So the firing of a transition can be considered as the occurrence of an event which then causes a state change. Note that there are some variations on the precise action taken by a transition when it fires. This definition is the normal one and the one used by the Petri net theoreticians.

Definition 8: A marking M_2 is called *reachable* from a marking M_1 if $\exists$ a sequence of transitions *t** such that $M_1 \xrightarrow{t^*} M_2$.

This concept of reachable is sometimes broken into two cases. The special case of sequences of length one is called *directly reachable* while the case of sequences of one or more are simply called *reachable*. As in other automata, the concept of reachability is very important. The logical behavior of the Petri net is properly described by the set of all reachable markings from some fixed initial marking.

Definition 9: The *reachability set S* is the set of all markings {M_i} which are reachable from some initial marking M_0.

Given the logical behavior of the Petri net, we can classify those behaviors in many ways by noting specific properties of the Petri net in terms of its reachability set.

Definition 10: A place p_i in a PN is said to be *bounded* if $\exists$ a finite number $k \in N$ such that $k \geq M(p_i) \forall M \in S$.

Definition 11: A PN is said to be *bounded* if each place p_i is bounded $\forall p_i \in P$.

So, a Petri Net is bounded if and only if it has a finite reachability set. However, being finite is often not sufficient in practice, since the reachability set can grow at exponential rate (2^n) where n is the number of places in the net.

Definition 12: A PN is said to be *safe* if it is bounded by one.

Definition 13: A transition t_i is said to be 'live' if for $\forall M_k \in S \; \exists$ a marking sequence M_j^* which enables t_i.

Liveness, unfortunately, has several different flavors. For example, one might consider a transition live if it was ever enabled. This definition, however, is the most widely used and meaningful. Other definitions do exist [*17*] and have been used in the past.

Definition 14: A PN is said to be 'live' if each transition $t_i \in T$ is live.

Note, that the enabling markings reachable from $\forall M_k \in S$ need not be the same. This means that not all markings in the reachability set of a live net need be reachable from each other.

Definition 15: A PN is called a *marked graph* or *decision-free Petri net* if all places have only one input and one output transition.

Although these types of Petri nets have very nice properties for analysis, you cannot model contention, since only one event (i.e., transition) can affect or depend on a particular condition (i.e., place).

Definition 16: A PN is said to be *conflict free* if, for every place which is an input of more than one transition, the place is on a self-loop with each such transition.

This implies that the firing of one transition cannot disable another transition. Therefore, although transitions may share places, conflicts are not possible. This limits the usefulness of the model since concurrent systems often contend for resources.

Definition 17: A PN is said to be *persistent*, if for any transitions t_1 and $t_2,(t_1 \neq t_2)$, and any reachable marking M which enables t_1 and t_2, firing either transition cannot disable the other.

This simply states that whatever the structure of the PN, no conflict can take place since firing a transition will not disable another transition. Note that this definition is made in terms of the reachable markings, so it is possible that a net is persistent for one marking and not for another marking. However, a PN is conflict free, if and only if, it is persistent for all markings [*19*].

Definition 18: A PN is said to be *free choice* if, for all arcs, either the output set of a place is single a transition or the input set of a transition is a single place.

In other words, any transition with more than one input place must be the only transition with those places as input places. This implies that when a marking enables some transitions with a common input place, then all transitions with the common input place are enabled. This class of nets allows some measure of contention, but restricts the types of conflicts to a simple selection.

Since the only topological restriction on the arcs in general Petri net is that the graph be bipartite (arcs may only connect places to transitions or transitions to places), the model has significant modeling power. (The Petri net with the addition of inhibitor arcs which test for zero tokens is equivalent to a Turing machine.) This fact is both a benefit and a curse. Since the model is powerful, very complex systems can be represented. However, the model also has several problems which are unresolvable in general, making it less interesting.

The models, called performance Petri nets (PPN), are variants of the original Petri net. The original Petri net is extended by associating some timing information with the Petri net. In the original model, only sequences of transition firings were of interest and no value of time between events was considered. The purpose of the original model was to explore all possible actions of the system, not the duration of events or the average behavior of the system. With the addition of timing to the model such calculations as delays, throughputs, and token distributions over time could be determined.

HISTORICAL PERSPECTIVE

The first attempt to form a performance Petri net was the addition of timing to the E-net model [20] developed by Noe and Nutt to model the CDC 6600 in 1971. The E-net model had many different constructs and modified firing rules. The model was used as a specification for the simulation of the actions of the hardware and could be considered a design language.

The first formal attempt to form a performance Petri net model was done by Ramchandani in 1973 as part of his Ph.D. thesis at MIT [6]. His model, the timed Petri net (TPN), was targeted at the problem of modeling the complex hardware being developed for new architectures. The model had associated a real value to the firing of a transaction so that the model could represent asynchronous circuits with various component delays. The value was either fixed, or restricted to a narrow range around a fixed value.

In 1975, Phillip Merlin presented a model for data communication protocols in his Ph.D. thesis at the University of California at Irvine which associated a range of time with a transition. This was used to model timeouts in a protocol and affected the possible states the system could obtain [21,22]. However, in 1977, a paper by Neil Jones, Lawrence Landwebber, and Y. Edmund Lien demonstrated that, for the timed Petri nets defined by Merlin, the reachability problem and even the boundedness problem were undecidable.

In the early 1980s a number of different models were introduced. The first Ramchandani model with a fixed value for the duration of transition firing was revived in the work of Ramamoorthy and Ho [7]. Zuberek restricted the value to integer values to represent a centralized clocked system [9]. At the other extreme the stochastic Petri nets (SPN) were introduced independently in the United States by the author [11] and in France by Natkin and Florin [10]. The SPN model associated an exponentially distributed random variable, not a fixed value, with each transition.

After the introduction of the stochastic Petri net model, several researchers adopted and extended the basic model. In 1982, researchers at the Politecnico di Torino in Italy introduced the idea of immediate transitions to SPN creating the generalized stochastic Petri net (GSPN) model [13]. These new models allowed priorities and random selection independent of time while retaining the Markov analysis methods. At about the same time, researchers at Duke University were using the basic SPN model with arbitrary distributions for firing times to develop the extended stochastic Petri net models [12] as a specification language for the hybrid automated reliability predictor (HARP) system. These models required the use of semi-Markov techniques or simulation for analysis.

Many groups still preferred the original timed Petri nets, so the discrete time stochastic Petri nets [23] were presented as a bridge between the two models. From the other direction, the generalized timed Petri nets [24] were introduced for the same purpose by Vernon and Holliday in 1985.

In the late 1970s, the European Petri net community was developing some new models. These new models, high-level Petri nets, were extended from normal Petri nets by allowing tokens to have values. In the case of colored Petri nets [25], the tokens have some identifier (or color). In the case of predicate transition nets [26], the tokens are strings of symbols. The transitions in these high-level nets are modified so that the enabling rules depend on the values of the tokens (i.e., predicates) and the firing of transitions are modified to change the values of tokens.

The existence of these new models led to the introduction of the corresponding performance Petri nets. Colored stochastic Petri nets were introduced by Alexandre Zenie [27] in 1985. Stochastic high-level Petri nets (based on predicate transition nets) were introduced by Lin and Marinescu [28] in 1987.

A TAXONOMY OF THE MODELS

The introduction of timing into the basic Petri net model can be accomplished in a variety of ways. The particular timing semantics provide a basis to categorize the different models. In this section, we describe the possible semantic differences and from that, form a taxonomy of the models presented in the literature.

The first distinction in the models is found in the type of Petri net used as the underlying model. Several different types of nets are described in the literature [17–19]. Several models are defined on a restricted Petri net mode, such as conflict free, marked graphs, or free choice nets.

The particular net object with which the timing information is associated is the second distinction we can find. Several models associate the timing with places (i.e., timed place Petri nets, TPPN) [8], while most associate the timing with transitions (i.e., timed transition Petri nets, TTPN) [6,7,9,11].

In the timed place model, tokens are output to a place and remain unavailable for some period of time. After this initial delay, those tokens change state to become available for enabling transitions with that place as an input place. You can construct a timed place model with a timed transition model by replacing every place in the timed place model with a timed transition to delay the tokens and a place to hold the tokens after the firing of the timed transition to enable the normal transitions in the original model. Given this mapping from timed place Petri nets to timed transition Petri nets, most work has concentrated on timed transition Petri nets.

The third and more subtle distinction is found in the semantics of transition firing when two or more transitions are concurrently enabled and share some input places. If tokens are not removed until the end of the transition firing time, then all competing transitions can be considered as firing concurrently. This implies that race conditions will exist and faster transitions may preempt slower transitions. If the timing is deterministic, then the preemption will be absolute and the logical behavior of the system is different. If only one transition is selected to initiate the firing delay and those tokens necessary for the firing are considered as unavailable for other transitions to initiate, then the semantics of transition firing includes a *preselection* rule. Preselection decouples the timing functions and the selection function for which transition to fire. Performance Petri nets that

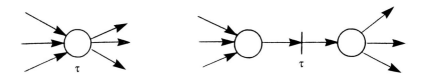

FIGURE 1   Mapping a timed place PN to a timed transition PN.

incorporate preselection in the transition firing semantics, can be subdivided into cases where preselection is done arbitrarily and where preselection is done based upon a probability function (Fig. 1).

The fourth distinction is based in how many concurrent firings of a single transition are allowed. If a transition is enabled at a moment in time when it is currently firing from a previous enabling, then there are two possible actions. Either a second concurrent firing may be initiated or the transition may be restricted to allow only one firing to be in progress at a time. In that case the tokens in the enabling places will simply queue until the current firing is complete. This distinction may be considered as a measure of the *internal parallelism* of a transition. If the rules for transition firing allow infinite parallelism, then tokens will not interfere with each other (i.e., no delays due to queuing). If the rules restrict the amount of parallelism, then tokens may interfere with each other. This same concept can be described as a load-dependent transition firing rule. It is like having as many replications of the transition as necessary to handle the enabling load.

The last distinction is based upon the timing values associated with a performance Petri net. There are three ways timing values can be associated with the net.

1. A single fixed value can be used (it may be real or integer); deterministic firing times
2. A range of values around some fixed valued can be used
3. A distribution of values can be used such that the time is a random variable; random firing times

Historically, the first two cases have been called timed Petri nets (TPN) and the last one has been called a stochastic Petri net (SPN). However, the first work on the stochastic Petri net [*11*] concentrated on the exponential distribution [*12–14*]. Later models relaxed that restriction [*12–14*], but retained the word stochastic in their name. Clearly, the idea of allowing an arbitrary distribution, as in the extended stochastic Petri net (ESPN) [*12*], would include the timed Petri nets as special cases.

EXAMPLES OF PERFORMANCE PETRI NETS

There are many different models in the literature that associate time with a Petri net in some way. There are also models which associate time with a directed graph which is equivalent to a Petri net. Many of the models are variants of the ones mentioned here. This list is by no means exhaustive, but is illustrative of the models currently in use.

Many models in the literature have identical properties to the models presented here. There is still a great deal of discussion about which particular specification structures would comprise a proper user interface. This discussion will avoid that issue since only the users can really determine which interface is the proper one.

The following examples of performance Petri nets should provide some indication of the diversity of the models presented in the literature. Each model has its advantages and disadvantages, and no one model has become dominant much to the frustration of its supporters.

E Nets

The evaluation nets (E nets) developed by Noe and Nutt [20] are very similar to Petri nets in appearance and operation. There are two basic differences in the operation of the two models. First, there is an additional place type that acts as a switch called a *resolution location*. Second, the firing rules are changed to allow a transition to be enabled only if the target places are empty.

There are five types of E-net transitions, which are all illustrated in Figure 2. In a T transition, when a token resides on location *b*, and no token resides on *c*, the transition fires. On firing, the token is removed from *b* and is placed on *c*. In the fork type F transition, the token is removed from *b* and tokens are placed on each of *e* and *f* only if both *e* and *f* were empty. The J transition is of the join type where tokens are removed from both *b* and *c* and one token is placed on *e* only if *e* was empty.

The last two types of primitive E nets use the resolution type of place. The state of the resolution place selects the output of the transition in the X transition case or the input of the transition in the Y transition case. If *r* contains a 1 in the X transition case, the firing of the

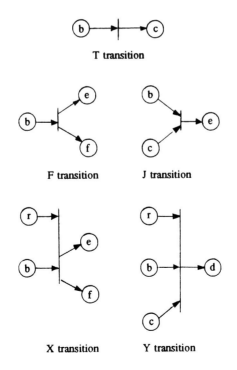

FIGURE 2.   Primitive E nets.

transition moves a token from b to f. In the Y transition case, a 1 in r would select c as the input for the transition so that the token would be removed from c and placed on d.

When the simulator was constructed, timings were associated with the transitions. To facilitate the construction of performance measures, a special object, called a resource, was introduced. A transition could specify a set of resources which were needed for the firing of the transition. That resource would then be considered as *in use* for the duration of the firing of the transition. The simulator would then keep track of the amount of total time a resource was in use. Postprocessing of the values associated with resource usages would allow the construction of complex performance measures.

Timed Petri Nets

Timed Petri nets were introduced by C. Ramchandani [6]. This model was later used by Ramamoorthy [7], Sifakis [8], Merlin [21], and Zuberek [9]. The basic idea of the extension was to simply add a label to each transition which indicated how long that transition took to fire. These time values were either a fixed (deterministic) value [6–9], or a fixed range around a value [6,21]. The underlying Petri nets were safe (1-bounded) and limited to a nonreflexive, conflict-free (decision-free) structure.

Consider the example from Zuberek [9] shown in Figure 3. This timed Petri net (TPN) is safe and decision free so that transitions cannot be disabled by other transitions.* The numbers in parentheses at each transition give the number of time units for that transition to fire. The timing diagram shown in Figure 4 gives a breakdown of the operation of the TPN. Note the cycle formed at time Step 4 which repeats at time step 14. The markings reached during the operation of the TPN before step 4 were transient markings because they would never recur.

Timed Petri nets enforce additional constraints on the reachability set. Markings reachable in the underlying Petri net may not be reachable in the TPN. First, since transition firing times may synchronize firings, the single transition firing rule of Petri nets is violated. Second, race conditions may always require one transition to fire before another transition can fire, effectively giving priority to the faster transition. As an example, in the TPN shown in Figure 3, the marking (0,1,0,1,0,0,0,1,0) will not occur, while it is in the reachability set of the underlying Petri net. This constraint on the reachability set may be viewed as an interlock phenomenon. Because of this interlock between the loops which keeps the loops synchronized in the TPN, the cycle time of any connected, safe,+ decision-free TPN is simply the time of the maximum cycle [7].

When additional tokens are placed on the net, two interpretations of the semantics of the transition operation are possible. First, a new token arriving after a transition has "started" could wait until the timing cycle of the transition is complete. Second, the new token may be allowed to start its own timing for that transition independent of any other tokens in use. The last interpretation was made by Ramamoorthy. It implies that transitions have an infinite internal parallelism available to tokens.

---

* Zuberek also allowed free choice Petri net models and assigned a probability to the firing of the transitions. He then gave an algorithm that analyzed the model using Markov analysis which doesn't work for all cases [24].

+Ramamoorthy allowed transitions to fire in parallel so the safety requirement was lifted. However, the result only holds for safe nets if a transition must complete a firing period before initiating a second one.

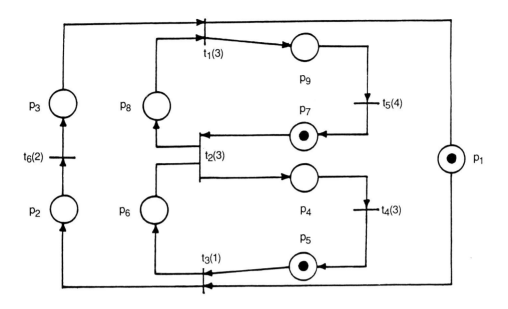

FIGURE 3. A timed Petri net

If the conflict-free restriction on the TPN is relaxed, some new issues arise. Consider two transitions enabled in the same marking. Then there are three ways to select which transition will fire. First, if the enabling tokens are not "committed" to a particular transition, then the transitions clock off their time values and the shortest time value always fires first. Therefore, a transition may never fire even though that transition is enabled. This creates a whole new series of deadlock detection issues. Second, a probability may be added to the selection of which transition to commit to, independent of the transition time. This complicates the performance calculations by requiring each dominant cycle possible to be calculated and then take the weighted average of these cycles. Third, the selection of which transition to commit to could be arbitrary, which is the method of Ramamoorthy.

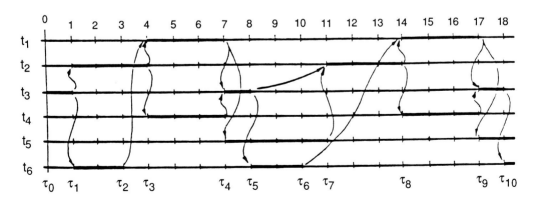

FIGURE 4. Timing diagram for TPN

The solution of such a system is very complex. Jones, Landwebber, and Lien [29] showed that even the reachability problem is undecidable in general for TPN of the type Merlin [21] described. In Ramamoorthy [7], a proof is given which shows that the TPN solution using cycle enumeration is NP-complete for general timed Petri nets. This is accomplished by constructing the TPN shown in Figure 5 where the calculation of the minimum cycle time is equivalent to a set enumeration problem. This certainly raises some interesting questions as to the usefulness of such models. So, with conflict, the solution is difficult or undecidable (depending on the model) and, without the ability to model conflict, the decision-free TPN cannot model contention for resources, which is one of the major reasons for using graph models. More recently, Jan Maggott [30] has looked at the complexity of intermediate models such as free choice nets.

The TPN model of Razouk and Phelps [31] is a hybrid of several different models. There is a decomposition of the firing of a transition into enabling times and firing delays. Enabling times are allowed to execute in parallel, so there is no preselection for enabling, but once the enabling times are complete, the tokens are dedicated to the transition and the firing delays are started. In a fashion similar to E nets, resources are associated with transitions to facilitate the generation of performance measures.

Generalized Timed Petri Nets

In the previous models, the underlying Petri nets were restricted to the class of safe (1-bounded) nets. Although several reports discussed the issues for k-bounded nets, their techniques were limited to the case of safe nets (or required infinite internal parallelism in transition firings). In the case of generalized timed Petri nets, k-bounded nets were allowed with the idea that transition preselection was done probabilistically (and independent of time), so that the underlying marking process formed a semi-Markov process.

The generalized timed Petri nets (GTPN) model [24] removes the restriction on safeness (but retains the restriction of boundedness) and the restrictions on conflict (such as

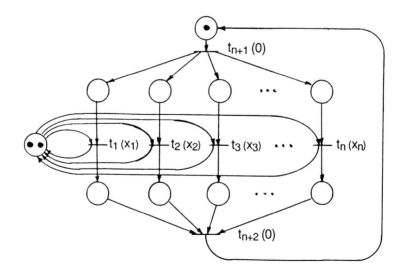

FIGURE 5.   A TPN requiring NP-complete analysis.

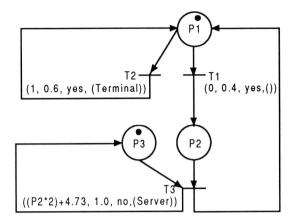

FIGURE 6.   An example generalized timed Petri net.

conflict free or free choice). Transitions have a 4-tuple, (t,p,q,R), associated with them. The first element t, is the time (an arbitrary, possibly state-dependent value) for the transition to fire. Firing assumes preselection and tokens are removed at the initiation of firing and are not available in the output places until the firing completes. The second element, p, is the probability that the transition will be selected to fire. This probability is easy to assign in the absence of conflict or in the case of conflict-free nets. In other cases, the construction of maximal subsets of transition firings is required and a computation from these probabilities is used to select which transition to fire. The third element, q, is a boolean which controls the construction of the probabilities when multiple enablings occur. The fourth element, R, is a set of resources (similar to those in E nets and Razouk's model) which are used to compute performance measures.

Note that the state of the GTPN now includes the marking and the remaining firing time (RFT) set for all currently firing transitions. In the case of multiple enablings (additional tokens), transitions will exhibit internal parallelism like Ramamoorthy's model. Therefore, the RFT set may contain multiple occurrences of a single transition with possibly different remaining firing times.

	$p1$	$p2$	$p3$	RFT Set	Resources
S_0	1	0	1	{}	{}
S_1	0	0	1	$\{(t_1, 0.0)\}$	{}
S_2	0	0	1	$\{(t_2, 1.0)\}$	{Terminal}
S_3	0	1	1	{}	{}
S_4	0	0	0	$\{(t_3, 6.73)\}$	{Server}

The embedded Markov chain, shown in Figure 7, corresponds to the GTPN shown in Figure 6 and is solved for the probabilities of being in particular states. With the addition of the timing information, the steady-state behavior for the semi-Markov chain can be determined.

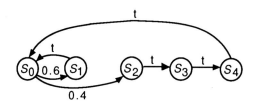

FIGURE 7.   The embedded Markov chain for the example GTPN.

This example did not have more than one transition firing concurrently. However, this is allowed in the model and it is possible to have several states with different remaining firing times for various combinations of transitions.

Stochastic Petri Nets

In the stochastic Petri net model [10,11], there is no preselection of which transition to fire. The firing of transitions is decided by allowing each enabled transition to begin firing. Since the firing time of each transition is a random variable with a range from zero to infinity, the particular sample values of the random variables may have any one of the transitions firing. So, the actual time until a transition fires is the minimum of the random variables for each enabled transition. If the random variables for the firing times are exponentially distributed, that minimum is again exponentially distributed with the sum of the firing rates. In addition, since the exponential distribution is memoryless, the remaining time for the firing of a transition (if it is still enabled) is again exponential with the original rate.

These transition firing semantics make the stochastic Petri net isomorphic to the class of homogeneous Markov chains. That means that the reachability set is the state space of a Markov process and that reachability set is identical to the reachability set in the underlying Petri net without timing constraints. Therefore, the analysis of a SPN model amounts to generating the state space of the underlying Petri net and constructing the equivalent Markov process for analysis using known techniques.

This equivalence of the underlying reachability set means that all the normal Petri net theory is applicable to SPN. However, as in the normal Petri net, the reachability set may be extremely large. In general, there may be a combinatorial growth in the size of the reachability set when the number of tokens in the initial marking is increased linearly. This is the major difficulty in using any of these models as analytical models of real systems.

Consider the 5 place, 5 transition continuous time stochastic Petri net shown in Figure 8. This SPN displays sequential operation (t_5,t_1), parallel operation (t_2,t_3), forking (t_1), joining (t_5), and contention (t_4,t_5). Include the expected firing rates of $\lambda_1 = 2$, $\lambda_2 = 1$, $\lambda_3 = 1$, $\lambda_4 = 3$, and $\lambda_5 = 2$. Assuming an initial marking of one token in place p_1 and no tokens in the remaining places, then solving for the reachability set, we find five states.

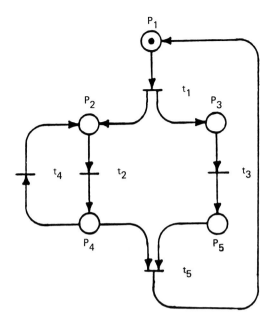

FIGURE 8.   An example stochastic Petri net.

	p_1	p_2	p_3	p_4	p_5
M_1	1	0	0	0	0
M_2	0	1	1	0	0
M_3	0	0	1	1	0
M_4	0	1	0	0	1
M_5	0	0	0	1	1

The reachability set along with the transitions rates forms the Markov chain corresponding to the SPN model (Fig. 9).

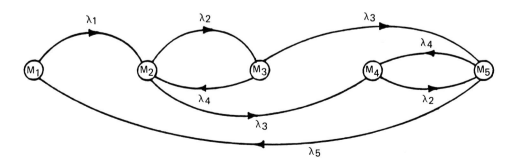

FIGURE 9.   The Markov chain for the example SPN.

Solving the ergodic Markov chain we obtain the following steady-state marking probabilities.

$$P[M_1] = .1163$$
$$P[M_2] = .1860$$
$$P[M_3] = .0465$$
$$P[M_4] = .5349$$
$$P[M_5] = .1163$$

Using the steady-state marking probabilities and the number of tokens in each place in a particular marking we can compute the steady-state probability of there being m_i tokens in each place for any marking. This is precisely the token probability density function.

$$P[m_1 = 0] = .8837 \quad P[m_1 = 1] = .1163$$
$$P[m_2 = 0] = .2791 \quad P[m_2 = 1] = .7209$$
$$P[m_3 = 0] = .7675 \quad P[m_3 = 1] = .2325$$
$$P[m_4 = 0] = .8372 \quad P[m_4 = 1] = .1628$$
$$P[m_5 = 0] = .3488 \quad P[m_5 = 1] = .6512$$

If we assume a different initial marking, then we obtain a different Markov chain. The more tokens we have in the system the larger the Markov chain. If we start with two tokens in place p_1 we would find 14 states in the reachability set. Similarly, if we started with three tokens in place p_1 we would find 30 states in the reachability set. This state space explosion is one of the major problems with using these models for complex systems.

The analysis of the delay in an arbitrary system yields to one of two techniques. First, if the equivalent Markov chain has trapping states, one can calculate the expected number of steps until one of the trapping states is reached. Second, if the chain is ergodic then the delay for components of the net may be calculated using Little's result and flow balance.

Consider the example of the small SPN in Figure 8. Let us apply Little's result to the subsystem made up of places p_2, p_3, p_4, and p_5 and transitions t_2, t_3, t_4, and t_5. Since t_1 is only enabled when p_1 contains a token the utilization of transition t_1 is 11.63 percent. Using the average service time of 0.5 units for t_1, the average rate at which tokens flow through p_1 is 0.2326 tokens per unit time.

By the conservation of flow, we know that the number of tokens entering the subsystem per unit time λ is 0.4652, which is double the flow through t_1 since t_1 is a fork transition. Since t_5 is a join transition, the flow in and flow out will be balanced. Since the subsystem conserves tokens (it neither destroys nor creates tokens) we may apply Little's result $\bar{N} = \lambda \, T$.

The average number of tokens in the subsystem is the sum of the average number of tokens in each place in the subsystem.

$$\bar{N} = \bar{m}_2 + \bar{m}_3 + \bar{m}_4 + \bar{m}_5 = 1.7674 \tag{3}$$

Therefore, on the average, the time until a token returns to p_1 after leaving is 3.8 units of time.

For the special case above, where the object is to determine the mean recurrence time of a marking M_i in a continuous time SPN, another method can be applied which does not need token conservation. By making the observation that the time until an enabled transition fires is the time spent in the marking, the mean time $\bar{\tau}_M$ is simply $(\sum \lambda_i)^{-1}$ for each enabled transition i, in that marking. After solving for the steady-state probabilities, $P[M_i]$, the mean time to return to the marking M_i is simply $\bar{\tau}_{Mi}/P[M_i]-\bar{\tau}_{Mi}$. Using the same values for the SPN as before, we find the same results $\bar{\tau}_{Mi}, P[M_i]-\bar{\tau}_{Mi} = 3.8$.

Extended Stochastic Petri Nets

Because the exponential assumption is very restrictive, several groups chose to relax that assumption. Relaxing the assumption forces the analysis to become more complex. The complexity of the analysis will depend on the precise distributions used for random variables representing the transition firing times. One extreme is the extended stochastic Petri net [12], where an arbitrary distribution for transition firing times is allowed.

By allowing an arbitrary distribution for firing times, the underlying stochastic process is no longer Markovian. It may be semi-Markovian, allowing the application of known techniques, or it may be so general that the only possible analysis is simulation. Simulation can be used to analyze the average behavior of almost any process (a generalized semi-Markov process to be precise [5]) and will not require the generation of the reachability set. By not generating the reachability set, the problem of state space explosion is avoided. However, since the state space is not evaluated, use of the model for verification purposes is no longer possible.

The ESPN are extended from the SPN by adding several features. First, the distribution of time for firing of transitions is now arbitrary. Second, the use of inhibitor arcs is allowed. Third, probabilistic arcs are added to ease the specification of alternate firings. Fourth, multiple (or weighted) arcs are allowed so that a simple arc with a multiplier, k, is equivalent to k parallel arcs in the Petri Net.

Generalized Stochastic Petri Nets

The difficulty of implementing priorities and non-time-dependent transition firing probabilities prompted another group of researchers to develop a different model which becomes a compromise between the complete generality of extended stochastic Petri nets and the original stochastic Petri nets. This model, the generalized stochastic Petri net [13], adds a new type of transition to the normal stochastic Petri net, the immediate transition.

In the generalized stochastic Petri net model, there are two types of transitions. The first type, the timed transition, is identical to the transition in the normal stochastic Petri net. The second type, the immediate transition, is a special transition which takes zero time to fire (an infinite firing rate). When an immediate transition is enabled, since it has an infinite firing rate, it will preempt any enabled timed transition. If more than one immediate transition is enabled, then there is no way to determine the probability from the relative rates that either transition will fire since both rates are infinite. Therefore, immediate transitions have a probability associated with them which determines the probability that the particular transition will fire when it is enabled concurrently with another immediate transition. This probability may be markedly dependent.

In the example of a GSPN, shown in Figure 10, the timed transitions are denoted by small rectangles, while the immediate transitions are denoted by narrow bars.

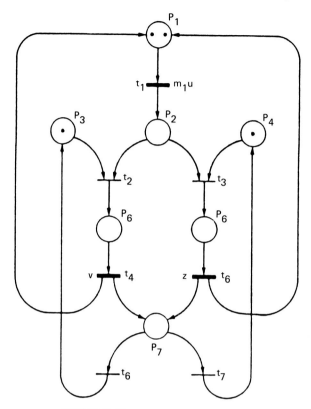

FIGURE 10.   An example GSPN.

$$prob(t_2) = \frac{M(p_3)}{M(p_3) + M(p_4)}$$

$$prob(t_3) = \frac{M(p_4)}{M(p_3) + M(p_4)}$$

$$prob(t_6) = \frac{M(p_3)}{M(p_3) + M(p_4)} \qquad \text{for } M(p_3) \neq 0 \text{ or } M(p_4) \neq 0 \qquad (4)$$

$$prob(t_7) = \frac{M(p_4)}{M(p_3) + M(p_4)} \qquad \text{for } M(p_3) \neq 0 \text{ or } M(p_4) \neq 0$$

$$prob(t_6) = prob(t_7) = \tfrac{1}{2} \qquad \text{for } M(p_3) = M(p_4) = 0$$

Unfortunately, the addition of the immediate transition also complicates the analysis. One of the goals of the GSPN was to maintain the ability to perform an analytic analysis of the model. However, the fact that some transitions fire at an infinite rate implies that some markings (states in the corresponding Markov system) will exist for zero time. That is different from a marking having zero probability (i.e., not occurring). So, the algorithm for generating the corresponding Markov chain requires the removal of the intangible markings (i.e., markings that occur but have a holding time of zero) which includes any reachable state in the underlying Petri net that enables one or more immediate transitions.

Tangible Markings

	p_1	p_2	p_3	p_4	p_5	p_6	p_7
M_0	2	0	1	1	0	0	0
M_1	1	0	0	1	1	0	0
M_2	1	0	1	0	0	1	0
M_3	0	0	0	0	1	1	0
M_4	1	0	0	1	0	1	0
M_5	1	0	1	0	1	0	0
M_6	0	0	0	0	0	2	0
M_7	0	0	0	0	2	0	0

Intangible Markings

	p_1	p_2	p_3	p_4	p_5	p_6	p_7
M_0	1	1	1	1	0	0	0
M_1	0	1	0	1	1	0	0
M_2	2	0	0	1	0	0	1
M_3	0	1	1	0	0	1	0
M_4	2	0	1	0	0	0	1
M_5	1	0	0	0	0	1	1
M_6	1	0	0	0	1	0	1
M_7	0	1	0	1	0	1	0
M_8	0	1	1	0	1	0	0

The removal of intangible markings does not increase the order complexity of the algorithm, but does give rise to some other more subtle problems. Since immediate transitions take zero time, loops of transition firings could proceed indefinitely and would not give rise to any tangible states. Finding and avoiding such loops is one of the significant algorithmic differences between normal SPN and GSPN. Another point that has been raised in the literature is the fact that the priority of the immediate transitions over the timed transitions gives rise to problems similar to those found in TPN where the reachability set (including the intangible markings) of the GSPN model is different than the underlying Petri net. In the example shown in Figure 10, the marking (0,2,1,1,0,0,0) cannot occur since tokens in p_2 can only come from firing transition t_1. Once t_1 fires, either t_2 or t_3 must fire before t_1 can fire a second time to increment $M(p_2)$ to a value of 2.

Regenerative Stochastic Petri Nets

A more recent use of stochastic Petri nets has been to specify the structure of a simulation. In the case of ESPN, the use of simulation was necessary to analyze the behavior of nets where the restriction of exponentially distributed firing times has been removed.

Regenerative stochastic Petri nets were suggested as a general framework to more formally describe a simulation program. Haas and Shedler [14] described a stochastic Petri net model where the firing times had a new better than used (NBU) distribution and showed that such models form a regenerative stochastic process. In a later, unpublished work, they showed that the relationship between RSPN and simulations (i.e., generalized semi-Markov processes) is even stronger than originally thought.

The RSPN model is slightly different from the SPN, GSPN, and ESPN models. The RSPN model adds inhibitor arcs to the SPN model in a fashion similar to the GSPN and ESPN models. Transitions are enabled in the usual sense. However, the firing rules are very unique. In an RSPN, when a transition fires, it removes tokens (one for each input arc) from a randomly selected subset of input places and places tokens on a randomly selected subset of its output places. Therefore, a transition may not remove a token which was required to enable it and similarly may not enable a subsequent transition whose input places include one of the output places of the firing transition.

This random selection of input places to remove from and output places to add to, is not a fundamental change for the model. If you replace a transition with an immediate transition for each possible subset of inputs and subset of outputs, assign that transition with the select probability, place a single token in a place which enables a timed transition with the appropriate distribution and output set, you have constructed an equivalent ESPN. Hence, the use of the random selection simply makes the model more compact. Note that the designer must still specify the selection probabilities which is equivalent to drawing out the different transitions in the case of the ESPN.

There is no preselection of transitions to fire, so the firing time delays may run concurrently. Simultaneous transition firings are not allowed, so only one transition will fire at any particular moment. However, since the distributions are more arbitrary, the time between transition firings can be arbitrarily small.

SUMMARY

These models have collectively become known as performance Petri nets. This is to distinguish them by their application domain from the more traditional Petri net models which are more directed toward verification and theory of computation. This area of research is changing rapidly and several recent results will have undoubtedly been overlooked in this survey.

Although there is some structure to the taxonomy presented here, the differences between the models are often subtle and extensive. It is important to try using each of the models to really understand some of their differences. Unfortunately, the examples given here are small enough to describe completely, but too small to illustrate many of the subtle interactions possible in the various models. Many of the models presented here are accompanied by a software tool, making the analysis of larger, more interesting problems practical.

To summarize, there are two major classes of performance Petri nets currently in use. The first class is the timed Petri net which refers to models with a deterministic firing time. The second class is the stochastic Petri net which refers to models with random firing times (based upon some distribution). An orthogonal distinction between various models is the use of preselection to decouple transition selection probabilities from the transition timings for any cases where conflict might occur.

At this time, no one model seems to dominate the applications, although TPN is gaining interest in flexible manufacturing. It is clear that each model has definite theoretical problems. However, at this time, there is no alternative which avoids all of the potential problems facing these models. Any technique that requires the construction of the state space (i.e., the reachability set) faces the state space explosion problem. Even the idea of enumerating cycles in the nets with restricted firing conditions is NP complete. Any technique that requires simulation avoids the state space explosion, but it also loses any verification capability.

The answer seems to lie in a technique which does not generate the reachability set, but draws upon the more theoretical work on special Petri nets. Unfortunately, application of those techniques will be extremely difficult for PPN that have firing rules such that their reachability set is different from the underlying PN reachability set used in the theoretical analysis.

REFERENCES

1. M. K. Molloy, *Fundamentals of Performance Modeling*, Macmillan, New York, 1988.
2. L. Kleinrock, *Queueing Systems: Vol. I—Theory*, Wiley and Sons, New York, 1976.
3. C. H. Sauer, and K. M. Chandy, *Computer Systems Performance Modeling*, Prentice-Hall, Englewood Cliffs, NJ, 1981.
4. S. Lavenberg, *Computer Performance Modeling Handbook*. Academic Press, New York, 1983.
5. D. L. Inglehart, and G. S. Shedler, *Regenerative Simulation of Response Times in Networks of Queues*, Springer-Verlag, New York, 1980.
6. C. Ramchandani, "Analysis of Asynchronous Concurrent Systems by Timed Petri Nets," Ph.D. thesis, MIT (1973) (Also: Project Mac report #MAC-TR-120 1974).
7. C. V. Ramamoorthy, and G. S. Ho, "Performance Evaluation of Asynchronous Concurrent Systems Using Petri Nets," *IEEE Trans. Software Eng.* SE-6 (5) (1980).
8. J. Sifakis, "Petri Nets for Performance Evaluation," in *Measuring, Modelling and Evaluating Computer Systems,* Proceedings of the Third International Symposium IFIP Working Group 7.3 (H. Beilner and E. Gelenbe, eds.) North-Holland Press, Amsterdam, pp. 75–93.
9. W. M. Zuberek, "Timed Petri Nets and Preliminary Performance Evaluation," *Proceedings of the 7th annual Symposium on Computer Architecture*, 1980, pp. 88–96.
10. S. O. Natkin, "Les Reseaux de Petri Stochastiques et leur Application a L'Evaluation des Systemes Informatiques," Ph.D. thesis Conservatoire National des Arts et Metiers (1980).
11. M. K. Molloy, "On the Integration of Delay and Throughput Measures in Distributed Processing Models," UCLA Technical Report No. CSD–810921 (September 1981).
12. J. B. Dugan, K. S. Trivedi, R. M. Geist, and V. F. Nicola "Extended Stochastic Petri Nets: Applications and Analysis," *Proc. of Perform. 84*, North-Holland Amsterdam, 1984, pp. 506–519.
13. M. A. Marsan, G. Balbo, and G. Conte, "A Class of Generalised Stochastic Petri Nets for the Performance Evaluation of Multiprocessor Systems," *ACM Trans. Comp. Systems*, (2), 93–122 (1984).
14. P. J. Haas, and G. S. Shedler, "Regenerative Stochastic Petri Nets," *Perform. Eval. 6* (3),189–204 (1986).
15. C. A. Petri, "Communication with Automata," Ph.D. thesis translated by C. F. Green, Information System Theory Project, Applied Data Research Inc., Princeton NJ 1966.

16. T. Agerwala, "Putting Petri Nets to Work," *Computer IEEE* 85–94. (December 1979)

17. J. L. Peterson, *Petri Net Theory and the Modeling of Systems*, Prentice–Hall, Englewood Cliffs, NJ, 1981.

18. W. Reisig, *Petri Nets*, Springer-Verlag, New York, 1985.

19. L. H. Landweber, and E. L. Robertson, "Properties of Conflict-Free and Persistent Petri Nets," *J. ACM*, *25*(3), 352–364 (1978).

20. J. D. Noe, "A Petri Net Model of the CDC 6400," in *Proceedings of ACM SIGOPS Workshop on System Performance Evaluation*, 1971, pp. 362–378.

21. P. M. Merlin, and D. J. Farber, "Recoverability of Communication Protocols—Implications of a Theoretical Study," *IEEE Trans. Comm.* 1036–1043 (September 1976).

22. P. M. Merlin, "Specification and Validation of Protocols," *IEEE Trans. Comm.* 1671–1680 (November 1979).

23. M. K. Molloy, "Discrete Time Stochastic Petri Nets," *IEEE Trans. Software Eng.*, *SE–11*(4), 417–423 (1985).

24. M. A. Holliday, and M. K. Vernon, "A Generalized Timed Petri Net Model for Performance Analysis," *IEEE Trans. Software Eng. SE–13*(12), 1297–1310 (1987).

25. K. Jensen "Coloured Petri Nets and the Invariant-Method," *Theoret. Comp. Sci.*, *14*, 317–336 (1981),

26. J. H. Genrich, and K. Lautenbach, "System Modeling with High-Level Petri Nets" *Theoret. Comp. Sci., 13*, 109–136 (1981).

27. A. Zenie, "Coloured Stochastic Petri Nets," in *Proceedings of the International Workshop on Timed Petri Nets*, July 1985, pp. 252–271.

28. C. Lin, and D. C. Marinescu, "On Stochastic High-Level Petri Nets," in *Proceedings of the International Workshop on Petri Nets and Performance Models*, August,1987, pp. 34–43.

29. N. D. Jones, L. H. Landwebber, and Y. E. Lien, "Complexity of Some Problems in Petri Nets," *Theoret. Comput. Sci.*, *4*, 277–299 (1977).

30. J. Magott, "New NP-Complete Problems in Performance Evaluation of Concurrent Systems," *IEEE Trans. Software Eng.*, *SE–13*(5) 578–581 (1987).

31. R. R. Razouk, and C. V. Phelps "Performance Analysis Using Timed Petri Nets," *Proceedings of the International Conference on Parallel Processing*, August 1984, pp. 126–129.

MICHAEL K. MOLLOY

PHIGS: PROGRAMMER'S HIERARCHICAL INTERACTIVE GRAPHICS STANDARD *

Fifteen years ago, sophisticated use of computer graphics existed only in the most highly funded high-tech institutions, such as national laboratories and scientific parks that provided research for the automobile, chemical, communication, and energy industries. Today, as a result of workstation advances, computer graphics technology is used in most aspects of engineering, scientific research, academic study, and daily business. Graphics products are widely available, and their price-to-performance ratio is constantly improving.

But many companies that now enjoy the efficiency and informational value of computer graphics are overwhelmed by the diversification and incompatibility of graphics solutions used within different groups in the same organization. For example, programmers within the same group develop similar applications based on different computer graphics software, because each is familiar and productive with his or her own favorite graphics tools. This type of problem is analogous to those in other advancing technologies. Try to imagine writing and publishing an encyclopedia with a staff of 30 writers, each using a favorite word processor—except for the one who prefers a typewriter. This type of chaos now exists in many organizations that use graphics tools, and it will only worsen unless the fundamental levels of computer technology and practice are standardized.

A DEVICE-INDEPENDENT STANDARD

Standards for programming languages and graphics tools have many benefits. Commmon practice can be taught, refined, and reapplied to subsequent projects, coordinated with other organizations, and easily interfaced to smaller or larger systems.

Device-independent standards let programmers concentrate their primary effort on developing applications. Many mundane tasks previously included in applications programs, such as data storage and manipulation, would be handled by the support system defined in such a standard. Further, and educated group of users becomes a long-term resource, maintenance of software becomes manageable, and new projects can be estimated, scheduled, and monitored with more accuracy due to relevant experience.

Developing a technology standard is similar to defining, building, delivering, and supporting a successful commercial product. Graphics standardization has been an ongoing activity on a national and international level since the 1970s. The ANSI and the ISO have specialized subcommittees whose charter is to develop the specifications for various functional levels of computer graphics.

The ANSI X3H31 committee, known as the PHIGS committee, has been working on a computer graphics specification that addresses three-dimensional modeling of hierarchically defined objects, rapid manipulation of geometric and rendering attributes, and interactive input. The committee members are employees of companies representing end users, applications developers, and suppliers of software tools, graphics hardware, and computers.

THE PHIGS SPECIFICATION

The Programmer's Hierarchical Interactive Graphics Standard (PHIGS) is a detailed description of graphics functions, error conditions, and the FORTRAN, C, and Ada language bindings. It is intended to provide a common programming base for graphics hardware and applications program developers to minimize time and energy lost dealing with incompatible systems and technology.

Currently, the draft proposed standard is being publicly reviewed for comment and completeness. Adoption of PHIGS as a standard by ANSI and ISO is expected in 1988.

Another group, the PHIGS + committee, is an ad hoc committee to develop compatible extensions to the ANSIPHIGS draft proposal. Its focus is to define extensions to PHIGS that address curves, curved surfaces, shading, lighting, direct color specification, and depth cuing. The PHIGS + committee, consisting of approximately 20 computer graphics experts, has been working since November 1986 to develop a detailed specification incorporating known practice in these areas.

ARCHITECTURE

PHIGS, as defined by the PHIGS standard, can be previewed in brief by subdividing it into the four major components shown in Figure 1: the control center, the data definition system, the data display system, and the interaction handler.

The control center maintains the state of the entire graphics system and monitors access to the other subsystems. The data definition system controls the construction, manipulation, editing, archiving, and retrieval of graphical objects called *structures*. The data display system controls access to the graphics display device (terminal, plotter, and so on) and manages the traversal (display) of the structures that have been designated for display.

The interaction handler is the most complex of the four PHIGS conponents. It manages interactive input processing and graphics hardware resources, and it provides instructions to the data display system to update the display. The interaction handler also supplies information to applications programs so that the data definition system can be used to modify structures.

CONTROL CENTER

The PHIGS control center maintains the global system state and the opening and closing of subsystems. PHIGS can be viewed simplistically as a finite state machine (see Fig. 2). The "Open PHIGS" control function initializes the system; the "Close PHIGS" function closes it. Open (graphics) workstation opens the connection to a graphics display device and initializes it for graphics output and input.

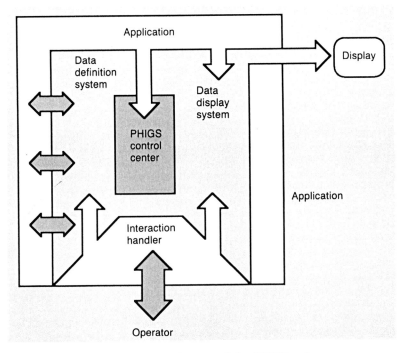

FIGURE 1.   A block diagram of the PHIGS subsystem.

On a engineering workstation, the graphics display device is usually a process window dedicated to graphics output and input. The control function "Close workstation" disconnects the graphics display device from PHIGS. Some implementations may choose to let the graphics image remain visible on a closed display. Others, such as engineering workstations, may close and release the process window dedicated to graphics, thus removing the graphics image from the physical display surface.

"Open structure" invokes the PHIGS graphical database editor and allows the passage of information to and from the data definition system. "Close structure" releases the editor and stops the passage of information.

The "Open archive" function permits the data definition system to read and write geometric models between the internal database of PHIGS and external permanent files maintained by the computer's operating system. The PHIGS archival subsystem also has a respective Close archive function.

DATA DEFINITION SYSTEM

The data definition system is the modeling and object-construction toolkit of PHIGS. The data definition system contains a central database, an editor, and archival utilities. The database consists of structures which iin turn are collections of atomic entities called *structure elements*—the fundamental building blocks of graphics objects.

Structure elements include three-dimensional geometric primitives, their respective primitive attributes, view specification indexes, modeling matrices, structure instances for

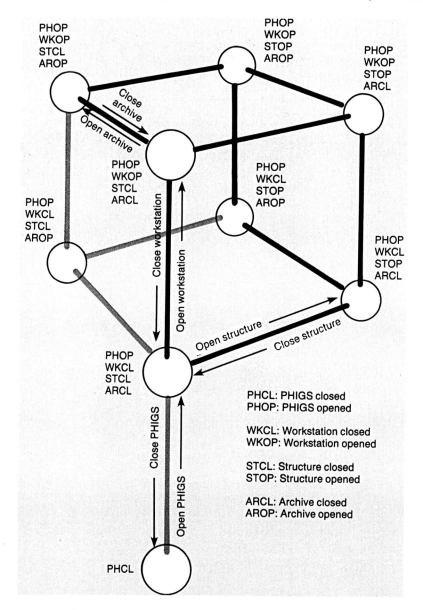

FIGURE 2.   A block diagram of a PHIGS control center.

creating hierarchical structure networks, labels, namesets (i.e., relational classification identifiers), pick identifiers, and applications data records.

GEOMETRIC PRIMITIVES

The geometric primitives included in PHIGS are polyline (a set of connected lines), fill area (a polygon, hollow or filled, without edge control), fill area set (a polygon, hollow filled,

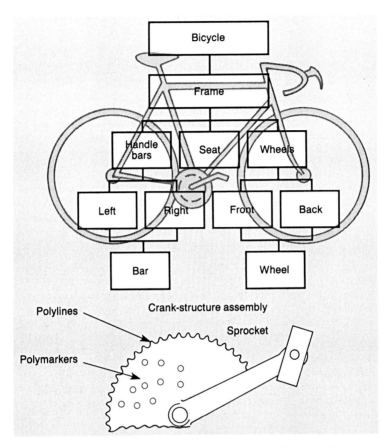

FIGURE 3. A hierarchical data organization, showing graphics primitives and structure elements

with edge control), polymarker (a set of locations, each indicated by a marker), text, and cell array (a rectangular grid of equal-size rectangular cells of a uniform color; see Fig. 3).

All primitives are three-dimensional; two-dimensional shorthand specifications are provided for applications that define planar objects. (The applications specify primitives in two dimensions, and PHIGS will automatically specify the third dimension by setting the z component internally to zero.)

The attributes for these primitives are segregated by primitive type. This means that attributes are not shared between primitives (see Table 1). In some graphics systems, for example, setting the color affects subsequent lines, polygons, and text. In PHIGS, setting the line color has no effect on text or polygons. Likewise, setting text color does not affect lines or polygons.

CENTRAL STRUCTURE STORAGE

The PHIGS graphical database is a simple file system called the *central structure storage* (CSS). The *structure editor* controls the passage of definitional information between an application and the CSS. The CSS contains all object definitions that can be displayed, modified, and archived.

TABLE 1.   Segregated Attribute Model

PHIGS employs a segregated attribute model to simplify and concentrate model construction on geometric primitives and not on the ordering and interaction issues of global attributes and primitives. Each geometric primitive in the PHIGS system has its own set of dedicated attributes that determine its appearance.

Polyline
    Set line color
    Set line type (line style)
    Set line-width scale factor (line width)

Polymarker
    Set marker color
    Set marker type
    Set marker scale factor

Fill area
    Set interior color
    Set interior style
    Set interior style index.

Fill area set
    Set interior color
    Set interior style
    Set interior style index
    Set edge existence flag
    Set edge color
    Set edge type (edge line style)
    Set edge-width scale factor (edge line width)

Text
    Set text color
    Set text font
    Set text precision
    Set text path
    Set text alignment
    Set character expansion factor
    Set character spacing
    Set character height
    Set character up vector

Cell array
    (no attribute settings)

For purposes of explanation, we can view the CSS facility as a simple text file system, view each structure (i.e., object) as a text file within the file system, and view each structure element as a line of text within a text file. Since structures are linear lists of structure elements (i.e., sequential lines in a text file), the structure editor is analogous to a simple text editor whose current line pointer can be positioned at any line (i.e., structure element), after which new information can be inserted and at which existing information is deleted.

BUILDING AN OBJECT

Building objects with PHIGS is a straightforward process. A complex object such as an automobile, airplane, or ship can be broken down into logical groups connected in a hierarchical manner. An application can establish the amount of detail to be defined at each level in the hierarchy and then begin to specify each accordingly. PHIGS permits both top-down and bottom-up construction of hierarchical objects.

For example, one application might choose to define an automobile by first defining all the atomic parts—nuts, bolts, flanges, rings, pistons—and then constructing large components, such as wheel assemblies, by instancing previously defined atomic parts. Another application might choose to define the automobile from the top down: defining the drive train, body exterior, body interior, and so on, then iteratively breaking down each group into smaller groups.

Defined structures can be archived so that they can later be retrieved by the same or other applications. The PHIGS archival utilities are part of the data definition system and manage the transfer of structures between the internal file system of the PHIGS CSS and the external file system maintained by the operating system.

Geometric parts libraries for automobiles, aircraft, and ships are excellent applications for PHIGS and its archival utilities. Applications can retrieve thousands of atomic parts easily and then construct a complicated object from atomic geometric components.

DATA DISPLAY SYSTEM

PHIGS separates the processes of data definition and data display. This separation permits the design of applications that only compute and build models using the PHIGS framework without displaying them.

Large mechanical analysis and molecular modeling applications can compute complex scenarios, build geometric models that reflect specific phases of the calculations, and archive these models. Smaller applications can then be specifically designed to retrieve the archived models, display them, and allow operator interaction with them. Other applications such as CAD systems tightly integrate the data definition and display systems. This is easily accomplished with PHIGS via the interaction handler.

POSTING

The process of displaying a structure and its descending network is called *posting*. The function "Post root" identifies a structure and its descendants that are to be traversed and displayed on a designated graphics display device. While a structure is posted for display, the interaction handler keeps track of activity occurring within the data definition system and the data display system. When an activity occurs that renders the current image of a posted structure network obsolete or out of phase with its hierarchical representation maintained in the CSS, a retroversal is requested to update the display.

The function "Unpost root" removes a specified structure network from the list being displayed and updated. During unposting, the image of the specified structure network is removed from the display. An additional function, "Unpost all roots," is a natural extension of "Unpost root."

INTERACTION HANDLER

The interaction handler controls several types of interactions. It controls interaction of workstation input peripherals, such as a mouse or keyboard. It controls the time that the image of an object is to be made current due to changes made within the data definition system or changes made to the data display system. It also manages available workstation resources, such as the color table, screen space, and interaction with the window manager.

The interaction handler controls physical input peripherals, such as a trackball, joystick, mouse, dial box, and keyboard, via a logical input mode. The PHIGS model defines six logical classes of input devices: Locator, Stroke, String, Choice, Valuator, and Pick. Each logical input device is mapped to a physical device.

The Locator and Stroke classes are logical pointing devices and return positional information to the graphics system and applications program. This information is of the form (x,y) ordered pairs or (x,y,z) ordered triples. The Locator device returns a single position. The Stroke device returns several positions.

A String device is used to return textual information to the graphics system and application. Usually, String devices are mapped to a physical keyboard on which the operator can type desired character strings. The Choice device is used to designate a choice from several available options. It is usually mapped to a function pad or button box and returns information of the form "button 13 was pressed."

The Valuator device is much like a light dimmer. It returns a value between a definable minimum, and maximum value. A Valuator device is usually mapped by the interaction handler to a dial box (a mouse-, joystick-, or light pen-actuated analog control, displayed on the screen).

The Pick device returns information regarding the part of an object, currently being displayed, at which the device is pointing. A Pick device is usually mapped to the physical device—such as a mouse, joystick, or light pen—and returns information of the form, "You are pointing to the left front tire of the car." Naturally, the returned information is encoded in more cryptic protocol.

INTERACTIVE INPUT MODES

Using this logical input model with these six classes of input devices, an applications program can control interactive input via three modes: Request, Sample, and Event.

Request requires the application's operator to take some action to trigger the input report. For example, a Request Locator would require the operator to press a mouse buttom berfore the (x,y) position pointed to by the mouse would be returned to the interaction handler. A Request String could require you to press a carriage return after entering text from the keyboard.

Sample mode input requires no operator interaction. In this mode, the applications program simply retrieves the current measure of the logical device. For instance, "Sample valuator" would return the current value of a dial immediately without any operator intervention. "Sample choice" would return which choices (i.e., buttons) are pressed down and which are not pressed. Both Request and Sample mode input are procedurally driven by the logic designed into the applications program.

THE EVENT MODE

Event is the most complex and powerful of the interactive input modes. In Event mode, the operator must take some action to trigger an input report. This action—an input event—is then placed in a first-in/first-out queue containing the class of input and a packet that includes the information the particular input class provides.

The application requests information from the event queue, determines from the event report which input class generated the event, and takes the appropriate action to process the information packet provided by that logical input device. Event mode is used to let an application be operator-driven rather than procedurally driven. Event-driven applications are usually more user friendly because input sequencing is defined by the operator and not the applications developer.

The interaction handler also assists the traversal (display) process. It detects when the display surface is to be updated because of changes in the object's definition or changes in the display system itself that affect a displayed image. Changes to definition could include, for example, the removal of the tires from a model of a car. The interaction handler would detect that the data definition system changed the object being displayed and would take the appropriate action to ensure that the displayed image correctly reflected the object's current definition.

Changes in the data display system can also cause traversal for the purpose of correcting an image on the display. For example, panning around and zooming in or out on an object can be accomplished by changing viewing information maintained by the data display system. In this example, the definition of the object has not changed, only the manner in which it is being displayed. The interaction handler detects the change and requests retroversal after internal transformations have been adjusted to yield the effect of pan and zoom.

WINDOW MANAGER

Engineering workstations require close integration with the window manager. An operator must be able to push and pop process windows, resize the graphics window, and move freely from one working process to another. The graphics system must be aware of the window manager and track changes in the workstation windowing environment. Window managers are classically event-driven systems from the operator's point of view. The graphics system needs to ensure that when events affecting the graphics environment occur, appropriate action takes place.

For example, an object is displayed within a process window dedicated to graphics; the operator resizes the repositions that window so that other work (e.g., editing a data file or document) can be done in another process window that requires more screen space. The interaction handler within the graphics system must detect that the physical screen space allocated for graphics has now changed; internal base transformations are adjusted and retroversal of the object is requested to correctly display the object in a smaller process window now located at a different position on the physical workstation display. The interaction handler manages this required interaction.

EXTENSIONS TO THE STANDARD

Graphics functions that address shading and lighting were not included in the original PHIGS specification. But many applications now require this capability, and several high-performance graphics workstations provide it: the Apollo 590, the Sun CXP series, the Hewlett-Packard SRX series, the Silicon Graphics Iris and 4D, and the Prime PXCL 5500.

The PHIGS + specification defines a set of compatible extensions to the ANSIPHIGS specification to address lighting and shading by incorporating additional geometric information. This information is in the form of vertex normals, vertex color specification, surface properties, and new geometric primitives that represent curves and curved surfaces. PHIGS + specifies lighting and shading models that let applications render realistic images of models defined using both PHIGS and PHIGS + primitives.

The PHIGS + primitives and attributes follow the philosophy of PHIGS and maintain the segregated-attribute mode. These new geometric primitives and attributes are structure elements much like the original PHIGS primitives and attributes. The PHIGS + primitives use the attributes of the original PHIGS primitives for Polyline, Fill Area, and Fill Area Set. This preserves the original PHIGS model and promotes migration of applications using PHIGS to PHIGS +.

The higher-order primitives included in the PHIGS + specification allow the parametric definition of curves and curved surfaces. The polynomial- and B-spline-based curve and surface primitives let applications most accurately approximate and render smooth shapes, such as pipes, car fenders, windshields, aircraft fuselages, wings, and smooth mechanical parts. The lighting and shading models combined with surface properties of polygonal and surface primitives allow the accurate simulation of illuminated objects by means of Gourand and Phong shading.

DESIGNING A PHIGS IMPLEMENTATION

Designing a graphics system to operate efficiently in multiple computing and graphics environments requires the definition of a conceptual computer and conceptual graphics device. These principles have existed for several years; device–independent graphics software is not a new topic. However, the developers of earlier systems used an interfacing philosophy that usually pivoted around the least common-denominator theory—that is, the definition of the software graphics device interface and software computer interface supported only those functions found on all systems to be supported. The rest of the required functions were performed in the device-independent kernel.

This philosophy worked well until graphics hardware became sophisticated and operating systems such an Unix and VMS could offload much of the work previously handled by the software product itself. Under the earlier philosophy, new high-performance graphics workstations would be treated as if they were film recorders connected to a large mainframe running a batch operating system.

Optimizing the interfaces between the major components of a computer- and device-independent graphics system requires that each subsystem understand the

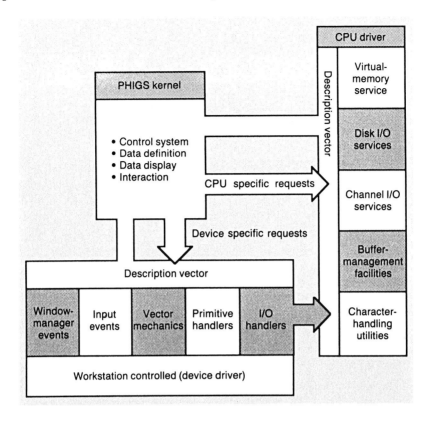

FIGURE 4. Figaro's CPU and device intelligence.

capabilities of the other to allow the migration of responsibility as a function of the capabilities of the graphics devices and the computing environment. In the graphics industry, this has been called "device intelligence." But the same philosophy and principles can apply to computing environments.

FIGARO'S ARCHITECTURE

Template Graphics Software's Figaro, a PHIGS implementation based on this theory, consists of three different software modules: the PHIGS kernel, the CPU driver, and the graphics device driver, called the *workstation controller*. The design of this system employs both device intelligence and computer intelligence. To promote efficiency, Figaro's designers defined description vectors and communication protocols between these systems so that the division of labor during execution of an application could be adaptive (see Fig. 4).

A simple example of this is the use of virtual memory. Both VAX/VMS and Unix support runtime allocation of virtual memory. But IBM VM/CMS and MVS/TSO do not. Rather than develop two distinct implementations of Figaro, one for IBM and one for VSM and Unix, the designers incorporated both. By establishing internal logic within Figaro to manage its own paging system once virtual memory was exhausted, the same code could be used on both IBM-based and VAX- or Unix-based computers.

On IBM systems, virtual memory is immediately exhausted because none can be allocated at run time; thus, Figaro would take over with its own paging system. On VMS and Unix systems, Figaro uses runtime allocation of virtual memory until it is denied access due to exceeding working size limits; it then rolls over into its own paging system using the existing allocated virtual memory as a cache.

Similar strategies are applied to optimizing disk and channel I/O. The computer-dependent subsystem has the internal knowledge of optimum buffer sizes and disk record sizes for the underlying operating system configuration. These are communicated to the Figaro kernel via description vectors. The kernel then has sufficient information to decide whether it should use the recommended parameters from the computer driver or override them.

Vector mathematics is another realm of optimization. Many of the new workstations have special functions used to multiply matrices. This can make significant differences in transformation, clipping, and rendering time of geometric primitives.

GRAPHICS ENGINE INTERFACE

These general principles were used to establish the Graphics Engine Interface (GEI). This interface is internal to Figaro and allows the flexible integration of a conformant PHIGS implementation with newly developed hardware, which may or may not be able to support all the PHIGS functionality in hardware directly.

The GEI establishes a multilevel graphics device interface for processing fundamental picture elements created during the traversal of the PHIGS CSS. Each picture element consists of a PHIGS or PHIGS + geometric primitive, its respective current attributes, and the composite, modeling, viewing, projection, and workstation transformation matrix.

Through this interface, a designer can easily determine if the picture element can be processed directly by the underlying hardware or if intermediate logic is required so that interfacing at a lower level is possible (see Fig. 5). The GEI was used to develop high-performance interfaces to the graphics workstations manufactured by Silicon Graphics, Sun Microsystems, Hewlett-Packard, Prime Computer, NEC, and Stellar Computer.

ACCEPTANCE OF PHIGS AND FIGARO

PHIGS is gaining momentum rapidly, Both the National Computer Graphics Association and the Association for Computing Machinery's Special Interest Group for Computer Graphics have sponsored tutorials at their respective national conventions to teach the concepts of PHIGS and promote graphics standards. Other technical committees such as the PHIGS + and three-dimensional X Window System groups have compatibly expanded upon the foundation set by ANSIPHIGS.

Putting theory of graphics standardization into practice requires industry commitment. Template Graphics Software began working on an implementation of PHIGS early in 1984. In 1985, TGS introduced Figaro, still the only commercially available implementation of the PHIGS proposed standard.

TGS has concentrated on satisfying the requirements of the top Fortune 100 companies requiring a three-dimensional graphics programming standard. These large corporations develop chemicals and build automobiles, aircraft, and power plants. They are

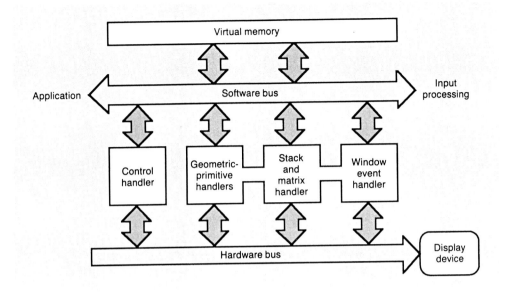

FIGURE 5. Figaro's graphics engine interface.

changing their technological methodologies to use the new engineering workstations in addition to existing mainframe computers. The establishment, availability, and delivery of PHIGS, operating efficiently in both the workstation and mainframe environments, simplifies some of the complex issues facing these companies during this transition.

Figaro is now fully supported on VAX/FMS, IBM, VM/CMS, MVS/TSO, Apollo Aegis and many major Unix workstations, including Sun, Silicon Graphics, Hewlett-Packard, Masscomp, Prime, Convergent Technologies, CalComp/Sanders, Celebrity, Motorola VME, and NEC. In addition to these workstations, Figaro also supports 200 graphics display devices, ranging from pen plotters, film recorders, and metafiles to interactive color terminals and monitors.

The cooperation between the hardware manufacturer and the software supplier will guarantee two critical components required to deliver a technology standard. First, it will ensure that product combinations function and perform to the expectations of current technology. Second, it will provide compatible product combinations on a variety of hardware platforms.

REFERENCES

Abi-Ezzi, S. and J. Bunshaft, "An Implementer's View of PHIGS," draft document, April 24, 1985.

American National Standard for the Functional Specification of the Programmer's Hierarchical Interactive Graphics Standard (PHIGS), ISO/DIS 9592–1: 1987 (E)

American National Standard Graphical Kernel System (GKS), *X3*, 124(1985).

Bunshaft, J., presentation on PHIGS, November 1984.

Bunshaft, J., "A Brief Introduction to PHIGS," *Computer Graphics '85 Conference Proceedings*, Vol. II (National Computer Graphics Association), Fairfax, VA, 1985, pp. 326–331.

Cahn, D. U., E. McGinnis, R. F. Puk, and C. S. Seum, "The PHIGS System", *Comput. Graph. World*, pp. 33–40 (February 1984).

Foley, J. D., and A. Van Dam, *Fundamentals of Interactive Computer Graphics*, Addison-Wesley, Reading, MA 1982.

Heck, M. and M. Plaehn, "PHIGS-Based Next Generation Graphics Software Development Tools," *CAE* pp. 55–62 (September 1985).

Newman, W. M. and R. F. Sproull*, Principles of Interactive Computer Graphics*, Second Edition, McGraw-Hill, New York, 1979.

"Status Report of the Graphics Standards Planning Committee of ACM/SIGGRAPH" (GSPC), *Comput. Graph. 13 (3)* (August 1979).

MARTIN PLAEHN

REAL-TIME COMPUTING

INTRODUCTION

Real-time computing is currently undergoing a revival. Many new and exciting applications are being developed, there is a wealth of new research results being produced, and the community of real-time experts is growing at a rapid pace. This revival is largely due to the demand for sophisticated real-time systems, such as space exploration, systems involving robots, and some systems involving *expert systems* programs [1]. Some common examples of real-time systems are command and control systems, process control systems, automated manufacturing, flight control systems, avionics, the space station, space-based defense systems such as SDI, visions and robotics, and teams of robots working in hazardous environments. More detailed accounts of these types of demanding applications can be found elsewhere [1–6].

The above examples of real-time systems are all large and complicated. However, real-time systems span a wide spectrum of applications from the trivial to the complex. For example, there are many trivial real-time systems such as a single microprocessor-controlled lab experiment or controlling an engine of an automobile. Other real-time systems are primarily data acquisition systems where data from multiple sensors are processed in a periodic fashion. The processing must often be very fast, but the complexity and functionality involved is usually limited. On the other hand, many real-time computer systems contain data acquisition subsystems as only a small part of the overall real-time system. These applications are special purpose and complex, require a high degree of fault tolerance, have timing requirements at all levels of functionality in the system, must exist for a long time, and are typically embedded in an even larger system such as a robot, a submarine, or a space station. Real-time systems usually have substantial amounts of knowledge concerning the characteristics of the application and environment built into the system. A majority of today's systems assume that much of this knowledge is available a priori, and hence these systems are based on *static* designs. The static nature of many of these systems contribute to their high cost and inflexibility. The next generation real-time systems must be designed to be *dynamic* and *flexible*.

Real-time systems are normally classified into soft real-time and hard real-time. However, there is no generally accepted definition of these terms. In fact, most real-time systems exhibit multiple characteristics making it difficult to clearly state a single term that classifies the system. Let us propose a definition for these two terms. Many real-time systems are characterized by the fact that severe (to various degrees) consequences will result if logical as well as timing correctness properties of the system are not satisfied. If a given task has no value to the system if run too early or too late, then we say that it is a hard real-time task. If the value of executing a task degrades the further it gets from its deadline, but it is still reasonable to execute the task, then we say that it is a soft real-time task. In other words, in soft real-time systems, activities have to occur in a timely fashion but still have merit if done late (and this implies that no catastrophic events occur by being late). For example, a task that must execute by time T to prevent a meltdown in nuclear power plant is a hard real-time task, but an accounting application running on an automated factory's computer might be required to be on-time, and causes irritation, but no major loss when late. In other applications, a late accounting program might cause severe financial loss and subsequent bankruptcy, and therefore, might be considered a hard real-time task. Consequently, it is the explicit timing constraint imposed on various tasks or collections of tasks which makes real-time computing different.

Real-time computing is often a misunderstood field. Some people erroneously equate concurrent programming with real-time computing. While, real-time computing is often highly concurrent, this feature alone does not make a real-time system. For example, timesharing systems can be highly concurrent, but they are not considered real-time because the task requirements have very loose average response time requirements, not explicit deadlines.

Another common misconception is that, too often, real-time is equated with fast computing. However, all systems prefer fast processing, but for non-real-time systems the performance requirement is usually stated as meeting some average response time, and not directly tied to the external or environmental timing constraints. On the other hand, real-time processing such as data acquisition and its subsequent processing may have to be done very quickly (i.e., more quickly than incoming data). This indeed gives rise to demanding and specific real-time constraints. That is, the speed of the processing is relative to the incoming data rates imposed by the physical features of the sensors and the environment.

For real-time systems, neither average response time nor high throughput are the primary metrics. For example, it is possible for a hard real-time system to have excellent average response time and high throughput, but yet not meet a single deadline. Two metrics that are of interest to real-time systems are minimizing task loss ratio and maximizing the value of executed tasks.

In summary, real-time systems differ from traditional systems in that deadlines or other explicit timing constraints are associated with tasks or collections of cooperating tasks, and faults including missed deadlines may cause catastrophic consequences. This implies that, unlike many systems where there is a separation between correctness and performance, in real-time systems correctness and performance are very tightly interrelated.

Many theoretical and applied results have been developed in real-time computing. This article provides an overview of the current state of the art in real-time computing, highlighting a number of open research issues. We divide the remaining parts of this article into nine technical areas as follows:

> Specification, design, verification, and analysis
> Languages
> Scheduling
> Operating systems
> Architecture and hardware
> Communication
> Fault tolerance
> Distributed databases
> Artificial intelligence

SPECIFICATION, DESIGN, VERIFICATION, AND ANALYSIS

Wirth [7] classified programs into three types: sequential, parallel, *processing-time dependent* (real-time). He showed that the difficulty of specification, design, verification, and analysis of programs increases as programs go from sequential to parallel, and increases further when real-time constraints are introduced. For example, in non-real-time systems we are interested in *safety* properties, defined as properties that deal with the requirement that nothing bad will happen, and *liveness* properties, which are defined as properties that deal with the requirement that something good will eventually happen. In real-time systems, we must also satisfy *timeliness* properties. Timeliness refers to the fact that a system is only considered correct if it is logically correct *and* results are produced on time.

Formal specification, verification, and analysis tools are being developed to deal with the special properties of time-critical applications [8–14]. A number of formal approaches have been used for the specification and analysis of traditional systems. These include:

1. Finite state machines
2. Petri nets
3. Hoare/Floyd/Dijkstra logic
4. First-order logic
5. Temporal logic

On the surface, temporal logic appears to be the most appropriate candidate for formally dealing with real-time systems since it already incorporates a notion of time. However, its notion of time is tied to the notion of *eventuality* rather than *timeliness*. While there is ongoing work on the use of temporal logic for specifying and analyzing real-time systems, the majority of current literature on real-time systems deal with approaches based on the other four types of formalisms.

Research questions that need to be answered include:

What is the worst-case response time of the system to a particular type of external event? Is the system performance under peak arrival rates adequate?

What is the effect of different operating policies, such as scheduling policies, on safety and timeliness?

Given the specification of the system, do the specifications conform to the safety properties of interest to the system?

Given an implementation, how can one ensure that the implementation conforms to the specifications?

What are the restrictions imposed on the external environment for the system to react safely? In particular, what are the rates at which stimuli can arrive at the system? What will be the effect of failures in the external environment?

In summary, the specification , design, verification, and analysis of real-time systems is a difficult and challenging problem. These technologies, when fully developed, need to be incorporated into an overall design methodology for real-time computing. What makes the problem especially difficult, is that the specification for a real-time system is a contract between the system and the environment, whereas in non-real-time systems the specification is usually environment and implementation independent.

LANGUAGES

Until recently, there has been very little work done on the design of languages for constructing real-time systems [15–19]. In most applications, time-critical parts of applications were (and still are being) implemented in machine code or assembler. Thus intimate knowledge of the underlying architecture is often a necessity for developing real-time software. This implies that the resulting software is quite often difficult to code, debug, modify, and maintain. Further, the low level nature of the code precludes the use of formal analysis techniques that are often applicable to more abstract levels of the system. In addition, any changes to the system hardware might necessitate a complete revamp of the software. All these factors point to the need for designing and using higher-level programming and specification languages to develop software for real-time systems.

Many current high-level languages that have been called real-time programming languages, although well-suited for systems programming, are not really suited for programming real-time systems. Berry et al. [15] portray the situation aptly when they say that "... the current so-called real-time programming languages do not provide any explicit means of correctly expressing time constraints. A forteriori, they provide no insurance that the constraints would be respected when executing the program." Most real-time languages available today are extensions to languages designed for non-real-time systems. Both imperative languages and equational dataflow languages have been extended in this manner.

New real-time languages are needed that (1) enable the specification of real-time properties such as periods, criticalness, deadlines, and resource demands; (2) have compilers that can impose rules and constraints on programmers, and can generate real-time information about the program object code running in a given environment (including the hardware and OS) such as worst case computation times; (3) have verification tools to prove logical and timing properties about the system; (4) have schedulability analysis tools that provide statistical information about the timing properties of the system in a dynamic environment.

The building of the next generation real-time systems requires a programming methodology that gives due consideration to the needs of meeting real-time requirements. The important issues include:

> Support for the management of time. First, language constructs should support the expression of timing constraints. For example, Ada tasking should have supported the raising of an exception when a task's deadline is missed. Second, the programming environment should provide the programmer with the primitives to control and to keep track of the resource utilizations of software modules. This includes being able to develop programs with predictable performance in terms of absolute time. Finally, language constructs should support the use of sound scheduling algorithms.
>
> Schedulability check. Given a set of well-understood scheduling algorithms, schedulability analysis allows us to determine if the timing requirements can be met. With proper support for the management of time, it may be possible to perform at least some aspects of schedulability checks at compile time.
>
> Reusable real-time software modules. The investigation of reusable software modules is an important subject, because it reduces the software development cost and enhances the quality of resulting software. Reusable real-time software modules have the added difficulty of meeting different timing requirements for different applications.

Support for distributed programs and fault tolerance. The problem of predicting the timing behavior of real-time programs is further exacerbated in the context of distributed systems. Special fault tolerance features might be added to the semantics of the language, e.g., various recovery mechanisms subject to timing considerations.

SCHEDULING

While specification and verification primarily concern the integrity of the system, scheduling theory addresses the problem of meeting the specified timing requirements. Satisfying the timing requirements of real-time systems demands the scheduling of system resources according to some well-understood algorithms so that the timing behavior of the system is understandable, predictable, and maintainable. For relatively simple systems, primary schedules and alternative schedules invoked due to failures, can be developed off–line. This static approach is inflexible and somewhat limited. Dynamic scheduling is required for more complex systems.

Scheduling theory has been developed and used in the study of manufacturing systems, transportation systems, process control systems, and so on [20]. Yet, it is important to realize that the real-time system scheduling problems are different from the scheduling problems usually considered in these and other areas of operations research. In most operations research scheduling problems, there is a fixed system having completely specified and static service characteristics. The goal is to find optimal static schedules which minimize the response time for a given task set. In many real-time computing systems, there is generally no incentive to minimize the response time, but rather the goal is to meet the deadlines. The system is often highly dynamic, resulting in continuously changing task sets. This requires on-line, adaptive scheduling algorithms. Such algorithms are usually based on heuristics since most of these scheduling problems are NP-hard. In these cases, the goal is to schedule as many of the more important jobs as possible, subject to meeting the task timing requirements. Alternative schedules and/or error handlers are required and must be integrated with the on-line scheduler.

Even the metrics by which the real-time scheduling algorithms are judged are not universally accepted. For example, one measure is the processor utilization level below which the deadlines of all the tasks can be met. For most real-time scheduling problems, the answer would be zero utilization, and, therefore this metric would not be useful. On the other hand, if tasks only need the CPU and they can be preempted, at zero cost, then it has been shown that the lower bound is 69% utilization. Such a result can serve as a useful rule of thumb in designing a system. Other measures include penalty functions which are defined according to the number of jobs that miss their deadlines, or a weighted success ratio which is the percentage of tasks that meet their deadlines weighted by the importance of those tasks, or yet another metric might be the minimum time to complete a collection of n tasks.

Many results in real-time scheduling are limited to cases such as: a single processor with a precedence relation over a set of sporadic jobs [21], two processors with a precedence relation over a set of identical sporadic jobs [22], and a set of independent periodic tasks on a uni-processor [23] or on a multi-processor [20,24]. Much of this work, while theoretically interesting, is applicable only to the simplest of situations. On the other hand, this more theoretical work did identify an important, often used algorithm, called the rate monotonic algorithm. The rate-monotonic algorithm assigns static priorities to tasks based on their time periods. It assigns higher priorities to tasks with shorter periods. It has been shown that this scheme is optimal among fixed-priority schemes. Optimal is defined as an algorithm that can schedule a set of tasks to meet their deadlines, if any algorithm can. This definition says nothing about what occurs if one or more tasks must miss their deadline. The theoretical difficulties encountered in real-time scheduling are described by Garey and Johnson [25], who show that the problem of scheduling tasks with unit computation times and arbitrary precedence relationships on two processors and one resource is NP complete; A polynomial time algorithm exists when the precedence relation is empty but arbitrary number of resources is present. But, for three processors and one resource, even with an empty precedence relationship, the problem is NP-complete. They prove NP-completeness results for generalized versions of the above problem and also point out the limited number of cases for which polynomial time solutions exist. In summary they show that resource-constrained scheduling is an NP-complete problem, and that the presence of precedence constraints exacerbates the problem. Again, most scheduling problems of interest to practical real-time systems are NP hard, hence heuristics are required.

Other recent scheduling work has attempted to minimize schedule length [26], dealt with specialized areas such as signal processing [27], or concentrated on concurrent programming [28]. Still other work has been addressing more complicated yet practical scheduling constraints, for example, scheduling of real-time tasks with resource constraints [29,30], distributed real-time scheduling [31], and the problem of stochastic execution time and transient overloads [32,33]. A great deal more needs to be done so that we can handle even more general and realistic situations. For example, the problem of *jointly* scheduling system resources such as CPUs, I/O devices, communication media, and secondary storage in order to meet the timing requirements of real-time tasks running on a distributed computer system is a realistic scheduling problem only now beginning to be addressed. Since most real-time systems have severe fault tolerance constraints, it is also necessary to integrate the scheduling policies with fault tolerance requirements. This work is sometimes based on off-line static scheduling algorithms and sometimes on-line dynamic schemes.

OPERATING SYSTEMS

It is often the case that existing real-time systems are supported by stripped down and optimized versions of timesharing operating systems. To reduce the run-time overheads incurred by the kernel and to make the system *fast*, the kernel underlying a current real-time system

> Has a fast context switch
> Has a small size (with its associated minimal functionality)
> Is provided with the ability to respond to external interrupts quickly
> Minimizes intervals during which interrupts are disabled
> Provides fixed or variable sized partitions for memory management (i.e., no virtual
>   memory) as well as the ability to lock code and data in memory
> Provides special sequential files that can accumulate data at a fast rate

> To deal with timing requirements,

> The kernel maintains a real-time clock
> The system provides special alarms and timeouts

Tasks can invoke primitives to delay by a fixed amount of time and to pause/resume execution

In general, the kernels perform multitasking; intertask communication and synchronization are achieved via mailboxes, events, signals, and semaphores.

A typical example of a commercial real-time operating system is VRTX [34] which is used in embedded microprocessor applications. This kernel supports primitives in the area of task management, memory management, I/O, and interprocess communication and synchronization. A main strength of VRTX is that it is quite independent of the hardware and runs on many different microprocessors. The VRTX kernel itself is cleanly separated from the file system called FMX and the I/O system called IOX. Recently, VRTX has announced support for 32-bit microprocessors and interprocessor communication support.

The features of current real-time kernels are designed to be fast. Fast is a relative term and is not sufficient when dealing with real-time constraints. Nevertheless, these features can be said to provide a basis for a good set of primitives upon which to build real-time systems. One problem with current technology that limits its extensibility to more complex situations seems to lie in the use of priority-driven or table-driven schedulers to schedule tasks with real-time constraints.

We now elaborate upon this problem. Of primary consideration in task scheduling today are the execution times, timing constraints, general resource requirements, fault tolerance requirements, precedence constraints, and criticalness factors of tasks. All of these factors must be considered and it is difficult to do that with a priority mechanism. For example, while the timing constraints are an indication of the *level of urgency* of a real-time task, the *criticalness* of the task is indicative of the *level of importance* that is attached to that task relative to other tasks. Mapping both of these concerns into a single metric causes some well-known anomalies. Nor is it effective to give a high priority to a task which, in turn, asks for a resource locked by some other task. The high-priority tasks just block and are likely to miss deadlines. Therefore, an integrated CPU scheduling and resource allocation scheme is needed. This is difficult to do using priorities. It is also difficult to solve the end-to-end scheduling problem with priority scheduling.

Another problem with priority-driven scheduling is that it usually involves a lot of code and priority tuning accompanied by extensive simulations to gain confidence in the system. Although priority scheduling has been used successfully in many real-time embedded systems, it is only at extremely high cost and inflexibility. Because the scheduling technique is not algorithmic, it is error-prone. For example, it is difficult to *predict* how tasks invoked dynamically interact with other active tasks, where blocking over resources will occur, and the subsequent effect of this interaction and blocking of timing constraints of all the tasks [35]. In addition, even a small change is subject to another extensive round of testing. Overall, this "design philosophy" forces designers and implementors to deviate from structured system development techniques whereby the resulting system is neither adaptive nor extensible. This makes maintenance and upgrading very expensive. But, since typical embedded systems, such as automated factories and air traffic control systems, have long lifetimes during which the systems evolve, incremental development and dynamic maintainability are of importance to these systems.

The key issue that has emerged is the need to provide predictability. However, more than lip service must be applied to this notion. Predictability requires clean, bounded, and low variance operating system primitives; some knowledge of the application; proper scheduling algorithms; and a viewpoint based on a team attitude between the operating system and the application [36–38]. The operating system must be able to perform integrated

CPU scheduling and resource allocation so that collections of cooperating tasks can obtain the resources they need, at the right time, in order to meet timing constraints. The cooperation requirement means that there is an end-to-end timing requirement, in other words, a collection of activities must occur (possibly with complicated precedence constraints) before some deadline. Using the current operating system paradigm of allowing arbitrary waits for resources or events, or treating the operation of a task as a *random process* will probably not be feasible in the future to solve this more complicated set of requirements. An important realistic and complicating factor to the integrated resource allocation problem is the need to be predictable in the presence of faults. This issue must receive more attention. See Ref. *37* for a description of the Spring kernel which addresses some of these issues.

It is also important to avoid having to rewrite the operating system (OS) for each application area. A library of real-time operating system objects might provide the level of portability required. We envision a Smalltalk-like system for hard real-time, so that a designer can tailor the OS to his application without having to write everything from scratch. As far as we know, there is no such system available, although some work is beginning on this approach.

ARCHITECTURE AND HARDWARE

Many real-time systems can be viewed as a three-stage process: data acquisition and filtering, application-dependent processing, and output to actuators and/or displays [*39*]. The complexity of each of these stages can vary tremendously. A real-time systems architecture must be designed to support these three components with high reliability and usually (but not always) high speed.

For the input and output phases, the architecture must provide extensive I/O support including special-purpose hardware for unique input devices such as acoustic, pressure, temperature, and other sensors. Sometimes the processing rates required to handle data acquisition are enormous. The processor(s) must be fast and reliable and sometimes directly support special application tasks and/or operating systems tasks that, in turn, are supporting the application. However, many current real-time architectures are based on dedicated hardware and software in such a manner that the architecture (and operating system) usually has to change with a change in applications or, worse, with a change in the current application. It is important to develop real-time architectures that are suitable for broader classes of real-time applications.

A typical architecture for real-time systems includes a system with many microprocessors, many memories (private and global), and multiple busses [*2,27,40– 44*]. There may also be high degree of functional and physical partitioning in the hardware, in the operating system, and in the application tasks. The system processors could be special purpose. Dedicated busses are also employed to reduce conflicts, enhance speed, and check for and be resilient to failures.

Any architectural design should adopt a synergistic approach where the operating system, the hardware, the programming language, and the application are all developed with the single goal of achieving the real-time constraints in a cost-effective and integrated fashion. This may require rules and constraints to be imposed on programmers and designers. Yet, the hardware and operating system should be providing some generic support so that minimal changes occur as an application evolves or as new applications are developed.

Open research issues in real-time architecture include; developing good interconnection topologies for processors and I/O, adding architecture support for error handling, developing architectural support for on-line scheduling algorithms and other operating system tasks, and directly supporting real-time language features.

COMMUNICATION

Communication in most current real-time systems is designed to be fast, but does not directly address timing constraints of individual messages. This approach is changing and many new protocols are appearing that explicitly address timing constraints [*45–55*]. In the new protocols, communication primitives used for programming real-time systems allow for the specification of deadlines or timeouts. Implementing these primitives is a nontrivial problem because of the variable message communication delays and the local nature of the clocks used in distributed real-time systems.

The communication media for next generation distributed real-time systems will be required to form the backbone upon which predictable, stable, extensible system solutions will be built. To be successful, the real-time communication subsystem must be able to predictably satisfy individual message level timing requirements. The timing requirements are driven not only by applications' interprocess communication, but also by time-constrained operating system functions invoked on behalf of application processes. Networking solutions for this context are distinguished from the standard non-real-time solutions with the introduction of *time*. In a non-real-time setting, it is sufficient to verify the logical correctness of a communications solution; however in a real-time setting it is also necessary to verify timing correctness. Timing correctness includes insuring the schedulability of synchronous and sporadic messages as well as insuring the response time requirements of asynchronous messages are met. Insuring the timing correctness for static real-time communications systems using current technology is difficult. Insuring the timing correctness in the next generation's dynamic environment will be a substantial research challenge.

The current state of the art and predominant practice for insuring network timing correctness is to use time-division multiplexing (TDM) techniques. This manifests itself as time-lines on busses and cyclical schedulers on rings. TDM approaches provide a strong systems solution for tasks/message sets with a single period or harmonically related periods like those found in phone systems. Experience with cyclical executives have found that as the task set periods grow in number and become relatively prime, the TDM schedule tends to be ad hoc in nature, painful to generate, very inflexible and difficult to modify [*16*].

A new high-speed fiberoptic transmission protocol called FDDI has been developed. The FDDI protocol guarantees a fixed communication capacity to each node in the system. This fixed capacity can then be applied to certain types of real-time traffic such as voice traffic. However, this protocol does not explicitly account for deadlines of individual messages.

In other recent work, IBM Federal Systems Division [*45*] and researchers at Carnegie-Mellon University [*50*] introduced a frame-level contention resolution protocol with message-based (as opposed to station-based) priority assignment. Researchers at Carnegie-Mellon University [*53*] are currently extending this work by developing techniques for applying recent advances in scheduling theory to the emerging local area network (LAN) standards. In this work, timing constraints must be mapped to message priorities.

As stated above, communication in real-time systems can be characterized by messages which must be received by a deadline. Explicitly using deadline information, protocol can determine the latest time to send the message (so that the message reaches its destination before the deadline). Several protocol designs exist to accomplish this form of message transmission including the virtual time carrier sense multiple access (VTCSMA) protocols [55] and a modified window protocol [54]. In the VTCSMA protocols, each node maintains two clocks: a real-time clock and a virtual time clock. Whenever a node finds the channel idle, it resets its virtual clock. The virtual clock then runs at a higher rate than the real clock. A node transmits a waiting message when the time on the virtual clock is equal to some parameter of the message. Using different message parameters in conjunction with the virtual clock, different transmission policies can be implemented. In particular, use of message arrival time, message length, latest time to send a message, and message deadline, implements first come, first served (FCFS), minimum-length-first-minimum-laxity-first, and minimum-deadline-first transmission policies, respectively.

In the modified window protocol [54], laxity is used as the metric for creating and modifying the transmission window. A number of other changes to standard window protocols are also required, but they are too detailed to describe here [54]. In the window protocol, as in the VTCSMA protocols, the idea is to maximize the number of messages which arrive by their deadlines. The window protocol is shown to work better than the VTCSMA protocols.

Additional research is needed to develop technologies that support the unique challenges of real-time communications which include:

Dynamic routing solutions with guaranteed timing correctness
Network buffer management that supports scheduling solutions
Fault tolerant and time-constrained communications
Network scheduling that can be combined with processor scheduling to provide system level scheduling solutions

FAULT TOLERANCE

Most real-time applications require a high degree of fault tolerance [6,56–60]. In these systems, fault tolerance is designed into the system from the start, and not added as an afterthought. This is necessary because of the highly interdependent nature of the application, the computer system, the environment, the reliability, and the timing requirements. On the other hand, many problems and solutions for fault tolerance are the same regardless of whether we are dealing with hard real-time systems or not. For example, triple modular redundancy (TMR) is often used, or in other cases n + 1 replicates of tasks (or resources in general) are created to handle n, fail-stop failures, or 2n + 1 replicates are created to tolerate Byzantine failures. In systems like SIFT [6], formal verification techniques are used to enhance the safety of the system by proving correctness and timing properties. However, there are some special, unique problems regarding fault tolerance caused by timing constraints such as hard deadlines and periodic tasks.

Many of the unique problems arise from the need to be able to schedule tasks to meet the timing constraints in the presence of errors. For example, TMR has to be scheduled to meet a deadline, similarly the n + 1 or 2n + 1 replicates haves to be scheduled to complete before a deadline (this includes time for voting). To solve yet other fault-tolerant scheduling problems, one approach is to a priori guarantee that a primary algorithm will make its deadline if there is no failure, and that an alternative algorithm (possibly of less precision) will be able to complete by the deadline if there is a failure. A nice feature of such an approach is that if the primary algorithm executes, then it is not necessary to run the alternative algorithm (or replicates) and the time set aside for the alternative is reused. Such an orderly scheduling approach is not always possible and some approaches require staggered schedules of task replicates such that an alternative task may begin execution on the chance that the first copy may fail. If the first copy fails then the alternate task is already partially complete and can continue. If the first copy completes successfully, then the alternate must be cancelled. However, techniques in scheduling fault-tolerant tasks are still primitive because such schemes are not general enough to handle periodic and nonperiodic tasks, preemptive and nonpreemptive tasks, tasks with general resource requirements (those resources may also have to be replicated), dynamic rescheduling and reconfiguration, all at low run-time overheads. For many applications, the run-time overhead is so important that precomputing schedules is a very common theme. These systems, however, are not very flexible nor adaptive. For more dynamic applications, for more intelligent, on-line decisions are made. For example, some current work [37] uses on-line schedulers which essentially plan the future execution of tasks to predict that timing constraints will be missed, enabling early action on such faults. This has many advantages in situations where it is very difficult to correct a faulty action once it occurs, but not as difficult to take some alternative action given that you can reliably predict that a missed deadline will occur.

Another difficulty in dealing with fault tolerance in a real-time system is recovery. Backward recovery techniques are generally too expensive. Most systems advocate some form of forward error recovery combined with an appropriate level of fault masking. Database systems have nice features for correctness and recovery. Work to use these techniques for real-time systems is beginning (see Distributed Databases).

Current research issues for fault-tolerance real-time computing include:

The formal specification of the reliability requirement
An understanding of the interaction of timing and fault-tolerance constraints
An integrated solution to fault tolerance: error detection, fault location, masking, scheduling of task replicas, formal verification, system reconfiguration, and recovery
Development of the necessary hardware support for fault-tolerance (see FMPT [56])
Study of the effects of real-time workloads on fault-tolerance including overloads
Reduce overhead of fault tolerance techniques

In summary, many embedded real-time systems have strong fault tolerance requirements. Difficult design tradeoffs must be made to build a fault-tolerant real-time system.

DISTRIBUTED DATABASES

Distributed databases have two primary requirements: correctness and reliability [61]. Many protocols have been developed to support these requirements. The real-time community is now trying to exploit the advantages of these protocols in a new setting.

In the database field, the notion of correctness is usually based on the concept of serializable schedules. Concurrency control protocols control the interleaving of concurrent transactions to give the illusion that they are executing serially. In other words, any interleaved execution whose effects are the same as those serial execution is called serializable. The main approaches to concurrency control are two-phase locking, timestamp ordering, and validation (optimistic concurrency control). Reliability is of extreme importance and correct operation in the presence of failures of transactions and/or processing nodes is usually supported. Many techniques are used to support reliability including undo logs and checkpointing. All the concurrency control and recovery protocols become more complex when replicated data must be supported and when physical network might be separated into two or more noncommunicating partitions due to failures.

In the real-time environment we must add another important requirement: timeliness. The timeliness requirement takes on many forms. For example, airline reservations, banking applications, and computer program trading on the stock market are examples of real-time databases with varying degrees of time constraints and various consequences as a result of missing these time constraints. Battle management or highly mobile and sophisticated teams of robots are applications that have even more stringent timing and reliability requirements. Only now do we find the research community attempting to apply the principles and protocols developed for database systems, to real-time database applications.

Let us consider some of the characteristics of real-time database systems. Often a significant portion of data in a real-time database is highly perishable in the sense that it has value to the mission only if used quickly. A significant portion of the data may be read-only or append-only. Transactions often have to perform statistical operations (e.g., correlation) over a large amount of data that is continuously updated and must satisfy stringent timing requirements. Often the timing constraints imposed are soft real-time constraints rather than hard real-time. Many, if not all, real-time transactions are probably known a priori and can be (largely) analyzed off-line with some degree of prescheduling. Serializability may not be a good criterion for the concurrency control of real-time databases because it may unduly limit the possible concurrency. Using semantic information to exploit maximum parallelism is probably needed in certain situations.

Since investigations into using database concepts in real-time systems is just beginning, questions can be found in all facets of distributed databases [62–66]. For example, how do we modify concurrency control protocols to account for deadlines, should we use a concurrency control protocol that might occur in deadlocks, what are the correct recovery strategies when time is critical, can we exploit techniques such as multiversion concurrency control to avoid blocking of real-time transactions, and what commit protocols should we use in a real-time environment?

ARTIFICIAL INTELLIGENCE

The current emphasis in real-time artificial intelligence (AI) research concerns reasoning about time-constrained processes and using heuristic knowledge to control or schedule these processes. Usually, the applications are large and complex with hundreds of interacting tasks and where the invocations of the tasks are highly dependent on the current environment and system state. A large number of real-time knowledge-based systems have been studied in areas as diverse as aerospace, communications, medicine, process control, and robotics [1,3,4,67,68]. To date many of them deal largely with passive monitoring of an environment and signaling error conditions. For example, there is an emergency procedures expert system to warn a pilot of problems and to initiate some simple corrective actions. As this system develops one could imagine more and more automatic control of the aircraft being done by the expert system. Other such warning systems exist for nuclear power plants, and monitoring of patients in intensive care, and for process control.

A key consideration in many of these applications is to provide the *best* available solution with a dynamically determined time constraint. This is approached by using a combination of monotonic functions (functions whose value strictly increases as more processing is applied), limiting search techniques as a function of available time before the deadline, and using general focus of attention techniques. Some AI applications combine the need for a high degree of sophistication with strict requirements for small size and speed. Such systems must operate safely on inaccurate or uncertain data inputs [68]. Special techniques must be developed here too.

Many open questions exist in the system support area for real-time AI. What programming language limitations should exist—unbounded loops, unbounded recursion, arbitrary invocation of garbage collection should not be permitted, and are LISP or OPS5 the correct languages for these applications? Other questions include what is the correct paradigm for the operating system (if there should even be one), what application semantics should be input to the OS, and what is the correct interface between the OS and the real-time AI application?

Like real-time databases, real-time AI is a new area of research providing many challenges and possibilities. It will be a driving force into the next generation of real-time computing.

CONCLUSIONS

Many real-time systems are large and complex, function in distributed and dynamic environments, include expert system components, involve complex timing constraints encompassing different granules of time, and may result in economic, human, and ecological catastrophes if these timing constraints are not met. New work on this type of real-time system is exciting and accelerating at a fast pace. Meeting the challenges imposed by these characteristics depends on a coordinated effort in many aspects of system development. On the other hand, simpler types of real-time systems are also valuable to society and are in use every day. These range from simple sensor monitoring to control of automobile engines. Even some very complicated real-time systems are in common use, however, their development is very costly and done in a more brute force manner than is desirable. Such systems include nuclear power plants, avionic systems, air traffic control. For the more complicated real-time systems of today and in the future, a more scientific basis for the conceptualization, specification, design, verification, implementation, maintenance, operation, and evolvability of real-time systems is needed.

ACKNOWLEDGMENTS

This article is a condensation of material found elsewhere [69–71]. I would especially like to thank Krithi Ramamritham, my coauthor of Ref. *71*, for his invaluable help on that work—which is then condensed here.

REFERENCES

1. M. L. Wright, M. W. Green, G. Fiegl, and P. F. Cross, "An Expert System for Real-Time Control," *IEEE Software*, *3*(2), 16–24 (1986).
2. G. D. Carlow, "Architecture of the Space Shuttle Primary Avionics Software System," *Comm. ACM, 27*(9), 926–936 (1984).
3. E. Durfee, and V. Lesser, "Planning to Meet Deadlines in a Blackboard-Based Problem Solver," Technical Report, University of Massachusetts, (1987).

4. H. Kasahara, and S. Narita, "Parallel Processing of Robot-Arm Control Computation on a Multimicroprocessor System," *IEEE Robotics and Autom. RA-1(2),* 104–113(1985).

5. J. D. Schoeffler, "Distributed Computer Systems for Industrial Process Control," *IEEE Computer, C-17*(2), 11–18 (1984).

6. J. H. Wenseley, et al, "SIFT-Design and Analysis of a Fault-Tolerant Computer for Aircraft Control," *Proc. IEEE, 66*(10), 1240–1255 (1978).

7. N. Wirth, "Toward a Discipline of Real-Time Programming," *Comm. ACM, 20*(8), 577–583 (1977).

8. S. B. Auernheimer, and R. A. Kemmerer, "RT-ASLAN: A Specification Language for Real-Time Systems," *IEEE Trans. Software Eng., SE-12(9),* 879–889 (1986).

9. J. E. Coolahan, and N. Roussopoulus, "Timing Requirements for Time-Driven Systems Using Augmented Petri Nets," *IEEE Trans. Software Eng., SE-9*(1), 603–616 (1982).

10. B. Dasarathy, "Timing Constraints Of Real-Time Systems: Constructs for Expressing Them, Methods of Validating Them," *IEEE Trans. Software Eng., SE-11*(1), 80–86 (1985).

11. V. H. Hasse, "Real-Time Behavior of Programs," *IEEE Trans. Software Eng., SE-7*(5), 494–501 (1981).

12. F. Jahanian, and A. K. Mok, "Safety Analysis of Timing Properties in Real-Time Systems," *IEEE Trans. Software Eng., SE-12*(9), 890–904 (1986).

13. J. S. Ostoff, and W. M. Wonham, "Modeling, Specifying, Verifying Real-Time Embedded Computer Systems," *IEEE Proc. 8th Real-Time Systems Symp.*,124–132 December 1987.

14. G. M. Reed, and A. W. Roscoe, "A Timed Model of Communicating Sequential Processes," *Proc. ICALP'86*, Springer, New York, 1986, pp. 314–323.

15. D. Berry, S. Moisan, J. Rigault, "Estrel: Towards A Synchronous and Semantically Sound High Level Language for Real-Time Applications," *IEEE Proc. Real-Time Systems Symp.,* 30–34 (December 1983) .

16. P. Hood, and V. Grover., "Designing Real Time Systems in Ada," SofTech, Inc. Waltham, MA, Technical Report 1123–1 (January 1986).

17. E. Klingerman, and A. D. Stoyenko, "Real-Time Euclid: A Language for Reliable Real-Time Systems," *IEEE Trans. Software Eng., SE-12*(9), 941–949 (1986).

18. I. Lee, and S. B. Davidson, "Adding Time to Synchronous Process Communications," *IEEE Trans. Computers, C-36*(4), 941–948 (1987).

19. R. A. Volz, and T. N. Mudge, "Timing Issues in the Distributed Execution of Ada Programs," *IEEE Trans. Computers, C-36*(4),449–459 (1987).

20. S. K. Dhall, and C. L. Liu, "On a Real-Time Scheduling Problem," *Oper. Res., 26*(1), 127–140 (1978).

21. J. Blazewicz, "Scheduling Dependent Tasks with Different Arrival Times to Meet Deadlines," *SIAM J. Comput., 6,* 416–426 (1977).

22. M. R. Garey, and D. S. Johnson, "Two-Processors Scheduling with Start-Times and Deadlines," *SIAM J. Comput., 6,* 416–426 (1977).

23. C. L. Liu, and J. W. Layland, "Scheduling Algorithms for Multiprogramming in Hard Real-Time Environment," *J. Assoc. Computing Mach.,* 20(1), 46–61 (1973).

24. R. R. Muntz, and E. G. Coffman, "Preemptive Scheduling of Real-Time Tasks on Multiprocessor Systems," *J. ACM, 17*(2), 324–338 (1970).

25. M. R. Garey, and D. S. Johnson, "Complexity Results for Multiprocessor Scheduling Under Resource Constraints," *SIAM J. Comput., 4*, 397–411 (1975).

26. J. Blazewicz, M. Drabowski, and J. Weglarz, "Scheduling Multiprocessor Tasks to Minimize Schedule Length," *IEEE Trans. Computers*, C-35(1), 389–393 (1986).

27. E. A. Lee, D. G. Messerschmitt, "Static Scheduling of Synchronous Data Flow Programs for Digital Signal Processing," *IEEE Trans. Computers, C-36*(1), 24–35 (1987).

28. D. Peng, K. G. Shin, "Modeling of Concurrent Task Execution in a Distributed System for Real-Time Control," *IEEE Trans. Computers, C-36*(4), 500–516 (1987).

29. W. Zhao, K. Ramamritham, J. Stankovic, "Scheduling Tasks with Resource Requirements in Hard Real-Time Systems,"*IEEE Trans. Software Eng., SE-13*(5), 564–577 (1987).

30. W. Zhao, K. Ramamritham, and J. Stankovic, "Preemptive Scheduling Under Time and Resource Constraints," *IEEE Trans. Computers, C-36*(8), 949–960 (1987).

31. J. Stankovic, K. Ramamritham, and S. Cheng, "Evaluation of a Bidding Algorithm for Hard Real-Time Distributed Systems," *IEEE Trans. Computers, C-34*(12), 1130–1143 (1985).

32. S. Biyabani, J. A. Stankovic, and K. Ramamritham, "The Integration Of Deadlines and Criticalness in Hard Real-Time Scheduling," *IEEE Proc. Real-Time Symp.,* 152–160 (1988).

33. C. D. Locke, "Best-Effort Decision Making for Real-Time Scheduling," Ph. D. thesis, CMU, May 1985.

34. J. F. Reddy, "VTRX: A Real-Time Operating System for Embedded Microprocessor Applications," *IEEE Micro* 6(4), 8–17 (August 1986).

35. R. R. Razouk, T. Stewart, M. Wilson, "Measuring Operating System Performance on Modern Microprocessors," *Performance 86,* 193–202 (1986).

36. K. Schwan, et. al., "High Performance Operating System Primitives for Robotics and Real-Time Control Systems," *ACM Trans. Comput.* 5(3), 189–231 (1987).

37. J. Stankovic, and K. Ramamritham, "Design of the Spring Kernel,"*IEEE Proc. Real-Time Systems Symp.,* 146–157 (December 1987).

38. H. Tokuda, J. Wendorf, and H. Wang, "Implementation of a Time Driven Scheduler for Real-Time Operating Systems," *IEEE Proc. Real-Time Systems Symp.,* 271–280 (December 1987).

39. K. G. Shin, C. M. Krishna, and Y. H. Lee, "A Unified Method for Evaluating Real-Time Computer Controllers and Its Application," *IEEE Trans. Automatic Contr., AC-30*(4), 357–366 (1985).

40. H. P. Baker, and G. M. Scallon, "An Architecture for Real-Time Software Systems," *IEEE Software,* 2(5), 50–58 (1986).

41. R. G. Arnold, R. O. Berg, and J. W. Thomas, "A Modular Approach to Real-Time Supersystems," *IEEE Trans. Computers*, C-31(5), 385–398 (1982).

42. H. D. Kirrmann, and F. Kaufmann, "Poolpo—A Pool of Processors for Process Control Applications," *IEEE Trans. Computers, C-33*(10), 869–878 (1984).

43. C. J. Walter, R. M. Kieckhafer, A. M. Finn, "MAFT: A Multicomputer Architecture for Fault-Tolerance in Real-Time Control Systems,"*IEEE Proc. Real-Time Systems Symp.,*133–140 (December 1985).

44. A. Pedar, and V. V. S. Sarma, "Architecture Optimization of Aerospace Computing Systems,"*IEEE Trans. Computers, C-32*(10), 911–922 (1983).

45. G. E. Dailey, "Distributed Systems Data Bus, External Audit PDR," 03J/04273/03, IBM FSD, Manassas, VA (May 1983).

46. FDDI Token Ring—Media Access Control, draft proposed, American National Standards Institute, No. ANSI X3T9. 5/83–16, (March 1985).

47. HSRB, SAE AE9-B High Speed Data Bus Standard, Society of Automotive Engineers, Subcommittee 9-b, Issue 1, Draft 2, January 1986.

48. P. Kermani, and L. Kleinrock, "Virtual Cut-Through: A New Computer Communication Switching Technique," *Comput Networks, 3,* 267–286 (1979).

49. J. F. Kurose, M. Schwartz, and Y. Yemini, "Multiple Access Protocols and Time Constrained Communication," *Comput. Surv., 16*(1), 43–70 (1984).

50. J. P. Lehoczky, and Sha, L., "Performance of Real-Time Bus Scheduling Algorithms," *ACM Perform. Rev.,* Special Issue, *14*(1), 44–53 (1986).

51. K. Ramamritham, "Channel Characteristics in Local Area Hard Real-Time Systems," *Comput. Networks ISDN Sys., 3–13* (1987).

52. K. C. Sevcik, M. J. Johnson, "Cycle-Time Properties of the FDDI Token Ring Protocol," *IEEE Trans. Software Eng., SE-13*(3), 376–385(1987).

53. J. K. Strosnider, Lehoczky, J. P., and Sha, L., "A Novel Scheduling Approach for Token Passing Media," submitted for publication.

54. W. Zhao, J. Stankovic, and K. Ramamritham, "A Window Protocol for Transmission of Time Constrained Messages," *IEEE Proc. 8th Int. Conf. on Distributed Computer Systems,* 384–392 (June 1988).

55. W. Zhao, and K. Ramamritham, "Virtual Time CSMA Protocols for Hard Real-Time Communication," *IEEE Trans. Software Eng., SE-13*(8), 938–952 (1987).

56. A. L. Hopkins, et al., "FTMP --A Highly Reliable Fault-Tolerant Multiprocessor for Aircraft," *Proc. IEEE,66*(10), 1221–1239 (1978).

57. A. L. Liestman, and R. H. Campbell, "A Fault-Tolerant Scheduling Problem," *IEEE Trans. Software Eng., SE-12*(11), 1089–1095 (1986).

58. C. M. Krishna, and K. G. Shin, "On Scheduling Tasks with a Quick Recovery from Failure," *IEEE Trans. Computers, C-35*(5), 448–455 (1986).

59. M. H. Woodbury, and K. G. Shin, "Workload Effects on Fault Latency for Real-Time Computing Systems," *Proc. Real-Time Systems Symp.*, 188–197 (December 1987).

60. J. A. Bannister, and K. S. Trivedi, "Task Allocation in Fault-Tolerant Distributed Systems," *Acta Informatica, 20,* 261–281 (1983).

61. P. A. Bernstein, V. Hadzilacos, and N. Goodman, *Concurrency Control and Recovery in Database Systems*, Addison-Wesley, Reading, MA 1987.

62. J. Stankovic, and W. Zhao, "On Real-Time Transactions," *ACM SIGMOD REC., 17*(1), 4–18 (1988).

63. M. Singhal, "Issues and Approaches to Design of Real-Time Database Systems," *ACM SIGMOD REC., 17*(1), 19–33 (1988).

64. U. Dayal, et al., "The HiPAC Project: Combining Active Databases and Timing Constraints," *ACM SIGMOD REC., 17*(1), 51–70 (1988).

65. R. Abbott, and H. Garcia-Molina, "Scheduling Real-Time Transactions," *ACM SIGMOD REC., 17*(1), 71–81 (1988).

66. L. Sha, R. Rajkumar, and J. Lehoczky," Concurrency Control for Distributed Real-Time Databases," *ACM SIGMOD REC., 17*(1), 82–98 (1988).

67. T. J. Laffey, P. Cox, J. Schmidt, S. Kao, and J. Read, "Real-Time Knowledge-Based Systems," *AI Magazine, 9*(1), 27–45 (1988).

68. V. Lesser, J. Pavlin, and E. Durfee, "Approximate Processing in Real-Time Problem Solving," *AI Magazine, 9*(1), 49–61 (1988).

69. J. A. Stankovic, "Real-Time Computing Systems: The Next Generation," Technical Report, TR 88–06, Dept. of Computer and Information Science, University of Massachusetts (1988).

70. J. A. Stankovic, "Misconceptions About Real-Time Computing: A Serious Problem For Next Generation Systems," *IEEE Computer 21*(10), 10–19 (1988).

71. J. A. Stankovic, and K. Ramamritham, *Hard Real-Time Systems,* Tutorial Text, IEEE Computer Society Press, Washington, D.C., 1988.

JOHN A. STANKOVIC

SPATIAL INFORMATION PROCESSING: REPRESENTATION AND REASONING

INTRODUCTION

Although there has been a great deal of research and development of symbolic and linguistic knowledge-based systems, spatial representation and reasoning are only beginning to be studied as an independent field [1]. Previously, these problems have been considered separate entities in computer graphics, computer vision, image processing, robotics, computer-integrated manufacturing, computational complexity, spatial databases, natural language processing, and expert systems. The following is quoted from *Building Expert Systems,* by F. Hayes-Roth, D. Waterman, and D. Lenat:

> Many design problems require reasoning about spatial relations. Reasoning about distance, shapes and contours demand considerable computational resources. Good methods of reasoning approximately or qualitatively about shape and spatial relations do not yet exist.

We are concerned with the systematic investigation of representation issues and reasoning schemes of spatial information and knowledge. Spatial information processing often requires novel ideas to deal with dynamic and complex data structures and hierarchical reasoning schemes. The advent of very large-scale integrated (VLSI), optical computing and storage, highly parallel computer architecture, and artificial intelligence (AI) workstations would certainly facilitate the development of this field.

First, some well known spatial object representations are reviewed [see Ref. 2 for other references]. Not all objects are representable by polyhedral and smooth surfaces, however. Natural objects of fractal character [3] are also pervasive. Thus, we consider also the collection of all compact, closed sets of R^3 as spatial objects [4].

Next, some general ideas of spatial information and knowledge are discussed. A hierarchy of spatial knowledge is proposed, including the world space, perceptual space, path space, and configuration space. The world space models the environment and objects in it. Perceptual space deals with various (visual, acoustic, tactile) sensory data and their understanding. The path space is concerned with motions in the world space, of either viewers or objects to be viewed. Configuration space describes states of a robotic system. States of different types may be in the joint space, path space, assembly space, or their various combinations, creating further hierarchies in the configuration space.

This research has been partially supported by the National Science Foundation.

Spatial information processing by computers is subject to three difficult bottlenecks: uncertainty, incompleteness, and complexity, although human cognitive processing is not subject to these impediments. Uncertainty and incompleteness are mainly due to the imaging and sensing process. Exponential complexity of algorithms arises sometimes due to the large scope of a spatial problem [e.g., the three-dimensional (3-D) path planning problem]. Two methods (1) active sensing and (2) topological and qualitative reasoning, which offer ideas to overcome these bottlenecks, are discussed. They are more flexible and robust than passive sensing and geometrical and quantitative reasoning, by avoiding most constraints while satisfying other constraints in an adaptive manner [5–7].

Our next concern is with several specific problem domains. In addition to the general reasoning paradigm, application domain knowledge is often needed. We describe some spatial reasoning issues in image understanding, robot exploration and map learning, spatial planning, autonomous mobile robots, automated assembly, tactical situation assessment, and spatial database management systems (DBMS). It is important to interrelate these application domains in a general system, requiring features from different fields and technologies, such as blackboard architecture, relational and spatial databases, reasoning with uncertainty, knowledge-base systems, temporal reasoning, and machine learning. The integration, management, and organization of spatial information and knowledge has been discussed [8].

It is impossible to give a comprehensive survey of this emerging field at the present time. In this report some of the general issues and ideas are discussed. Omissions include parallel computer and storage architecture, highly parallel processing techniques (such as neural processing), the vast literature of computer vision, and robotics.

SPATIAL REPRESENTATION

Spatial representation depends on coordinate systems in the world space R^3. Around each object, we have a local map based on a local coordinate system that describes the local behavior of the environment. In the case of robotic manipulation, this local coordinate system is the task coordinate system. Different coordinate systems are integrated in a global coordinate system of the world space R^3 (Fig. 1).

Several different spatial representation schemes are described in the literature. Not all spatial objects are 3-D with smooth or polyhedral boundary surfaces. They may be 0-D points, 1-D curves, 2-D surfaces, and even sets of quite strange nature, such as fractal sets [3]. In general, we require them to be compact and closed sets in the world space R^3, and collectively for them to be a compact family in the topology of sets of R^3. *An important problem is to find efficient algorithms that will transform one representation to another.* For example, we like to find fast algorithms to change an octree to a polyhedral boundary representation and vice versa.

Constructive Representation

The constructive representation of spatial objects is provided by a collection of 3-D volumetric (or solid geometric) primitives and a collection of set theoretic Boolean operations: union, intersection, and complementation. The representation is called the constructive solid geometry (CSG) method in the literature. Usually, the collection of 3-D volumetric primitives includes blocks, cylinders, cones, spheres, and superquadrics. The data structure is a binary tree whose leaves are instances of primitives and the branching nodes are Boolean operations and positioning information. This method is quite efficient at

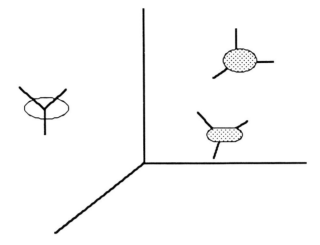

FIGURE 1.   Different local coordinate systems in a global world space coordinate system.

representing complex objects in terms of a small number of primitives and operations and, consequently, is commonly used in CAD and CAM. However, its expressive power is limited in general curved surfaces, such as the human face. This method is not convenient for mathematical analysis, such as finite-element analysis, and spatial reasoning schemes.

Spatial Decomposition Representation

The spatial decomposition representation is to decompose the 3-D world space, or the region surrounding the objects of interest, particularly into nonoverlapping subregions such that objects are represented by subregions of suitable resolution. The octree structure is the most commonly used representation. It is a hierarchical representation of an object by a tree of cubes of different sizes. Each cube is decomposed into eight octants (or cubes). This recursive scheme provides a fine structure of the 3-D world space or the region of interest. Any cube is shaded black, gray, or white according to whether it is occupied fully, partially, or not at all. Although the octree structure represents spatial information efficiently in the rectangular coordinates, it is only suitable for orthographic viewing in computer vision.

For perspective viewing, the octree structure is extended to spherical octree structure in Ref. 9. This data structure divides a solid sector in the perspective projection into eight octants. This sector is limited by the shortest radial distance of the object to the viewing position. Each octant is recursively decomposed into eight octants. The hierarchical tree is the same as the rectangular one. One significant improvement is the localization of these spherical octrees around objects in space. For each cluster of objects, a spherical octree is constructed. Different spherical octrees may be related to each other on the viewing sphere (Fig. 2).

Surface Boundary Representation

An object is represented by its boundary surfaces in the 3-D world space. In the polyhedral case, a boundary surface may be represented as a polyhedron whose faces are polygons, such as triangles and squares. In the smooth case, a boundary surface may be approximated

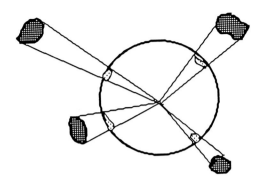

FIGURE 2.   Different spherical octrees are related on the reviewing sphere.

by triangle or polyhedral faces to any degree of accuracy. In the topological case, the boundary of a set is defined as the intersection of its closure and exterior in set theory.

Sometimes, it is convenient to represent the boundary surface by smooth surface patches. In algebraic geometry, a surface is expressed by the set of points (x,y,z) in R^3 that satisfy $F(x,y,z) = 0$. Usually, the function F is a polynomial or a differentiable function of x, y, and z. A more convenient approach is the parametric surface representation: $x = f(u,v)$, $y = g(u,v)$, and $z = h(u,v)$, $(u,v) \varepsilon D$, a region in R^2, where f,g,h are smooth functions of u and v. Specifically, a Monge patch is given by $x = u$, $y = v$, and $z = h(x,y)$, where h is the height function. The Monge patch is suitable for orthographic viewing, but not for perspective projection [10]. In Ref. 10, the spherical patch $\rho = \rho(\theta,\phi)$ is used to represent the surface patch, spanned by the solid viewing angle in θ and ϕ. The radial value ρ is assumed to be a smooth function of the angles θ and ϕ (Fig. 3).

Generating Representation

The generating representation generates an object by a spatial curve as the axis. For instance, a cylinder is generated by rotating a line segment around an axis in space. Equally, it is generated by sweeping a circle along the same axis. In the literature, generating representations are often called generalized cones and sweeping representations. A related representation scheme is the skeleton representation, which uses the axis or the spline to represent the skeletal shape.

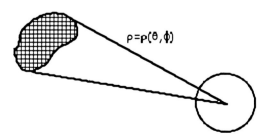

FIGURE 3.   The radical value ρ as a function of angles θ and ϕ.

Multiframe Representation

A spatial object is represented by several 2-D projections in different orientations. Some results use 2-D silhouette projections and line drawings. The characteristic views method is a more complete approach. All the 2-D projections are categorized into a finite number of topological equivalence classes. Different views in the same equivalence class are related by linear transformations. Others use shading information in 2-D image frames to reconstruct the 3-D object. The reconstruction is usually based on the orthographic (or parallel) projection.

Fractals (Fractal Sets)

Many important spatial patterns of nature are either irregular or fractal [*3*]. The usual geometry is no use to the study of these sets. For example, the coastline of an island or the boundary of clouds are classic fractals. The best known fractals arise from the geometric model of Brownian motion. The term "fractal" was coined by B. Mandelbrot; however, the basic fractals were known to mathematicians such as Weierstrass, Sierpinski, and Hausdorff for some time. Mathematically, a fractal is defined as a set for which the Hausdorff dimension strictly exceeds the topological dimension [this is related to the Hausdorff measure of Ref. *4*]. Since random dot diagrams play an important role in computer vision, we may speculate that *fractals are useful to computer vision and spatial reasoning also.*

A HIERARCHY OF SPATIAL INFORMATION AND KNOWLEDGE

The World Space

Our world is full of objects. Not all objects in space are 3-D with smooth or polyhedral boundary surfaces. They may be 0-D points, 1-D curves, 2-D surfaces, and even sets of quite strange nature, such as fractal sets of Mandelbrot [*4*]. Certain objects, such as cloud and smoke, are even dissipative. The world space $\mathcal{W}$ is the collection of all spatial objects.

In most cases, objects are compact in the world space R^3. However, highway or airport runways may not be considered compact if their lengths are very long. Then, a *local* octree structure is set up around each compact object, associated to a local coordinate system. Moreover, they may be topological, and are more general than the traditional, global, rectangular octrees.

A qualitative shape description of objects is given by the topological equivalence of objects. Two objects in $\mathcal{W}$ are homeomorphic if there is a homeomorphism (generalization of a rigid transformation) between them. Therefore any cube is topologically equivalent to a solid ball, not a donut or a cup (Fig. 4). This equivalence may be too weak, thus more restrictive (than topological) equivalences must be defined. For instance, all chairs with a back and four legs are equivalent under a suitable polyhedral equivalence, which preserves the back and four legs.

Well known set theoretic relations, such as intersection, union, complement, betweeness, to-the-right-of, etc., are defined in the topological model of the world space $\mathcal{W}$ of objects. Thus, a theory of spatial relationships may be established in $\mathcal{W}$. We have subtheories for familiar categories and equivalences. The metrical category uses rigid motions and isometric equivalence. The polyhedral category uses polyhedral preserving mappings and polyhedral deforming equivalence. In any case, we have a shape space S,

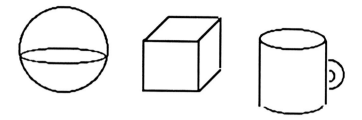

FIGURE 4. Topological equivalence of objects.

which is the quotient space of $\mathcal{W}$ under a given equivalence relation $\mathcal{R}$. What it means is that an object under different equivalences has the same shape: $S = \mathcal{W}/\mathcal{R}$.

Probability measures may be defined on the space $\mathcal{W}$ of objects, or its shape spaces S under different shape equivalences. From the probability distribution functions, we are led to Bayesian, Dempster–Shafer, and other approaches to semantic spatial knowledge.

The Perceptual Space

The perceptual space $\mathcal{V}$ consists of the space of sensory (not necessarily visual) images. However, images are also sets in the perceptual category. In Ref. *18* a spherical visual model is developed. The spherical perspective eliminates some limitations of the flat perspective model and provides a mechanism for temporal sensory data fusion on a single image sphere (Fig. 5).

The perspective projection π is a transformation from the world space $\mathcal{W}$ to the perceptual space $\mathcal{V}$. This is the model of *image generation*. The reverse process is *image understanding* which is concerned with recognizing the objects whose images are to be understood. Image understanding is a major kind of spatial reasoning. If we denote reasoning by arrows, image understanding is denoted by vertical arrows, while reasoning in $\mathcal{V}$ and $\mathcal{W}$ is denoted by horizontal arrows (Fig. 6). In the world space $\mathcal{W}$, we have local topological octree structures around objects. A second kind of octree structure, the

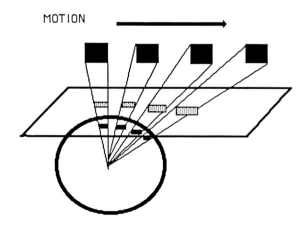

FIGURE 5. Temporal sensory data fusion.

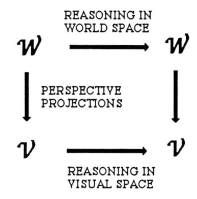

REASONING IN
WORLD SPACE

$\mathcal{W}$ $\longrightarrow$ $\mathcal{W}$

PERSPECTIVE
PROJECTIONS

$\mathcal{V}$ $\longrightarrow$ $\mathcal{V}$

REASONING IN
VISUAL SPACE

FIGURE 6.   Spatial reasoning mechanism.

viewer-centered spherical octree structure, is introduced for treating the reasoning scheme: image understanding between $\mathcal{V}$ and $\mathcal{W}$. Moreover, the viewer-centered spherical octree structure supplies a single representation scheme for the following:

1. (In world space) spatial arrangements of objects (with respect to the viewer)
2. (In perceptual space) visual and other perceptual images
3. (In path space) path planning, robotic navigation and collision avoidance
4. (In configuration space) motor control, sensor-controlled spatial manipulation (for instance, the viewing angular sector is compatible with the motor control angle)

This local viewer-centered spherical octree structure is further integrated with all local topological object-centered octrees which are constructed in regions bounded by

$$\rho_1 \leq \rho \leq \rho_2,\ \theta_1 \leq \theta \leq \theta_2,\ \text{and}\ \phi_1 \leq \phi \leq \phi_2,$$

the smallest volumetric enclosure of an object, with respect to the spherical coordinate system. We note that a global octree for the scene is not needed as required in the literature [1]. Each local viewer-centered spherical octree integrates all of its *visible* topological object-centered octrees. Local octrees may have different resolutions in (θ, ϕ) and different radial (range) data. These local substructures of the objects as well as the free space form an irregular *tessellation* in the spherical viewer-centered *hierarchical structure* of a finite and compact universe U in R^3. What we have in the world space $\mathcal{W}$ of R^3 may be projected onto the visual (perceptual) image sphere, say S^2, creating images (sets) in $\mathcal{V}$, under the central (perspective) projection. The Hausdorff distance in R^3 is projected to the Hausdorff distance of S^2 [4]. The organization of object-centered spheres and the viewer-centered sphere is given in Figure 7.

Chen [4] indicated that spatial relations in R^3 may be interpreted in terms of knowledge about the angles θ and ϕ and range (radial) data ρ of the spherical data structure. We should note that, in our models, the range ρ and angles θ and ϕ may not be *exact*, but only rough and approximate. For instance, we are able to attach the so called "uncertain manifolds" (sectors) around any fixed point set in (ρ, θ, ϕ) in a consistent way, for both the

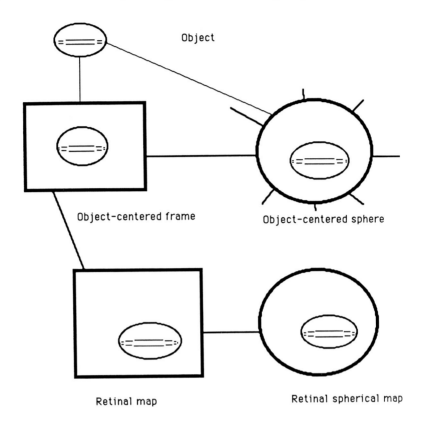

FIGURE 7. Object-centered sphere vs. viewer-centered sphere.

world and perceptual spaces. In the literature, only uncertain manifolds in a 2-D world space are considered.

The Path Space

For autonomous mobile robots [6, 7, 11, 12], path planning, navigation and collision avoidance are basic problems. Path planning has been treated traditionally by optimization of a certain set of cost functions. As indicated in Refs. 6 and 7, accurate metrical maps are not readily built; inaccuracy in sensory input and miscalibration or slip in motor output will lead to metrical inconsistency and cumulative errors. The qualitative approach is to consider paths in the path space $\mathcal{P}$ and landmarks in the world space $\mathcal{W}$ (often sensed in the perceptual space $\mathcal{V}$ only) in the form of arcs and nodes of graphs, respectively (Fig. 8).

The mathematical theory of *topology* provides the tools—"general topology" and "homotopy" for the qualitative theory of paths and landmarks. General topology is the study of topological spaces (landmarks and their surroundings) and their homeomorphisms (used in the world space); and "homotopy theory" is the study of equivalence between paths or higher dimensional free regions in space. In particular, "homotopy theory" considers the space $\mathcal{P}$ of paths in space.

If a journey or a robotic manipulating task consists of several steps, these steps are represented by certain nodes in space, the landmarks. They are qualitatively characterized by the topological equivalence classes (homeomorphic classes) in $\mathcal{W}$. In fact, a landmark,

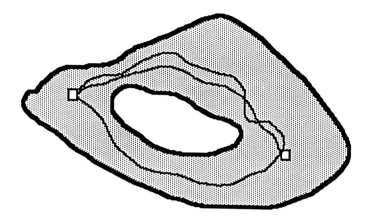

FIGURE 8. Qualitative path space.

such as a hill or a building or a car, is shrunk (homeomorphic) to a point. Between two nodes, a great number of paths pass through them. From the starting node to the goal node, we examine the space of all paths connecting them.

How to define an equivalence relation between two such paths? Homotopically, they are equivalent, if one can be deformed into another by a continuous function. Intuitively, if one does not mind a little walk, two homotopic paths are really not different paths. Therefore, we define a path qualitatively as the whole equivalence class of arcs which are homotopically equivalent between two nodes (Fig.9).

After the qualitative reasoning, a relaxation technique is needed to find the optimal or near-optimal paths and to recognize the optimal or near-optimal landmarks. Using a potential function, a hill-climbing technique will give a solution of landmarks [6, 7]. The desired path should be the minimal one in the equivalence class with respect to a certain metric in the universe U. It is a geodesic (the shortest curve between two points) under the given metric. There is a standard approach to find geodesics by solving a differential equation.

The path space $\mathcal{P}$ and the perceptual space $\mathcal{V}$ may be linked in many ways. In the spherical representation, navigation and collision avoidance may be considered as an intersection problem in the spherical data structure. An efficient algorithm [4], the "walk-around" algorithm, guides the autonomous mobile robot to avoid obstacles, to find a suitable path to go around obstacles, and to return to a planned path. The input to the system is the collection of continuous observables from the spherical vision system which

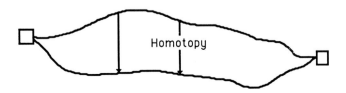

FIGURE 9. Homotopy of two equivalent paths.

constructs *local* octree structures for objects in the environment. The building and updating of the spherical data structure and its *local* octree structures constitute a dynamic spatial information system. This system is computation-intensive. The qualitative approach to *local* viewer-centered and object-centered octree structures will alleviate somewhat the difficulty.

The path space $\mathcal{P}$ is further related to the velocity space and other physical spaces. We do not discuss them here.

The Configuration Space

The configuration space C contains the world space $\mathcal{W}$ and the path space $\mathcal{P}$ as subspaces, and is controlled by inputs from the perceptual space $\mathcal{V}$. If only motion is considered, C may be reduced to the space of motion parameters, such as motions around various joints of a collection of hinged bodies (say robotic arms), within a region bounded by a collection of polyhedral walls. Algebraically, the position of a single rigid body is given by a rotation matrix R_1 and a vector A in R^3. If a second rigid body is hinged to the first, then the overall position is described by $[A, R_1, R_2]$ of two rotations R_1, R_2 and a vector A. These motion parameters form a vector in $R^{3+3+3} = R^9$. If we have a collection of n hinged bodies, the motion parameters form a vector in $R^{3(n+1)}$. The set of constraints satisfied by these parameters is described by algebraic equations. The resulting configuration space is an algebraic manifold in $R^{3(n+1)}$. Although computational algorithms are available, their complexity is enormous. The qualitative theory of that configuration space is the topological modeling of spatial transformations. By freeing the dimensions, some of the constraints are eliminated. A generalization of Lie groups, such as rotation and translation groups, is given elsewhere [*13*]. The category of generalized Lie groups keeps the basic characteristics of Lie groups, but consists of a wider class of topological homeomorphisms.

If there are tasks in a plan to be carried out, the configuration space C is a "fiber" space over the world space $\mathcal{W}$, namely over each set X in $\mathcal{W}$, a subplan P(X) of tasks $\{T_{X,1}, \ldots, T_{X,n}\}$ (the fiber at X) is attached (Fig. 10). The notion of a fiber space is borrowed from topology also. The fiber space C is not necessarily representable by the parameter (euclidean) space R^α. A hierarchy of heterogeneous data structures arises in the configuration space C.

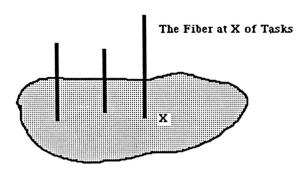

FIGURE 10.   Fiber space of tasks.

EXAMPLES

Exploration and Map Learning [*6, 7*]

An environment that generates spatial information and knowledge is usually captured by a map. Around each distinctive object or location, a local map is constructed. A global map integrates all of those local maps that are being considered. The construction and learning of these maps of an unknown environment is one of the most important questions of spatial reasoning. While the goal is to construct and to learn geometric and metrical maps which give exact distances, sizes, and other quantitative information, a qualitative and topological approach is similar to human cognitive maps of new environments. It is more robust because of its capability of managing uncertainty, error, and noise. As we acquire more knowledge, a topological map may be given the correct metric to become a geometric map.

This approach is valid in other tasks, such as designing a house and making a sculpture. First, we come up with a conceptual and abstract picture of what we intend to build. This initial picture is more topological, although the final product may be measured up to metrical accuracy. Thus, both the metrical and topological methods are useful. They are complementary to each other in the process.

The basic topological equivalence is a homeomorphism which sets up the topological equivalence between two topological spaces. For instance, a circular disk is topologically equivalent to a square. There are many topological invariants of any topological space that may be used to characterize the given space. That is, we may classify an infinite number of different topological spaces into a finite number of essential classes according to each topological invariant. For instance, the circular ring is equivalent to the circle in the "homotopy" theory, although they are of different dimensions, thus topologically not equivalent. This "weaker" invariant than the topological equivalence provides a smaller number of different classes. Basically, the weaker is a criterion, the large is the collection of objects that satisfy the criterion. The topological model in Ref. *6* is actually a homotopy model, because a path which has a width is represented by nodes and arcs which form a 1-D complex.

Spatial Semantic Networks and Frame Systems

Spatial knowledge representation and its inference are usually handled by semantic networks, equivalently frames or first-order predicate calculus [*14, 15*]. Knowledge is organized into IS-A and SUBSET hierarchies, together with relations and constraints. The knowledge should include both generic object models and specific instances of object. For spatial reasoning, it is useful to have active procedures attached to the semantic networks so that numerical values may be dynamically computed.

Most spatial reasoning systems are for image understanding. Among them, ACRONYM [*14*] is the best known model-based system. It uses explicit representation of generic objects, representing its geometric objects in a hierarchy of frames. Spatial relations between objects are represented as quantified algebraic inequalities, and interpretation is performed by an external graph-matching procedure. For matching, strong domain models are used. The matching is independent of the data, thus, the search is done without any flexibility. The quantifiers are also quite rigid in reasoning. A multilevel geometric reasoning system for vision has been developed by others which has a hierarchical organization of both object knowledge and knowledge about spatial reasoning. Algebraic constraints from the perspective projection are combined with additional constraints from the model to derive equations describing a family of interpretations for each object.

The 3-D FORM system [*15*] is being developed by Kanade and others. It uses frames to represent its objects and relations among objects. Active procedures (demons) are attached to the system arguments so that they are hypothesized or computed as needed. Primitive objects have demons to compute missing parts of their descriptions from other parts. Since both object and relation knowledge are explicitly represented, extension of the system to additional domains involves only adding new frames, without modifying the codes that manipulate the frames. The reasoning process is controlled by accessing objects, so the representation is amenable to top-down and bottom-up processing. Despite some nice capabilities of these systems, a classic problem of AI, referred to as the frame problem, still is a major difficulty for spatial reasoning systems. The complexity due to the dynamics of spatial reasoning is enormous. This kind of system certainly cannot emulate the human capability of spatial reasoning.

Spatial Database Management Systems [*16*]

Because of the enormous size of spatial databases and complexity of the search requirements, conventional relational database management systems (DBMS) can represent a processing bottleneck in spatial reasoning systems. Object-oriented representations offer an alternative approach that provides a conceptual framework for both the static and dynamic domain knowledge. One explores the search space reduction and potential of an object-oriented database. If, in addition, both the object-oriented and spatial-oriented representations are hierarchical, additional reductions in search space size and improvements in problem-solving efficiency are achieved through the use of recursive and multiple resolution reasoning.

In a DBMS with host-resident software and disk-resident data, access time depends on the search space size and disk retrieval time. The general approach consists of three steps. First, a fully integrated object and spatial-oriented database organization is developed to support efficient access and manipulation of the knowledge base. Second, a distributed processor implementation is used to allow the entire active knowledge base to be resident in random access memory to support concurrent search. Third, low-level spatial reasoning schemes, including Boolean operations, path planning, and metric computation, are implemented to exploit the rich structure of the spatial DBMS. A hybrid data structure consists of vector, pyramid, quadtree, octree, and frame-based components for representing uniformly and nonuniformly sampled point, line, and region object attributes.

Automated Assembly [*17-19*]

An important problem in robotics is automated assembly of mechanical parts. Automated assembly requires an information processing and control approach that describes the process, the workpieces, and the assembly equipment. The modeling of mechanical assembly processes is one essential step. The process flow language and knowledge representation of assembly processes are another. Backstrom [*7*] proposed a static and dynamic logical modeling of assembly processes. The model should have the expressive power of important geometric aspects of the assembly process, such as the composite structures of objects. Some are elementary bodies, holes in bodies, contact between bodies, and attachment of bodies, and constraints in relative movability and attachment. Using first-order logic, object domains, functions, primitive predicates and derivable predicates, and constraint axioms are expressed. Dynamic representation requires an extension of first-order logic to dynamic or modal logic. This faces the classic *frame problem* that dynamically updating rules are practically infeasible. One approach is to introduce some operators in the dynamic logic which represents the assembly process. This direction needs further research. Other work [20] uses the procedural approach in geometric models. However, the procedural approach is not suitable for spatial reasoning.

Tactical Situation Assessment [21]

Tactical situation assessment is the problem of analyzing incoming military intelligence data about enemy activities, to produce estimates of their intentions and capabilities. An important requirement is the analysis of the terrain for finding militarily significant features, such as cover and concealment, avenues of approach, and obstacles. One can construct a terrain analysis graph that describes the features. Significant features change only occasionally, so the results can be used repeatedly for detailed analysis of a particular area. In order to understand the enemy's intentions, these features are matched with intelligence reports. A complete solution to the problem requires solving several major AI research areas, including planning and plan learning. So far, most of research results are finding militarily significant features. Two classes of algorithms are region segmentation based on military knowledge and line-of-sight calculations. The visibility analysis provides potential attack routes in a certain region.

Spatial Information Management in a Mobile Robot [7, 8]

The objective is to establish a central information manager for an autonomous system. Strat and Smith define the common requirements. First, each should have the capability of perception of its environment and understanding of visual, sonar, and radar images. Whatever the source of data, each needs to perform image understanding, match image data with stored expectations, and build a model of its surroundings incrementally. Second, each system is expected to operate in an unstructured environment. Highly adaptable procedures that use novel representations of natural form are needed. Model-based approaches are not sufficient. Fractal and topological models are more practical. Third, the environment is dynamic. The mobility of the autonomous system is not the only source of change. Other objects are moving also.

Fourth, perception, planning and execution monitoring require knowledge-intensive processing. Domain-specific knowledge must be encoded and made available for use in every stage of processing. Finally, information must be available from a variety of sources. The incompleteness and uncertainty of information need multisensor fusion and information integration in real time. In Ref. 8, the Core Knowledge System Architecture is proposed, focusing on spatial and relational organization and its implications for integrating information from multiple sources. Many technologies, including blackboard architectures, relational and spatial databases, uncertain reasoning, epistemic logic, computer graphics, and knowledge bases are applied.

Spatial Planning [11, 12, 22]

Motion planning has been studied by many researchers. The general schemes for solving the pathfinding problem in robotics and computational geometry can be characterized by the manner in which the approaches represent the free space. There are two basic approaches. One represents the obstacles explicitly as geometric shapes (polygons) and the free space is defined implicitly as being outside of those obstacles. The shortest path in a 2-D space can be found by searching the visibility graph. The extension to the 3-D shortest path problem is very expensive computationally. The other represents the free space explicitly and finds the path directly inside the free space. For example, the free space may be described as generalized cones where the central axes for these cones form a connected graph of passing channels. The pathfinding problem is to search for the path on the connectivity graph. The path is a collision-free path, but may not be the optimal one. The Voronoi diagram is another method of describing the free space. It characterizes the skeleton or passing channels of the free space between adjacent obstacles. The Voronoi diagram partitions the 2-D plane into disjoint regions. Meng [12] derived an algorithm for pathfinding under location uncertainty. Other algorithms can be found [4, 22, 23].

Spatial planning does not restrict to motion planning. VLSI design and floor space planning in architectural design are two commonly mentioned applications [18, 22]. The problem is concerned with a rectangular dissection of a rectangular space into nonoverlapping rectangular subspaces. The inference rules are used to determine constraints from a constraint graph.

REFERENCES

1. A. C. Kak, and S. Chen (eds.), *Proceedings of AAAI Workshop of Spatial Reasoning and Multisensor Fusion,* Morgan Kaufmann, Los Altos, CA, 1987.

2. P. J. Besl, and R. C. Jain, "Three-Dimensional Object Recognition," *ACM Comput. Surv., 17*(1), 75–145, (1985).

3. B. B. Mandelbrot, *Fractals: Form, Chance and Dimension,* W. H. Freeman, San Francisco, 1982.

4. S. Chen, "A Geometric Approach to Multisensor Fusion and Spatial Reasoning," in *Proc. AAAI Workshop of Spatial Reasoning and Multisensor Fusion,* Morgan Kaufmann, Los Altos, CA, 1987, pp. 201–210.

5. D. H. Ballard, "Eye Movements and Visual Cognition," in *Proc. AAAI Workshop of Spatial Reasoning and Multisensor Fusion,* Morgan Kaufmann, Los Altos, CA, 1987, pp. 188–200.

6. B. J. Kuipers, and Y. T. Byun, "A Qualitative Approach to Robot Exploration and Map-Learning," in *Proc. AAAI Workshop of Spatial Reasoning and Multisensor Fusion,* Morgan Kaufmann, Los Altos, CA, 1987, pp. 390–404.

7. T. S. Levitt, D. T. Lawton, D. M. Chelberg, P. C. Nelson, and J. W. Dye, "Visual Memory Structure for a Mobile Robot," in *Proc. AAAI Workshop of Spatial Reasoning and Multisensor Fusion,* Morgan Kaufmann, Los Altos, CA, 1987, pp. 99–106.

8. T. M. Strat, and G. B. Smith, "The Management of Spatial Information in a Mobile Robot," in *Proc. AAAI Workshop of Spatial Reasoning and Multisensor Fusion,* Morgan Kaufmann, Los Altos, CA, 1987, pp. 240–249.

9. S. Chen, "Multisensor Fusion and Navigation of Mobile Robots," *Int. J. Intell. Sys.,2,* 227–252, (1987).

10. M. Penna, and S. Chen, "Spherical Analysis in Computer Vision and Image Understanding," in *Image Understanding in Unstructured Environment,* World Scientific, 1988, pp. 125– 177.

11. T. Lozano-Perez, and M. A. Wesley, "An Algorithm for Planning Collision-Free Paths Among Polyhedral Obstacles," *Comm. ACM, 22,* (1979).

12. A. C. C. Meng, "Free Space Modeling and Geometric Motion Planning Under Location Uncertainty," in *Proc. AAAI Workshop of Spatial Reasoning and Multisensor Fusion,* Morgan Kaufmann, Los Altos, CA, 1987, pp. 430–439.

13. S. Chen, and R. Yoh, "The Categories of Generalized Lie Groups," *Trans. Am. Math. Soc., 199,* 281–294, (1974).

14. R. A. Brooks, "Symbolic Reasoning Among 3-D Models and 2-D Images." *Artif. Intell., 17,* 285–348, (1981).

15. E. Walker, M. Herman, and T. Kanade, "A Framework for Representing and Reasoning About Three-Dimensional Objects for Vision," in *Proc. AAAI Workshop of Spatial Reasoning and Multisensor Fusion,* Morgan Kaufmann, Los Altos, CA, 1987, pp. 21–23.

16. R. Antony, "Spatial Reasoning Using an Object-Oriented Spatial DBMS," in *Proc. AAAI Workshop of Spatial Reasoning and Multisensor Fusion,* Morgan Kaufmann, Los Altos, CA, 1987, pp. 42–51.

17. C. Backstrom, "Logical Modelling of Simplified Geometrical Objects and Mechanical Assembly Processes." in *Proc. AAAI Workshop of Spatial Reasoning and Multisensor Fusion,* Morgan Kaufmann, Los Altos, CA, 1987, pp. 52–61.

18. J. E. Hassett, "Automated Layout in ASHLAP: An Approach to the Problem of General Cell Layout for VLSI," in *Proc. 19th Design Automation Conference,* 1982, 00. 777–784.

19. J. L. Nevins, and D. E. Whitney, *Assembly Research, Automatica,* Vol. 16, No. 5, Pergamon Press, New York, 1980.

20. M. A. Wesley, T. Lozano-Perez et al., "A Geometric Modelling System for Automated Mechanical Assembly," *IBM J. Res. Dev., 24,* 64–74, (1980).

21. D. McDermott, and A. Gelsey, "Terrain Analysis for Tactical Situation Assessment," in *Proc. AAAI Workshop of Spatial Reasoning and Multisensor Fusion,* Morgan Kaufmann, Los Altos, CA, 1987, pp. 420–429.

22. S. Kundu, and R. Singh, "Spatial Reasoning in Rectangular Dissection," in *Proc. AAAI Workshop of Spatial Reasoning and Multisensor Fusion,* Morgan Kaufmann, Los Altos, CA, 1987, pp. 82–89.

23. F. P. Preparata, and M. I. Shamos, *Computational Geometry,* Springer-Verlag, New York, 1985.

SU-SHING CHEN

STATISTICAL AND SCIENTIFIC DATABASE
MANAGEMENT SYSTEMS

INTRODUCTION

Statistical and scientific databases (SSDB) are generally defined as databases that support statistical and scientific applications [1–4].

In particular, the term "statistical databases" (SDB) refers to databases that represent statistical or summary information and are used for statistical analysis [5]. Many application areas include examples of SDB: for instance, socioeconomic databases (e.g., population or income counts, energy production and consumption, health and medical statistics, etc.), business databases (e.g., financial summary reports, sales forecasting, etc.), and so on.

Generally there are two broad classes of statistical databases (SDB): *micro* and *macro* SDBs [6]. The former refers to SDB containing disaggregate data (or microdata), that is records of individual entities (e.g., patients' medical records in hospitals, or various census data regarding the single citizen, etc.). Its utilization is directed mainly to statistical analysis. The latter refers to SDB containing aggregated data (or macrodata), typically the result of the application before simple "count" or "sum" functions on the microdata, and eventually other more or less complex statistical-mathematical functions (with the aim of obtaining, for example, *Mortality tables* per "sex," "type of illness," and "year," or tables with the *percentage* relative to *Consumption of products for the production of energy* per "type of product," "year," and "state," or tables with the *average Remuneration* per "type of industry," "employee qualifications," and "year," etc.).

The term "scientific databases" refers to databases that include scientific data, most of which result from *experiments* and *simulations*; we call both of them "experiment data." In addition, there exist data in *support* of the experiments and data that are *generated* from the experiment data; referred to collectively as "associated data" [7].

Statistical databases management systems (SDBMS) may, instead, be defined as database management systems able to model, store, and manipulate data in a manner suitable for the needs of the statisticians and to apply statistical data analysis techniques to the stored data. Most of the commercial systems available today were designed primarily to support transactions for business applications (e.g., banking or marketing), while statistical and scientific applications have different data structures, characteristics, and properties operate over such data and processing requirements [8].

We describe now the main characteristics of such data, the research topics of the area, the obtained results, and the main problems existing, at present, in the field of the SSDBM.

CHARACTERISTICS OF SCIENTIFIC DATABASES

As already stated, there are two types of scientific data: experiment data and associated data.

Experiment data are generally classified in data from experiments and data from simulation. The former are usually measurements of some physical phenomena (e.g., the collision of particle beams or the spectra generated by molecules in a strong magnetic field). The latter typically result from complex computations derived by using values from the previous time interval. Both can be classified according to two important characteristics: regularity and density. The former refers to the pattern of the points or coordinates for which values are measured or computed (e.g., in physics experiments, detectors are placed in a specific configuration; if the configuration describes a regular grid or some other geometric structure, the experiment is said to have *spatial* regularity). In general, regularity implies that a mapping between the coordinates of the measured values and the storage locations of these values can be made by means of a computation. When, instead, spatial irregularity exists, it is necessary to enumerate the data points, and store their identifiers with the data values. The latter indicates whether all the potential data points have actual values associated with them (e.g., simulation data of fluid motion computed on a regular grid would have data values (for velocity, direction, etc.) computed for each point of the grid, and therefore the data are considered dense). on the other hand, in many experiments a large number of measurements that are below a certain threshold are discarded and not recorded. Sparsity implies a large number of null values which may be compressed out [9].

The associated data are generally classified in data in *support* of the experiments, and data that are *generated* from the experiment data. The former fall into two types: configuration data and instrumentation data. The latter fall into three types: analyzed data, summary data, and property data.

Configuration data describe the initial structure of an experiment or simulation. Usually they do not change in the course of the experiment or simulation, while they can change between experiments and simulations. In this last case it is important to keep track of these changes, associated the correct configuration data with the corresponding experiment data.

Instrumentation data (crucial for the correct analysis of the experimental data) are descriptions of different instruments used in an experiment and their changes over time.

The analyzed data are data generated by the analysis of experiment data; the analysis process that produces such data may require several steps. It is important to capture the analysis process, the input and the output databases of each step, and the relationships between the steps.

Scientific databases, similar to statistical databases, which deal with statistical summaries (aggregations) of data sets, are often aggregated. As in the case of statistical databases, there is a need to organize, search, and browse collections of summary data, and to preserve their relationship to lower level data from which they are derived.

Property data represent a substantial amount of work devoted to the organization and classification of properties referring to materials, phenomena, substances, etc.; they are the summary of information learned over the years, but, unfortunately, many property databases cannot be accessed on-line. Property data are not uniform: they contain numeric data, images, graphs, and istograms, as well as text and bibliographic data; they are often called "multimedia" data.

Some of the more important conclusions are [9]:

Multidimensional data are prevalent in scientific databases and methods for efficiently managing, accessing, and compressing multidimensional data are desirable

Although scientific databases are usually very large, often they can be partitioned into small independent units; this implies that parallel processing can be applied

Scientific databases include a variety of support data that describe that instruments and the configuration of experiments; some configuration data need special capabilities found in engineering database systems

The analysis of scientific data generates many summary data sets; special techniques for handling analyzed data and summary data are required in order to manage their meta-data, to keep track of several data sets, and to handle nonscalar data types (such as vectors and matrices)

Historical aspects of scientific databases (e.g., time series of measured data, historical sequence of generating different summaries of data, etc.) are important

Many of the above-mentioned points concern aspects that are similar in statistical databases (in particular, supporting the multidimensional aspects of the data, historical aspects, and handling of summary data). For this reason, and for the inadequacy of commercial database management systems to support in a suitable manner both statistical and scientific applications, often the researchers merge the problems of their field in a single area [*3,4,7*].

CHARACTERISTICS OF STATISTICAL DATABASES

It is essential that a number of characteristics are built into the database for it to be useful for statistical analysis; characteristics which involve an adequate description of the quantitative information in the database (e.g., a suitable 'metadata,' as defined below, should in included). This description is absolutely necessary for understanding the inferences which emerge from data analysis. Certain kinds of description or definition are nearly always included in the database, but other information is almost never included. A detailed analysis will reveal subtleties which are correlated with this description, and often cannot be modeled without it [*10*].

It is important, however, to characterize the data, the informative nature of which can either 'aggregate' or 'disaggregate.' To be more exact, we can distinguish [*6*] between microdata, that is, records of individual events (e.g., data obtained from censuses, sampled surveys, or simply data relative to individual employees of a given firm, data-bank clients, etc.) and macrodata [*11*], that is, data which are the result of the application of statistical–mathematical functions on microdata contained in traditional databases (e.g., mortality tables per illness, year, sex, and region, or time series relative to occupation per working area, region, and year, etc.).

In everyday situations, a statistical user often does not have disaggregate data directly at hand. These users generally have to refer to already aggregated data (at various levels of aggregation, dependent on various factors, such as the source of information, how private the disaggregate data is, etc.), data which are normally provided by institutes created for the purpose of gathering and issuing information or industries, banks, other public or private organizations which publish or issue, on request, statistical information about their activity: we generally use the term 'data owners' for these sources of information.

Macrodata regarding a certain field of interest are normally distributed between various data owners; therefore, the activity of a statistical user is, in its first phase, characterized by the homogenization of the data which came from these various sources of information, and checking, where possible, the semantic consistency and the comparability between the different levels of data aggregation which are available to the user. We will examine the problem in the section Heterogeneous Data Sources.

As regards microdata, there are a number of more than satisfactory solutions relative both to the logical (and conceptual) representation of the data which one wishes to describe and to their manipulation and management [*12*]. Instead, it is generally agreed that conventional DBMS are in many ways inadequate to manage efficiently macrodata and to support statistical (and scientific) applications [*5,8*].

Let us now take a look at the characteristics which distinguish statistical macrodata from microdata, and the problems which arise in their acquisition, logical and conceptual representation, memorization, querying, elaboration, and more generally, their management.

Among the main points which characterize statistical macrodata, we can list the following (subsequently we will use the terms "macrodata," "summary data," and "quantitative data" as synonyms):

1.   They are stable, in the sense that they represent events consolidated in time; in fact, a table which represents car production in Europe, contains data classified according to the variables which describe it (e.g., car company, model, cubic capacity, country of production, year of production, etc.), but the data relative to car production always refer to events which have already taken place (car production refers to years or months in the past and therefore to data which in general can no longer be altered). The 'dynamism' in this case, consists of the enlargement (with new data) of the database. For example, if the memorized data relative to a certain phenomenon came to a halt in June 1986, new data (on the same phenomenon) relative to the subsequent period of time (July 1986, . . ., February 1988, . . can be added; therefore the instances of the domains of some of the variable which characterize the summary data are increased.

2.   In these tables two variable (implicitly or explicitly expressed)–"temporal" and "spatial"–(e.g., when and where the phenomenon took place) are always present.

3.   The quantitative data which appear in the tables always have a unit of measure (e.g., tonnes or hectoliters, but also a simple number, as in the case of 'number of').

4.   The macrodata, in general only numeric, always have a data type (which can be simply 'number of' but also 'rate,' 'average,' etc.) which is dependent on the function which has been applied to the original microdata.

5.   Each numeric value (instance) which appears in a table (summary attribute) is characterized by an ennupla (or tupla) of instance of variables which describe it (category attributes); thus, for example, in the table in Figure 1, the *number of cars produced* (the phenomenon described) during the year "1980" of the *model* 'Dyane' (by the *car company* Renault) was 85,400. This fact demonstrates the distinction made between 'quantitative values,' that is, the macrodata which appear in the table and the 'qualitative values,' that is, the metadata which describe the summary attribute (this distinction is not made in conventional DBSM).

6.   It is not uncommon to have 'missing values' or 'sparse data' in these tables; regarding the former, this is a direct consequence of the *cross product* of all possible values of category attributes. In fact, this can happen either because the data were not taken for all the instances of a category attribute (e.g., in Fig.1, the production of the car model 'Dyane' in 1986 and 1987 has not been recorded) or because they would not have any meaning (if one thinks of a mortality table described per sex, type of illnesses, etc., the data relative to deaths by tumor of the prostate gland of the female sex are missing because they are meaningless). Proper statistical treatment of missing data usually depends on the reason for the missing data and, as we have seen in the previous example, such as with questionnaires, the logical structure may influence the interpretation of a missing value.

No. of cars produced (in thous.)		Year				
	Model	80	81	82	....	
Renault	Dyane	85,4	86,7	88,1	...	
	....	...	...	...	...	
Toyota	Corolla	107,3	112,6	114,2	...	
	Corona	72,8	74,1	77,2	...	
	....	...	...	...	...	
Honda	Civic	91,3	93,8	97,5	...	
	....	...	...	...	...	
Alfa Romeo	America	24,9	27,1	29,4	...	
	Spider	9,4	10,0	11,3	...	
	....	...	...	...		

Car-builder

FIGURE 1.

We will speak of representing and interpreting of null values in statistical tables in item 7.

With reference, however, to the sparse data, in many data sets there are structured patterns of missing data. This is particularly the case for designed experiments where the 'design' is an optimum sparse coverage of the independent variable levels. Research is in progress on the handling of sparse data to find ways to economize storage, to describe metadata, and to optimize retrieval while keeping the logical description independent of storage considerations.

7.   The operations on these tables are conceptually different with respect to those carried out on microdata (e.g., if one thinks of a reclassification of a category attribute: the instances of the new attribute could be obtained by regrouping a certain number of instances of the original attribute; for example, passing from 'January,' 'February,' and 'March' to 'First Trimester'). The traditional operations of cancellation, insertion, and modification are rare or not even permitted.

8.   The variety of data treated is much larger than in conventional DBMS (matrices, vectors, time series, relations, time-ordered sets, etc.)

9.   The number of data involved in the management operations is often large and the database itself is large (sometimes containing hundreds of millions of records).

The above demonstrates the difference between commercial and statistical DBMS in both the properties of the data and the operations on the data, as well as the difficulty which a user faces when working with tools which are not entirely suitable (hybrid systems obtained by interfacing a conventional DBMS with statistical package are often defined as SDBMS).

MULTIDIMENSIONAL DATA STRUCTURE AND METADATA

Multidimensionality is a dominant feature in SSDBs. Many of the characteristics and requirements of SSDBs can be traced to this feature. The phenomenon described (e.g., level of employment in the United States 1970-1980) is generally a multidimensional phenomenon, where the numeric values which appear, for instance, in a statistical table, are usually distinguished by a set of categories or parameters. As an example, the terms exporting country, importing country, commodity, year and month can be used to identify trade data, while the terms temperature, acidity, salinity, length of exposure, and material used can describe a corrosion experiment.

In such examples, there exists naturally a multidimensional space for which measured data are collected. We will examine later how this is reflected at the physical and the logical level.

The difficulty of dealing with multidimensional spaces is further compounded by the fact that each dimension can itself have a complex (usually hierarchical) structure; in other words, each category attribute which describes the summary data can be further broken into subcategories; energy can be subcategorized into oil, coal, and gas. This subcategorization of a single dimension can continue into many levels, and sometimes overlapping occurs. Representing such complexity requires special facilities at the logical and user interface levels [9].

The property of multidimensionality makes multidimensional data structures, such as grid files, quad trees, or K-D trees, attractive data structures for SSDBs. These data structures are especially effective when several data values in a region of the multidimensional space are needed at the same time [14].

With regard to the importance of metadata in SSDBs, we can say that "metadata is necessary to specify information about statistical data for both human beings and computer programs. It can provide definition of logical models as well as more mundane documentation details for both database administrators and users. Well-defined and differentiated metadata is necessary to permit software linkages between different logical and physical representations; between statistical databases, application programs, and user interfaces; as well as between multiple distributed and heterogeneous systems" [2]. Then they "are essential in an interactive environment where the output of any routine can immediately serve as input to another" [11].

Moreover, "statistics metadata contain some numerical functions (perhaps vector valued) of observed data, which can be used to compute other statistics" [15].

"Many researchers in SDBMS have rediscovered that metadata can play a vital role not only in data description but also in enhancing statistical processing of the data [16].

McCarthy provided an excellent overview of metadata, including statistical metadata, as it is known to the researchers in DBMS. According to McCarthy, metadata are data about data, i.e., systematic descriptive information about data content and organization that can be retrieved, manipulated and displayed in various ways. "His definition of statistical metadata includes default specifications at the database level, error expansion, aggregate or disaggregate expressions, suppression expressions, etc" [15].

It is necessary to organize and manage metadata, just as is the case with data. However, metadata typically contains much text, and its structure can be more complex than just text strings. It is necessary, therefore, to manage metadata with tools that can handle text. Most data management systems and statistical packages have very limited capabilities in this area.

The requirements of metadata management include special data and manipulation languages which contain the right set of data types and structures such as variable length text, hierarchical attributes, vectors, and matrices. Other facilities should include automatic fixing on keywords of the metadata, querying tools on metadata, and browsing capability for the user to find out the subject matters stored in the database [6].

According to DBMS researchers, metadata have two broad kinds of properties: functional (based on usage) and operational (based on the objects actually used and stored). With regard to the first property, metadata is used for the following purposes:

1. Storage and retrieval of data; e.g., if one wishes to analyze particular census tracts, the metadata must be examined in order to select the data items of interest as well as the definitions of the variables to be examined as data.
2. Presentation and display of data; this category might include the documentation and display of a table. In this case, metadata would include variable definitions, case names, and other title and footnote information (indicating, e.g., the source of the data).
3. Analysis of data (which includes any calculations that might be performed on the data, such as aggregation, comparison, reclassification, etc.).
4. Physical manipulation of the data files.

With regard to the second property, the approach is to look at those kinds of information most commonly included in various database manipulation systems [17]. In general, systems that are heavily oriented toward computation seem to be less capable in the area of metadata management than systems that are oriented more heavily toward data management. Database systems that are oriented primarily toward textual data have generally better metadata capabilities, although they usually compensate by having little in the way of analytical or computational capabilities [17]. At present, no widely available commercial system for the organization and manipulation of statistical databases has comprehensive and adequate facilities for handling metadata, even though some of the advantages of the use of metadata have been shown in manufacturing test environments and in interactive informations display systems [15].

HETEROGENEOUS DATA SOURCES

Heterogeneous data may cause problems in the ability to access or understand data, or the ability to establish consistency in structure or meaning with other data [18]. Such heterogeneity among data may include:

Changes in classification scheme, collection method, etc.
Differences in physical format, units or levels of resolution or parameters.
Undetected disparity in meaning due to insufficient description.
A possible research topic seems to be the use of "correspondence graphs," an effective tool for relating alternative classifications and solving a certain

number of problems (matching, merging, interaction, compatibility, and derivability) [19].

Different methods of data definition and different data structures add to the complexity of doing an analysis. Additionally, data (and metadata) may be lost in going from one system to another because of differences in capabilities. The need to use different computer systems may further compound these difficulties [18].

Among the different approaches which may help to avoid or solve problems of dealing with heterogeneous data, we can list: more complete metadata, better metadata management, and the imposition of standards (an unpopular but often effective approach to avoiding problems of dealing with heterogeneous data is to impose standards). In fact, a serious impediment to the integrated use of summary data sets produced by different data sources is the use of different classification systems [19].

The most obvious way to minimize the problems of connecting data that differ in source is to provide complete data documentation. Some or all of this information (metadata) will be required to establish if fields or records originating in different data sets can be validly linked and, if so, how (source integration) [20].

Correspondence graphs (or labeled bipartite graphs) are an effective tool for relating alternative classifications and solving a certain number of problems (matching, merging, interaction, compatibility, and derivability); however, while work is progressing in the area of dealing with heterogeneous data (and systems), we are far from a solution to these problems.

DATA MODELS

Data models are tools to describe reality. They provide a way of managing different concepts that belong to the real world but which are difficult to manipulate in a computer environment. The power of a model and its completeness are measured by the degree of accuracy it achieves in describing the external world. Data models use abstraction to hide detail and concentrate on general common properties of data objects. For that reason, the data model is strongly related to the type of objects found and the type of data collected in an application. For statistical databases, it is necessary to keep in mind that the raw data is different from commercial data and thus requires models different from those available for commercial data [21].

Let us briefly deal with the subject; first on a conceptual, and then on a logical level. A case apart is the semantic model SAM* [22], in which the author proposes a network structure (as a means of representing the conceptual design of a database) and a tabular structure for representing the implementation design of a database; this model introduces a set of restructuring operations and algebraic operations.

Conceptual Models for Summary Data

Conceptual data models are instruments for describing reality: every model uses for such a goal a limited collection of representation structures. Abstractions represent a powerful mechanism in modeling reality. An abstraction is a mental process that we use when we select some characteristics and properties of a set of objects and leave out other characteristics which are irrelevant to the application.

A conceptual statistical model (CSM) is discussed elsewhere [23], and a methodology for conceptual design of statistical applications, using two different data models for elementary and summary data is described which uses representation structures and corresponding symbols as shown in Figure 2.

In conceptual statistical models, the methods and guidelines of general methodologies for conceptual database design (to specify issues of statistical applications) have been adapted and the approach used consists of the following three points:

1. The choice of two different yet complementary data models for the description of elementary and summary data (for improving the expressiveness of the representations at the two levels): the E-R model of Chen and a redefinition of the Grass model [*10,24*].
2. A use (in the methodology) of the conceptual schema of elementary data.

Abstraction	Symbol
Class of objects	S
Category attribute	C
Statistical classification	X
Statistical computation	E
Generalization	G
Aggregation	A
Grouping	✳

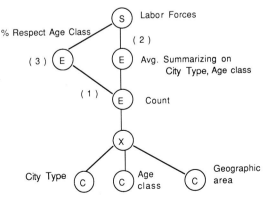

FIGURE 2.

3. A strategy for the design of the statistical schema which consists of an effective tradeoff between topdown and bottomup activities. Typical topdown activities are the design of the draft elementary schema, of the skeleton statistical schema, and the aggregation subschemas. A bottomup activity can be the design of the statistical schema through incremental merging of aggregation subschemas.

As already mentioned, in the semantic model SAM* (semantic association model), a table structure is defined: the generalized relation (or G-relation), which employs two types of attributes (category and summary) [27], and the relation of the relational model is a particular case of such a structure. This model follows two general types of concepts: atomic or nondecomposable concept and nonatomic concept. An "association" is instead, defined as "the grouping of atomic and/or nonatomic concepts to describe another nonatomic concept." Seven association types are defined, which are useful for the conceptual modeling of databases. In describing such associations, the author uses a network representation, with labeled nodes and arcs. If the same nonatomic concept is seen by different users as having different semantic properties, the concept will be labeled with more than one association type name.

The semantic properties of each association type are given defining the 'structure,' the 'operations' that can be performed on an attribute occurrence, and the 'constraints.'

The algebra defined in SAM* is formed by operators able to carry out statistical queries, plus operators of the relational algebra (suitably redefined). The graphic representation shows only the important properties of the association types and an example is shown in Figure 3. Chan [25] also defines and illustrates a number of restructuring operations and relational algebraic operations, as we will see in the following section. The author explains that a G-relation can be nested in other G-relations, forming a hierarchical structure. Furthermore, the data type is automatically treated for the aggregation and disaggregation operations. The basic idea of a G-relation is that a statistical user needs the 'record logic' concept to describe and manipulate his or her data, since this enables him or her to manage the table as a single entity. Then the category attributes and the summary attribute are connected together in a uniform way. Nevertheless, the term G-relation characterizes a collection of data formed by different concepts, without this being evident to the user; furthermore, this requires that the summary attribute is denoted in imprecise terms (e.g., the name of the statistical-mathematical function). A statistical user will find that the G-relation is not easy to use. This is mainly due to the difficulty of the use of the operators, specifically the necessity to verify the conditions of applicability, and the complexity in the semantics of the conditions themselves.

Unsuitability of Existing Models

As mentioned previously, and a matter on which a number of authors agree, is that a number of existing models are unsuitable for representing and manipulating correctly statistical and scientific macrodata.

In particular, the relational model brilliantly resolves both the formal correctness and the method of representing (by means of 'relations') and manipulating (by means of relational algebra operators) information (i.e., traditional database microdata) for the user. This has led many researchers to propose the same model (and the same algebra) for the representation and manipulation of statistical database macrodata. For the manipulation of such data, it has become increasingly necessary to extend the relational algebra, by introducing other operators capable of carrying out the typical queries of a statistical environment (and

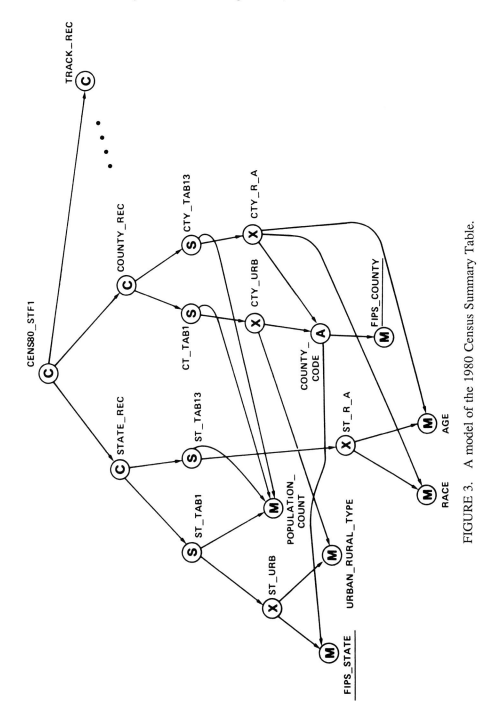

FIGURE 3.   A model of the 1980 Census Summary Table.

ENERGY CONSUMPTION	Country			
	Italy		France	
(In Percent)	Year		Year	
	1979	1980	1979	1980

Type		1979	1980	1979	1980
	Solid fuel	7.2	13.8	11.4	26.2
	Hyd. geoth.	6.8	6.3	3.6	5.8

FIGURE 4.

of the relative database), as well as by redefining that traditional operators of the algebra itself.

If, in fact, a statistical table is represented by the relational model, then applying a number of the relational algebra operators to the relation which represents the above-mentioned table, we obtain a summary data, the informative significance of which is often falsified. One of these operators is, for example, projection. If, we consider the table in Figure 4 (represented by means of two tables for convenience) and applying the following projection operator:

$$\Pi_{\text{type of source, country, absol. value}} \text{ENERGY CONSUMPTION}$$

to the relation R_1 = Energy Consumption in Figure 5 which represents the above-mentioned two tables with a relation, we obtain a new relation (represented in Fig. 6) whose summary data have lost their informative value. In fact, the consumption of solid fuel in Italy in 1982 assumes two different numeric values (and this is true, in this particular case, for any nation and any year); the ambiguity depends on the elimination of the attribute 'years,' which was one of the attributes which characterize the original numeric data, without distinguishing between the various roles–descriptive and summary–which the two attributes (years and energy consumption) have. It can be deduced from this example that the relational algebra presents limits in correctly manipulating statistical database data, in that its operators can generate relations which no longer represent statistical tables. Furthermore, such a model gives rise to an enormous redundancy in the tuples (see the table in Fig. 2), as regards the instances of category attributes, in that it represents monodimensionally a structure (the statistical table) which is in itself multidimensional [24]. This monodimensionality is to be understood in the sense that, in a relation, the instances of a summary attribute are reported

Type	Year	Country	Percent
Solid fuel	1979	Italy	7.2
Solid fuel	1979	France	11.4
Solid fuel	1980	Italy	13.8
Solid fuel	1980	France	26.2
Hyd. geoth.	1979	Italy	6.8
Hyd. geoth.	1979	France	3.6
Hyd. geoth.	1980	Italy	6.3
Hyd. geoth.	1980	France	5.8

FIGURE 5.   Energy consumption.

along the direction of one column; in reality these instances must be considered as points in a multidimensional Cartesian space, having the category attributes as the axes.

We will see in the paragraph on Operators and Query Languages for SSDBs how researchers in the field have responded to this unsuitability.

Logical Model for Summary Data

In formulating a logical data model suitable for statistical databases, there are two different approaches. One tries to extend a traditional data model to include concepts that are common in statistical manipulation. Examples of this approach appear in Hebrail [26] and Tan-

Type	Country	Percent
Solid fuel	Italy	7.2
Solid fuel	France	11.4
Solid fuel	Italy	13.8
Solid fuel	France	26.2
Hyd. geoth.	Italy	6.8
Hyd. geoth.	France	3.6
Hyd. geoth.	Italy	6.3
Hyd. geoth.	France	5.8

FIGURE 6.   Energy consumption.

sel [27], where the concepts of summary sets and time are added to the relational model (often such data are called "historical").

A second approach is to develop new models which will facilitate the use of the data by the end user. Chan's [25] influential work in this area introduced two types of abstraction to organize the statistical information: category attribute and summary attribute.

It is worth noting that practitioners make a distinction between parameters (which correspond to category attributes) and variables (which correspond to summary attributes) because it provides a better understanding of the content of the database and how it was established. One of the main benefits of modeling the semantics of category and summary attributes is the capability of automatic aggregation. It is the ability of the system to infer the subset of values over which an aggregation (or statistical function) should be applied [28].

A possibility is to have these semantic concepts represented internally, so that they are invisible to the user. An example of a system that takes this approach is SUBJECT [25], in which these semantic concepts are represented as a graph. There are two kinds of nodes: a 'cross product' node (x) and a 'cluster' node (c). The nodes can be connected by arcs to form a directed acyclic graph. Cluster nodes represent a collection of items. Cross product nodes are used to represent composite keys of category attributes.

An example of a subject graph is shown in Figure 7.

As can be seen, cluster nodes are used to represent a hierarchy of parameters. This is a way of representing complex category attributes. Cluster nodes are also used to represent the collection of summary attributes under the node labeled 'variables.'

This graph structure is invisible to the user and is used to support a menu-driven interface. The user does not need to know the types of nodes, but the system can make use of them to provide automatic aggregation. The graph can be either browsed by moving up and down the nodes, or searched directly with keywords. The sharing of nodes provides the capability to use the same clusters (e.g., state names) across data sets, and to avoid confusion of names. One main advantage of this representation is that the user can be shown the content of the database by gradually revealing more detail when requested [28].

An extension of SUBJECT is GRASS (graphical approach for statistical summaries) [24,29]. This model is realized by means of a direct, acyclical, orientated, and connected graph; it gives the statistical user an easy and immediate instrument to get to know, by working this way inside, the structure of the statistical database on a logical level. GRASS introduces five types of node, which are 'marked,' to distinguish type and 'labeled,' to distinguish each node within the limits of the same type. The marks which distinguish the node types are S, T, A, C, and t_n and their semantic description follows:

> An S node represents the conceptual relation which exists between different nodes (of the S or T types) on a lower level of aggregation; this grouping, in a sole higher level phenomenon, depends on the particular conceptual view which the statistical database designer has toward these phenomena. This means that more conceptual representations of the same statistical database can exist by means of node S.

> A T node represents the summary data physically present in the databases; the label expresses the phenomenon described (and, at times, some implicit category attributes, as already seen) and the types of data itself.

> An A node and a C node represent, respectively, the concepts of "aggregation" and "category attribute."

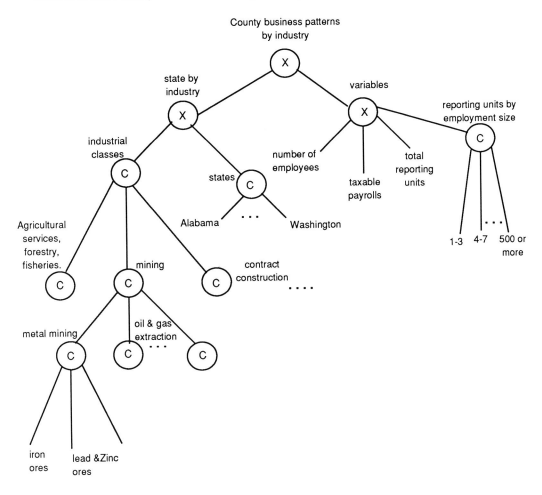

FIGURE 7.   SUBJECT graph.

A t_n node represents one of the assumable values within the limits of a domain datum of category attribute definition (this domain, in order to distinguish it from the primitive domain already introduced, is sometimes called C domain; it will be a subset of the primitive domain, from which it is extracted, and can obviously coincide with the primitive domain itself).

A T node is a "well" both with respect to the part of the graph made up of the S nodes (i.e., the upper part of the graph with respect to the level of the T nodes), and with respect to the table trees formed by nodes C, A, and t_n (which make up the lower part of the GRASS graph).

We can have the same labels for different nodes (A and C) as long as the nodes are not in common with respect to the same table tree (that is have the same T node as a well).

Figure 8 shows an example of statistical data representation made using the GRASS model. This graphic representation is part of a functional model, Mefisto [*30*], which is based on the simple statistical table concept (SST), a data structure obtained by applying an

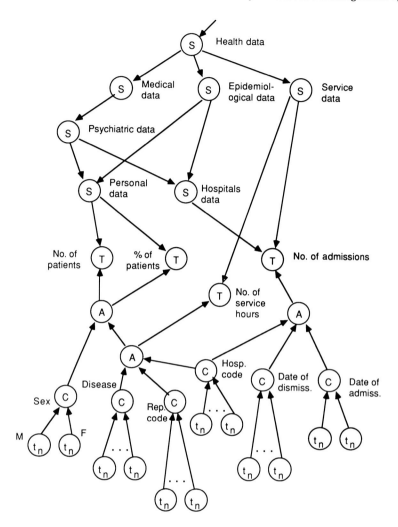

FIGURE 8.

aggregation function (usually SUM or COUNT) to microdata (i.e., disaggregate data). Therefore, an SST is a data structure characterized by:

a. A single summary attribute (the quantitative or calculated data), which represents a property of the statistical phenomenon described in SST; its instances are the numerical values in the table

b. A set of category attributes (qualitative data), i.e., the variables which unequivocally describe the summary attribute

c. A set of values, which we will call variable domain of the table, corresponding to each category attribute; these values are generally strings of alphanumeric characters

d. A specific data type, dependent on the particular aggregation function which gave rise to the summary attribute; e.g., the function COUNT produces the data type 'absolute values' (e.g., number of), the function PERCENTAGE produces the type 'percentage,' etc.

Each instance of the summary attribute is characterized by the combination (cross product) of instances of category attributes. An SST allows the user to have an exact knowledge of both the structure of the original microdata and the aggregation activity carried out on these to obtain an SST.

In the Mefisto model, an SST is a complex data type which can be represented by a couple (R,g) where R is a relation, whose attributes are the SST category attributes and g is a function which maps the category attributes which describe the macrodata to the same macrodata.

The formalism of the structure chosen to represent an SST is based on the mathematical function and the label of the SST characterizes the content of the same.

The Mefisto model is capable of describing an SST by means of: (1) a data structure; and (2) a set of operators capable of manipulating the data.

Recently a new model has been proposed, STORM (STatistical Object Representation Model) [31], in which the authors, starting from the previous models, define a new statistical entity, called "statistical object" (SO), and introduce three different representation levels and two different representation spaces.

Briefly, a statistical object (SO) is a complex structure of data, defined by a triple $\{u, c, f\}$, where: u is the name of the SO, which defines the universe of the phenomenon described (e.g., if the name of the SO is "Car production in USA in 1988," the universe will be made up of the number of cars produced in the United States in 1988); c is a finite set of category attributes, each with its own definition domain (the instances of which can be of a set-valued type); each category attribute has a certain number of *modalities* (called "domain cardinality") which corresponds to the number of instances of the domain for that category attribute or for that SO; f is a function which maps from the Cartesian product of the category attributes relative to the SO (or from one of its subsets) to the summary values of the SO itself.

A certain number of parameters can be tied to each SO name; these are the category attributes of the SO which have only one value (e.g., "statistical source," sometimes "place" and/or "period of time," etc.) in the definition domain.

The Storm model defines three representation levels, called, respectively, the "Topics" level ($\mathcal{T}$ level), the "Statistical Objects" ($\mathcal{S}$ level), and the "Base" level ($\mathcal{B}$ level).

Only T-type nodes appear in the first level (T level).

A $\mathcal{T}$ node represents a topic, that is a subject according to which one or more SOs or one or more T nodes are classified or aggregated. The structure, at this level, is that of an oriented, acyclic, connected graph.

This is a "conceptual" level, in the sense that the T nodes (or the S nodes of the underlying level) can be grouped together according to criteria which can vary from designer to designer.

The statistical user can redesign the "view" according to his or her own point of view (which, in any case, will be "personal," similar to a subscheme of a relational DBMS).

All the lower-level T nodes will point toward one or more S nodes.

Three types of nodes (S, A, and C) appear in the second level (S level). The $\mathcal{S}$ node represents all the SO summary attribute values; each S node always has a name (or label).

The eventual parameters, the data source, the data type, and the unit of measure are linked to the name.

The $\mathcal{A}$ node represents the aggregation of the category attributes which describe the above summary attributes; this aggregation is, in fact, the Cartesian product of the instances of the definition domain of each one of the above category attributes. An A node can even not have a name.

The C node represents a category attribute; a definition domain is associated with each C node. Each C node has a name; C nodes belonging to various SOs can have the same name (whereas homonyms in the same SO are not allowed).

Examples of Storm graphs are shown in Figure 9 (T level) and Figure 10.

The root of the tree, which represents an SO is always an S node.

Under the S node there is always an A node which is pointed at it. This A node is, in turn, the root of two or more C nodes. These can point directly at the A node or form a classification hierarchy.

Finally in the third level (B level) only C and A nodes appear.

The C nodes represent the "base" (or primitive) attributes from which all the S-level category attributes are extracted. The definition domains of the latter are included in the (or equal to the) definition domain of the base attributes.

The Storm model resolves the ambiguity in distinguishing between category attributes and the instances of those attributes by introducing, both at S and at B level, two representation spaces. At the S level, such spaces are called Space of the SOs and Space of the Category Attributes Instances (or, simple, Instances Space).

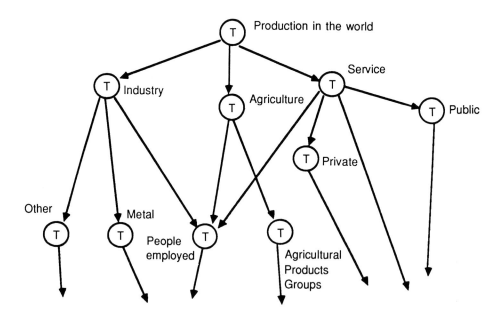

towards S Nodes

FIGURE 9.

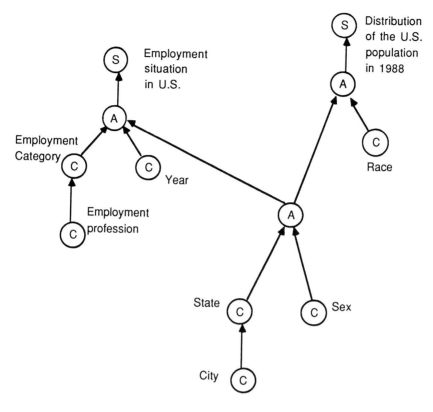

FIGURE 10.

At the B level, such spaces are called, respectively, Base Categories Space (intensional form) and Base Category Instances Space (extensional form).

The solution proposed for the S level is illustrated in Figure 11.

The Storm model resolves other problems which arise in different situations (which are frequent in statistical reality). For instance, it labels the edges when particular dependencies (ID, multivalued, etc) appear in the graph or when different "levels" of classification (the problem of graph "symmetry"), or different "types" of classification (the problem of graph "homogeneity"), or different "units of measure" (the problem of graph "uniformity:), or even any combination of the three above-mentioned cases appear in a statistical object (SO). We will use the term "classification properties" for the above-mentioned conditions of (non)-symmetry, (non)-homogeneity, and (non)-uniformity.

For example, the problem of the nonhomogeneity of an SO arises when the instances of a category attribute are, in turn, different classifications.

For example, the category attribute "Empl. Type" of the table in Figure 12 has as its instances "Secretary," "Scientist," and "Blue-collar Worker." Each of these instances is, in turn, classified with regard to different criteria.

Such criteria can be thought of as category attributes, respectively, "Years experience," "Degree," and "Type," whose instances belong to completely different domains.

In fact, "Years experience" has as its instances "1–3," "4–7," etc., while "Degree" has as its instances "Engineer," "Physician," etc., and "Type" has as its instances "Metal worker," "Plumber," etc.

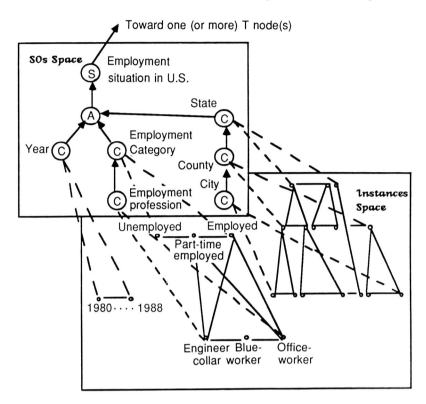

FIGURE 11.

Empl. Type	Secretary	Years Experience	1–3 4–7 ...	. . . .
	Scientist	Degree	Engineer Physician . . .	. . . .
	Blue-collar worker	Type	Metal worker Plumber . . .	. . . .

FIGURE 12.

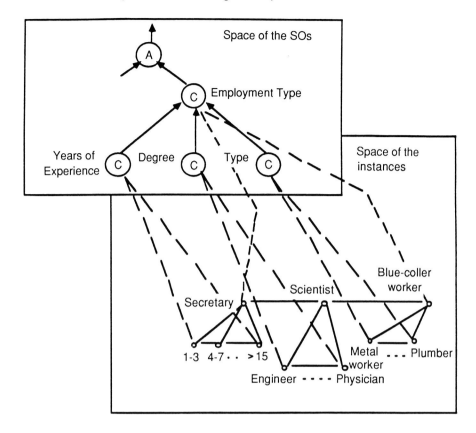

FIGURE 13.

The solution proposed by the Storm model is to represent such a situation, in the space of the SOs, by means of a *partitioning graph*, whose meaning is obvious and whose shape is shown in Figure 13.

Often a change of category attributes occurs with time. For example, the political structure of a region or of a state can change with time. The Storm model resolves the problem in the following way.

If, for example, the two states CA and NE, at time t_0, were formed by the territorial areas identified, respectively, by CA.0 = <CA.1, CA.2, CA.3> and NE.0 = <NE.1, NE.2> and if, at the time t_x a new state NEW_NE has been created, so that CA.0 is transformed into CA.x = <CA.1, CA.2>, NE.0 is transformed into NE.x = <NE.1>, while the new state is defined by NEW_NE = <CA.3, NE.2>, then the change in semantic significance of a category attribute or of an instance is resolved (at S level) by labeling the edge which comes from the C node with a "T" (time) and, at B level (both intensionally and extensionally) as shown in Figure 14.

The situation described can be easily understood by means of the representation of a bipartite graph like the one in Figure 15.

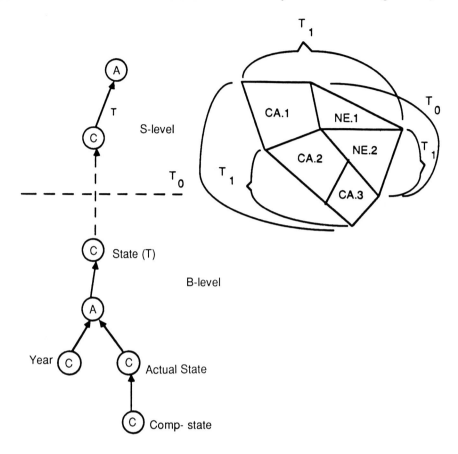

FIGURE 14.

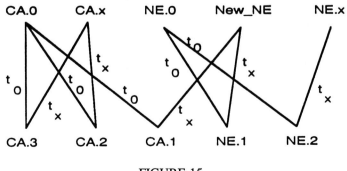

FIGURE 15.

REPRESENTING AND INTERPRETING NULLS IN STATISTICAL TABLES

The presence of scarce data or null values is frequent in the statistical tables. In the case of statistical databases, the refined subdivision made in the theory of null values [*32,33*] is not necessary. In fact, the statisticians basically use only two types of null values: Unknown (or nonavailable) and nonexisting (the latter are often called "structural zero entries" [*34*]). An example of the null value "unknown" arises when in a statistical table only the data relative, for example, to the production of fruit in the United States are reported; if (in this case) the data relative to the state of California for the years "80, 81, 82" are missing, they will be "unknown" (presumably not recorded after a survey and, in any case, not available).

An example of "nonexisting" data, instead, can be found in a statistical table where the data relative to the reports of illness subdivided into illness and sex are illustrated; in this case the missing data regard "cancer of the prostate gland" for "sex = female" or "breast cancer" for "sex = male" (the value will be zero, but it will be a *structural zero*, in that it can never assume a value which is different from zero). In Figures 16 and 17, a simple case of these situations is shown. It should be noted that there is an important difference between the two types of null values, especially with reference to the relative *marginal value* (the total with respect to the category attribute). In particular, in the former (unknown) case the total with respect to the category attribute, for which there are unknown values, is not the total of the attribute itself (in the case of Fig. 16, the total of fruit produced in the U.S. is not the total of the category attribute "state," because only some of the states of the U.S. are listed in the statistical table). In the latter (nonexisting) case, although it is true that, with regard to Figure 17, the total of cancer of the prostate cases in Italy in 1988 is the total reported in the marginal (summarizing with respect to "sex"), in this way, the information that these cases are the total of males alone and not the entire Italian population is lost.

Production of fruit in the US (in tons)	STATE		
	Alabama	California	Nevada
80	1,889	U	785
81	1,977	U	823
YEAR 82	2,099	U	878
83	2,120	34,046	818
88	2,378	36,392	911

FIGURE 16.

Number of people dead of cancer in the U.S.	Site of the Cancer			
	Lung		Breast	Prostate
	Sex		Sex	Sex
	Male	Female	Female	Male
80	1,749	2,285	5,267	12,459
81	1,827	2,411	5,343	12,943
YEAR 82	2,004	2,780	5,421	13,521
...	......	.....	......	.....
88	2,399	4,392	5,501	16,230

FIGURE 17.

OPERATORS, QUERY LANGUAGES, AND USER INTERFACES

In most statistical analyses, the data are organized into tables (flat files), not only in the computer, but also in the analyst's mind. Reports generated also take this form. For this reason, many of the statistical analysis systems accommodate only this form of organization.

Operators must exist at the appropriate level of abstraction for the user so as to spare the user having to program operators in an unnatural manner [35];moreover, other operators are useful to enforce the logical rules of the operation. As has been noted, a data model is characterized by; a data structure and a set of operators capable of manipulating this structure and well defined in their semantics.

Starting, in fact, from the limitations of the relational algebra operators in the case of aggregate data (such as statistical data), a number of authors have tackled the problem. A good review of traditional operators, useful in SSDBs, is made by Shoshani [8]. Researchers have followed two different paths: (a) to extend the relational model (and the algebra on which it is based) to adapt it to the new reality; (b) to study and introduce a new model, that is a new data structure and new operators with their own semantics to manipulate them, which are perfect for this type of reality.

From the former point of view, different proposals have been made. In particular, Johnson [36] defines the query language STRAND which allows the user to formulate queries involving aggregate functions without conceptualizing the query in terms of aggregation. He also introduces the concepts of summary set and category attributes, and the operations of 'summarization' and 'restriction' on summary sets. Furthermore, he adds to the existing model (the Entity Relationship Model), the semantics of the above concepts.

Using the framework of the entity relationship model, an additional type of entity is allowed, called a summary set, which is simply database views, generated by using aggregate functions, and which captures the semantics of category attributes. In addition, an attribute which is designated as a summary attribute, can have an aggregation function (e.g., sum, average) or any other desired function (defined as a program) associated with it.

In the SAM* model [22], as already seen, Su proposes a data structure in which two types of attributes are recognized (category and summary) and in which the relations is a special case of the already mentioned G-relation. The relative algebra is redefined from the relational algebra and established in such a way (by particular conditions of applicability) as to avoid those situations in which the application of an operation would generate data that cannot represent a correlation and, at the same time, when such operations are applied to relations, they behave in a way that is analogous to that of relational algebra operations. We note that, for example, in the projection description there are three conditions of applicability and this fact brings with it a greater difficulty in their use.

In particular, the author introduces both a number of restructuring operations (denoting and promoting operations, aggregation and disaggregation), and relational algebraic operations, redefining the classic operators of projection, selection, join (plus the traditional set operations of union, intersection, difference, and extended Cartesian product) for the G-relation. The redefinition of the operators is carried out in such a way that situations in which the application of an operator leads to data which cannot represent statistical tables are avoided, and at the same time when these operators are applied to the relations, they exhibit a behavior similar to that of relational algebra. It follows that the algebra operators are redefined according to the type of attribute on which they will operate; this requires that in the definition of each operator, applicability conditions are inserted. This fact implies a greater difficulty of use for the users.

Another proposal comes from Ozsoyoglu [37], who puts forward both extended relational algebra (ERA) and relational calculus [38] (an extension of the proposal of Klug [39], and a statistical DBQL) [40,41]. The latter article reviews the proposals made for SQL; in particular, ABE, a screen-oriented language similar to query-by-example is discussed [42]. Elsewhere [37], the passage from the flat representation of the relational model to a representation through tables, called primitive summary tables (PST), with 'forests' of line and column attributes, is obtained by means of two new operators: relation formation and primitive summary table formation. The PST aims to overcome the limitations of the relational model with respect to multidimensionality, by giving a two-dimensional view of the structure; in fact, a PST is described with a formalism, on a logical level, in the way in which a user wishes to see it in output; it must be kept in mind, however, that in the model, two PSTs having the same category attributes, but in which some 'line' attributes are exchanged with the same number of 'column' attributes, are different structures (even though on a logical level, they have the same information content).

By the relation formation, an "information equivalent" relation is obtained from a statistical table; on such a relation it is then possible to apply all the operations of the extended relational algebra. From the PST formation, it is possible to produce a statistical table from relations that satisfied predefined constraints (the functional and embedded join dependencies). The filtering done by such operations allows the removal of the inconsistent data only a posteriori.

In Ozsoyoglu [38], three new operators are also introduced (pack, unpack, and aggregation by template), and a fixed volume of relations $<R_1, \ldots, R_2>$ is considered, on which a set of operations (including those mentioned above) are formally and semantically defined (i.e., restriction, set union, set difference, etc.).

Ghosh [*43,44*], too, proposes both new operators, based on statistical relational tables (SRT) and a new query language (which has some similarities with query by example). In particular, he redefines the projection operator and introduces the 'aggregate' operator for aggregating the macrodata associated with the different cells of the SRT (an operation similar to a union operation).

All these proposals, as already mentioned, refer to the extension of the relational model and to the introduction of some new operators.

Other authors have preferred to follow another path: that of defining ex novo a model and a new algebra. A first proposal was made by Chan [*25*]. In this report, the authors proposed SUBJECT (which we spoke about before). The proposal made in Rafanelli and Ricci [*24*] is also based on the two concepts of 'clustering' and 'cross product'; here the authors propose the GRASS model, and introduce the already mentioned concept of simple statistical table (SST). On such concepts a new algebra for statistical data is proposed by Fortunato [*45*].

In order to schematically represent the elements which constitute such algebra and the way they are connected, we use the graph in Figure 18, where the oriented edge goes from the input data structure to the output data structure, with regard to the operators associated with the edge itself.

The algebra operators can have one or two tables in input, or the 'relation-table' couple; output is generally one table, except for the comparison operator (in which it is a relation).

In particular, with regard to the previous figure, we can give an example of application on a table of the 'summarization' operator.

This operation provides in output a table in which a category attribute of the starting table is deleted and the values of the summary attribute are recomputed. Let us consider the table quantity of fruit production (T_1 of Fig. 19), characterized by "region" and "year" as category attributes; if we wish to have the total quantity of fruit production in the years 1981–1983, that is, a new table in which the production of fruit is divided only by 'region,' we apply the summarization operator rather than the category operator 'years.' All the values (relative to each region) with respect to all the years (which will therefore disappear from the table) will be aggregated automatically. The result of the operation is shown in Figure 20.

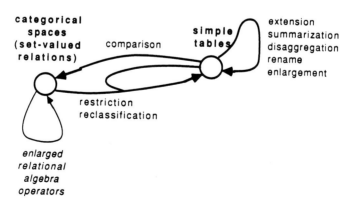

FIGURE 18.

Quantity of fruit produced (in tons)		Year			
		1980	1981	1983	....
	Lazio	127	132	139	....
Region	Piemonte	68	72	71	....
	....	.....	.....	.....	....

FIGURE 19.

A statistical query language (STAQUEL) [46] based on relational algebra was first proposed, followed by its extension toward the user interface aspect, VISTA (visual statistical query language) [47].

The latter is a recent proposal which "immerses" STAQUEL in a multiwindow visual interface, based on the GRASS representation of a table.

The user operates on the graphic representation of the tables to be manipulated by working with the elements constituting the graph, by suppressing variables of the table, by joining tables, and by defining new classification criteria. The interface allows the graphical and interactive definition of the GRASS scheme of the output tables, while the procedures needed for calculation are completely transparent to the user. In addition, dialog procedures have been defined that guide the user in the definition of those commands which require multiple interaction (consider those needed for the definition of a time series). The resulting interface is a multiwindow environment in which the definition and execution of a command can be controlled in various ways, and which allows: the formulation of complex queries starting from simpler queries, the definition of the printer output format using example output templates, and preview or definitive printing of the results.

A good figure that sums up the major issues in the interface between five major system elements (1) the end use (U); (2) data management application (DM); (3) data analysis

Quantity of fruit produced (in tons)		
	Lazio	398
Region	Piemonte	212
	.....	.....

FIGURE 20.

application (DA); (4) machine-computer and end-user peripherals (M); (5) storage disks, db machines, etc. (S) is reported in Cable [*48*] and reproposed in Figure 21.

The only other proposal of a graphical interface is GUIDE [*49*], a graphical user interface for database exploration.

The article describes a system which uses graphics devices as tools to interface to complex data (such as statistical data). The system offers a graphics interface to the user. The database schema is displayed as a network of entity and relationship types. Queries can be expressed as traversal paths on this network. Partial queries (called 'local queries') can be formulated and represented graphically and database retrieval results of any local query are available at any time. Local queries can be linked together to form larger queries and provide the basis for building queries in a piecemeal fashion. Parts of the schema can be selectively made visible or invisible and provide the basis of representing levels of details of the schema [*49*].

PHYSICAL ORGANIZATION OF DATA

The need to compress the data in a SSDB, while permitting fast access, is one of the main problems in this area. There are a large number of known compression techniques varying from coding to intricate text compression; some of these techniques are particularly applicable to SSDBs and are discussed by several authors [*28,50,51*].

Although the SSDBs are usually characterized by having a large content of numerical data, they are usually supported by a great deal of textual metadata [*11,16*]. Different types of compression techniques can therefore be applied to the different types of information.

As Bassionni notes [*51*], "the effectiveness of data compression in any system largely depends on the characteristics of data in that system. For instance, numerical fields tend to have large clusters of zeros or missing data indicators. This sparseness of SSDBs [*28*] is an important property that has a significant impact on the overall compression ratio achieved. integer numbers for many attributes tend to have a distribution over a wide range of values, usually with a skewness toward the lower end. Thus many values can be stored using a smaller number of bytes (or bits) than the maximum length in the distribution."

In this latter work, as in Ref. *52*, an analysis of the most significant compression techniques is made; the particularly significant ones are discussed by others [*53–55*]. The tendency for clustering of null values often occurs within a single column (representing a single summary attribute). This suggests that from a compression point of view, it is advantageous to transpose files (i.e., to store values by attribute, rather than as records or tuples). Another situation arises (as we have already seen) when not every possible combination of the category attributes is valid; i.e., for the combinations that are not valid, the values for all the summary attributes are null. In such a case, the entire entry is missing from the database. This situation is referred to as the "partial cross product."

Is there a way to compress these 'partial cross products'? Replies to this problem, which has not yet been completely resolved, are given by several authors [*54,56,57*].

SECURITY

Security problems in statistical databases arise from the wish to provide statistical information without compromising sensitive information about individuals [*28*].

	end user U	data analysis DA	data management DM	machine M	storage S
U	•Natural Languages	•Statistical Analysis Packages •Exploratory Data Analysis (EDA) •Graphics	•Query languages •Report Generators	•Human Factors •Voice •WIMPS (windows, Icons, Mice, pull–down Menus)	•Security
DA		•Language Standards •File Formats	•Integration (where to draw the line)	•Portability (of data and software) •Device Drivers •Operating Systems	•Optimization
DM			•Distributed Databases	•Ditto (as DA above)	•File Systems •Access Control •Data Structures
M				•Communications Standards	•Database Machines •Communications •Data Capture
S					•Backup/ Archiving •File Transfer

FIGURE 21.

Another way of defining the security is: an SDB is said to be secure if it is impossible to deduce confidential information exclusively from the 'story' (knowledge) of the query accepted.

The problem of security in statistical databases (SDBs) is fundamentally that of limiting the use of the database in such a way that no sequence of statistical queries is sufficient to deduce, directly or indirectly, confidential or private information of an individual type [58–60].

Statistical database security is a difficult problem. It has been demonstrated that simple techniques, such as restricting the number of individuals that qualify in an aggregate query to be above a chosen threshold, do not work. Thus a variety of other techniques were proposed. They include keeping track of previous queries, prepartitioning the data sets into cells whose boundaries cannot be crossed by aggregate queries (this method is most popular for census data), estimating the aggregate values from samples over the data, and perturbing either the input or output values [8,29].

Let us now define the 'compromisability' of a statistical database. An SDB is said to be compromised if the user succeeds, with direct or indirect methods, in violating the privacy of individual values relative to the information (aggregate and/or disaggregate) present in the SDB [61–63]. This compromise can be of two types: positive, if the user succeeds in getting to know the values of a particular datum; negative, if the user succeeds in getting to know that a datum does not have a certain value.

Obviously an SDB is secure if it cannot be compromised either positively or negatively. A good mathematical treatise on the conditions of 'compromisability' of an SDB is given in Ref. *61*.

We can distinguish two types of security control: internal and external. The external security controls regard operations which take place outside the authorized management system, for example, personal screening, limited access to the computer for certain people, fire protection, etc.

The internal security controls regulate the operations of the SDB management system by subdividing it into four areas: access to objects memorized in a file; flow of information from one memorized object to another; deduction of the confidential values memorized in the SDBs; cryptographic code of confidential data memorized in files and transmitted over communication lines. Here are some examples:

In Figure 22 regarding access, Mr. Smith can be allowed to read file X and write on file Y, but he has no access to file Z.

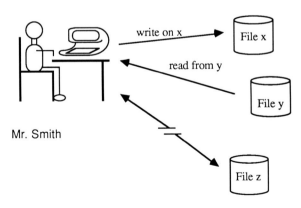

FIGURE 22.

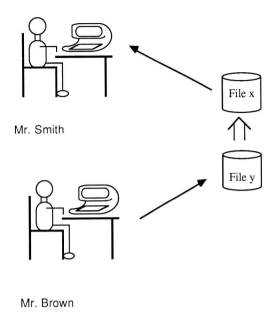

Mr. Smith

Mr. Brown

FIGURE 23.

In Figure 23, as his access is denied to file Y, Mr. Brown teams up with Mr. Smith who makes him a copy; flow control can prevent this.

In Figure 24, an examiner uses previous knowledge to deduce confidential information from a statistical summary; deduction control can prevent this.

In Figure 25, Mr. Smith illegally obtains a copy of file X, but its cryptographic code ensures that the contents remain meaningless to him.

The efficiency of access controls is based on three assumptions. The first is the correct identification of the user; identification based on the use of passwords is simple and widely used, but needs accurate safeguards to prevent code identification [64,65]. Identification schemes based on personal characteristics (voice or even signature recognition) are clearly safer but more expensive. The second assumption is that of denying access to a user who has not been previously introduced. Regular safeguarding makes use of the cryptographic code. The third assumption is that the privileged information is heavily protected. No user program can write in those segments which are heavily protected.

The deduction controls are probably the most complex part of the problem and therefore attract the most attention from researchers.

We can call: $P_c(0)$ the set of 'confidential' propositions of an abstract object 0 defined on a class of C_I individuals (inside a data relation R of an individual database), so that the values of a sublist A_I of attributes satisfy a certain relation R_I; these propositions are therefore the ones of which the user U should not have any knowledge; D(0) the set of queries which can be expressed regarding 0; $D_u(0)$ the set of admissible queries for the user regarding 0.

A "characteristic attribute" is one whose values can appear in a "characteristic formula" [66].

FIGURE 24.

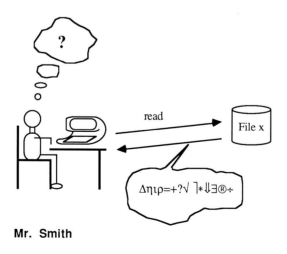

FIGURE 25

A query is called "admissible" (that is, $d \in D(0)$ in P_c (0), if it does not violate the information which the Database Administrator (DBA) has defined as "confidential":

$$d \,/\!\!\to P_c \,(0).$$

We call "logical inference process" of confidential information the following succession of queries

$$(d_1, \ldots, d_s)$$

with $(d_i \in D_\cup (0) \,\forall\, i)$, which allows the violation of the confidentiality of any proposition P_j belonging to set P_c (0).

A general mathematical model of the inference type which can be used to violate the privacy of a SDB is proposed by Beck [67]. Actually the "acceptance query problem" presents a very difficult solution problem, because it should not be based on the analysis of the knowledge produced by the accepted queries only. If a user knows some of the properties characterizing a record, he may obtain the other properties if he also knows whether other hypothetical records exist or not. Briefly we list only a few control methods of the logical inference; more and detailed information can be found in the reports in the bibliography.

These methods can be classified into two basic types (1) methods which act on the admissibility of the query (restrictions); (2) methods which act on the memorized values or on those supplied in answer to the query (perturbations) [59,66,67]; the first type includes all those techniques used to prevent or control whether a query can compromise the SDB; the second type includes the techniques which do not place limitations on the admissibility of the queries, but supply as an answer, modified values, with a reasonably good statistical reliability.

Among the methods which refer to query control, we can quote the following:

(a)   Table restriction techniques [59]
(b)   Order control [68]
(c)   Table size control (S_m/N criterion) [69]
(d)   Explicit risk estimate [68]
(e)   Existence of data exchange (determines transformability) [70]
(f)   Cell restriction techniques
(g)   Query set size control [71–73]
(h)   Implied query control [74]
(i)   Query overlap control [75,76]
(j)   Auditing

A second class of deduction controls is based on the distortion of the replies; some are known as 'Methods of Protection and Output Modification,' for example:

(a)   Cell suppression
(b)   Grouping (or rolling up) [59]
(c)   Partitioning [77,78]
(d)   Table perturbation techniques [79]

others are known as 'record-based perturbations,' for example:

(a)   Random sample queries [*60,68,72,80*]
(b)   Random data perturbation [*60,67,81*]

and others as 'Rounding techniques' in which we can include;

(a)   Systematic rounding and systematic range
(b)   Random rounding and random ranges
(c)   Controlled rounding

and finally the 'cryptographic controls' are also important.

Cryptographic coding (encryption) is a common safeguard for data memorized in DBs (or memorized temporarily, i.e., 'in transit' in the DB), the security of which is not sufficiently guaranteed by other types of control (especially in the above mentioned cases) [*80*].

In traditional cryptographic systems there is a security channel, at a slow transmission speed, by means of which the 'transmitter' can inform the 'receiver' of the key k used to codify the message.

This message, transmitted at a high speed, is as secure as the key is secret. The technique is called [*82*] symmetrical cryptography, since the same key is used at the two ends of the channel. The code is violated if an 'intruder' can deduce the key by analyzing the cryptographic texts.

The key is usually changed with a certain regularity so that the time interval is less than the time necessary for the cleverest intruder to identify the key itself.

EXPERT SYSTEMS ON SSDBS

Before discussing the impact of expert systems on statistical database management, it is necessary to give some brief informal definitions. First of all, we can identify a subclass of general computer systems, called knowledge-based systems.

A knowledge base consists of highly structured symbolic data representing a model of the relationships between data elements and their uses. Thus a knowledge-based system contains a discernible knowledge structure and the mechanism for its application. A particular subgroup of knowledge-based systems is the field of expert systems. A prerequisite for an expert system is a domain of activity in which there exist human experts. The knowledge base of an expert system is designed to capture the expertise of its human counterpart [*83a*].

The expert system, in order to emulate a decisional process, needs three kinds of information:

(a)   Regarding the domain of application
(b)   Regarding the method of identification and use of the information necessary to resolve the problem
(c)   Regarding the problem examined

An expert system is formed from three components:

(a)   The long-term knowledge base which is constituted by the concepts and specific rules of the field of application
(b)   A general algorithm, the inferential motor, which is the implementation of the method of reasoning

(c) The short term knowledge base (facts base) constituted by the information, that is, the facts on the individual case

The expert system works as follows: the motor starts from hypotheses or from initial facts (present in the short-term knowledge base) and, manipulating the concepts and the fragments of knowledge (making up the long-term knowledge base) decides which new facts to acquire through conversation with the user or through deduction, and values the credibility of the single hypotheses, giving a "certainty factor" for each hypothesis.

The interest of statistics toward expert systems, and more generally toward the techniques of artificial intelligence, derives from the opportunity which these techniques offer for the study of data analysis strategies, to be understood as a structured and integrated system of techniques for the description and the treatment of data and the interpretation of results.

From a brief analysis of the existing literature we can identify three major statistical areas in which expert system applications are found:

STUDENT [*83b*] is an expert system designed to help the user choose and apply a technique and to allow the construction and the use of knowledge-based consultation systems applied in data analysis techniques and to acquire 'by examples' strategies of analysis, to be carried out by interfacing with other systems. This system uses the S language and is used as an interface with statistical programs.

MUSE (MUltivariate Statistical Expertise) [*84*] is an expert system designed to be used in an industrial environment, which is proposed as a system of aid for the choice of statistical methods which are most suited to determine sets of data, in order to carry out statistical programs and interpret the results.

ADONIA [*85*] is an expert system of assistance for management of data analysis. The system uses an already existing library of statistical programs written in FORTRAN and is founded on a knowledge base which includes the methods of use of the analysis programs and the explanation of the results. The basic idea of ADONIA is the distinction between 'local' knowledge of the data and the phenomenon and the knowledge of techniques of analysis: in this way the system is presented as a 'supervisor' for the use of data analysis techniques.

Expert Systems in Inferential Statistics

The other major field of application of expert systems is inferential statistics, which is based on the a priori assumption of statistical models, relative to the data structure.

Among the expert systems which are included in this type of application is the REX system (Regression EXpert) proposed by Pregibon and Gale [*86,87*] for the analysis of regression.

The system guides the analysis, testing the regression assumptions, suggesting the appropriate transformations, if these assumptions are not respected, and justifying the suggestions given. Furthermore, it helps the user in the interpretation of the intermediate and final results. The STUDENT expert system, as we have seen, is derived from REX.

EXPRESS (EXPert system Relying on Existing Statistical Software) [*88*], is another expert system which aims to integrate the calculation potential of known statistical packages with the statistical capacity of evaluate, according to a stepwise procedure, the results of the analysis before moving on to the subsequent applications.

STAT 1 and the subsequently improved STAT 2 [*89*] are expert systems in which the main aim is to help researchers in the field of social sciences who are not experts in the statistical field, to choose suitable statistical methods of analysis, even simple ones, as hypotheses tests, correlation measures, etc.

Another system, which is difficult to fit in either of the two previous classes, is ESTES (Expert System for Time Series), proposed by P. Hietala [90]. This expert system is designed to help the user in the analysis of time series. The system is a guide for a user who is not an expert in statistics and time series analysis for the identification of a number of essential properties of the time series: trend, seasonality, level of movement, outliers. The system is characterized by the fact that it can analyze data and give instructions, without assuming any decision, leaving the user the task of choosing from possible alternatives indicated.

Other experimental systems include STATPATH [91], GLIMPSE [92], CLAVECIN [93], and PANOS [94]. These all concentrate on providing the user with advice on an appropriate analysis model or hypothesis test. Some of them, like GLIMPSE, are linked to analysis packages while others are freestanding components with no direct links to the statistical database. Most of the above systems were constructed using techniques that have become standard in building expert systems. Rules and heuristics are taken from textbooks and incorporated into a knowledge base as production rules or frames. This is combined with a standard shell to handle the control strategy (backward or forward reasoning) and a natural language interface to communicate with both experts and users [83a].

TEMPORAL DATA

Temporal data, often representing a collection of information over time [95], are vitally important for SSDBs. The time element of measurement data can usually be modeled as another dimension in the multidimensional space which is formed by other parameters. This is true especially if regular measurements are taken over time. Dealing with temporal data becomes especially difficult when events occur in discrete but irregular sequences, such as the breakdown or replacement of detectors. The other problem is that different data sets may vary at different rates, and even worse, the rate for the same commodity can vary of different time intervals and from country to country. During the data analysis process, it is necessary to correlate both kinds of measurements, as Shoshani declares [8]:

> In general, modeling temporal data requires the integration of static data, data that change in regular intervals, and data that appear as irregular discrete events. From a logical point of view it is necessary to model the various types of temporal data, so that their semantics are clear to the user. It is also necessary to provide query facilities that permit users to specify conditions in the time dimension, as well as correlate data that may be varying at different rates.

CONCLUSIONS

The area of statistical and scientific databases represents a stimulating field of research, but there are still many problems to be resolved (both theoretical, and from the point of view of the builders and especially of the user). A reference point on the state of research in the area is represented by the Proceedings of the Congress on SSDBs which is held every two years [1–4].

REFERENCES

1. *Proc. 1st Int. Workshop on Statistical Database Management,* Menlo Park, CA, 1981.
2. *Proc. 2nd Int. Workshop on Statistical and Scientific Database Management*, Los Altos, CA, September 1983.
3. *Proc. 3rd Int. Workshop on Statistical and Scientific Database Management*, Luxembourg, July 1986.
4. M. Rafanelli, J.C. Klensin, and P. Svensson (eds.), *Statistical and Scientific Database Management, Lecture Notes in Computer Science*, Springer Verlag, New York, 1989.
5. H.K.T. Wong, "Statistical Database Management," *ACM–SIGMOD* (1982).
6. H.K.T. Wong, "Micro and Macro Statistical/Scientific Database Management," *First Int. Conf. Data Engineering*, Los Angeles, March 1984.
7. A. Shoshani, F. Olken, and H.K.T. Wong, "Characteristics of Scientific Databases," *Proc. Tenth Int. Conf. Very Large Data Bases*, Singapore, August 1984.
8. A. Shoshani, and H.K.T. Wong, "Statistical and Scientific Database Issues," *IEEE Trans. Software Eng., SE*–11, (10) (1985).
9. A. Shoshani, F. Olken, and H.K.T. Wong, "Data Management Perspective of Scientific Data," in *"The Role of Data in Scientific Progress"* (P.S.Glaeser, ed.), Elsevier B.V., Amsterdam, 1985.
10. D. E. Denning, W. Nicholson, G. Sande, and A. Shoshani, "Research Topics in Statistical Database Management," *Bull. IEEE Computer Soc. Tech. Comm. Database Eng., 7* (1) (1984).
11. J. McCarthy, "Metadata Management for Large Statistical Databases," *Proc. 7th Int. Conf. VLDB*, Mexico, Sept. 1982.
12. P. Chen, "The Entity-Relationship Model em Toward a Unified View of Data," *ACM Trans Database Sys., 1* (1) (1976).
13. E.F. Codd, "A Relational Model of Data for Large Shared Data Banks," *Comm. ADM, 13*, (6) (1970).
14. H. Samet, "The Quadtree and Related Heirarchical Data Structures," *ACM Comput. Surv., 16* (2) (1984).
15. S.P. Ghosh, "Statistics Metadata," in *Kotz-Johnson Encyclopedia of Statistical Science,* Vol. 8, John Wiley & Sons, New York, 1988.
16. Y.M. Bishop, and S.R. Freedman, "Classification of Metadata," in *Proc. 2nd Int. Workshop in Statistical Database Management.*
17. R.T. Lundy, "Metadata Management," *IEEE Computer Soc. Tech. Comm., 7* (1) (1984).
18. S. Heiler and T. Maness, "Connecting Heterogeneous Systems and Data Sources," *Bull. IEEE Computer Soc. Tech. Comm., 7* (1) (1984).
19. F.M. Malvestuto, M. Rafanelli, and C. Zuffada "Many-Source Databases: Some Problems and Solution," Tech. Report of IASI-CNR, R.218, June 1988.
20. F.M. Malvestuto, and C. Zuffada "The Classification Problem with Semantically Heterogeneous Data," *Proc. IV Int. Work. Conf. on SSDBM, Lecture Notes in Computer Science,* Springer Verlag, New York (in press).
21. C. Riano and D. Rotem, "Data Models for Statistical and Scientific Database Management," *Statis. Software News., 13* (1) (1987).
22. S.Y.W. Su, "SAM*: A Semantic Association Model for Corporate and Scientific-Statistical Databases," *Inform. Sci., 29* (2–3) (1983).

23. Di Battista, and C. Batini, "Design of Statistical Databases: A Methodology for the Conceptual Step," *Inform. Sys., 13* (4) (1988).

24. M. Rafanelli, and F.L. Ricci, "Proposal of a Logical Model for Statistical Database," in *Proc. 2nd int. Workshop on SDBM*.

25. P. Chan, and A. Shoshani, "SUBJECT: A Directory Driven System for Organizing and Accessing Large Statistical Databases," *Proc. 7th Int. Conf. on Very Large Data Bases,* Cannes, France, Sept. 1981.

26. G. Hebrail, "A Model of Summaries for Very Large Databases," *Proc. 3rd Int. Workshop on SDBM,* 1983.

27. A. Tansel and M. Arkun, "HQUEL, A Query Language for Historical Relational Databases," *Ref. 3.*

28. A. Shoshani, "Statistical Databases: Characteristics, Problems and Solutions," *Proc. 8th int. Conf. VLDB,* Mexico, Sept. 1982.

29. M. Rafanelli, "A Management System for Statistical Database," in *The Role of Data in Scientific Progress* (P.S. Glaeser, ed.), Elsevier, (North Holland), Amsterdam, 1985.

30. M. Rafanelli and F.L. Ricci, "A Statistical Functional Model for Statistical Tables," *Proc. Int. Symp. Modelling, Identification and Control*, Acta Press, Grindelwalk, Switzerland, 1988.

31. M. Rafanelli, and A. Shoshani, "STORM: A Statistical Object Representation Model," Tech. Rep. L.B.L., University of California (in press).

32. "ANSI/X3/SPARC Study Group on Data Base Management Systems Interim Report 75–02–08," *EDT-Bull. ACM SIGMOD, 7,* 2 (1975).

33. Y. Vassiliou, "Functional Dependencies and Incomplete Information," *Proc. 6th Int. Conf. Very Large Data Bases,* Montreal, 1980.

34. Y.M.M. Bishop, "Discrete Multivariate Analysis,' MIT Press, Boston, 1984.

35. J.E. Gentle and J. Bell, "Special-Data Types and Operators for Statistical Data," *Bull IEEE Computer Soc. Tech. Comm. 7* (1) (1984).

36. R.R. Johnson, "Modeling Summary Data," *Proc. ACM-SIGMOD, Int. Conf. Managing Data,* Ann Arbor, MI, April 1981.

37. G. Ozsoyoglu, and Z.M. Ozsoyoglu, "An Extension of Relational Algebra for Summary Tables," in *Proc. 2nd Int. Workshop on SDBM*.

38. G. Ozsoyglu, Z.M. Ozsyoglu, and V. Matos, "Extending Relational Algebra and Relational Calculus with Set-Valued Attributes and Aggregate Functions" *ACM Trans. Database Sys., 12* (4) (1987).

39. A. Klug, "Access Paths in the ABE Statistical Query Facility," *Proc. ADM-SIGMOD, Int. Conf. Managing Data,* Orlando, FL, June 1982.

40. Z.M. Ozsoyoglu, and G. Ozsoyoglu "STBE: A Database Query Language for Manipulating Summary Data," *Proc. IEEE COMPDEC Conf.,* Chicago, Nov. 1984.

41. G. Ozsoyoglu, and Z.M. Ozsoyoglu, "Statistical Database Query Language," *IEEE Trans. Software Eng., SE-11* (1a) (1985).

42. A. Klug, "ABE —A Query Language for Construction Aggregate-by Example," in *Proc. 1st Int. Workshop on SDBM*.

43. S.P. Ghosh, "Statistical Relational Table for Statistical Database Management," *IEEE Trans. Software Eng., SE-12* (12) (1986).

44. S.P. Ghosh, "Category Numerical Relational Operations for Statistical Database Management," Research Report IBM RJ 5780 (November 1987).

45. E. Fortunato, M. Rafanelli, F.L. Ricci, and A. Sevastio, "An Algebra for Statistical Data," *Proc. 3rd Int. Workshop in Statistical and Scientific Database Management.*

46. M. Rafanelli, "Security in Statistical Databases" (in Italian),Tech. Rep. IASI-CNR, RI.35, Feb. 1985.
47. L. Meo Evoli, M. Rafanelli, and F.L. Ricci, "Visual Interface for Queries on Statistical Databases," *Proc. 8th Symp. Computational Statistics* (short paper), COMPSTAT '88, Physica Verlag, Copenhagen, 1988.
48. D. Cable, "Interface Issues," *Stat. Software News., 13* (1) (1987).
49. H.K.T. Wong, and I. Kuo "A Graphical User Interface for Database Exploration," *Proc. 8th Int. Conf. VLDB*, Mexico, Sept. 1982.
50. D. Batory, "Physical Storage and Implementation Issues," *IEEE Computer Soc. Bull. Database Eng., 7* (7) (1984).
51. M.A. Bassiouni, "Data Compression in Scientific and Statistical Database," *IEEE Trans. Software Eng., SE-11* (10) (1985).
52. H. Reghbati, "An Overview of Data Compression Techniques," *Computer, 14 (4) (1981).*
53. D. Batory, "Index Coding: A Compression Technique for Large Statistical Databases," in *Proc. 2nd Int. Workshop on Statistical Database Management.*
54. S. Eggers, F. Olken, and A. Shoshani, "A Compression Technique for Large Statistical Database," *in Proc. 7th Int. Conf. on Very Large Data Bases,* Cannes, France, Sept. 1981.
55. K. Hazboun and M. Bassiouni, "A Multi-group Technique for Data Compression," *Proc. ACM SIGMOD Int. Conf. Management of Data,* 1982.
56. P. Svensson, "On Search Performance for Conjunctive Queries in Compressed, Fully Transposed Ordered Files," in *Proc. Int. Conf. Very Large Databases,* 1987.
57. P. Svensson, "Database Management Systems for Statistical and Scientific Applications: Are Commercially Available DBMS Good Enough?" in Ref. *4.*
58. F.Y. Chin, "Security in Statistical Databases for Queries with Small Counts," *ACM Trans. Database Sys., 3* (1) (1978).
59. D.E. Denning "A Security Model for Statistical Database," Computer Sciences Department, Purdue University, West Lafayette, IN, 1983.
60. J. Schlorer, "Query Based Output Perturbations to Protect Statistical Databases," Klinische Dokumentation, University of Ulm, Ulm, West Germany. Oct. 1982.
61. Z. Michalevicz, "Compromisability of a Statistical Database," *Inform. Sys., 6* (4) (1981).
62. F.Y. Chin, and G. Ozsoyoglu, "Statistical Database Design," *ACM Trans. Database Sys., 6,*(1), (1981).
63. G. Ozsoyoglu, and F.Y. Chin, "Enhancing the Security of Statistical Databases with a Question-Answering System and a Kernel Design," *IEEE Trans. Software Eng., SE-8* (3), (1982).
64. R.S. Gaines, and N.Z. Shapiro "Some Principles and Their Application to Computer Security," *Foundations of Secure Computation*, Academic Press, New York, 1978.
65. J.H. Saltzer, and M.D. Schroeder, "The Protection of Information in Computer Systems," *Proc. IEEE, 63* (9), (1975).
66. J. Schlorer "Insecurity of Set Controls for Statistical Databases," *Inform. Proc. Lett., 18* (1984).
67a. J. Schlorer, and D.E. Denning "Protection Query Bases Statistical Output in Multipurpose Database Systems," *Proc. IFIP 1st Sec. Conf.,* North Holland, Amsterdam, 1983.
67b. L.L. Beck, "A Security Mechanism for Statistical Databases," *ACM Trans. Database Sys., 5* (3) (1980).

68. D.E. Denning, J. Schlorer, and E. Wehrle "Memoryless Inference Controls for Statistical Databases," Computer Sciences Department, Purdue University, West Lafayette, IN, 1982.

69. H. Block, and L. Olsson, "Bakvagsidentifiering, *"Statistik Tidsrift, 14* (1976).

70. S.P. Reiss, "Practical Data-Swapping: The First Steps," *Proc. 1980 Symp. Security Privacy,* April 1980.

71. D.E. Denning, P.J. Denning, and M.D. Schwartz, "The Tracker: A Threat to Statistical Database Security," *ACM Trans. Database Sys., 4* (1) (1979).

72. D.E. Denning, "Secure Statistical Database Under Random Sampling Queries," *ACM Trans. Database Sys., 5* (8) (1980).

73. J. Schlorer, "Disclosure from Statistical Databases: Quantitative Aspect of Trackers," *ACM Trans. Database Sys., 5* (4) (1980).

74. A.D. Friedman, L.J. Hoffman, "Towards a Fail-Safe Approach to Secure Databases," *Proc. 1980 Symp. Security and Privacy,* April 1980.

75. R.A. De Millo, D. Dobkin, and J. Lipton, "Even Database That Lie Can Be Compromised," *IEEE Trans. Software Eng., SE-4* (4) (1978).

76. D. Dobkin, A.K. Jones, and R.J. Lipton, "Secure >Databases: Protection Against User Influence," *ACM Trans. Database Sys., 4* (1) (1979).

77. C.T. Yu, and F.Y. Chin "A Study on the Protection of Statistical Databases," *Proc. ACM Sigmod Int. Conf. Management of Data,* 1977.

78. F.Y. Chin, and G. Ozsoyoglu, "Security in Partitioned Dynamic Statistical Databases," *Proc. IEEE Compsac,* 1979.

79. R. Conway, and D. Strip "Selective Partial Access to a Database," *Proc. ACM Annual Conf.,* 1976.

80. D.E. Denning, "*Cryptography and Data Security*, Addison–Wesley, Reading, MA, 1982.

81. D.E. Denning, and J. Schlorer "Inference Control for Statistical Databases," *IEEE Computer, 16* (17) (1983).

82. G.J. Simmons, "Symmetric and Asymmetric Encryption," *Comp. Surveys, 11* (4), (1979).

83a. A. Elliman, and K. Wittowski, "The Impact of Expert Systems on Statistical Database Management," *Statist. Software News., 13* (1) (1987).

83b. D. Pregibon, and Gale W. "REX: An Expert System for Regression Analysis," in *Proc. COMPSTAT* 84, Physica-Verlag, Heidelberg Wien, 1984.

84. E. Dambroise, and P. Massotte, "MUSE: An Expert System in Statistics," *Proc. COMPSTAT* 86, Physica-Verlag, Heidelberg Wien, 1986.

85. P. Malvache, and S. Reissian "ADONIA: un systeme expert d'aide a la conduite d'une alayse de donnees, in *Les systemes experts & leur applications,* 6èmes journées internationales Avignone, 1986.

86. W.A. Gale, and D. Pregibon, "An Expert System for Regression Analysis," *Proceedings of the 14th Symposium on the Interface,* (Heiner, Shcer, Wilkinson, Eds.), Springer-Verlag, New York, 1982.

87. W.A. Gale, "Student Phase 1—A Report on Work in Progress," in *Artificial Intelligence & Statistics, (Gale W.A., Ed.),* Addison-Wesley, Princeton, 1986.

88. F. Carlsen, and I. Heuch, "EXPRESS— An Expert System Utilizing Standard Statistical Packages," in *Proc. COMPSTAT 86,* Physica-Verlag, Heidelberg Wien, 1986.

89. D.J. Hand, "The Application of Expert Systems in Statistics," in *Interactions in Artificial Intelligence and Statistical Methods"* (Phelps, B. ed.), Gower Technical Press, Aldershot, 1987.

90. P. Hietala, "How to Assist an Inexperienced User in the Preliminary Analysis of Time Series; First Version of the ESTES Expert System," in *Proc. of COMPSTAT* 86, Physica-Verlag, Heidelberg Wien, 1986.

91. K.M. Porter, and P.Y. Lai, "A Statistical Expert System for Analysis Determination," Proc. ASA Statistical Computing Section, 1983.

92. J.A. Nelder and D. Westenholm, "An Expert System for GLIM," in *Statistical Expert Systems* (R. Haux, Ed.) Fisher, Stuttgart, 1986.

93. E. Demonchaux, J. Quinqueton, and H. Ralombondrainy, "CLAVECIN: Un System-Expert en Analyze des Connes," INRIA N.431, Rocquencourt, France, July 1985.

94. K.M. Wittkowski "Generating and Testing Statistical Hypotheses: Strategies for Knowledge Engineering," in *Statistical Expert Systems* (R. Haux, Ed.), Fisher, Stuttgart, 1986.

95. A. Segev, and A. Shoshani, "The Representation of a Temporal Data Model in the Relational Environment," in Ref. *4.*

MAURIZIO RAFANELLI

VISUAL THINKING

INTRODUCTION: VISUAL THINKING IN COMPUTING

Its ability to deal with visual information is one of the mind's most powerful capacities. Visual thinking, high-level manipulation of visual information, is important to computer science because, with the flowering of computer graphics and image processing, it provides the basis for a rich and intuitively satisfying channel of man–machine interaction. Just as writing evolved to help the verbal mind, so various media have evolved to help the visual mind. Computer graphics is potentially the most powerful of these visual media.

However, in considering visual thinking in relation to computer science, we face a problem. Consider, for example, the icon-based desktop metaphor for graphically organizing the man–machine interface. We know that it provides a very effective style of man–machine interaction. While we have experimental techniques that allow us to explore aspects of that effectiveness, we are a long way from having a theory of human visual thinking that we can use exactly and deeply to understand how and why that interface works. There is a large conceptual gap between what we understand about visual thinking and what, out of practical necessity, we need to do in order to develop more effective ways of interacting with the computer. This doesn't mean that, in thinking about the creation of graphics interfaces, we must do so without intellectual guidance. It does mean, however, we are going to have to accept some relatively informal and speculative thinking.

THE METHOD OF LOCI

The *locus classicus* for any discussion of visual thinking is the method of loci, a technique for aiding memory invented by Greek rhetoricians and which, over a course of centuries, served as the starting point for a great deal of speculation and practical elaboration—an intellectual tradition which has been admirably examined by Frances Yates [1]. The idea is simple. Choose some fairly elaborate building, a temple was usually suggested, and walk through it several times along a set path, memorizing what you see at various fixed points on the path. These points are the loci which are the key to the method. Once you have this path firmly in mind so that you can call it up at will, you are ready to use it as a memory aid. If, for example, you want to deliver a speech from memory, you conduct an imaginary walk through your temple. At the first locus you create a vivid image which is related to the first point in your speech and then you store that image at the locus. You repeat the process for each successive point in the speech until all of the points have been stored away in the loci on the path through the temple. Then, when you give your speech you simply start off on the imaginary path, retrieving your ideas from each locus in turn. The technique could also be used for memorizing a speech word for word. In this case, instead of storing ideas at a loci, one stores individual words.

The method of loci has become a central part of our "memory improvement" lore. Further, the effectiveness of this technique has been verified in psychological laboratories.

According to Ulric Neisser [2], a cognitive psychologist, it works even for people who deny that they have mental images.

Although we know that the technique works, we don't know why or how it works, so it is with the desktop metaphor for the man–machine interface, so it will be for future computational extensions of our capacity for visual thinking. Our capacity to invent is beyond our capacity to understand our inventions.

UNDERSTANDING MOLECULAR STRUCTURE: THE WORK OF IRVING GEIS

Notice that, while the method of loci employs visual thinking, it is not fundamentally a technique for thinking about visual objects. As an example of thinking in a visual domain, consider the work of Irving Geis [3], a scientific illustrator who during the past thirty years of his career created illustrations of large biomolecules. Geis's earliest illustrations along this line appeared in a 1961 *Scientific American* article written by Sir John Kendrew, the Nobel Laureate who worked out the molecular structure of myoglobin.

Geis's task is to create paintings or drawings of these large molecules, which have many constituent parts—myoglobin, for example, had about 2500 atoms—whose configuration must be accurately depicted. In a very few cases, Geis works from a three-dimensional model (as he did when working on myoglobin), but in most cases he starts with (computer-generated) stereo pairs.

In a personal interview, Geis indicated that, in studying a molecule's structure, he uses an exercise derived from his training as an architect. Instead of taking an imaginary walk through a building, the architectural exercise, he takes an imaginary walk through the molecule. This allows him to visualize the molecule from many points of view and to develop a kinesthetic sense, in addition to a visual sense, of the molecule's structure. Geis finds this kinesthetic sense so important that he has entertained the idea of building a model molecule large enough that people could enter it and move around, thereby gaining insight into its structure. Geis has pointed out that biochemists, as well as illustrators, must adapt this kind of thinking. To understand the functional structure of a molecule, biochemists will imagine various sight lines through the image they are examining. If they have a three-dimensional image on a cathode ray tube (CRT), they can direct the computer to display the molecule form various orientations. It is not enough to understand the molecule's shape from one point of view. In order intuitively to understand its three-dimensional shape one must be able to visualize the molecule from several points of view.

There is a strong general resemblance between Geis's molecular walk and the method of loci. In both cases we have not only visual space, but motoric space as well. The rhetorician takes an imaginary walk through an imaginary temple; Geis treats the molecule as though it were an environment and imagines how it would be to walk through that environment. The strong resemblance between these two examples suggests that they call upon the same basic cognitive capacity.

In his discussion of the method of loci, Ulric Neisser suggests that it is derived from the schemas used for navigating in the world. The rhetorician uses these navigational schemas as a tool for indexing the points in a speech; Geis uses them to explore the complex structure of large molecules. To use an analogy from computer science, it is as though Geis took a program for navigation and applied it to data derived, not from the immediate physical environment, but from molecular biology. Similarly, the rhetorician applies the program to the points of a speech he or she wishes to memorize. The program is the same in all three cases. Only the data on which the program operates is different.

Before we can make imaginary walks through molecular structures, however, it is necessary also to create basic conventions for visualizing molecules. There is no way of directly illuminating these molecules with visible light and thereby observing them; the wavelengths of visible light are too large to usefully interact with the molecules to produce an image. A common convention is to treat the atoms as balls and the interatomic bonds as sticks. This convention, often adopted in constructing mechanical models, is one which Geis has used often. What is important is the fact that this mode of depiction *is a convention.*

Furthermore, various conventions can be used for various purposes. In order to elucidate the functional structure of these molecules, it is sometimes necessary to adopt conventions which simplify the image in a way that calls attention to molecular function. That is, an image which shows all of the atoms and all of the bonds may be too complex to show clearly how the molecule's structure enables it to function.

Let us return to Geis's work on myoglobin. Myoglobin binds oxygen molecules in the muscles. It is difficult to see just how this is achieved if the image shows all 2500 atoms, including the lone oxygen molecule at the center. In 1968, Geis had the idea of simplifying the image by putting an imaginary tube around the main chain of the myoglobin molecule and then depicting only that tube, and not the atoms within it. This simplified the myoglobin image in the same way that wrapping a tree with fabric would simplify the shape of the tree. The effect is to emphasize the functional structure of the myoglobin molecule, to make it easier to see and analyze the folding which allows the molecule to capture and to hold an oxygen molecule.

Just as we do not understand how the method of loci works, so we do not understand the psychological mechanisms by which visualization conventions are created. But an examination of art history can give us some clues about the nature of the conventions which have been invented for the depiction of our ordinary visual world, where, it turns out, visualization conventions are as necessary as they are for the invisible world of macromolecules.

VISUAL THINKING IN ART

Sir Ernst Gombrich [4,5] has been interested in the techniques and conventions by which Western artists have constructed realistic images. Contrary to what many, including the artists themselves, have thought, artists don't simply paint what they see. Rather, artists have had to invent representational conventions for constructing realistic images.

One of Gombrich's most amusing examples concerns the depiction of the rhinoceros. In 1515, Albrecht Dürer, the famous printmaker, created an image of a rhinoceros which showed it to be covered with armorlike plates—a feature not present in any real rhinoceros. In 1790, one James Bruce published a drawing of a rhinoceros, drawn from life, which he said corrected many mistakes present in Dürer's rendition. But this drawing clearly depicted armorlike plates. It may have been drawn from life, but Gombrich points out, the influence of Dürer's image was so powerful that it was able, in some ways, to triumph over observation. It is as though the representational conventions in Dürer's image were a conceptual device through which other artists understood and interpreted the rhinoceros.

The techniques of perspective drawing provide a more general example of such representational conventions. We are so used to coherent pictorial perspective that we tacitly assume that artists create such images simply because that is what they see when they set out to paint a scene. However, Greek, Roman, and Medieval artists could not manage coherent perspective. Those techniques developed only during the Renaissance. But, once those techniques had been developed, they were codified and became part of the culture's artistic lore.

Examining a wide variety of paintings and drawings, Gombrich has analyzed many such conventions. He argues that these conventions of realistic rendering indicate that the mind apprehends and interprets the world through mental objects which he calls schemas. These schemas are tuned to various kinds of visual relationships, relationships between lines, forms, and colors. The various representational conventions work because they allow the artist to create images which preserve the visual relationships which are captured in these schemas. Thus, for example, the conventions of perspective rendering work because they capture visual relationships important to our schemas for depth perception.

There is an important difference between the conventions of pictorial representation and mental schemas for visual representation. We can imagine that the visual schemas exist only in the visual system. But conventions for pictorial representation must be executed by the motor system. The artist holds the pencil, the pen, or the brush in his hand and moves it over the drawing surface. Not only must these conventions satisfy visual schemas, they must also be such that the motor system can execute them. The motor program through which a convention is realized is, in effect, a motoric reconstruction of the visual schema satisfied by the convention.

This relationship between the motor system and the visual system is not something which Gombrich discusses, but it is clearly important to the thinking process involved in creating a drawing or a painting. Somehow there must be a way of deriving a plan for motoric action from the visual schemas which represent a scene. The general point is that, just as the method of loci involves visual and motor interaction, so does the creation of images. Visual thinking is not simply a matter of what the eye sees. It also involves how the body and the hand move in visual space.

A SPECULATIVE PROPOSAL

Given that visual thinking has a motor component, I offer the following speculative proposal: visual thinking involves the internalization of visuomanipulative activity and of movement through the environment. We move through the physical environment, sometimes in a familiar place, sometimes in a strange place; we handle objects, sometimes to accomplish a specific task, sometimes simply to inspect the object. Visual thinking involves imagined locomotion in imagined settings, imagined manipulation of imagined objects. The settings and objects may be real, but not present, or they may exist only in imagination. In defining visual thinking in this way I am aligning myself with an approach to thinking which derives from Lev Semenovich Vygotsky's [6] seminal analysis of the relationship between thought and language.

Vygotsky was a developmental psychologist who argued that thinking involves the use of inner speech to control mental activity. To simplify matters a great deal, he investigated a developmental sequence which goes like this: (1) First, the young child is subject to speech from adults, who use it to direct the child's activity, pointing out things to see, telling the child what to do. (2) As the child learns to speak, he or she learns to direct his or her own activity by talking, aloud, to himself or herself. (3) After a while, external speech becomes unnecessary. Inner speech is stable enough so that the child can use it to direct action and perception. This inner speech is the stuff of thought.

What is important about Vygotsky's account is that it involves the internalization of an external action. External speech required physical activity, moving the vocal musculature, which has physical effects, the propagation of sound waves. These sound waves reach the ear where they are detected by the auditory apparatus and decoded. Vygotsky's theory (and the observations behind it) clearly implies that, at one stage in the child's development, the brain is using an external communication channel—the propagation of sound from mouth to ear—to manage its operations. After a while, however, it becomes possible to communicate the same information through an internal channel. External speech has become internalized.

In order to construct a similar account of visual thinking we can turn to the work of Ulric Neisser [2]. In common with many psychologists, Neisser believes that perception is an active process. The mind does not passively accept the impress of external stimuli as a wax tablet accepts the impress of a stylus. Rather, the mind actively structures sensory input. This process involves a *perceptual cycle* in which internal *schemas* representing objects direct exploration of the environment for information about objects. The information thus obtained is being continuously used to guide further exploration of the environment.

Images are said to exist when the perceptual cycle is activated with schemas for which no external objects are available. Thus, one may be looking for one's gloves. The "gloves" schema is activated, but the gloves aren't visible. In this situation one has an image of the glove. But, for Neisser, this image is not so much a picture in one's head as it is perceptual preparation to see and recognize the gloves whenever and wherever the environment makes them available. Both the perception of an object and the mental image of that object are grounded in the perceptual cycle; both arise through the activation of the mental schema for that object.

For Neisser, what needs to be explained about mental images is how they get detached from immediate perceptual activity. That is, how do we activate schemas in a context where there is no external support for them (that is, no external objects corresponding to the activated schemas)? One possibility, Neisser suggests, is locomotion. Perception is rapid, but locomotion is relatively slow. Consequently, as we move about in a familiar environment we are constantly anticipating things which we cannot yet see. This anticipation entails the activation of schemas in the absence of objects to which they correspond. We anticipate the appearance of the corner drugstore before we actually reach it; we anticipate the appearance of the pharmacist before we actually give her our prescription; and so forth. Neisser does not provide any explicit mechanism for how we activate these images, but his discussion makes the existence of such a mechanism seem plausible.

It is in this context which Neisser discusses the method of loci. For Neisser it is a clear example of the activation of visual schemas in the absence of external stimuli to support those schemas in the perceptual cycle. The schemas created by walking through an environment have become so thoroughly learned that they can be set in motion in the absence of that environment and be used to activate other schemas (the images associated stored at the various loci).

We can now work our way back to Vygotsky [6] by considering Neisser's account of language. Most of our schemas will be multimodal, we can see, hear, touch, smell, and taste things. If we hear a dog barking, we expect that by looking in the direction of the sound, and perhaps moving, we will see the dog. Seeing the dog, we know that by moving even closer we can smell it and touch it. Thus the arousal of a schema in one sensory mode can prime the perceptual cycle for perception in other sensory modes. According to Neisser [2], when the child is first learning language, the names of things become assimilated to the general schemas for those things. Thus, when a young child sees a dog and hears it called "dog," the child assimilates that (linguistic) sound to its general schema for the dog. Just as the multimodal dog has an appearance, an odor, a texture, and a touchable shape, and makes characteristic noises, so it also has this peculiar auditory attribute "dog." Just as the appearance of a dog can activate the complete multimodal schema, leading the child to anticipate certain odors and tactile sensations, so hearing this special auditory attribute, "dog," can also activate the complete multimodal schema.

Perhaps the most peculiar property of the name is that it is the part of the complete schema which comes under the child's direct control. The child can, by moving the vocal musculature, utter the sound, "dog," and thereby activate the dog schema in the complete absence of any external stimulus. In this way language gives us the capacity arbitrarily to manipulate our perceptual schemas. We generate words, aloud, or, later, silently, and the schemas are aroused and manipulated according to the structures of words which are generated.

Obviously we can use inner speech to call up and to manipulate visual images, yielding a form of visual thinking. Neisser's account of the mental image, including his treatment of the method of loci, suggests that we may have some visual thinking which does not depend on inner speech. In both cases internalized motor activity (whether locomotor and manipulative, or vocal) is involved in visual thinking. The important point is that thinking is virtual action. This implies that, if we want to think about how computer graphics extends visual thinking, we have to consider, not only what kind of images can be created, but how those images are manipulated. In a sense, visual thinking is always visuomotor thinking.

THE CONTROVERSY OVER MENTAL IMAGES

To this point we have, for the most part, assumed that mental images exist. This is not, however, an unproblematic assumption. There has, in fact, been a great deal of controversy over whether or not mental images are real, and, if so, whether or not they play a significant role in thinking. Do we think in words, or at least in some quasiverbal, or propositional, code? Or do we think in images? That, propositions or images, is the primary distinction, though it is qualified and elaborated with almost endless subtlety and sophistication.

Many of the central issues have been discussed by John Anderson [7], Stephen Kosslyn, and Zenon Pylyshyn [9,10]. While the results of psychological experimentation play a large role in these discussions, much of the disagreement concerns fundamental issues about just what kinds are inferences are permissible. Perhaps, since computing has provided many of the concepts and metaphors which inform this debate, the easiest way to approach these fundamental issues is to begin with an extended analogy from computing.

Imagine, on the one hand, the CRT of a CAD system which is displaying a pleasing shaded image of, for example, a gear assembly. On the other hand, we have another CRT, linked to the same system, which is displaying a fragment of the code for a program which controls some numerically controlled device used in making one of the gears in the assembly displayed on the first screen. Obviously, one of these displays is an image and one is not. Yet, both displays have been generated from the same database and the software generating those displays could well have been written in the same language. Thus, at bottom, both of these displays offer information which is coded in a propositional form.

The fact that the displays are quite different, that one is an image arrayed in two-dimensional space and the other consists of one-dimensional string of "words," obviously is not inconsistent with the fact that both are implemented in systems which use a propositional coding. Regardless of the display format, all of the computation is propositional. Those who argue against mental imagery make much the same argument with respect to the human mind. The basic processes are more or less verbal and propositional and mental images, where they exist, are mere epiphenomena playing no deeper a role in thinking than blinking lights play in the operations of a computer.

A counter argument could be constructed in the following way: We know that, from a theoretical point of view, any conceivable computation can be carried out in any language which meets certain fairly simple criteria. A bit more practically, anything which can be programmed at all, can be programmed in Fortran, or Lisp, or C, or Pascal, or APL, whatever. But, when you get down to it, not all languages are equally suited to all programming tasks. The theoretical equivalence of Lisp and Pascal does not translate into equivalent practical utility. Or, moving into the hardware domain, the fact that, theoretically, any computation which can be executed on a parallel machine can also be executed on a serial machine has little force in a physical world where all real computations take place at finite speeds. In this world there are computations which are so large that serial execution would take days or weeks. Where it is possible, there is real practical value in breaking such computations into many pieces, each assigned to its own processor, with all of the processors running in parallel.

So, the counter argument would go, it might be with the mind. In theory all mental activity could be implemented in some sort of verbal code, but, in practice, it is not. For there are some activities where an imagistic code is more efficient.

This kind of argument has some formal justification in Miriam Yevick's [11] work on holographic logic, which was inspired, in part, by Karl Pribram's [12] advocacy of holography as a model for neural processing. She is interested in the relationship between the complexity of an object and the complexity of a representation adequate to identify the object. For geometrically simple objects, such as squares, triangles, crosses, and circles, a propositional formalism of some sort is quite adequate. But for geometrically complex objects, such as Chinese ideograms or faces, an adequate holographic representation is simpler than an adequate linguistic representation.

A holographic representation of an object or a scene is certainly not, in any simple sense, an ordinary image of that object or scene. But it is not unreasonable to think of it as a very special kind of analog representation and it is certainly quite different from the sort of propositional representations favored by the opponents of mental imagery. The basic point, however, is simply that the fact that anything *can be* linguistically encoded *need not imply* that the mind, or the brain, *does in fact do so*. Most objects in the natural world—human beings, animals, trees and bushes, and so forth—are not geometrically simple. It is thus worth considering the possibility that vision uses a representation scheme which is more appropriate to such objects than propositional schemes seem to be. At the very least Yevick (and Pribram) offer an alternative to both simple mental images and propositional formalisms.

A simple empirical argument, and one which has been quite influential in recent thinking, comes from experiments performed by Robert Shepard [13] and his colleagues. Subjects would be shown a target figure and another figure similar to it but having a different orientation. They had to compare the figures and determine whether or not they were identical. What Shepard discovered is that the length of time subjects took to reach a decision was proportional to the angle through which a figure had to be rotated so that it had the same orientation as the target figure, thus allowing a direct comparison. If one figure had to be rotated 40 degrees and another had to be rotated 60 degrees, then it took one and a half times as long to reach a decision in the second case as it took in the first. Shepard interpreted this as support for the idea that subjects were mentally rotating a mental image of the figure. Mental rotation would thus be one basic operation in visual thinking. Other types of operation, such as scanning and zooming in, are suggested by the work of Stephen Kosslyn [8] and his colleagues.

Operations such as rotation, scanning, and zooming might well be the primitive operations of visual thinking, with higher level processes being organized by structures such as the method of loci or by inner speech. The argument about mental imagery is about whether such operations are, in fact, primitive, or whether they are implemented in some as yet undiscovered propositional form of neural coding.

SOME EVIDENCE FROM NEUROPSYCHOLOGY

The visual system is one of the most thoroughly studied systems within the brain (and has recently been reviewed by David Hubel [14]). Roughly, the system begins with the retina, continues into the midbrain, and then into the cerebral cortex. The optic nerves, which connect the two retinas to the brain, each contain about a million fibers. The primary visual cortex occupies about 3 percent of the area of the cerebral cortex, but it contains about 10 percent of the estimated 50 billion neurons in the cortex, and is surrounded by secondary and tertiary areas which are heavily implicated in visual processing. It is estimated that each neuron is directly connected to 1000 to 10,000 other neurons. The various regions of the visual brain are connected by massive bundles of fibers which are constructed so that there is a topic mapping from one region to another, from retina to midbrain to primary visual cortex, to secondary and even tertiary cortical regions. That is, neurons which have a certain spatial relationship to one another in one region project to neurons in other regions which have the same spatial relationship to one another. (Note: According to Gordon Mountcastle [15], such mapping may be typical of all cortical regions, not just visual regions.)

Sensory information from the right half of the visual field is processed in the left hemisphere, while information from the left visual field is processed in the right hemisphere. We should keep this in mind as we consider one of the most dramatic bodies of evidence in neuropsychology, evidence which indicates that, roughly speaking, the dominant cerebral hemisphere (which is the left hemisphere in righthanded people) seems to be specialized for verbal tasks while the nondominant hemisphere (which is the right hemisphere in righthanded people) seems to be specialized for visual tasks. Since both hemispheres are involved in visual perception, it seems reasonable to believe that this evidence is about how the brain *elaborates on* the results of perception, that it is germane to questions about visual thinking and not about visual perception.

Much of this evidence comes from work on split-brain subjects begun by Roger Sperry [16]. While there are a few cases of people who are born without direct connections between the right and left cerebral hemispheres, most of these are people who have undergone split-brain surgery as a treatment for very severe epilepsy. Once the cerebral hemispheres have been disconnected from one another it is possible to present information selectively to either hemisphere, thus investigating the different capacities of the two hemispheres. Generally speaking, in this situation, one hemisphere does not know what the other is doing. It is almost as though one person now had two more or less independent minds.

The dominant hemisphere has proven to be better at speaking, writing, and calculation. The nondominant hemisphere has proven to be more adept at visual tasks. For example, if a simple line drawing of a cube is presented to a subject's left hemisphere, the subject will not be able to draw a very accurate copy of it. If the same drawing is presented to the right hemisphere, the subject has little trouble making a good copy of the cube, despite the fact that the subject has to execute the drawing with his left hand, which is not normally used for such tasks. The nondominant hemisphere is also superior at discriminating between items by touch and at matching tactile and visual stimuli, which would seem to be important in the visuomanipulative aspect of visual thinking.

In this context it is useful to return to the method of loci. The obvious speculation is that it involves interaction between the two cerebral hemispheres. The mental loci are established in the nondominant, the visual hemisphere. These loci are then linked to ideas in the dominant, the verbal, hemisphere through vivid images which are associatively related to the appropriate verbal concepts. This method thus uses the visual hemisphere as a system for indexing and retrieving material in the verbal hemisphere. The method of loci is thus an example of how visual and verbal thinking can interact.

Metaphor is another example of such interaction. Metaphors generally conjure up images. Consider a statement such as "Achilles was a lion in battle." The point of this metaphor is that Achilles and the lion are alike in their fighting style; swift, impassioned, and furious. Benzon and Hays [*17,18*] have argued that the process by which that style is conceptually isolated is a visual one in which a mental image of Achilles fighting is "filtered" through an image of a lion fighting. However, the mechanism by which this process is controlled is a verbal mechanism, the sequence of words "Achilles was a lion in battle." In this case we have a verbal process controlling a visual process.

As a final example of verbal/visual interaction, consider the process of describing an object or a scene. Components of the scene must be named, relationships between them must be specified, and appropriate properties attached all around—"the sky was blue, the pine trees tall and green, and the eagle cast a shadow on the surface of the pond as it flew across the fiery sun." Such sequences of words are verbal reconstructions of visual objects. Something in one representational form, visual, is reconstructed in a different representational form, verbal.

These last examples, the method of loci, metaphor, and description, all seem to involve interaction between verbal and visual processes, between the dominant and nondominant hemispheres. Such interaction may well be essential to all but the simplest forms of thinking with, about, and by means of visual objects.

Finally, to do justice to those who question the existence of visual imagery, we should realize that none of the evidence on hemispherical differences really addresses their questions about what is absolutely primitive in mental processes. This evidence tells us only that the two hemispheres are specialized for tasks in different domains. It tells us nothing about how those tasks are implemented in either hemisphere. The visual hemisphere could well be using a propositional code to do its work. The fact that the two hemispheres are constructed of the same types of neurons arranged into the same types of assemblies suggests that both implement the same primitive operations. That is something which both the proponents and opponents of mental imagery will have to consider.

VISUAL THINKING, SCIENCE, AND CREATIVITY

Since science has been constructed in the kingdom of reason, a number of thinkers have been intrigued by cases in which the intuitive ways of visual thinking have been important—as though there were something odd about rational theory having its origins in "irrational" intuition. One of the most famous examples concerns Kekulé's discovery of the structure of benzene in 1865. The crucial idea, that benzene is organized in a ring, came to Kekulé in a dream in which he saw a snake biting it own tail. There is no reason to doubt this story, nor, I assert, even to doubt the soundness of the lesson usually derived from it, that both visualization and unconscious thought processes, such as dreaming, are important in scientific creativity. However, we do not at all understand how Kekulé's unconscious mind produced the dream image nor how Kekulé's conscious mind got from a recollection of the dream image to the solution of the problem at hand, the structure of benzene.

Consider another example, a letter from Einstein to Jacques Hadamard, who was investigating the creative process and queried many mathematicians and scientists about their mental processes. Einstein asserted:

> The words or the language, as they are written or spoken, do not seem to play any role in my mechanism of thought. The psychical entities which seem to serve as elements in thought are certain signs and more or less clear images which can be "voluntarily" reproduced and combined. . . .The above mentioned elements are, in my case, of visual and some of muscular type. Conventional words or other signs have to be sought for laboriously only in a secondary stage, when the mentioned associative play is sufficiently established and can be reproduced at will.

Note that Einstein talks, not only of visual elements, but of muscular ones as well. As was the case in the method of loci, or Geis's thinking about molecular structure, visual thinking is also associated with motoric thinking.

More recently, Arthur I. Miller [20] has been interested in the role which visual imagery played in the development of physics in this century. His discussion of the development of quantum mechanics is particularly interesting since considerable controversy developed over the issue of appropriate visualization. How does one visualize things which sometimes act like waves and sometimes act like particles? The Bohr atom was readily visualized as a miniature solar system. That visualization, however, became untenable and work in subatomic physics proceeded without appropriate visualization for about two decades until, in 1949, Richard Feynman introduced diagramatic conventions for visualizing quantum mechanical events. Miller makes the point that the Bohr atom is a visualization derived from the ordinary perceptual world (simple mechanical objects in motion) whereas Feynman diagrams are visually abstract and unrelated to ordinary phenomenal reality. The development of quantum mechanics thus involved an abandonment of one set of conventions for visualization, purely formal and mathematical elaboration, and then a return to visualization, but with new conventions.

Neither Hadamard nor Miller have provided a practical manual of scientific creativity—that isn't what they were after. They were interested in the role of nonverbal, often visual, thinking in science. However, others such as William Gordon [21], Kurt Hanks [22], and Robert McKim [23], have been interested in promoting exercises in visual thinking as a means to creativity. In one way or another these exercises, often derived from classroom and consulting practice, are intended to get around verbal and/or logical thought processes. One may be asked to imagine the various things one can do with a brick, or to construct a bridge with a stack of cards. Betty Edwards [24] is mostly concerned with teaching people to draw by using exercises designed to keep verbal processes from interfering with visual work. In one exercise a person is asked to copy a picture which is upside down, making it impossible readily to identify (i.e., name, verbalize) the components in the image. In this way one is forced to draw what one sees, rather than what one knows. Edwards has, however, developed some exercises which are more directed toward general ideation. For example, one can draw abstract images expressing a particular mood or emotion.

Two other thinkers advocate a specific visual technique. Tony Buzan [25] talks of *mind maps*, while Gabriele L. Rico [26] talks of *clustering*. The idea is the same in both cases. Rather than organizing one's ideas and notes in outline form, make free-form diagrams depicting associative relationships between one's ideas. Write a term down (or even, in Buzan's case, make a small sketch), then write associated terms, phrases, concepts nearby, connecting closely associated ideas with lines. The result is a spider's web of associatively linked ideas. This form of note taking and ideation is much more flexible than creating and refining outlines, which impose a fixed hierarchical structure on one's thinking.

It is not hard to see that this technique is similar in spirit to the method of loci. But, where the method of loci used an imaginary fixed path as a mechanism for storing and retrieving a sequence of ideas, this technique arranges ideas in a way which allows you to explore and contemplate many paths through the ideas. These diagrams also have a loose resemblance to the cognitive network structures which have been proposed as models for cognitive organization by a many researchers in the cognitive sciences. If one assumes a cognitive network model for natural language semantics, then clustering and mind maps would seem to be a technique for visually representing and exploring the structure of one's verbal and propositional universe. This suggests, finally, that an important aspect of creativity may be, not simply visual thinking, but the capacity efficiently to move back and forth between visual and verbal modes.

IMAGES AS TOOLS FOR THOUGHT

Perceiving and thinking about the visual world is one thing. Creating imaginary visual worlds and thinking about them is a bit different. But in both cases we are thinking about objects deployed in space. But images are used as tools for thought in more abstract ways.

The basic idea is simple. Many very simple visual images have been used to express ideas. Each of these images can be considered a kind of "visual proverb," a visual image which can be variously applied in different conceptual realms much as we call on ordinary proverbs. For example, consider the triangle. A linguist might use a triangle to visualize the relationship between a word, the object designated by the word, and the perceptual schema used to recognize the object. But for the Christian theologian, the triangle is likely to be used to visualize the relationship between the Father, the Son, and the Holy Ghost. These are very different conceptual realms, but the triangle has conceptual value in both of them. The triangle is thus the vehicle for a "visual proverb." What are the visual properties which make it a useful image to think with? What about other simple geometric forms, squares, crosses, circles, or spirals? Beyond these simple forms, what about more complex images—for example, William Butler Yeats, the Irish poet, was deeply impressed with an image which consisted of two interpenetrating cones.

These forms are, of course, common in the visual symbols used in all cultures for religious, artistic, and decorative purposes. The question we are asking now is how these forms help us organize experience and ideas which may not be inherently visual, which may not be directly linked to perceptions of the external world. How do we think with these forms? Is this at all similar to the "more or less clear images" which Einstein asserted to be at the root of his own thought processes? Can we think of Feynman's quantum mechanical diagrams as a rigorous development of imagery of this sort? In a different vein, these visual forms are the substance of much of the apparently aimless doodling which many of us do. But is doodling aimless, or is it a form of visual thinking?

At least one place to begin looking for answers to these questions is in the development of drawing skill in children. Howard Gardner [27] reports that, before they try to make representational drawings, children will spend a great deal of time drawing simple geometric images—circles, squares, crosses, arrows, and so forth—and combinations of them. This activity is concerned only with the creation and elaboration of graphic forms, not with using graphic forms to represent objects and scenes. In Gardner's view the child is learning the properties of the graphic medium. Not only must the child learn how to control the movement of the drawing implement, but the child must also learn the correlations between what is seen in visual space and what is done in motor–tactile space.

It is possible that the figures drawn are those which are pleasing in both visual and motor space. For example, the circle is visually elegant—an enclosed boundary with uniform curvature—and motorically pleasing—a smooth continuous motion which ends where it started. The repertoire of simple geometric forms might thus be a basic "vocabulary" of equivalences between visual and motor space.

These visuomotor equivalences could then be the seeds around which the later conceptual use of graphic images can be built. The child first uses these correlations in the process of combining lines and circles and squares to represent people, houses, dogs, and so forth. Later, the adult can take these correlations into other, often abstract, conceptual realms. In fact, once the adult thinker shifts his or her thought away from the phenomenal world, what else is there to think with but words and simple intermodal conceptual objects—visuomotor triangles, squares, circles, crosses, etc.—which in themselves, do not represent anything?

THE GRAPHICS INTERFACE

While the internal operations of computers are managed by propositionally structured codes, graphics has proved to be the basis of an intuitively satisfying man–machine interface. During the early 1970s, a research team headed by Alan Kay [28] was interested in making computers more accessible to children. As part of this effort they developed a graphic interface, drawing on the previous work of Ivan Sutherland (Sketchpad), Douglas Engelbart (NLS, standing for on Line System), and the Rand Corporation's GRAIL system. The result of this effort was a way of interacting with the computer through pointing at graphic objects rather than through typing commands. With the visual interface the user no longer has to remember all of the available commands. Instead, the computer displays the names of the available options on the CRT screen and the user simply chooses among them. That difference may seem like a small thing, but it is a small thing which makes an enormous practical difference. It is very much easier for people to use a mouse to select from a set of displayed options than it is for people to type in commands.

Once again, a comparison with the method of loci is in order. Instead of the memorized path through a building one has the visual objects on the CRT—windows, menus, icons, and so forth. Instead of (mentally) walking through a building one points at these visual objects with a mouse, and presses buttons on the mouse. However, in both cases one is using a visual structure to index the content of some conceptual world.

Work on visual interfaces continues. People in the field of artificial intelligence (AI) are interested in visual interfaces because AI systems involve very complex information structures and even the expert user needs all the help he or she can get. Such systems typically contain large structures of information about the system's application domain. These knowledge structures are easier to work with if they can be examined visually, for the visual representation provides a better sense of large scale structure. The meaning of any given conceptual unit depends heavily on its linkage to other units, whose meaning, in turn, depends on their linkage to other units, and so forth. This structure of linkages can't be easily grasped while looking at the contents of unit after unit as they are called to the screen. Visual representations allow one to grasp the ways these units are linked together.

Most graphics interfaces are only two dimensional. The display is two dimensional and one interacts with it two dimensionally, by moving some pointing device (mouse, puck, or stylus) over a two-dimensional surface. There are application domains, however, where one would like a three-dimensional interface. It is not easy to provide a three-dimensional display, but it is certainly possible to operate with two-dimensional projections of a three-dimensional domain. That applies, however, only to display. Providing three-dimensional input is a different matter. Here one would really like to be able to move some input device in three dimensions and have the coordinates directly entered into the computer. James Foley [29] has reviewed a number of possibilities.

The most interesting device is a glove with sensors that pick up information about hand and finger movement, allowing hands and fingers to move freely in three-dimensions. This information can then be used to guide the movement of a "virtual hand" within the computer. Work is also being done on providing tactile feedback for such a glove. Force feedback would also be useful, though it is a more difficult problem.

There are many applications where a three-dimensional interface would be valuable. The most obvious examples involve design. An engineer who is working with a solid modeling system could benefit from an interface which permits him or her directly to manipulate shapes rather than issuing commands from a keyboard. With an appropriate 3-D interface, the engineer would be able to "grasp" the geometric primitives (spheres, cylinders, cones, cubes, and so forth) from which he must construct his shapes, combine them manually, and then stretch, fold, and compress the resulting solid to the desired shape.

A pharmaceutical chemist using a computer graphics system to test out possible structures for a new drug has a similar need for direct manipulation. The process of creating a drug is essentially one of synthesizing a molecule whose shape allows it to act as a biological "key" in the appropriate biological "lock." It would be easier for a chemist physically to manipulate a (proposed) molecule than to enter shape manipulation commands from a keyboard.

A three-dimensional interface might also be useful in exploratory data analysis, where a statistician is exploring the structure of a data set which is organized in 3, 4, 5, 10, 15, 50, or more dimensions. Exploring high dimensional data sets is fundamentally difficult because it is extremely difficult effectively to present data organized in more than four dimensions, with three dimensions being mapped onto the three spatial dimensions and one dimension being mapped onto time. The purpose of exploratory data analysis is to create techniques for analyzing high dimensional data sets. Having a three-dimensional interface obviously wouldn't increase the number of dimensions directly available to the senses, but it would make it easier to explore and manipulate data which has been suitably collapsed onto three spatial dimensions.

Video technology provides a different way of getting three-dimensional information into the computer. One uses a video system though which the user's motion in physical space is picked up and projected into a visual world which exists only inside a computer and which is viewed on a CRT or a projection screen; appropriate software analyzes the moving image for information about motion in three dimensions. An image of one's hand, or of one's whole body, could appear on the CRT, moving about and manipulating objects in the virtual world defined in the computer. Myron Kruger [30] has been working with such environments, using them primarily as forms of interactive art. Such environments obviously could be used for any application where motion and manipulation in three dimensions would be useful. One might, for example, use such technology to enable one to "walk" through the structure of a biomolecule in the way that Geis has described. Or, an architect might use it to "walk" through a building being designed.

At this point, the computer has become a "theater" into which the mind projects its images. These images are created, manipulated, and explored, however, by physical action which is picked up and projected into the computational theater. We now have a curious inversion of the idea that visual thinking is the mental imitation of physical motion and manipulation. Now physical action is being used for the manipulation of purely imaginary objects and the exploration of purely imaginary spaces.

THE VISUAL NATURE OF
THE WORLD OF COMPUTING

Few conceptual domains are more intensely visual than the world of computer science. Consequently, visual thinking is necessary to understand this world in greater depth, and conventions for visualizing this world are important—and they are ubiquitous. One particularly interesting aspect about the world of computer science is that it is both physical (hardware) and abstract (algorithms and data structures), and conventions of visualization exist in both domains.

At the most concrete level we have very complex physical devices—semiconductor chips, circuit boards, disk drives, and so forth—which must be designed, a task which is fundamentally, though certainly not exclusively, a visual one. More interestingly, visual imagery informs the more abstract material of computational theory. Turing's metaphor of a device which reads and writes to an infinitely long paper tape is a visual one, and it is fundamental to the idea of computation. The distinction between serial and parallel processing is another fundamental idea which invites visualization.

Less abstractly, we have logic diagrams for visualizing the basic functional structure of the computing elements which are realized in circuitry and software. While the physical shape of computing circuits varies according to the technology in which they are implemented, the logical structure of the circuit is independent of the details of those physical structures. That logical structure is captured in logic diagrams. Diagrams are also important for software. Flow charts depict algorithms while trees and networks depict data structures. From several levels of hardware organization through several levels of software organization, computing technology is visually rich.

But much of this richness cannot be grasped simply in spatial terms, no matter how many dimensions exist in the space. Computing is, irreducibly, a process; it takes place in time as well as in space. Adequate visualizations must, therefore, be animated. Consequently, researchers such as Marc Brown and Robert Sedgewick [31] have been developing animation techniques for visualizing the dynamic behavior of algorithms. These techniques have obvious educational applications, for the animations can help students gain an intuitive feel for how different algorithms work. These same techniques are of potential value in the design and analysis of algorithms and as tools for programming and debugging.

Finally, we should consider the work of Seymour Pappert [32], who has been interested in teaching children about programming and mathematics through a highly visual and interactive environment constructed in the LOGO programming language. He discovered that students enjoy working in such an environment and that they learn rapidly and effectively. Even students who had shown an antipathy toward mathematics respond well to the opportunity to move graphical "turtles" around on the CRT screen by issuing commands to the computer. The experience gained by students in watching and controlling the movement and creation of graphical objects on the CRT screen sows the seeds from which more abstract knowledge can grow.

Thus, just as computing is a highly visual world, so it contains within it techniques for the visualization of that world. To borrow a phrase from John Barth, the novelist, the key to the treasure is the treasure. The world of computing is new, and, to most people, deeply strange. To the extent that this world can be grasped visually, computing can itself provide the means for constructing the visualizations.

BACK TO THE FUTURE

Predicting the future is notoriously difficult and generally thankless. In the case of visual thinking there are two interrelated futures to predict, the future development of our understanding of visual cognition and neuropsychology and the future development of computer graphics and image processing. I see little point in broad speculation about what the future might bring in these two areas, or in their interaction.

If, however, we wish to contemplate that interaction and the possibilities it opens for the computational extension of visual thinking, we should consider another issue: cultural context. Visual thinking may take place in the minds of individuals. But those individuals exist in a culture. And cultures all have their characteristic ways of doing things, their characteristic ways of thinking.

We must face the fact that we are inheritors of an intellectual culture which is deeply ambivalent about visualization. That ambivalence will certainly influence the computational extension of visual thinking.

Western culture is doubly rooted in ancient Israel and ancient Greece. At the center of our religious traditions we have the Old Testament prohibition against graven images. In the Medieval Christian church there was a great deal of controversy over whether or not churches should be decorated with images and sculptures of religious figures. Our philosophy is similarly biased. However glorious Greek art was, their philosophy doubted that glory. Plato held that art is an imitation of an imitation of reality; consequently, it is so unreliable that art must be considered, in effect, a species of lying. Ever since, art, in whatever mode, visual or verbal, has had to justify itself, to show that it is not fundamentally a species of deception.

However, as Ernst Gombrich has pointed out in *The Story of Art* [5], the ancient Chinese had quite a different attitude toward images. They made meticulously accurate sculptures of religious figures—intended accurately to depict them in various contemplative states—and used paintings of natural scenes as objects for meditation. Thus we cannot argue that our ancient ambivalence about visual images is inherent in the nature of images. Rather, it is an ambivalence which existed in the ancient roots of our culture, but which did not necessarily exist in other cultures.

This ambivalence is not dead. Art is as much a problem for contemporary philosophers as it was for Plato. The skepticism with which intellectuals treat motion pictures and television probably has as much to do with ambivalence about images as it has to do with the content of programming in these media. And, as Larry Smarr [33] has pointed out, scientists who use computer graphics to depict the results of numerical simulations must contend with colleagues who believe only analytic methods are valid. While these colleagues talk of numerical methods as being "inelegant" and worry about the approximate nature of such solutions, one cannot escape the feeling that they are also manifesting suspicion of this work precisely because it depends so heavily on visual thinking, as though the abstract images, which are often quite pleasing, had the power to seduce us into untruth and so must be resisted. Finally, in an article reviewing the applications of computer graphics to biochemistry, J. E. Dubois, D. Laurent, and J. Weber, have noted that skeptics doubt the value of graphic presentation, preferring to emphasize the role of the underlying computational model. They are quite confident the skeptics are wrong; that graphic presentation is essential. It would seem that the skeptics are only echoing the long-standing cultural prejudice against visualization.

An examination of the circumstances in which modern science originated suggests that such skepticism is mistaken. It is generally accepted that the first flowering of the Renaissance was in the visual arts, during the fourteenth and fifteenth centuries, and that the final flowering gave us modern science, culminating in the work of Isaac Newton. Both J. Bronowski [*35*] (in an essay on Leonardo da Vinci) and Irving Geis [*3*] (in an essay about the history of anatomy) have suggested that it was the artists who first turned the culture's attention toward a rigorous examination of the natural world. Ancient and medieval science were not empirical disciplines; scientific laws were deduced from philosophical first principles, such as uniform circular motion, rather than from an examination of natural phenomena. The practice of basing one's understanding of the world on close observation entered into Western high culture through the efforts of Renaissance artists. Scientists acquired the practice from then and then forgot where they learned it. It is not an idea that we are comfortable with—that science should owe a significant debt to art.

This prejudice is unfortunate for it limits our capacity imaginatively to exploit the possibilities which computing offers for visual thinking. In order to realize these possibilities we will have to confront our ambivalence about images and to rethink our conceptions of how we come to know and to act in the world. This kind of cultural reassessment is not a well-defined task and it is not likely to be undertaken in a straightforward way. While we may talk of the need to undertake this reassessment as though we could appoint a committee to study the problem and to make recommendations for further committees and further studies, this reassessment is most likely to happen, if at all, as a side effect of the deployment of graphics-based applications. As more and more people find that graphics-based computing is essential to their work, they will come to form a cultural constituency which is willing to entertain, support, and undertake such a reassessment. Perhaps in the context of that cultural activity we will at last see a full flowering of our capacity for visual thinking.

REFERENCES

1. F. A. Yates, *The Art of Memory*, University of Chicago Press, Chicago, 1966.
2. U. Neisser, *Cognition and Reality*, W. H. Freeman, San Francisco, 1976.
3. I. Geis, "Beyond the Naked Eye," *Print 29*(3), 33–48 (1975).
4. E. Gombrich, *Art and Illusion*, Princeton University Press, Princeton, 1961.
5. Gombrich, *The Story of Art*, Phaidon, London, 1951.
6. L. S. Vygotsky, *Thought and Language*, MIT Press, Cambridge, 1962.
7. J. R. Anderson, "Arguments Concerning Representations for Mental Imagery," *Psychol. Rev., 85*, 249–276 (1978).
8. S. Kosslyn, S. Pinker, G. E. Smith, and S. P. Shwartz, "On the Demystification of Mental Imagery," *Behav. Brain Sci., 2*, 535–583 (1979).
9. Z. Pylyshyn, "What the Mind's Eye Tells the Mind's Brain: A Critique of Mental Imagery," *Psychol. Bull., 80*, 1–24 (1973).
10. Z. Pylyshyn, "Computation and Cognition: Issues in the Foundations of Cognitive Science," *Behav. Brain Sci., 3*, 111–169 (1980).
11. M. L. Yevick, "Holographic or Fourier Logic," *Pattern Recog., 7*, 197–213 (1975).
12. K. H. Pribram, *Languages of the Brain*, Prentice-Hall, Englewood Cliffs, NJ, 1971.
13. R. N. Shepard, "Form, Formation, and Transformation of Internal Representations," in *Information Processing and Cognition* (R. L. Solso, ed.), Lawrence Erlbaum, Hillsdale, NJ, 1975, pp. 87–122.
14. D. H. Hubel, *Eye, Brain, and Vision*, Scientific American Books, New York, 1988.
15. V. B. Mountcastle, "An Organizing Principle for Cerebral Function: The Unit Module and the Distributed System," in *The Mindful Brain* (G. M. Edelman and V. B. Mountcastle, eds.), MIT Press, Cambridge, 1978.

16. R. W. Sperry, "Lateral Specialization in the Surgically Separated Hemispheres," in *The Neurosciences: Third Study Program* (F. O. Schmitt and F. G. Worden, eds.), MIT Press, Cambridge, 1974, pp. 5–19.

17. W. Benzon and D. Hays, "Metaphor, Recognition, and Neural Process," *Am. J. Semiotics 5*, 59–80 (1987).

18. W. Benzon and D. Hays, "Principles and Development of Natural Intelligence," *J. Soc. Biol. Structures, 11*, 1–30 (1988).

19. J. Hadamard, *The Psychology of Invention in the Mathematical Field*, Dover, New York, 1954.

20. A. I. Miller, *Imagery in Scientific Thought*, MIT Press, Cambridge, 1986.

21. W. Gordon, *The Metaphorical Way of Knowing*, Synectics Education Press, 1960.

22. K. Hanks, L. Belliston, and D. Edwards, *Design Yourself!*, William Kaufman, Los Altos, CA, 1978.

23. R. McKim, *Experiences in Visual Thinking*, Brooks/Cole, Monterey, CA, 1972.

24. B. Edwards, *Drawing on the Artist Within*, Simon and Schuster, New York, 1986.

25. T. Buzan, *Use Both Sides of Your Brain*, E. P. Dutton, New York, 1983.

26. G. L. Rico, *Writing the Natural Way*, J. P. Tarcher, Los Angeles, 1983.

27. H. Gardner, *Artful Scribbles*, Basic Books, New York, 1980.

28. A. C. Kay, "Microelectronics and the Personal Computer," in *Microelectronics*, W. H. Freeman, San Francisco, 1977, pp. 125–135.

29. J. D. Foley, "Interfaces for Advanced Computing," *Sci. Am., 257*(4), 126–135 (1987).

30. M. W. Kruger, *Artificial Reality*, Addison-Wesley, Reading, MA, 1983.

31. M. H. Brown and R. Sedgewick, "A System for Algorithm Animation," *Comput. Graphics 18*(3), 177–186 (1984).

32. S. Pappert, *Mindstorms*, Basic Books, New York, 1980.

33. L. L. Smarr, "An Approach to Complexity: Numerical Computations," *Science, 228*, 403–408 (1985).

34. J. E. Dubois, D. Laurent, and J. Weber, "Chemical Ideograms and Molecular Computer Graphics," *The Visual Computer, 1*, 49–63 (1985).

35. J. Bronowski, "Leonardo da Vinci," in *Renaissance Profiles* (J. H. Plumb, ed.), Harper & Row, New York, 1965, pp. 71–87.

WILLIAM L. BENZON